2013
PUSHCART
PRIZE XXXVII
BEST OF THE
SMALL PRESSES

EDITED BY BILL HENDERSON
WITH THE PUSHCART PRIZE EDITORS

Note: nominations for this series are invited from any small, independent, literary book press or magazine in the world, print or online. Up to six nominations—tear sheets or copies, selected from work published, or about to be published, in the calendar year—are accepted by our December 1 deadline each year. Write to Pushcart Fellowships, P.O. Box 380, Wainscott, N.Y. 11975 for more information or consult our websites www.pushcartprize.com. or pushcart press.org.

Acknowledgments
Selections for The Pushcart Prize are reprinted with the permission of authors and presses cited. Copyright reverts to authors and presses immediately after publication.

Distributed by W. W. Norton & Co.
500 Fifth Ave., New York, N.Y. 10110

Library of Congress Card Number: 76-58675
ISBN (hardcover): 978-1-888889-66-6
ISBN (paperback): 978-1-888889-65-9
ISSN: 0149-7863

For
Hugh Fox (1932-2011)
a Founding Editor of The Pushcart Prize

INTRODUCTION

I T'S THE MOST GHASTLY of times and the most glorious of times.

First the ghastly: politicians; lifestyle; consumers; a culture of celebrity glitter; an internet tsunami of instant facts, factoids and nonsense that obviates knowledge and wisdom; a 'greed is good' oligarchy; vanity publishers taking over the commercial publishing empire; legitimate and terrified publishers in a race to the best-seller bottom; bookstores collapsing; Kindle in charge; profiteers cashing in on wannabe authors with zero talent — the result? A new censorship of clutter. Everybody into the pool and you don't have to know how to swim. A cacophony of drowning shouts.

Yet it is also the most glorious of times: of course there are thousands of examples — for instance, the authors of the stories, essays, memoirs and poems reprinted and mentioned in this PPXXXVII. In all my years of editing this series, with lots of help from hundreds of people (this year Bob Hicok and Maxine Kumin wonderfully co-edited the poetry), I've never been so happy with our literature. There is simply too much talent, insight, wisdom, empathy and skill out there in small press land to be included even in a volume of this heft—the largest ever. The Word survives indeed thrives in the ruins.

To further lift your mood — consider that Edith Pearlman (her stories appeared in PPXXV and PPXXXIII) recently won the National Book Critics Circle Fiction Award for *Binocular Vision*, a story collection from tiny Lookout Books. The NBCC Board declared that Lookout's publication is "a triumph for Pearlman's distinctive storytelling."

At the same ceremony Laura Kasischke (our co-editor of poetry for last year's Prize) won the poetry award for *Space, In Chains* (Copper Canyon) and Geoff Dyer won the criticism award for *Otherwise Known As the Human Condition: Selected Essays and Reviews* (Graywolf Press).

In other words half of the NBCC's most recent nods went to small presses. A record.

Plus, this just in, Tracy Smith won the 2012 Pulitzer Prize for Poetry for *Life On Mars*, (Graywolf again).

In last year's PP we noted that Paul Harding's commercially rejected novel *Tinkers* won the Pulitzer Prize for fiction thanks to the insight and energy of the editors at Bellevue Literary Press, and Jaimy Gordon's novel *Lord of Misrule* won the National Book Award for fiction due to the efforts of Bruce McPherson, the one man band behind her publisher, McPherson & Company.

As the commercial world (vanity and traditional) marches behind the bean counters our independent presses carry the flag of what's truly valuable and enduring.

Feel better?

❊ ❊ ❊

Almost forty years ago many editors helped found this series — some internationally famous, others stalwarts of the small press scene at the time. One such stalwart, Hugh Fox, put his name behind this project when it was still just a glimmer in my imagination. Hugh died last year. He was a poet, novelist, archaeologist and teacher who published over one hundred works.

Hugh spent his entire working life teaching American literature and writing at Loyola University in Los Angeles, the Instituto Pedagogico in Caracas, the University of Sonora in Mexico, the University of Santa Catarina in Brazil and Michigan State University. He was founder and a Board of Directors member of COSMEP, the organization of independent publishers. He was also editor of *Ghost Dance*—the international quarterly of experimental poetry—and contributing reviewer for *Smith/Pulpsmith* and *Choice*.

Hugh took a chance with us at the very start. We miss and honor him for his support when it counted.

❊ ❊ ❊

My friend and occasional dining partner, Barney Rosset, who died this year at age 89, was not generally recognized as a small press guy. He drove Grove Press into the commercial stratosphere and descended rather rapidly, but in his early days, just after he bought the struggling Grove for $3000, he was a literary hero who opened the world to previously censored work by Henry Miller, D.H. Lawrence, John Rechy and

60 plus others like Frank O'Hara, Allen Ginsberg, Jack Kerouac, Lawrence Ferlinghetti and Samuel Beckett.

Barney's discovery of Beckett was a classic small press saga. It started in Paris with a little mag called *Merlin*. (In the 1950's *Merlin* and George Plimpton's *Paris Review* were rivals of sorts.) Enter a young recent college ex-pat, Richard Seaver, living in a cheap Left Bank hotel who discovered Beckett's work when he was a 45 year old unknown, and became his one man fan club.

But Beckett himself was shy, hard to find. Here's Seaver's account of how they finally met:

> We'd all but given up hope of ever hearing from Beckett when, one dark and stormy early evening in late November . . . a knock came at the door. The noise of the rain on the glass roof up above was so deafening we barely heard the knock. When finally I answered, there, outlined in the light, was a tall gaunt figure in a raincoat, water streaming down from the brim of the nondescript hat jammed onto the top of his head. From inside the folds of his raincoat he fished a package, not even wrapped against the downpour: a manuscript bound in a black imitation-leather binder.
>
> "You asked me for this," he said, thrusting the package into my hand. "Here it is."

It was the manuscript for his novel "Watt." Beckett disappeared into the night.

[Note to writers: no literary agent was involved in this transaction. No mention of money or an advance or rights. Just an editor who loved Beckett's writing and an author who was willing to walk through a rainstorm to hand it to him.]

Seaver comments in his recent memoir of those years, *The Tender Hour of Twilight* (FSG, 2012), Samuel Beckett was "the most exciting writer I have read since I've come to Paris . . . for god's sake and nobody was reading him."

Seaver set out to rectify that oblivion in the pages of *Merlin*. Meanwhile, in New York Barney Rosset happened on a copy of *Merlin* #2 and flew to Paris to meet and eventually hire Seaver for his new press.

Their association at Grove would last over a decade, revolutionize the literature of the 20th century, and lead to the Nobel Prize for literature for Beckett.

Seaver and Rosset kept the faith and we all owe them a big chunk of our current literary heritage.

❖ ❖ ❖

The Pushcart series also owes much to our endowment contributors. You will find them listed at the rear of this volume. Their generosity insures that this series will continue as long as the spirit of literary independence thrives. Join them if you are willing and able. Your name will be enshrined in every future volume. Immortality, indeed.

❖ ❖ ❖

Every year I ask our poetry co-editors to comment on their selections.

Maxine Kumin's most recent book, *Where I Live: New & Selected Poems 1990-2010*, won the 2011 L.A. Times award. A former U.S. poet laureate, her honors include the Ruth Lilly and Pulitzer prizes.

Maxine Kumin comments:

> From the breadth and heft of the possibly 2,000 submissions that UPS delivered, I found too many really, really fine poems cluttering my head and desk, making the selection process an ongoing struggle. My choices are of course quirky and subjective but I hope they reflect an array of temperaments and passions: lyrical, political, narcissistic, meditative, elegiac, as well as a broad assortment of journals and online sources, several previously unknown to me. I was surprised to find almost no poetry in the old forms and not surprised by the number of poems written in the first person. I am not drawn to opacity whether intentional or accidental and I am drawn to musical and metrical deftness. When I had whittled the possibles down to sixty, the final cutting was painful; when the group had reduced to thirty it was excruciating to decide which were Pushcart Prizes and which were Honorables. The latter in my opinion are just as deserving as the prize-winners and I hope that readers of this anthology will take the time to ferret them out.

❖ ❖ ❖

Bob Hicok's seventh collection of poems, *Elegy Owned*, is forthcoming from Copper Canyon Press. A recipient of five Pushcart Prizes, a Gug-

8

genheim and two NEA Fellowships, his poetry had been selected for inclusion in seven volumes of *Best American Poetry* and he was a finalist for the National Book Critics Circle poetry award in 2001.

Bob Hicok comments:

> Eighteen pounds of poetry in a box. That's how it begins when you edit the Pushcart prize, followed by another eighteen pounds a few months later. Maxine Kumin had her own thirty-six pounds of poetry, so between us, there's something of a small child by weight we've read down to what you'll find in this book. Out of our thirty-six pounds, we each selected fifteen poems, we were given fifteen yeses and what felt like infinite nos. So from thirty-six pounds I chose not even a few ounces of poetry, maybe a bird's worth, a thrush or sparrow. And while I like my thrush of poetry, my starling, I make no claims for its value beyond its appeal to me, my fresh-hatched crow of poetry.

❉   ❉   ❉

Thank you, honored reader, for sampling our collection. (May I suggest you start with Rasheda White's poem "A Shadow Beehive" from *Ecotone* on page 182? Rasheda is in the Fourth Grade.) So much that is worthy has been listed in the "Special Mention" section. And even more can be found through a subscription to the little mag of your choice or a purchase at your local, independent bookstore.

We depend on you. Without you, the theater goes dark.

BH

THE PEOPLE WHO HELPED

FOUNDING EDITORS—Anaïs Nin (1903-1977), Buckminster Fuller (1895-1983), Charles Newman (1938-2006), Daniel Halpern, Gordon Lish, Harry Smith, Hugh Fox (1932-2011), Ishmael Reed, Joyce Carol Oates, Len Fulton, Leonard Randolph, Leslie Fiedler (1917-2003), Nona Balakian (1918-1991), Paul Bowles (1910-1999), Paul Engle (1908-1991), Ralph Ellison (1914-1994), Reynolds Price (1933-2011), Rhoda Schwartz, Richard Morris, Ted Wilentz (1915-2001), Tom Montag, William Phillips (1907-2002). Poetry editor: H. L. Van Brunt

CONTRIBUTING EDITORS FOR THIS EDITION—Kim Addonizio, Dan Albergotti, Dick Allen, Carolyn Alessio, John Allman, Idris Anderson, Susanne Paola Antonetta, Antler, Philip Appleman, Tony Ardizzone, Renee Ashley, David Baker, Jim Barnes, Kim Barnes, Ellen Bass, Rick Bass, Claire Bateman, Charles Baxter, Bruce Beasley, Marvin Bell, Molly Bendall, Pinckney Benedict, Marie-Helene Bertino, Linda Bierds, Diann Blakely, Marianne Boruch, Michael Bowden, Betsy Boyd, John Bradley, Krista Bremer, Geoffrey Brock, Fleda Brown, Kurt Brown, Rosellen Brown, Michael Dennis Browne, Christopher Buckley, Andrea Hollander Budy, E. S. Bumas, Richard Burgin, Stephen Burt, Sarah Busse, Kathy J. Callaway, Bonnie Jo Campbell, Richard Cecil, Kim Chinquee, Jane Ciabattari, Suzanne Cleary, Michael Collier, Billy Collins, Jeremy Collins, Martha Collins, Lydia Conklin, Robert Cording, Stephen Corey, Lisa Couturier, Michael Czyzniejewski, Phil Dacey, Claire Davis, Stuart Dischell, John Drury, Karl Elder, Angie Estes, Ed Falco, Gary Fincke, Ben Fountain, H. E. Francis, Alice Friman, Joanna Fuhrman, John Fulton, Richard Garcia, Scott Geiger, David Gessner, Gary Gildner, Linda Gregerson, Marilyn Hacker, Susan Hahn, Mark Halliday, Jeffrey Hammond, James Harms, Jeffrey Harrison, Michael Heffernan, Daniel L. Henry, William Heyen, Bob Hicok,

11

Kathleen Hill, Jane Hirshfield, Jen Hirt, Daniel Hoffman, Caitlin Horrocks, Maria Hummel, Joe Hurka, Karla Huston, Colette Inez, Mark Irwin, David Jauss, Bret Anthony Johnston, Laura Kasischke, Joy Katz, George Keithley, Brigit Pegeen Kelly, Thomas E. Kennedy, Kristin King, David Kirby, John Kistner, Judith Kitchen, Richard Kostelanetz, Maxine Kumin, Wally Lamb, Caroline Langston, Don Lee, Fred Leebron, David Lehman, Sandra Leong, Dana Levin, Philip Levine, Daniel S. Libman, Gordon Lish, Gerald Locklin, Rachel Loden, William Lychack, Paul Maliszewski, Dan Masterson, Alice Mattison, Tracy Mayor, Gail Mazur, Robert G. McBrearty, Nancy McCabe, Rebecca McClanahan, Erin McGraw, Elizabeth McKenzie, Wesley McNair, Brenda Miller, Nancy Mitchell, Jim Moore, Micaela Morrissette, Joan Murray, Steve Myers, Kent Nelson, Kirk Nesset, Michael Newirth, Aimee Nezhukumatathil, Josip Novakovich, Risteard O'Keitinn, Joyce Carol Oates, Lance Olsen, William Olsen, Dzvinia Orlowsky, Peter Orner, Alan Michael Parker, Edith Pearlman, Benjamin Percy, Lucia Perillo, Patrick Phillips, Donald Platt, Joe Ashby Porter, C. E. Poverman, Sara Pritchard, Kevin Prufer, Lia Purpura, Amanda Rea, James Reiss, Donald Revell, Nancy Richard, David Rigsbee, Atsuro Riley, Jessica Roeder, Jay Rogoff, Gibbons Ruark, Vera Rutsala, John Rybicki, Maxine Scates, Alice Schell, Brandon Schrand, Grace Schulman, Philip Schultz, Lloyd Schwartz, Salvatore Scibona, Maureen Seaton, Anis Shivani, Gary Short, Floyd Skloot, Arthur Smith, Anna Solomon, David St. John, Maura Stanton, Maureen Stanton, Gerald Stern, Pamela Stewart, Leon Stokesbury, Terese Svoboda, Chad Sweeney, Ron Tanner, Katherine Taylor, Elaine Terranova, Susan Terris, Robert Thomas, Jean Thompson, Melanie Rae Thon, Pauls Toutonghi, William Trowbridge, Lee Upton, Laura van den Berg, Dennis Vannatta, G.C. Waldrep, BJ Ward, Don Waters, Michael Waters, Marc Watkins, Charles Harper Webb, Roger Weingarten, William Wenthe, Philip White, Joy Williams, Marie Sheppard Williams, Naomi J. Williams, Eleanor Wilner, S. L. Wisenberg, Mark Wisniewski, David Wojahn, Carolyne Wright, Robert Wrigley, Christina Zawadiwsky, Paul Zimmer

PAST POETRY EDITORS—H.L. Van Brunt, Naomi Lazard, Lynne Spaulding, Herb Leibowitz, Jon Galassi, Grace Schulman, Carolyn Forché, Gerald Stern, Stanley Plumly, William Stafford, Philip Levine, David Wojahn, Jorie Graham, Robert Hass, Philip Booth, Jay Meek, Sandra McPherson, Laura Jensen, William Heyen, Elizabeth Spires, Marvin Bell, Carolyn Kizer, Christopher Buckley, Chase Twichell,

CONTENTS

REGENERATION AT MUKTI

fiction by JULIA ELLIOTT

from CONJUNCTIONS

Call me a trendmonger, but I've sprung for a tree house. My bamboo pod hovers amid galba trees, nestled in jungle but open to the sea, the porch equipped with hemp hammocks. A flowering vine snakes along the railings, pimping its wistful perfume. With a single remote control, I may adjust the ceiling fans, fine-tune the lighting, or lift the plate-glass windows, which flip open like beetle wings. My eco-friendly rental has so many amenities, but my favorite is the toilet: a stainless basin that whisks your droppings through a pipe, down into a pit of copro-phagic beetles. These bugs, bred to feast on human shit, have an en-zyme in their gut that makes the best compost on the planet—a humus so black you'd think it was antimatter. The spa uses it to feed the or-chids in the Samsara Complex. As visitors drift amid the blossoms, we may contemplate the life cycle, the transformation of human waste into ethereal petals and auras of scent.

"Orchids are an aphrodisiac," said a woman at lunch today, her unagi roll breaking open as she crammed it into her mouth, spilling blackish clumps of eel. She had crow's-feet, marionette lines around her mouth, a porn star's enhanced lips.

"Yes," said a man in a sky blue kimono, "I think I read something about that on the website."

"They have orchid dondurma on the menu," I said, scanning the man's face: budding eye bags, sprays of gray at his temples, the gouge of a liver line between his green eyes. I placed him in his early forties.

"Fruit sweetened," he said, "fortified, I believe, with raw mare's milk, if you do dairy."

"Colostrum," I said. "Mostly goat. But I don't ingest sweeteners or juices, only whole fruits."

"My philosophy on dairy," said the woman, waving her chopstick like a conductor, "is that milk is an infant food. I weaned myself ten years ago." Her lush bosom actually heaved, hoisted by the boning of a new-fangled corset.

For some reason (maybe it was the way the woman shook her dead blonde hair like a vixen in a shampoo commercial), I found myself smirking at the man over the centerpiece of sculpted melon. I found myself wondering what he'd look like after completing the Six Paths of Suffering. I couldn't help but picture him shirtless, reclining on a rock beside one of the island's famous waterfalls, his skin aglow from deep cellular regeneration and oxygenation of the hypodermis.

"I'm Red," he said. And he was: flushed along his neck and cheeks, the ripe pink of a lizard's pulsing throat.

The powers that be at Mukti—those faceless organizers of regeneration—have designed the spa so that Newbies don't run into Crusties much. We eat separately, sleep in segregated clusters of cottages, enjoy our dips in the mud baths and mineral pools, our yoga workshops and leech therapy sessions, at different times. As Gobind Singh, our orientation guru, pointed out, "The face of rebirth is the mask of death." And this morning, as I walked the empty beach in a state of above-average relaxation, I spotted my first Crusty crawling from the sea.

Judging by the blisters, the man was in the early stages of Suffering. I could still make out facial features twitching beneath his infections. He had the cartoonish body of a perennial weight lifter, his genitals compressed in the Lycra sling of a Speedo. He nodded at me and dove back into the ocean.

I jogged up the trail that curled toward my tree house. In the bathroom, I examined my face again. I studied familiar lines and folds, pores and spots, ruddy patches and fine wrinkles, not to mention a general ambient sagging that's especially detectable in the morning.

Out beyond the Lotus terrace, the ocean catches the pink of the dying sun. A mound of seaweed sits before me, daubed with pomegranate chutney and pickled narcissus. My waitress is plain, as all the attendants are: plump cheeks and brown skin, hair tucked into a white cap, eyebrows impeccably groomed. Her eyes reveal nothing. Her mouth neither smiles nor bends with the slightest twist of frown. I'm wondering how they train them so well, to be almost invisible, when I note a shadow darkening my table.

"Hi," says the man from yesterday. "May I?"

"Red, right? Please."

The bags under his eyes look a little better. His helmet of hair is losing its sticky sheen. And his bottom lip droops, making his mouth look adorably crooked.

"Just back from leech therapy." He grins. "A bit freaky to have bloodsuckers clamped to my face, but it's good for fatty orbital herniation and feelings of nameless dread."

We laugh. Red orders a green mango salad with quinoa fritters and mizuna-wrapped shad roe. We decide to share a bottle of island muscador. We drink and chat and the moon pops out, looking like a steamed clam.

Though Red is a rep for Clyster Pharmaceuticals, he's into holistic medicine, thinks the depression racket is a capitalist scam, wishes he could detach himself from the medico-industrial complex. I try to explain my career path (human-computer interaction consulting), how the subtleties of creative interface design have worn me out.

"It's like I can feel the cortisol gushing into my system," I say. "A month ago, I didn't have these frown lines."

"You still look youngish," says Red.

"Thanks." I smile, parsing out the differences between *young* and *youngish*. "You too."

Red nods. "It's not that I'm vain. It's more like a state of general depletion. The city has squeezed the sap out of me."

"And life in general, of course, takes its nasty toll."

"Boy does it." Red offers the inscrutable smile of an iguana digesting a fly.

I don't mention my divorce, of course, nor my relocation to a sun-deprived city that requires vitamin D supplementation. I pass the wine and our fingertips touch. Red's wind-mussed hair is a significant improvement, and I imagine kissing him, forgetting that in two weeks we'll both be covered in weeping sores.

I've opened my tree house to the night—windows cranked, jungle throbbing. My blood's up from Ashtanga yoga. A recent dye job has

21

brightened my hair with a strawberry blonde, adolescent luster. Wine-glass in hand, I pace barefooted. And Red: seated on my daybed, his face feral from a five-day beard, lips so pink I've already licked them to test for cosmetics.

Between thumb and index finger he's rolling a globule of sap. Now he's inserting the resin into the bowl of his water pipe. And we take another hit of ghoni, distillate of the puki bloom, a small purple fungus flower that grows from tree frog dung. We drift out onto the porch and fall into an oblivion of kissing.

We shed our clothes, leaving tiny silken mounds on the bamboo planks. Red's penis sways in the humid air. Shaggy thighed, he walks toward the bedroom, where vines creep through the windows, flexing like tentacles in the ocean breeze.

He reclines and smiles, his forehead only faintly lined in the glow of Himalayan salt lamps. We've been hanging out religiously for the past seven days, are addicted, already, to each other's smells. Every night at dinner we begin some delirious conversation that always brings us back to my tree house, toking up on ghoni, chattering into the night. Earlier, discussing the moody rock bands that moved us in our youth, we dis-covered that we attended the same show twenty-seven years ago. Some-how we'd both been bewitched by a band of sulky middle-aged men with dyed black hair who played a broody, three-chord pop. Now we can't stop laughing at how gravely we'd scowled at them from the pit, our gothic costumes bought from the mall.

We've already been infected. Both of us received the treatment two days ago, Red at eleven, me at three. And we met for a lunch of shrimp ceviche between appointments.

All week long, Lissa, the lactose-free blonde, has been chattering about the Hell Realm, wondering, as we all are, when our affliction will begin. She's the kind of person whose head will explode unless she opens her mouth to release every half-formed thought. Her perfume, derived from synthetic compounds, gives me sinus headaches. Just as I sus-pected, she's an actress. I'm almost positive she has fake tits. Even though Red and I beam out a couple vibe, huddled close over menus and giggling, she has no problem plopping down next to him, lunging at the shy man with her mammary torpedoes. And he always laughs at her lame jokes.

This afternoon I have a mild fever and clouds stagnate over the sea.

The meager ocean breeze smells of sewage. I feel like a fool for ordering the monkfish stew, way too pungent for this weather. And Lissa won't stop gloating over her beef kabobs. Red, sunk in silence, keeps scratching his neck. I'm about to exhale, a long, moody sigh full of turbulent messages, when Lissa reaches over her wine flute to poke Red's temple with a mauve talon.

"Look," she says, "bumps."

I see them now: a spattering of hard, red zits. Soon they'll grow fat with juice. They'll burst and scab over, ushering in the miracle of subcutaneous regeneration.

"And my neck itches." Red toys with his collar.

According to the orientation materials distributed by Guru Gobind Singh, the Hell Realm is different for everyone, depending on how much hatred and bitterness you have stored in your system. All that negativity, stashed deep in your organic tissues, will come bubbling to the surface of your human form. The psychosomatic filth of a lifetime will hatch, breaking through your skin like a thousand minuscule volcanoes to spit its lava.

"Time for my mineral mud bath," says Red. And now I see what I could not see before: a row of incipient cold sores edging his upper lip, wens forming around the delicate arch of his left nostril, a cluster of protoblisters highlighting each cheekbone like subtle swipes of blusher.

The Naraka Room smells of boiled cabbage. Twelve of us squat on hemp yoga mats, stuck in the frog pose. Wearing rubber gloves, Guru Gobind Singh weaves among us, pausing here and there to tweak a shoulder or spine.

According to the pamphlet, Gobind Singh has been through the Suffering twice, without the luxury of gourmet meals, around-the-clock therapies, or hands-on guidance from spiritual professionals. Legend has it that he endured the Hell Realm alone in an isolated tree house. Crumpled in the embryo pose for weeks, he unfurled his body only to visit the crapper or eat a bowl of mung beans. His skin's as smooth as the metalized paint that coats a fiberglass mannequin. His body's a bundle of singing muscles. When he walks, he hovers three millimeters off the ground—you have to look carefully to detect his levitational power, but yes, you can see it: The bastard floats.

I can't help but hate him right now. After all, this is the Hell Realm and hatred festers within me. My flesh seethes with blisters. My blood suppurates. My heart is a ball of boiling pus. As I squat in meditation, I tabulate acts of meanness foisted upon me over the decades. I tally betrayals, count cruelties big and small. I trace hurts dating back to elementary school—decades before my first miscarriage, way before my bulimic high school years, long before Dad died and my entire family moved into that shitty two-bedroom apartment. I recede deeper into the past, husking layers of elephant skin until I'm soft and small, a silken worm of a being, vulnerable as a drop of dew quivering on a grass blade beneath the summer sun.

"Reach into the core of your misery," says Gobind Singh. "And you will find a shining pearl."

The pamphlet, *Regeneration at Mukti*, features a color photo of a pupa dangling from a leaf on the cover. Inside is an outline of the bodily restoration process. My treatment has borne fruit. I suffer (oh how I suffer!) from the following: urushiol-induced dermatitis (poison oak rash), dermatophytosis (ringworm), type one herpes simplex (cold sores), cercarial dermatitis (swimmer's itch), herpes zoster (shingles), and trichinosis (caused by intramuscular roundworms). Using a blend of cutting-edge nanotechnology and gene therapy, combined with homeopathic and holistic approaches, the clinicians of Mukti have transmitted controlled infections into my body through oils, fungi, bacteria, viruses, and parasites. As skilled therapists work to reroute my mind-body networks to conduct more positive flows, my immune system is tackling an intricate symphony of infections, healing my body on the deepest subcellular levels: banishing free radicals, clearing out the toxic accumulation of lipofuscins, reinstalling hypothalamus hormones, and replacing telomeres to revitalize the clock that directs the life span of dividing cells.

I itch so much that I want to scrub my body with steel wool. I want to roll upon a giant cheese grater. I'd love to flay myself and be done with the mess. According to the pamphlet, however, not only does scratching interfere with the healing process, but the mental discipline required to refrain from scratching strengthens the chakra pathways that enhance positive mind-body flow.

I have a beautiful dream in which I'm wallowing in a patch of briars. I worm my naked body against thorns, writhe ecstatically in nests of prickly vines. I cry out, convulsing with the sweet sting of pleasure. I wake before dawn, pajamas stuck to my skin.

For me, consciousness is nothing but the seething tides of itchiness, hunger, and thirst, a vague sex drive nestled deep in the misery. I live like an animal from minute to minute, appointment to appointment— breakfast, lunch, and dinner.

Morning: a bowl of oats with flax seeds and blueberries, followed by a kelp bath and castor oil massage. After that: a cabbage poultice administered by experts, who then slather my body with shea butter and wrap it in sea-soaked silk. Before lunch I must descend into the bowels of the Samsara Complex for blood work and nanotech nuclear restructuring. Then a lunch of raw vegetables and fermented organ meats, kombucha with goji and spirulina.

Postlunch I do a volcanic mud bath, then hydrate with a goat milk and basil soak. Next comes a green-tea sensory-deprivation session, then kundalini yoga with Gobind Singh. Staggering from this mind fuck, I head straight for the Samsara Complex for stem-cell work and injections of Vita-Viral Plus. Then a light coconut oil massage and I'm good to go.

At supper I'm startled by Red's appearance. Yes, I've been monitoring his Incrustation. But I wasn't prepared for the new purple swellings around his eyes or the dribbling boils on his chin. Ditto the lip cankers and blepharitis. Of course I'm aware of my own hideousness. Of course I recoil each time I see my face in the mirror (think rotted plums and Spam). And the itching is a constant reminder of my state. Nevertheless, deep in the core of my being, I feel unscathed, as though the process were happening to someone else.

Though Red and I haven't touched each other in weeks, we eat together most nights, fresh from soothing therapies and tipsy on our allotment of organic, sulfite-free wine. We have about an hour until the itching becomes unbearable, then we slump off to our respective tree houses.

Tonight we're enjoying the fugu sashimi with pickled dandelion greens. The humidity hovers around fifty percent, great for our raw skin. And the ocean looks like pounded pewter. Though we're both disgusting, it's like we're mummy wrapped in putrid flesh, our real selves tucked down under the meat costumes.

"I was thinking about the hot springs," says Red. "Since our infections seem to be stabilizing."

25

"Quite a hike," I say. "It'd be hell on our swollen feet."

"You can do most of the way by ATV."

"What?" says Lissa, who's hovering over our table, wearing a full-body catsuit of black spandex, only a few square inches of her polluted flesh visible through eye and mouth holes.

"I wanna go," she says, sitting down on the other side of Red. "I hear the springs help with collagen reintegration."

"And improving the flow between throat and brow chakras," says Red, smiling idiotically.

"Really?" says Lissa. "The third-eye chakra? Cool."

A waitress appears. Lissa orders kway teow with fermented beef. The patio's getting crowded. The music's lame, all synthesized sitars and tabla drum machines. But Red bobs his head in time to the tunes. And Lissa slithers up next to him, gazes raptly at a pic on his iPhone.

"That's you?" she shrieks.

"That's me."

"A mullet. No way!"

"It's an alternative mullet, not a redneck mullet."

"Let's not mince hairs," quips Lissa.

"Ha! Ha! Ha!" cries Red.

And then Lissa flounces off to the bathroom, but not without tousling his hair.

"God." I take a sip of water. "She's dumb."

"She's not as stupid as she puts on," says Red.

"What does that mean?"

"You know, the whole ingenue act."

"She's got to be at least thirty-eight."

"Chronologically, maybe, but not biologically."

I want to drill Red for a more precise number—Does she look thirty-two? twenty-six? nineteen?—but I don't. I grab my purse, a practical satchel that slumps on the table beside Lissa's glittering clutch.

"Don't go," says Red. "I haven't swilled my allotment of vino yet."

"That's OK." I manufacture a yawn. "I'm sleepy."

I weave through the tables without looking back, skirt the rock garden, and stomp down the jungle trail. Deep in the forest, male kibi monkeys howl, adolescents looking for mates. The small nocturnal monkeys spend their days dozing in the hollows of trees, but at night they hunt for insects and baby frogs. They eat their weight in fruit, sip nectar from flowers, sing complex songs that throb with vitality and longing.

26

After a four-mile ATV jaunt, Red and I finally steep neck-deep in a steaming spring. Though Lissa invited herself along, I scheduled our jaunt for a Tuesday, well aware of her strenuous nanotech routine. For the first time in weeks, the itch has left me, and my body flexes, supple as a flame. The hot springs stink, of course, a predictable rotten-egg funk, as sulfur dioxide leaks into the air. But it's worth it. My skin's sucking up nature's beauty mineral, strengthening collagen bundles, improving cellular elasticity. Plus, mist-cloaked mountains swell around us. And though Red's facial blebs have started to ooze, he radiates boyish optimism.

"Look what I brought." He smiles, leaning out of the pool to dig through his rucksack. "Sparkling apple cider. Organic. Though I forgot glasses."

"That's OK. We can swig from the bottle."

"Exchange HSV-1 fluids?"

"And ecthymic bacteria."

"Ugh."

We sit in the mystical vapor, sipping cider and touching toes. The haze softens the hideousness of our faces. Our disembodied voices dart like birds in a cloud. We talk about Red's ex-wife, whose weakness for fey hipster boys is partially responsible for his sojourn at Mukti. I tell him about my money-obsessed ex-husband, who once updated his stock portfolio while I was in the throes of a miscarriage. Through the bathroom mirror of our hotel room in Bali, I could see him in the other room, smirking over his Blackberry. And then I heard him talking to his broker on the phone.

"I'm sorry," says Red.

"I'm over it."

I find his hand under the water. We sit floating in a state of semicontentment. Then we start up with the cider again.

Exceeding our daily allotment of alcohol, we drink until the bottle is empty and the effervescence inside us matches that of the bubbly spring. A plane flies over. The sun infuses our mist shroud with a pearly glow. And then a man steps into the pool, emerging from the steam as from another dimension, clad in dingy cutoff shorts. By all appearances, he's not a patient. His skin has photoaged into a crinkled rind. He's got senile cataracts and wisps of long, gray hair. And when he cracks a smile, we see a wet flash of gums, like a split in a leathery desert fruit.

"I have company today," he says, his accent Californian with a hint of Caribbean patois. "I'm Winter." He extends a gnarled hand. I'm thinking he must be an ancient hippie who retired here before Mukti took off.

"You folks up from the spa, I reckon." He sinks down into the pool.

"How'd you guess?" says Red, and the old man chuckles.

"And you?" I say.

"I'm from around. Got a little cottage up over the way."

Winter tells us he keeps goats, sells cheese and yogurt to Mukti, plus fruit from his orchard and assorted herbs. He asks us how the healing's going. Inquires about the new post office. Wonders what's up with the pirates who've been plaguing the Venezuelan coast.

"Pirates?" says Red.

According to the old man, pirates usually stick to freighters, but have recently drifted up to fleece Caribbean cruise ships.

"Thought I heard something about yachts getting hassled near Grenada," Winter says.

"This is the first we've heard about any pirates," I say, imagining eye-patched marauders, dark ships flying skull-and-crossbones flags.

"Probably just talk," says Winter.

Red checks his watch, says our soak has exceeded the recommended span by four and a half minutes. We say good-bye to Winter, speed off on our ATV.

Seventy-five percent humidity, and the boils on my inner thighs have fused and burst, trickling a yellow fluid. My neck pustules are starting to weep. Choice ecthymic sores have turned into ulcers. I spend my downtime pacing the tree house naked. I shift from chair to chair, day-bed to hammock, listening to the demented birds. A plague of small green finches has invaded the island. They flit through the brush, squawk, and devour berries.

This morning I've neglected my therapies. Though I'm due for nan-otech restructuring in thirty minutes, the thought of putting on clothes, even the softest of silk kimonos, makes my skin crawl. But I do it, even though I know the fabric will be soaked by the time I get to the Samsara Complex. I slip on a lilac kosode and dash down the jungle trail, gritting my teeth.

I pass a few Crusties. I pass a dead turtle, its belly peppered with black ants. I pass an island assistant, lugging her sea-grass basket of eco-friendly cleaning chemicals. Though she, like all the assistants, is a broad, plain-faced woman, the beauty of her complexion startles me. But then I remember that in a few weeks, my sores will scab over. I'll crawl from my shell, pink and glowing as the infant Buddha. I'll jet to the mainland and buy a fleet of stunning clothes, get my hair cut, meet Red for one last rendezvous before we head back to our respective cities. We'll revel in our sweet, young flesh—and then, well, we'll see.

Another evening in paradise and I pick at my grilled fig salad. The ocean is gorgeous, but what's the point? It might as well be a postcard, a television screen, a holographic stunt. Red's pissy too, grumbling over his lobster risotto. And don't get me started on Lissa.

Lissa won't shut up about the pirates. Keeps recirculating the same crap we've heard a hundred times: The pirates have attacked another Carnival cruiser; the pirates have sacked yachts as close as Martinique; the pirates have seized a cargo ship less than ten miles offshore from our very own island. Angered by the resale prospects of boutique med supplies, they've tossed the freight into the sea.

"I always thought pirates were the epitome of sexy," says Lissa, crinkling her carbuncular nose at Red.

"They won't seem so sexy if you run out of Vita-Viral Plus," says Red.

"Unless you think keloid scars are the height of chic," I add.

"But medical supplies are worthless to them," whines Lissa. "What would they gain from another attack?"

"They might attack out of spite," I say.

"Mukti keeps emergency provisions in a cryogenic vault," says Lissa, "in case of hurricanes and other potential disasters."

"Or so the pamphlet promises," says Red, gazing out at the ocean, where a mysterious light beam bounces across the water.

"You think they'd lie to us?" Lissa widens her enormous eyes and runs an index finger down Red's arm. She's a touchy person, I tell myself, who hugs people upon greeting and pinches shy waitresses on the ass.

"I wouldn't be surprised." Red smiles at her and turns back to the sea.

Both Red and I are in the latter stages of contraction when the pirates seize another cargo ship. Our flesh has crisped over with full-body scabbing. We're at that crucial point when collagen production stabilizes, when full-tissue repair and dermal remodeling kick into high gear. Of course, the powers that be at Mukti have not acknowledged the pirate incident. The powers that be have given no special security warnings. They've said nothing about waning provisions or shortages of essential meds. Though the therapists and medical staff carry on as usual, I detect a general state of skittishness—sweat stains in the armpits of their white smocks, sudden jerky movements, faintly perceptible frown lines on faces hitherto blank as eggs.

Rumors spread through the spa like airborne viruses. And one day, a day of high humidity and grumbling thunder, the kind of day when your heart is a lump of obsidian and you wonder why you bothered to get out of bed at all, it becomes common knowledge that the pirates have seized a freighter, that they're negotiating a ransom with Mukti, asking a colossal sum for the temperature-sensitive cargo.

Red and I are on the Lotus Veranda eating zucchini pavé with miso sauce, waiting for poached veal. The waitress slinks over, apologizes, tells us that the dish will be served without capers. Red and I exchange dark looks. We imagine jars of capers from Italy stacked in the belly of a cargo ship, the freighter afloat in some secret pirate cove. And deeper in the bowels of the boat, in a refrigerated vault, shelves full of bio-medical supplies—time-sensitive blood products and cell cultures in high-tech packaging.

All around us, scabby patients whisper about the pirates, reaching a collective pitch that sounds like an insect swarm. Hunched in conspiratorial clusters, they flirt with scary possibilities: spoiled meds, botched stage-five healing, full-body keloid scarring, an appearance that's the polar opposite of that promised by *Regeneration at Mukti*. "Shedding your pupal casing," the pamphlet boasts, "you will emerge a shining creature, renewed in body and spirit, your cell turnover as rapid as a ten-year-old's. Skin taut, wrinkles banished, pores invisible, you will walk like a deva in a pink cloud of light."

I'm in the Samsara Complex for cellular restructuring. There's a problem with the nanobot serum. They keep rejecting vial after vial, or so I've gathered through several hissing exchanges between the bio-med doc and her technicians. When Tech One finally shoots me up, he jabs the needle in sideways, apologizes, then stabs me again.

I stagger into the Bardo Room, where a half dozen Crusties mill among orchids, the floor-to-ceiling windows ablaze. Nobody speaks. The endless ocean glitters beyond, a blinding, queasy green. The light gives me a headache, an egg of throbbing nausea right behind my eyes. I collapse into a Barcelona chair. My skin tingles beneath its husk. I stare down at my hands, dark with congealed blood and completely alien to me. I wonder if I should have stayed as I was—blowing serious bank on miracle moisturizers, going to yoga five times a week, dabbling in the occasional collagen injection.

Of course, it's too late to turn back now. I must focus on positive affirmation, as Guru Gobind Singh so smugly touts. I must not allow my mind to visualize a body mapped with pink, puffy scars. With such an exterior, you'd be forced to hunker deep in your body, like a naked mole rat in its burrow.

Red, fresh from bee-sting therapy, joins me under the shade of a jute umbrella, our eyes protected by wraparound sunglasses. It's too hot to eat, but we order smoked calamari salads and spring rolls with mango sauce. Red's incommunicative. I'm trying to read *Zen and the Art of Aging* on my iPhone, but the sun's too bright. We don't talk about the pirates. We don't talk about our impending Shedding. We don't talk about the chances of scarring, the jaunt to the mainland we've been planning. I tell Red about the monkey I spotted from my tree-house porch last night. I try to discuss the ecological sustainability of squidding. We shoo jhunkit birds from our table and decide to order a chilled Riesling.

More and more Crusties crowd onto the patio. Waitresses hustle back and forth. They no longer inform us when some ingredient is lacking. They simply place incomplete dishes before us with a downward flutter of the eyes. Certain therapies are no longer offered—sensory deprivation and beer baths, for example—but we strive to stay positive.

Although we keep noticing suspicious changes in medical procedures, we prevent cognitive distortions from sabotaging our self-talk. When a bad thought buzzes like a wasp into the sunny garden of our thoughts, we swat the fucker and thump its crushed corpse into the flower bed. And, most importantly, we spend thirty minutes a day visualizing our primary goal: successful mind-body rejuvenation and an unblemished exterior that radiates pure light.

Nevertheless, it's hard to sustain mental focus when your spring rolls lack almonds, when your wine's third-rate, when your dermis burns beneath its crust. It's hard to envision yourself floating in a bubble of celestial light when you look like you've been deep fried. I'm having trouble picturing the crystalline features of the deity. I can't help but notice that the sea smells of sewage, that our table is sticky, that our waitresses are contemptuous, smooth skinned, and pretty in their way, with decades of insolent youth to burn. When Lissa alights at our table in a translucent white kimono, my misery is complete.

But Red only nods at her, keeps staring out at the empty sea.

I'm studying his profile when I spot a dark figure lurching from a clump of pink hibiscus. Black skin, green shorts, ammo vest. The man lugs a Kalashnikov. He's yelling in Spanish. Other pirates emerge from the landscaping, waving guns and machetes. One of them screams fragments of English: *Surrender, you scab-covered dogs.* Lanky, with a dramatic cheek scar, he tells us to put our wallets on the table, along with all cell phones, iPods, Blackberries, handheld gaming devices, and jewels. Random pirates fire their guns into the air.

In one convulsive movement, patients start rifling pockets and purses, removing rings and bracelets, plunking valuables onto tables. Then we sit with hands behind our backs as the bandits have instructed. We don't flinch as they rip designer sunglasses from our faces. We squint with stoicism at the boiling sea while they fill their rucksacks with treasure. Shadows grow longer. The sun sinks. The jhunkit birds, emboldened by our immobility, descend upon the tables to peck at canapés.

When the pirates finally creep off into the jungle, crouched in postures of cartoonish stealth, the waitresses spring into action. They bustle about distributing bottled water. They assure us that security has been summoned. They fill our wineglasses, wipe bird shit from our tables, spirit away our dirty plates. The sky flushes pink. Lissa trembles like a Chihuahua until Red drapes a friendly arm over her back. He's just being courteous, I tell myself, as I wait for this contact to end.

A woman weeps quietly at the edge of the patio, then she blows her nose and orders shrimp dumplings in ginger broth.

According to the pamphlet, the final days before Shedding should be days of intense relaxation—no medical procedures, no exhilarating therapies, no excursions. Even extreme dining is discouraged. It's difficult to drift like a feathery dandelion seed when Mukti's security forces have crawled out of the woodwork into our sunny paradise.

They've always been here, of course, lurking in the shadows, monitoring the island from subterranean surveillance rooms, but now they loiter openly in their khaki shorts, handguns only partially concealed by oversized tropical shirts.

Yesterday, while enjoying an aloe vera bath in the Bodhi Herb Garden, I heard a crude snicker. I gazed up through a tendril of sarsaparilla to glimpse the smirking face of a security guard. There he was, licking an ice-cream cone, his mustache dotted with pearls of milk. And now, as I float in the Neti Neti Lagoon, stuck in step two of the Instant Calming Sequence, I hear a security guard barking into her cell phone. I count to six and wait for her to finish her conversation. When I start over with a fresh round of uninterrupted breathing, her ringtone bleeps through the gentle thatch of birdsong. So I switch to Microcosmic Orbit Meditation, envisioning a snake of light slithering through my coccyx. Now the security guard is laughing like some kind of donkey. I open my eyes. Gaze up into palms and spot a tiny camera perched next to a cluster of fruits. Its lens jerks back and forth like the head of a nervous bird.

In addition to the dread of pirates charging through the bush, in addition to the distraction of security guards and fears of type-I scarring, we must also worry about the weather as the island's now on hurricane watch—or so the powers that be informed us this morning. The ocean breeze has become a biting, sandy wind. A weird metallic scent blows off the sea, and I get the feeling that the island's swathed in bad karma. Plus, a few Crusties, having shed their husks, have been jetted to the mainland without the Rapture Ceremony—a ritual designed to reassure remaining Crusties that their golden time will come, that they too will walk in flowing robes, their silky necks garlanded with narcissus.

Yesterday afternoon, instead of gathering on the beach to watch the smooth-skinned devas depart in the Ceremonial Boat, we crowded into the lobby of the small airport. Through a plate-glass window, we observed two devas dashing from flower-decked golf carts toward a commuter jet, their faces shrouded by scarves and sunglasses. Security guards swarmed, their tropical shirts easy to spot. And rumor has it that one of the devas, a famous movie star, was being whisked off to California where she'll resume her career as a romantic comedy queen—blonde icon of feminine joie de vivre, laughing in the sun.

Red, in the final throes of his remodeling phase, has a TSF of 99.6 percent. His exterior has the golden huskiness of a pork rind. And now, as he scans the endless ocean, his beautiful green eyes burn behind his scabby mask. He's barely touched his scrambled tofu. He takes long, dreamy slurps of mango smoothie. I know he'll be jetting off to the mainland soon. Once there, he won't be able to contact me by phone or e-mail, the Mukti contract dictates, so we've made arrangements, booking reservations at the Casa Bougainvillea.

I keep picturing that moment when we'll meet by the pool at sunset. I keep picturing Red reclined beside the waterfall featured on the hotel's brochure. First he'll look startled. Then he'll smile as his eyes run up and down my body. He'll bask in the vision of a female epidermis refortified with type III collagen and glowing like the moon. Though I haven't worn jewel tones for years, I'll highlight the infantile pallor of my skin with a scarlet sheath dress. I'll wear a choker of Burmese rubies. Dye my hair auburn, paint my nails crimson, wear lipstick the color of oxygenated blood.

After we revel in the softness of a ten-minute kiss, we'll drink Romanée Conti under the stars.

Yesterday I stood in the airport lobby, watching Red hop from a flower-decked golf cart and then scurry through strong wind to Mukti's commuter jet. Kaffiyeh-style headgear and huge sunglasses concealed his face. When he turned from the platform to wave, a shadow passed over him, and then he dipped into the jet with a sly smile. I have no idea how his Shedding went. I have no idea what his refurbished carnality looks like, though I've seen his Facebook pics, his high school yearbook photos, a few snapshots of the young Red rock climbing in Costa Rica.

Lissa too has been spirited away—nubile and golden, I fear. Though she was obscured by a chiffon Lotus robe, I have the sick suspicion that she's gone through her Shedding unscathed. That she looks gorgeous. That she'll stalk Red at the Casa Bougainvillea, appearing naked and luminous beneath his balcony in a courtyard crammed with flowering shrubs.

And now, as the few remaining Crusties huddle in the basement of the Skandha Center, awaiting the wrath of a category-four hurricane named Ophelia, Gobind Singh lectures us on the Deceptive Singularity of the Self.

"The Self you cling to," says Gobind Singh, "is an empty No Self, or Shunya, for the True Self does not differentiate between Self and Other, which is not the same, of course, as the No Self."

Gobind Singh sighs and takes a long glug of spring water, for we are the Stubborn Ones, unable to take pleasure in the Shedding of Others, greedy for our own transformation. According to Gobind Singh, the True Self must revel in the Beauty of the Devas, even if we ourselves do not attain True Radiance during this cycle, because the True Self makes no distinction between Self and Other.

According to Gobind Singh's philosophy, I should delight in the divine copulation of Red and Lissa, which is probably taking place right this second on one-thousand-thread-count sheets. I should yowl with joy at the thought of their shuddering, simultaneous orgasm. I should partake in the perkiness of Lissa's ass as she darts from the bed, turning to give Red a full-frontal display before disappearing into the humongous bathroom to pee. According to Gobind Singh, their ecstasy is my ecstasy.

Glowing with self-actualization, floating a few millimeters above the bamboo flooring, Gobind Singh weaves among us. We sit in full lotus, five sullen earthbound Crusties, slumped in our own hideousness. We fidget and pick at our flaking shells. The second the guru turns his back, we roll our eyes at each other.

And when the winds of Hurricane Ophelia pick up, shaking the building and howling fiercely enough to blot out the throbbing of electronic tablas, we can't control the fear that grips us. All we can think about is literally saving our skins. As the electricity flickers and the storm becomes a deluge, Gobind Singh tells us that all men, no matter how wretched, have a Buddha Embryo nestled inside them, gleaming and indestructible as a diamond.

I wake alone in the basement of the Skandha Center, calling out in the darkness for the others. I bang my shins against their empty cots. Upstairs in the dim hallway, I discover sloughed Casing, shreds of what looks like crinkled snakeskin littering the jute carpet. I pick my way toward the light. Hurricane Ophelia has shattered the floor-to-ceiling lobby windows, strewing the floor with shards of glass.

Out on the wrecked patio, windblown chairs have been smashed against the side of the building. And birdcalls whiffle through the air.

"Hello," I yell, but no one answers.

The Samsara Complex is empty. So is the Lotus Lounge; both buildings battered by the storm.

I jog down a jungle trail toward the Moksha Jasmine Grove. There, a natural spring trickles from the lips of a stone Buddha. Pink birds flit through the garden. The statue squats in a pool, surrounded by trellises of Arabian jasmine that have miraculously survived the hurricane. Raindrops sparkle on leaves. The garden is a locus of peace and light.

From the deepest kernel of my being, I crave water. My throat's parched. My skin burns. And I know that my time has come. I feel pregnant with the glowing fetus of my future self.

I shed my robe. I step into the blue pool. I sink neck-deep into the shallow water, mimicking the pyramid structure of the seated Buddha, face-to-face with his stone form. I drink from the spring until my thirst is quenched. And then I breathe through my nose, fold my hands into a Cosmic Mudra. Counting each inhalation, I become one with the water.

My body is like a pool's surface, its brilliance dulled only by a skin of algae.

My body is like a fiery planet, casting off interstellar dust.

Slowly, I rub myself, chanting the Bodhisattva vows:

I vow to liberate all beings, without number.
I vow to uproot all endless blind passions.
I vow to penetrate, beyond measure, the Dharma gates.
And the Great Way of Buddha, I vow to attain.

My Casing begins to pull away. I don't look at my uncovered flesh. I squeeze my eyelids shut to avoid temptation and keep on chanting, focused on the radiance pulsing within. In my mind's eye I see a glimmer of movement, a hazy form with human limbs, a new and improved woman emerging from the murk—glorious and unashamed.

On the count of three, I open my eyes.

Nominated by Conjunctions

WE ARE ALL OF US PASSING THROUGH*

by HARRY CREWS

from THE GEORGIA REVIEW

I came through Monarch Pass in Colorado, fifteen thousand feet high and fourteen miles out of the nearest town—I came through on a 650cc Triumph motorcycle about dusk dark in late September of 1958. It was snowing lightly. I was freezing. I had been on the road for a little over a year, driven there by what you call your higher educational system.

I have never cared what horse a man was riding, only how he rode him. Because that is the pretty and human thing. I got out of the Marine Corps in 1956, and went to the University of Florida and found it full of granite men riding granite horses. Deliver me from men who are without doubt. Doubt makes a man decent. My most steadfast conviction is that every man ought to doubt everything he holds dearest. Not all the time, but now and then. *Sometime*. With rare exceptions, though, professors treat their disciplines as closed subjects, as though nothing had been written or discovered or reevaluated about their disciplines since the day they were awarded their PhDs. Consequently, universities have become communities of men with answers instead of—as they should be—communities of men with questions.

Anyway, I couldn't bear it after my sophomore year. There didn't seem to me to be any difference at all between, say, a professor of history and a sergeant in the Marine Corps. Both men's worlds were carefully proscribed; both men knew exactly what you ought to do and say, and where you ought to squeeze your juice. So one fine spring day I

---

* From "Take 38," an unpublished collection of Harry Crews's autobiographical writings in the Harry Crews Collection, Hargrett Rare Book and Manuscript Library, University of Georgia.

got on a Triumph motorcycle and left. Eighteen months later I limped back into the University of Florida purified and holy, ready to continue with what society expected of me.

But that evening coming through Monarch Pass, freezing, I was still being tried and purged. I was not pure, and even though I was hurt bad, I had not yet developed the limp by which every saint is known. About every two miles I had been getting off the bike, going around behind the machine and holding on to the twin exhausts with my gloved hands. My fingers were numb, had been numb for the last twenty miles. Coming from Georgia, I knew something about frostbite, and I thought that was what was in my fingers. It scared me. I kept thinking of myself handless. So I stopped the Triumph every two miles until it got so cold that when I stopped I couldn't get off. I literally could not swing my leg over the seat. A freezing, driving wind was roaring right into my face and eventually it simply benumbed me to the point that when I tried to talk to myself (you know the kind of thing: "Come on now! Not much further. Don't be such a pussy, suck it up and go!") I couldn't say the words. I couldn't feel my lips. I could make sounds, but not words.

There was no place to stop. It was straight down off the mountain toward the little town whose lights I could already see. But like everything else it did end, and when I got down into the town, it was much warmer, though it must have been snowing for days because snow was banked on the trees and against buildings and over the curbs. I cruised through that warm place feeling good.

You have to be on the road seventeen hours with no place to stop to know what it means to drive between neon-lit storefronts and see houses, side by side and permanent as taxes, to realize how warm *images* can make you. Never mind what the weather was; this was where people lived—you see their windows, see their cars parked in carports and driveways. I tooled around for probably an hour, feeling good just knowing I wasn't going to die, frozen in some Midwest wilderness.

I didn't know exactly where I was going. I had a sleeping bag and a coffee-pot rolled behind me on the bike. But I wasn't about to risk myself in that snow again. I was in an alien land, and I was scared. I wanted to go where it was safe. I could go to a hotel, but that cost money, and I was headed for Mexico with the little score I'd made working for Hunt's Foods Inc. in Hayward, California, which is right down the road from Oakland, which is right down the road from San Francisco. I didn't want to spend any more than I had to. There were missions, but I had unpleasant memories of all the missions I had stayed in, because they made you pray for your breakfast. I mean you didn't *have* to pray, but you did unless you wanted to hurt some religious freak's feelings. And since I have never been a basically cruel person, I've always shown whatever respect I could muster when the old lady (sometimes an ancient gentleman, but for some unknowable reason usually an old, old lady in some sort of uniform you did not recognize) would get you together in the morning—whiskey drunks, winos, pill heads, runaways, syphilitic wanderers, retards, and whatever else had wandered in during the night—and make you go through obsequious, cowardly, belly-crawling rituals where you told Jesus that you hated yourself and would gladly kill yourself, stamp out the vermin of your life with knife, gas, long fall (anything above the tenth floor) if only it was not a sin against His Holy Person.

That left the YMCA. The worst thing that could happen to you at the YMCA was that you'd get sucked off. I wonder how many people who contribute to the Young Men's Christian Association (of course the people who contribute to the YMCA never stay there) know that if you are a young man, you dare not go to the Young Men's Christian Association unless you are willing to take it in the ass or give it in the mouth?

I am not easily provoked to outrage, but I say categorically now, once-and-for-all, that my *general* experience with YMCAs around the country is that if you drop your soap in the shower, don't pick it up. You do, and at least three guys will be injured in the rush that will result from them storming to violate your asshole.

None of which kept me from staying in them. The YMCAs' great attraction was that they were incredibly cheap and you didn't have to pray for your breakfast. So I was cruising through those warm streets of that little town, looking for a YMCA. And found one. They advertise well. The one I found was on a busy corner downtown housed in what looked like it had once been a private home that was a kind of mansion, a huge pile of marble with columns. And in the back of the thing two wings had been added—low ugly modern brick structures built onto the original house.

I went up on the sidewalk under a tree—I remember it as a kind of oak, but I don't know if they have oaks in that part of the world—and there I shut the Triumph down, the first time it had been shut down that long day of riding, and covered it with a poncho. With some difficulty I got off, untied my bedroll, and went inside. A tall, thin, pale young man stood behind a desk and watched me come across the lobby.

When I got to him he said: "You can't bring fresh meat in here."

"What?" I said, truly not hearing him.

My ears were ringing from the wind, and would ring on into the next day. If you rode every day your ears always had the sound of the wind in them, because that was before the day when every motorcycle rider by law had to wear a crash helmet. I wore a knitted black navy watch cap and it did nothing against the wind, so I had a lot of trouble hearing what was being said to me.

"What?"

"You can't bring fresh meat in here."

Now I thought the guy was talking about a woman. I thought he was telling me that I couldn't bring a woman to my room. I was trembling and exhausted, and taking a woman to my room was the last thing I had on my mind. After seventeen hard hours on a bike you can't even jerk off, much less confront a woman.

So I told him: "Oh, I'm not thinking about that. Honestly, that's the last thing I'd do. I'm new here, I don't even know anybody."

"What?" he said.

"I'm not from this part of the world," I told him. "I don't know anybody. Where would I get a woman?"

"Where would you get a what?" he said.

We went on about ten minutes like that there at the desk, and I won't inflict all of what we said on you. Enough to say that he thought I was a hunter. Apparently there are a lot of people that time of the year who shoot—I don't know, deer, bear, and other such—and he thought I was one of them. He meant by fresh meat exactly that: freshly killed animals from the woods, and if I had any or was going to have any, I couldn't bring'm into the YMCA.

I guess he had every right to think that. Here is what I looked like coming across the lobby of the YMCA toward him:

At that time I'd been on the road about ten months, working at whatever jobs I could find, washing dishes in Cody, Wyoming, mining salt just outside of Redwood City, California things like that. My hair was down to my shoulders, and I had not shaved since I left the university. Under the knitted black watch cap I had a pair of World War Two goggles to keep the wind out of my eyes. These, when I walked into the YMCA that night, were pulled down and strung from around my neck. I was wearing a sheepskin-lined flight jacket that I'd bought out of a surplus store, a great jacket that I got cheap because the zipper didn't work. I had it held together with four enormous safety pins, the kind used in laundries, about three inches long. The leather of the jacket

40

was peeling and had a tear in the shoulder that let the sheepskin show through. My Levi's hadn't been washed in weeks and were stiff with motorcycle grease and dirt from the road. The inside of the right leg of the Levi's had been pretty much eaten away—ragged holes from knee to ankle—by battery acid from the bike. The engineering boots I had on made me walk even stranger than I ordinarily walk—and I walk pretty strange anyway—because the left boot had a sole made out of a quarter of inch of lead from the time when I raced the Triumph in Northern California—just outside Sacramento—on a dirt track anytime I could pay the entry fee to it. On a track you always run counterclockwise, and the lead sole on the left boot is so you can put that foot down and keep it down while turning the track without getting it maimed, and while it helps you in a race, it had no function at all once you left the track but I had kept it on for no other reason than all the other misplaced macho bullshit that was coursing through my blood in those days.

It made me feel good, invincible, to limp down a sidewalk with that left boot shooting a few sparks and making a loud and unseemly noise. Too, in the back of my mind, I think I had the notion that I might stomp some son-of-a-bitch's face in with it, somebody who really deserved stomping. To this day I've never stomped anybody and, I'm pleased to say, no longer want to. But for years I was always on the lookout for the possibility. I was nothing if not a violence freak. But then you've got to understand this was before Peace and Pacifism had become respectable. I mean you didn't kill or mutilate indiscriminately, but for those who deserved it (and I don't remember how one determined who deserved it in those days and who did not, I only remember it was an issue)—for those who deserved it, you always finished off with a good stomping.

"What is the difference in the room and the dormitory?" I asked.

"Difference," said the pale young man.

"Price," I said.

"The room is four dollars. The dormitory is a dollar and a quarter."

"The dormitory," I said.

I got the key and the directions to one of the ugly wings behind the house I mentioned earlier. The dormitory turned out not to be a true dormitory at all. It was a moderately large room, maybe twenty feet by twenty feet, with double-decker beds lined cheek to jowl down both sides so that only a small aisle was left. At the end of the aisle was a cheapo chest of drawers with a small mirror on top. The light in the ceiling was uncovered. A film of musty odor—not entirely unpleasant—hung over the room. None of the beds were occupied.

The clerk in the lobby had given me towels and directions to the showers, but I was hurt too bad from the day's ride to care about a shower. I dropped my stuff on the floor, stripped down to some sour drawers that had really seen a lot of action, hit the light by the door and was asleep almost before my head touched the pillow, which, incidentally, was covered with a white case with a green legend stenciled across one end that read: STOLEN FROM THE YOUNG MEN'S CHRISTIAN ASSOCIATION.

Even exhausted, I'm a light sleeper. Anything brings me instantly awake. The room I was in was utterly dark, and I must have opened my eyes simultaneously with the wedge of yellow light splitting the room, followed for the briefest instant by the silhouette of a man. He didn't turn on the light, which I took for a courtesy, and half asleep again already, I heard him drop a shoe, another one. A belt buckle hit the floor. He was directly across the narrow aisle from me, but the room was so dark not even an outline of him was evident as I heard the springs give under his weight.

I was just about to slip under and be asleep again when I heard a sound like a tire had been punctured by an ice pick: SSSSSSsssssssssss! My eyes popped open. My heartbeat jacked up a notch. I wasn't sure if I had heard what I thought I heard or not. Maybe I'd been dreaming. I tentatively closed my eyes and was beginning to relax when I heard a sound a child might make imitating a train whistle: OOOOOOoooooooooOOOOOOoooOOOOOOO!

Now there was no mistake. I *had* heard something, and it clearly came from the guy across the aisle. I turned slowly and strained to see him but the room was hermetically sealed in darkness. My whole body drew tight. I became aware of sounds I had not heard before: pipes banging somewhere through the walls, a creak now and again as though the building was settling, a car horn.

Nothing else came from across the aisle though. I was beginning to convince myself that there was a reason for the guy doing whatever he had done, and that I ought to ignore it and go on to sleep because he was through now and it wouldn't happen again, when a series of grunts rocked the air around my head. UUnnt! UUnnt! TURCH! KaGUNK! Then silence. I was half-sitting in my bunk by the time the grunts stopped.

"Something wrong over there?" My voice had a little trembling croak in it, and it was only when I heard it that I realized I was scared. There was no answer to my question. Instead, I heard deep regular breathing. I eased down on the pillow and waited. When it came, it was the imitation of a machine gun. Uh-uh-uh-uh-uh-uh-uh-uh-uh-uh!

"Hey fella," I said. No answer. "Hey, fella, what's your trouble?" To that, I got as a reply the original sound, that of a tire being punctured.

"Hey," I called. And then in a kind of scream: "Hey!"

"What is it?" The voice came out of the dark not more than three feet from where I lay. "What's the matter with you?"

I don't know what I expected, but whatever it was, it was a long way from what I got. The voice was not much more than a whisper and almost without inflection. But it was more than antagonistic. It was venomous. Evil. I felt cautiously over the side of the bed for my boot with the lead sole. But I couldn't find it. I couldn't even find the boot that didn't have the lead sole. And from across the aisle there now came a kind of air raid, full of diving planes and sirens and whistling bombs.

I figured I had to be firm with him, but even thinking that firmness was what was needed, it was with tremendous misgivings that I said, rather loudly: "All right, *you*, knock off the goddam bullshit!"

I knew I'd made a mistake the moment it was out of my mouth, because the silence following my voice was filled with a great in-suck of breath, ending in a strangled gasp. And I knew I was locked in the dark with madness.

"What did you say?" the voice asked, so filled with passion it could hardly speak.

I had eased to a sitting position, getting ready to bolt for the door, when I heard the springs on the top bunk stretch and recoil as if they were being used like a trampoline. Then I heard two naked feet hit the floor half a room away by the door.

"I asked you what it was you said?"

"Look," I said, "I'm just passing through, and . . . "

"We are all, *all* of us passing through," the voice said, "but . . ."—the voice had taken on a malicious smile—". . . I just happen to be between you and the door. You ain't passing nowhere."

I probably would have been afraid anyway, but the darkness made it much worse. I only had the voice to go on. I wished I knew what he looked like, something about him. But all I had was the voice and the certain conviction that he was crazy.

"What do you want?" I said. "What the hell *do* you want?"

43

I was still being firm, or trying to.

"Ah, my friend," said the voice, "it is you who want. I do not want. I have never wanted."

"Then why are you between me and the door?" I said. "Why did you say I wasn't passing *anywhere*?"

"Your problem is questions," the voice said.

He was coming toward me. I retreated along the aisle, toward the rear of the room. He was a big mother. Although *actually*, I could see nothing; nonetheless I was being stifled and overwhelmed by what I could feel in the aisle in front of me. I thought I could smell him too. I *could* smell him: something hairy, full of wood-musk, the sweet suffocating smell that only wild things have.

"You just keep on asking them questions, don't you," the voice said.

My back touched the wall. There was no place to go.

"Look," I said, trembling. "What do you want?"

"What I want, you can't give."

This is not easy to say, even this long time after the fact, but I was nearly weeping from terror. It all seemed so silly that I had come this long way to be summarily butchered in a dark room by a man I did not know, had never seen, against whom I had no grievance, and who could not possibly have a grievance against me.

"I've never done anything to you," I said.

"Oh, but you have. You have."

"You don't know my name," I said.

"I did not say I knew your name."

"*My name is Harry Crews! My name is Harry Crews!*" I screamed my name out of a hysterical compulsion, because I suddenly knew that he must think I was someone else.

"Is that really your name?" the voice asked.

"Yes," I cried, "yes. You've got the wrong man. You've come for the wrong man."

"No," the voice came back, "it is for you I've come. You and all your kind."

My kind? My *kind*? I thought wildly. What can that mean? What *can* it mean?

"I don't know what you mean," I said, pressing into the wall, my sweat making it slick. "I don't understand."

"I don't expect you to understand." The voice was patient now, quieter. "I only expect you to believe."

And I believed. I believed it was dark and I was going to die. I believed I'd never know the face of the thing that killed me, its name, or why. *They'd* know who it was. *They* would catch it, name it, discover its secret. But I, alone and ignominiously weeping, would have death fall from its hand onto my blind head, knowing nothing.

It was too much to bear, and in a spasm of cowardice, I charged away from the wall, my eyes squeezed shut, straight down the aisle toward the door. I expected to hit something—someone—but didn't. To this day, I do not know why I didn't, because the aisle was too narrow to pass anyone without touching him. I jerked open the door and raced down the hall without ever looking back. I had some thought that he might be behind me, and if he was, I sure as hell didn't want to know if he was gaining on me.

The lobby was empty. I saw no clock but I could *feel* that it had to be three or four in the morning. The desk clerk was dozing in a metal chair behind the desk. And I scared him every bit as bad as I'd been scared by vaulting the desk and landing more or less straddle of his lap. His eyes popped open and he started yelping and slobbering and struggling to get up but he was too thin to be able to move me. And I, dressed only in my moldy shorts, hair and beard tangled, twisted across my face, had him half by the shirt-front and half by the throat, yelping and slobbering too, nose to nose with him.

He finally did in desperation unseat me from his lap but couldn't get loose of my hands, so that we hopped, skipped, and grotesquely danced from behind the desk and out into the lobby and around the lobby, screaming and talking at once, both of us trying to find out what was happening here in the middle of an otherwise quiet night at the YMCA. Ultimately, we calmed enough to talk.

"Who?" he said.

"In my room," I said again.

"It's you," he said in disgust.

"Damn right it's me—what's left of me after what you put in my room."

"How dare you come out here like that," he said. "You can't behave like this at the YMCA."

"You put a crazy man in there with me?" I said.

"You didn't bathe," he said, a little sour anger settling on his mouth.

"I'm going to kill you if you don't listen," I screamed.

He had been bouncing around on the balls of his feet, full of nervous gestures, his thin arms and legs jerking about, but then he got very quiet and said in an even voice: "What did you say to me?"

45

I had the awful sense of a distorted funhouse mirror where you see the same image retreating into the glass, perfectly reproduced and growing smaller and smaller into infinity.

"I'm trying to get you to go out there and take that person out of my room."

"You threatened me," he said.

"I've *been* threatened," I said. "This whole place is a threat."

"The YMCA is not a threat," he said. "And I'll have to ask you to get out of the lobby dressed like that."

"Do you know who's in my room?"

He thought about that and then said: "No."

"I don't either," I said.

He pinched his chin with his pale, rather blue fingers. "I believe you're in the dormitory" he said.

"That's right," I said. "That's where I am."

He spoke with numbing rationality: "A dormitory by its very nature will have *many* people. They may not live up to your expectation. I never said they would."

"But will they try to kill me?"

"Did someone try to kill you?"

"Yes."

"How did he try to accomplish this deed?"

"Well," I said, "he didn't actually *try* to kill me."

"I see," he said. "Did someone at the YMCA threaten to kill you?"

"No," I said, sensing already I was defeated.

"I thought not," he said.

"But there was a guy in there making strange noises and when I tried to ask him what was wrong, he started shouting and hemmed me up." I sounded like such a weak stick, it shamed me.

"Hemmed you up?" he said.

"Got between me and the door," I said.

"And you came to *me* for help?"

I could see his point, had already *seen* his point. I outweighed the clerk by about forty pounds. I was also hairy and had a dangerous sole on my left boot.

I waved my hand off vaguely toward the wing where the madman was. "Are you going to see about it or not?"

"Of course I'll have a look if you like." He was enjoying himself immensely. "Besides," he said, "it seems the only way I'll get you out of the lobby." He added as an afterthought as we were going down the hall, "You really ought not to come out here dressed like that."

When we got to the room the light was on. The clerk turned to me and said: "Is that the man who had you cornered and threatened?"

A man about the size of a jockey sat on the bed opposite mine. His legs, skinny as a child's and marked with blue veins, were hardly long enough to let his toes brush the floor.

"I don't know," I said. "But I don't think so."

"You don't know?" said the clerk.

I could feel myself blushing. "The light was turned out," I said. "I never saw him."

The little man sat watching us. A sharp pale tongue kept darting over his lips. And the light seemed to hurt his eyes, which he had shaded now with a paper-thin hand.

"Billy," said the clerk, "do you know this man?" He pointed at me.

The little man said: "He turned on the light. And he went away. So I prayed for him."

"See?" I demanded. "That's crazy."

"That's Billy," said the clerk with a kind of sighing patience which seemed to imply it was something I should have known all along. He took me by the elbow and led me out in the hall. "We don't even register Billy," he said. "He just comes and goes as he will. I can assure you he's harmless."

"How is it you're able to tell me that?" I wanted to know.

"He thinks he's Jesus Christ," said the clerk.

"Christ," I said.

"Right," he said.

"I was swearing" I said.

"Don't swear," he said, "this is the YMCA."

"Right," I said.

I didn't want to tell him, inasmuch as this *was* the YMCA, that the fact that the little man thought he was Jesus Christ was no assurance to me at all. When I think of Jesus Christ, I think of the Byzantine Christ, He of the hooked nose and burning eyes. Let others think of Him as a gentle God-Man with a palm leaf and a donkey, if they can. For my part, I can't.

Obviously I couldn't tell all of that to the clerk. It would not have applied. Most of what I think usually doesn't. I don't know what the point is, but whatever it is, I'm usually not on it, but beside it.

"Now go on back in there and have a good night's sleep," said the clerk, "and don't ever come into another lobby of a YMCA unless you're properly dressed." This last was delivered harshly, sternly. Quite clearly, he was no longer intimidated by me, if he had ever been.

I went back into the room where the little man still sat on the side of the bed. I looked at him, he at me. We said nothing. I was embarrassed, and furious with myself because of it. I had been properly shat upon by everybody concerned, and here I was embarrassed.

"I'm turning out the light," I said.

The little man didn't answer me. Instead he lay down in his bed and stretched out flat on the covers, his hands folded funeral-like on his skinny chest. I watched to see if his eyes were going to close. They didn't. They didn't seem to be blinking either. He was lying unnaturally still and straight. I turned out the light anyway and went to my bunk.

No sooner had I lain down than The Voice said: "They think I think I'm Jesus, but I don't think I think I'm Jesus."

"Shit," I said, and jumped for the light. I never took my eye off him as I jerked into my clothes and grabbed up my bedroll.

"I let'm think it," he said as I was going out the door. "But I haven't said who I am yet."

As I was going by the desk, the clerk, who was dozing again in the metal chair, looked up.

"You leaving *now*?" he asked.

"He doesn't think he's Christ," I said, "and you're a goddamn fool."

It was still dark, but it had quit snowing. I dug the Triumph out from under the snow-covered tarp, and spent thirty minutes kicking the engine before it caught. I was bone tired. My head hurt. My eyeballs felt pitted, and there was a skin of fuzz on my tongue and teeth. I had had no shower and my armpits under the sheepskin jacket were sticky and lined with a dirty rash. There was no place to go to rest. I went to an all-night diner and ate two bennies with a cup of black coffee, and sat there thinking how the night had been wasted.

As soon as the bennies got my heart cranked up and my eyeballs rushing, I'd go south through Raton Pass into New Mexico and on into El Paso and from there straight through the desert a little over a hundred miles to the town of Chihuahua, in the state of Chihuahua, Mexico. Sitting in the diner, I could see it clearly, the bennies burning the road clean in my head, lying straight between sand and cactus after you left Ciudad Juarez, but I was angry and would remain angry for weeks because I thought that everything had been wasted and undone and

48

that I had given up a night's rest and no inconsiderable part of my manhood for nothing there in the YMCA.

But of course nothing is ever wasted. Ten years later, when I would start the first novel I was able to publish, *The Gospel Singer*, the little man in the YMCA sat up in his bed and up in my head as alive and immediate as he had ever been, and out of his skinny legs and maniacal voice I made the character of Didymus, and it was in the person of Didymus that I first felt the miracle that keeps fiction writers writing fiction, the miracle of the alphabet turning into blood.

If not better than wine, it's at least as good.

Nominated by The Georgia Review

BEYOND AND BEYONDER

by MATT HART

from SMARTISH PACE

Beyond and beyonder, appearances and depths.
The vision looking out is the same as looking in
and what one sees depends on the eyes: who's looking?
Philosophy, it kills us, but it also lifts us up. Geometry

at angles, without cutting, through smoke, and physics
and wonder do we even exist at all? There are
a thousand ways, and more, to sing and to song. Some days
the heart alights in a tree, and others the tree is already

on fire. It comes as no surprise, then: what's beautiful
is always both crash site and landing, memorial
and monument, lighthouse and warning. The sense
of our senses both exuberant and dire. In us

the wildest bewilderment glistens. The wilderness
transforms as the architect explodes. Every single one
of us a hymn to achievement, so weird with potential,
so wired to wolfish-ness, illimitable goodness. In life

as in art, what's important are the choices, the actions
that follow and the forms as they glow. Let us consider
the past as we go, and let us consider the future
at our fingers. What do we want for the next generation,

and the next generation's next generation? When they listen
to our music, when they open our books, remember
our wars and treaties and image, will they find there
a lightness or an absence where we fluttered? An elegy

in which to drown? An ode to something better? This
isn't in darkness, but in love, it's a promise. The human
predicament is nothing short of marvelous. We get to decide
how it goes.

Nominated by Smartish Pace, Chad Sweeney

PUNCHLINE

fiction by ERIN MCGRAW

from THE KENYON REVIEW

And this our life, exempt from public haunt,
Finds tongues in trees, books in the running brooks,
Sermons in stones, and good in everything.

—*As You Like It*, William Shakespeare

When Father Phil Castor counseled his parishioners, he advised them to pay attention to the things they didn't want to think about—the shadows, the echoes, the uneasy feelings. "That place where your mind skids away? The thing you won't even get close to? That's where your trouble is. That's the thing to notice." Seeing the complacent look seep across the face of whoever sat in his office that day, Phil would bear down. "Don't imagine that you think about everything. You don't. No one does. And your downfall is going to come from that thing you don't want to see."

He knew better than to share his own experience, even if hearing a few stories about the real lives of priests might do prissy Mary Holt a world of good. The kind of parishioner who came to her priest for guidance did not want to hear about the small, shameful lapses of charity—the way Phil had blurted, "I thought you were on a diet," when he saw the church's two-hundred-pound secretary, Dorothy, ferociously eating a Blizzard at her desk; the dog he'd kicked when it barked, advanced on him, and lifted its leg. Ashamed of himself, Phil apologized to the secretary and put out some leftover hamburger for the dog, but his penitent actions were not the point. The point was the way Phil still let his mind tiptoe away when he saw that skinny, rough-looking mutt stalking around the church parking lot. His lazy mind was willing to let him think he was a genial man, full of unforced kindness, and it was up to him to remind himself otherwise, whether or not he shared his hard-won wisdom.

Today's parishioner was Wendy Markham, a twitchy woman who

52

writhed with prayer during Mass. Phil had to force himself to listen to her mousy whisper and not the din from the street outside—a new office complex had recently gone in, and no one had figured out what to do with the sudden step-up in traffic. Twice Mass had been interrupted by accidents, and Wendy had complained about that, too, as if Phil could have stopped them. He already knew that she would leave today's session trying with all of her might to find the thing that she was not thinking about, and he also knew that she would never come a mile near it. What Wendy needed was not spiritual counseling but a bathtub-sized bottle of Xanax. "When did your sense of anxiety begin?" he said loudly, to overcome the honking.

"Last Sunday, during your sermon, when you said that God is a trickster. Now I look at everything that I used to hold as holy and wonder, 'Is this just a joke? A trick from a trickster God?'"

"I was making a larger point. Our ideas of holiness are constricting. God's holiness is larger than our ideas can ever be."

"Trickster, you said."

"I'm very sorry if my choice of words was misleading or upsetting."

"I haven't slept since. Is my marriage a trick? Are my children tricks?"

Phil closed his eyes against the monumental temptation to tell her yes. He had no memory of talking about the trickster God from the pulpit. What had possessed him? If she complained to the bishop, Phil would be called to the chancery office in record time. "Are you chastising me, Wendy? I did apologize."

"Of course I'm not chastising you. You're a priest."

"Good to know," he said.

This was the second time someone had recounted a point from his own sermon that he did not remember. Two weeks ago Matt Maynard had mentioned Louise, Phil's sister, dead at the age of fourteen from a water-skiing accident. Phil had been nine and had loved Louise beyond reason. His mother often said that he never would have joined the priesthood if he hadn't lost Louise, which might have been true, but carried overtones that made Phil nervous. Although he dreamed of her often and restlessly, he didn't like to mention Louise's name, which even now felt like letting cold air onto a wound. Hearing Matt talk about her made him furious, though he knew he was not being fair to Matt, the kind of stalwart who showed up at the rectory after a big snowfall ready to plow the parking lot.

"It's just like you said, Father—the loss of innocents is hardest of all," Matt said. Surely in his sermon Phil had said "the loss of innocence."

53

Did it matter? Now Louise was part of the parish conversation. Phil's brother, Gary, called two nights later, and Phil was surprised the news had taken that long to travel. "Leave me off your pulpit."

"No problem. You don't present good homily material."

"Honestly, Phil. What were you thinking?"

"I have no idea."

Gary laughed. He always did, eventually. "You make me worry for the future of the church."

"Stand in line, bro." Phil hoped that he had not mentioned the rope of chestnut hair that Louise had bribed him to brush for her. The bright, sweet smell of that heavy hair.

He had used to be a disciplined preacher, faithful in applying the homiletics principles he'd learned in the seminary. He did not come to the pulpit unprepared, and he studied scriptural commentary to supplement his never-sufficient knowledge. He could not remember when he started to veer from his scripts, only that he began to get more enthusiastic responses from parishioners after Mass. "What a helpful sermon that was, Father. Thank you." Sometimes the parishioner thanking him was a young and pretty woman, and Phil liked that, of course. But he wasn't setting out to flirt. It just happened lately that while he was giving his prepared remarks, something would occur to him—a useful example, a demonstration of a principle. Not an inspiration, nothing like that, but the tardy arrival of an idea that should have occurred to him when he was writing out his notes two days before. A thing, you might say, that he hadn't been paying attention to.

He had not thought much about these on-the-spot additions until parishioners started quoting back to him words he had no memory of using. Louise, for instance. Or what had apparently been a pretty long analogy involving mortgage debt. Or, now, a trickster.

His computer screen was bright with waiting e-mails, but he did not look at them. Tonight was his night to go downtown and do a lock-in with at-risk youth, a ministry he liked. The boys taught him phrases, not always vulgar, that he hadn't heard before, and they were a tonic break from overwrought self-appointed saints in the parish. The at-risk youth would be just what Phil's doctor would have ordered, if Phil had had a doctor. The at-risk youth would be down with a trickster God.

He knew that he needed—soon—to think hard about what was happening in his preaching. He had slipped out of control, and out-of-control people did harm. He would find an hour to contemplate before he finished writing next Sunday's sermon.

* * *

The sermon wrote itself, which should have made Phil suspicious. It did make him suspicious, but he didn't have time to sit and track down what was troubling him. One of his at-risk youth, Jeff, called Pelicano because he liked to carry things in his mouth, had collapsed during Phil's shift. He fell without making a sound, and he was dead before the ambulance even arrived. At the hospital, ER doctors guessed that Pelicano had shot up a speedball before wandering into the youth center; all Phil knew was that suddenly the boy was gray and still on the tile floor. The other boys had waited for Phil to do something, but what was he supposed to do? He wasn't an EMT, and he wasn't Jesus. He held the boy's heavy head in his lap and felt tears spill out of his eyes. "Pussy," one of the boys said.

That was Wednesday night. Thursday was taken up with reports to the hospital, to the police, and to the three separate boards that oversaw the program. "This terrible incident shouldn't jeopardize the entire program," Phil said in a phone call to one of the board heads. His voice was a little desperate. "The program does great good."

"The program isn't in any danger," the man said. "You need to calm down."

Thursday night: a wedding rehearsal followed by dinner with the bride's extended family. Friday: he was late for hospital rounds after nearly getting clobbered by a pickup truck shooting through the intersection on the last second of a yellow light. Then he paid a visit to the nursing home where Mary Otis, a Holy Name founding member, was living. Her daughter was in town, and Mary had called three times to make sure Phil would come and meet the girl. He entered the sunny room already smiling. Mary, a tiny creature who looked like a cocoon after the butterfly had departed, beamed. "Do you go to visit your own mother, Father?" she said, while Phil shook hands with the daughter, a rumpled, tired woman who would look exactly like her mother in thirty years.

"I wish I could. She died at fifty-two, of cancer."

"How sad. But your father?"

"He died a year later. I still have a brother."

"So the two of you are all alone. The stained glass, eh?"

"I'm sorry—I don't follow."

She looked at him sharply. "Your own words, Father. Our lives as stained as glass."

"Of course," he said.

On his way back to the rectory, Phil stopped at Liquor Barn, bought a small bottle of Stoli, and tried to remember when he could have talked about stained glass to Mary Otis. Nothing came back to him. He could hardly remember the last time he'd seen the woman.

That night, after appointments, a meeting with the Worship Committee and dinner with the Men's Club, he seated himself at his desk with the lectionary, a Bible, and a pile of commentaries to write Sunday's sermon. The reading was the Good Samaritan. For once, an interpretive path opened right up and Phil gratefully followed it. He wrote for two hours, rewarded himself with a belt of Stoli, and went to bed.

Recent history being what it was, he looked carefully at the sermon before Mass the next evening, but nothing looked exceptional. *Stay on script*, he warned himself as he vested. *Don't make me have to tell you twice*. That was a shout-out to his mother.

The Good Samaritan! "We know that we should try to model ourselves on him, and that is true. We should help the people who need us. But the parable also invites us to consider the pleasure of giving comfort. The traveler was naked and bleeding; he would die if someone didn't help him. Imagine the consolation the Samaritan felt as he cradled that poor man's head and wiped the blood from his eyes. Imagine the pleasure that came from saving someone." He was crying. Tears were off script.

We should wish for the chance to save someone, he thought suddenly. We should hope for violence and devastation, if we can bring some measure of healing. Well, no—that wasn't right.

"We should give thanks," he said lamely, and hurried on to the Creed.

After Mass, Phil couldn't shake the sense that he had nearly closed his hand around a profundity. This was a new feeling for him; he had been a so-so seminarian, a plodder who did not exactly earn the Bs he received in philosophy. When he went to see his teacher for the third time about Aquinas and the *Summa*, his teacher had said, "Let it go. There's not much call for scholasticism in most parishes." That had proved to be true. Phil would have been better off taking accounting.

Now he felt a realization breaking upon him, nearly visible, and he tried to keep it before him as he shook hands after Mass, greeted Mrs. Parcell's sister, here to visit for the week, and promised a group of boys a basketball game. When he finally closed the rectory door behind him, giddy excitement washed through him.

Drawing the blinds in his study, he sat in the armchair and closed his eyes. He turned his thoughts to the Good Samaritan, moved to pity by the beaten, dying man. Phil tried to imagine himself into the scene: the road covered with dusty yellow dirt, the blazing sun and the sweat running into his eyes and beard, the scrubby bushes at the wayside that gave off a hot, sharp scent. The beaten man, flies lighting on his sores, moaned through broken teeth. Seamlessly, Phil's thoughts moved to Pelicano, whom he had not particularly noticed on Thursday night. If he had, Phil would have forced Pelicano to leave; the shelter forbade drugs or any obvious signs of using. What the hell had Phil been doing, not to notice a two-hundred-pound gangster high as a kite, carrying cotton balls in his mouth?

It was only too easy to imagine himself on the footpath beside the man beaten and robbed. Helplessly, Phil saw himself—his robe clean, his new sandals making a pleasant slapping sound on the dirt—approach the man, look at him, then straighten up and walk past. A dense smell of incense rose from the soft linen of his robe. Light caught on the tapered silver leaves of an olive tree, and a bird's song sounded like tumbling water. Sitting in his stiff armchair, listening to the rattle of the air conditioner, Phil cried as if knives were slicing through him.

"Don't you think you're making yourself out to be just a little important?" said Gary. "You're getting above your pay grade, Phil. The kid O.D.'d. You didn't kill him."

"I sure didn't save him."

"You were there to supervise a roomful of teenagers, right? What were you doing when the kid collapsed?"

"I was talking to some of the other boys. There was going to be a job fair downtown, and they wanted to know whether they'd be taken seriously if they didn't show up wearing suits."

"Good question. Deserved an answer."

"I think a person can answer dress-code questions and still notice if a kid is about to collapse."

"The kid could bench-press 350 and he was jacked out of his mind. Do you think he was going to let you give him a hug?"

"He deserved to have somebody notice," Phil said doggedly. "Anybody deserves that much."

Gary sighed and shook his head, and they settled into SVU. "No way is that guy the perp," Gary said. "The killer was a runner. Look at this guy's arms."

"You don't run with your arms."

"Shows how much you know." Gary put in thirty miles a week and liked to poke Phil's paunch. "You figure your spare tire gives you more cred with the gang bangers?"

"They told me I look just like a priest."

After the show was over, Phil hugged his brother, watched his car turn the corner, then turned off the TV and rinsed out their glasses. He waited for the satisfaction that usually came when he checked the locks and turned off the back-porch light, those sweetly fussy evening gestures. Instead, he remembered Pelicano, and barely made it to the kitchen before he vomited.

His sadness was devastating and physical; in the days that followed Phil felt as if body parts were being pulled out of him. By the middle of the week people were starting to ask him if he was all right. "Did something happen? You look gut shot," said Matt. He was better than Grace Mattea, who laid her hand sympathetically on Phil's arm and said, "I can see your pain. I am praying for you."

"Thank you, Grace, but I'm just a quart low on sleep."

She smiled at him and shook her head. "Not everything can be talked about, I know."

But priests were supposed to talk. That was their job description. All day long Phil was expected to talk to committees, talk to engaged couples or kids in trouble, talk to the sick and bereaved, talk from the pulpit, talk on the phone. Now his mouth felt like sand and words refused to take shape; when Otto Mersing hauled his son who had just been arrested for joyriding to Phil's office, all Phil could manage to say was, "Was it worth it?"

"Yes," the boy said, earning him a pop from Otto.

"We grab at what we think will make us happy," Phil mused. "Sorrow— grief—is insupportable, so we do whatever we can to push it back."

"I was bored," the boy said.

"Talk to him about jail," Otto said to Phil.

Things did not improve that night when he emceed the wine auction, a fund-raiser that was rowdy by church standards and for which he needed to adopt a light tone. He scoured his joke books and found a few acceptable stories to tell, but he could feel the ghastliness of his smile as soon as he arrived in the parish hall. He had printed out six jokes, stopped after the second, and no one protested when he handed over the microphone to Matt, auctioneer for the night.

Sitting in the back of the hall while Matt made the kind of racy jokes a priest shouldn't laugh at, Phil felt grief move through him in waves. He could not even say what, exactly, he was grieving. Gary was right about Pelicano, a boy whom Phil had barely known by sight. He grieved because he was a priest, and because he had been in that room, and he had seen no reason to stop talking to teenage boys about covering their tattoos. He grieved because Pelicano had shot up. Jesus, that was a good enough reason.

By Saturday evening he thought of Mass with actual panic. He xeroxed a sermon from one of his source books, choosing a talk about finding the face of God in the people around us. The sermon had nothing to do with the readings, but Phil thought he could get through it without breaking down, which right now was his only criterion.

And he was wrong. He had read the sermon in his office, of course, but he hadn't read it aloud, and it turned out that there was a tremendous difference between silently looking at and actually saying sentences like "God is before us every day, in the people we love best as well as those we pass on the street." Phil's voice broke in half, and he stood, trying to recover himself, his shoulders shaking, for over a minute before he could say, "Let us stand and pray." After Mass parishioners fled.

He could get his doctor to prescribe Paxil. He was probably the only priest in the diocese not taking the stuff. And in the meantime he would exercise and think positive thoughts. Watch *Mr. Rogers*. Whatever it took. Nobody objected if their priest had a little bit of existential angst going on—it made him interesting, like a movie priest. But crying in the pulpit, like bringing up irrelevant stories during homilies, unnerved people. Another month of this and he'd be handling serpents.

He went for a long walk and had worked himself into a pretty decent mood by the time he got back to the rectory. There he listened to the single message on the voice mail: Gary was in the hospital, the victim of a hit-and-run. He was in ICU. One of the attending nurses had recognized his last name and called the rectory.

Phil was in the car before he could think and had pulled into the surging traffic before he could feel. Or rather, he felt a keen wind filling his rib cage. Gary, an early-morning runner. So easy to imagine him dreamily moving along, hardly bothering to check for traffic at six on a Sunday morning. A driver who might have been drunk or just sleepy or as relaxed as Gary himself, because when you're up at six on a Sunday morning the world belongs to you. Phil let out a noise, an awful sound.

ICU was, of course, a nightmare. Phil had to force himself to look at his brother's swollen face, the bruise that closed one eye and the gash across his forehead, and the tube jammed into his neck. Gary's throat would feel like sandpaper once the tube came out, if it came out.

"You can talk to him," the nurse said. "He's sedated, but he's not completely out. He can hear."

Phil nodded. He would have preferred that Gary not be able to hear the miserable beeps and clicks that monitored the movements of his heart and lungs, both of which had been injured. He had been thrown fifteen feet and landed face first on an ivy embankment. A homeowner shuffling out to get his newspaper saw Gary on his ivy and thought first to call 911 and indignantly report a drunk on his property. Then he heard the rattle of Gary's breath and saw the curious shape of his body, and the man's hands shook so badly that he spent over a minute punching buttons on his phone before he could get the ambulance to come.

"That call saved his life?" Phil said.

"Yes," said the nurse carefully, and in the pause before that word Phil realized how far Gary still had to come back. Sitting beside his brother's bed, Phil mechanically moved through prayers but did not listen to his own words. Gary's bony face did not look serene and did not, thank God, look suffering or ill. To tell the truth, he looked annoyed. "Is there anything I can do to help?" Phil said to the nurse.

"Pray."

"Anything else?"

"I could use a sandwich."

Phil left ICU and came back half an hour later with the biggest sandwich he could find. The nurse laughed and thanked him. At the end of the visiting time, the sandwich was still wrapped up at the nursing station, weeping lightly into its wax paper.

Through the week Phil stayed at the hospital as much as he could, watching his brother drift in and out of consciousness. The doctors were having trouble keeping Gary's lungs inflated, so his blood-oxygen levels kept plummeting. He had two operations to repair his torn heart. Phil brought more food to the ICU nurses. On his ninth day there, when Phil was at church, Gary died.

"He was very quiet, Father. He didn't look like he was suffering at all. He just let go of whatever he'd been hanging onto. An embolism— it's painless." Phil stood in front of the doctor and wept without covering his face, like a child. The doctor shifted his weight and said softly, "He's in a better place."

60

"How did he get there?"

"Pardon me, Father?"

"How did he get to the better place? He doesn't know the way. Who showed him?"

"You'd better sit down," the doctor said. By the time Phil left the hospital, he was holding a prescription of his own. "I don't feel good about letting you go," the doctor said.

"Nothing happens to me," Phil assured him.

Priests from three neighboring churches, friends, or close enough, came to Holy Name and said Mass in Phil's place for two Sundays. The worship committee put together services, the budget committee compiled the accounting statement, and every morning Phil opened his front door and found more casseroles and plates of brownies. Should he be concerned that no one wanted to come in and talk to him? Maybe people had heard the ululations he sometimes made at night. A sound like that would be enough to keep him from knocking on a door.

His mind was a gluey sludge of platitudes and prayers, none of them useful. *God does not give us more than we can handle. God is closest to us in our brokenness.* What did that even mean? When the bishop called and reminded Phil that he could not have kept his brother alive, Phil said, "That does not help."

"I'm sorry. It's time for you to get back on your feet."

"I'm not lying down."

"Fathers Campbell and Martinson have been happy to step in for you, but their parishes need them. As Holy Name needs you."

"Are you saying that I'm being selfish because I'm grieving my brother?"

"Yes."

Gary's laugh would have rung out. He often said that priests were the most heartless people in the world. After hanging up on the bishop, Phil dropped to his knees and crawled back and forth across his study. He scraped his face against the rough carpet and cried until he was gasping, one shuddering wave followed by another. He had no idea how much time passed before he finally stopped and lay panting gently beside his desk. If he were a drinker, this would be the time to start a bender. The bottle of Stoli, so little it was cute, still stood in the high kitchen cabinet, missing only one drink. He wished he could offer the rest to Gary, who had liked vodka martinis.

After a while, numb, he pulled himself back to his feet. He was too old and had counseled too many people to expect a breakthrough, just as he had long ago given up expecting God to walk forward and offer divine aid. Phil's faith had taught him to hear God's voice in the voices of people around him, and to see God's hand behind the three dishes of lasagna filling up the refrigerator. God used people, a phrase that could be heard more than one way, and that was typical of God. God was close by but invisible like any good prankster, maybe leaning against the pantry door, smiling at Phil expectantly, waiting for him to catch on. A whole world of suffering, and only God seeing the funny side. Maybe Gary was part of the joke now. Maybe Gary and God were splitting their sides. "Honestly?" Phil said aloud, facing the place God might be standing. "I'm done." He hit the lights on his way out of the room.

The next day a clean wind blew in from the west. The weather had been sticky, and now Phil, standing at the end of the rectory driveway to get the newspaper, tipped back his head and inhaled this new air that brushed over him like a feather. It had a sharp, refined edge, and Phil imagined it sliding across his skin, shaving off the thinnest imaginable layer, leaving him just a little smaller. When he opened his eyes, he nodded at the sky, blue as the cornflowers Dorothy had put in a squat pottery vase on his desk.

He could preach about the beauties of nature, he thought, and looked back into the impassive sky. One torn cloud rippled like a slow banner, its edges dissolving. Another, sheer as a veil, rearranged itself over his head.

From the maple behind him, recently pruned into a lollipop by Matt, a mockingbird broke into a torrent of chatter. No other birds answered, and after a moment, the bird recommenced its speech. "You should consider the priesthood," Phil said, and the bird flew irritably away.

Resisting the habit of prayer—thanks or praise or acknowledgment—was easier than he expected. The wind felt good against his face, and he stood at the end of the driveway for another few minutes, long enough to wave at Matt when he drove by. Matt looked startled at Phil's thumbs-up. He must have thought that grief is a nonstop process, a shroud that the griever dragged to every corner of his life. Phil had used to think that, too.

Another car went by, and then another. Phil was looking at the tree, hoping the mockingbird would come back. Then a shriek of brakes, and a crash. Phil took off like a dart.

Halfway onto the curb at the edge of the intersection, a silver convertible, top still up, was smashed into the side of a beater Honda. Phil heard his own rough breathing as he ran, and he heard an engine's warning bleat, but no screams or calls for help. The scene was calm, which made him run faster. Bits of glass that caught the morning sun crunched under his feet and the bitter smell from the air bags, bad as burned hair, swept over him. Why was no one else coming? Why weren't the drivers crying out?

By the time Phil got to the cars, the driver of the Honda—a young man in a Hawaiian shirt—had already slid free, coughing a little. The silky red shirt was covered with powder. He smiled weakly and held up a hand. "Are you OK?" Phil said.

"No. My car was just wrecked."

"I'll help you."

"Do you have another car?"

"I'll call the police."

The man pointed at the convertible. "He's doing that."

Sure enough, the driver of the convertible, still wearing his seat belt, was on the phone. Catching Phil's eye, he nodded, as if he and Phil were agreeing to something. The man touched the phone's screen, then called through the window, "Can you open the door? It won't work on my side."

Phil pulled the handle and heard something in the mechanism move. The whole front end of the car was buried in the Honda—no surprise that the door wouldn't work. The surprise lay in the fact that nothing was on fire, and both drivers seemed not just unhurt but unruffled. The driver of the convertible would have been more upset if he'd taken a fall on a basketball court. Now, in this intersection, the only heart juddering in its chest seemed to be Phil's. He yanked harder at the door and heard another frustrated mechanical noise. Then a muscle in his shoulder ignited, the door shot open, and its window tipped out, exploding on the asphalt.

"Fuck," said the driver, another young man, this one with hair cropped to the skull and a minute goatee.

"Sorry," Phil said.

"That will be one more thing to replace."

"I think you're going to have to replace the car. You're lucky to be alive."

"Not lucky. I paid for good engineering. But thanks for coming over."

Phil pointed at the rectory. "I live there. Do you want me to get you some coffee or anything while you wait for the police?"

"No, man. I'm good." He looked away. Stubbornly, ignoring the plain invitation to leave, Phil remained until the police arrived. "Are you a witness, sir?" the officer said when he finally pulled up.

"No," Phil and the two drivers said.

"Then I'll ask you to step back." The officer was probably fifty, like Phil. His gut spilled over the top of his splayed belt, and he kept running his hand over his hair and sighing. He directed all of his questions to the two drivers. Eventually Phil shrugged and walked back to the rectory. They knew where to find him.

At the edge of the driveway, he paused underneath the tree. The mockingbird had returned and was belting out its borrowed tunes. Phil recognized this near-joke, its punch line that never fully arrived. It reminded him of Gary, who had been a practical joker when he was a boy. A few months after Louise's death, Phil had gone to her room, lain across her yellow bedspread, and fallen asleep. When he woke up, his fingers were laced together with ribbon Louise had used in her hair and Gary was snickering behind the door. Phil got up to chase him, but he couldn't hit him hard because his fingers were wrapped in ribbon.

A sound crowded Phil's throat, either laughter or agony. He knew that as soon as he made noise, the bird would fly away. But when he started to laugh, the bird stayed.

Nominated by Jay Rogoff, Melanie Rae Thon

THE SEVENTY-FOURTH VIRGIN

fiction by M.C. ARMSTRONG

from THE GETTYSBURG REVIEW

In *The Seventy-Third Virgin*, Colonel Ali Al-Khan played an American woman. He stood naked in a garden in the movie's most famous moment. He faced a warrior also played by himself, and this warrior was also naked. He was lost. He had lost count. He, like the viewer, had been through virgin after virgin, the variety in flesh slowly lost in the sameness of the scenery, the same lock of legs, the same leopard curling through the floral thickets, the same bluebird always on the shoulder of the postcoital corpse, for in the colonel's interpretation of heaven, the virgins must die. There must be a moment where the warrior, discharged of his nacreous nectar, can walk empty and alone into the arms of the one everlasting creator, also played by the colonel.

Bill Caesar used to blow leaves for a living. When the war began he was a detailer, a cleaner of cars and a part-time thief. He was a scavenger, a hoarder of parts. He was addicted to pornography and crystal meth. Bill Caesar had given up on Christianity and America, just as he felt America and Christ had given up on him. Bill still went to church with his grandmother every Sunday, but he often fell asleep during service.

"America wants you dumb," Bill told me. "They're happiest when you just get fat and tired and don't ask any questions. It's good for business."

One day he pulled back a cracked mirror in his bathroom, revealed a medicine cabinet that was full of vials containing antidepressants, amphetamines, barbiturates, erectile dysfunction medication, and several different prescriptions for stomach and heart problems.

"Before you guys, I was on more pills than my grandmother. I was sick. America was sick."

But things have changed. Bill Caesar has lost sixty pounds, and so can you.

There's been an awakening. Kovach, West Virginia, was once the site of the most serious fighting in the war. Here is where you found the privately armed militias, the fundamentalists with the underground bunkers. They called themselves "rednecks," a term used to describe an unfashionable tan line. There are rumors that many of the people in this region are inbred and addicted to drugs, just as Bill was. Yet the prevalence of violence and drug abuse did not create a dissonance in the "hearts and minds" of these believers. Around the necks of the countless corpses from the first battles were crucifixes.

"We would talk about peace, but look at history," Bill said.

He opened an encyclopedia that once belonged to his grandfather. Bill doesn't watch much TV anymore. He's now an avid reader. He shows me a painting from antiquity, a picture of women burning alive. "Witches."

"We executed more people than anybody else in the world. Right up there with Pakistan and Iran. Whether it's women, poor people, retarded people—I don't know. You'll hear people talk about the sermon on the mount and compassion, but that's just not the way Christianity played out in America."

Bill told me the story of a friend who lived in another country, one of the millions of refugees. His name was Russ. He was molested by a Catholic priest. He committed suicide last month.

"Before you guys, it was gay this and gay that," Bill said. "You turn on the TV and we're either watching some gay guy trying to convert a straight guy or watching a girl cheat on her husband, making everybody just hate women. I mean it makes sense if you think about it."

Bill looked away for a moment. The room went silent. Bill is thrice divorced. His last wife left him for the minister of a megachurch, the infamous Reverend Todd Hostetler. For Bill, this was "the straw that broke the camel's back."

The control tower at Dulles Airport resembles a minaret. We arrived on the tarmac to greet Colonel Ali Al-Khan. It was an exciting time. There was intelligence of a forthcoming attack on Washington, one that could possibly change the course of the war. Before the plane touched down, there was a period of quiet conversation.

"Allen Dulles was the director of the CIA," Bill told me. "I'm not sure if it's him or his brother they named the airport after, but they were both very secretive men, responsible for countless acts of terror. They assassinated leaders left and right, overthrew countless governments that were trying to establish democracies in both Africa and South America, not to mention the Middle East. We had good dudes for awhile, like Eisenhower—guys who knew that we were on the verge of turning tyrannical, but nobody could do anything. Guys like the Dulles brothers held all the cards, these men behind the scenes. The military-industrial complex. Corporate terrorism. Which is kinda what terrorism is all about, right—corporate? If it's national, government sponsored, then it's not terror, right? That's why the CIA was so dangerous. They hid our armies in corporations until the corporations became indistinguishable from the armies."

Colonel Khan's plane touched down at midnight. Khan had been in Kashmir, finishing a film. There were rumors he wanted to do a movie about the war, the first wave of American suicide bombers, but I was told by his agent that his visit was purely patriotic. Apparently he'd received countless letters from the troops. His work as a soldier, thespian, and Muslim businessman had earned him an international reputation.

"I just want to see the war for myself," he told me, as we drove through Virginia, the oldest colony in the country.

We passed the ashes of the ambiguous American companies. We saw horses in fields, fires on the mountain. We passed by an old drive-in theater where Colonel Khan wanted to stop. He wanted to walk around in the weeds and the gravel, take pictures of the blank screens, the old, rusty microphones posted on their poles, the merry-go-rounds and the slides, the old popcorn booth.

Bill and I stood back. We watched as the movie star danced in the moonlight. This is the country where movies began. The drive-in theater was where people parked their cars and engaged in acts of premarital sex while watching movies in the country's "heyday."

"I have hope for this country," Colonel Khan said, as we returned to the road.

He told me that he believed people were starting to "come out of the closet," a phrase often used in America to describe the announcement of homosexuality. The soldiers chuckled at this phrase, but Colonel Khan was serious.

"Christianity is dead," he said. "I have listened to Reverend Todd. I have seen the ATMs in the sanctuaries. I have seen the churches converted to gymnasiums and discotheques and police stations and museums. You cannot have a faith that can be so easily converted to so many things. This is the essence of Christianity. It is like capitalism. It is like the chameleon, and, therefore, the American was like a chameleon. Whatever shape or color he needed for a given situation he assumed. This is why so many great actors and actresses come from here—this tendency. One must be experienced in his craft in order to juggle the identity of the chameleon with the true identity of the believer."

Perhaps Colonel Khan was that "rare bird," as Americans say. We stopped at a checkpoint. Colonel Khan signed the bicep of a soldier with his knife. We took pictures in front of a burned-out Mustang.

Colonel Khan struck his famous pose: a drunken face coupled with slouched shoulders and a distended stomach. His ability to impersonate, to actually embody the American, was uncanny. The stomach muscles required to maintain such an appearance over the course of an entire film are beyond comprehension, perhaps the result of intense military training. According to insiders, Colonel Khan never uses a stunt double and always refuses the moulage of the makeup artist. He does everything himself. When we returned to the base, there was a fire to greet him.

Suicide was the issue for Bill Caesar. I watched him strip the flanks of a buck deer with a horn-handled knife his grandfather gave him. I watched him give a speech on leadership and patience, his hands steady as he circled the fire.

People listen to him now. They respect his skills. But it wasn't always like this for Bill. Before the war, West Virginia was like much of America. Drug abuse was on the rise. Divorce rates had doubled. The rate of clinical depression had tripled over two generations. The percentage of children born to unmarried parents had gone up sevenfold. Suicide rates among the young people in the state had quadrupled. And this is to say nothing of the rates for adults and soldiers.

"Colonel Khan saved my life," Bill told his men. "Y'all remember channel six-seventy-six?"

It was now late. The men had finished their meal. They were sitting "Indian style," sipping chai tea. Bill was the only one standing. The embers of the fire were glowing.

"I was watching Mr. Khan at two in the morning," Bill said. "It used to be that I'd just watch that channel when I was stoned. There was something weird about seeing the 'terrorists' praying, but I don't know. That night it was like God commanded me to stop. Just something in my gut. Maybe some of y'all saw the same program."

This was a month after Bill's third wife left him. Bill described an infomercial, a promotion for a new online interactive translation of the Koran. He described Khan talking about the wisdom of Allah, his cautions about hasty decision making, a short dramatization of the world's creation.

"The word was *deliberation*," Bill said. "Colonel Khan told me to wait three days before I made a big decision. He told me God didn't just make the earth like that. He said God needed six days. Even though that's not a lot of time, it shows the wisdom of deliberation. So I didn't kill myself just then. I waited and I watched more of the programs on that channel and I realized: people in this country kill themselves for themselves, which if you play it out like a math equation—like the colonel did—the whole thing equals nothing. When you don't kill yourself for something bigger than yourself, you just cancel yourself out, and maybe worse. Maybe you even destroy the people you leave behind. My grandmother is still alive. I remember on the second day thinking about her and how much pain she'd feel, how she wouldn't have anybody to walk her across her bridge in the winter, nobody to eat her cookies or watch Jeopardy with—and then it really dawned on me. She wouldn't have anybody to talk to. She'd be alone. All by herself."

Bill's oldest brother was executed by the American government. His youngest brother killed a Chinese woman "just so he could play video games all day in the pen," Bill told me. Although his mother was still alive, living somewhere in California, Bill hadn't heard from her in years.

"Colonel Khan taught me about love," he said to his men. "He taught me that dying for something is better than dying for nothing."

Bill snapped the elastic waistband on his pants. He hugged Colonel

Khan as his men applauded and fired their guns into the night, causing leaves to fall, birds to fly. When the fire finally died, Bill helped Colonel Khan to his feet. He led him through the network of bunkers. I kept a respectful distance, allowing Bill some time to ask questions. After awhile, I noticed something you never would've seen in America five years ago: two soldiers holding hands.

Bill Caesar wore a mullet, a hairstyle often mocked in America. Distinct from the long hair of those who were once called "hippies," the mullet is in some ways the "negative" of the "hippy hairdo." Just as the conservatives of America saw the longhaired hippies as the sign of sentimental idealism, many of the liberals I've spoken to see the mullet as the sign of inveterate ignorance. They associate it with the indentured servants from Mexico. One form of long hair as a sign of wealthy nostalgic rebellion, another as a sign of poverty and machismo.

I watched Caesar from a distance with the leader of the Iraqi special forces, a lieutenant whose identity must remain secret. We watched Caesar's mullet flap in the wind as he fired through targets and dug trenches. We stood back as he looked under the hood of one of the white trucks our military had donated. He raised his arms in a sign of victory after successfully replacing a spark plug.

"Good," said the lieutenant. "Now let's go find some bad guys."

Bill started the truck. Despite the pleas of the lieutenant, Colonel Khan insisted on riding "shotgun," a term Bill explained to us as we drove down the road.

"One man drives, other man shoots. Can't shoot if you're driving."

When Bill was growing up, the man riding shotgun shot deer and stop signs, random acts of destruction. We approached the town of Kovach. We passed a baseball stadium and a diner. We waved to a family of Negroes sitting on a porch; their son Horace was on Caesar's SWAT team. He always drove the lead vehicle in the convoy. Prior to the war, Horace worked at a call center selling information to international corporations. His wife bought popular words from search engines before being downsized into a mechanical turk.

"He had an 'Amazing Grace' moment," Caesar told Colonel Khan. "Horace thought he was living the good life. Then he lost his home and his wife. She went off with a soldier. Same old story."

We passed through a classic American neighborhood: Empty, identical, oversized homes with white plastic siding; meticulous gardens now wild with weeds; the face of a middle-aged woman in a red silk dickey posted on the real-estate signs that stood in every yard.

"How 'bout the seventy-third real-estate agent?" Horace remarked over the CB.

"Everybody wants to live in the big city," Caesar said. "Most people have forgotten there's a war out here—judging by the news."

"Why have you not killed your wife?" Colonel Khan said.

The truck went silent. Colonel Khan's question seemed full of compassion, a genuine empathy with the suffering of Bill Caesar. Yet I wondered, even then, if it was all part of a character study, if Colonel Khan would one day wear a mullet and drive a truck through a simulated American landscape, the love of a faithless woman still tearing at his heart.

"Americans are a little different than Arabs," Bill said.

"Is that right?" Colonel Khan said.

"I sent the reverend a pipe bomb, but it didn't go off," Bill said.

"That was cowardly."

"I know."

"This is the sign of America's sickness," Colonel Khan said. "You have forgotten the original source of evil."

"I know," Bill said. "You're right."

"If I'm right, why is she alive?"

Bill looked like he wanted to respond to the supercilious tone in the colonel's voice. His eyes "bugged" with intensity. But then he took a deep breath, as if suddenly reminded of the virtues, the program on deliberation that had started it all.

Moments later, the colonel grew unsettled, perhaps unsatisfied with the exchange. I listened to him speak in Arabic. I understood his command. We changed course. I could see Bill stiffen in his seat as we drove across a tall bridge where lower-middle-class Americans used to simulate suicide. They would harness a large rubbery band to the beams of the bridge and then dive toward the river.

I looked down at the eutrophic waters, suddenly aware that this was not just another "celebrity embed." We took a left a kilometer after the bridge, wound our way down a loose gravel road, passing crosses in the ditches, the river getting bigger and bigger.

I could smell fire and fermentation, the loamy breath of the river mingled with the smoking of meat and the cool leaves of sycamore trees and blackberries. We slowed down on a flat muddy road that ran parallel to the water. There were trailers and cabins, discarded machines in the yards, naked children blowing bubbles. I saw a little girl swing from a tire tied to a vine. She disappeared into the summer water and then reappeared with her hair slicked back, now looking like a boy.

The convoy stopped in front of a metal mailbox shaped like a fish. This was the home of Bill's third wife, Polly Colfelt-Whitacre-Hostetler. The house rested on wheels. There was a pink truck in the driveway, a bridge made of compressed grocery bags in the front yard, a bridge over nothing, leading from one plot of fallow dirt to another. There was a red-white-and-blue sign that read Vote Yes for Kids.

Bill led us up the front steps. Horace and his men stayed with the vehicles. Bill knocked on the door. We heard the sound of wild steps, a fluttering in the floorboards.

The door opened. Polly appeared before us. She was wearing a white rubber sun dress. When she first stepped into Bill's arms, I expected the garment to immediately redden. I thought he had stabbed her with his grandfather's knife. I looked at the colonel. His eyes were wide and blank, like a bird of prey. It took me a moment to see that Polly was "overcome with emotion," and so was Bill.

He made a show of releasing his hands from her waist, but this did not change the fact that they instinctively went there in the first place. Polly had hair like hay. She checked her purse, sniffed her armpits. She directed us into the house with her forefinger to her lips.

She led us to a bathroom door. Bill made a signal with his finger. The colonel sent close to a hundred rounds through the door, and there, on the ground, behind the shattered particle board, was the Reverend Todd Hostetler, one of the most radical clerics in the country and thus one of our high-value targets, breathing his last wheezy breath.

Polly immediately called for the children. They came spilling out of two rooms in the back. There were at least a dozen of them along with three dogs and five cats, and on the shoulder of the oldest boy, perhaps fifteen years old, was a red-tailed boa constrictor, the design down its spine like the injected lips of a starlet.

I watched the colonel finger the snake and assess the situation in the living room. I admired his deliberation. He saw what I saw: the children were fascinated. They ran skipping circles around the soldiers. Khan told all of them except for the youngest girl to go outside, where I could hear them imploring Horace to let them toy with his gun.

"Kilby sure has grown up," Bill said to his ex-wife, as the door closed.

Kilby, who wore a red mullet and freckles, was Bill's son, the only of the children who belonged to him.

"Have a seat, young lady," the colonel said, directing Polly's daughter to his knee.

The colonel was sitting in a white Naugahyde recliner, which seemed an accessory to Polly's sundress. The child, a brunette of about ten, did as she was told. She even smiled, ran her hands down the colonel's legs, reverse cowgirl.

Bill and Polly were commanded to sit on the matching couch. One of the dogs took a seat at Bill's feet, began to clutch and thrust at his leg. The colonel smiled.

"Here we go," he said, bouncing the child on his knee. "Everybody having fun now, just like dogs, no?"

Bill released an uncomfortable laugh, a sound like he'd been punched in the stomach.

"She would make a fine actress, would she not?" the colonel said to me.

The colonel moved his hands up her ribs and blew on her neck, making her giggle. I must admit, I was a bit taken aback. I was uncomfortable with the way he bounced the child on his knee. It felt inappropriate *in the moment*. I wanted Bill to stand up and do something. I remember how he looked me in the eye at one point, as if he expected *me* to do something.

But it is precisely in moments like these where the colonel teaches us most poignantly. What we see as a sin in the moment is a mere stone removed from the road of the final path, the ever unfolding path of the truth.

"Marriage, Bill, is a sacred institution, yes?"

"Yes, sir."

"No, Bill. No. Not anymore. This is old hat. This is my first video."

"I'm sorry, sir."

"Yes, you are. What does *sharia* mean, William? Show me that you have paid attention to the basics. What does the word mean?"

Bill sat up straight for a moment, then fell into a crouch, his fingers laced in his lap. He shrugged his trapezius muscles. The colonel removed the shirt of the young girl. He threw it atop Bill's head, quickening his memory with anger.

"The path to the watering hole," Bill shouted.

"Yes," the colonel said. "Yes. This is the meaning, the path to the watering hole. Just as the law of Christ is living water, so is the law of Muhammad the path to the water. Water, Bill. Water. Constancy, change. Always there, always changing. There is nothing sacred, yet everything is sacred. So hard to discern the sky from the sea after awhile. Everything is the same, right?"

"Yes, sir."

"No, you fucking idiot. Look at this girl, Bill. Do you want her to be the seventy-fourth virgin?"

"No, sir."

"Why?"

"Because she's just a child. She's too young, sir."

"Too young to be split like a piece of fruit? Like a fresh peach?"

"Yes, sir."

"Why, if the most sacred vow between two people means nothing, should she mean something? She, who you have made no vow to?"

"Because she's a child."

"Bill, have I not taught you how to think? What did I discuss in volume twenty-three?"

"The sacred."

"And what makes something sacred?"

"God's word."

"Yes. God's word. You *know* what it is, yet you ignore it. You treat it like water. You let it pass, and just like water and the salt it bears, you don't miss it until it's gone. Abuse, abuse, abuse, until the salt and the water become nothing more than a field of hollow stones. In America I have witnessed wondrous things, William. I have held the saxifrage, the flower that bursts through the rocks. Yet I know there is no water in rock, William. I know, just as you know, where the water is and where it isn't. Yet smell the underwear of this child, William! Tell me if it wouldn't be easy to get lost in this world."

The colonel tossed the child's panties at Bill. I noticed Polly's fingernails buried in the canvas thighs of Bill's pants. We were all tense, all one. The cameras were always rolling, but still! What was he doing sniffing the underwear of a child? Nobody could gauge his sincerity from one moment to the next. Bill, like the rest of us, was confused, afraid, perhaps more than a bit faithless, drifting back and forth like a pendulum.

"Wait," he said.

"Yes, Bill?"

Bill's head returned to his hands, a gesture of prayer. The child was completely naked on the colonel's thigh, and not entirely unhappy. Like most fools of the earth, like everyone in that room, she was oblivious to design, to God's will. Or perhaps her smile indicated the very opposite, that American notion of the child's wisdom.

"Polly," Bill said. "The colonel's right. I know what the law requires. Colonel, you yourself argue that we must adapt God's law to our land, that the stoning of a faithless woman is, to some degree, figurative, yes?"

"To some small degree, Bill, yes."

"A hail of bullets is a form of stoning, yes?"

"Yes, Bill. Yes."

"Okay. Children don't need to do or see certain things, yes?"

"Yes, Bill. Yes."

"Okay. Can we do this my way, without the girl?"

The colonel's smile was more demonstrative than it had been all day. There was a feeling of great relief among the men, myself included. The colonel had taken us to the brink, and, as is always the case, the mind tastes God in this place. What is necessary becomes clear.

We followed Bill outside. He called his son down from the turret of the truck, said he wanted to teach the child a lesson. But he told the other boys to stay. He had his rifle poised behind Polly's head. One could tell, walking behind her, that she was wearing a Saran Wrap thong. She kept flashing the other soldiers.

We walked along the river road, cut a path into the woods, walked past chimneys of broken stone, the riparian landscape dense with foliage, bloated roots like nerves in the earth, the American landscape more alive than anything I've ever witnessed.

"It's easy to get lost in this country," Bill said, the two men walking side by side in front of the other soldiers.

"Yes, Bill," the colonel said. "I know this has been a tough year for you. But I'm glad you have found strength. I must admit, I was a bit worried, as they say."

"It's all of this," Bill said, sweeping his hand across the canopy of leaves. I followed his hand. It was hard to see the sky, hard to see anything but what was right in front of us.

"It's like you say in volume eighteen," Bill said. "Our strength is our weakness. I mean, I'll grant you: You're a smart guy, but think about this country and how easy it is to be dumb when you're walled in by so many trees, so much mystery around every corner. This isn't the desert where you can always see things so far and clear, where you can make sense out of miles. In America, it's the opposite, Colonel. Everything's covered. You really have to know things to see things clear. It kinda struck me when you were talking about saxifrage. Just that word. The way it reminded me of my granddaddy and all the things he used to teach me, what berries to eat, what berries not to eat, what flowers did what. You know what I mean?"

"Yes, Bill. I do."

"Colonel, this is me, this is my country, but I've been afraid of it, like everybody else. We all want to see things clearly. We don't want a desert, but we do. It's out here she'll feel the fear, the terror. Not in there."

The colonel said nothing. He merely shook his head, clapped Bill on the back. We arrived at a small clearing at the top of a rise, the river perhaps a full kilometer behind us.

"Face against the tree, bitch!" Bill screamed.

The colonel turned toward Bill's men, spoke into the camera.

"Do you see what he's doing? There are a million faces of Zina. We need not indulge her sentimental incarnations. For Zina, as the woman of a million faces, is the woman without any true face. Bill, may your bullets bore into the back of her skull as permanent empty eyes for all to see."

For those Americans unfamiliar with our teachings, Zina is our name for adultery, and also the name of a recurrent woman in the colonel's films. Polly Colfelt-Whitacre-Hostetler responded to the colonel's words with yet another flip of her white rubber sundress, showing us all her backside and the transparent thong, what appeared to be a tattoo of a middle finger on her left buttock.

The colonel smiled, took a brief bow for the boys. Bill Caesar pushed the muzzle of his gun into Polly's head, said a few choice words. He stepped back into the center of the clearing—his son, his men, myself, and the colonel but a few steps behind him in a crescent formation.

"Kilby," he said.

With his left hand steadily holding the rifle, he motioned his son forward with his right. It seemed to me that he wanted his son to learn, to see what was happening. Of all the children, there was but this one that was his, and when Bill fired his gun, his son ran toward his mother's body, but Polly, instead of sliding down the trunk, seemed to stagger. As Bill and the boy reached her body, she fell in alongside them, and they ran down the rise, into the trees.

The men ran left and right and into the middle of the clearing, firing up a mist. The colonel raised his hand, stilling the soldiers who were so eager to give chase. He turned to me with a patient smile, swept his hand across the land.

"Bill lost his will," he said. "But he was right, was he not?"

"How do you mean, sir?" I said.

"This. All of this. This land *is* different. But it will not always be. Write this down, my friend: The desert is coming as a sea. The sooner we tear down their forests, the better off they'll be."

I followed the colonel back to the village, to the trailer by the river. I stood on the edge of the living room with the lieutenant and the cameramen and the other soldiers, the child once again on the colonel's knee. Within seconds of completion we sent the movie out to the entire world. This, I believed, would be the final movie, the last of his cautionary tales, the story of how the American retreated to his cave, the woman who led him astray, the child that brought him home.

But here's the thing, as they say in America.

Bill Caesar did not come home.

And perhaps I became impatient. Perhaps I lost my faith. Or maybe, in between takes, standing by the river with the colonel, I was merely letting my mind wander as we sometimes do when we think we're not working.

"Think he'll come back?" I asked.

I heard the horn of a train in the distance, the bark of a dog. The colonel shrugged his shoulders. We watched the huts along the river light up, the silhouettes of Americans eating dinner and watching television, playing with their children. I remember seeing cars pass over the bridge, the sound of crickets like bells, an old woman sweeping off her porch. It was then that I turned to the colonel and offered what, at the time, was truly nothing more than idle chatter. I was not suggesting an idea for another movie. I was merely asking a question, part of my ongoing curiosity about Bill Caesar, a man whose story now seemed on the verge of ending—if only he would've faced the consequences of his actions!

"Is his grandmother still alive?" I asked.

Nominated by The Gettysburg Review

DO THE DO

by ELTON GLASER

from SOUTHERN POETRY REVIEW

When the drummer tattoos his snare
And puts the hammer down on the high hat,
Taking a stick to the blues,

The band kicks in, Uptown Louie and the Regulators,
Brawl of piano and a foghorn sax, gitstrings
On rhythm and lead, with a fat bass at the bottom.

This ain't no martini music, chanteuse
In a throaty hush, smoke wrapped around her
Like a foxhead stole, brushes soft on the tight skin.

This is mayhem in the neighborhood, rimshots and beer.
It brings the ladies out
Like a hard knuckle knocking at the back door.

It gets the mopes and the gimps and the bedridden up
And slips their sockets loose
Until they do the do with a shaky strut.

Louie's looking good tonight in a Hong Kong suit.
He's got the hair and the sneer
And a voice rough as creosote on a telephone pole.

Skeeter can make his left hand
Slap the scales around until they scream
And leap like the Holy Ghost boogie of Jerry Lee.

That's "Night Train" you hear, Bad Alvin on the honk and slur—
Ten years on the road to earn his scars
In a dozen duck-for-cover bands.

It's all jism and jungle, late love and cheroots,
Sweat equity on the dance floor.
Somebody lies about his rusty heart. Somebody don't.

And now it's "Harlem Nocturne," low in the gut,
Time split down the middle
By a midnight clock, air going blue on a slow drip.

Louie nods once at the tired room
And lets the last chord linger, so sweet, so sad
That even the dim light trembles at the end of the song.

Nominated by Southern Poetry Review, Phil Dacey

ON "BEAUTY"

by MARILYNNE ROBINSON

from TIN HOUSE

It has seemed to me for some time that beauty, as a conscious element of experience, as a thing to be valued and explored, has gone into abeyance among us. I do not by any means wish to suggest that we suffer from any shortage of beauty, which seems to me intrinsic to experience, everywhere to be found. The pitch of a voice, the gesture of a hand, can be very beautiful. I need hardly speak of daylight, warmth, silence. When I was a girl too young to give the matter any thought at all, I used to be overcome by the need to write poetry whenever there was a good storm, that is, heavy rain and wind enough to make the house smell like the woods. I wrote in a style both tragic and passé. If I had known the word, I would have probably titled all my poems "Threnody." They were inevitably lamed by my inability to think of enough good rhymes. I knew there were things amiss with them, and I hid them under my mattress and never looked at them again. I cannot claim to have been the Emmeline Grangerford of northern Idaho, because there were other serious contenders for that title in my personal acquaintance. No matter. I felt, when the fit was upon me, the purest desire to interpret into language whatever it was I felt in the storm. Nothing remarkable in that, but for me the experience was important if only because I've never really outgrown it. The old passion is gone, and the poetry, and I am no longer quite so exclusively under the spell of Edgar Allan Poe, God rest his soul. But that old sense that I must try to be an interpreter of the true and absolute world, the very planet, that has remained. I once attempted a rather melancholy poem about Being Itself, but was stymied once again by the insufficiency of rhymes.

80

I was supported in all this by a lingering romanticism, by Wordsworth and Keats at school, and, at my grandparents' house, by a far too lovely painting of the moon. Remarkable as it seems to me in retrospect, the only students in my high school who were given the skills they would need to be employable were the ones who were not considered to be up to much else. My own education was sublimely impractical, and therefore it encouraged me, always implicitly, to feel that my way of thinking about things had value. Not that anyone encouraged aspiration in me; not that I aspired; it was all much purer than that. I had, in a stuffy and provincial form, cultural permission to be attracted to what seemed to me to be beautiful. I memorized so much poetry, most of it dreadful, of course, and no one ever asked me why. They would have known why—because most of it seemed beautiful to me. I went to college and was instructed in more rigorous standards, and I am very grateful for that, needless to say.

The word *beauty* has always seemed to me unsatisfactory. I have often felt there is an essential quality for which we have no word, and that therefore I am driven back on *beauty*, or *elegance*, which has the same problem. It is interesting that both these words are French, that they displaced Old English precursors. In any case, the word *beauty* has never seemed to me quite suited to the uses I have had to make of it, as though it were never really naturalized into my interior language, or what I might call my aesthetic experience. If that did not oblige me to use the word *aesthetic*. Why this awkwardness? Why must we lapse into French or Greek to speak of an experience that is surely primary and universal? Perhaps the awkwardness of the language refers to the fact that the experience of beauty is itself complex. We all know we can be conditioned to see beauty where our culture or our generation tells us to see it. Not so very long ago, fashionable American women carried little vials of arsenic along with their powder and hairpins, a dose that gave them a pallor that was considered to be lovely at the time, though to an objective eye it must have resembled death. And we know beauty can be fraudulent, compromised. Whenever power or privilege wishes to flaunt itself, it recruits beauty into its service, or something that can at least pass as beauty and will achieve the same effect. So it is entirely appropriate to regard beauty with a critical eye. But the point should be to discover an essential beauty, not to abandon the intuition altogether.

American literature, back in the days when we still remembered the Revolution, aspired to an aesthetic of simplicity, of common speech,

81

common circumstance. These things seen under the aspect of very grand thought, of course. Eternity is as far as to the very nearest room. Then plain speech in our literature became the sign of plain thought, mental and spiritual entrapment, and, after that, this grievous state of soul came to be seen as all that plain language can possibly render. This lowered evaluation seems to have become entrenched about the time of the Depression, and to have become the condescension that mistakes itself for fellow feeling. I generalize too broadly. Faulkner is one great exception, and there are others. But American realism and naturalism seem to me to have broken speech into two dialects: an authentic speech that addresses simple thought and immediate experience, often victimized or degraded experience, and an artificial and essentially suspect speech for those who express ideas. We have educated a larger proportion of our population than any civilization in history, yet a candidate for president can be pilloried for letting slip a word the press considers vaguely recondite. The prejudice against learned language reinforces the notion that those who speak ordinary American English can't have much on their minds. More recently, the flood of faux French into universities has certainly compounded the problem, since it encourages the use of a jargon that would be laughable in a novel, or on the editorial page, or in conversation with a friend. In any case, we do not now have a dialect that allows us to speak naturally about ideas, at least in fiction. Whether this is less true for other areas of discourse, I cannot say since the attempt seems to be made so rarely.

The nineteenth century was right. Ordinary language can do as much as the mind can ask of it, and do it with extraordinary integrity. What we have lost with this awareness is respect for people in general, to whom we condescend, as though we were not all ourselves members in good standing of people in general. We explain others to ourselves without reference to what were once called their souls, to their solitary and singular participation in this mystery of being. We are not much in awe of one another these days. We do not hesitate to deprive each other of dignity or privacy, or even to deprive ourselves of them. In saying this, I am speaking of the media, journalism, and publishing, which, for all anyone knows, are no true gauge of what public feeling is, or what it could be if it formed under other influences or had other choices. The problem I am describing is not local and it is certainly not new. The emergence of democracy awaited the rise of respect for people in general, and it will not outlive its decline. What reason can there be for protecting the privacy and freedom of conscience, or even the franchise, of anyone, if we assume nothing good about those whom we are protecting and enfranchising? There is much talk about the polarization of this country. Most disturbing, I think, is the way both sides are of one mind, and they are of one mind in this: neither acts in a way that acknowledges the beauty and complexity of individual human experience. Neither treats the public—the people—with real respect. Lately, there has been talk to the effect that science has lowered humankind in its own estimation. This notion has a very long history, going back to the time when grave damage was thought to have been done by the discovery that the earth was no longer the center of the universe.

There are those who believe we have outlived every beautiful notion about what human life must be because this is the age of science. These people must not have been paying attention. Science, being one of the unequivocally human undertakings, describes humanity to itself, for weal and woe, in everything it does. Mathematicians and physicists have a habit of using the words *beautiful* and *elegant* to endorse theories that are likelier to cleave to the nature of things because of their efficiency and soundness of structure. I would like to see language brought to a similar standard. If this were at all a philosophic age, we might be wondering why it is that beauty can test reality and solve its encryptions in the modest, yet impressive, degree our humanity allows. For me, this is a core definition of beauty: that it is both rigorous and dynamic and that it somehow bears a deep relationship to truth. If I seem to be brushing up against logical positivism, I assure that you that in taking statements that science produces as norms of proof, I mean only that we are part of a mystery, a splendid mystery within which we must attempt to orient ourselves if we are to have a sense of our own nature. I say this knowing that contemporary science suggests, with its talk of unexpressed dimensions of reality and the effect of the observer on what seems to us to be autonomous and objective reality, that the apparent lawfulness of nature can seem to be what the old philosopher Jonathan Edwards said it was: a courtesy to our limitations. I believe that there is a penumbra of ignorance and error and speculation that exceeds what might be called the known world by a very large factor indeed. I believe this penumbra is as beautiful in its own way as what I have called truth because it is the action of the human consciousness. It is most human and most beautiful because it wants to be more than consciousness; it wants to be truth.

Admiring the cosmos carries certain risks in these contentious times. It sounds like piety. It sounds, more specifically like an argument for intelligent design. Oddly, great areas of science are closed off from consideration by people who take themselves to be defenders of science, precisely because it is impossible not to marvel at the things science reveals. Controversy has not gone well in this country for some time, and there could be no better illustration of that fact than that, at this moment, when gorgeous hypotheses bloom day after day, when the heavens should be as wonderful to us as to the Babylonians, we refuse to look up from a quarrel we've carried on now for 150 years. Anyone who reads an occasional article on genetic research knows that both change and stability are more mysterious than the simple mechanisms of Darwin, championed by writers such as Richard Dawkins, can by any means acknowledge. On the other hand, anyone who has read a little good theology, or encountered a devout mind, is perfectly aware that religion does not hang on the question of the origin of species. I have read that there are great spiral structures in space so vast that no account can be made of them, no hypothesis made to describe their formation, and they appear somehow to have their own weather, so to speak. To what can we compare these things but to the mind that discovered and described them, the human mind, which, over the centuries, has amassed by small increments the capacity for knowing about them. Planet earth is not even a speck of dust in the universe, and how uncanny it is that we have contrived to see almost to the edge of what time and light will allow, to look back billions of years and see suns forming. When I read about such things, I think how my own heroes would have loved them. What would Melville have done with dark energy, or Poe with spooky action at a distance? Whitman could only have loved the accelerating expansion of the universe. Dickinson probably knew already that our sun is atremble with sound waves, like a great gong. It is a loss of the joy of consciousness that keeps us from appropriating these splendors for the purposes of our own thought.

Religion, or at least those religions that derive from poor, battle-weary Genesis, has believed that humankind holds a privileged and central place in the created order. I am very far from suggesting that by this privilege was meant so trivial a thing as the capacity of knowing on a scale almost commensurate for grandeur with the universe in which we are so trivial a presence. I'm no believer in proofs. John Ames and I are very much of one mind on that point. But perhaps we should note in the insights of the ancients another thing at which to marvel. They recognized a special destiny for humankind, when grueling labor and early death would have consumed most of them. The destiny we have made for ourselves may well be the end of us; we all know that, and they seem to have known it too. Still, there is magnificence in it all. So the supposed conflict of science and religion is meaningless, because these two most beautiful ventures of expression of the human spirit are reduced to disembodied fragments of themselves with no beauty about them at all, which is a great pity since their beauty should have been the basis for harmony between them.

When I wrote *Gilead*, I used the plain voice suited to the place and character. I've been very gratified by the responsive readers who found the language moving and at the same time noticed how ordinary it really is. Plain language has a strong, subtle music in it, which is intimately related to its capacity for meaning. I think every significant American poet before the modern period set out to prove this point. The fad for too long now has been to try to find the hermeneutics of practically everything, to find the agenda behind what is said, which in general seems to mean a scheme to enhance the interests of one's demographic. One hears the phrase "a hermeneutics of suspicion." All this brings to a text a reading that exists apart from the text, so whatever a writer might attempt or intend can be dismissed as self-distraction or camouflage. Then why listen for a distinctive music in the language? Why watch for a characterizing gesture? I have read that literacy has fallen among college graduates, that they are less capable of taking in the explicit sense of an editorial, for example. I suspect they were only practicing their hermeneutics: deconstructing, prying out an agenda, since attending to an explicit meaning would be like tossing the coffee and eating the paper cup. Quite simply, to approach any utterance as if its meaning is separable from its presentation is to disallow art in every positive sense of that word. It is to strip away the individuation that might make a work a new witness, and it is to violate the bond of reader and writer. The essence of our art lies in creating a lingering dream, good or bad, that other souls can enter. Dreaming one's soul into another's is an urgent business of the human mind: the dreaming itself, not whatever agenda can supposedly be extracted from it. As art, it plays on the nerves and the senses like a dream. It unfolds over time like a dream. It makes its own often disturbing and often inexplicable appeal to memory and emotion, creating itself again in the consciousness of the reader or hearer. There have always been people for whom all this makes no sense, but the refusal to take literature on its own terms somehow came to seem sophisticated and swept the universities. Stranger things have happened, I suppose.

In any case, fiction has the character of a hypothesis, or it is written in an implied subjunctive, because it means that reality is greater than any present circumstance. It says, "I will show you how that past or other or potential reality might feel, how it might look." And here I wish to say again that the beauty of language is rigorous and exploratory: it creates consent to, and participation in, a sense of coherency that is something like the fabric of experience itself. Anyone who makes the effort can find four or five scientific cosmologies, all of them substantially wrong, no doubt, and all perhaps in some part right. They are webs of possibility fashioned from conjecture and observation, and every one of them is human consciousness projected on that starry void from which humankind has never been able to turn its gaze. How strange it is that no new thought comes from these new heavens. Copernicus and Galileo moved the world, so to speak, with ideas that were fundamentally far less astonishing than those that have come in the last few decades. The effect of this abeyance of beauty of which I have been speaking is very general in contemporary experience. Everything we are asked to look at is abrupt, bright, loud, in the visual sense of the word, especially the evening news. We are expected to react to it, not to consider it. It is addressed to our nervous systems, never to our minds. I know the assumptions at work here, and none of them is a compliment to the public or, to employ older language, to the people. There is no inevitability in any of it. The visual technologies are blamed, but in fact no more beautiful studies of the human face exist than those made in film while it was still possible for the camera to pause for a moment.

I spoke before about the epic battle between parody science and parody religion. Anything stripped of the beauty and dignity proper to it is a parody. Public life itself is now entirely too vivid an instance of this phenomenon. We are losing an atmosphere that is necessary to our survival. We are losing the motive and the rationale that supported everything we claim to value. But the solution is everywhere around us, and is as simple as seeing and hearing. We are a grand and tragic creature, humankind, and we must see ourselves as we are, quite possibly the greatest wonder of creation, alone in our capacity for awe, and in that fact altogether worthy of awe. We know that humankind has sat around its fires from time immemorial and told its tales and told them again, elaborating and refining, and we know that certain of these tales have become myth, epic, fable, Holy Writ. Now, because we have devoted so much ingenuity to the project, we have devised more ways to tell ourselves more stories, which means only that an ancient impulse is still so strong in us as to impel the invention of new means and occasions for telling and hearing to satisfy this appetite for narrative. At the most fundamental level, narrative is how we make sense of things—that is, our experience of ongoing life is a story we tell ourselves, more or less true, depending on circumstance. I believe this narrative is the essential mode of our being in the world, individually and collectively. Maintaining its integrity—maintaining a sense of the essentially provisional or hypothetical character of the story we tell ourselves— is, I will suggest, our greatest practical, as well as moral and ethical, problem. Fiction is narrative freed from the standard of literal truth. In effect, it is the mind exploring itself, its impulse to create hypothetical cause and consequence.

I know there is nothing fashionable about putting active consciousness at the center of a discussion of what we are. I know phrases like "our being in the world" are considered extremely suspect, if they are considered at all. If my language is somewhat romantic, it is so in reaction against an inappropriate reductionism that especially afflicts the discussion of consciousness, and which cannot at all address the experience of reading, hearing, or creating narrative. Nor can it, for that matter, address thought. There is, of course, the honorable strategy of inquiry called reductionism, which narrows a question in order to clarify it, and there is a very bad habit, also called reductionism, which is a tendency to forget that the question has been narrowed, and narrowed provisionally, in service to the understanding of the complexity in which it is in fact embedded.

Yes, we share consciousness with cats and dogs. They can interpret the sound of the refrigerator door opening, and we can interpret a ballad or a mathematical formula. However, with all respect to animals, there are real limits to the usefulness of the analogy they provide. Our extraordinary complexity is not only our distinction among the animals and our glory but also our tragedy, our capacity to do extraordinary harm. We may have most of our genome in common with the higher primates, as well as with pigs and fungi, it seems, but we are the only creatures who would ever have thought to split the atom. This is an instance of our unique ability to get ourselves in the worst kind of trouble, to create trouble this seismic world, left to itself, would have spared us. To err is human; to err catastrophically is definitively human.

Our capacity for error at its most beautiful can be seen as the ability to make tentative models of reality and then reject them. We are certainly unique in our drive to know very much more than we need to know, and this capacity for making and rejecting has been crucial through the unfathomable amount of learning we have done since it first occurred to us to fashion a primitive weapon. Reductionism that would make us unique chiefly for our upright stance and our opposable thumbs sounds tough-minded. But I suspect its great appeal lies in its exclusion of the data to be drawn from our unique history as the makers and products of civilization. The neo-Darwinists insist that we and our behavior are formed around the project of ensuring our genetic survival. History should be a sufficient rebuttal.

I tend to draw analogies from science because I believe that our sense of the world is always hypothesis, and we are sane in the sense that we understand this. To proceed by hypothesis is the method of modern science, ideally. It is one of the dominant assumptions of modern culture that science by its nature drives back the shadows of error. It is this confidence that very often leads science to forget skepticism and to take itself for the unique domain of truth. Many of the darkest shadows of the modern period have been the products of science, and there is no reason to call it by any other name than science simply because it was grossly in error. Racial theory and eugenics are cases in point. I say this because I wish to assert that all thought always inclines toward error. The prejudices that would exclude one tradition of thought from this tendency, be it science or be it theology, are simply instances of the tendency toward error.

Narrative is the strategy of the mind for putting things in relation. I know I assume many things by using such a term as "the mind," or by suggesting that it could by its nature have such a thing as a strategy. I believe I am proceeding at least by analogy with things science tells us: for example, that heart cells beat, and that brain cells seem to be independently capable of cognition. I have never read an account of the processes by which healing occurs in the body or pathogens are dealt with by the immune system that did not invite the use of the word tactic or strategy. The ability to put things in relation—to say, "If this, then, that," or even, "And then and then"— is as essential to our survival as the ability to heal. Therefore, in speaking of the mind, I think it is reasonable to assume an intrinsic purpose and complexity of the kind that one finds in every other physical system. Of course, failure is the snake in the Garden in every one of these systems, brilliant as they are. Just so, the mind is prolific in generating false narrative. Like the immune system, it can turn against itself, defeat itself.

It has lately been fashionable to say, quoting Nietzsche, that there is no fact, only interpretation. This itself is an interpretation of the fact that in our efforts to understand the world, we ordinarily get things a little wrong, sometimes very wrong. Fact does break through interpretation when it startles us, shames us, or kills us. I would say that every utterance, except the very slightest one, feels the pull of error, a sort of impalpable and irresistible gravity exerted on it by habit, assumption, fear, by the mass of presumed knowledge that is itself shaped by the same pull of error. I would say also that this bias away from truth is reinforced by the character of language itself. Language makes sense without reference to the truth, or with an oblique or even an inverted reference to it. So why have we sat around our fires these last dozen millennia, telling each other stories? What are we doing when we write fiction? What is the value of intentional untruth, acknowledged as such by teller and hearer, writer and reader? Granting that, at its best, fiction can be said to express a higher truth— I will not for the moment attempt a definition of that phrase—the great majority of the tales we tell have more modest aspirations, or they rehearse and reinforce conventional notions, or play on prejudice or fear. If, as I have said, narratives are always false in some degree, then perhaps fiction might be called the creative exploration of the tendency of narrative toward falsification, or toward the inevitable primacy of mind and language over objective fact in any account we attempt to make of the unfolding of the phenomenal world. Fiction might also be called the creative exploration of the power of narrative to enlist belief, even in the absence of what we ordinarily call credibility. Or, if we are at ease in the world of fabrication, perhaps this is so because every construction we make of the world is, or should be, hypothetical. It is a story we tell ourselves. Being hypothetical, it is also at best falsifiable. We believe we understand someone; we find we've been wrong when we hurt them or they hurt us. We think we know how we are perceived and valued, and learn that those around us have quite another view of us, far better or far worse. I might suggest that we are sane in the degree that our internal narrative retains the character of hypothesis, permitting editing, necessary adjustment, the assimilation of new understanding. Fictional narratives consistently employ surprise, reversal, irony, hidden identity. The wandering Ulysses is continually confronted with prodigies that alter the effective terms of survival. Only his shrewdness, his ability to respond to urgencies that constantly change, allows him to return alive to Ithaca. Disrupted hypothesis is structured into fiction of all kinds, from *Don Quixote* to "Casey at the Bat." Freud used Sophocles to illustrate his thesis, and so will I. Oedipus the king understands himself as wise, virtuous, and fortunate. In the course of the tragedy, he learns that in every way he has considered himself to have been fortunate, virtuous, and wise, he has in fact lived out a destiny that can only lead him to misery and exile, to something worse than disgrace. He was doomed to misunderstand, to live by an utterly false hypothesis, so perfect in its seeming consistency with experience that it was destroyed all at once, suddenly, catastrophically. For the rest of us, at best we remind ourselves that there are always limits to what we can know, that things are not always as they appear to us. These fictions I have described are in fact multiple narratives, the one that has the initial appearance of truth, the truer narrative that disrupts it, and then the overarching narrative that tells us that the best of us and the wisest of us can sometimes be very wrong. At our worst, we fall into inappropriate certainty. In individuals, this can be anything from irksome to pathological. In societies, it can be literally atrocious.

Perhaps one function of fiction is to train us in the fact of the intrinsic plausibility of narrative, that is, to practice us in acknowledging the fact that plausibility is no guarantee of truth, that plausibility can be merely an effect of intelligibility compounded by fantasy, or fear, or worse. Elvis is alive and bussing tables in a truck stop in Arizona. Extraterrestrials take an uncivil interest in the anatomy of earthlings. Jesus eloped with Mary Magdalene to the south of France. These narratives flourish as they do under a thin pretense of journalism and a thinner pretense of scholarship. Clearly, acknowledged fiction does not teach us the lesson well enough, that we are inescapably error prone, and that what strikes us as plausible has no necessary relation to truth. We need only consider the potency of the blood libel against the Jews or the impact of the Protocols of the Elders of Zion or, more recently, the British document that seemed to confirm the suspicion that Saddam Hussein possessed weapons of mass destruction.

I have a theory about this moment in American history. We have all forgotten what ought to be the hypothetical character of our thinking. I know I have described the ability to absorb and modify as the mark of sanity, and I wish only to underscore this view. The problem at the most obvious level is the much-noted disappearance of the art of compromise. In general, we are inappropriately loyal to our hypotheses, rather than to the reality of which they are always a tentative sketch. This is a special problem in a climate of urgency and anxiety. In the privacy of the classroom, as aware as they are of the afflicted state of the world, my students sometimes ask me if I have any explanation for what we are doing there. Why write fiction, they ask, and why read it? What does it mean, why does it matter? They are themselves engrossed in the art as writers and readers, and yet they ask these questions, and I have had to give a great deal of thought to their questions in order to feel that I can reply in a way that can do them any kind of justice. It might never have occurred to me to answer these questions if my students had not expected me to know the answers. I tell them we are doing something so ancient, so pervasive, and so central to human culture, that we can assume its significance, even if we cannot readily describe or account for it. There is no reason to suppose the invention of narrative is in any way a marginal activity. Narratives define whole civilizations to themselves, for weal or woe. It surprises my students a little to find themselves placed in continuity with humankind, since they have been encouraged to believe, as I have also been encouraged to believe, that, as moderns, we are on the far side of a rupture in the history of civilization that makes all that we do different in kind from all that went before. I am telling them that they should follow the grain of their humanity, that words are beautiful and thoughts are shapely, and that they participate in the mystery of these facts as surely as Shakespeare ever did. They have been taught, as I was taught also, that the modern experience has brought with it certain disillusionments, typically unspecified though sometimes invoking the First World War, that curtail aspiration or even embarrass it. The wisdom we have supposedly acquired in the course of our disillusionment has given us to know that the great questions are closed, and they are closed not because they have been answered but because we now know they were meaningless to begin with, no matter how handsomely they may have figured in *The Epic of Gilgamesh* or *Paradise Lost*. Fond as I am of the old great ideas and persuaded as I am that they did not die from the excesses of the twentieth or nineteenth or seventeenth centuries, and that they did not perish under the razor of logical positivism, I really do not believe that they are the only great ideas of which the species is capable. It is because we have isolated them as illusions and imagined ourselves to be beyond illusions, that, in putting them aside, we have—

by no means inevitably—foreclosed the possibility of new grand thought. There has been a pronounced tendency for the last four centuries or so to demystify the mind and the self. It was a project of early modern science, and it is a tendency still vigorously present, not much changed by the passage of time and the advance of neuroscience. Not coincidentally, it is very much in harmony with the neo-utilitarianism of our cultural moment, as well as with the fads of illness and cure or of dysfunction and reformation that seem always to entrance our public, caught forever, as they always seem to be, between anxiety or self-disparagement and undashable hope.

There is an economic rationale at work here, favoring a demystified view. If the operations of the mind are assumed by the public to be simple and standard, these fads can of course be mass-marketed. And there is the belief that Americans in particular are in fact a bit stupid, that their emotions are few and primitive. It is this belief that led to our own recent oddly Maoist cultural revolution, the intentional dumbing down of everything in our collective life that requires or reflects intelligence and even minimal education, except, perhaps, for tax forms and the fine print on the back of credit card applications. Stupid is not a dialect that can tell us anything we need to know, and we have installed it as the language of journalism and public life to truly regrettable effect. Who would deny this? Yet the prejudice that insists on finding an essential simplicity in the human brain, sometimes called the most complex object known to exist in the universe, retains its authority.

The human situation is beautiful and strange. We are in fact Gilgamesh and Oedipus and Lear. We have achieved this amazing levitation out of animal circumstance by climbing our rope of sand, insight and error, corrective insight and persistent error. The working of the mind is astonishing and beautiful. I remember two lines from a poem I learned in high school: "Let not young souls be smothered out before / they do strange deeds and fully flaunt their pride." That poem protested poverty, as I recall, but privilege can smother too, and the best education can smother if the burden of it is to tell the young that they need not bother being young, to distract them from discovering the pleasures of their own brilliance, and to persuade them that basic humanity is an experience closed to them.

My theory of narrative as a fundamental act of consciousness implies to me that paranoia might be entrapment in a bad narrative, and depression may be the inability to sustain narrative. I believe we are collectively putting ourselves at risk of both paranoia and depression. In an earlier paragraph, I put the question of the higher meaning that can sometimes be achieved in fiction. I would say that meaning is essentially a new discovery of the joy of consciousness—and, of course, the perils of it. We live in uncertainty, which means that we are always exposed to the possibility of learning more, for weal and woe. I would call this awareness humanism, an ultimate loyalty to ourselves that we are all too ready to withhold.

Nominated by Tin House

THE FALL OF PUNICEA

fiction by PAUL STAPLETON

from J JOURNAL

I pulled open the city gate with my white flag unfurled, billowing out above my head. Outside the walls the Volsci were lined up in ranks on the Campus Martius, maybe a thousand of them in battle gear. I prayed to Fish they would honor the sign of ceasefire. The minute they saw me, their choruses were quelled, and their drumming was tamped to a muffled beat.

"Vive Pax Tiberna!" I shouted.

The Volsci campfires crackled in the wind. Some of the soldiers laughed, "The Pax is dead."

I ignored them. "I come as an ambassador to King Victorrex Gloriosus, sacker of cities, breaker of stone, brave son of Hedd." I knew I would get him at the mention of his father.

Victorrex signaled, and three Volsci ran towards me. I drew in my breath and tried to remain as wooden as a statue. Still I trembled. When the soldiers reached me, one snatched my flag and the other two my arms, tugging me forward into the Volsci crowd. I figured I was a dead man, but I suppressed my fear and trusted in Fish. The soldiers tossed me before Victorrex, who stood stone-faced, his cheeks covered in war paint. We were close in manly age.

"Sextus the Learned," he said. I must admit I was flattered by his recognition. My reputation had been growing in the region ever since my royally funded sabbatical to the library in Alexandria. I fancied myself a philosopher by trade. "Why does King Tarquin not come himself?"

"The King does not wish to offend you with his coarse speech." I bowed obsequiously.

"Well spoken," he said. "What is your message?"

"King Tarquin sees your tremendous army. At your martial chorus terror shakes the marrow of our bones. Proud you must be of your unmatched weapons of modernity." I continued on like this with line after line of pure pulp. I knew he would eat it up. One thing I've learned is that people can't resist flattery, especially imperialistic egomaniacs.

"You speak the truth," Victorrex said. "But what is your mission? Is it that you sue for peace?"

"Certainly not. King Tarquin knows that to sue for peace from a man such as you, the image of Mars, is an insult."

Victorrex hacked out a clam of sputum and expectorated on the ground between us. "Then why do you come?" he asked.

"King Tarquin knows the battle is over even before it has begun, but he also deems it unworthy of your honor not to put up a fight. Confident in your confidence in the confidence of your soldiers . . ." It was a mouthful, and I admit I was nervous, but the king could not hide his disdain, which spread across his face, clear as his war paint.

"Please, hurry up," he said, "my soldiers are impatient to slaughter your troops and rape your women."

"I fully understand," I said. "To get straight to the point, King Tarquin would like to challenge three warriors from your army to fight three of ours, three on three, so to speak. Surely, you will not fear such a contest."

A cry rose up from the Volsci, "Bring it on!" But Victorrex raised his hand and silence returned. "You challenge three of my soldiers?" he asked.

"Unless, of course, you are afraid, in which case, we can go ahead with the full-scale battle."

"Victorrex Gloriosus fears nothing," the dupe said.

"King Tarquin knows this, but if you are, shall I say, uncomfortable with our request, we can go ahead . . ." It went on like this a half-dozen times before we finally negotiated the terms: three of our men, the Horatii, would fight to the death against three of their men, the Curiatii. If the Horatii won, the Volsci would return to their homes in the next town over, and if the Curiatii won, the Volsci would in short order raid, pillage, and sack Punicea. It was not exactly a bargain, but I knew a good deal when I heard one. We shook hands, and I strutted back to the city with my white flag blazing above my back.

After Regi blew his trumpet, and King Tarquin announced the terms, the mustered Puniceans let loose a sigh of relief. The youthful Horatii even leaped a bit in anticipation of the competition. The priests were called out of the temple with the golden statue of Fish, and a pious sacrifice of clams was offered to our favorite god in thanksgiving for the delay of death. The priests also chanted petitions seeking victory in the coming combat. Their song was a solemn one:

> Fish, source of our life,
> Swimmer and lord of the sea,
> Give us victory in the coming strife,
> And we will sacrifice hoards of clams for thee.

The Horatii knelt before Fish and offered a silent votive prayer, and then the priests hauled Fish back into the temple with the women and children. I stood atop the city tower with King Tarquin, and he allowed me to address the troops: "Puniceans, if the Volsci should prove victorious in the match, our martial plan is to run for our lives. If you want to stick around and fight, you're welcome to, but I advise against it." The faces of my fellow citizens blanched, ashen with fright, and I realized this was no way to rally their spirits. "Warriors, do not fear," I continued. "The Horatii are the fiercest men in the Tiber Valley and perhaps the world." A little hyperbole could not hurt. "We shall triumph behind their strength."

Cheers rose up, and I decided I should end on the high note. I gave a simple benediction of Fish and nodded to the King, who gave a thumbs-up and ordered the city gate opened. Then we all stomped out into the broad plain of the Campus Martius, led by Tarquin and me, with the three Horatii right behind us. The Volsci had swept away their campfires to make room for the contest and were now lined along the far side of the plain in front of our wheat fields, which extended several hundred yards back to the sylvan overgrowth of the thick brimming forest. When the Volsci saw us fully assembled, a trumpet sounded, and the three Curiatii strode forth from their midst, identical triplets, the only difference among them their colored mantles, gold, silver, and white. As radiant as the sun, they were beauteous and strength-filled, rumored to be lovers of ladies, and not truly of Volscian stock, or even Mediterranean, but foundlings, left in the Tiber to drown by a roaming tribe of the warlike peoples of the North. But this was no time to contest their genealogy.

As the Curiatii reached the middle of the plain, King Tarquin stared as if stunned by their beauty, and a gasp of wonder heaved out from our soldiery. But the Horatii were not to be intimidated and gallantly marched forth to face their illustrious foes. The sets of triplets met at centerfield, shook hands, and then counted off ten paces in either direction. The crowd on both sides joined in the count, "One, two, three, four . . . " At ten, the Horatii wheeled to face their opponents, who had already turned on nine, the cheats, eager to fight. Spears flew, dirt spewed up, and, faster then you could say, "Victorrex Gloriosus," one of the Curiatii was dead. A swift spear had torn straight through his comely face, and his body flipped into a tumble as the life force gushed out in gore. A cheer rushed forth from the Punicean onlookers. It was now a three on two.

Emboldened by success, our three champions fell into pursuit, and the Curiatii fled in the opposite direction. Victorrex cast his sullen eye upon the cowardly retreat of his fighters and uttered castigations which could be heard above the tumultuous din. "Turn around and fight, you venereal minions of Mars!" Shamed by their leaders disapproval, the two Curiatii halted their flight, spun, and met their foe head on. Swords clashed, sparks flashed, and one of the Curiatii collided against two of the Horatii. Reeling, the Volsci fighter whirled his steel and with a lucky blow lopped off both their Punicean noggins. Their headless forms slumped into a heap, and the Volsci crowd roared with glee. At the sight of his lifeless siblings, our final warrior raised up his sword so as to give himself some legroom and high-tailed it out of there, across the Campus Martius, aiming himself for the wheat fields and, I guessed, the woods beyond. But the Volsci throng stretched itself out to barricade his escape. When our hero realized he was blocked, he reversed himself and scampered towards our side of the field, but the two Curiatii cut him off. He turned like a frightened rabbit and bolted for the far end of the campus. King Tarquin fell to his knees, and all of us did the same. Together we begged Fish for a miracle.

The Curiatii closed in on their prey like panthers on a deer, and the Volsci cheered in wild waves as our warrior sprinted away. The Curiatii outstripped each other in their thirst to catch Horatius, and the three combatants, strung out on the plain, looked as if they were vying in an Olympic foot race. The clamor of the armies echoed across the heavens, then, suddenly, at the far end of the campus, our man struck. He rotated on his heels and, with a lunging poniard, skewered one of the Curiatii before the poor bastard had time to react. The Curiatius's sword dropped from his hand, and his blood-splattered body shivered to its death in the dust. The other Curiatius stumbled into his dead brother, and he too met the Punicean's plunging poniard, which became fastened in the crook of his neck. A cheer pealed from our leaping ranks. The wound, however, was not fatal, and the enemy writhed in the grass. Our hero snatched up the sword which had killed his own two brothers, and our battalions responded with merciless applause. Then raising high into the air the murderous blade, Horatius finished off his foe with a vengeful thrust. The Curiatii were defeated, and our city was saved.

King Tarquin and I bounced into each other's arms, and our troops shouted halleluiahs to Fish. We all lifted Horatius to our shoulders, and a bunch of our men began clapping their hands in a steady rhythm, chanting, "Punicea, Punicea, Horatius the Warrior." On the other side, the Volsci were already filing away, disappearing into the woods as suddenly as they had come. Victorrex Gloriosus and some stragglers, more stunned than anything else, stared at the battlefield, dumbfounded, as if they had been turned to stone. The fallen bodies lay scattered in the field like sloughed-off snakeskins, two Curiatii on the far side of the campus, the third, the silver-cloaked, near the Horatii, not far from the city gate. I grabbed King Tarquin and told him it would be right to shake Victorrex's hand, suspecting that Victorrex was probably not too keen on our victory. A little sportsmanship could go a long way in keeping him from reneging on the terms of engagement. Besides, it was just good form. The King agreed, so we jogged over to Victorrex and exchanged handshakes. He congratulated us on the fight.

"King," I said, "why the Fates wove us this victory, I cannot fathom. But the people of Punicea are thankful to you for honoring the terms of battle. May the gods bless you, and hold you, and keep a strong wind at your back." It was an old seafaring blessing that came in handy sometimes.

A tear appeared in Victorrex's eye, and he pointed to the bodies in the battlefield. "King Tarquin, I request permission to retrieve my fallen soldiers." I was surprised at his humility and at the very request itself. I mean I didn't think he needed permission to gather the corpses of his own men. Fish knows, we didn't want them.

"By all means," King Tarquin answered him, "piety demands it."

Victorrex ordered some men to fetch his fallen soldiers. We wanted to return to the celebrations but also knew that tact was necessary. King Tarquin was trying his best to remain solemn, but the fact was he was ebullient, quietly tapping his side to the rhythm of the victory songs. This is when the real trouble began.

The women and children were spilling out of the city, and the priests set Fish in the middle of the campus, so everyone began dancing like bacchanalians around our favorite god. It was pandemonium. The only Puniceans not celebrating were Mother Horatia and her buxom daughter, who were kneeling beside the deceased Horatii, crying their womanly eyes out. Our hero too had disengaged from the hullabaloo and joined his mother and sister in their grief. The Volsci pallbearers were hauling away their corpses on makeshift stretchers slapped together with spear shafts and battle flags. When the young Horatia caught sight of them, surprisingly, she rose from her knees and dashed across the field, wailing at the top of her lungs, "My beloved is dead, my beloved is dead." At first, I thought she intended to attack the Volsci, hysterical at the slaughter of her brothers. In a way, I found it touching, although I have to admit, I wondered at the word "beloved." But when I saw her kissing and clutching the silver-cloaked Curiatius, it was obviously not the first time she had ever felt him stiff, if you get my drift, and I realized something was awry.

Her brother must have realized too because he jumped up, sword flailing above him, and rushed towards his sister, red-faced with fury. Some revelers caught wind of what was happening and raced after Horatius like a swarm of bees on a bear. King Tarquin and I hurried to whisk Horatia away, and even Victorrex and the remaining Volsci tried to shield her, but to no avail. Horatius was still raging with the fervor of combat, and not a phalanx of Spartans could have stopped him. With one fell swoop of his sword, Horatia's pretty head was bounding in the dust. I could not believe my eyes. Horatius towered above his sister's empty shoulders, panting with mania in his face, and, to be honest, for a minute there I thought he was going to slay the whole lot of us. King Tarquin, to his credit, shouted, "Stop, Horatius!" and grabbed the madman's arm. Horatius dropped his weapon, and then everyone, me included, jumped in to restrain him. Victorrex and his men scooped up the last Curiatius and hustled off into the wilderness. They had seen enough of Punicea for a day.

The entire population now formed a circle around the murder site, all of us silent with disbelief. The sun had dropped to the horizon like a red ball of blood, and twilight crept into the sky. The priests pressed through the crowd with Mother Horatia, and, when she saw her daughter slain on the ground, she shrieked from the lowest depths of her soul. Her lament echoed across the plain, and the pathos was so overwhelming that all of us began to weep. The priests transported the remains of the deceased on a ceremonial litter, leading a somber cortege to the statue of Fish. Tarquin and I grabbed Horatius by the arms and followed the procession. No one said a word, and our crying and shuffling feet were like the march of the dead into the netherworld.

The priests set down the remains of Horatia and the corpses of her brothers and ordered the clam diggers to bring out three times the normal allotment for the ensuing rites. Everyone waited in silence. The clam diggers returned from the sacred cistern with barrels teeming and poured the clams on the ground before Fish. We all kneeled in supplication, and the mounds of clams were set aflame. In silence, I begged Fish to accept our offering for the dead souls, but at the same time I was thinking about the laws that applied to the situation and the complexity of the case. You see, some years back, I had convinced King Tarquin to issue an imperative for me to "co-author" a civil law code for Punicea, based on rational principles of justice, and nothing else, not custom, not politics, not even religion. It was remarkably enlightened of him to give me the go-ahead, and it later provided me with a steady income when he designated me as the official civic adjudicator, in other words, chief justice, an appointment which came as no surprise since no one else in the city could read or write.

On the one hand, Punicean law clearly defined this situation as murder, or more specifically, sororicide. We were a community that had always emphasized familial piety, and we viewed all forms of violence against the family as intolerable. In fact, if I may say so myself, we were the first city in the Tiber Valley to condemn all domestic violence, even against women. The truth was that in most cities around the Mediterranean crimes against women were regarded less seriously than those against men. We were the only polis I knew of to make sororicide unequivocally punishable by death. On the other hand, Horatia was practically a traitor, a capital crime itself, although I realized the evidence was somewhat circumstantial. The king was probably going to call a general meeting of the citizenry, and it would be my duty to sort out the legal issues. To say the least, the circumstances portended a long night.

The sun disappeared, black night descended, and torches were stationed around the funeral gathering. After the preliminary offerings, the priests announced that Fish had swum the souls of the dead into the river of shadows. It was time now for the cremation— my least favorite part. The priests laid the bodies atop the smoldering cinders of clams, prayers were recited, hymns sung, fresh wood was set down. Then torches were applied to the corpses. The firelight flickered across our faces, and the stench of burning flesh smoked away from the remains. I felt as if I had wandered into the darkest realm of Orcus.

As I suspected, once the funeral had ended, King Tarquin called for a general meeting to be held around the central tower within the city walls. The priests transferred Fish into the city, followed by the mass of people. Once inside, the gate was closed, the women and children ordered home, and Tarquin and I accompanied Horatius to the top of the tower. Regi blew the trumpet, and Tarquin addressed the crowd. "Citizens of Punicea, this day will be remembered for ages to come. Today we survived the onslaught of the mighty Volsci. Thanks to the wits of Sextus the Learned, the courage of Horatius, and, of course, the benevolence of Fish, our city was saved." Applause rippled across the gathering. "But citizens, our joy was short lived, our triumph defiled by a heinous deed—sororicide." A collective gasp rose into the night. It was the first time anyone had actually spoken the word aloud, and I think the pronouncement made the crime seem all the more horrific. Tarquin pointed to Horatius. "The man who was our hero has become the agent of abomination."

Shouting fragmented the crowd. "But she was a traitor!" someone yelled above the others.

Tarquin raised his hands for silence and continued speaking. "Punicea is a city governed not by the whim of a king or people or priesthood, but by the rule of law. It is the law that provides order and liberates us from anarchy. Therefore, tonight we seek justice by means of our law." Again the crowd broke into shouting, and Tarquin waited for silence to return. "Before we apply that law, however, we will afford every citizen the opportunity to express his opinion."

A debate broke out that plodded through the night and into the wee hours of the morning. Seemingly every male voice in Punicea was heard, but still division reigned. King Tarquin told the crowds that a decision had to be made, and that ultimately it was his responsibility as king, chosen by the people and ordained by the priests of Fish, to execute that decision. But first he wanted to hear the advice of the civic adjudicator.

This was one speech I could have done without. I canvassed the faces of my fellow citizens and then Horatius. I had witnessed him defeat the Curiatii and save our city, but at the same time, the lunatic had murdered his own sister. "Puniceans," I said, "the law mandates death for this crime." The crowd grumbled, and I contemplated Horatius, who stared fixedly into the night. "By crucifixion," I added. It was a method we had learned from the Etruscans, although we had never actually put it into practice—we never had the need. It was the latest technology and supposedly more humane than the traditional methods: flaying, gutting, drowning in a sack with monkey, cock, dog, and snake, or even decapitation. I don't know how many stories I had heard of bungled beheadings that ended with executioners hacking away at a neck like an overgrown milkweed.

The citizens were in a frenzy, some screaming approval, some cursing the law. "Where would we be without Horatius!" someone yelled. I asked Regi to blow the trumpet. He let loose a high piercing C-note, and everyone grabbed their ears. Silence returned.

"I understand the case is a nuanced one," I said. "Yet it is not my duty to express my own opinion but to explain the law. I will address what I see as the basic positions of our citizens, and for each I will explain how the law applies." People actually applauded. "One opinion claims that all violence is wrong and opposed to the true spirit of the Pax Tiberna. These people, mostly the tree keepers, believe violence has no place whatsoever in the civil law code."

"Tell it, Sexy!" one of the tree keepers yelled. I really did not like these guys and their steadfast pacifism. I had spent years co-writing the civil code to establish a lasting justice in our city and to make Punicea a model for the Tiber Valley, the Mediterranean, and even the world. Then I risked my life to save our hides by negotiating the three-on-three with the Volsci, yet all these jerks had to say was that everything I had done was antithetical to the Pax Tiberna. To hell with them.

"Nonetheless, the law is what it is, and unless we rewrite the whole code, we have to stand by what it says. Even if it were changed this very night, the rule of *ex post facto* still applies."

"What does that mean?" It was one of the tree keepers.

"It means if you don't like the way I've written the laws, you should have beaten your spear into a stylus, not a pruning hook." I got a mild laugh with that line, but someone shouted, "Mercy before justice!" and hissing and catcalls punctuated the general din. I resumed speaking, but was muted by arguments and shouting. Then Horatius himself called out, "Citizens of Punicea!" Only a few listened until he shouted again, "Citizens of Punicea!" When they realized it was the man himself who was speaking, everyone came to order. "Citizens," he said. "Today I have committed an unforgivable crime. I have killed my own sister. I stand guilty before you and before the law. My punishment is death, and I accept my fate with equanimity." His display of fortitude was altogether admirable, but then he added, "But, please, think of my mother."

Think of his mother. From an objective standpoint, a mother in these circumstances would normally evoke pity, compassion, even outright pardon, but anyone who knew Mother Horatia knew otherwise. Mother Horatia was probably the least-liked woman in all Punicea. She was renowned for her bitter personality and penchant for insult, and not a woman in town had ever spent an afternoon with her, laundering clothes in the river or picking berries on the outskirts of the Campus Martius or gathering crops at harvest time, without coming away battered by her sarcasm and brusqueness, if not, in fact, her fists. She was a feisty, combative shrew, obnoxious beyond reason, to the extent that no one marveled when her husband Horatius wandered off and was "lost" at sea. Who could endure her daily abuse? The three Horatii boys had been so emotionally battered at the hands of their sadistic mother that they could not help being what they were: the nastiest sons of a bitch and the fiercest fighters our people had ever seen. Over the span of the years, not a Punicean kid their age had not been bullied by them, and to be honest, a compelling reason for establishing the civil law code in the first place was to keep the Horatii in check, because in their manhood, most of us were downright terrified of them. Young Horatia was another matter altogether. Rather than nasty, she had turned needy, seeking the affection she did not receive at home in every Tom, Dick, and Harry who stumbled her way. To put it mildly, the Horatii children were damaged goods, and Mother Horatia was to blame. Think of his mother? Fish forbid, and I said as much, more or less: "The law does not consider emotions, good or bad, Horatius. The law is blind to personal feelings. Otherwise it becomes subjective, which leads to the rule of caprice, not justice. No, the law must be impartial."

The whole crowd paused and communally stared at me. Many nodded their heads in agreement, but soon there was a ruckus again, screaming, hollering, a clamor of confusion. King Tarquin raised his arms. Regi blew his trumpet until his ears were red. Finally, somehow, the crowd settled down to where I could speak again.

"The next opinion calls for Horatius's complete exoneration on two counts, first, because Horatia was a traitor, and, second, because he is the savior of our city." I held up two fingers for dramatic effect. "What we saw on the Campus Martius suggested Horatia may have been, shall we say, allied with one of the Curiatii. But what of it? So the girl slept around. That's no news to anyone around here." I darted my eyes from man to man, the many I knew who had partaken of Horatia's charms. "Furthermore, at this point in time, we have no statute equating carnal knowledge with treachery. Yes, it may be in poor taste to sleep with the Volsci, but it's no crime."

The cads all cheered.

"As for Horatius, he did indeed save our city, but there is no law which grants immunity to anyone in Punicea, not even the king. If Horatius were to be exonerated, not only would the law against sorori- cide be jeopardized, but the very law code itself. Once an exception is allowed, it opens the door for all kinds of excuses, and then the law is nothing. We're right back to the arbitrary decisions of kings and priests that we wanted to eradicate in the first place." There were murmurs of dismay. "In other words," I said, "according to the law, we would have to execute Fish himself if he slew his sister."

I understand now it was the wrong choice of words. The crowd did not like the comparison at all, not one little bit, and I should have known better. The priests shook fists at me, shouting, "Blasphemy!" Again I asked Regi for a trumpet blast, but this time skirmishes broke out, and several men hooked their hands on the stanchions of the city tower and began rocking it back and forth. It was pretty obvious that a full scale riot was about to break loose. King Tarquin signaled Regi again, but the rocking sent me falling into the trumpeter, knocking him off the tower. I was trying to hold on, praying to Fish for a way out of this jam, when I heard the sound of cracking wood. The legs of the tower had given out, and Tarquin and Horatius and I plummeted. Be- fore I knew it, I was on the ground, snatched up by my shirtsleeves, socked with a right cross, trapped in a melee. The entire populace was pummeling away at each other in a free-for-all. I lost sight of Tarquin, and soon I was flinging punches myself, at first in self-defense, then I noticed the tree keepers, and even I was on the offensive. It was mad- ness.

In the middle of it all the priests seized Fish and dragged him into the midst of the fracas. In retrospect, it was a shrewd move, because, as soon as we all saw Fish, we held onto our fists in fear of striking the deity himself. I'm sure none of us had any idea what the consequences of such a blow would be, but I guarantee no one wanted to find out. In a matter of minutes, the fervor of the fight was lost, and we stood around, ashamed, our eyes sharpened on the priests and Fish. We had no idea what was going to happen next, but it was pretty obvious that for the moment the priests were in charge of Punicea. King Tarquin was tangled beneath a pile of beams and broken planks from what had been the city tower, and to my relief, he was all right. A few priests yanked him to his feet and escorted him to Fish. Then the eldest priest, Father Nupa, beckoned his younger brethren to lift him onto their shoulders so he could see above the crowd.

Nupa was very old. In fact, according to popular belief, he was 273 years old. I had always wondered about this, but not a soul of us could recall a time when Nupa was not alive. The grandparents of the oldest of the original settlers could not even remember a time when Nupa was not a priest. He hailed from the days in Carthage before King Tarquin's father had sailed from the homeland with colonists in search of a more peaceful existence. Nupa could speak of the early days of the cult of Fish, before it was an organized religion, when Fish himself swam the depths of the watery world, more of a tyrannical, vengeful, almost pathological Pisces than the fatherly Fish we all knew and loved. Some claimed Nupa had actually seen Fish himself with his own eyes, and it was commonly known that at one time he had personally sacrificed offerings of much more than clam innards. To put it nicely, in my generation the life expectancy of firstborns had improved dramatically, though there was still a faction of zealots who looked upon the old days as the good old days.

Now Nupa began to speak, but he was so old, and his voice so brittle, that no one could hear a word of what he was saying. Still, we dared not interrupt his speech. He surveyed the crowd and rambled on until he fell into a deep sleep. We had been awake the whole night. At 273, I could understand why he was sleepy, but no one seemed to know if his speech was finished or not. Everyone was afraid to ask, so we stood sheepishly, waiting. In the east the black steed of night began to flee from the chariot of Apollo. A rooster crowed. The sound startled Nupa, who awoke and peered at us, his eyes creeping from face to face. Then he croaked out in a voice like a cackling bird, "Fish fangs, shark bites, dangerous seawater," or something to that effect. He repeated this litany at least a half dozen times, then slumped on the sacerdotal shoulders of his brethren and fell asleep again. That was it.

We all turned to one another in puzzlement. What in the name of

Fish did that mean? No one seemed in any hurry to offer an interpretation except some of the priests, that is. Without warning six of the clowns tramped into the crowd and grabbed the civic adjudicator—yeah, me!—by the shoulders. Then one of them announced in a voice terribly easier to understand than Nupa's that Fish demanded a penitential offering. He was not at all pleased with the way we had been behaving, and the sacrifice required the flesh of the author of the civil law code. Sextus the Learned must die. How he got this out of the fish-fang business was beyond me, but none of my compatriots seemed to think it too far-fetched. I screamed to King Tarquin to do something. After all, we were co-authors of the civil law code, weren't we? But it was too late. The case was beyond his jurisdiction. It had become a priestly affair, and I was the sacrificial clam.

The priests bound me with ropes woven by their wives for ceremonial use, flattened me out supine, and fixed me to stakes before the statue of Fish. Prayers were offered, and a flaming torch was presented by one of the priests as the others partook in a solemn ritual of spitting in my face. Then the scrolls of the civil law code, having been removed from the city archives, were placed beside me.

"Go ahead, burn me, but not the law code," I cried. "Please, it took me years to compose."

A section was torn off and shoved into my mouth as a gag. The priest approached me with the fiery torch, ready to ignite his sacrifice. I was about to die. The situation was so surreal that I could actually hear infernal drums greeting me from the underworld. They were getting louder and louder. One of the priests glanced around in perplexity. Oddly, he seemed to hear the drumming, too. Soon flaming arrows and catapulted stones were pelting us like hail in midsummer, and it became altogether clear that the underworld had nothing to do with any of this. The Volsci were back.

Within minutes, the city was in flames, the walls breached, and the citizens of Punicea were scrambling for their lives. I wriggled in vain to break free, pegged to the ground, and when the massive statue of Fish wobbled over in the chaos, I thought I was a goner, but remarkably the statue fell over me, but not on me, the lateral curvature between the pectoral and caudal fins creating a snug little niche for a skinny little bookworm like me. There I lay throughout the entire sack of the city, safe and sound, protected by Fish, discovered only after the last Punicean had been slaughtered and all the women carried off, when Victorrex Gloriosus ordered the "big flounder" hoisted up and to his astonishment found me and the civil law code preserved and basically intact. Call it what you will, chance, serendipity, a miracle, and though the opportunity for negotiations had passed, at least on a municipal scale, arrangements for an individual philosopher were another matter. Apparently, the civil law code and I were known commodities, whose value could be appreciated even by a man masked in war paint. As the conquerors paraded in triumph across the Campus Martius and into the woods, battle trophies were raised up in front of Victorrex Gloriosus: the statue of Fish, Regi's trumpet, the scrolls of the law code, and me. Elevated above the throng, I gazed back at what only a short time before had been Punicea, now a rubble of wood, bones, and dead men—and clams. Before a single tear could well up in my eye, however, a spear shaft prodded my nose forward in the direction we were headed, towards the city of the Volsci and my new home.

Nominated by J. Journal

NOTES FOR MY DAUGHTER AGAINST CHASING STORMS

by MATT MASON

from NEBRASKA POETS CALENDAR

Tornadoes swing through like a kid
playing hopscotch, rip one house to splinters
and leave the neighbors unmussed,
up and down, here and there,
they flatten churches on Easter Sunday,
take up whole towns by the roots,
drive a piece of straw into a tree,
stick a single two by four into a roof
and declare it "art," stack a car
on a car on a motorcycle,
call it a night.

And that, my daughter, is how teenage boys approach love.
I don't say that it is
evil, more like an amoral force of nature,
they look all pleasant showers before they
tear your roof off and leave
your trees in shreds.
So you may dream of his blue
eyes, cloud-free compliments, the music
he likes, the motorcycle he drives,
the great tattoos on his neck, but

when the skies turn that yellow, that green,
when the hail starts popping through air

fit to boil, you listen
to my forecast, you leave the car
parked, grab a flashlight
with one hand, a blanket with the other, go
for the basement, now you run.

Nominated by William Trowbridge

IT ISN'T DEAD, JUST DIFFERENT

by SOMMER BROWNING

from SPORK and EITHER WAY I'M CELEBRATING (BIRDS, LLC)

Across from my mother and me, in the Roy Rogers
at the James Fenimore Cooper travel plaza
on the New Jersey Turnpike, an old man

with Flirt stitched onto his visor
gives us a nod good evening. No offer to buy

a drink. No wink. He's flirting with flirting
how a one-legged bird flirts with walking.
My mother and I order chicken sandwiches,

and try to reswallow our hearts. Earlier,
we stopped dead in front of a car on fire.
Careening across four lanes of Turnpike. Backwards.

Even if she straightens out, she's still on fire.

At night the Turnpike is lit like a wet snake.
Any direction you travel, you know you're headed
for fangs. Only the golden oil refineries

nestle in its coils. Yet we
scale the ridge of its back, flirt with tons
of speeding metal, even fire. Like two geniuses

dispelling a myth, we clutch tight what we say:
You're fucked even if you aren't fucked.
Clear our plastic trays. Get back on the highway.

Nominated by Spork

AMERICAN JUGGALO

by KENT RUSSELL

from N+1

I'd been driving for seventeen hours, much of it on two-lane highways through Indiana and then southern Illinois. Red-green corn sidled closer to the road until it stooped over both shoulders. That early in the morning, a mist was tiding in the east.

I figured I had to be close. A couple of times I turned off the state road to drive past family plots where the houses were white, right-angled ideals. On many of these plots were incongruous strips of grass—homespun cemeteries. I wondered what it would be like to grow up in a place like this. Your livelihood would surround you, waving hello every time the wind picked up. You wouldn't be able to see your neighbors, but you'd for sure know who they were. You'd go to one of the Protestant churches seeded in the corn, take off your Sunday best to shoot hoops over the garage, and drink an after-dinner beer on your porch swing, certain of your regular Americanness. And one day you'd get buried feet from where you lived, worked, and died.

Doubt about the trip unfurled inside me as the odometer crawled on. I couldn't have told you why I was doing this.

Back on IL-1 I looked to my right and saw an upside-down SUV in the corn. It must've flipped clear over the stalks nearest the road, which stood tall and undamaged. The SUV's rear right wheel—the whole wheel—was gone, but the axle still spun. Stumbling alongside the wreck was a dazed kid in a Psychopathic Records fitted cap. The fingertips he touched to the side paneling seemed to keep him from pitching over.

When midwestern bugs hit your windshield, they chink like marbles. When I'm feeling indecisive in a car, I mash the accelerator.

When the hip-hop label Psychopathic Records released its seventeen-minute trailer for the 11th Annual Gathering of the Juggalos, a four-day music festival, five people I knew sent me links to it. I suppose that for them it was a snarker's Holy Grail: everyone involved in the video had such a boggling lack of self-awareness that the whole thing bordered on parody. "The Gathering has fresh and exciting shit to do all around the fucking fizzuck," the trailer went. "One hundred rap and rock groups! Helicopter rides! Carnival rides! Seminars! . . . And if you like midgets, we got midgets for you." Mind you, I had no idea who or what any of this was.

The trailer featured bedraggled and unkempt white folks. "Fresh-ass" was used as a compound modifier denoting quality. Willis from *Diff'rent Strokes* would be there, and Vanilla Ice was going to sign autographs. There would be wrestling all night, four nights in a row. I understood that some could find joy in making fun of these people and their "infamous one-of-a-kind" admixture of third-rate fun fair and perdition. But I was also impressed by the stated point of the thing: "The real flavor, what separates the Gathering from every other festival on the planet, is the magic in the air. The feeling of 10,000 best friends around you. The camaraderie. The family. And the love felt everywhere throughout the grounds. You'll meet people, make future best friends, you'll probably get laid. And you'll realize that the family coming together is what all of this is really about."

I did some hasty groundwork on that boon the internet and found that juggalos are: "Darwin's biggest obstacle." "A greasy, fat teenager with a Kool-Aid mustache and no friends who listens to songs about clowns in his stepmother's double-wide mobile home when he isn't hanging out at the mall food court." "They paint their faces, are aggressive, travel in packs, abide (supposedly) by a simplistic code of rules, and tell all those non-juggalos that juggalos live a happier and freer life." Saturday Night Live spoofed their last Gathering trailer. There's a band called Juggalo Deathcamp. "Illegal Immigrants Can Stay, Deport the Juggalos" is a statement that 92,803 people on Facebook agree with.

Why didn't I know about these people? Why does everyone hate them?

Juggalo Etymology is this: Insane Clown Posse, founders of Psycho-pathic Records, were performing in front of 1,800 at the Ritz in War-ren, Michigan, in the early '90s. Violent J, one half of the Posse, was doing "The Juggla," a song off *Carnival of Carnage*, and when he rapped the chorus, "You can't fuck with the Juggla . . . " he asked, "What about you, Juggalo? Are there any Juggalos in here?" The crowd went nuts and the term stuck.

No definition exists. Nowhere in Psychopathic Records' discography do any of their artists—neither ICP, nor Twiztid, nor Blaze Ya Dead Homie, nor Anybody Killa, nor Boondox—attempt to delineate what a juggalo is or believes. The artists themselves self-identify as juggalos, but when they rap about juggalos, they do so with awe, incredulity, and more than a little deliberation. From ICP's "Welcome to Thy Show": "We just glad we down with them, hate to be y'all / and have a juggalo shatter my skull for the Carnival." From Violent J's interview with *Murder Dog* magazine: "Juggalos started with ICP and now it's grown into its own culture. It's still very much a part of ICP, but there are other groups that Juggalos follow. A Juggalo is not just a fanbase of ICP. A Juggalo is a way of life. . .. The juggalos is very much like a tribe. It's like this wandering tribe who gather every year at a sacred place to have a ritual. It's an ancient thing for humans."

ICP are Violent J and Shaggy 2 Dope, the juggalo patriarchs, two white minor felons from the working-class suburbs of Detroit who dropped out of high school, donned clown face, and around 1992 created both Psychopathic Records and a mythology called the Dark Carnival. Without getting too deep into it: the Dark Carnival comprises six studio albums, known as the Joker's Cards. In each Joker's Card—*Carnival of Carnage*, *The Ringmaster*, *Riddle Box*, *The Great Milenko*, *The Amazing Jeckel Brothers*, and *The Wraith*—ICP describes more of the Carnival and its murderous personalities and attractions. The Carnival is a travel-ing inquisition during which racists are blown up, wife beaters tortured, pedophiles bled dry, and the wealthy consigned to hell.

From Violent J's memoir, *Behind the Paint*, which reads a lot like Bukowski's *Ham on Rye*: "Every kid who came through the line was just like us. They looked like us, dressed like us, talked like us and all that. NO!!!! I'm not saying that we influenced them and their style; I'm say-ing that they already had the same style as us. We were all just different forms of SCRUB!!!! We were all the same kind of people! We were all the world's UNDERDOGS. We were all pissed, and ready to do something about it."

In the early days, this "something" sounded a lot like class warfare. This, for instance, comes from the liner notes to *Carnival of Carnage*, ICP's first studio album:

> If those of the ghetto are nothing more than carnival exhibits to the upper class, then let's give them the show they deserve to see. No more hearing of this show because you can witness it in your own front yard! A traveling mass of carnage, the same carnage we witness daily in the ghetto, can be yours to witness, feel and suffer. No longer killing one another, but killing the ones who have ignored our cries for help. FREE PASS FOR THE GOVERNOR'S FAMILY! Like a hurricane leaving a trail of destruction, the ghetto on wheels! My views may be ugly, but so are the bloodstains on the streets I roam. If there is no change soon tickets will be issued to . . . The Carnival of Carnage.

This is more or less of a piece with the greater gangsta rap ethos of the early '90s, albeit espoused by two white clowns. But after *Carnival of Carnage*, ICP focused on inventing more characters and set pieces for their Dark Carnival, and gory righteous murders took precedence over politics. The clowns became like superheroes (at one point producing their own comic book series), and their slant-rhymed torture fantasies stood in for mobilization. If anything, their political beliefs could now be classified as apocalyptic. The Dark Carnival is, basically, a rapture that one can't prepare for, aside from making sure not to be too wealthy to get through the needle's eye. In the meanwhile, Utopia comes once a year, at the Gathering.

Perhaps the most enduring element of that early ICP ethos is the violence. In 2006, a juggalo named Jacob Robida attacked three men in a Massachusetts gay bar with a hatchet and a gun, fled to West Virginia, kidnapped a woman, and drove to Arkansas, where he killed her, a police officer, and himself. In 2008, two Utah juggalos armed with a knife and a battle-ax attacked a 17-year-old and stabbed him twelve times. A juggalette from Colorado got her juggalo boyfriend to stab her mother to death. Two Pennsylvania juggalos took a boy into the woods and slit his throat in 2009. Police in Utah, Arizona, Pennsylvania, and California consider juggalos a criminal gang.

The man in the Ticketing Trailer told me someone would be by shortly with my press pass, which I had lied to get. Nobody assigned me to go to the Gathering of the Juggalos, and I couldn't have said why I was standing there in the buzzing heat at the entrance of Hogrock Campground, a hundred-plus acres of cleared land in the Shawnee National Forest just outside tiny Cave-In-Rock, Illinois. Next to me was a shirtless kid named Squee. I'd helped him carry a gunnysack down the steep declivity that connects the overflow parking to the campground. I'd said, grinning conspiratorially, "Let me guess: This shit's full of beers, right?" He'd said, "Fuck your beers, dude, we're smoking that weed. This shit's full of Powerades. Gonna sell these shits."

Squee rapped on the trailer's window ledge and told the ticketing man, "Uhh, I lost my car." "You lost your what?" the ticketing man asked. "My hoopty." "Can't help you." Squee turned to some other kids who were getting their bags checked at the gate and said, "Shit, I was in a tent with four juggalettes—sounds good, right?—Camry keys in my pocket, getting my drink on, my brain on. Now I can't find that shit." He glared at the kid next to him and said, "I told you it was a stupid idea to get that fucked up on the very first night, Randall."

Sandy the PR agent, my age and attractive in a round-featured midwestern way, rode shotgun in a golf cart that skidded to a halt in the dirt in front of the ticketing trailer. She handed me a lanyarded, laminated card that had the dimensions of a child's placemat at a chain restaurant. It was emblazoned with the Psychopathic Records mascot, the Hatchetman, and the letters "VIP." I'd never been credentialed before.

"Charmed, I'm sure," Sandy said, and reached her right arm, which was sleeved with tattooed leopard spots, over her left shoulder for me to shake from the back of the golf cart. At the wheel was a freckled child. "This is Justin. He works here, kind of." Justin turned to me slowly; his smile was wide and shingled with milk teeth. He floored it and the cart reared onto its back wheels, jumped forward once, and took off at speed.

We bounced down the dirt pathways that web Hogrock. "This is normally a biker camp," Sandy said, "but sometimes also a Baptist kids' camp. This is the third straight Gathering here. Every Gathering's been in Michigan, Ohio, or Illinois. Seven thousand went to the first, twenty thousand went to the last. This thing's a day longer than Woodstock."

Tents sprouted from every inch of open flat land on either side of the path. Pup tents, two-person tents, bivouacs, walk-in affairs with air-conditioning. Back in the woods, red tarp domes showed between trees like pimples under hair. Next to most were dusty American cars filled with stuff: beers, empty motor oil bottles, liters and liters of Detroit's bottom-shelf Faygo cola, pallets of Chef Boyardee, chips, chocolate, powdered Gatorade. Ruddy juggalo faces poked out from tent flaps at the approaching burr of the golf cart, adding to the surreal feeling of touring an encamped American diaspora.

We drifted past the seminar tent, the second stage, the autograph tent, the freak-show tent, the carny food booths. The sky was as dully off-white as the inside of a skull. I'd read that these four days would range in temperature from 96 to 100 degrees. Sweatwise I was already through the looking glass. "I did the whole Gathering last year," Sandy said. "I'm not staying past sundown tomorrow. I hope you brought something green, or an orange." Justin slalomed around shirtless jug-galos. Seen from behind, most had broad, slumped shoulders and round, hanging arms. These people were not stout. Their torsos were grubbed with fat. They looked partially deflated. You think I'm being cruel, but these were the most physically unhealthy people I've ever seen. "Because if not, you're shit out of luck. Unless you especially love carnival burgers, or fried curds from out the back of someone's RV."

We visited a swimming hole nicknamed Lake Hepatitis that was the kelly green of putt-putt hazard water; a waspy helicopter you could ride in for $40; a trailer full of showers; a wrestling ring; and the half-mile-long valley that held the main stage on one end and a small carnival at the other. It turned out that Justin was the son of Psychopathic Re-cords' VP. My credential flapped and whined in the false breeze like a musical saw.

Justin braked hard on a narrow bridge that spanned a parched creek. There was a backup of cars looking for open campground. Not more than twenty-four inches in front of us sat twin girls on the rear bumper of a white minivan. They couldn't have been a day over 14 or a biscuit under 225. They wore bikini tops, and the way they slouched—breasts resting on paunches, navels razed to line segments—turned their trunks into parodies of their sullen faces.

The air here was dry and piquant. Cigarette and pot smoke con-vected, chasing out oxygen. One of the girls called out to Sandy "You're really pretty," emphasizing the *You're* as if being pretty were suspect. Juggalos swarmed the bridge, and when the traffic stopped they closed in, hawking whatever they had. Hands shot into the cart holding cones of weed for $15, glass pipes for $10, bouquets of mushrooms for I don't know how much, Keystone Lights for $1, single menthols for $1. A clutched breast was pushed through the fray and jiggled; from somewhere a disembodied voice demanded a dollar.

Then somebody screamed, "WHOOP, WHOOP!"

Understanding how this sounds is important, as it forms a refrain to the entire Gathering. A single "WHOOP, WHOOP!" is like a plaintive, low-pitched train whistle dopplering from afar. The Os are long, and there's a hinge between the first WHOOP and the second. You sort of swing from one syllable to the next.

The crowd fortified the call, returning it deeper and rounder. "WHOOP, WHOOOOOOOOP!" Sandy overturned her handbag, found oversize sunglasses, and put them on. "Just say it. Just do it," she said. Thinking myself a funny guy, I did a kind of Three Stooges "Whoop whoop whoop!"

Which I now know was wrong. "WHOOP, WHOOP!" is juggalo echolocation. It not pinging back means trouble.

The twins screamed, "Show us your titties, bitch!" at Sandy. A tall man with a massive water gun screamed, "Man, fuck your ride!" and sprayed us with a stream of orange drink the pressure and circumference of which would've made a gelding head-shy. A "FUCK YOUR RIDE!" chant went up and around the crowd, and garbage was thrown. I would describe what kind of garbage, and how it felt to be the object of such ire—but I had so much garbage thrown at me at the Gathering of the Juggalos that showers of refuse became commonplace, a minor annoyance, and describing one would be like describing what it's like to get a little wet on a winter's day in Seattle. Justin, bless his soul, floored it, parting the crowd with the derring-do one is capable of when one's father is running the show.

"Shit," Sandy said. "Shitbagging shit."

Justin grinned. "That was your first Faygo shower, dude."

They dropped me off in an open field, and I never saw them again. Thenceforward I returned every "WHOOP, WHOOP!" with gusto.

Blender named ICP the worst artists in music history. I'm sure you won't find many music fans or journalists who disagree. And yet, according to Billboard's independent album charts—and ICP has been independent since they left Island Records in 2001—their album *Forgotten Freshness Vol. 3* peaked at number 10, *The Wraith: Shangri-La* at number 1, *Hell's Pit* at number 1, *The Calm* at number 1, *Forgotten Freshness Vol. 4* at number 4, *The Wraith: Remix Albums* at number 9, *The Tempest* at number 2, and 2009's *Bang Pow Boom!* at number 1. Twiztid has had one number 1, two number 2, and one number 3 independent albums. Dark Lotus, the quasi-mystical supergroup made up of ICP, Twiztid, and Blaze Ya Dead Homie, has charted at number 3, number 4, and number 6.

ICP alone have two more number 1 independent albums than Arcade Fire and Elliott Smith; three more than Arctic Monkeys and the National; and four more than the Yeah Yeah Yeahs and the White Stripes. I understand that may be hard to believe. You likely can't name a song by any Psychopathic Records artist (except maybe ICP's "Miracles"). They don't have singles that play on the radio, in hip boutiques, or on the stirring trailer for *Where the Wild Things Are*. Only Insane Clown Posse have been on the Billboard Hot 100—in 1997, when they spent five weeks on the charts, peaking at number 67, with "Santa's a Fat Bitch."

Psychopathic Records peddles horrorcore, a hip-hop genre that originated in the early '90s. Horrorcore narratively and figuratively incorporates all kinds of horror-film tropes: hyperviolence, gore, moralism, and inventive Rube Goldberg-style faces of death, all set to samples of, say, the *Creepshow* or *Zombi 2* sound track. Jamie Madrox of Twiztid: "Think of it as if there was a *Halloween* or *Friday the 13th* on wax and Jason and Michael Myers could actually rap, this is what their vibe would sound like." The germ of horrorcore can be traced to the Geto Boys, influential beyond their appearance on the *Office Space* sound track, several of whose lesser-known songs integrated the aforementioned stuff. But Esham, a Geto Boys contemporary from Detroit, was the first MC to build his persona exclusively around the horrific, and thus is considered the true progenitor of horrorcore. He inspired Insane Clown Posse, who in turn inspired the Psychopathic family.

Horrorcore had its big national moment in the mid-'90s, when the Flatlinerz and Gravediggaz were charting and ICP's *The Great Milenko* went platinum. But the sound still defines Metro Detroit and much of the Rust Belt. There's Esham and the Clowns, King Gordy, Prozak, Twiztid, Marz, Blaze Ya Dead Homie, J Reno, Rev. Fang Gory, Freddy

Grimes, Troubled Mindz, Defekt—even Eminem can be considered horrorcore-influenced, on account of Slim Shady's chainsaw revs and gore-focused gaze.[*]

Since ICP, many if not most horrorcore acts have been white, as has been their audience. All but one of the artists on Psychopathic, which is based in Farmington Hills, come from Michigan. All are white or Native American. Psychopathic pulls in $10 million a year and has its own wrestling federation, energy drink, and film division.

Wending my way to the park entrance from where Sandy and Justin dropped me off took three hours. The golf cart had created a compact and navigable illusion. The site was shaped like a bone-in top loin, its paths marbling it as randomly as fat. I realized I hadn't packed any water, or bedding.

I had imagined, what with the Gathering being a music festival, that I'd be able to slink around anonymously. I was immediately disabused of this. I was the only person not wearing black or red. I was the only person who did not have Psychopathic Records iconography tattooed somewhere on his body. My hair, ridiculous as it was, both fro'ed out and sopping in the humidity, marked me as exceptional. The juggalos who hadn't shaved their heads completely had shaved everything below their crowns and braided the rest into rigid tendrils that zagged upward like the legs of a charred insect.

Everywhere I went, juggalos stopped what they were doing to track me with spotlight eyes. Their heads moved in time with my stride, the way man or beast will do when a threat is sensed. For four days I would have to fight a strong urge to break into a jog.

I decided to follow one of the dry creeks that no longer reach the Ohio River. I moved between trees on a rise above the bank and walked until I realized I was amid a dozen people facing the creek in a staggered formation of lawn chairs. Somehow I hadn't noticed what they

---

[*] ICP and Eminem had a long-running beef that began in 1997, when Eminem was a little-known battle rapper about to release The Slim Shady EP. He was passing around a flyer at a club regarding his release party. The flyer read, "Featuring appearances by Esham, Kid Rock, and ICP (maybe)." Eminem handed one to Violent J; this being the first time the two had ever met or spoken, Violent J objected to Eminem's presumptuousness. After that, barbs went back and forth. Eminem called ICP talentless; ICP contended that Eminem was a commercial product made by Dr. Dre and MTV, and recorded a parody of "The Real Slim Shady" entitled "Slim Anus."

were watching: one man breaking tube after fluorescent glass tube on the back of another man who lay prone on the dead leaves in the creek-bed. When the tubes popped and tinkled they released jinnish poofs of talc. I thought maybe the other guy was drunk. Then the assailant mo-seyed to the back of a rusted panel van that canted down the bank. He pulled out a T-ball bat vined with razor wire. I actually said, "Oh, no!" He knelt over the other guy, pulled his head up by the hair, and started gouging his forehead. Someone in the chairs finally said, "Pin his ass, Darryl." I moved on.

I walked by a pavilion whose purpose I couldn't immediately discern. Women danced naked in cages, and there was a stage fronted by picnic tables. Both stage and picnic tables were being stood on by a lot of people. A master of ceremonies emerged from the onstage crowd, screaming a station identification into a microphone—WFuckOffRa-dio, Psychopathic's internet radio station—and that it was time for the contest. I didn't see any hands go up. It was just: two beer bongs were handed to two dudes who put the hoses to their mouths before two other dudes poured a plastic 750 milliliter bottle of gin into each fun-nel. I found myself shaking my head no while applauding slowly. After the bottles were finished the dudes were allowed fifteen seconds to recoup. The naked ladies had stopped dancing and were gripping their bars tightly. Only cicadas zapped the silence. Then began the second leg of the contest, which involved a third dude—this time chosen from a show of eager hands—jumping onstage to kick one of the gin-drinkers in the crotch, and then the other, and so on, best-of-three-falls style. The last man standing was given a goodie bag smaller than the medio-cre goodie bags I received at the end of grade-school birthday parties. The crowd lined up to high-five both contestants, "WHOOP, WHOOP!"s all around.

When I finally arrived at my rental car, panting and glazed with sweat, I threw it in reverse, feeling a most acute despair.

The Hardin County sheriff stopped me at the Hogrock egress. Ca-prices and Grand Marquises illustrated with Psychopathic Records de-cals sat passengerless on the shoulder. Two deputies were ducking juggalos into a paddy wagon. The sheriff ambled up to my window, leaned in to appraise me, and waved me on. I was still full of paranoia and phantom guilt when the wind whipped my VIP badge across my neck, drawing a faint line of blood. I drove to the next town over to buy beer.

A few words on horror, and why some people like it:

I've never seen *Citizen Kane* and don't care to, but Kane Hodder is the best and only Jason Voorhees in my mind. I have no idea what *Casablanca* is about, but I can give you rundowns of *Cannibal Holocaust*, *Cannibal Ferox*, *Sexo Canibal*, and *Anthropophagus*, or if cannibals aren't your thing, *Demoni 1* and *2* or *Demonicus*. I need to scan down to number 14, *Psycho*, on the American Film Institute's list of our hundred best movies to find one I've actually watched.

"Serious" film strikes me as absurd. It's bowdlerized life. Filmic drama asks me to care about loves, losses, and supposed triumphs, which together amount to the chiseled dash connecting my birth to my death on my tombstone. To me, the modern horror film has more to do with first-world existence as it is lived today. In the modern horror film, we no longer come together to defeat a beast, gaining knowledge of and confidence in ourselves along the way. Altruism is no longer rewarded. Even the most self-sacrificing character will be killed off, often for laughs. One protagonist, if any, survives by becoming more brutal than the monster. He trades debasement for survival, which is short-lived— because the monster of course comes back, for the lucrative sequels.

In horror, characters are stripped of everything they think they know and believe they are. Education and privilege mean nothing. Security is a delusion; today is the last day of your life. You, what you think makes you you, your blemishes and singular characteristics, will disappear in an instant. Stalking everything you do is death, and all that matters is how furiously you go out.

Back at the gathering, with my quivered tent on one shoulder and a book bag full of water and Luna bars on the other, a suitcase of Natural Light in hand, I went looking for a spot to camp. I had picked up a map and program from the ticketing trailer, so I knew where I was going this time. On the way, I took note of the license plates I saw: Illinois, Wisconsin, Michigan, Indiana, Ohio, Iowa, Nebraska, Kentucky, Missouri, Kansas, Oklahoma, Colorado, New Mexico, West Virginia, Pennsylvania, Massachusetts. Over the course of the Gathering I did not see any plates from Florida, which is where I'm from, nor did I meet anyone from Miami, which is where I grew up. I encountered dozens of juggalos from Ohio, many of them from Akron, my dad's ancestral home. My mom's side of the family hails from New Castle, a cluster of mining concerns and fireworks factories in western Pennsylvania, which was also well represented at the Gathering. I myself had never been this deep into the Midwest before. As I was driving here, thumping regularly over I-71's asphalt panels, not quite equidistant from cultural capitals on both coasts, I imagined my rented red Kia a blood cell not driven but recalled to a heart.

One enterprising juggalo asked if I'd like to touch his testicles for $5. I hastened my search for a campsite. Finally I picked a spot next to the parking lot in the "Lost Ninja Clan" area. (*Ninja*, I learned, is the diminutive form of *juggalo*, e.g., "What up, ninja?") Having never camped before, I spent twenty minutes flexing tent poles and accidentally launching them like javelins. I heard a soft voice behind me ask, "Need any help?" I turned and met Adam.

Adam was from Detroit. He was shorter but more solidly built than me, and as pallid as the disinterred, with fine black hair and black eyes. He pronounced short a's with the nasal-pirate accent Michiganders swear they don't have. His red and black Blaze Ya Dead Homie basketball jersey exposed an homage to horror-movie serial killers tattooed over powerful arms. A full-color Leatherface tattoo swelled on his right biceps while he put my tent together, a Kool puckered throughout.

Adam was camping with his brother twenty feet away in a canvas lean-to. They both worked irregular shifts at an auto plant, which was why they could come. This was Adam's third Gathering. He was disappointed the rest of his friends couldn't make it. "That's OK, though," he said, "because I've got ten thousand friends here."

I knew then and there that I should have stuck to Adam like a journalistic remora, but it was hot and I'm awkward, so I shook his hand, told him I'd catch up with him later, and crawled into my tent, happy to have a space that was mine alone.

I turned on the lantern end of my emergency flashlight and started jotting impressions. The heat, light, and cicadas made the experience not unlike lying inside an incandescent bulb. It wasn't long before I dozed off. A "FUCK YOUR FACE!" chant roused me from half-sleep; I checked the program and couldn't be sure if it was coming from the Psychopathic Records Karaoke Tournament or the wet T-shirt contest hosted by Ron Jeremy. Then I was asleep.

In 1992, my parents went into real estate and began making money. Almost instantly—my mother had been in the business three weeks, my father a little longer—I was pulled out of Boys and Girls Club baseball and enrolled in a tennis academy on a private island. I received a new wardrobe of tiny white shorts, white polos, white loafers. My parents bought a conversion van, with a TV and VCR in the back, to take on family vacations. There were art lessons. A family portrait was taken and mailed out with seasons greetings, four months ahead of Christmas.

We were at our first Dolphins game, a preseason game, marveling at the champagne and chicken fingers in the luxury suite, when one of the many TVs cut in with news that Hurricane Andrew had made an unanticipated 90-degree turn to the west. It was going to intensify into a category 5 storm between the Bahamas and Miami.

Police cruisers rolled through the neighborhood and ordered evacuation as Biscayne Bay crawled over the seawall. Except for what fit into duffels, we each wrapped our favorite belongings in a heavy-duty garbage bag that was left on top of our beds. They're eerie even in memory, polypropylene sarcophagi. We piled into our van with our dogs and raced a black and fast sky inland to my grandfather's.

We rode out the storm in my grandfather's bathroom, the safest part of his cinder-block house. We took turns standing on the lip of the filled bathtub to look through the thin window. First came a five-hour block of destruction, after which my family, along with the rest of the city, went outside to tour the damage. Miami was leveled, cast yellow, and it quavered uncomfortably under the sun. There were thirty minutes' worth of anxious peace. At 7 years old, desperate to run from building to building and sample the damage, I felt a kind of fluorescent joy, the liberation of disaster. Then came five more hours of bookending storm. When it ended, my parents drove me and my sisters straight to the airport.

My mother had called in a favor from her extended family in New Castle. My sisters and I were going to live there for a while. Before we boarded the plane to Pittsburgh, we had no idea we had cousins. They were the family my grandmother left when she and my grandfather, a local boy back from World War II, moved to Miami, where they'd heard there were jobs for fishermen.

My sisters and I stayed in the drafty empty nest of my great aunt, a fierce nonna recently widowed of her long-haul-driving husband. She was the cook at the restaurant and bar my cousins collectively owned and operated. They pitied us as if we had fallen to them from a higher station. They went out of their way to treat us as they thought we were accustomed—they bought me a GameBoy a New York Yankees hat, and Michael Jackson tapes. September in Pennsylvania was too cold for the clothes I had, so they took me to the consignment shop and bought me a Teenage Mutant Ninja Turtles sweatshirt on which Raphael challenged any and all to CM'ON, TRY IT! I asked my cousins how that first word read, and they said it was "cee-mon."

It wasn't until I got back to Florida that I understood our home had been destroyed. Thirteen feet of storm surge had washed over it. Only half of what remained was habitable. When school started, the district mandated that I be taken out of class once a week and put in a support group, where I colored in pictures of newer, better homes. For Christmas we covered the water damage with gift wrap; my dad was jobless within the year. We rebuilt our house with insurance money, sort of, and my folks lived in it for two more decades, leaks, mold, and zoning codes be damned. We never lived as high as we did before the hurricane or as low as immediately after it. When I got back from the Gathering, I learned that my parents had closed on a deal to sell the house to the neighbors. They then put their stuff in the van and lit off for California. The neighbors demolished the house posthaste.

I was awake and jackknifed in my tent after a juggalo screamed "WHOOP, WHOOP!" right outside it. Everyone in the vicinity returned the call, and it redoubled on the trails, an aural telegraph relaying the A-OK. Security stayed near the front entrance; juggalos were very much in charge here. Adam and his brother were gone. I'd slept for five hours, and now it was early evening. The bigger acts were beginning their sets, and everyone was making their way to the main stage.

The setting sun made candy floss out of the clouds. A kid leaned against a tree and faced the procession with this sign: "Need coke? Show me your open butt crack, girls." The helicopter had not stopped nor would it stop buzzing 'Namishly overhead.

I stopped at a carny food booth to buy a cheesesteak. I took my sandwich to a large wooden pallet to sit and eat, but I was shooed by a child huckster who was using it as a stage. "What up, fam. Help a juggalo get home. Three dollars for one kick, five dollars for two." He wore a red jumpsuit and had braids like dead coral. On the back of his jumpsuit was the Hatchetman, Psychopathic Records' logo and kokopelli. The Hatchetman is the cartoon profile of a guy with a big head, the afore-mentioned braids, and a goatee, and who is running with a hatchet in one hand. Over four days, I saw the Hatchetman stitched onto shirts, pants, cheer shorts, bikini tops, beanies, caps, and shoes; shaved into heads and chests; and tattooed on so many pounds of lacquered flesh— on arms, shoulders, forearms, over the avian bones on the backs of hands, across necks and asses, in the lee of breasts, on calves, clavicles, and feet.

A topless woman wrapped in the Canadian flag walked up next to me to watch, her boyfriend behind her. She noticed the VIP signboard around my neck.

"What makes you so special?" She was pale, but her eyes were so blue they looked colorized.

I stammered something about maybe trying to write about the Gath-ering. Then I asked if they'd met any other international juggalos.

"Fuck yeah we have," the boyfriend said. He was bullish, with a shaved head. "Finns, Australians, English, Japanese." He was from Windsor, Ontario, right across the border from Detroit. He'd been waiting ten years to go to a Gathering. He wanted to know: "You going to shit all over us like every other newspaper?"

"They want to shut us down," the woman added. "If this was political, they'd shut us down."

Her boyfriend leaned in: "Look, dude, there've always been juggalos. It's just, before ICP, nobody gave us a name. We were just walking around in Bumfuck by ourselves, you know? But get us all together? Tens of thousands of us? And everybody wants to shut us down." At this I nod, but I don't know who "everybody" is; overall the Gathering seemed more ignored than persecuted. "Just tell everybody the truth, ninja. Tell them what we're like. Maybe when they read it, they'll be, like, 'That's me, that's where I belong.'"

A non-carny working a barrel grill paid his $3 and had his kick. The kid didn't even need to catch his breath before reprising his spiel. "Man, I was a punter in high school," the griller said, shaking his head. "I heard them shits pop."

The valley that held the main stage and carnival was filled with jug-galos. After sunset, the only light came from the stage and the winking bulbs of the Octopus, the Swinger, and the Hustler. I lingered in the light of the rides, scribbling notes and drinking the Nattys I'd brought. Several worse-than-mediocre acts came and went from the stage, and the juggalos chanted "FAM-I-LY" at the ones they liked.

I felt it necessary to get more than a little buzzed that night. The nigh-illegible notes I took in the rides' glow became suffused with a false and beery insight. After one of the cars in the Hustler rained solid waste upon me, I wrote, "In another time, I still don't believe these people would've belonged to unions or the Elks." When a group of teens who hid their faces with bandannas passed by, I wrote, for reasons that remain inscrutable, "Ohio is SHAPED LIKE AN ANCHOR!!" and underlined it hard enough to tear the page.

I also wrote that juggalos seem far more comfortable around black people than your average middle American, and I still think that. There were a handful of blacks at the Gathering who weren't performers, and their interactions with the juggalos (though I might have expected tension, going in) were some of the most natural white-black interactions I've ever observed. It was just dudes talking to one another.

By the time Naughty by Nature took the stage, I was good and drunk. They kept spouting malapropisms like "We're glad to be at the juggalo!" and "Much love to the ICP posse!" Like the rest of the non-juggalo rappers performing at the Gathering—including Tone Loc, Warren G, Rob Base, Slick Rick, and Coolio—they were in it for the money. All I wanted was to hear "Hip Hop Hooray," but first they kept demanding that I and everyone else chant "WHITE BOYS!" first.

This might have been the clearest indication that NbN misunderstood their audience. They saw the crowd as another mass of white boys, same as at every other concert they'd performed over the past two decades, and they betrayed a little passive-aggressive weariness. The juggalos around me seemed mostly confused. Their collective grumbled response could be summed up as: "These guys don't understand that we're just like they are, or like they used to be before they made money."

I was a white, middle-class teenager, but where I'm from I was the exception. My Miami high school was five times the size of the average Florida school and 80 percent Hispanic, 10 percent black, 10 percent other. Most of the student body qualified for free or reduced-cost lunch. My friends were Cuban, Nicaraguan, Haitian, Brazilian, Panamanian, Colombian, Bahamian, Mexican. Few of their families could be considered solidly middle class. They were working-class immigrants, born overseas or first-generation American.

Assimilation is a fascinating thing to watch happen. The metaphor of the melting pot is very often spot-on. Over time, immigrants' original cultures are rendered and take on the essence of ours. That's what stewing does—it takes disparate ingredients and imbues them with a single general flavor. In Miami, most people I knew assimilated. They put on polo shirts and said "dude" and drove circles around the mall on weekends. They affected middle-class white adolescence, with quite a few cultural tics. As an American you have to believe that's something everyone strives for, becoming the "we." You feel good seeing it. You're a little affronted if someone doesn't strive for inclusion. In my high school, the kids who assimilated had a derisive term for those who didn't: *ref* short for *refugee*. Fashion could be reffy, as could hair, mannerism, inflection, you name it.

The assimilated kids picked on refs, who were considerably poorer. They screamed "INS!" and waved lit matches around refs' oiled hair. The refs never protested. They shoaled along walls and stared straight ahead, always maintaining the same imperturbable expression. Me, everyone mostly ignored. Sometimes I got pushed into the hydrangea bushes and called white boy. Sometimes Latinas feigned interest in me while their unseen *novios* busted guts behind lockers. But mostly I was an anomaly. And, at the risk of sounding ridiculous, I never felt white, except by default. White America was very far away. It was a nation my parents expatriated from; like my Cuban friends, I figured one day I'd visit my homeland. The glimpses I caught on TV or in movies were bewildering. Ski teams? Blond cheerleaders? Battles of the bands? We had a hip-hop showcase, with the final coming down to a Hot Boyz clone vs. a Dead Prez ripoff. Our school's homepage looped Trick Daddy's "Let's Go." Our senior class song was "Tipsy" by J-Kwon.

In the night I was roused by three juggalos attempting to enter my tent. I struggled to hold the zippers together, hissing "Go away!" until it became an incantation. "The fuck is up with this ninja?" said one of them. "We just want to pass out, ninja," said another. Sometime later I woke up needing badly to go to the bathroom. The tent's zippers, now broken, wouldn't budge. I guzzled a bottle of water and used it as a receptacle; this I would do every hour for three hours. I missed Coolio's

4:30 AM set but could hear it anyway. The juggalos finally came to rest at dawn. The cacophony they made—burps, coughs, hacks, pukes—sounded like a bodily orchestra tuning up. A sleepy "WHOOP, WHOOP!" followed someone's long brown note.

After tearing a hole in and birthing myself from the tent, I went on an early-morning circuit of the grounds. The nearest Port-o-Potty had been blown up in the night. RVs that also served as mobile tattoo parlors were opening their doors at seven thirty. The treetops in the distance made a rampart against the sky.

I stopped at the Spazmatic Energy Sauce pavilion to mix a tube of coffee crystals into a bottle of water. Juggalos in various stages of undress slumped everywhere over everything. A young mother led her son to the other end of my picnic table. He sat down to breakfast on an elephant ear and grape Faygo. His mother pulled the tab on a can of beef barley soup. She rubbed an eye with the heel of one hand and sipped from the can with the other. Hanging from her neck was a homemade advert scrawled on torn cardboard that read, $2 for big Ass Titties, $1 if your a down ass ninja. She lit a menthol and took a swig from her son's Faygo.

The mother was in a bikini top and her son was shirtless, yangs of black paint smeared on his face. They were probably a combined 30 years old, yet stretch marks mottled their bodies. Fat dangled off them in dermal saddle bags as empty as the calories that made them. Again, I bring this up not because I'm body-snarking but because I've only ever seen these physiques in places—the Bronx; Liberty City, Florida; New Castle—where dinner comes either from Burger King or the convenience store.

The son razzed me with a tongue full of violet pulp. I smiled at him. Then he "WHOOP, WHOOP!"ed and pollocked his remaining Faygo all over me.

Whether my open notebook had triggered some kind of antischolastic mania in the child, I don't know. But he managed to soak it so thoroughly that only days later, after several hours under a blow-dryer in a Washington, Pennsylvania, motel room, could the notebook be opened again. The rest of this essay's grist was scribbled in a cryptic shorthand on folded paper towels in a goddamn hurry.

I went to the Boondox, Insane Clown Posse, Anybody Killa, and Blaze Ya Dead Homie seminars. "Seminar" is the official name for these sessions, but it's maybe the wrong term. They're more like shareholder meetings. The artists stood on a dais and explained themselves to hundreds of juggalos under a tent sweltering in hay dust and pot smoke. Boondox set the tone, saying, "We wouldn't be shit without you." Audience participation stretched for hours; comments ranged from "When are you coming to my town?" to "Can I have a hug?" to "You don't even know the names of your own songs, you cock," to "I'm proud of the way your attitude has improved." Juggalos challenged artists to onstage chugging competitions and beat them. Glass pipes of innumerable colors and fungal shapes were passed from the crowd to the stage. Someone fired roman candles into the tent's folds, an exceptionally bad idea. In front of me among the crowd behind the tent, two men explained to a third how they had just hitchhiked their way back from the Hardin County jail. A range-finding water balloon popped in the dirt a few feet behind me. Violent J of ICP summed up my predicament: "You could have a camera crew, or documentary people running around, you could take pictures, interview ninjas, but you can't possibly know what it's really like to be part of this family unless you're a part of this. That's like, that's like, hearing about love, and actually being in love. Those are two different ma'fucking things, right? Well this is love, right here. This is real love amongst each other in this bitch." As he spoke this, some juggalos fifty yards away on a hillside with a trebuchet pegged me right in my face with a Faygo-filled balloon.

I had hoped to find Adam at the campsite around lunchtime, maybe have a few brats, laughs. No sign of Adam. I ate a few chocolate Luna bars, soft and fecal-looking in the heat; immediately regretted it.

There was one ATM on the premises. It might've been the only ATM in Cave-In-Rock. It was the plastic stand-alone kind you get flaccid bills out of at bodegas and strip clubs. I saw no one else use it. It was its own little island in a field that included the Psychopathic Records merch tent. The usage fee was $5.

For twelve hours every day, the merch tent thronged with juggalos. I watched them buy T-shirts and CDs, but also caps, cowboy hats, ski masks, hoodies, basketball, football, baseball, and hockey jerseys, tongue rings, comics, posters, wallets, belt buckles, fingerless gloves, flip-flops, shorts, and dresses, all in every conceivable size and color.

Except "Property of Psychopathic Records" onesies; those were available only in black.

I wondered, How is the merch tent doing such a brisk business without anyone having to use the ATM?

The answer is that the Gathering of the Juggalos is a free market in every sense. Aside from Drug Bridge—which even the security guards called Drug Bridge—juggalo wares were on sale anyplace you looked. RVs doubled as tattoo parlors and greasy spoons. Cardboard signs affixed to tents advertised kush, chronic, and 'dro. I still don't know what ketamine is, but I said it out loud once and was pitched to immediately. Reese's Cups, fan fiction, electronic cigarettes, oil paintings. I saw gasoline bartered for acid tabs. The juggalos I spoke with clearly believed that making money this way was preferable to having a real job, despite their living demonstrably worse lives than people with real jobs. Still, one juggalo told me, "Dog, I came here broke and hustled $1,000."

The second evening, I locked myself out of my rental car. I asked the first person I saw if he had a slim jim. He did, and fifteen seconds and $35 later, I was back to getting waters out of my trunk. As I headed to see Warren G, a guy driving roughshod in a golf cart spotted me and pulled a U-ey. A handpainted sign read TAXI RIDES $2. "Hey my man!" the guy said, pointing to my VIP pass. "Where'd you get that?" I explained that I emailed ahead of time and made arrangements with Sandy, the disappeared PR agent, and that actually the VIP pass entitled you only to free golf-cart rides on the first day of the Gathering. "Yeah, I don't care about all that. I'm riding in this golf cart, you know what I'm saying? Which I stole, you know what I'm saying? And they see that shit around my neck? Dog, I could get in anywhere!" Off in the distance, Warren G was launching into "I Want It All." "Dog, I'll make it worth your while. Money . . . or, you know, drugs." I declined. When I reached the main stage and took a water out of my book bag, a horrifically sunburned albino limped up to me, squinting, and asked, "How much?" I didn't know how to explain that I wasn't selling my waters, and he was in a bad way, so I charged a dollar, because the bottle was still hot from the trunk.

I took my vip pass off once to blend in, maybe get the juggalos to open up. Within three minutes security guards in a golf cart drove up and threatened to take me to "juggalo jail." Standard admission was $150, and juggalos were sneaking in, they told me. Where was my wristband, or my commemorative sheriff's badge celebrating the release of Psychopathic's Western homage, "Big Money Rustlas"? I stammered and jangled my VIP lanyard. Then they all bought balloons filled with nitrous oxide from a guy.

The nights at the gathering were black as space. If you didn't have a flashlight to sweep trails with, you were bound to twist an ankle. On the plus side, I could plop down with the burnouts and scrawl blind notes without anyone noticing.

That second night a carny stabbed another carny in the stomach, Tila Tequila got pelted with debris until she bled, and I saw Tom Green perform in the seminar tent. Before he came on, two juggalos in the audience fist-fought for half a minute before onlookers chanted "FAM-I-LY! FAM-I-LY!" The fighters stopped and slinked away, shamed.

Tom Green got hit with a hot dog and was offered two separate bong hits, one of which he accepted; the chant was "TOM SMOKES GREEN!" Any joke that required a setup was interrupted. Someone shouted something about Drew Barrymore that seemed to hurt him. A juggalette to my left started to laugh at a joke, paused to vomit, and resumed laughing. Tom tried to do a bit about technological dehumanization, with gags about text messages and porn, but he was chanted down. It was very uncomfortable in there. More things were thrown. Juggalos had power over a famous person and they knew it. Eventually he was performing like a jester, quick to start one joke only to abandon it for another before his audience assaulted him.

He ended with a monologue about how everyone on Twitter had begged him not to come, but that since his postcancer philosophy is carpe diem, he wanted not only to come but to prove everyone wrong about juggalos. This was answered with raucous "WHOOP WHOOP!"s.

I heard that later he would try to save Tila Tequila from bombardment with objects both vile and dangerous by jumping onstage to draw juggalo fire, to no avail.

After sleeping for maybe two hours, I got up on the third day and went to see the actual Cave-In-Rock. It's a cave fifty-five feet wide and a hundred deep, scoured out of a cliffside by the Ohio River. For more than 200 years pirates, counterfeiters, horse thieves, and murderers used it as a natural refuge and ambush. The river floods the cave from time to time, which may be why it's so cool and loamy inside, smelling of equal parts fecundity and decay.

I was reading the teen inscriptions (VINCE DID ALLIE X RIGHT HERE), not finding any that were juggalo-related, when a mother and her two daughters entered the cave. The mother, who spoke with a deep Midwest twang, said she lived forty-five minutes away but had never brought the girls here. We're wont to do that, she said—spend our lives missing the beautiful things right in front of us. She had the blue eyes and curdled face of a 4-H beauty queen gone to seed. I lied and said I hadn't heard of the Gathering but was passing through on my way home from a friend's. She offered to pray with me right then and there, "Right here and right now to know you are saved," was how she put it. "This wasn't a coincidence. You and me here today. Don't write it off as one." My nods were bogus, like a drinking bird's. Behind her on the Ohio the *Shawnee Queen* puttered by, and some old folks waved. She said she was sorry to say it but I could die just as easily as her sister did at 17. Wherever I was going to I could just die. "You will stand before Jesus Christ. You will." She squeezed her girls' hands, and they said, "You will be judged by our Lord and Savior." The woman asked me to consider living a life like hers, said she'd leave a CD for me on my rental car's windshield, and then she left.

My clothes were geologic with overlapping sweat rings. I smelled like trench foot. The shower trailer at the Gathering was out of the question. I took off my boots and jumped into the Ohio River. I promised the woman I'd listen to her CD, but I don't know what I did with it.

On the third night of the gathering I finally found a perk associated with the VIP badge: access to the handicapped persons' viewing platform. I stood behind paraplegic juggalos, juggalos on crutches, a little-ette (his term) with a prosthetic leg signed by the entire Psychopathic roster, a blind juggalo, juggalos suffering from various twists and sprains. One woman tore her meniscus during Brotha Lynch Hung but joined us on the platform rather than go to the infirmary; she refused to miss Blaze Ya Dead Homie. Her face, and the faces of her husband and two children, were painted in the style of ICP's Shaggy 2 Dope.

The handicapped used the height advantage to rain Faygo on those below. I used it to watch the crowd in the minutes before the sun set. Every third face was painted. Juggalos flew homemade banners announcing their area codes. They did drugs, they moshed, they diced the air with their hands while rapping along to Axe Murder Boyz, two Colorado brothers signed to Psychopathic's sublabel Hatchet House. Amid the thousands someone was waving a used car lot-size American flag with the Hatchetman sewn over the fifty stars.

The good liberal definition of the underclass is something like: black and brown, struggling but persisting, dignified, systematically disadvantaged, living for the dream of becoming We. Americans don't have a hard time explaining white poverty because Americans rarely try, even though most poor people in this country are white. If you're white in this country, it's taken for granted that you're part of We.

Not all juggalos are poor. Many bristle at the accusation. But a lot, maybe most, are. In the last decade, the Midwest experienced the largest upswing in poverty in the US. A third of the country's poor now live in suburban Middle America. Still, you'll never hear a juggalo use the term "white trash." "White trash" is an old term, older than the United States of America. Its roots lie in the 17th century, when "lubbers" and "crackers," formerly indentured and escaped white servants, formed their own communities on the outskirts of the Chesapeake tidewater region. These whites flouted the colonists' nascent cultural mold, disrespected their ideas of property, color, and labor. The majority thought of them as boondock curios, except during political and economic crises, when they considered them criminal savages. "White trash" nowadays is a contemptuous term, because it implies that one had all the privileges of whiteness and squandered them; one's poverty is one's own fault. It's a shocking term, because it suggests that even without unions and factories, class in America is real and cuts across racial lines. But mostly it's a useful term, because it has no set definition. It's protean. It's for when the majority of white people want to delineate what they are by saying, "What we are not is them."

Juggalos say anyone's free to become a juggalo, but I don't know about that. I think it's more like they weren't born into the respectable middle class and didn't see a path that led there, so they said fuck it. They tattooed the Hatchetman on their necks and allied themselves with a fate they couldn't escape. They would be stigmatized for this white poverty, this woeful inability to move and change, to be free radicals, so why not embrace it, make it known permanently and up front? You can be a juggalo, or you can be white trash—the first term is yours, the second is somebody else's.

One juggalo in particular caught my attention right before it got dark. On stage the Axe Murder Boyz were closing out their set, rapping the coda to their modest hit "Body in a Hole":

And it ain't no friends, and it ain't no girls 'cuz I'm by myself, and I
    got this hole in my backyard
I've been digging it for a year
I can't cope with my own fear
Voice I hear has all control, so
I beat you in the head with a hammer and leave it stuck in your skull
    then I put your body in a hole.

The juggalo was threading his way laterally through the back of the crowd like an unraveling hem. He was decked out in Axe Murder Boyz merch, and he carried with him a milk crate brimming with plastic 1.5-liter bottles. The bottles were uncapped and filled with gray water. Periodically he set the crate down, grabbed a bottle, and chucked it skyward as hard as he could. A liter and a half of wastewater weighs 3.3 pounds. Some of that streamed off in flight, but not much. Fellow juggalos in the front were packed too tightly for any of the bottles to miss. If they weren't knocked to the ground, the victims reacted the same way: First, they took a few moments to allow their eyeballs to recenter, and to consider what just happened. Then they looked around for the cause of the pain. Finding no evidence, they picked up the leaking bottle and hurled it in a cardinal direction. The kid in the AMB gear skipped close enough to the platform that I could hear him yelling "FUCK THE FRONT! FUCK THE FRONT!" as his bottles netted the air. The Axe Murder Boyz closed their set by shrieking, "Fuck the whole world except the motherfucking juggalo family!"

I was disappointed with myself for having missed both nights of Flashlight Wrestling despite the program's adjuration to "FUCK YO SLEEP grab a six pack a bag of that fluffy green a flash light and join us ringside." But I was ready for BloodyMania 4, the biggest event of the Juggalo Championship Wrestling circuit.

I showed up early, a few minutes before 1 AM, but the three sets of bleachers were already full. When I sat down on the grass, I was quite surprised to find I was next to Adam and his massive twin brother.

"Adam!" I said. "Where've you been all week?"

"You are so uncomfortable, ninja," he said. The floodlamps were chaffed with bugs, so light flurried about his face like TV static.

"Dog, we know you're uncomfortable." He didn't look at me directly; his eyes were strabismic. He was probably quite high. He had a sweating phalanx of beers on the dead grass in front of him. "We seen you walking around all the time, never sitting down. The Orbiter's what we call you."

"It's because I'm writing about this. I'm going to write the good juggalo story, give you dudes a fair shake." I pulled out my wad of etched Brawnys. "I want you to help me. Like, will you ever stop being a juggalo, or is it like the mafia? How come when you guys start listening to Psychopathic, you stop listening to everything else?" A bit of a gulp and then, "Why does everyone hate you?"

"Nah man, I'm not going to speak for us. I'm not going to be no spokesperson. There are so many juggalos, and, like, you don't know me."

The Weedman and Officer Colt Cabana entered the ring. Officer Cabana was the heel, so he took it to the Weedman in the early going.

"Do me a solid, dude. No juggalos will talk to me because I'm not a juggalo." Officer Colt was using his baton on the Weedman whenever the referee's back was turned, and the crowd demanded redress.

"Bet it's not that they don't like you but 'cuz of this," and Adam flicked the enormous VIP pass around my neck.

Contrapuntal chants flared up, "YOU'RE A BITCH!" and "WE WANT BLOOD!" Adam's brother keeled over onto the grass.

"It's like, we'll never read whatever you write about us. You can write whatever you want about us, and everyone's going to believe it. What difference does it make what I say? You've got the power. Plus, I give no shits."

In the bleachers, juggalos stood and gestured at Officer Cabana. Each painted face sang its own curse. None was comprehensible, but all together the juggalos looked like a frontlit audience of nattering holy fools.

Officer Cabana climbed the top rope and told the crowd, "I am the law!" Juggalos hailed him with anything at hand. Full beers, chicken wings. A dead fish landed several feet short. I watched a mother take a shitty diaper off a baby and hand it to a man who spun it like a discus over the ring.

"What you should write, though," Adam went on. "Why do, like, motherfuckers in New York or whatever, how do those motherfuckers

136

think they're better than me if, like, making fun of me is still OK with them? You know what I'm saying? It's like they think they know me, and, like, know what's best for me, is what pisses the fuck out of me. Motherfucker, not everyone wants to be you, you know what I'm saying?"

The Weedman began his comeback when someone hustled him a joint from the bleachers to the ring. I was exhausted.

"You know, I always wanted to be a professional wrestler," Adam said.

A juggalo on a bicycle shadowed me on the ten-minute walk back to my tent. Out here the night sky was unlidded. The moon seemed zambonied. Did you know our moon is the only one in this solar system to have been created out of its captor planet? It's true. Billions of years ago, something the size of Mars slammed into proto-Earth and kicked up detritus that conglomerated into the moon. Much of the detritus came from that Mars-size projectile, but the moon and the earth are more alike molecularly than they are different. The moon's an ashen doppelgänger. They say it smells like spent gunpowder. Before I turned off the path, the juggalo on the bicycle kicked me in my ass and said, "Fuck off!"

That third night a huge midwestern thunderstorm finally rolled in and inveighed. I had to sprawl out like a starfish to keep my tent on the ground. Purple lightning lit the inside of the tent like thoughts in a head. Three guys from Rochester sat around a sheltered fire talking about the juggalette they had slept with in succession. "I fucked the shit out of that bitch," went one. "Listen to me, I sound like a proud dad, but that preteen pussy was doing some very fucking adult shit," went another. I don't think I can convey how terrified I was of them seeing the coal of my cupped flashlight as I transcribed their conversation. I consider myself a connoisseur of low-pressure systems, and I was impressed with this storm. Serious midwestern thunder unfurls. It made me think of dead fists blooming.

At dawn I pulled up my stakes in the rain. The moon was still visible. I would miss the Insane Clown Posse concert that caps every Gathering. On my way out of the grounds, four juggalo hitchhikers ran into the path of my rental car. I did not slow down, and they jumped out of my way.

The teenage girl behind the counter at the lone two-pump station in Cave-In-Rock had angled a boombox so that it blasted Taylor Swift at the door. I lurched in, sopped and rank, my legs sheathed in mud. She was all freckles and crinkled church dress. After so many juggalos, I thought she was a seraph.

"The pump won't stop, so be honest," she said. "Are you part of that thing? Are you honest?"

I told her I was leaving it.

"We don't like those people," she said. "Those people aren't like us here." +

Nominated by N + 1, John Kistner, Paul Maliszewski, Amanda Rea

MUDGIRL SAVED BY THE KING OF CROWS. APRIL 1965.

fiction by JOYCE CAROL OATES

from BOULEVARD

In Beechum County it would be told—told and retold—how Mudgirl was saved by the King of the Crows.

How in the vast mud-flats beside the Black Snake River in that desolate region of the southern Adirondacks there were a thousand crows and of these thousand crows the largest and fiercest and most sleek-black-feathered was the King of the Crows.

How the King of the Crows had observed the cruel behavior of the woman half-dragging half-carrying a weeping child out into the mud-flats to be thrown down into the mud soft-sinking as quicksand and left the child alone there to die in that terrible place.

And the King of the Crows flew overhead in vehement protest flapping his wide wings and shrieking at the retreating woman now shielding her face with her arms against the wrath of the King of the Crows in pursuit of her like some ancient heraldic bird-beast in the service of a savage God.

How in the mists of dawn less than a mile from the place where the child had been abandoned to die there was a trapper making the rounds of his traps along the Black Snake River and it was this trapper whom the King of the Crows summoned to save the child lying stunned in shock and barely breathing in the mud-flat like discarded trash.

Come! S'ttisss!

Suttis Coldham making the rounds of the Coldham traps as near to dawn as he could before predators—coyotes, black bears, bobcats —

tore their prey from the jaws of the traps and devoured them alive weakened and unable to defend themselves.

Beaver, muskrat, mink, fox and lynx and raccoons the Coldhams trapped in all seasons. What was *legal* or *not-legal*—what was listed as *endangered*—did not count much with the Coldhams. For in this desolate region of Beechum County in the craggy foothills of the Adirondacks there were likely to be fewer human beings per acre as there were bobcats—the bobcat being the shyest and most solitary of Adirondack creatures.

The Coldhams were an old family in Beechum County having settled in pre-Revolutionary times in the area of Rockfield in the Black Snake River but scattered now as far south as Star Lake, and beyond. In Suttis's immediate family there were five sons and of these sons Suttis was the youngest and the most bad-luck-prone of the generally luckless Coldham family as Suttis was the one for whom Amos Coldham the father had the least hope. As if there hadn't been enough brains left for poor Suttis, by the time Suttis came along.

Saying with a sour look in his face—Like you're shake-shake-shaking brains out of some damn bottle—like a ketchup bottle—and by the time it came to Suttis's turn there just ain't enough brains left in the bottle.

Saying—Wallop the fuckin' bottle with your hand won't do no fuckin' good—the brains is all used up.

So it would be told that the solitary trapper who rescued Mudgirl from her imminent death in the mud-flats beside the Black Snake River had but the mind of a child of eleven or twelve and nowhere near the mind of an adult man of twenty-nine which was Suttis's age on this April morning in 1965.

So it would be told, where another trapper would have ignored the shrieking of the King of the Crows or worse yet taken shots with a .22 rifle to bring down the King of the Crows, Suttis Coldham knew at once that he was being summoned by the King of the Crows for some special purpose.

For several times in his life it had happened to Suttis when Suttis was alone and apart from the scrutiny of others that creatures singled him out to address him.

The first—a screech owl out behind the back pasture when Suttis had been a young boy. Spoke his name *SSSuttisss* all hissing syllables so the soft hairs on his neck stood on end and staring up—upward — up to the very top of the ruin of a dead oak trunk where the owl was perched utterly motionless except for its feathers rippling in the wind and its eyes glaring like gasoline flame seeing how the owl knew *him*—a spindly-limbed boy twenty feet below gaping and grimacing and struck dumb hearing *SSSuttisss* and seeing that look in the owl's eyes of such significance, it could not have been named except the knowledge was imparted—*You are Suttis, and you are known.*

Not until years later came another creature to address Suttis and this a deer—a doe—while Suttis was hunting with his father and brothers and Suttis was left behind stumbling and uncertain and out of nowhere amid the pine woods there appeared the doe about fifty feet away—a doe with two just-born fawns—pausing to stare at Suttis wide-eyed not in fright but with a sort of surprised recognition even as Suttis lifted his rifle to fire with a rapidly beating heart and a very dry mouth—*Suttis! SuttisSuttisSuttis!*—words sounding inside his own head like a radio switched on so Suttis was given to know that it was the doe's thoughts sent to him in some way like vibrations in water and he'd understood that he was not to fire his rifle, and he did not fire his rifle.

And most recent in January 1965 making early-morning rounds of the traps, God damn Suttis's brothers sending Suttis out on a morning when none of them would have gone outdoors to freeze his ass but there's Suttis stumbling in thigh-high snow, shuddering in fuckin' freezing wind and half the traps covered in snow and inaccessible and finally he'd located one—one!—a mile or more from home—not what he'd expected in this frozen-over wet-land place which was muskrat or beaver or maybe raccoon but instead it was a bobcat—a thin whistle through the gap in Suttis's front teeth for Suttis had not ever trapped a bobcat before in his life for bobcats are too elusive—too cunning —but here a captive young one looked to be a six- to eight-months-old kitten its left rear leg caught in a long spring trap panicked and panting licking at the wet-blooded trapped leg with frantic motions of its pink tongue and pausing now to stare up at Suttis in a look both pleading and reproachful, accusatory—it was a female cat, Suttis seemed to know— beautiful tawny eyes with black vertical slits fixed upon Suttis Coldham who was marveling he'd never seen such a creature in his life, silver-tipped fur, stripes and spots in the fur of the hue of burnished mahogany, tufted ears, long tremulous whiskers, and those tawny eyes fixed upon him as Suttis stood crouched a few feet away hearing in the bobcat's quick-panting breath what sounded like *Suttis! Suttis don't you know who I am* and drawn closer risking the bobcat's talon-claws and astonished now seeing that these were the eyes of his Coldham grandmother who'd died at Christmas in her eighty-ninth year but now the grandmother was a young girl as Suttis had never known her and somehow—Suttis could have no idea how—gazing at him out of the bobcat's eyes and even as the bobcat's teeth were bared in a panicked snarl clearly Suttis was made to hear his girl-grandmother's chiding voice *Suttis! O Suttis you know who I am—you know you do!*

Not for an instant did Suttis doubt that the bobcat was his Coldham grandmother, or his Coldham grandmother had become the bobcat —or was using the bobcat to communicate with Suttis knowing that Suttis was headed in this direction—no more could Suttis have explained these bizarre and improbable circumstances than he could have explained the "algebra equations" the teacher had chalked on the blackboard of the one-room school he'd attended sporadically for eight mostly futile years even as he had not the slightest doubt that the "algebra equations" were real enough, or real in some way that excluded Suttis Coldham; and so Suttis stooped hurriedly to pry open the spring-trap fumbling to release the injured left rear leg of the bobcat kitten murmuring to placate the spirit of his girl-grandmother who both was and was not the elderly woman he'd known and called Gran'maw and the bobcat bared her teeth, snarled and hissed and squirmed and clawed at his hands in leather gloves shredding the gloves but leaving Suttis's hands mostly unscathed and raking his face only thinly across his right cheek and in the next instant the bobcat kitten was running—limping, but running—on three swift legs disappearing into the snowladen larch woods with no more sound than a startled indrawn breath and leaving behind nothing but a scattering of cat feces and patches of blood-splattered silver-tipped fur in the ugly serrated jaws of the trap and a sibilant murmur *S'ttus! God bless.*

And now it was the King of the Crows summoning Suttis Coldham unmistakably—*SSS'ttissss! SSS'ttiss!*

Suttis froze in his tracks. Suttis stood like one impaled. Suttis could not hide his eyes and refuse to see. Suttis could not press his hands over his ears and refuse to hear.

SSS'ttisss come here! Here!

The King of the Crows was the largest crow Suttis had ever seen. His feathers were the sleekest and blackest and his wingspread as wide as any hawk's and his yellow eyes glared in urgency and indignation. Like a hunted creature Suttis made his way along the river bank, as the King of the Crows shrieked in his wake, flying from tree to tree behind him as if in pursuit. For it would not be true as Suttis would claim that he

142

had followed the King of the Crows to the child abandoned to die in the mud-flat but rather that the King of the Crows had driven Suttis as a dog might drive cattle. Suttis could not hide, could not escape from the King of the Crows for he knew that the King of the Crows would pursue him back to the Coldham farm and would never cease harassing and berating him for having disobeyed him.

Suttis stumbled and staggered along a three-foot-high embankment that jutted out into the vast mud-flat. Not long ago the last of the winter snows had melted and the mud-flat was puddled with water, as the Black Snake River was swollen and muddy and swift-rushing south out of the mountains. Everywhere was a buzzing-thrumming-teeming of new life, and the rapacity of new life: black flies, wasps, gnats. Suttis swatted at the air about his head, a cloud of new-hatched mosquitoes. Underfoot was the ruin of a road. Ahead was the ruin of a mill. Suttis knew the mud-flats—the Coldhams hunted and trapped here—but Suttis had no clear idea what the purpose of the mill might have been at one time, or who might have owned it. His grandfather would know, or his father. His older brothers maybe. The ways of adults seemed to him remote and inaccessible and so their names were blurred and of little consequence to him as to any child.

Come here! Come here S'ttis come here!

SSS'ttisss! Here!

On the narrowing embankment Suttis moved with caution. The King of the Crows had so distracted him, he'd left his trapping gear behind— the burlap sack which bore the limp broken bloodied bodies of several dead creatures—but still he had his knife, sheathed in his jacket which was Amos Coldham's Army-issue jacket of a long-ago wartime, badly stained and frayed at the cuffs. On his head he wore a knit cap, pulled down onto his narrow forehead; on his lower body, khaki workpants; on his feet, rubber boots from Sears, Roebuck. Passing now the part-collapsed mill with its roof covered in moss that made him uneasy to see—any building, however in ruins, Suttis Coldham was inclined to think that something might be hiding inside, observing him.

In the mountains, you might be observed by a man with a rifle, at some distance. You would never know how you were viewed in a stranger's rifle-scope even as the stranger pulled the trigger and for what reason?—as the Coldhams liked to say *For the hell of it.*

Suttis cringed, worried that he was being observed and not by just the King of the Crows. Entering now into a force-field of some other consciousness that drew him irresistibly.

Broken things in the winter-ravaged grasses, rotted planks, chunks of concrete, a man's single boot. A shredded tractor tire, strips of plastic. In the vast mud-flat tracks ran in all directions with a look of frenzied determination—animal tracks, bird tracks—and on the embankment, what Suttis identified as *human-being footprints*.

Suttis's eye that gazed upon so much without recognition, still less interest, for instance all printed materials, seized at once upon the *human-being footprints* on the embankment which Suttis knew to be, without taking time to think, not the footprints of his brothers or any other trapper or hunter but *female footprints*.

Suttis knew, just knew: *female*. Not even the boot-prints of a young boy. Just *female* boot-prints.

There were other prints, too—mixed with the *female*. Possibly a child. Suttis knew without calculating, with just-seeing.

Not that these tracks were clear—they were not clear. But Suttis understood that they were fresh for no other tracks covered them.

What was this! Suttis whistled through the gap in his front teeth.

A piece of cloth—a scarf—of some crinkly purple material, Suttis snatched up and quickly shoved into his pocket.

SSS'ttisss! Here!

Atop a skeletal larch the King of the Crows spread his wings. The King of the Crows did not like it that Suttis had paused to pick up the crinkly-purple scarf. For the King of the Crows had flown ahead of Suttis, to bade him to hurry to that point, to see.

And now Suttis saw—about twelve feet from the base of the embankment, amid a tangle of rushes—a doll?

A child's rubber doll, badly battered, hairless, unclothed and its coloring mostly flaked off—too light to sink in the mud and so it was floating on the surface in a way to cause Suttis's heart to trip even as he told himself *Damn thing's only a doll.*

Was he being mocked? Had the King of the Crows led him so far, to rescue a mere *doll?*

Suttis drew nearer and now—he saw the second figure, a few yards from the first. And this, too, had to be a doll—though larger than an ordinary doll—discarded in this desolate place like garbage or trash.

Pulses beat in his head like spoons against some wooden vessel. A doll! A doll! This had to be a doll, like the other.

As so much was tossed away into the Black Snake mud-flats that were an inland sea of cast-off human things of all kinds. Here you could find articles of clothing, boots and shoes, broken crockery, plastic toys, even shower curtains opaque and stained as polyurethane shrouds. Once, Suttis had found a pair of jaws in the mud—plastic teeth—he'd thought were dentures but had had to have been Halloween teeth and another time the wheel-less chassis of a baby buggy filled with mud like a gaping mouth. Mostly these cast-off things accumulated at the edge of the mud-flat where borne by flooding water they caught in exposed roots with the debris of winter storms, skeletons of small drowned creatures and the mummified remnants of fur with blind pecked-out eyes like gargoyles fallen from unknown and unnameable cathedrals while farther out in the mud-flats such objects were likely to sink and be submerged in mud.

Lurid tales were told in Beechum County of all that was "lost" —discarded and buried and forgotten—in the mud-flats.

Bodies of the hated and reviled. Bodies of "enemies."

Humped outlines of dead logs in the mud-flat like drowsing crocodiles.

Cries of smaller birds silenced by the furious shrieking of crows.

Was this a doll, so large? It looked to be the size of a small child — Suttis had no clear idea how old—two years? Three?

Weak-kneed Suttis approached the very edge of the bank.

The King of the Crows shook his wings, jeering, impatient.

SSS'ttisss! Here!

The King of the Crows was very near to speaking, now. Human speech the great bird could utter, that Suttis could not stop his ears from hearing.

As the wide black-feathered wings of the King of the Crows fluttered wind and shadows across Suttis's slow-blinking eyes.

"Jesus!"

A little girl, Suttis thought, but—dead?

Her head was bare as if shaved—so small! So sad!

Nothing so sad as child's bare head when the head has been shaved for lice or the poor thin hair has fallen out from sickness and it seemed to Suttis, this had happened to him, too. Many years ago when he'd been a small child.

Lice, they'd said. Shaved his head and cut his scalp with the razor cursing him as if the lice were Suttis's fault and then they swabbed the cuts with kerosene, like flames too excruciating to be registered or gauged or even recalled except now obliquely, dimly.

Poor little girl! Suttis had no doubt, she was dead.

Maybe it was lice, they'd punished her for. Suttis could understand that. The small face was bruised, the mouth and eyes swollen and darkened. Blood-splotches on the face like tears and what was black on them, a buzzing blackness, was flies.

Only the head and torso were clearly visible, the lower body had sunk into the mud, and the legs. One of the arms was near-visible. Suttis stared and stared and Suttis moved his lips in a numbed and affrighted prayer not knowing what he was saying but only as he'd been taught *Our Father who art in heaven hallowed be thy name bless us 0 Lord for these our gifts and help us all the days of our lives 0 Lord thy will be done on earth as it is in heaven! Amen.*

Suttis had seen many dead things and was not uncomfortable with a dead thing for then you know, it is dead and cannot hurt you. Only a fool would lay his bare hand upon a "dead" raccoon or possum and that fool would likely lose his hand in a frantic rake of sharp curved claws and a slash of razor-teeth.

A dead thing is a safe thing and only bad if it has started to rot.

The poor little girl in the mud-flat had started to rot—had she? For something smelled so very bad, Suttis's nostrils shut tight.

It was a wild extravagant prayer of Suttis Coldham, he'd never have believed he could utter:

God don't let her be dead. God help her be alive.

For cunning Suttis knew: a dead child could mean that Suttis would be in *trouble*. There were Coldhams who had been in trouble being in the close proximity of the dead and these dead adult men, women. And Suttis had been beaten for staring at children in a wrong way, or a way deemed wrong by others, by the children's mothers for instance who were likely to be his Coldham relatives—sisters, cousins, young aunts. Staring at his own baby nieces and nephews when they were being bathed in the very presence of their young mothers and such a look in Suttis's face, of tenderness mixed with brute yearning, Suttis had somehow done wrong and been slapped and kicked-at and run out of the house and in his wake the cry *Nasty thing! Pre-vert! Get to hell out nasty pre-vert Sut-tis shame!*

And so now if this little girl is naked Suttis will turn and run—but it looks as if on what he can see of the little body is a nightgown — torn and grimy but a nightgown—isn't it?—for which Suttis is damned grateful.

The King of the Crows has been screaming for Suttis to bring the little girl to shore. In a crouch half-shutting his eyes groping for something—a long stick, a pole—a piece of lumber—with which to prod the body loose.

Suttis has it!—a part-rotted plank, about five feet long. When he leans out to poke at the doll-figure in the mud he sees—thinks he sees—one of the swollen eyelids flutter—the little fish-mouth gasping for breath— and he's stricken, paralyzed—*The little girl is alive!*

A terrifying sight, a living child—part-sunken in mud, a glint of iridescent insects about her face—has to be flies—suddenly Suttis is panicked, scrabbling on hands and knees to escape this terrible vision, moaning, gibbering as the King of the Crows berates him from a perch overhead and like a frenzied calf Suttis blunders into a maze of vines, a noose of vines catches him around the neck and near-garrots him the shock of it bringing him to his senses so chastened like a calf swatted with a stiff hunk of rope he turns to crawl back to the edge of the embankment. There is no escaping the fact that Suttis will have to wade into the mud-flat to rescue the girl as he has been bidden.

At least, the sharp stink of the mud has abated, in Suttis's nostrils. The most readily adapted of all senses, smell: almost, Suttis will find the mud-stink pleasurable, by the time he has dislodged and lifted the mud-child in his arms to haul back to shore.

Suttis slip-slides down the bank, into the mud. Makes his way to the mud-child lifting his booted feet as high as he can as the mud suck-suck-sucks at him as in a mockery of wet kisses. Above the mud-child is a cloud, a haze of insects—flies, mosquitoes. Suttis brushes them away with a curse. He's shy about touching her—at first. He tugs at her arm. Her exposed shoulder, her left arm. She's a very little girl—the age of his youngest niece Suttis thinks except the little nieces and nephews grow so quickly, he can't keep them straight—can't keep their names straight. Lifting this one from the mud requires strength.

Crouched over her, grunting. He's in mud nearly to his knees — steadily sinking. Rushes slap against his face, thinly scratching his cheeks. Mosquitoes buzz in his ears. A wild sensation as of elation sweeps over him—*You are in the right place at the right time and no other place and no other time will ever be so right for you again in your life.*

"Hey! Gotcha now. Gonna be okay."

Suttis's voice is raw as a voice unused for years. As it is rare for Suttis

147

to be addressed with anything other than impatience, contempt, or anger so it is rare for Suttis to speak, and yet more rare for Suttis to speak so excitedly.

The part-conscious child tries to open her eyes. The right eye is swollen shut but the left eye opens—just barely—there's a flutter of eyelashes—and the little fish-mouth is pursed to breathe, to breathe and to whimper as if wakening to life as Suttis carries her to shore stumbling and grunting and at the embankment lays her carefully down and climbs up out of the mud and removes his khaki jacket to wrap her in, clumsily; seeing that she is near-naked, in what appears to be the remnants of a torn paper nightgown all matted with mud, slick and glistening with mud and there is mud caked on the child's shaved head amid sores, scabs, bruises and so little evidence of hair, no one could have said what color the child's hair is.

"Hey! You're gonna be okay. S'ttis's got you now."

Such pity mixed with hope Suttis feels, he has rarely felt in his life.

Carrying the whimpering mud-child wrapped in his jacket, in his arms back along the embankment and to the road and along the road three miles to the small riverside town called Rapids murmuring to the shivering mud-child in the tone of one of his young-mother sisters or cousins—not actual words which Suttis can't recall but the tone of the words—soothing, comforting—for in his heart it will seem a certainty that the King of the Crows had chosen Suttis Coldham to rescue the mud-child not because Suttis Coldham happened to be close by but because of all men, Suttis Coldham was singled out for the task.

He was the chosen one. Suttis Coldham, that nobody gave a God damn for, before. Without him, the child would not be rescued.

Somewhere between the mud-flats and the small town called Rapids, the King of the Crows has vanished.

The sign is RAPIDS pop. 370. Suttis sees this, every time Suttis thinks there's too many people here he couldn't count by name. Nor any of the Coldhams could. Not by a long shot.

First he's seen here is by a farmer in a pickup truck braking to a stop and in the truck-bed a loud-barking dog. And out of the Gulf gas station several men—he thinks he maybe knows, or should know their faces, or their names—come running astonished and appalled.

Suttis Coldham, Amos Coldham's son. Never grew up right in his mind, poor bastard.

Now more of them come running to Suttis in the road. Suttis carrying the little mud-girl wrapped in a muddied jacket in his arms, in the road.

A little girl utterly unknown to them, the child of strangers—so young! —*covered in mud?*

Amid the excitement Suttis backs off dazed, confused. Trying to explain—stammering—the King of the Crows that called to him when he was checking his traps on the river . . . First he'd seen a doll, old rubber doll in the mud-flat—then he'd looked up and seen . . .

Quickly the barely breathing mud-child is removed from Suttis's arms. There are women now—women's voices shrill and indignant. The child is borne to the nearest house to be undressed, examined, gently bathed and dressed in clean clothing and in the roadway Suttis feels the loss—the mud-child was *his*. And now—the mud-child has been taken from him.

Harshly Suttis is being asked where did he find the child? Who is the child? Where are her parents? Her mother? What has happened to her?

So hard Suttis is trying to speak, the words come out choked and stammering.

Soon, a Beechum County sheriffs vehicle arrives braking to a stop.

In the roadway Suttis Coldham stands shivering in shirt-sleeves, trousers muddied to the thighs and mud-splotches on his arms, face. Suttis has a narrow weasel-face like something pinched in a vise and a melted-away chin exposing front teeth and the gap between teeth near-wide enough to be a missing tooth and Suttis is dazed and excited and trembling and talking—never in his life has Suttis been so *important*—never drawn so much *attention*—like someone on TV. So many people surrounding him, so suddenly!—and so many questions . . .

Rare for Suttis to speak more than a few words and these quick-mumbled words to a family member and so Suttis has no way of measuring speech—a cascade of words spills from his lips—but Suttis knows very few words and so must repeat his words nor does Suttis know how to stop talking, once he has begun—like running-sliding down a steep incline, once you start you can't stop. Lucky for Suttis one of the onlookers is a Coldham cousin who identifies him—insists that if Suttis says he found the child in the mud-flat, that is where Suttis found the child—for Suttis isn't one who would take a child—Suttis is *simple and honest as a child himself and would never do harm, not ever to anyone—Suttis always tells the truth.*

In a Beechum County sheriff's vehicle the nameless little girl is taken to the hospital seventy miles away in Carthage where it is determined that she is suffering from pneumonia, malnutrition, lacerations and bruising, shock. For some weeks it isn't certain that the little girl will survive and during these weeks, and for some time to follow, the little girl is mute as if her vocal cords have been severed to render her speechless.

Beaver, muskrat, mink, fox and lynx and raccoons he trapped in all seasons. How many beautiful furred creatures wounded, mangled and killed in the Coldham traps, and their pelts sold by Suttis's father. And it is the child in the mud-flat Suttis Coldham will recall and cherish through his life.

In bed in his twitchy sleep cherishing the crinkly-purple scarf he'd found on the embankment, still bearing a residue of dirt though he'd washed it with care and smoothed it with the edge of his hand to place beneath the flat sweat-soaked pillow, in secret.

Nominated by Boulevard, H.E. Francis, Christina Zawadiwsky

APRIL

by ALICIA OSTRIKER

from POETRY

The optimists among us
taking heart because it is spring
skip along
attending their meetings
signing their email petitions
marching with their satiric signs
singing their give peace a chance songs
posting their rainbow twitters and blogs
believing in a better world
for no good reason
I envy them
said the old woman

The seasons go round they
go round and around
said the tulip
dancing among her friends
in their brown bed in the sun
in the April breeze
under a maple canopy
that was also dancing
only with greater motions
casting greater shadows
and the grass
hardly stirring

What a concerto
of good stinks said the dog
trotting along Riverside Drive
in the early spring afternoon
sniffing this way and that
how gratifying the violins of the river
the tubas of the traffic
the trombones
of the leafing elms with the legato
of my rivals' piss at their feet
and the leftover meat and grease
singing along in all the wastebaskets

Nominated by Marilyn Hacker, Joan Murray, Eleanor Wilner

THE FLOATING LIFE

fiction by SARAH CORNWELL

from THE MISSOURI REVIEW

We cluster around the radio in the teachers' berth. I twist the dial to 16, the hailing and distress channel, and Dave holds a hand up for silence, even though nobody's talking. Most of the message is static, but it sounds bad. Ports are closed all along the northern coast of Puerto Rico, Haiti, the Virgin Islands. The throaty, Spanish-inflected voice of the Coast Guard broadcaster tells us to switch to 22A, and we do, straining for specifics of the attack, or whatever it is. I can make out snatches only: *stay at sea . . . hazards . . . we don't know . . . repeat stay . . . as it comes in.* The distant sound of hip-hop drifts from the dormitory berths; the students are enjoying a normal afternoon belowdecks, unaware. The satellites are down. The computers and the handheld devices search endlessly for signals.

Dave is trembling. He clamps one meaty hand over the other on the tabletop. "Do we tell the kids?" he asks. Dave is our history guy, but his graduate degree was in ethics.

"Tell them what?" I ask. "That we don't know what's going on?"

There are four of us down here, the core teachers: Dave, me and the two women, Beth and Audrey, who huddle together tearfully. Beth is a Catholic, and she stares out a porthole at the dark reddish line of the horizon, racked no doubt by fictional horrors—the four horsemen bearing down from the cloud cover. Captain Ho and the crew are above, engaged, I assume, in some immediately useful work. As a biologist, I can say that Captain Ho is a good example of evolved human behavior; he navigates, he adapts, he survives. His wife is the cook. He has everything he needs onboard the *Demeter*, our 140-foot steel-hull brigantine.

We four are lesser examples, lonely men and women who for various reasons have chosen to live life afloat, teaching spoiled, wealthy children, none of whom we will know for more than one semester. This is our summer trip, a ninety-day southern odyssey. We leave in May from San Francisco straight for the Great Barrier Reef, head north to the Indian Ocean and then down the coast of East Africa, around the tip and across the South Atlantic to Argentina, then shoot back up toward home base in the Florida Keys in August. Most of us missed a mark somewhere: career, family, dream.

The hatch opens with a wet squeak, and Captain Ho appears on the stairs—his sockless boat shoes and the cuffs of his jeans. He climbs down, looking tired already, a sheen of sweat on his forehead, ham radio clutched in his hand. "Nothing," he says. "Nothing on VHF, nothing on single sideband or satellite, and this thing—" He smacks the radio down with a force that speaks of tightly lidded pressure, "Even this fucking thing. Nothing."

"So what do we do?" I ask him.

"What can we do?"

"Right."

Our situation seems to me like an ethics test question, a hypothetical dilemma. If you were stranded on a boat full of high school students during some kind of catastrophe—say, terrorist attack, nuclear detonation, apocalypse—would you *a, b, c* or *d*? Would that Dave could offer us multiple choice. The unlimited field of options for response feels, right now, like no options at all.

At dinner, I watch the kids—thirty of them—shoveling canned peas into their mouths, cutting fat off the thick steaks we've been eating ever since Rio. I can see in their easy conversation that end-of-semester shipmate bond, a weathered good nature that will surprise their parents when they tramp down the gangway at Key West.

If they tramp down the gangway at Key West.

Stop it, I tell myself. This is dangerous and weak-minded thinking, and I should stop. But Jesus Christ, what if we have to start a new race on an island somewhere, out of view of the aliens or al-Qaeda or whoever? I can't help darting a glance at Lisa, who is demonstrating something for the boy next to her with a piece of bread she holds in the air, then slowly tilts. She looks at him as if to say, *Understand*?

Lisa is my best student, maybe ever. She is a junior. She comes to all my study sessions and extra-credit dives, and her fascination with the systems of the world reminds me of my purpose. She will be very beautiful, though for now she chews the ends of her sandy hair, and constellations of pimples shift like the turning sky on her forehead and the places to either side of her chin. I would like her for a daughter-in-law instead of the bleached-blond bimbos my sons are sure to pick.

Dave, beside me, spills a glass of water down the front of his shirt, I help him mop the plastic table. He spears his steak and holds it up to drip-dry. "Nolan," he says, "how can you eat?"

I shrug. Actually, I'm really hungry. Should I lose my appetite in the face of the looming unknown? I have been more afraid of saltwater crocodiles and box jellyfish. At least with those guys, I know the danger is real. A few years ago, in Australia, I was bitten through my wetsuit by a venomous blue-ringed octopus. They massaged my heart until it worked again. That's about what it takes for me to lose my appetite.

The truth is, very little could divert my attention from tomorrow's dive. Right now, we are twenty-four hours from the offshore bank reef where I will take the kids down to see massive coral spawning. There is only about a half-hour window of time, annually, when the elkhorn coral releases its infant polyps into the ocean. Year after year I have seen the kids' eyes widen inside their masks as the water around them fills with bright, tiny planulae that rush toward the light. A vast night snowstorm of life.

The planulae—little packages of egg and sperm—will gestate as they float on the ocean's surface, and then they will drift back down to reattach and start new colonies. Elkhorn coral is on the endangered list, and each year I catch thousands of planulae and ferry them north to a lab on Key West, where I am helping to build a coral nursery. The conservationists there will nurse my polyps into adulthood and then release them back into the Atlantic to rebuild the dying reefs. Coral polyps—the tiny animals that twine together to form what you'd recognize as coral—are all stomach, mouth and tentacle. Instead of a brain, they have a nerve net. They are beings of appetite and sensation. I admire them.

I clap Dave on the back as I get up to bus my dishes. He scowls at me. He doesn't want reassurance; he'd rather wallow. Lisa has left the dining hall, I pass her on deck on the way to the teachers' berth. She is pressed against the railing, watching the horizon through binoculars. When she lowers them, I see circular impressions around her eyes.

"What do you think it is?" she asks. "The red stuff?"

I am honest. "No idea."

"Could it be some kind of aurora?"

"Sure."

When I squint, the horizon looks like a slack, fuzzy length of maroon yarn looped around the world. Clouds hang low and bright, and the sun, almost set, casts light across the water in glancing horizontals. I put my hand out, and Lisa lays the binoculars in it. Magnified, the red horizon *is* alarming. I can see striations in the color—dark, light, dark—as if the redness in some places is rolling toward us.

"Can we still go on the dive?" Lisa asks.

"Absolutely."

"Mr. Harrity?" she asks. I hand the binoculars back. "When we get to Key West—" My breath catches in my throat. I think of a place I know that has the best soft-shell crab and margaritas.

"Do you think you could write me a recommendation? For college?"

I tell Lisa of course I will, and I hurry past her and down to my berth, where I lie in bed for a while, trying to straighten myself out. My feelings for Lisa are purely professorial. Someday maybe I will eat soft-shell crab with her parents to celebrate her college admission, and she will still not be old enough to order a drink. Actually, I'm sure I would hate her parents. They're New Yorkers, probably rich and overprogrammed. I bet the mother wears a fur coat.

Maybe the redness is an atmospheric illusion. How could it appear the same in the west—where Puerto Rico lies just thirty-some miles off—as it does in the east, where the ocean stretches to distant Africa?

Later, in the teachers' berth, I play scrabble with Audrey. She keeps spelling out things like *doom now* on her tile rack and flipping it around to show me, giggling. *No moon g. Go x soon.*

"You just keep picking up O's," I commiserate.

Dave lies on the padded fold-out bench we call the sofa, pretending to read a biography of Eisenhower. "Ten bucks says Beth can't keep a secret." Beth is on babysitting duty tonight, supervising the girls' dormitory. I think Dave's wrong, though; if anyone can put on a happy face for the kids, it will be studious little Beth, our Classics teacher. If she can convince kids that Latin will serve them well, she can convince them of anything.

Audrey grows serious, watching me. "Are you thinking of your kids?"

"Oh, they're fine. They have no idea."

"No, I mean, *your* kids."

"I'm sure they're fine, too," I say. I'm sure everyone is fine.

It's no use thinking about my sons. They're both installed at state universities, but even if the radio worked, I couldn't reach them. My sons were eight and ten when my wife and I split, and they chose to live with her full-time. I will never understand it. When we offered them the decision, I thought it would mean summers or winters, weekends or weeks. Their defection is the hinge on which my life swung away from ordinary concerns. I lasted a year alone in that landlocked city where we'd lived together, and then I found this dream of a job. I see the boys for holidays, but they are barely recognizable as the children they were—they drive SUVs; they like action movies; I have heard them use the word *faggot*.

Audrey rearranges her letters thoughtfully. She says, "I keep thinking of my ex-boyfriend. I guess that means something, right? I guess I'm having an epiphany." Audrey isn't even thirty yet. I don't know exactly what she's doing on this boat; she talks every now and again about library school, and she seems like the kind of sweet, smart woman who would enjoy marriage and a good job in a real town somewhere. I don't mean that in a sexist way; she's welcome to the floating life if it suits her. I just think she's a little bit stalled, as I was at her age, stuck in dead-end lab jobs where the only biological phenomena that crossed my path were in drops of blood squished between glass slides.

Dave is fiddling with the radio, but now it's nothing but static on every channel. We're on our own.

I wake up thinking of the reef, damselfish lurking in recesses in the coral, reef sharks soaring above like happy kites. I have three teaching blocks to get through before I can prepare for tonight's dive. We will hit the water at nine o'clock so we can reach our depth by nine-fifteen and watch through the half-hour window for spawning.

Captain Ho is on deck, showing some freshmen the best way to coil line. They should know this by now. A few older boys shuffle past and yell the old joke, "Heave, Ho!" He smiles and waves them off. It is hot already. The red horizon encircles us, exhausting to consider, like a practical joke gone on too long.

"Any news?" I ask him.

"No," he says. "No change." My reflection looms fisheyed on his sunglasses. He guides me a few steps away from the kids. "I'm thinking about heading back to where we picked up the last transmission."

An anxious muscle flutters in my chest. "Why? You think we'll get radio there?"

Captain Ho chews his lip, and it strikes me: this is not a safety measure—this is some psychological thing. He wants to feel like he's doing something. "Hmm," I say, and pretend to consider this option seriously. "Staying on course seems like the best bet. When the radio comes on, they'll know where to find us."

"I just thought . . ." Captain Ho takes his sunglasses off, wipes them methodically with the hem of his T-shirt, doesn't finish the sentence.

"You're doing all the right things, John," I tell him, and I turn and make for my classroom. If he needs my permission to change course, I'll make it my business to lie low until it stops mattering, until I'm sitting tight with my tanks full of planulae.

Lisa is in my third block. She is still distracted by the red horizon, which is ever-so-slightly thicker this afternoon, and she watches it bob through the portholes of our lab classroom. Most of the kids seem oblivious, but a few, like Lisa, are on edge. For a moment I am alert to a bright screen under a desk—news!—but it is only a battery-powered game. "Put it away," I tell the kid, and he scowls.

I am teaching them about the ecosystem of the reef. If we had Internet access, today I would show them streaming video of coral masses releasing planulae. But this might be even better: to let them come to the dive with blank minds and be amazed. Each student has prepared a brief report on a species we could see on tonight's reef dive. We've had manatee, angelfish, moray eel, barracuda. When it's Lisa's turn, she punches up a PowerPoint presentation, and I hear a few groans. She clears her throat. I wouldn't have liked her when I was her age. I would have missed out.

She says, "The *Hippocampus*, or seahorse, is one of the few genera on earth in which the male releases young. The female seahorse deposits eggs into a brood pouch on the male, and he fertilizes and carries the eggs. If we see a seahorse tonight, it is most likely to be of the species *zosterae*: a dwarf seahorse. But remember, kids," she says, hamming it up unsuccessfully, "size doesn't matter."

I love her.

One of the greatest mysteries of my life is how the coral know so precisely when to spawn. Bleached and broken and ravaged by human interference, they still know, down to the half hour, when their infant polyps will have the best shot at life. And it is the same year in, year out, despite the ceaseless change of the world.

At eight o'clock I am ready to go. The plastic funnels I use to gather planulae, the cameras, gear and suits for ten kids and a couple of teachers are all laid out on the stern deck. Since I can't bring thirty kids with me on each dive, usually we rotate. But I set up the coral dive as our finale—an end-of-semester reward for the top GPAs from each class. Certain kids have clawed their way up from B to A averages just to get a spot.

I make my way through the narrow hallway from my classroom to the teachers' berth to find some coffee. I like to dive caffeinated—not something I recommend to my kids. As soon as I step inside, I am sorry I did. Dave is laid out on the sofa, breathing hard and fast, Audrey perched beside him. I have no time for this.

Audrey looks up at me. "Panic attack," she whispers. "He keeled over on deck."

"Were there kids around?"

Audrey nods.

"Jesus Christ." Mass hysteria is something I *do* know how to fear. "Hey, buddy," I say to Dave as I turn on the one-cup percolator. "You okay?"

He nods once and goes on gasping. Audrey leans across him to lift the sweaty brown curls from his forehead, and her T-shirt gaps at the neck. Dave shuts his eyes, ever the gentleman.

I beckon to Audrey, and she gets up. I whisper, "Are you still coming tonight?"

"Something came up," she says, rolling her eyes toward Dave.

"Okay," I say, ignoring her tone. "And if any of the kids ask, we'll say he has low blood sugar." If I were free tonight, I'd sit with Dave and help him collect himself, too, but even then, it would only be an exercise. Dave doesn't need me. If I were asked to choose between my reef and Dave, and I guess I *am* being asked to choose, I'd choose my reef.

So I do; I choose my reef.

I join the kids as they suit up on the stern deck. In the darkness, the horizon looks as blue-black as ever. Beth is in her wetsuit, doing pressure checks on all the tanks. I am surprised to see her here. I thought Audrey would be the hardy one.

"I couldn't keep on doing nothing," Beth says, a new brassiness to her voice. "So why not?" She works her long brown hair into a ponytail in a few expert moves. "Where are the girls?"

Only the boys have shown up—seven of them. My three girls are missing. I tell Beth I'll be right back, and I dash belowdecks. I can spend minutes only on this. The girls are in their dormitory berth, where I am not supposed to go. I climb down the ladder, and girls in boxer shorts recoil into their bunks like mollusks. I ask for Lisa, and they point me toward a bottom bunk with a drawn canvas curtain, behind which I hear whimpering. I've never heard such a little-girlish sound come out of Lisa. I squat by the curtain.

"Lisa?"

A hand pulls the curtain back, and there is Lisa with my other two missing divers, who have been comforting her. I am in the inner sanctum. Lisa sits up and lets out a long breath, composing herself. There's my girl.

"Something is really, really wrong, isn't it?" she asks me. Tears have left delicate marks like dried-up rivers on her cheeks. "Satellites don't just all stop working at once. Radios don't go dead."

One of the other girls, a Tanya, picks up the thread: "And Mr. Sheehan fainted."

We all sit for a moment, paralyzed by not knowing. But I am the adult, and I have to offer them *something*. "If it were anything serious," I lie, "we'd know by now."

Tanya sucks her teeth. "Really? You don't know anything? We're so fucked."

"Please don't tell the other kids you think so, Tanya."

Lisa is watching me closely. "What if something happens while we're on the dive?"

"Nothing's going to happen." Below us, the coral is ripening. These few moments of delay could ruin everything, and as they tick by, I realize how badly I need Lisa down there with me. I fix my disciplinarian-eye on her, and it works its magic; she drops her gaze to my collar. "If you miss this, you're going to be sorry for the rest of your life." I widen my focus to include the other girls. "All of you."

They squirm, but I still haven't won them over. I am desperate. I say, "I don't know how I could write a recommendation for a student who would pass this up." I reach out and tug on Lisa's arm. "Up."

She wipes her eyes on the shoulder of her T-shirt and swings her feet out onto the ground, one and then the other. "I was just worried about my parents, you know. In New York. If it's, like, a terrorist thing."

She's using the past tense. This is good. "I'm sure they're just fine, Lisa. We have to get going," I say. The girls communicate in a female language of glances, and then they get up and follow me.

I slip into the warm ocean, and it is as soothing as sleep after the hardest day. The moon is gibbous, and from beneath, the surface of the ocean glows. Around me in the dark, bright shafts of bubbles appear where my students' headlamps illuminate the areas of disturbance caused by their less graceful entries into the water. Beth floats beside me. She turns the spotlight toward the kids, and I count them: ten. We descend.

Halfway down we stop for a bubble check, scanning each other's tanks for leaks. There is a sense, as we continue down, of infinity: endless depth on all sides. Some divers find that feeling of space uncomfortable, but I love it. I am weightless in the womb of the earth. I am part of an endlessly beautiful system.

Particles drift in the silver beams of our headlights. A school of gray snappers darts below me. I have gone ahead, and I trust that Beth is bringing up the rear, counting our kids again and again. My eardrums pop. The ocean here is twenty-five meters deep, and it is not long before I make out the dark topography of the reef: the hulk of a brain coral, the jutting shapes of the elkhorns. It is a fantastic night city: spires and high-rises and caves full of sleeping things. Small fish lurk in bending grasses. I feel an impulse to announce myself: I am here! I have missed you!

I pass over the reef, looking for the best view. I find a concentration of elkhorn coral and set about preparing my funnels as the kids join me, swinging their headlamps around in search of action. We have about fifty minutes of air. My regulator mouthpiece tastes vaguely sulfurous, and I wonder what was used to clean it, or if the whole atmosphere is full of the horizon's toxic red dust, settling invisibly on all surfaces. I spit it out and swish it around in the sea, and the taste is gone.

We wait. Lisa floats at my side, her blond ponytail fanning out like something alive. Whenever we see a fish, she looks at me as if I could somehow signal her the species name. I just nod. It is so dark and so quiet. Anemones bend in the sea breeze. From down here, everything feels improbable: the red horizon, Dave breathing into a paper bag, our little bobbing ship. Land itself begins to feel improbable. When I think of my sons, they are five and seven, playing in a sandbox, not the disappointing young men I know are out there somewhere, making do. We swim in lazy circles around the elkhorns. I beckon the kids over to see a nudibranch—a tiny, neon purple sea slug—clinging to the coral. A huge moray eel ribbons by. But the coral holds out.

I watch the passage of time on my dive watch, and I start to worry. *Come on*, I think at the coral. *Now*. When my ex-wife used to dive with me, she could never stay down for more than half an hour. Pressure headaches. I check in with Beth and the kids, exchanging A-OK hand signals. They grin around their regulator mouthpieces to show me they are still feeling gung ho. They are not disappointed; they see stoplight parrotfish and blue tang. They swim a few meters off after a shadowy stingray and then come back. They don't know what the coral spawning would look like. They don't know what they're missing.

Maybe it already happened. Is it possible that the coral know more than I do about the situation on land, that they've decided to hold on to their eggs? Have I simply miscalculated? Or is this the way living things change—threatened again and again by God only knows what? I feel a little sick from the coffee and the pressure and the dropping weight in my gut: it's not going to happen.

I've missed the spawning. Goddamn it.

Beth swims beneath me, and I am blinded for a moment by her spotlight. She gives me a thumbs-up to say *time to go up*. She's right; we have only enough air left for ascent and decompression. This year, my reef will die faster than it can grow. I am heartbroken for my polyps.

We ascend at the rate of our spent breath, the carbon dioxide rising from our regulators like slow silver balloons. A few meters beneath the surface, we stop for decompression. We can see the shadow of the ship. Some of the kids have mastered neutral buoyancy; others sink and twist, trying to keep their bodies level. I watch them and feel a different pang; at least I should have succeeded here, as a teacher. We surface into cool air and sound. A handful of students are waiting for us on deck, playing cards and sipping tea. "Hey!" someone shouts, "There they are!"

We climb the ladder up to them, and I hear kids saying, "Did you see the eel? Oh my God, that thing was fucking huge!" Beth wrings saltwater out of her ponytail.

I slide my mask up onto my forehead and look around for Lisa, who will understand the depth of my disappointment. In their suits in the moonlight, my divers glimmer wet and black like seals. They stumble and hold each other up, peeling off flippers. I can't tell which one is Lisa.

"Lisa?" Everyone looks at me and blinks.

"Oh my God," says Tanya, and then all the kids are saying it. Beth takes frantic headcounts: *Onetwothreefourfivesixseveneightnine. Onetwothree fourfivesixseveneightnine.*

I unscrew my regulator and slip my rig onto a fresh tank as fast as I possibly can. Thank God there are fresh tanks. Mine is an octopus rig, with a spare hose and demand valve for a second diver. I've never had to use it before. I slide down the ladder. Above me, the kids' faces appear dark over the rail.

"Nolan!" Beth is shouting. "Wait!"

I know she's trying to come with me, but she's taking too long. Lisa doesn't have the air for this. I dive.

My legs burn, my breath thunders in my head. I'm going too fast and there is nobody to check my gear. If I get the bends, I'll deserve them. I forced Lisa on the dive. She was distraught, and I did not listen. Anything that happens to her will be my fault.

I'm about fifteen meters down when I see the snowstorm coming.

I feel a lump in my throat and bite down on my regulator mouthpiece. It's happening after all. Planulae shine in the beam of my headlamp. Little fragments of light, little diamonds. I left my funnels on deck. I swim down, down, down, and they are all around me, flying upward toward the vague moonlight. If I had pockets, I would fill them. If I could point these baby polyps toward safety, God knows I

163

would do it. Most will be eaten by fish. Those that mature in these waters and drift back down to form new reef will be bleached and poisoned by our heat and our chemical runoff, or choked out by sewage-fed algaes. *I'm sorry*, I think to them. *I'm so sorry*. I only have time for Lisa.

I push down against the upward traffic, pressing my lips together so as not to swallow planulae. I retrace our swim. I can see only a few meters ahead in the dense, spawning rush. Minutes pass. I am not sure exactly when Lisa would, or will, or, God forbid, *has*, run out of air; exact timing depends on a set of variables: breath and pressure and so on. I swim as close to the reef as I can. Something big catches my eye, but it is only a dark, swaying sea fan. I see angelfish gulping planulae. I find that brain coral we first saw, and then I make my way to the elkhorns.

Something takes shape in the darkness ahead, and as I get closer, I swim for it with all my might. It is Lisa, floating like an empty suit in the storm. Even before I check her vitals, I find her tank gauge and see that she is out of air. I rip the regulator off her, and a tiny flower of blood blooms from her mouth into the water; I have torn her lip. I shove my secondary mouthpiece into her mouth. Only now do I put my finger to her slender neck. I feel a pulse. Her throat trembles. Her lungs hiccup, and then she looks at me through the swarming life.

All around us the world is dark. If you had no lights, you would feel the spawning only as a gentle current buoying you up. I hold Lisa by both arms. We stare at each other, each in the spotlight of the other s headlamp, as she shudders and flails, searching for the pattern of her breath. Planulae rise through the light between us. She has cried inside her mask; water pools in the curved plastic below her eyes. She bears it out; she finds her breath. She grows calm. I know what she is feeling because I have felt it myself: she has been returned to life. She is astonished.

We float together as the spawning slows, and though I am looking at Lisa, I see all my children. I see every kid I ever taught, unaging, crowded on the stern deck of our old ship, suiting up to follow me into the dark. I pass my hands over dead reef, and it comes back to life, the polyps strong and hungry. I see my sons, my beautiful boys, lying prone amidst the rubble of a destroyed America. I nestle regulators between their lips, and I watch as they, too, open their eyes, find their breath.

I give a thumbs-up sign to Lisa, and she shakes her head no and holds out a finger, the signal for *just a second*. We stare at each other in perfect understanding. We both want to stay here as long as we can. We are afraid to go up.

We are afraid of everything.

Nominated by Missouri Review, Ed Falco, Wally Lamb, Ron Tanner

THE MERCIES

by ANN PATCHETT

from GRANTA

Long before any decisions have been made about where or when she might be moving, Sister Nena starts combing the liquor stores early in the morning looking for boxes. She is breaking down the modest contents of her life into three categories: things to keep, things to throw away, things to donate to Catholic Charities. Sister Melanie is doing the same.

'What's the rush?' I ask, picking my way past the long row of boxes that lines the front hall, everything labelled and sealed and neatly stacked. It is August, and the heat and humidity have turned the air into an unbearable soup. I think they're getting ahead of themselves and I tell them so. Sister Kathy, who is responsible for assessing their situation, won't be coming from the mother house in North Carolina for weeks.

'We've got to be ready,' Sister Nena says. She does not stop working. Her state of being is one of constant action, perpetual motion. A small gold tennis racquet dangles from her neck where on another nun one would expect to find a cross. 'I won't pack the kitchen until the very end.'

Not that the kitchen matters. I suspect that the nuns, who are small enough to emulate the very sparrows God has His eye on, should be eating more, which is why I've brought them dinner. Sister Melanie is going to Mercy, the nuns' retirement home, but she doesn't know when. Some days she is looking forward to the move, other days she isn't so sure. She stops and looks in the bag at the casserole I've brought, gives me a hug, and ambles off again.

Sister Nena is certain that she doesn't want to go to Mercy. She regards it as the end of the line. She's hoping to land in a smaller apartment by herself, or maybe with another sister, though finding a new room-mate at the age of seventy-eight can be a challenge. 'It's up to God,' she says, then she goes back to her boxes.

Sister Nena was born in Nashville, the city where we both live. She was eighteen when she entered the convent. Sixty years later the convent is gone and the Sisters of Mercy who are left in this city are largely scattered. For almost twenty years, Sister Nena and Sister Melanie have lived in a condo they once shared with Sister Helen. The condo, which is within walking distance of the mall, is in an upscale suburban neighbourhood called Green Hills. It isn't exactly the place I would have pictured nuns living, but then everything about my friendship with Sister Nena has made me re-evaluate how life is for nuns these days.

'It's like that book,' she said, summing up the best-seller, 'First I pray, then I eat.'

'That leaves love,' I said.

'That's it. I love a lot of people. Pray, eat, love, tennis. I'm in a rut. I need to find something else I can do for others.'

I guess I always thought the rut was part of it. A religious life is not one that I associate with great adventure. But now that change is barrelling towards her, Sister Nena is restless for its arrival. Day after day she is standing up to meet it and I can see she's had a talent for adventure all along. It seems to me that entering the convent at the age of eighteen is in fact a great act of daring.

'I didn't always want to be a nun,' Sister Nena said. 'Not when I was younger. I wanted to be a tennis player. My brothers and I knew a man who let us play on his court in return for keeping it up. It was a dirt court and my brothers would roll it out with the big roller and I would repaint the lines. We played tennis every day.' Nena, the youngest of three. Nena, the only girl, following her brothers to the courts every morning of summer on her bicycle, racquet in hand.

When I asked her what her brothers thought of her joining the convent, she said they thought she was crazy, using the word crazy as if it were a medical diagnosis. 'So did my father. He thought I was making a terrible mistake giving up getting married, having kids. I liked kids,' she said. 'I babysat a lot when I was young. I had a happy life back then.

167

I had a boyfriend. His family was in the meat-packing business. My father called him Ham Boy. It was all good but still there was something that wasn't quite right. I didn't feel comfortable. I never felt like I was living the life I was supposed to.'

What about her mother is what I want to know. What did her mother say?

Sister Nena smiled the smile of a daughter who had pleased the mother she loved above all else. 'She was proud of me.'

There will never be enough days for me to ask Sister Nena all the things I want to know, and she is endlessly patient with me. She can see it plainly herself: it hasn't been an ordinary life. Some of my questions are surely a result of the leftover curiosity of childhood, the quiet suspicion that nuns were not like the rest of us. But there is another way in which the questions feel like an attempt to gather vital information for my own life. Forget about the yoga practice, the meditating, the vague dreams of going to an ashram in India: Sister Nena has stayed in Tennessee and devoted her life to God. She has lived with her calling for so long that it seems less a religious vocation than a marriage, a deeply worn path of mutual acceptance. Sister Nena and God understand one another. They are in it for life.

The Sisters of Mercy was started by Catherine McAuley in Dublin. She recognized the needs of poor women and girls and used her considerable inheritance to open a home for them called Mercy House, taking her vows in 1831. Committing your life to God was one thing, but I think that choosing an order would be akin to choosing which branch of the military to sign up for. Army? Navy? Dominicans? From a distance it all looks like service but the daily life must play out in very different ways. 'The Mercies taught me in school,' Sister Nena said.

I nod my head, of course. I was also taught by the Mercies in school. I was taught by Sister Nena.

'They never manipulated me,' she said in their defence. 'But I admired them, their goodness.'

I spent twelve years with the Sisters of Mercy and I am certain, in all that time, no one ever suggested that I or any of my friends should consider joining the order. Nuns have never been in the business of recruitment, which may in part account for their dwindling ranks. What we were told repeatedly was to *listen*. God had a vocation for all of us and if we paid close attention and were true to ourselves, we would know His intention. Sometimes you might not like what you heard. You might think that what was being asked of you was too much, but at that point there really was no getting out of it. Once you knew what God wanted from your life, you would have to be ten different kinds of fool to look the other way. When I was a girl in Catholic school I was open to the idea of being a nun, a mother, a wife, but whenever I closed my eyes and listened (and there was plenty of time for listening — in chapel, in maths class, in basketball games — we were told the news could come at any time) the voice I heard was consistent: be a writer. It didn't matter that writing had never been listed as one of our options. I knew that for me this was the truth, and to this end I found the nuns to be invaluable examples. I was, after all, educated by a group of women who had in essence jumped ship, ignored the strongest warnings of their fathers and brothers in order to follow their own clear direction. They were working women who had given every aspect of their lives over to their beliefs, as I had every intention of giving my life over to my belief. The nun's existence was not so far from the kind of singular life I imagined for myself, even if God wasn't the object of my devotion.

In her years as a postulant and then a novice, Sister Nena moved around: Memphis, Cincinnati, Knoxville, finishing her education and taking her orders. When I asked her when she stopped wearing a habit, she had to think about it. '1970?' Her hair is now a thick, curling grey cut close to her head. 'I liked the habit. If they told us tomorrow we had to wear it again I'd be fine with that. Just not those things that went around the face. There was so much starch in them that they hurt.' She touched her cheek at the memory. 'It got so hot in the summer with all that stuff on, you couldn't believe it. But if it got too hot I'd just pull my skirts up.'

It was around 1969 that Sister Nena came back to Nashville to teach at St Bernard's Academy, about the same time I arrived from California and enrolled in first grade late that November. This is the point at which our lives first intersect: Sister Nena, age thirty-two, and Ann, very nearly six.

The convent where we met was an imposing and unadorned building of the darkest red brick imaginable. In those days it sat on the top of a hill and looked down over a long, rolling lawn dotted with statuary. It was there I learned to roller-skate and ran the three-legged race with Trudy Corbin on field day. Once a year I was part of a procession of little girls who set a garland of roses on top of the statue of Mary while singing, 'Oh Mary, we crown thee with blossoms today', then we would file back inside and eat our lunches out of paper sacks. The cafeteria was in the basement of the convent; the classrooms were on the first floor. On the second floor there was a spectacular chapel painted in bright blue. It had an altar made from Italian marble and a marble kneeling rail and rows of polished pews where I would go in the morning to say part of the rosary and then chat God up in that personal way that became popular after Vatican II. My mother worked long shifts as a nurse and she would take me and my sister to the convent early and pick us up late. The nuns would let us come into their kitchen and sort the silverware, which in retrospect I imagine they mixed together just to give us something to do. My sister and I were well aware of the privilege we were receiving, getting to go into their kitchen, their dining room, and, on very rare occasions, into the sitting room on the second floor where they had a television set. Still, in all those years, I never set foot on the third or fourth floor of the building. That was where the nuns slept, where Sister Nena slept, and it was for us as far away as the moon, even as it sat right on top of us.

How did we find each other again?' Sister Nena asked me recently while we were in the grocery store.

'You called me,' I said. 'Years ago. You were looking for money.'

She stopped in the middle of the aisle and shook her head. 'I forgot. It was for St Vincent's School. Oh, that's awful. It's awful that that's why I called you.'

I put my arm over her shoulder while she steered the cart. Sister Nena likes to steer the cart. 'At least you called.'

Sister Nena lived in the convent at St Bernard's until she was sixty years old. That was when the order sold the building. The parcel of land, which sat smack in the middle of a hip and crowded neighbourhood, was valuable. A large apartment complex was built in the front yard where we had played. They ripped out the giant mock orange trees first. Picking up mock oranges, which were smelly and green and had deep turning folds that were distressingly reminiscent of human brains, was a punishment all the girls sought to avoid. It surprised me how sorry I was to see the trees go.

The convent had an interior window over the doorway to the chapel that could be opened on to the third floor so that the nuns who were too infirm to come downstairs could sit in their wheelchairs and listen to mass. When I was a girl I would try to glance up at them without being noticed. From my vantage point down in the pews they were tiny in their long white dresses, which may have been the uniform of advanced age and may have just been their nightgowns. After the sale of the convent, the sisters who were retired or needed care were sent to Mercy, which was then a new facility twenty miles outside of town. The grade-school students were moved next door into the building that had once been the high school (the high school, never as successful as the grade school, was now defunct) and the convent itself was converted into office spaces. Every schoolroom and nun's bedroom found another use: a therapist's office, a legal practice, a Pilates studio. The altar was given to a parish in Stone Mountain, Georgia. It had to be taken out through the back wall with a crane. The pews were sold. The empty chapel was now rented out for parties.

'That was hard,' Sister Nena said in the manner of one used to taking hard things in stride. 'We had a lot of fun there, especially in the summers when everyone would come home, the sisters who taught in other towns would all come back. We'd sit up and tell stories and laugh, have a glass of wine.'

I went back to St Bernard's once, years later, and climbed the back stairs to the fourth floor and stood in an empty bedroom/office to look out of the window. It was like looking down from the moon.

The vows for the Sisters of Mercy are poverty, celibacy and obedience, service to the poor, sick and uneducated, with perseverance until death. Obedience is another way of saying that you don't complain when your order decides to sell the place where you live. You don't get a vote. Sometimes this strikes me as ridiculously unfair ('You should have told them no,' I find myself wanting to say, even though I have no idea who 'them' might have been). Other times, when I can manage to see outside the limitations of my own life, I catch a glimpse of what the move must have been for Sister Nena: another act of faith, the belief that God has a plan and is looking after you. It must be the right thing because you had turned your life over to God and even if you didn't understand all the intricacies of the deal, He wasn't about to make a mistake.

After the sale, the younger sisters, the ones who were still teaching, were relocated to rented apartments around town so they could have an easier commute into work. 'It was all right,' Sister Nena said. 'We'd all still get together on the weekends and have dinner.' Sister Nena, who taught reading in grades one through three, and Sister Helen, my maths teacher for those same grades, and Sister Melanie, the lower-school principal, lived together in a rented condo, the three bedrooms making a straight line off of the upstairs hallway. They were happy there. They continued to work until the time came to work less. They semi-retired, retired, tutored children who needed tutoring, helped out at Catholic Charities. After she left St Bernard's, Sister Nena volunteered at St Vincent de Paul's, a school for underserved African-American children in North Nashville that remained in a state of constant financial peril until it finally went under.

Then, in 2004, Sister Helen had a stroke. After she got out of the hospital she was sent to Mercy. For a long time Sister Melanie and Sister Nena thought that she'd come home and take up her place again in the third bedroom, but Sister Helen only got worse. Day after day, Sister Nena would drive the twenty miles out to Mercy to visit her friend and try to get her to do the puzzles in the children's maths work-books that she had taught from for years, and sometimes Sister Helen would, but mostly she would sit and watch television. Over time she recognized Sister Nena less and less, and then finally not at all. It was because of the stroke that I started seeing more of Sister Nena. We would have lunch after she played tennis or have coffee in the after-noons. She would talk about her friend and sometimes she would cry a little. They had, after all, been together for a very long time. It was during one of those conversations that she mentioned Sister Helen's last name was Kain, and I wondered how I could have never known that before.

Sister Nena and Sister Melanie stayed on in Green Hills, but by 2010 Sister Melanie was growing increasingly fragile, forgetful. It was the consensus among the other nuns, and of Sister Melanie herself, that she was ready to go out to Mercy.

The question then was what should be done with Sister Nena? She was, after all, still playing tennis like one of the Williams sisters three times a week and didn't seem like a candidate for the retirement home. Still, while one spare bedroom could be overlooked, the rented condo was $1,400 a month and there were no extra nuns to fill up what would now be two spare bedrooms. It was decided that Sister Nena could stay out of Mercy, but she needed to find an apartment that was significantly less expensive. For the first time in her life she would be on her own.

I like to take Sister Nena to Whole Foods. It is a veritable amusement park of decadence and wonder to one who has taken a vow of poverty. Her ability to cook is rudimentary at best and she doesn't like to shop, so I advocate prepared foods from the deli. Sister Melanie, who adored the grocery store, made her pilgrimage to Kroger every Sunday. It was not a habit Sister Nena planned on picking up, claiming her Italian heritage would save her: as long as she had a box of pasta and a jar of sauce she was never going to starve. I could usually convince her to let me get a few things now that I knew what she liked. She was greatly enamoured of the olive bar. After Sister Kathy had visited and the decision about everyone's future was settled, I took Sister Nena to the store and we got some coffee and went to sit at a small table by the window to discuss the details. She told me she'd found a place in a sprawling complex called Western Hills on the other side of town. I didn't like the sound of it. I knew the neighbourhood, and the busy street was crowded with fast-food places, cheque-cashing centres and advertisements for bail bondsmen. She was set on getting a two-bedroom so that she could have a little office for her computer and the chair where she says her prayers in the morning. I argued for a smaller place in the neighbourhood where she lived now, but for once in her life the decision was Sister Nena's to make and she intended to get what she wanted. 'It's all going to be fine,' she said, trying to reassure me, to reassure herself. 'Sister Jeannine lives out there. She likes the place. I've got it all figured out. Sister Melanie's helping me work on a budget. They gave me a bank account, a credit card and a debit card.'

There in the cafe at Whole Foods, amid the swirl of mothers with strollers and young men with backpacks, my friend was not out of place, a slightly built Italian woman in a tracksuit. I stared at her blankly, unsure of what we were talking about.

'I got a chequing account,' she said again.

'You've never had a chequing account?'

She shook her head. 'Melanie handled all the finances. She paid the bills. 'Then Sister Nena leaned in, moving her cup aside. 'What exactly is the difference between a credit card and a debit card?'

I tried to outline the differences as clearly as possible; explaining the different ways either one of them can trip a person up. 'When you use the debit card you have to write it down in the registry the same way you would a cheque. You need to write everything down and then subtract it from your balance each time so you'll know how much you have.'

She took a sip of her coffee. 'I can do that. I'm smart enough.'

'You're perfectly smart,' I said. 'But I don't know if you know all of this already. Once a month you get a statement from the bank. You have to balance your chequebook against the bank statement.' I never thought much of the intellectual content of my secondary education, which was weighed down by a preponderance of religion classes and gym. But while the nuns may have been short on Shakespeare, they were long on practicality. By the time we were in high school we had learned how to make stews and sauces and cakes. We knew how to make crêpes. We could remove stains and operate a washing machine. We were taught not only the fundamentals of sewing, but how to make a budget and balance a chequebook, how to fill out a simple tax form. Down at the grade school, Sister Nena had not received the benefits of any of these lessons.

She puzzled over what I was saying about bank statements for a long time. When I got to the part about how she was supposed to mark off her cancelled cheques in the tiny column in the registry, she suddenly perked up as if she had found the answer to the problem. Then she started laughing. 'You shouldn't tease me like that,' she said, putting her hand on her heart. 'You scared me to death. You shouldn't tease a nun.'

'I'm not teasing you,' I said.

By the slight flash of panic that came across her face I could tell that she believed me. Still, she shook her head. 'I don't have to do that. I never saw Sister Melanie do that.'

All the Sisters of Mercy living in their separate apartments submit a budget to the mother house, estimating the cost of their electric and phone bills, food and rent. What they came up with for their monthly stipend was a modest number at best. The order picks that up, along with all medical expenses and insurance. When Sister Nena was hit two years ago by a car that ran a red light, her car was totalled and the order agreed that she could have a new car. I drove her to the Toyota dealership. All she had to do was sign a piece of paper and pick up the keys. 'I hope it's not red,' she said on the way there. 'I don't like red cars.'

The car, a Corolla, was new, and it was red. Sister Nena walked a slow circle around it, studying, while the salesman watched. It wasn't every day a car was purchased over the phone for someone who hadn't seen it. 'I take it back,' she said to me finally. 'The red is nice.'

When Sister Nena was a young nun teaching at St Bernard's, around the time that I was her student, she received an allowance from the order of twenty dollars a month. All of her personal expenses were to be covered by that sum: Life Savers, shoes, clothing. Any cash gifts from the parents of students that came inside Christmas cards were to be turned over, as was any money from her own parents folded into birthday cards. It wasn't a matter of the order leeching up the presents; it was the enactment of the vow. They were still to be poor even when a little extra cash presented itself. I couldn't help but wonder if there was ever a small temptation to take a ten-dollar bill from one's own birthday card, but the question seemed impolite. 'What if your mother sent you a sweater?' I asked instead. I was not being wilfully obtuse. I was trying to figure out the system.

'Oh, that wasn't a problem. You got to keep the sweater.'

It is possible that the only reason any of this makes some limited sense to me is because these were the lessons I was taught as a child. The notion of a rich man's camel not being able to make its way through the eye of the needle was a thought so terrifying (my family was not without means) it would keep me up at night. I believed then that turning away from the material world was the essence of freedom, and someplace deep inside myself; someplace that very rarely sees the light of day. I still believe it now. I imagine that no one who has spent sixty years embracing the tenets of poverty thinks to herself, I wish I'd had a $200 bottle of perfume. That said, after our coffee and the perilous conversation about chequing accounts, we went into Whole Foods to do some shopping. Sister Nena was adamant about wanting to go to Kroger, a less expensive grocery store a few blocks away, because the weekly nun dinner was going to be at her house that night and she'd promised to make pork chops. I told her no, I was buying the pork chops where we were. I believed that pork chops were not an item that should be bargain-hunted.

'When did you get to be so bossy?' she said to me.

'I've been waiting my entire life to boss you around,' I said. I filled up the cart with salads and bread and good German beer while Sister Nena despaired over how much money I spent.

In the check-out line I was still thinking about the twenty dollars a month, a figure that she told me was later raised to one hundred. 'I worked almost fifty years and I never once saw a pay cheque,' she said, and then she shrugged as if to say she hadn't really missed it.

175

Sister Melanie had moved out to Mercy the week before Sister Nena moved to her new apartment, but she came back to help. Sister Nena's eighty-year-old brother, Bud, was there along with two of his children, Andy and Pam, and Sister Nena's friend Nora came. Together we loaded up our cars with everything Sister Nena didn't want to leave to the two movers. It was 6:30 in the morning and had just started to rain.

'We can probably take all the boxes in the cars,' she said. 'That way the movers wouldn't have to bother with them.'

'They're movers,' I said, trying to remember if I had helped a friend move since I was in graduate school. 'That's what they do.' I went to take apart Sister Nena's computer, which was a series of enormous black metal boxes with dozens of snaking cables coming out the back. It looked like something that might have come out of NASA in the seventies. I was very careful putting it in my car.

Western Hills was actually set farther back from the busy street than I had realized, and the complex was so big that it had the insulated feel of a small, walled city. Once our caravan arrived and the contents of our cars were emptied out into the apartment's small living room, the rest of the group went back to their lives and Sister Nena, Sister Melanie, Sister Jeannine and I begin to put the food in the refrigerator and the clothes in closets while the movers brought in the furniture and the boxes. The three nuns, all in their seventies, did hard work at a steady pace, and while I might have been tempted to sit down for a moment on the recently positioned sofa, they did not, and so I did not. I told the movers where to put the television.

'I'm sorry,' the young man said to me. 'I know you told me your name but I don't remember.'

'Ann,' I said.

'Sister Ann?' he asked.

It was true that in a room with three nuns I could easily pass for the fourth. We were all dressed in jeans and sweatshirts. We had all forgone mascara. I shook my head. 'Just Ann,' I said. I thought about my mother, who, like the nuns, is in her seventies now. She was and is a woman of legendary beauty, a woman with a drawer full of silk camisoles and a closet full of high-heeled shoes, who never left the house without make-up even if she was just walking the dog. My sister and I often wondered how her particular elegance and attention to detail had passed over us, how we had managed so little dexterity where beauty was concerned.

But as I talked to the mover, a Catholic kid with a shamrock tattooed inside his wrist, I thought of how we would arrive at the convent very early in the morning and how we would stay sometimes until after dark. Maybe what rubbed off over the years was more than faith. Maybe the reason I felt so comfortable with Sister Nena and the rest of the nuns was that I spent the majority of the waking hours of my childhood with them.

That first time Sister Nena called me all those years ago, when she was looking for someone to help her buy school supplies for the children at the St Vincent de Paul School, she told me she had prayed about it for a long time before picking up the phone. She wasn't happy about having to ask for money, but the children didn't have paper or crayons or glue sticks and she knew I'd been doing well over the years. She'd read some of my books. 'I taught you how to read and write,' she said.

'You did,' I said, and didn't mention that she had in fact done a great deal more for me than that. Sister Nena had been the focal point of all of my feelings of persecution, the repository for my childish anger. I knew that she had thought I was lazy and slow, dull as a butter knife. I watched the hands of other girls shoot up in class while I sat in the back, struggling to understand the question. While having no evidence to the contrary at the time, I was certain that I was smarter than she gave me credit for being, and I would prove it. I grew up wanting to be a writer so that Sister Nena would realize she had underestimated me. I have always believed that the desire for revenge is one of life's great motivators, and my revenge against Sister Nena would be my success. When I was a child I dreamed that one day she would need something from me and I would give it to her with full benevolence. It was true that she had taught me how to read and write, but what she didn't mention on the phone that day, and what she surely didn't remember after nearly fifty years of teaching children, was what an excruciatingly long time it had taken me to learn.

My parents divorced in Los Angeles where I had started first grade at the Cathedral of the Incarnation. In late November of that year, my mother took my sister and me to Tennessee for what was going to be a three-week vacation to see a man she knew there. We never went back. I had not yet learned to read in California and when I was eventually enrolled in St Bernard's, I landed on Sister Nena's doorstep. I remember her well. She was child-sized herself, wearing a plain blue polyester dress that zipped up the back. She had short dark hair and the perpetual tan of a person who played tennis on any passable day. She moved through the classroom with enormous energy and purpose and I could all but see the nonsensical letters of the alphabet trailing behind her wherever she went. I was perilously lost for all the long hours of the school day, but I had yet to conclude that I was in any real trouble. It was still a time in my life that I believed we would go home again and I would catch up among the children and the nuns I knew in California. In Nashville, we stayed in the guest room of strangers, friends of my mother's friend. These people, the Harrises, had daughters of their own who went to St Bernard's and the daughters were not greatly inclined to go to school, nor were the Harrises inclined to make them. Many days we all stayed home together. It was 1969, a fine year for truancy.

I started second grade at St Bernard's as well, having learned very few of the lessons that had been laid out in my first year. The enrolment at the school was small and we had the same teachers for grades one through three. Again, Sister Helen was there with the maths I didn't understand. Again, Sister Nena rolled up her sleeves, but the making of letters eluded me. We left the Harrises' house and found our own apartment, and then moved again. After Christmas we moved to Mufreesboro, a less expensive town thirty minutes away where I was enrolled in public school, but we didn't stay. A few months into third grade we were back in Nashville and I was back with Sister Nena. I still couldn't read whole sentences or write the alphabet with all the letters facing in the right direction. I knew a handful of words and I did my best to fake my way through. Sister Nena, seeing me turn up for a half year of school for the third time in a row, had had enough. She kept me in from recess and after school, badgering me with flashcards and wide-ruled paper in which I was expected to write out letters neatly over and over again. If I was firmly wedged between the cracks I'd fallen into, she had plans to pull me up, by the hair if necessary. She would see to it that I wasn't going to spend the rest of my life not exactly knowing how to read or write. Cursive was waiting just ahead in fourth grade, she told me. I had better get up to speed. She might as well have said that in fourth grade-classes would be conducted in French (a confusion that came from a Babar book my sister had. Because it was both in cursive and in French I believed that cursive *was* French.) I was terrified of all there was to do, of how far behind I had fallen, and somehow I convinced myself that I was terrified of Sister Nena. I wouldn't be in trouble if it wasn't for her because no one else in my life had noticed I couldn't read.

The only thing interesting about my anger and blame of Sister Nena was my willingness to hold on to it without any further reflection until I was in my thirties. I had let my seven-year-old self, my eight-year-old self, make my case against her. How much happier I would have been to never learn anything at all! It wasn't until I sent her a cheque for school supplies that I found myself wondering how often I was in her classroom those first three years and how much work she had in front of her every time I wandered in. It isn't often the past picks up the telephone and calls, affording the opportunity to reconsider personal history in a way that could save countless thousands of dollars in therapy had I been inclined to go. I found myself thinking about my childhood, my education. It is a pastime I am particularly loath to engage in, but I was struck that all I had remembered was her exasperation with my epic slowness, not her ultimate triumph over it. To overstate the case, it was a bit akin to Helen Keller holding a grudge against Annie Sullivan for yanking her around. The next time the children of St Vincent de Paul ran out of glue sticks and Sister Nena called me again, I suggested that we go shopping together and buy some.

She was standing outside her condo in Green Hills when I arrived, waiting for me. Sister Melanie and Sister Helen, still in good health, were home as well. Tennis and prayer and a habit of eating very little must agree with the human body because Sister Nena seemed to have foregone the ageing process completely. She was exactly the person I had known when I was a child and she was nothing like that person at all. She opened up her arms and held me. I was one of her students, one of who knows how many children that had passed through her classroom. That was what she remembered about me. I was one of her own.

There have been very few things in my life that have made me as happy as taking Sister Nena shopping. When we started it was all school supplies, though eventually she confessed her longing to buy small presents for the teachers at St Vincent's who were every bit as poor as their students and paid a sliver of the wages a public-school teacher would have made. She picked out bottles of hand lotion and boxes of Kleenex, staplers and Life Savers, gifts too modest to embarrass anyone, but her joy over having something to give them all but vibrated as we walked up and down the aisles of Target piling things into our cart. It turned out the real heartbreak of the vow of poverty was never being able to buy presents for the people who were so clearly in need.

Despite my constant questions about what she might need for herself, it was years before Sister Nena let me buy anything for her. She wouldn't dream of letting me take her to the olive bar back then. That came later in our friendship, after Sister Helen had her stroke, after her best friend Joanne died of cancer, which was an inconceivable loss. We inched towards each other slowly over many years. At some point I realized that the people she was closest to were dying off or being sent away. Over the course of years there was a place for me.

'You're at the top of my prayer list,' she tells me. 'And not because you buy me things.' She has come to understand that letting me buy her things makes me ridiculously happy, and my happiness, instead of the things themselves, is the source of her joy.

'I know,' I said.

'It's because I love you,' she said.

So ferocious is my love for Sister Nena that I can scarcely understand it myself. Hers is the brand of Catholicism I remember from my childhood, a religion of good work and very little discussion.

'I like the Catholic Church,' she says to me sometimes.

'Good thing,' I say, which always makes her laugh. I think that she is everything I had ever loved about our religion distilled down to fit into one person, the part of the faith that is both selfless and responsible: bringing soup to the sick, going to visit the widower husbands of her friends who have died, sticking with the children who are slow to learn and teaching them how to read, because it wasn't just me, it turns out there are legions of us. She babysits for two Haitian girls, Islande and Thania, and helps them with their reading and their maths. They ask their mother to bring the phone to their beds before they go to sleep so they can call Sister Nena and say goodnight, tell her they have said their prayers. I think of how Sister Nena spoke of the Mercies who taught her in school and how she had admired their goodness. I think of how it took me half my life to comprehend the thing she had discovered as a child (I have no doubt that she had been a better student than I was).

She is happy in her new apartment, though she probably could have set up her camp in a closet somewhere and been fine. Happiness is her mindset, her decision, and while she often reminds me that God will take care of things, she is also determined not to trouble Him if at all possible. It's a little bit like wanting to move all the boxes before the movers come. She will take on the work of her life quickly, do it all herself when no one is watching so that she can show God how little help she needs.

Any worries she has these days are focused on Sister Melanie, who is adjusting slowly to her new life at Mercy. Sister Melanie is shy and had long relied on Sister Nena for her social skills. 'She stays in her room all the time,' Sister Nena said. 'Whenever I go out to see her, there she is. I tell her, no one's going to find you in here. You have to get out.' She is reaching down into that place where Sister Melanie has wedged herself. She is trying to pull her up.

We got together the day after the funeral of her friend Mary Ann. Mary Ann was the other Catholic in her tennis group. 'I'm fine. I'm not sad,' Sister Nena tells me when I call. I know better than to believe her. 'You don't have to take me out.'

'What if I just want to see you?' I say.

Over lunch she tells me that the last time she saw her, Mary Ann was very peaceful. 'She looked at me and said, "Nena, I'm ready. I want to see God."' Then Sister Nena shook her head. 'I'm wrong. That was the time before last. The last time I saw her she couldn't say anything. When I went to her funeral and I saw the urn there and I thought, where is her soul?' Sister Nena looks at me then, hoping that I might know 'Is it with God? I want to believe her soul is with God. She was so certain. I'm just not sure. I shouldn't say that.' She puts her hand flat out on the table. 'I am sure.'

'Nobody's sure,' I say.

'Sister Jeannine is sure.' She shakes her head. 'I don't know. I'm contradicting myself. I know God made us but I'm not so sure about what happens afterwards.'

'What do you want to happen?' I ask her.

This she knows the answer to immediately. It is as if she has been waiting her entire lifetime for someone to ask her. 'I want God to hold me,' she says.

You above all others, I tell her. You first.

Nominated by Granta

A SHADOW BEEHIVE

by RASHEDA WHITE

from ECOTONE

I hear an old man and woman playing chess
for some false teeth. I hear a tree knocking
in the sand and the sand flies up and down
and it sounds like a window. I hear cold
old shadows chattering their teeth in the winter.
I hear my sister polishing the shadows' fingernails.
I hear shadow kids playing with a shadow beehive
in the yard and a shadow kid gets chased by the bees
and all the bees are gone so a homeless man comes
down and gets some honey. I hear my mother
in the kitchen drying out the darkness.

Nominated by John Rybicki, Genie Chipps

A FAMILY RESTAURANT

fiction by KAREN RUSSELL

from CONJUNCTIONS

WELCOME TO "A FAMILY RESTAURANT"!
OWNED AND OPERATED BY THE BAKOPOULOS FAMILY SINCE 1929

This morning, my father approached me waving the new menu from **RAY'S ITALIAN FEATS**, our rival across the street, and demanded that I type this up for you.

"Write the story. It's a menu, Leni, it's supposed to have the story."

"Which one?"

"Jesus, I don't know, the story, our story! The family story!"

I.

OUR STORY:

In 1929, my great-grandmother, Demetria Bakopoulos, boarded a boat from Kalymnos, Greece, with her first husband, Hektor Bakopoulos, and their four small children and followed a dotted line across the Atlantic, which I will try to draw for you on this revamped menu if Frank gives me the green light, and sailed into the coastal waters of southern Florida until they arrived at the island of: New Kalymnos. Hektor worked as a sponge fisherman until he had enough money saved to lease the storefront that became **A FAMILY RESTAURANT** and then, courteously, died. Permitting Demetria to make the business deal of a lifetime and remarry a cook from the merchant marines who could devein and butterfly shrimp like a Lilliputian surgeon. Demi's squirrel-faced eldest daughter, Eleni Bakopoulos, survived her mother and her stepfather and her three brothers and took over the business in 1952. For many years she was married to "an American investor," Richard "Rocky" Spry—our oldest patrons at **A FAMILY RESTAURANT** always

183

speak about Rocky's investing in finger-quotation marks—and when Richard Spry left her, she reverted to her maiden name and let her sons know that their American surnames had magically, elastically snapped back into the Old Country: Now they were Frank Bakopoulos, age seven, and Ed Bakopoulos, age four.

Frank is my father—you might catch a glimpse of him if you are sitting in the booths against the wall. That seventy-year-old man who keeps slapping his neck, in the apron that comes down to his calves? My dad. He's only making me write this to compete with that steaming load that eponymous Ray of RAY'S ITALIAN FEATS put on the back of *his* new menu, in which he lists all the cataclysms that his Sicilian ancestors survived en route to New Kalymnos—"Centuries of *la miseria*! Earthquakes, fire, typhus, hurricanes, shipwreck, famine, scurvy, mallpox." I think Ray forgot a letter there, All this they endured to deliver their "famous" pizza sauce to the Americas. That crappy sauce comes out of a box. Ray is a known defroster, a rat-faced liar who uses tomato paste and Kraft. We have no respect for Ray. I think he even enjoys that. Sometimes he eats with us on Sundays, when his restaurant is closed, and we heckle him; we've spent the last twenty years sharing our customers, volleying the families of New Kalymnos back and forth between our restaurants like the world's slowest game of tennis. Ray, a bachelor, has mimeographed a daguerreotype of someone else's enormous Italian family onto the front of his menu in beautiful sepia inks. You know I wouldn't take an oath that Ray is Italian? He does have that mustache, and he puts some spin on the ball when he pronounces words like *"arrabbiata,"* but I swear I would not be surprised if his obituary informs us that he was born in Milwaukee.

If you ate here between the years of 1971 and 1979, you remember this line from the old menu:

BE SURE TO SAVE ROOM FOR DESSERT: OUR "WORLD-FAMOUS" FROSTY TREAT, MAMA'S DEATHBED SHERBET!

If that's what you came for, I'm afraid you're out of luck. We haven't been able to serve that in decades. Not since my family forfeited our access to the secret ingredient.

Rocky Spry, my grandfather, chose our name, A FAMILY RESTAU-
RANT. Hand painted the sign, olive-green letters on dandelion wood.
(Prior to this the place was a Greek speakeasy: a blank door and an
umbrella.) Rocky assured Eleni that American diners would respect
their restaurant for its candor—"Look, why not call a spade a spade,
right? We could put on airs, call ourselves a 'bistro.' But let's face the
music here: We're a goddamn family restaurant. A squat-and-gobble.
So why not say, one family to another: You can eat here. Bring the kids,
put the baby in a booster seat, have an onion straw, here's a damn
crayon and gin is on the way for old dad and mom."

Apparently, Rocky left the family one month after the new sign went
up. It's what you walked under to get inside here. By now, I should have
brought your water. My apologies if it's a busy night and it's taking a
little while.

How did Mama explain my grandfather's disappearance to her boys?
She didn't. She invented a new menu item, "Mama Bakopoulos's Good-
night Waffle," because Eddy, after his father disappeared from the restaurant and the house, began demanding breakfast at night. Every
night, for nearly a year: breakfasts. Into adulthood, my uncle Ed would
go on strange gluttonous sprees where he squirted strawberry syrup
onto all foods, "like a dog pissing the house during a thunderstorm,"
was how my father explained it to me. This was decades before the
self-help lexicographers defined my humongous, furious uncle Ed as
an "emotional eater." But you know, I've been working in A FAMILY
RESTAURANT for my entire lifetime and it seems to me that very few
people are eating on "neutral."

Frank has an animal's nonchalance about his past. My father, on his
father: "Leni. I really don't remember him. The guy could walk in here
today and order a dog and I wouldn't recognize him."

"And what did Mama think about his leaving?"

"How the hell should I know?"

Ed and Frank were doomed by the restaurant to be Mama's Boys
deep into adulthood: big-eared teenagers and then bearded men on the
streets of New Kalymnos, but ageless in the warm restaurant lights. You
and Mama Bakopoulos have already met—that's her shooting darts at
you from the front of this menu. See? The lady in the cowl, with the
face like a split baked potato? The small guy on her knee is my father,

Frank, age eleven, man of the house by the time that picture was taken in 1961. The slightly cross-eyed kid whose furry homemade "sweater vest" appears to be a bunch of sewn-together bath mats? His brother, Eddy. And all of the decor in A FAMILY RESTAURANT belongs to her childhood: "Mama's Broken Victrola," "Mama's Bonnet That Looks Like a Detonating Pineapple," "Mama's Scary Wooden Toy from Oilikos."

Irene caught my father at a rare moment, when he was living away from home for the first time in his life, twenty-two and working for the electric company in Lefferts, New Jersey, on a contract job. Saving money, for a future that never quite came into focus. She fell in love with Frank before she'd heard word one about the family restaurant. She caught his eye at a no-name gas station, where he was standing in front of one of those big refrigerators—just to cool off, it seemed. This is my parents' "how we met" story. It was the single memory from their shared lifetime that could cause them both to light up. It's a lot more succinct than their second story, how they ceased to know one another.

"Oh my God!" Frank pretended to scream when he saw Irene, a fake scream so acoustically similar to the real deal that she screamed too, and dropped her car keys.

"No, dummy, I'm screaming because of how you *look*, see?" he'd explained in a slightly embarrassed new register. "You shouldn't be around the pumps, it's a fire hazard. You're, uh, you're dangerously hot."

"Huh?"

Later my father admitted to my mother that he'd flunked out of high school chemistry.

"You might react with the gas—and combust!"

"That doesn't even make sense."

Two months later, they were engaged.

"Be my wife?" He'd had blue chewing gum in his mouth when he asked her. Irene had never felt so happy in another human's company. When they kissed, they'd swapped the wad of gum back and forth with the goofiest solemnity until Frank swallowed the gum and had a coughing fit.

One night about a week later, she found her fiancé sitting with red eyes, Indian style, underneath the pay phone in her dormitory. His mother was very sick. Would Irene maybe take a leave of absence from the junior college, come with him to Florida? His brother had called him home to help take care of her.

"Yes," my mother said, quicker than a miner can strike a match, and unwittingly committing the next decade of her life to A FAMILY RESTAURANT. "Can we get married first, though?" In Irene's imagination the air of Florida was boiling, its waters thronged with dinosaurs. A part of her was afraid that if they didn't marry now, Frank's offer would dissolve in the shimmering Florida heat. They were flying back in time to Frank's childhood, a zone in which he hadn't made her the offer, where she did not yet exist.

(They'd had a bit of a Who's On First routine when Frank tried to explain the restaurant to her: "Yes, but what's it called?" "A Family Restaurant . . ." "Frank! Stop teasing! OK: What is the name on the door of the freaking restaurant?" "That's the name, Irie, it's A *Family Restaurant*. . .." "Oh my God, Frank.")

"I can't cook, you know," she told Frank on the bus ride to the airport. "My cooking is for shit." The ring was blue zirconium. On the flight down, Irene crooked her ring finger as if beckoning their future, shooting light all around the airplane cabin. *We are a married couple, in the sky*. Frank had paid for their tickets, God alone knew how.

A stewardess poured them a tomato-juice toast on the honeymoon Delta flight to Frank's home, *To us*, Irene waited for him to say.

"To Mama's health."

"To Mama." Irene twirled her celery through the bloodred cup. When the seat-belt sign lit up she straightened in her chair as if electrocuted. Who the hell was Mama? What did she really know about any of these people, the Bakopouloses or Bakopouli, with whom she'd just agreed to share her life? Now that the plane was in the air she could clearly see a stretch of questions, whole cities of questions that she should have asked before takeoff.

"Your mother knows about me?"

Frank shrugged. "Not exactly."

"You didn't tell her you got married?"

Sometimes when Frank argued with her it was like watching a bear jogging to keep its balance on a rolling barrel. There was something antic and hilarious in the timbre of his voice. Something dangerous too.

"Of course not! Mama just *had* a heart attack!" Frank stared at Irene incredulously, as if his new wife were the one with a weak heart. "We'll tell her in person. Easy does it. She'll like you."

It was hate at first sight. "Mama!" Frank had shouted up to his mother's window from the driveway when they got in late that night. "Come down! I'd like to introduce you to the new Mrs. Bakopoulos!" This was

187

breaking the news gently? Irene wondered. She felt as if she were watching a wrecking ball smash into the side of the split-level house.

I don't know the details, but apparently this introduction went so disastrously that my mother crept upstairs, settling herself on the spaceship-themed coverlet on Frank's childhood bed while, downstairs, her new husband explained her presence in Mama's house to Mama; Irene closed her eyes and counted to two hundred while she listened to a hailstorm of pots, followed by the sound of a groaning man hurling a discus.

"That?" shrugged Frank the following morning. "Yeah. Mama threw that there. I tried to stop her. It can't be good, you know, for her heart." There was a mop lying in the middle of the Bakopoulos lawn. Irene stepped delicately over it; the handle appeared to have struck and dented the Bakopouloses' mailbox. The mop looked like an effigy of Irene to Irene, with its pale hair askew on the grass. She shared this observation with Frank.

"That's nuts," said Frank. "That's a crazy way to think. Mama doesn't even know you yet. Now, hurry to the car, Irene. I'm the prep cook, you're the dishwasher. Mama's orders. She'll kill us if we're late."

DAY ONE AT A FAMILY RESTAURANT:

"Go help Mama clean," Frank said. "She'd like that."

"*I* clean!" Mama said, as if she were shouting out her own name, instead of merely volunteering to do the next verb on the chore wheel. Mama turned on the Porta Power vacuum and, without perhaps exactly intending to do so, chased Irene out of the restaurant like a bull charging a matador. Irene stood dazed in the sun, still holding a napkin. Days 2 through 182 were very much the same. In dreams Irene wiped the dishes and watched her own face shriveling, the young and vibrant layers of her life falling away like flower petals, all of the color and particularity draining out of her as she merged with the bleak, blank face of Mama.

No one lives forever. Irene gave herself this pep talk on Saturday nights, bunning sea dogs near the window with the big fan, straining to see the actual sea. Black waves tugged away from her, as if the world were on a wire, and the night would jump, retreat, jump again. Her eyes could only see so far into the twinkling mist that separated the island from the peninsula, but she had faith that it was there, Twenty minutes by boat. They could get back to it.

Frank bought Irene an old-fashioned green bicycle with a wide gray seat, an antique piece that I now own and ride around town. She tooled around the parking lot, waiting for his shift to end, her long legs whacking into the handlebars. Between her bruised knees and the green bicycle and the paint-blue island sky, Irene felt like a peacock trailing colors around the lot. She felt twelve, eleven, younger still, orbiting A FAMILY RESTAURANT on the bicycle and waiting for Frank to exit through the back doors and turn her into Mrs. Bakopoulos, his wife.

"Those are *hickeys*?" Mama accused her one day, peering out of the back door of A FAMILY RESTAURANT and pointing at Irene's knees.

"What? Mama, no—"

"They are *hick-eys*," she affirmed before Irene could explain her bruises, and tossed a bucket of steaming orange broth into the parking lot. The scene felt biblical, Irene later told Frank.

"If there had been a big rock next to the Toyota, your mother would have stoned me."

Frank made a face. "She's sick. Give her time."

The plan was that my parents would stay on the island for three or four weeks, just until Mama was back on her feet. But Mama was on her feet all the time, chasing down Frank and Irene. Belatedly, many months after their wedding day, she threw rice at Irene. "You make these ones? Is *sticky*," Mama charged, and Irene, whose face now resembled the cover illustration of *Beowulf*, covered by a golden chainmail of long-grain rice, could not acquit herself. Irene gave Mama half a year. More. Not once in all that time, according to Irene, did my grandmother volitionally meet her daughter-in-law's blue eyes, although sometimes Irene would look up from clearing a table to find Mama's eyes boring a hole into her shoulder, as if she were trying to amputate Irene's arm with an invisible mentally controlled laser. "Because my bra strap was showing, Leni. That's how she was."

Goddamn it. Frank said I had to get Our Story told in eight hundred words. So that it would fit on the back of the menu. I still have to tell you about the sherbet, with its radioactive glow; the secret ingredient. The days when Mama died and I was born.

Well, maybe I can staple pages.

Is it Happy Hour? Get the Shiver-Me-Timbers cocktail. It's on me, compliments of the house. Blame me for delaying your meal, and Frank will give you a generous pour and bring it out with a complimentary dish of mixed nuts. Growing up in A FAMILY RESTAURANT I made anything my toy—the forks, the foiled toothpicks. I was a lewd kid or something was wrong with my head and I thought these mixed nuts looked like naked sunbathers. Little nudist colonies of cashews. I used to line them up on the sunny windowsills while my parents fought about Frank's secret—"Shh, keep sleeping," I told them.

Did my mother pray for Frank's mom to die? Not in so many words. "Take her soul, Lord," she prayed vaguely, figuring that God was no dummy, he could read into that. Sometimes she intoned the prayers like a movie mobster—"Send Mama on a *long* vay-*cay*-shun."

Mama, meanwhile, appeared to be losing her mind. Her pain medications made her dotty. She wore a shower cap instead of her hairnet, brought a red bowling ball to work, terrified the Happy Hour crowd by bursting through the kitchen door with a bouquet of knives.

"You!" she told Irene in a low vibrato. "You look like an anteater pissing through its nose!"

What did that even mean?

"It's just an expression," said Frank wearily. "It's a shame that you don't speak Greek. In Greek, she is a comedian."

As Mama Bakopoulos weakened, my mother became bolder. "When are we leaving, Frank?" Right in front of Mama she would discuss her plans to raise her future children in California, to return to school.

"Frankie will never go with you there," she'd say with maddening confidence. "No. To that place, with you, never." She took her eldest son's hand and held it to her belly, and Frank inclined his head toward her; Irene shuddered. His posture was an eerie inversion of a father-to-be waiting for the kick. "Frankie will stay here with his mother."

"I'm not leaving you, Mama," Frank mumbled with a pained and apologetic smile. Weeks to live, was her doctors' latest assessment.

As Mama's health failed, so did the family business. Frank and Ed hired someone to do the cooking, a small, polite, slightly lethargic Portuguese woman named Domitila, who one night stole all the money in the till, two ten-pound sacks of crinkle-cut fries, the dainty ketchup spout, and a bottle of Johnny Walker Black.

Frank moved Mama to the cardiac ward; Irene learned that A FAMILY RESTAURANT was five months behind on rent. *We're closing down*, Irene thought, her heart speeding. Frank and Ed would be freed from the ten-block radius that hemmed the Bakopoulos men inside their childhood. She and Frank would start a family of their own.

Meanwhile, grief was doing strange things to Frank, who was after Irene for the first time in months with a new kind of intensity, mutely squeezing her and licking her next to the ice machine, cornering her against the freezers, corralling her between the stacked towers of baby booster chairs. His grip around her waist was almost suffocatingly tight. In the past, whenever they closed together, he'd lift her onto the bar, slide a hand up her skirt under the fulgurating pink and emerald lights of Mama's seashell sconces. But Irene would no longer fool around with Frank inside A FAMILY RESTAURANT. When Frank leaned in to kiss her, it was Mama's face that Irene saw leering at her.

"Outside," she said.

Gross. I'm so sorry about that—I know, you came here to eat—I too find other people's earnest sex lives extremely unappetizing. Particularly if the braid of legs in question belongs to one's parents. But, unavoidably, this too was part of the story of A FAMILY RESTAURANT.

II.

In the hospital, in her death throes, Frank's mother began to gurgle in odd syllabic patterns that he swore belonged to a foreign tongue. Pain-inflected utterances. Not just gibberish, but *language*—although nothing that sounded remotely close to Greek or English.

"You're right—it's the medication," Nurse Florentz said generously, giving my father the opportunity to allege something sane.

Moans rose from his mother's veiled bed, shimmering waves of sound that might mean anything. The curtain danced on its silver rings.

"Wait—hear that?"

"I'll see about the morphine levels," said Nurse Florentz.

But Frank knew his mother. He didn't agree with Nurse Florentz. He sat at the edge of her bed with a tape recorder, pausing only to gulp red gelatin cubes in the hospital cafeteria. Near the end of the tape he called his brother, Ed.

Ed said he couldn't hear much over the blenders—it was Happy Hour. "Happy Hour," said Frank, staring down at their mother's dark face. She was snoring lightly, exposing a tiny row of teeth that made him think for some reason of marshmallows dissolving in cocoa. How did anybody alive survive a parent's death? His mother, awake now, smiled weakly at Frank—an unrecognizably gentle smile—and in her final minutes she spoke real words to him, whispery but distinct, in Greek. Frank waited for a little while, then hit PAUSE on the tape.

Frank and Eddy held the funeral on the island but had Mama buried in Greece, in a Kalymnos plot, a few miles from her ancient home. Frank found a special translator in Kos who was able to help him with Mama's last instructions. It was a recipe that she had given him.

III.

The business was saved.

"You can cook now?" Irene asked him. "Since when?"

"I'm just following orders."

"Whose!"

Prior to Mama's death, A FAMILY RESTAURANT served the same innocuous American beach grub that you see listed inside this menu: Cokes and Sprites, cole slaw, hot dogs with mustard and a catarrh of green relish. "Looks like somebody sneezed on a weiner," Mama used to complain darkly. "What the Americans want to eat, though." She'd inherited the incredulity and Old World horror of her mother, Demi; like Demi, she read off the menu items as if she were reciting the terms of a humiliating war treaty: Hamburgers. Bacon Cheeseburgers. Clam Basket. Shrimp Basket. Chicken Fingers. (A macabre name that used to make me picture Foghorn Leghorn's amputated hands.) Prior to Mama's death, the only desserts on the menu were chocolate pie, apple pie, and the "Dieter's Delite Fruit Plate"—basically an unripe whole cantaloupe that Mama sometimes tossed disgustedly at skinny people like a basketball. Overnight, the menu changed to include: SPECIAL OF THE DAY #6: MAMA'S DEATHBED SHERBET.

"I'd like to order number six, the Special—'Ma's Deathbed Sherbet.'"

"Number six, please."

Some people were shy about ordering it.

"Fries and a Coke. And, ah . . . how's that number six?"

"Yes, I'd like the number six. Mama's, ah, Mama's . . . right, that's the one."

Frank served the sherbet so shockingly cold that it numbed the tongue. Whatever he was putting in it caused the dish to glow. The color was never quite the same—it was always pale orange, like a bowl of emulsifying sunshine, but sometimes a new batch would have these radishy-pink streaks, sometimes it could look almost minty. Adults who ordered the sherbet reported tasting the usual suspects—nutmeg, cloves, cinnamon, anise, raspberries, peach syrup, vanilla—and, invariably, Something Else. Their children only smiled; they looked like they were spooning up light.

I should clarify here that Mama's Deathbed Sherbet did not curse our customers or confer magical powers (at least, not to my knowledge). Nobody left their tables with X-ray vision or a beautiful new singing voice or an invulnerability to cancer. It was just a really good dessert.

Frank refused to tell anybody the "famous ingredient." How strange, I used to think, that a secret could achieve such notoriety—this hole that everybody on the island could see. Inside our house, Frank's secret was something round but empty, like the number zero—swallowed air. "It was her Will and Testament," he told my uncle. "She left it to me because I'm the oldest, Ed. Her executor." He'd shake his head almost theatrically, still trying to protect his kid brother. "Believe me, if you knew what I had to do to make the sherbet you wouldn't be jealous."

"Just *taste* it, Irene," my father was still begging her in those early days. "It's the best batch yet, honest to God."

Irene learned that she was pregnant on the same day that Mama died. At first, my mother refused to touch Mama Bakopoulos's dessert. One spring night, though, in her last trimester, when Frank was on another trip to Greece to procure the ingredient, Irene broke down and ate bowl after bowl of the orange sherbet; driven to it, I imagine, by the same spasms of hunger that can launch any pregnant woman into the streets in search of root beer and dill pickles, and by something even stranger. A rage that I can really only guess at here, cannibalistic, to consume her mother-in-law's last traces. Expunge Mama Bakopoulos from the kitchen.

Then I was born. Irene stared into the blanket that the nurses handed to her, jolted out of her wooziness. My mother, I'm told, began to wail with me. *No.* Even enervated from a forty-hour labor, Irene had to fight down a reflexive impulse to thrust me back at the nurse. She gritted her teeth, held on to me with all her strength. (And later the nurses would joke that the frightened new mother had clenched her jaw and splayed her palms across my back as though she were trying to keep her hands from flying off a hot stove top! A pretty girl with an ugly baby.) She looked again: There was my face, which was also the puckered, miniaturized face of Mama Bakopoulos. A little wailing red bud in the blue blanket.

Reincarnation, why rule it out?

"Frank?" my mother asked that first night. "Do you think the sherbet could . . . bring her back?"

Frank stared at her. "That's not funny, Irene."

Frank demanded that I be named for his mother; my mom viciously refused; many knock-down fights ensued; "Leni" was their compromise. That's me.

My first days were black ones for my mother. At times she was certain that I was an anchor, flung overboard by Mama from beyond the grave, intended to secure her permanent mooring at A FAMILY RESTAURANT. Some caul covered my face so that she couldn't see it—all she saw was Mama. Babies, what person alive is repelled by their smell, but Irene swore I smelled like Mama in her last days, vinegary and aged. Whenever she breast-fed me, she saw Mama's Deathbed Sherbet melting into spectacular colors in its glass dish. When she rocked me, she had to swallow back the singsong Greek melodies that Mama used to croon while sweeping out the kitchen. How had so much of Mama gotten absorbed into her bloodstream? Antibodies, didn't she have any of those against Eleni Bakopoulos? Those were the days when Irene grieved for her own mother more powerfully than she had since she was a teenager.

"Hush, little baby," she sang, and flipped the portrait of Mama that Frank had set on my nightstand. All night she sat by my crib, watching me sleep. Sometimes I wish I could dream those earliest dreams again, whatever I used to see in the time before I could recognize my own face. Yellow, red, and blue shapes swung on wires above me, a zoo mobile, while through the crib bars my mother's hand stroked my black hair. Mama Bakopoulos's curls were already coming in. Irene watched me like a mirror, waited for her blue eyes to open in my face, for her face to surface in my flesh. But I failed, I couldn't repeat any part of her. Frank says that our biological stalemate made him feel, for different reasons, as stunned and helpless as Irene did. He watched her watching me at the nursery's edge, both of them frozen.

194

Now my mother was in a sort of Chinese finger trap: She was never leaving Frank, and Frank was never leaving A FAMILY RESTAURANT. Several times a year, and never during the winter months, we all noted, my father flew to Kalymnos, Greece, for two weeks to retrieve more of the "secret ingredient." Whatever substance Frank was bringing back was compact enough to fit inside his beat-up blue duffel. He once let slide to Irene during an argument that he froze the ingredient, to preserve it, and that he only needed "a pinch" of it to make a batch of the sherbet.

By this time I was three or four years old and already on the clock, carrying a horseshoe tray of blue marine salt and quartered limes to the drunks, walking on tipsy feet myself. I remember feeling small as a cat as I moved between the trouser legs at the bar, peanuts bouncing off my head, bathed in the lush sour stench of our patrons' underarms. Once a big, gesticulating drunk brushed my earlobe with his lit cigarette and I howled so terribly—and salted the man, apparently—that Frank had to comp his hundred-dollar bar tab. In my earliest memories, my parents are always shouting to be heard over the happy din of other couples, other families. Their arguments peppered the air in the kitchen:

"Look at this!" Irene. "America is one of the fattest nations in the world. Maybe we should serve something else, Frank. Steamed zucchini! Carrots, raisins! Perhaps a slaw of some kind—"

"Sherbet is not a fried donut, honey, it's healthy! It's healthy for business, that's for sure." Frank shook his head. "You could thank me, you know. Do you think it's easy to make the stuff? Do you know how much money I've turned it into?"

"Change the menu," she hissed. "Serve something else. Anything else, Frank."

"Ed and Lisa are going to buy a home, did he tell you? Their mortgage payments start next month. And I've been thinking about private school for Leni. A new car to replace that shitbox LeBaron you drive." Frank paused. "I leave for Kalymnos tomorrow."

"And when are you coming home?"

"Soon."

Sherbet—to make it does not require the Rosetta Stone. Here is the ingredient list for ordinary sherbet:

- 7 ounces sugar
- 1 ½ tablespoons finely grated orange zest
- ¼ teaspoon salt
- 2 cups freshly squeezed orange juice
- 1 tablespoon freshly squeezed lemon juice
- 1 teaspoon vanilla extract
- 1 ½ cups very cold whole milk

As a child, I couldn't imagine where my father went for weeks at a stretch. Lisa was the first to broach the subject in the dining area. Lisa was Ed's girlfriend, my babysitter, and mom's sort of de facto sister-in-law, a lanky woman with wide-set, spacey eyes and incorrigible red curls who was so beautiful to me. She seemed like an alien as she floated beneath all of the framed Bakopoulos portraits that Mama had nailed to the dark walls. Lisa hostessed and waited on tables and bitched pleasantly about almost every aspect of the restaurant's operations.

"OK, Frank!" Lisa exploded one day, still trembling from the dinner rush. "Please just tell us: What are you keeping in that freezer? Are there perhaps some fucking bodies in the freezer? Are we all going to jail?"

"Yeah, is this some Soylent Green bullshit? Because *kids* eat that sherbet."

"I eat it," I said.

"Maybe it's an endangered animal. Like a rhino." Uncle Ed made himself hysterical. "Frank: Are you crushing up rhino balls or something? Is it a panda? I don't want to spend my days in a federal penitentiary because the secret ingredient is some eye-of-newt shit, only the newt is, you know, a goddamn panda."

Lisa and Irene stared at Ed.

Lisa took Ed's hand. "I was just teasing before—I'm sure Frank's just picking weird mushrooms somewhere. I don't think he's out in the bamboo strangling pandas." She frowned. "Or people. Can you picture your brother hurting *anybody*?"

Everybody looked at my mother. Who was staring at Frank. Gazes used to ricochet like bullets inside A FAMILY RESTAURANT.

"Where is Daddy going?" I asked that night.

"Away."

"But where?"

"Greece. He says."

196

"Why?"

"To make his mother happy."

This reason satisfied me. It seemed to satisfy almost everybody. To make a mother happy, she told me bitterly, was a perfectly satisfying reason for doing anything. That Mama Bakopoulos had been dead for seven years seemed immaterial to the conversation. I told my mother that I thought Frank's reason was a plenty good one; at least, I understood it; every night, to please my mother, I was praying for a different face.

During the nine years we served Mama's Deathbed Sherbet, A FAMILY RESTAURANT never had to advertise: no church bulletins, no radio spots. We never had to change our underwhelming name. We were doing so well for that period that we'd been able to hire strangers to bus the tables, not kids from the high school (I'd begged my father) but a few slim, fickle men whom my father located with newspaper ads. They rarely stuck around our restaurant for long, I'm not sure why. During the interviews, my father seemed completely at a loss: "So do you steal?" he asked the applicants. "Do you work hard? You, ah, you like hot dogs?" I think he lacked the ability to judge the character of non-Bakopouloses.

Once Irene came downstairs to find Frank holding on to the phone with both hands, staring into the backyard—someone at Pepsi-Cola who vacationed on New Kalymnos and was a self-professed "number six addict" had just made him a high-six-figure offer for the recipe. "No, thank you," Frank said. He hung up with a sigh. The scale was wrong, Frank explained to my mother.

"We can't sell out. There's not enough of it to go around."

"Of what?"

"Of the secret ingredient. I can barely keep *us* supplied now!"

My dad wasn't interested in talking to reporters. He wouldn't even discuss it with a Tallahassee talk-show host, a TV laureate with a grin like a Halloween pumpkin whose message on our machine said he'd heard about the sherbet's "reputation for causing elation!"

"Come over, OK, we'll serve you a dish," Frank told the telephone. "My God, what part of 'secret ingredient' don't you people understand?"

We expanded; now we had two kitchens. Kitchen 1, anyone could walk into; Kitchen 2 was a galley-sized annex with a door to which only my father had the key. Through the porthole in the door to the public kitchen, I'd watch him assemble the sherbet's public ingredients: sugar, milk, and fruit. Zesting lemons, Frank smiled like a Buddha statue. I've never seen a grown man look happier performing any activity than my father did, zesting. Kitchen 2 had no windows.

Like everyone, I loved the glowing stuff. That first bright bite seemed to make your hunger huger, like a lit match dropped into a well. I liked to eat Mama's dessert in secret, under the tablecloth, with the bowl on my lap, the sweating glass sticking to my bare thighs. Going down, the sherbet burned. It slid along my throat until I clutched my ribs and rocked with the pleasure of it. I had nothing in my small world to which I could compare the flavor. Sometimes it seemed to contain whole orchards, and sometimes it was a single taste.

Happiness, it seemed, was one secret that our customers were eager to keep. You'd think the customers would demand to know Mama's ingredient, and perhaps they traded guesses in private, but I can't remember anyone asking me about it. We garnished number six with orange rinds and fat red strawberries, and if people commented at all that's what they chose to remark on—"Big strawberries, huh!" they'd say. Now I think that the families we served were wary of chasing the flavor off their tongues. Often the entire room of diners fell silent for an hour or more, a hundred spoons clinking musically on glass. "Fragrant," "piquant," "robust," "bittersweet"—none of that Zagat's argot came even close to describing its taste. As ever, Mama Bakopoulos had the last word.

"What a nice dessert," families said, and then left two hundred percent tips.

Once I overheard a wire-thin teenager covered in red and black wolf tattoos, a guy who did not look like he had a sweet tooth in his skull, whisper, "It's better than drugs."

Today I have some new theories about the popularity of our dessert at A FAMILY RESTAURANT. What we gave them was only disguised as food, I think. It seemed to nourish some hidden mouth, some universally parched place. Just writing about it here, I can feel that spot in me beginning to salivate. I don't know what to call it, but it's what I spent my early lifetime catering to at A FAMILY RESTAURANT.

Forgive me, I see we're approaching seventeen pages here. You must be starving. I'll finish up so you can order. Whatever you do, avoid the fish taco, Frank can't get that one right—it tastes like a sea kayak that sprang a leak. Are you maybe considering defecting to Ray's Italian Feats? Chucking our menu to read Ray's Family Story, a glib four hundred words printed underneath that grinning cartoon of a Roma tomato, with the arms and the legs? I don't blame you for that preference, but just remember—those laminated pictures of his *nonna* in her white twill mantelet, his handsome wife, the perfect children arrayed like a string of garlic bulbs around the rustic dock? It's complete bullshit, of course. Nobody has a family like that. And why is that tomato wearing Keds?

Nineteen seventy-five: A restaurant opened up across the street from us. Ray's Italian Feats.

"Italian Feats? What, he's turning Dago cartwheels over there?"

"I think it was supposed to be 'Feast.'"

This was confirmed by Ray: a misprint on the awning. "I plan to sue," he said genially. Back then his menu was just a list: garlic rolls and spaghetti marinara and several of the more convoluted pastas. It was devoid of any history or chummy cartoon tomatoes.

There was no open aggression between us, but sometimes we opened our back doors and let warring smells duel and tangle in the street between our restaurants. It was like the Sharks and the Jets, only olfactory.

One dusk I caught Ray staring into Kitchen 1, doing a pull-up onto our window ledge, his whole body tensed into the furious shrug of a cactus. I guess I should have called the police. "Scram, you trespassing defroster," is what I should have said. "You should be ashamed."

Instead, I led Ray around to the small back entrance to Kitchen 2. I watched him use his crowbar to jimmy the door. We stood breathing softly on the threshold, like some low-budget sci-fi movie—here we were, about to enter the spaceship, a dirty Chevy sedan inconveniently in the shot. I realized that I was holding Ray's hand—how had that happened?—my fingers gloved together with his sweaty stubs, pepperoncini wafting almost imperceptibly out of Ray's skin. Incredibly, Ray didn't curse at me or shake loose from my grip. I don't even think he was trying to steal our recipe necessarily—I think his hobbies just included petty crime. We entered the room. My father was standing with his back to the door, and I glimpsed something orange fluttering from his hands into a large mixing bowl.

I had never set foot in Kitchen 2. It was clean and orderly, a dollhouse version of Kitchen 1. Ray was already backing outside. Slowly, as if sensing our gazes falling on him like a net, my father stiffened and began to turn. "Is it you, Mama?" he said, softly but unmistakably.

We fled.

"How was work?" Irene asked Frank later that evening.

"Work was work," Frank smiled, the phrase he always used to double-knot his day. I studied his thick fingers with their blunt, clean nails, half expecting to see orange stains there. I never breathed a word about what I'd seen and heard that day to either of them. If my father was haunted, that was his problem. I was so tired of being mistaken by everyone for the ghost of Mama Bakopoulos.

One afternoon, Irene pulled my hair into a ponytail and put on sapphire earrings and walked us over to Ray's Italian Feats. Ray was wearing a bookie's visor indoors, stinking of hairspray and garlic, with a pompadour that never moved—I wondered if Aquanet could seep into your brain and paralyze the rest of you. The man was some kind of paradox, an original stereotype. Everything about him seemed inauthentic, but I couldn't tie this deception to any clear purpose. Where he was honest, it turned out, was when it came to his ingredients.

"What's in this?" she asked Ray. "And this?"

He narrowed his eyes. "You one of those that's allergic to wheat? Don't bring me any lawsuits." But he listed every ingredient for her.

"Ladies, you're gonna explode!" Ray said, bringing my mother her fourth dish, a densely layered fusilli. The tuna fusilli contained tuna, fusilli, black olives, tomato sauce, and oil. "Leni, look how delicious," she said, and punctured something that could only be a noodle. She smiled up at Ray. "Are you married?" Ray grinned back. "Who's asking?"

"So let me get this straight," Ray said, much deeper into the evening. "You're jealous of the ice cream?"

"It's sherbet."

"You're in some kind of fucked-up love triangle with your husband and a bunch of fruity creams?"

Which was better, I wondered, to frame it in Ray's terms or to say, "I'm in a love triangle with my dead mother-in-law?" What my mother said was, "I'm in a love triangle with a mystery." My ears perked up. I knew that Ray had seen my father sprinkle the orange substance into the bowl. Would he tell her? "A family secret."

"Does she know?" Ray said. "Your daughter?" And they both stared at me. Ray coughed. "I think she maybe does. She looks like she was probably born knowing the recipe. It's eerie, Irene. Kid's the spitting image—"

"I know *that*," I said, pulling at my face with my hands, and pushed away from the table.

As I grew older. Mama Bakopoulos began to surface out of my face like a galleon. My skin tone darkened from pink to olive; my eyes dulled to a somber green the exact shade of Swiss chard. Mama cracked her knuckles and so did I; Mama was mildly dyslexic, like me, always swapping numbers and vowels on the chalkboard menu; Mama had my crooked smile, my tree-trunk ankles. At school most of my friends dreamed of having a doppelganger sister, but I'd missed her by a generation, my twin, my dead grandmother. Sometimes I fantasized that Mama Bakopoulos was still alive; she'd mother me better than this stranger with the flashing eyes, Irene.

"Your face is . . . ungrammatical!" Irene shouted at me once, and I knew what she meant. There was nothing horrifically wrong with it— basically, it was intelligible as a face—but it looked foreign, asymmetrical. "Un-American," she told me on another occasion. If I had known more of the story of A FAMILY RESTAURANT—if my mother had taken the time to inscribe our story on the menu, like I'm doing for you—I might have told her, "Mom, I'm not *her*." I am not the reincarnation of your mother-in-law, and I too wish I could get a do-over on my bone structure. Don't judge a book, Mom. I'm begging you. I'd stare at Mama's mulish face on the cover of our menus and have the oddest sensation, as if I were reading my obituary from the future.

This March will mark my forty-seventh spring as an employee of a family restaurant. On Saturday nights I catch sight of my face in the wine-glasses that I polish and I cannot believe that I'm still here.

When they were kids, imprisoned in the Bakopoulos kitchen while schools of other boys went glinting past the restaurant windows on bicycles, Frank and Ed had a favorite joke, a real eye roller about a head of romaine lettuce trapped in a fridge—

201

Knock! Knock!

Who's there?

Lettuce!

Lettuce who?

Let us out, it's freezing in here!

"Where are *you* going?" I asked my mother one night. Frank had left for Greece a week ago. She was tugging at the half-zipped lips of her bulging suitcase, trying to make it swallow the delicate bone of a white stiletto. I had never seen those shoes before. I had never seen my mom in makeup, red lipstick and blue eyeliner that looked clownishly super-fluous on her beautiful face. When she turned to me, I saw how tired her eyes looked. Anybody could see how hungry she was, how deeply thirsty, and this seemed to be the rotten joke at the core of A FAMILY RESTAURANT—that its hostess and waitress and cook and barmaid, the woman who had spent a decade in its kitchen, could wind up fam-ished.

"I haven't been sleeping, Leni," she told me simply. "I'm going to find your father. If he doesn't tell me this time—"

"Take me with you," I'd shouted. A test.

I knew then that she really was afraid of me. I've heard people com-plain, of their mothers, "Well, she looked at me as if I were a stranger!" But Irene looked me dead in the eye, as if she knew my exact dimen-sions, my past and my future, and was all the more terrified. Her fear was so convincing that I was persuaded too—I was a monster, a change-ling daughter, Mama Bakopoulos risen from the dead. "It's a cloning," Frank laughingly acknowledged when patrons held up the cellophane-green menu with Mama Bakopoulos's portrait to my face. Don't judge a book. Don't judge a book. I wished I'd been born a boy. Had I looked like Frank or Ed, whose faces were only mildly traumatized by Mama, it might have been different for us. Decades later I am still trying to figure out what to say to my mother to let her know that I was locked in a prison too, staring out at her through the cage bars of my face bones.

To her credit, my mother didn't lie to me. She didn't say, "It's OK" or "See you soon" or "I'll be back."

"I've got to find out what it is, Leni."

I nodded, feeling that for once I was very close to my mother. I'd inherited her hunger. A cramp sent me lurching against the banister; suddenly I was dying to know the answer too. It did seem incredible, didn't it, that we'd been swallowing and digesting this ingredient for years without having the slightest clue what it was?

"Goodbye, Mom!" I called down. "Good luck!"

With my parents gone, Frank in search of the secret ingredient and Irene in search of Frank, I lived with Uncle Ed and Lisa. I had just turned eleven. That was the summer they were trying for a baby, a process Lisa related to me in cheerful, indelible detail ("and that is why your uncle Ed follows me into the shower!"); it made me wonder why I didn't have a brother or a sister. (Later Frank would tell me that Irene had refused to have another child, terrified that any future son or daughter would be "contaminated" with Mama.)

Lisa didn't believe that the orange sherbet was some kind of extra-genetic mechanism of heredity; she thought my mother was crazy. And I tried to believe Aunt Lisa; only I could feel my grandmother inside my body, see her curling through my black hair and hear her cracking out of my knuckles, a sound as awful as footsteps on ice. She was coming back to life. While my parents were gone, I cut my hair as short as a boy's and streaked it freakishly with lemon juice, read magazines about plastic-surgery options. One night, at Ed and Lisa's place, I scoured my face in the bathroom mirror with steel wool from the restaurant kitchen, trying to escape Mama's hex, until Lisa walked in on me and shrieked, applied peroxide to the pulpy mess I'd made of my skin.

Finally, emboldened by Ray's criminal ease with the crowbar, I broke into my father's secret larder. Kitchen 2 smelled like nothing at all: It was polished, the tiles almost blinding in the ticking light. I turned on the faucet, watched my hand blur under the jetting water. I stared at the quiet blades inside the blender and imagined putting my face inside it. I took the crowbar and began to hit the lock on the freezer, experimentally at first and then with all my might. When the lock fell away, I whistled—I honestly had not been expecting my anger to have any outcome whatsoever. The door opened with a little gasp. Inside was an enormous mixing bowl full of the orange sherbet, surrounded by tiers of bare and humming shelves. I hardly remember what I did next—I don't even think I stopped to get a spoon, my fingers sinking into the cream—but when I looked up, Uncle Ed was standing over me—it was six o'clock. Family sedans were honking at one another from the lot.

"Leni," was all he said, and from the curious, besotted, half-frightened way he was looking at me I guessed that he was watching his mother rise out of my odd green eyes. I stood up and let the empty bowl fall from my hands; it didn't break, and I remember staring down at my reflection in it with a stab of disappointment. It spun like a planet on the kitchen tiles.

"I'm so full, Uncle," I mumbled. I wiped at the liquid trickling out of my eyes and the corners of my lips. I didn't know this then, but

I'd just eaten the last-ever batch of our family recipe. For the next seven nights, I had dreams where I rinsed the suds from a thousand plates in the restaurant sink and saw Mama Bakopoulos regarding me somberly out of each one. That summer, only my father returned from Greece.

What astounds me now is that my father still defends my mother— more than that, he accepts the blame for her "sickness": her refusal to come back to New Kalymnos again, her inability to see me as separate from Mama. Even today he'll talk about Irene with the gentlest kind of sorrow, as if acknowledging that it was his cough that set her off, sent the germ of the infirmity somersaulting toward my mother.

"When did it start to go wrong, Dad?" I asked him recently.

"Oh," said Frank, thinking backward. Doing the etiology. "When I kissed her, I guess? That first time?" He shook his silver head. "Nah, I think we were still OK then. I think it must have been when I asked her to marry me."

He looked right at me, his gray eyes as steadily unsteady as the sea, and I imagined that my mother must have been about this same distance from him when he made the proposal. "When I asked her to become a part of the family. Maybe that was the cough that got her sick."

When Frank stopped making number six, customers begged him for an explanation, and no one was satisfied with his gruff response.

"There's none left."

"None of *what*?"

"The secret ingredient. I ran out of it."

"You can't find more? Grow some more!"

And Frank would avert his eyes, give his head an angry shake. Like everyone, I hounded him:

"What *was* it, Dad?"

"Leni," he said, touching my cheek gingerly. "I'm sorry. Really, it won't grow anymore. It got, ah"—he frowned, rummaging for the word he'd found in the dictionary to explain what had happened to it after Irene divorced him—"*extirpated.*"

And I don't even think he was sorry, in a way—we stayed on at A FAMILY RESTAURANT but my father was always home now, and no longer a slave to the recipe, no longer the kitchen automaton of his dead mama. For years I burned with an anger that I found easiest to direct at my father, the paterfamilias who had cursed me with this face, the secret hoarder, who wouldn't even try to ease the beating pain in me by drawing me closer, telling me the whole recipe. For years the ingredient remained a permanent blank in Our Story. Gradually I came to accept that Frank was telling the truth on one count: Whatever glue had held the three of us together, the bloodred epoxy that makes a family, was gone.

And that's Our Story—I'm sure your order will be up soon, if I haven't brought it out already. I wish that I could bring you a sample of Mama's Deathbed Sherbet; forgive me for taking so much time describing a choice that isn't even on the menu. I suppose it's only fair, if you made it this far, to share the secret ingredient. Not too long ago, my father had a scary bout with pneumonia, in the same hospital where Mama died and I was born, and one night his gray eyes flew open on the hospital pillow and clapped on to my face; he began to give me, very slowly, in English, the entire recipe.

The flowers growing on her grave in Kalymnos, Greece, had been planted by my father—his mother's last wish. They were narcissus blooms, with brilliant orange coronas. Every few months he returned to harvest them. My mother's plane landed in Kos and she took the Kalymnos Star ferry to Pothia, arriving in the middle of the night, and asked everyone at the docks about my father's whereabouts until she was escorted by the single cab driver traveling the streets at that hour to the gates of the cemetery—the very spot, the driver confided, where he had only recently deposited her husband, Mr. Bakopoulos. All those years ago, Ed and Frank had paid a fantastic sum to have their mother interred here (for a dying woman, that Mama sure managed to croak out a lot of requests). Irene went crazy when she found Frank there, kneeling on the woman's grave and plucking up the blooms. The narcissus petals glowed a familiar orange, budding out of the soil that served as Mama's ceiling. Something unspeakable happened to them that night, something that is still humming, entirely unknown to me, behind the simple scroll of the recipe. Whatever words flew between them under the moon of Old Kalymnos must have been terrible, I think, and it's easy for me to imagine my mother pulling the flower beds up by their roots, like hair, clawing at the orange petals that she'd been forced to serve and swallow for more than a decade, and my father calling her crazy, crazy, trying to pin her arms behind her back. The following night she came back to the grave site, he told me, and salted the earth.

Nominated by Conjunctions

SOCANASETT

by CHRISTINE GELINEAU

from PATERSON LITERARY REVIEW

My mother used to insist
that living next door
to the penitentiary and state reform schools
was a good thing, reasoning
that escapees' first priority
would be distance between themselves
and the confines they'd left behind.
That's the story she would try
to sell us kids but we knew better, knew about
the boys who'd ducked from the shower line
at Socanasett, slipped newborn and naked
out of sight of the guards, freedom
came that naturally to them.
When the clothes went missing
from a neighbor's line we understood the boys
were not cold, or suddenly shy but
crafty, looking to blend back in
with those of us who didn't yet know what they knew:
the true worth of one's own skin
and what it can cost to own it.

Nominated by Paterson Literary Review, Lee Upton

TWO NIGHTS

by ANTHONY DOERR

from FUGUE

Winter in the mountains of central Idaho and the snow has let up. A
slim horn of moon hangs in the gap between two peaks. I zip up my
sleeping bag, pull on mittens.

It's maybe twenty degrees. The lake I'm camped beside is just beginning to freeze—paper-thin sheets of ice are interlocking above the shal-
lows. The clouds have peeled away. The sky travels through a long
spectrum of purples.

Everything seems poised to become something else. Silhouettes of
trees on the ridgelines might become men; boulders might stand and
stretch and slink away. I am at 7,800 feet, five miles from a road, forty
miles from a town, and yet here come whispers, six or seven syllables,
carrying across the water.

I blink into the dimness. My heart roars. The lake I'm camped beside
is still. The mountains glow. Nothing. No one.

Welcome to Idaho. We have ten major rivers, eighteen ski resorts, and
fifteen people per square mile. We have hidden valleys where the wind
pours through seams of aspens and makes a sound in the leaves exactly
like the sound of rain falling on a pond. We have forests where the
growing season is so short that fifty-year old trees are only four feet tall,
and get so rimed with ice in January that they look like gardens of oversized, glittering cauliflower. We also have an escalating methamphet-
amine crisis, looming water disputes, massive agribusiness feedlots, and
hour-long lines to eat dinner at The Cheesecake Factory.

Forget tourist brochures, forget airbrushed photos of sunsets, forget travel magazine spreads of flyfishermen at dawn casting into a smoking bend of Silver Creek. Idaho is bigger than eighty Rhode Islands and most of its boundaries are entirely arbitrary. Some parts get hardly any snow and some get eight feet. Vast stretches of the state are arid and yet inside these borders are almost 116,000 miles of rivers.

In January you can stand in a polo shirt outside a Starbucks in Boise and call somebody in Madagascar on a cellular telephone while 150 miles away a mountain goat stands on a mountaintop in the River of No Return looking down over an unbroken desert of snow twenty feet deep. Nothing I will ever write could do this place justice.

Among the quantities of peoples and tribes who have traveled, slept, and died in the topographical anomaly that is presently called Idaho, among the 12,000 years of their successive, unknowable generations, the great bulk of them marking time in ways we would only vaguely understand, was a small group of people who lived in the sprawling mountains surrounding the Salmon River.

They've been known by lots of names: Tukudeka, Sheepeaters, Toyani, Snakes, Arrow Makers. There probably weren't ever more than a couple of thousand of them. They lived in caves, in clefts in the rocks, and in wickiups made of sticks. They wore snowshoes in winter, and their furs were expertly tanned. Sometimes, supposedly, they hunted while wearing the decapitated heads of animals. Their bows, painstakingly crafted by heating and laminating sections of sheep horn, were renowned: one witness describes one of these bows sending an obsidian-tipped arrow through a nine-inch pine tree at a distance of fifteen paces.

That any human beings raised children in this rugged, shattered country, so close to timberline, stupefies me. In winter, the temperature rarely climbs above freezing and it's not uncommon for trees to snap in the cold. Summer is no picnic, either: not with bears and cougars, thunderstorms and forest fires; not with insects rising from the meadows in huge, throbbing clouds.

These people, these Tukudeka, have been called hermits, skulkers, and scavengers. A party of explorers who encountered them in 1819 described them as "truly wild men of the mountains. . . dressed in sheepskin garments, living among rocks in caves." The 1937 WPA guide to Idaho called them "wily and treacherous, though cowardly.

I'd call them old-school, bad-ass. Intrepid. Remarkable. I'd say they were more involved in the natural world than any of us could ever hope to be.

A whirlwind history: In 1805, when Sacagawea led Lewis and Clark into what is now called Idaho, the explorers found legions of beavers. Back in Europe, top hats made of felt were getting unreasonably popular. And guess which kind of animal fur makes the best hat felt?

For the next forty years, fur trappers slew Idaho's animals by the hundreds of thousands. In one season in the 1830s, the Hudson's Bay Company recorded taking 80,000 beavers from the Snake River.

On the heels of trappers were missionaries, and on the heels of missionaries were settlers. By the mid 1840s, by the time fashionable Europeans preferred hats made of silk, the Snake River had become a 'fur desert' and an east-west highway called the Oregon Trail had been established.

One by one, the people whose ancestors had been hunting, fishing, and digging up roots in this country for centuries were displaced, excluded, or eliminated. By the middle of the nineteenth century, of Idaho's original tribes, only the Tukudeka, with their hunting dogs and rabbit-skin blankets and year-round snows, could have remained fairly isolated.

But in 1862, prospectors found gold in the Boise Basin. Dozens of strikes were made. Boomtowns sprouted like mushrooms. Soon gold-seekers were working up every creek in every mountain range, no matter how inaccessible.

Meanwhile diseases carried by domestic sheep were decimating native herds of bighorn. Smallpox was doing the same to native humans. Survivors were being relocated systematically. When they resisted, they were forced off their land.

It's a familiar story: emigrants, eager to let livestock graze the camas meadows, depicted native people as bloodthirsty terrorists. Native people, hungry, desperate, watching cows and hogs chew up roots their families depended on for generations, said they were only protecting their way of life.

The summer of 1877 saw the Nez Perce War. The summer of 1878 saw the Bannock War. Subduing troublesome Indians became an American machinery unto itself. Military careers depended on it. Merchants in Boise were said to dread the prospects of a peaceful summer.

At the beginning of 1879, decimated by illness, their primary source of food vanishing, and their ancient hunting grounds invaded by armed prospectors, how many Tukudeka could have been left? Maybe thirty or forty families? They still dressed in hides, wove baskets, and cooked in clay pots. They still fitted their weapons with stone points. They were, perhaps, the last native Americans in the contiguous United States to live in a way their ancestors would immediately recognize.

And yet they had to know what was coming. In February of 1879, five Chinese miners were found murdered in an abandoned town twenty-three miles north of present-day Stanley. Not long afterward, two white ranchers were found dead on the south fork of the Salmon River. In both instances, the Tukudeka, accused of harboring renegades from previous Indian wars, were blamed. Settlers roared for protection.

So on the last day of May, Troop G, First Cavalry, soldiers of the United States Army, rode out from Boise to hunt down the last free-roaming native people in Idaho. The cavalcade did not have an easy time of it. Swollen creeks swept away mules and horses. They were assailed by lightning, snow, and hail; their animals were plagued by wood ticks and mosquitoes. Seemingly every day a mule pitched off a precipice and tumbled hundreds of feet into a rocky drainage.

It wasn't until mid-August, seventy-nine days after leaving Boise, that the soldiers in Troop G saw any real traces of their quarry: several empty wickiups, one of which had some firewood stacked beside it.

Two days later, reinforced by several dozen mounted infantrymen, they climbed to a diamond-shaped expanse of sawgrass and sagebrush, hemmed in by mountains, that is now a backcountry airstrip called Soldier Bar. There, at the base of a rocky slope, their scouts found a hastily-evacuated camp. There were ten wickiups, buckskin, beads, blankets, pots and pans.

Among the cavalrymen of Troop G was a private named Edgar Hoffner, a novel-reading, pipe-smoking cavalryman who kept a daily diary. "We turned our horses out after getting to this camp, to await developments," he wrote. "Gathered up every thing that we could find and consigned to the flames."

So casual! So nonchalant! How do things get to the point where a person would think so little of burning the possessions of eight or nine families?

Any time you look for evil in an individual person, though, you'll al-

211

most never find it. In his diary, Hoffner is often funny, often wistful. He misses home; he gets in snowball fights with other soldiers; he pines "for a cottage by the sea, for a cabin in the wood." When he has no food, he says he eats "wind pudding" for supper. Indeed, when he's not burning the possessions of Tukudeka families, Private Hoffner behaves much as any of my friends might in similar circumstances, if my friends were better with horses and significantly tougher about missing meals. He is kind to his fellow soldiers; he manages to keep a sense of humor in any weather.

And what about the settlers who demanded the Tukudeka be brought in? Isn't it folly to judge them, too? They lived deep in snowed-in valleys in houses they had built by hand: purlin roofs, log walls, cold decanting through cracks and knotholes. The wind-wracked faces of big mountains stared down at them all day. And maybe once a year some utterly foreign man emerged from the snows in animal furs with a few possessions tied to the back of a dog? Surely that'd be enough to make any of us sleep with a shotgun under the bed.

All their lives they'd pumped each other full of terrible stories: Indians were attacking wagon trains and burning children in front of their mothers; Indians were ruthless and inhuman assassins. By the late 19th century, the Tukudeka were probably more legend than reality, anyway; they were yetis, sylphs, bogeymen. Anything happened—a rancher was murdered, a horse was stolen, a pie disappeared off a windowsill—and who were you going to blame?

It's snowing; it's freezing cold; you wrap your sleeping children in blankets and listen to the wind pour off the mountains. You think: The winter, the darkness, the fastness beyond my front door—it's populated.

On the morning of August 20th, 1879, squads of cavalrymen started up the steep inclines surrounding Soldier Bar. Twenty men stayed behind with the pack train as a rear guard. By the time the riders were five miles away, they heard gunfire. They sprinted back, many on foot, as the slopes were too steep for horses. There had been an ambush. One of the men in the rear guard was shot through both legs and soon died.

That night the soldiers went to sleep in the grass at intervals of ten feet, clothes on, carbines loaded.

"The hostiles," wrote Private Hoffner, "have signal fires on the mountains on two sides of us."

That was August 20th, 1879. More and more lately, I am haunted by that night. Twin fires burn on the mountainsides. Six dozen cavalry-men—panicky, keyed-up, pissed off—lay down to sleep in the grass, They had just buried a comrade and they were nearly out of food.

Above them on the rocky slopes, maybe forty or fifty Tukudeka—toddlers, adolescents, women, men—tried to keep the babies quiet. They were among the last of their people, among the last free native people in the entire United States. The Civil War was over, Edison had invented the phonograph, and these people were still living outside, still making their homes in what any of us would call the middle of nowhere.

Maybe they were scared; maybe they were furious; maybe they were resigned. Probably they were hungry. Probably there were some refu-gee Bannocks or Nez Perce with them, men who had so far avoided the reservation, men who had rifles, men who had known little in their lives besides deracination and subjugation.

It'd be another couple of hours until dawn. If the sky was clear, the Milky Way would have been huge and dazzling, a sleeve of light draped across the sky. And in all that immensity, there was *nowhere* for the Tukudeka to go, no retreat, no quarter, the world had left them behind, somehow they had become strange and wrong, scattered amongst the hills, and everything was on the line: their idioms, their legends, their ancestors, their kids.

Maybe they slept; maybe one or two managed to forget their situa-tion long enough to whisper to each other and smile, before the crystal-line night reasserted itself and their aches and injuries came back and they were reminded again of the soldiers camped in the field below, bent on chasing them down.

One hundred and twenty-eight years later, I'm camped beside an alpine lake in December, not terribly far from Soldier Bar. For me nothing is more compelling in this country than the night skies: on winter nights the stars flicker white and red and blue, twisting and glittering in their places. In the same moment they can seem both astonishingly close and impossibly far away. This is not typically comforting: you feel the size of the Earth beneath your back, which is massive enough to hold all of its cities and oceans and creatures in the sway of its gravity, and on the far side of the Earth is the sun, 300,000 times more massive than the Earth, and slowly your thoughts begin to bump up against the enormity of the Milky Way, in which our entire solar system is merely a mote.

I close my eyes; I think of the brook trout in the lake beside me, quick and sleek, little sleeves of muscle suspended in the black water, their fins and bellies fringed with orange, their backs aswarm with patterns. The snowy peaks gleam in the moonlight. In a few days this lake will be frozen over, and I wonder if the fish turn up their eyes, if they watch the lights traveling through the sky, if they sense that this could be the last time they will be able to see them.

There are claims the Tukudeka may have been a distinct cultural group for 1,000 years. Some of the sites they used suggest a cultural continuity that stretches back as far as 8,000 years. But by August 1879, there were only a few families left, trying to get some sleep among the rocks.

A December night in 2007. An August night in 1879. Between me and them stretches an abyss, the automobile and the airplane, penicillin and the microchip, plastic furniture and space travel. Did the Tukudeka understand how fragile memory can be? Did they bury their memories on the hillsides around them, hoping someday someone might return to dig them back up?

"The conquest of the earth," wrote Joseph Conrad, "which mostly means the taking it away from those who have a different complexion or slightly flatter noses than ourselves, is not a pretty thing when you look into it too much."

Territory and gold, civilization versus wilderness, Rome versus the barbarians. Out of the history of Idaho comes the whispers of the Tukudeka; comes Private Edgar Hoffner with his tobacco and rifle; comes the relentless brooms of progress.

Fifty-one native Americans from that area eventually surrendered to the United States Army in October of 1879. The following year they were moved to the Fort Hall reservation, a good 200 miles from the Salmon River country. Whoever remained in the folds of the mountains might have hidden there another ten years. But the Indian Wars were over, and the last of Idaho's tribes had been relocated.

The Northern Pacific laid rails across the panhandle in 1882 and the Union Pacific sewed up the southern part of the Territory in 1884. In 1890, Idaho became a state.

Even to neighboring tribes, some historians say, the Tukudeka had seemed like druids, gnomes, elves. They were blamed for bad luck and big storms and lost objects. They were the Old Way, the hard way, the unknowable. They lived a life that was hard to believe.

Sometimes, in the winter, I stop at an intersection in Boise and watch the sleet coming down in slow sheets, raking across the foothills, all browns and whites, the cars splashing past around me—even the trees looking miserable, dormant, waiting, uncomfortable—and I think: thank God I don't have to sleep outside tonight.

And Idaho? Many of the places the Tukudeka knew are still here: cold green forks of rivers and here-and-there copses of cottonwoods and great broken slopes of volcanic scree aglow with lichen, and clouds like vast men-of-war dragging tentacles of rain across the ridgelines. Idaho still has the most roadless land in the Lower 48 and the largest single designated wilderness area, too. We have two gorges deeper than the Grand Canyon. We have sagebrush prowled by skinny foxes with the pilfered eggs of songbirds clamped gingerly in their teeth, and whole hillsides skittering with grasshoppers the color of straw.

Every life here, no matter how sequestered, no matter how im-pounded, is still informed by the land, for better or worse. And that for me is what Idaho continues to be about, this territory, this state, this country, the stripe of the Milky Way printed across a velvet sky and the silhouettes of mountains strobing in and out of view during lightning storms.

I live here because, even if I only have one afternoon, a few hours between obligations, I can ride a bike up into the hills above Boise, into cooler, more watered places, where wildflowers color the hillsides and the remains of old burns are still plain—the great blackened skeletons of sentinel ponderosa, granite blocks half-tumbled on the hillsides, spring creeks carving through the gulches. After twenty minutes of pedaling, the city of Boise will be far enough below that its features will have faded and become a wide green blur, bedded between mountain ranges, a haze over it, maybe the first evening lights winking on.

The history of our planet is one of absolutely relentless change. "There is nothing stable in the world," wrote Keats. "Uproar's your only music." Everything—mammoths, short-faced bears, western camels— eventually goes extinct. For about two million years, every August, tens of thousands of salmon poured into the rivers of Idaho. Redfish Lake, 900 miles from the Pacific, supposedly turned crimson with sockeyes. Last summer, only four fish made it back, and they were born in a hatchery. And there's no reason to think it won't happen to us, too; that, someday, some final band of humans will build signal fires among the rocks, and look down at who or whatever has come to finish us off.

The country the Tukudeka lived in, craggy, hazardous, hammered by snow, near-holy in its beauty, is still here. A person can go see the Saw-tooth Mountains and the Salmon River and even hike to Soldier Bar, where Private Hoffner helped bury his comrade, and where some of the last free Tukudeka rested among the rocks; and there are even less-traveled places, like the Lost River Range, or the Lemhi Mountains, which are about as far as you can get nowadays, in the Lower 48, from anybody.

A person can still go into the country and find a few ghosts, some pictographs, a stone hunting blind, a stick or two from a forgotten sheep trap.

"You people of low lands," wrote Private Hoffner in 1878, "have no idea how loud thunder can roar or how bright flashing the lightning is on the mountain tops."

A person can still walk into the mountains and stare up at the welter of stars.

Nominated by Fugue, Kim Barnes

WRITS OF POSSESSION

fiction by BENJAMIN PERCY

from VIRGINIA QUARTERLY REVIEW

1.

When Sammy knocks, when she says, "Sheriff's office," she stands to the side of the apartment door. No one has tried to shoot her, not yet. But you never know. The peephole darkens. She waits for the door to rattle open, and when it doesn't, she knocks again. "I know you're in there," she says, and the apartment manager, a man with bony arms and shoe-polish black hair, leans close to her and says, "I know he's in there."

This is the River Side Apartment Complex, and Sammy is a deputy with the civil division of the Deschutes County sheriff's office. Every day people are falling behind—every day there is a taller stack of evictions, small claims notices, repossessions of property, wage garnishments for unpaid debts—and every day there is another address to visit, a door to knock on, sometimes to kick down.

The carpet is a burnt orange. The walls are pine-paneled. The fluorescent light above them buzzes on and off. She hates her job, hates that she spends most of her day trudging through dumps like this, delivering subpoenas, hurrying people out their doors and down staircases with garbage bags full of clothes, cardboard boxes spilling over with frozen food. In the three years she has worked in the civil division, only once has someone been happy to see her—and she was serving him divorce papers. She seized her baton as he hugged her.

She knocks again, this time using the side of her fist, booming at the door. "Hello," a voice, a man's voice, says. "Okay. I'm opening."

She supposes she feels bad for people. When they cry or beg or point to their grubby children and say, you're doing this to *them*. Maybe pities them, maybe that's a better way of putting it. But then a dog will come padding out of a back room or she'll spot a video game console, a pool table, a cappuccino machine. And she'll decide from their carelessness that they're getting what they deserve. She'll want to say, "How much you spend on dog food a month?" or "How much you think you could have sold that Xbox for?" But she won't. Instead, when people show their teeth or kick over chairs or get down on their knees and take her hand and beg, she simply says, "I'm no judge, no jury," so that people contain their anger and sadness, bottle it up for someone else.

Every one of these addresses is like a hole—the same hole, many-chambered—and sometimes, when she thinks back on all the addresses she's visited, she feels as though she is falling through them, through their living rooms and kitchens, seeing hundreds, thousands of faces all twisted in an upset expression directed at her.

At her hip she carries handcuffs, a telescoping baton, a .40 caliber Glock. She keeps her hair short—ever since, seven years ago, when she was working patrol, a drunk yanked her ponytail, grated her cheek against the asphalt—and she knows her square face, her broad shoulders make her look a little like a man. People blink a few times when they first meet her, trying to make sense of her.

That's the case now, when the door clicks open and she moves into the dim light of the apartment and faces an old man, mid-seventies, wearing pale blue jeans and a ribbed white tank top. His head is bald except for a horseshoe of white hair. His feet are bare—their skin spotted and knotted with veins, the toenails a chalky yellow.

"Frank Ridgeway?"

"Yeah." His square-framed glasses take up most of his face. He peers at her through them and they are thick enough that she can't distinguish the color of his eyes.

"I have a court order," she says and holds out the paper, folded twice as if to better contain the secret. "Notice of eviction."

She steels herself, ready for him to plead his case—like all the others—to smack his fist into an open palm, shout so loudly spittle flies from his lips. To say that he has rights, that this is an illegal eviction. To say that he's been cheated, that the landlord has been cashing his checks all long.

But he doesn't. "Okay," he says and waves both hands as if to clear a bad smell from the air. "Okay. All right."

218

They are standing in his kitchen. The counter is bare except for a brown mug and a plate dirtied with crumbs. The smell of old coffee and cigarette smoke. Beyond the kitchen, the living room. Same pine-paneled walls and orange carpeting as the hallway. Dirty light seeping in through the tan curtains. A wooden box of a television playing Fox News with the sound off. She wonders if he has children, even grand-children, who could help. She doesn't see any photos magneted to the fridge, hanging on the walls. Everything is bare.

Frank still hasn't taken the paper. She shakes it at him and he snatches it from her and says, "Fine." He unfolds it and folds it up again without reading, drops it on the counter. "I suppose you want me to leave?"

"Now."

"How long do I have?"

"Now."

"Fine." He departs her, walking toward a blackened doorway that must lead to his bedroom, where he pauses. "While you wait, don't suppose you want a glass of water? Or some milk?"

No one has ever asked her this before, so it takes a moment to reply: "No. Thank you."

"I'll only be a minute." He coughs, his cough sounding like pennies rattling at the bottom of a paper cup. "I got to warn you, though. I die sometimes. I been dying all day."

"Excuse me?"

He taps his chest. "My heart stops beating. My lungs stop breathing. I die. Not officially but it's death all the same. Then I wake up. I'm telling you this because I feel a spell coming on. Wouldn't want to alarm you." His smile is damp and pink—he hasn't put in his teeth yet—but she doesn't sense a joke.

She looks to the manager for help, but he is in the hall, muttering into his cell phone, chewing his thumbnail. "What should I do?" she says to Frank. "If you die? Do you want me to call an ambulance?"

"Don't do nothing. Give me a couple minutes—I'll come back." He picks at a splinter in the doorframe. "Doctor calls it a heart condition. I call it a Korean condition." His chest hair is as white as dandelion fluff. He reaches into it, under his tank top, and withdraws his dog tags, and rattles them at her.

Normally she doesn't talk to tenants during repos or evictions except to say, "Hurry," or "I don't care." But Frank is old. And alone. And though she is used to dealing with people who have made the wrong choices, they are, almost all of them, young and furious and seemingly capable of rectifying whatever ruin has come to them. He is different. A lone cloud coming apart in gray filaments, a few drops of rain. She feels, no other word for it, sad.

She calls to him, "Frank?" just as he clicks on the light in his room. His eyes are thin black slits behind his glasses. "You don't mind me asking, what does it feel like? When you die?"

He considers this a moment before answering. "You feel like you're falling," he says. "You feel like you're falling down a very deep hole." His hand makes a falling motion. "Every time I keep expecting to hit bottom. But so far, no bottom."

2.

John peels up the duck-patterned Linoleum in the bathroom and lays down tile. He rips away the aquamarine carpet in the guest room and pliers out the hundreds of tacks and staples to reveal the hardwood gleaming beneath. He scores the floral wallpaper in the kitchen and sprays it with DIF and scrapes off damp shreds of it and gouges the drywall so that he must mud and texture before splashing the walls over with paint. He unscrews the light fixtures—all white orbs with brass collars—and replaces them with wrought iron. He hangs new gutters. He trades out the appliances for stainless steel. He installs new hardware on all the cabinets. He removes the cracked and yellowed switches and outlets and screws in white plates.

Now the house looks like the house he imagined when, five years ago, he walked through it and laid his hands on its walls and said, "I can see the potential." Five years and he hasn't flipped open his toolbox until now—now that he has to move. His marriage is falling apart. His daughter is starting to bring home college brochures. His boss at the biodiesel company where he works ordered a thirty-day furlough for all employees. So he spends his evenings and weekends alone—his wife has moved in with her parents and his daughter spends all her time in her room—restoring the house, his house, which he has come to hate, to think of as a kind of grave, for someone else to enjoy.

The back porch overlooks a hillside crowded with big pines. For the decorative posts—staggered every ten feet along the railing, squared and beveled, as tall as a rifle and as thick as a thigh—the builder didn't use the treated fir or cedar he should have, and dry rot set in. When John pulls off the old sheathing, tearing into it with a hammer and a short crowbar, he reveals their hollow core, and in it, the skeletons of four birds along with their rotten wig of a nest.

John uses the crowbar to claw them from the post, for ten years their tomb. Bones and branches and broken bits of shell scatter at his feet. He toes at a skull and it crumbles into a white powder. He guesses the birds were nesting when the house was being framed, maybe up in the rafters, and the builder climbed a ladder and cradled the nest in his hands and cooed and whistled at the baby birds and then tossed them inside the post before hammering on its cap and whispering goodbye.

3.

For more than a month they have lived here. A month is the longest they have ever gone before getting caught—the owners walking in on them watching television, taking a shower, knifing mustard across bread. Then they run—they have learned to be fast—and eventually find another house.

They look for a subdivision with brickwork driveways and three-car garages, with columns flanking the front doors and maple saplings struggling to grow in the front yards. They find a four- or five-story house with no dog toys or playground equipment in its backyard. They discover an unlocked window or a sliding glass door. In a guest room in the far corner of the walkout basement, they drop their backpacks. They wait.

The first few days, they spend a lot of time listening to the footsteps thumping overhead, the muttered conversations overheard through the heating ducts and thinly insulated walls. They take note of the owners' patterns. If there are no children and no pets, that usually means the couple spends their days, sometimes their nights, working, these doctors and lawyers and engineers. What little time they do spend at home, they spend in their room.

After the shower hisses, the door slams, the Lexus growls to life, the garage door rumbles closed, the house is empty and will typically remain so until evening comes.

So the two of them—the boy and the girl, brother and sister, homeless for more than two years after running away several times over from foster care—they steal the clothes from the edges of the closet, the backs of drawers. They pawn the jewelry and cameras and DVDs. They slip money—just a few bills, not enough for anyone to notice unless they were really looking—from wallets and purses. They walk on the sides of their feet so that they don't leave tracks in the white carpet. They hide from the maid when she comes on Mondays and Thursdays. But mostly they just hang out, watch television, raid the fridge for treats.

One morning, they are in a master bedroom with a vaulted ceiling, a four-poster king-size bed, and two walk-in closets, each of them bigger than any bedroom they've ever called their own. An archway leads into the bathroom, where the toilet rises up on a pedestal, where the counters are marble and the shower is surrounded by glass bricks and the tub is a deep cauldron with two dozen jets.

She, the sister, rummages through the closet and climbs into a suit seven sizes too big, while he, the brother, pulls on a black cocktail dress that won't zip up his broad back. A flat screen television hangs on the wall. They punch through the channels, finally settling on VH1— a Best of the 80s countdown—and leap from one side of the bed to the other, playing air guitar, yowling along with the big hair bands.

They are laughing, hitting each other with pillows, when the screen goes dark, when the music falls away. They stand in a mess of sheets, breathing heavily A man is watching them. His face is a severe shade of red. He has small eyes and a small, pinched mouth. He is as tall as a doorway. They recognize him from the photo albums shelved in the living room, from the wedding photo hanging in the hallway.

The brother and sister look at each other— neither of them knowing what to do. He is blocking the door. And the nearest window drops twenty feet into a thorny hedge, a broken leg.

"Who are you," the man says, not yelling, not yet, "and what are you doing in my house?"

In another story, they might have told him their names. They might have told him about their father running off, their mother drinking heavily—the social workers with their tired eyes and sleepy-sounding voices, the cat piss-stinking foster homes decorated with crosses and strangely colored paintings of Jesus petting sheep. And the man might have listened. His eyes might have softened. His posture might have relaxed. He might have even smiled briefly when they told him about the week they spent living in a Super Wal-Mart.

And when they finally said, "We're sorry. We'll leave now," he would have yelled, "No!" his arms outstretched to block their way. "No," he would say, his voice softer this time. "Stay. Please." And the brother and sister would shrug at each other when he motioned them downstairs, when he led them to the kitchen, where they would make sandwiches and pour tall glasses of milk and eat together in the breakfast nook that overlooked the green expanse of lawn that ran into a pond with a concrete swan vomiting an arc of green water in the middle of it.

When they were finished eating their sandwiches, when they licked their lips and settled back in their chairs, he would look out the window and quietly ask them if they would like to stay. They would say, no, they couldn't, they had to move on, and he would say, stay, really, I mean it—and they would know that he meant it, that he wasn't going to trick them and call the police, that maybe the house felt a little too big for him, that maybe he needed them as much as they needed him, and they would all smile and finish their glasses of milk.

But that is another story

4.

Mr. Peterson has taken a job in Seattle with a software company. As part of the hiring bonus, if the house doesn't sell within the next two months, the company will offer him x amount of money and assume the title.

The Petersons try. Some of the neighbors will admit to that—that they do try. They install new countertops, new carpeting, new sinks and faucets. They brush paint on the walls. They remove all of their family photos and hide all of their toys so that the house could belong to anyone, so that the couples who follow high-heeled, lipsticked realtors through the rooms, up and down the stairs, their fingers lingering on the railings and doorknobs, can imagine the house as their own.

They list the home for $599,000—a fair price, everyone agrees. A price that will reflect well on the neighborhood. But the months pass without an offer. And the Peterson's garage fills steadily with cardboard boxes sealed with tape. And then one day the Bekins trucks pull up to the curb and the movers—the sweating, thick-waisted men with mustaches—leap out to haul away all of the furniture and books and wedding china. They leave the house vacant of everything except the window treatments, the dimples the couches crushed into the carpet.

Now the original realtor sign comes down and another one goes up listing the house at $399,000. The neighborhood, red-faced and narrow-eyed, hates the Petersons for this. Over the past few years they have watched property values climb—doubling, tripling, and they have counted on that equity—they believe in their houses as investments more than as places to live. So they scowl at the empty house as if it is to blame. They call the realtor—they call the Petersons—to express their outrage. They encourage their dogs—their yellow labs and golden retrievers and Siberian huskies—to shit in the front yard. Someone spray-paints *fuck you* in black swirling letters across the garage door, but the next day it is painted over. Someone rips the realty sign from the front yard and shoves it into a nearby storm drain, but the next day it is up again—and within a week it is topped by a red banner that reads SALE PENDING.

In this neighborhood, a subdivision called Swan Ridge, no one can paint their houses anything but earth tones. Nor can they plant vegetables or store play equipment in their front yards. They cannot park RVs and boats in their driveways for more than twenty-four hours. And when you live in a neighborhood like this, there are certain expectations of you. There are rules you must abide by, and now the rules have been broken.

So they wait until it is night. The streetlamps buzz to life. The garage doors rumble open. People collect red three-gallon jugs of gasoline and carry them sloshingly down the block and gather in the driveway of the house, the empty house. There are twenty people altogether, mostly members of the neighborhood association. Others watch from their front porches. The moon is out and its reflection glows in the living room window like a spectral eye. The siding is vinyl and the porch-boards are made of recycled plastic and nobody knows how well these will burn. They want inside—they want the house to burn from the belly up.

They try to kick open the front door, but it is deadbolted and no one can make it splinter inward like the cop shows on TV. So they circle the house and try the windows and find one of them unlocked and rip off the screen and boost a middle-aged woman named Susan Pearl through it so that she can unlock the front door and allow them to rush inside, to splash gasoline along the walls, to soak pools of it into the carpet, waterfall it down the stairs. Their eyes tear over. The fumes make them dizzy. They cough and laugh at once.

They make a trail of gasoline—gasoline they would have otherwise used to power their riding lawnmowers across lawns of Kentucky blue grass—they make a trail of gasoline down the porch, along the brick-work path, to the driveway, where Susan sparks her pink rhinestone

Zippo and lights a menthol cigarette and takes a deep drag off it and flicks it in a sparking arc.

Her lipstick has made a red collar around the filter that matches the red ember at its tip. It spins through the air and bounces off the cement and comes to a stop in a pool of gas that ignites with a huff. A tongue of blue and orange flame licks its way speedily toward the house.

It isn't long before the windows explode and the flames rise through them and the siding around them blackens and buckles and melts and runs like tears. Sparks swirl up into the night, lost among the stars. The roof vanishes in a snapping crown of flame. The street appears sunlit. The heat is tremendous. Everyone staggers out of the driveway, into the street, with shadows playing across their faces, making them appear as strangers to each other.

5.

There is a knock at the door. At first Brent doesn't hear it because of the TV—the game show that doesn't require talent, only luck, the contestants choosing among the fifty beautiful women who stand on stage holding silver briefcases full of money. Brent is yelling when he first hears the knock, throwing up his arms and condemning the greed of the man who could have gone home with 100,000 grand but decided to keep playing. "The idiocy," Brent says. "The fucking idiocy people are capable of." And then the knock.

Brent punches the mute button and rises from the couch to open the door, wondering vaguely who it might be, maybe the Jehovah's witnesses he saw prowling the neighborhood earlier? Or maybe Papa Johns—had he ordered a pizza? He had, hadn't he? It is so hard to remember anything anymore, every day bleeding into the next, a weekday the same as a weekend, night no different than day, ever since he lost his job.

Under the yellow cone thrown by his porch light stand two men. They wear black boots and black jeans and black T-shirts. Their hair is buzzed down to their scalps like a wire brush. Their shoulders are rounded with muscle. Behind them stands a cop—black windbreaker with a yellow star on the breast. A woman, he realizes, only when she speaks, when she hands him a piece of paper, a repossession notice, she explains.

He looks at the paper, but doesn't really read it. The men shoulder their way past Brent, while the woman tells him they are here to retrieve the 55-inch HD plasma he bought on an installment plan at Best Buy. He was $1,000 into his $3,000 payment plan when he lost his job as a financial consultant at Wells Fargo. He has not, as he advised so many others to do, nested away his money. For the first three months he lived off his severance pay. He sent out queries for jobs that did not exist. He has not applied for unemployment. He has not asked his parents for help, has not even told them about losing his job. He has not written a check in six months, doesn't answer the phone when the creditors call, will not listen to the messages that go from stern to snarling.

The woman remains on the porch as the men approach Brent's television, which rests on a two-tiered glass console with black metal legs. One of them hits the power button and shoves the remote in his pocket. Then they rip the wires from the wall and wrap them around their fists like tangles of hair. They station themselves at either side of the television and say, "Ready?"—and lift it without any trouble. It ought to weigh more, Brent thinks, considering how much it cost. He is folding the repossession paper in half and then in half again, and then again, making a square he can fit in his pocket. He does not feel much of anything. These past few days he has spent mostly on the couch, his mind empty except for simple needs, the next diet soda he will drink, the next program he will watch.

Their invasion of his condo does not bother him, not particularly, even though they act like the television is theirs, like their employer is a parent and they are its vengeful children. He is too tired to care. It isn't until one of the men bumps into him and says, "Move, loser," that something sparks inside him, something electric, as he remembers the weight of his manager's hand on his shoulder—the sad smiles of his co-workers when, in a daze, he packed up his desk—the Wal-Mart bag he found on his front porch the next day, big-bellied with the things he left behind, his Trailblazers coffee mug, his calculator from college, the M. C. Escher calendar.

On the coffee table sits a half-empty bottle of Budweiser. The glass is warm in his hand when he picks it up. The men are not looking at him. They are looking at the open doorway, taking baby steps toward it, taking care not to trip over a magazine rack, to knock against the edge of the coffee table. And the cop is already gone, walking toward the black sedan parked in the street.

Brent doesn't say anything when he approaches the men, doesn't scream a wild animal scream. He simply snaps his arm—the bottle spiraling through the air, the beer twisting and fizzing from it—into the gray and watchful eye of the television.

<h2 style="text-align:center">6.</h2>

Tonight the mother reads the little boy the story of *Harold and the Purple Crayon*. They lay side-by-side in his bed, and when she finishes, when she snaps shut the book, he asks her to stay a little longer. "To cuddle, Mama." She tells him no. She has to go. He has to sleep. "Just for a minute," he says. "A mini-minute," she says and remains curled up by him for a few breaths before climbing out of bed, pulling the covers up to his chin. "Don't leave," he says and she says she has to and kisses his forehead and lets her lips linger there another moment before she snaps off the light, says goodnight, closes the door.

He's not scared of the dark. He's not worried about monsters beneath his bed or aliens at the window. It's his mother—whose eyes are red-rimmed, whose hair is going gray at the roots because she hasn't been to the beauty parlor in months—who worries him. He hears her crying through the walls. He hears her on the phone: "We're underwater," she keeps saying, along with that word, foreclosure. They are going into foreclosure.

One night he asked her where it was, foreclosure. "I'm sorry?" she said and he said, "We're going there. You keep saying we're going there. Foreclosure." Her lips flattened and her eyebrows came together and she asked him if he wanted to watch cartoons—would he like that?

He has heard at Sunday school the story of Noah and the ark that survived the great flood. And he has seen on the news the waters that rose up from a river to swallow towns in a place called Iowa. This is what his mother is worried about, he feels certain. This is why she is packing all of their things into boxes, suitcases. A flood. A flood is coming. And its waters will be black and roiling with terrible fish, their eyes white, their fangs thin and crooked. He imagines the first wave of the flood surging along the street, splashing against the side of their house, foaming and reeking of the terrible fish that wait outside, gnawing at the wood. The water will seep under the doors and lick its way down the hallway, rising, rising.

He needs to work quickly. And he knows his mother might notice the light under his door, so he pulls the shades instead, allowing the moon into his room, its light silvering over his walls. Slowly he slides open his closet. From a shelf devoted to art supplies he pulls a box of crayons and fumbles through them until he pulls out one he thinks to be purple, though it could just as well be black in the uncertain moonlight.

And there, on the wall, he begins to draw a boat, one big enough for the two of them, to carry them away to foreclosure.

7.

The neighborhood is empty. it has always been empty. It was built by a custom homebuilder that has developed subdivisions in three different states. Since the market crashed, the company has laid off most of its employees in its building and land development divisions. It is working with financial advisors and legal counsel on vendor payments and other cash obligations.

Construction has stopped. All the signs and sales trailers have been hauled away. No sod has been laid; the yards are made of mud. The farther you travel into the neighborhood, the more unfinished it becomes. Houses that are naked of siding—the sheets of felt paper stapled to their exterior coming loose to flap in the wind like rotten skin. Houses that are missing windows and doors. Houses that are nothing more than a skeletal frame and lots that are nothing more than an excavated hole, a muddy cavity collapsing inward.

The neighborhood runs up against a pine forest. And it isn't long—after the payloaders and bulldozers and trucks stacked high with lumber grumble away—before the animals begin to creep from the shadows, to explore the houses and consider them a kind of nest or burrow.

A great horned owl sails into an attic—through the octagonal hole cut for a gable vent—and makes it his roost. Crows blacken the rafters of an unfinished frame. A black bear claws aside the latticed frame of a porch and roots and burrows beneath it. Feral cats wander the streets. Wasps and swallows mud over the eaves.

Beyond the subdivision's river-rock entryway—Swan Hollow, the gold lettering reads with etched cattails rising around it—stands a model home, a design known as the Apex IV, with its 2900 square feet, its hardwood flooring and enameled woodwork, its formal and informal dining rooms, study, great room and a kitchen bigger than most restaurants' with granite countertops, a center island, and custom maple cabinetry throughout.

Months ago, a realtor left the back door unlocked, and tonight it comes unstuck when a hard wind sucks it open. It groans and swings on its hinges, as though beckoning the forest. And the forest answers. From between its trees, like shadows come to life, steals a pack of coyotes that noses through the door and into the kitchen, where they pause and lick their chops and sniff the air. No one has been here for a long time: the house is theirs. They yap and growl and set off through the many rooms, their paws thudding across the carpets, clicking across the tiles and hardwood. They pee in the corners. They gnaw at the legs of the dining room table. They leap onto the beds and leather couches and snap playfully at each other.

One day a teenager in a Ramones T-shirt with nothing better to do hurls a brick through the Apex IV's picture window. It shatters, crashing inward, leaving behind a square shadowy mouth framed by fangs of glass. The teenager stands in the front yard, grinning widely, pleasuring in the music of destruction, the crash and tinkle of broken glass still biting the air, soon replaced by snarls and yaps that come from inside the house and that come together into a terrible howling, the howling of a dozen coyotes, growing louder and louder like a siren that sends the teenager stumbling back, into the street, where his bike lies on its side.

He pulls the bike upright and climbs onto it and kicks at the pedals to get them turning, to get the bike moving, just as the pack of coyotes pours through the broken window, a surging gray wave of them, all jabbering and clacking their teeth as they pursue him for his trespass.

8.

Her hearing isn't what it used to be, but Gertie can still hear the knock at the door, even from upstairs. She doesn't like to be bothered, likes to keep to herself. When the phone rings, she lets the answering machine pick up. And at church—her only destination these days besides the doctor's office—the First Baptist church where she serves as a deaconess, where she has hardly missed a Sunday in fifty years, she shakes hands during the sharing of the peace and lingers afterwards for coffee, but doesn't go out of her way to say much except, "Lovely day," or "Lovely to see you." So when she hears the knock at the door, she goes to the window of her bedroom, pulls aside the lace curtain, peers down at the front porch.

Nobody knows about her troubles. Nobody asks how she is getting along, and even if they did, she likely wouldn't tell them. She has never been one to complain. Not about the arthritis chewing at her fingers and not about the cataract that fogs over her left eye and not about how badly she misses Harry, how empty the house feels without him. And not about the crooks—though she'd like to give them an earful, maybe crack them over the head with a can of soup—who convinced her to take out a 30-year, 6.4 percent mortgage for $37,000, along with a $10,000 line of credit.

She and her husband had owned the home since 1951, had raised their son here, his height still faintly sketched in the kitchen cupboard door, the pencil marks like the broken blood vessels that trail down her legs. She couldn't keep up with the payments. Over and over the writs of possession have been posted on her door. Over and over she has ripped them down and folded them in half, and in half again, and again, until they are tiny white squares she places at the bottom of her garbage can, as if the dark truth contained in them might decompose along with the coffee grounds, dissolve like a communion wafer on her tongue and absolve her.

On the porch stands the policeman—no, a woman, Gertie realizes, when the figure moves into a slant of sunlight, peering into the living room through the bay window, a big woman with the haircut and bow-legged stance of a man. She knows Gertie is home—her Buick is parked in the driveway. The policewoman isn't going away this time. She isn't going to post another notice and clomp down the porch and grumble away in her unmarked car. She hammers at the door again and then forcefully tries the knob, so that Gertie imagines she can feel the force of the hand on her, shaking her, strangling her.

Gertie withdraws from the window and the lace curtain falls slowly into place like a spider's web. Her husband is dead. Her son is dead, too. So many of her friends and neighbors. Everyone is dead. She says this out loud—everyone is dead—her voice a metallic rasp as she pulls open the drawer of the night table and pulls out the revolver, the .357 her husband kept around the house for security. It is heavy—she holds it in a two-handed grip, the muzzle drooping, aimed at the floor between her legs. She sits on the edge of the bed. The springs moan. The policewoman hammers at the door again—and then yells something, Gertie doesn't know what.

She can't recall if Harry ever took the gun to the shooting rang or out to a gravel pit to blast pop bottles. As far as she knows, it has never been fired. She wonders vaguely how old the bullets are, whether they can expire, when she brings the muzzle to her breast—not her mouth, that would be too much trouble to clean up, too much ugliness to look at for whoever found her—and pulls the trigger.

9.

Sammy can't dwell on the sad stories. The family that moved into their van. The man who says his store has been empty ever since the second Wal-Mart opened up. The woman who says her husband has cancer, says their insurance dropped them, says they had to put all their medical expenses on their credit cards. The rank piles of laundry in the corners, the stained pizza boxes and crumpled soda cans decorating the floor, the child wearing a T-shirt as a dress, clutching a one-armed teddy bear.

Sometimes she wishes she lived in a world without doors. There's too much hurt out there, and every time she opens a door, she opens herself to it, their collected voices, their collected failure—all powered by voices that scream and whine and blame and beg and reason—punctuated now by a gunshot on a summer afternoon.

She does not want to open this door. She does not want to pound up the stairs. She does not want to face the body she knows is waiting for her inside. She drops the eviction notice and it flutters to the porch like a broke-backed bird and she stares at it for a long time before stepping out from the shadow of the porch, into the sun, heading back to the car where she will radio an ambulance before roaring off to the next neighborhood, the next address, the next door to drag her knuckles across, dreading what waits for her.

Nominated by Virginia Quarterly Review, Bret Anthony Johnston

ON A SPRING DAY IN BALTIMORE THE ART TEACHER ASKS THE CLASS TO DRAW FLOWERS

by MARY SZYBIST

from THE KENYON REVIEW

I.

I can begin the picture: his neck is bent,
his mouth too close to her ear as he leans in
above her shoulder—to point
to poppies shaded in apricot, stippled
just as he taught her. Class is over.
They are alone in the steady air—

Through the window, a jump rope's tick.
An occasional bird. High voices.
Perhaps, so caught up in composing her flower,
she doesn't feel his fingers
there and there, her neck exposed
to the spring air—

II.

There are only a few lines in the paper: her grade, his age, when the
police arrived. J. calls to say he doesn't believe the girl. *Girls that age,*

he says—*you know how this goes. Hey, if there's a trial, you could be a witness.*

    What kind of witness?

    Character witness.

III.

Yes I knew him. One summer we lounged in the backyard sun and listened to songs about *wouldn't it be nice.* On the swing, on the lawn, I posed for him, leaned my head against the picnic table. That was when I did not have enough, could not have enough looking at.

That summer he carried his sketchpad everywhere and on those slow, humid afternoons, I felt him elongate, shade, and blur. Above us the sky was like a white rush of streetlights, and I wanted to be nothing but what he shaped in each moment—

I closed my eyes, felt the sunlight on my thighs. To be beheld like that—it felt like glittering.

IV.

What should be remembered, what
imagined?

She shifts in her chair. Her uncertain fingers
trace, against the sky—how many times?—
the red edges of the petals, caress
the darkening lines, trying to still them—
though she cannot make the air stop
breathing, cannot make cannot
make the shuddering lines stay put.

Nominated by David Baker, Molly Bendell, Marianne Boruch, Michael Collier, Maxine Scates

SIGNS

fiction by BESS WINTER

from AMERICAN SHORT FICTION

It is after a series of nubile young researchers have begun to parade through Koko the gorilla's life that she learns the sign for *nipple*. She draws her heavy arms close to her chest, and her leathery pointers spring out toward the unsuspecting graduate student. A look of expectation settles onto her simian face. Sometimes her gaze rests on the soft-sloping clavicle that betrays itself from beneath an unbuttoned collar, sometimes on the ponytail that rests coyly on one shoulder like a thick tassel, and sometimes on the face of Dr. Thomas, senior supervising researcher, as if she's asking him whether she's doing it right.

Inevitably, the student looks to Dr. Thomas. *What should I do? What should I say?*

Nipple, signs Koko.

Inevitably, Dr. Thomas tells her it is her duty, as a paid researcher, not to interfere: that she should indulge Koko's fetish, that this, too, should be researched.

Inevitably, there is a long moment while the student struggles with the request. Dr. Thomas fumbles his pencil, tapping it against his notepad, twirling it between two fingers. He does this until the student takes in a long, reedy breath, looks down to unbutton her blouse with shaking hands.

Then there is the moment when she peels off her blouse and unhooks her bra, and the moment when she sets the bra beside her on the table or hangs it by one strap over the edge of the chair.

Dr. Thomas knows there are two types of graduate students: the ones who put their bras beside them on the table and the ones who hang them up on the chair. They may be further categorized by type of bra: underwire, sports. Then there are those who don't wear bras at all. He can never predict which students will not be wearing bras, except that these young women are usually small-breasted, gamine.

And there is the inscrutable moment between woman and beast when the researcher, breathing fast, sits half-clad in front of the gorilla, and the gorilla does not sign at all. When the researcher tries to avoid a direct gaze into the gorilla's eyes lest she provoke her, she cannot; Koko seems to address her directly and without words. Dr. Thomas jots down notes, but he cannot understand why, in this moment, Koko reaches out to take the student's hands. He can only hypothesize about why some graduate students cry at the slightest touch and why some smile at the gorilla, why some curl into Koko's arms when she opens them. Why some allow her to touch and gentle them, to trace their eyes and nose and soft neck with her rough fingers. Why some nod knowingly, and why the gorilla nods back, and why he feels a sudden shift in the room, as if he's the unwelcome guest at a sacred rite.

He can only guess at this, too: why, after each student leaves for the day and it's just Dr. Thomas and Koko, the gorilla regards him with a withering look. Why she pokes at her fruit and then looks up at him like a wife waiting to broach a touchy topic at dinner.

And why, when she finally signs to him *nipple*, he searches her earth-brown eyes for some silent instruction. But if there are words in those eyes, he can't find them. Those eyes are deep and ripe. They're unmapped territory. He doesn't know whether to remove his shirt or call back a graduate student. With a shy hand, he touches his collar and makes to open it. But before he completes the gesture, the moment passes, or he has done the wrong thing already. Koko looks away.

Nominated by American Short Fiction, Michael Czyzniejewski

EMISSION

fiction by JOSHUA COHEN

from THE PARIS REVIEW and FOUR NEW MESSAGES (Graywolf Press)

This isn't that classic conceit where you tell a story about someone and it's really just a story about yourself.

My story is pretty simple:

About two years after being graduated from college with a degree in unemployment—my thesis was on Metaphor—I'd moved from New York to Berlin to work as a writer, though perhaps that's not right because nobody in Berlin *works*. I'm not going to get into why that is here. This isn't history, isn't an episode on The History Channel.

Take a pen, write this on a paper scrap, then when you're near a computer, search:

www.visitberlin.de

Alternately, you could just keep clicking your finger on that address until this very page wears out—until you've wiped the ink away and accessed nothing.

However, my being a writer of fiction was itself just a fiction and because I couldn't finish a novel and because nobody was paying me to live the blank boring novel that was my life, I was giving up.

After a year in Berlin, with my German-language skills nonexistent, I was going back home. Not home but back to New York, I was going to business school. An M.B.A. It was time to grow up because life is short and even brevity costs. My uncle told me that, and it was his being diagnosed with a boutique sarcoma that—forget it.

Yesterday by close of business was the first time my portfolio ever reached seven figures, so if every author needs an occasion, let this be mine. Sitting in an office when I should be out celebrating my first million—instead remembering these events of five years ago to my keyboard, my screen.

But as I've said this is not about me—no one wants to hear how I'm currently leveraged or about my investments in the privatization of hospitals in China.

I met Mono—I'll always think of him as Mono—only once, a week before I left Neukölln forever. Left the leafy lindens and sluggish Spree, the breakfasts of sausages and cheeses and breads that stretched like communist boulevards into late afternoon, the stretch-denim legs of the artist girls pedaling home from their studios on paint-spattered single-speeds, the syrupy strong coffees the Kurdish diaspora made by midnight at my corner café and its resident narcoleptic who'd roll tomorrow's cigarettes for me, ten smokes for two euros.

I was at a *Biergarten*, outside on its patio overlooking the water. The patio was abundant with greens: softly flowing ferns, flowers in pails, miniature trees packed into buckets to cut down on the breeze from the brackish canal. It was summer, still the evenings sometimes blew cool. Not this one. This evening was stifling. A few punks, scuzzy but happy, sat mohawked, bare chested, feeding decomposing mice to their domesticated ermine. I was about to follow suit, had my shirt halfway up my beer gut when he sat down—just when the sun was coming down.

Prose descriptions are safer than photographs (pics) and movies (vids). No one would ever identify the hero of a novel, if he'd come to life, solely by his author's description. Let's face it: Raskolnikov—"his face was pale and distorted and a bitter, wrathful and malignant smile was on his lips"—is not being stopped on the street.

Across from me Mono sat reading that novel, in English of course. And English led to English—he asked what beer was I drinking, an Erdinger Dunkel, and ordered the same.

To make conversation I said, Too bad we're being served by the Russian. The Turk—turning my eye to the eye of her hairy navel—is way hotter.

This is not to my credit. To his he just smiled.

It was a tight smile, lips chewing teeth, as if he wasn't sure how fresh his breath was.

I don't know why Mono made an impression on my premillionaire self—maybe because when you're young and life's a mess, the world is, too: young and messy. It could also have been the beer, hopped on malt, its own head turning my head to foam.

I was in my mid-twenties, actually in that latter portion of my twenties, spiraling, like how a jetliner crashes, to thirty.

But Mono was young.

He had his decade in front of him.

We covered thirty: scary, scary.

Also we discovered we were both from Jersey—me from South, he from Central, but still.

Why here?

It was important to deliver this offhand. All expats worry about coming off spoiled or ludicrous, insane.

Why I came here was to write a book, I offered, which isn't working out.

He brought his mouth to his beer, not the other way around. The beard was still growing in.

He swallowed, said, *Achtung*, and as the sun disappeared, told me this story.

Back in Jersey—this was only two months before the time of his telling but anything Jersey felt like years ago, amenitized among diners and turnpikes—Mono was a deliverer.

Like a priest: delivering from sin?

Or a recent arrival from Fujian with the fried rice, the scooter?

No, what Mono brought were drugs.

Drugs paid well but only for those actually supplying. Mono merely supplied the supply. This was not *the ideas economy*—whatever was supposed to save this country once we'd stopped physically making anything of value.

This was effort, was pick up, drop off, keep all names out of it and deal exclusively in cash. (FYI, Benjamin Franklin is one of only two people featured on bills never to have been U.S. President.)

Mono worked for a man—and he was a man with multiple children and women and not a lost lanky kid like Mono—who called himself Methyl O'Nine (as in cocaine, benzoylmethylecgonine, also zero and nine were the last two digits of his retired pager).

He was a short, slim but muscled, comparatively black man with a ritually dyed henna fleck of a goatee discreet beneath voluminous dreads, like plumbing gone awry.

Mono spent weekends moving his product.

Methyl was a hushed seclusive type—not just careful but temperamentally dervish in his sandals and gangsta hoodies—and never wanted his deliverers to know where he lived or with whom he supplied, and so he'd meet Mono as he'd meet all the others who did Mono's job, on discrepant dim corners in Trenton.

Whenever he called, Mono went and Mono went wherever Mono was called, which meant a lot of driving the Ford from near campus to fields and wharves and the parking lots of mid-priced restaurants.

Ford: bad brakes, transmission with the shakes, used to be his mother's.

Campus: a fancy private university approximately an hour south of New York.

Methyl's customers were mostly students—the idle rich, studiously clubby douches and athletic fratters, the occasional slumming neo-Marxist—but there were also the professors both adjunct and tenured. Some needed the drugs to write the papers, others needed the drugs to grade the papers, all needed the drugs—which they'd snort from atop the papers with rolled paper bills.

The students lived in student housing, the faculty lived in faculty housing (most student and faculty housing was identical), but Mono lived just outside Princeton—sorry, my mistake—in a collapsing bleachers of an apartment complex tenanted exclusively by the lowest-paid support staff: the sad diabetics who mopped up the home-game vomiting and this one security guard who protected the academics on weekdays but on weekends was regularly arrested in spousal disputes.

Mono hated being thought of as a dealer, as a danger. No respect for his opinion, no regard for his mind. And so he'd intimate deadlines, make allusions to debt, often just outright say it.

Enrolled but in another department.

Grothdyck? I snoozed through his seminar last spring.

I'm not sure if any of the students believed him, though I'm not sure what reason they'd have not to believe him and anyway it wasn't exactly a contradiction to be both enrolled and an impostor, a fine student and seriously druggish, deluded.

Mono's father had taught mathematics at the university—he'd made major advances in knot polynomials, applied them to engineer a tamper-proof model for voting by computer—and so was sure his son's application would be accepted, despite the crappy grades.

But it wasn't, it was rejected.

When he finally sold the house and moved away to chair the math department of a school in California—this was about six months before

239

Mono and I sat together over beers in Berlin—Mono decided to remain.

Mono's mother had died—an aneurysm after a routine jog, a clean body in a bloodless bath—three years before these events. Her death was why his father had wanted to move, though Mono thought his failure to have been admitted to school had an influence—his father's professional humiliation (Mono was a professional at humiliating his father).

And the car his mother left behind precipitated Mono's fight with his father—when the professor began dating a former student or began publicly dating her. She'd brought the largest veggie-stix-'n'-dip platter to the gathering after the funeral.

She was also from Yerevan—super young and super skinny and tall with curly red hair curled around a crucifix that oscillated between the antennal nipples of her breasts—and as long as we're confusing ourselves with chronology, she was just two years older than Mono.

His mother's ailing Ford became his because his father already had a convertible.

Then one afternoon his father asked, Could you lend Aline your car for the day? She wishes to consolidate her life before the moving.

Mono said he said nothing.

His father tried again, Could you drive her yourself, to assist with the boxes?

Mono explained:

That was his father's way of telling him that Aline was coming to Cali.

My mother's car? Mono finally asked.

But you can forget about Aline. She's pregnant with Mono's half brother in Palo Alto and this is her last appearance.

At the time Mono's name was not yet Mono. That name was as new as Berlin.

Like monolingual, he'd said when we shook hands (his hand was sweaty).

Whereas the surname he'd been given was much more distinctively foreign. Not that he was supposed to divulge that name to his customers—to them, until he ruined himself, he was only *Dick*.

To get him to loiter outside your dorm or stand around licking fingers to count bills on the rickety porch of an off-campus sorority, you dialed

Methyl, who'd say, He be calling a minute before he shows. Name of Dick.

Dick would usually show up within a half hour and though he was supposed to only get paid and leave, he never followed Methyl's instructions.

Instead he'd play older brother, stacking used plastic cups, making troughs of new ice, holding class presidents steady upside down for keg-stands, reveling in free drinks and ambient vagina until recalled to work with a vibrating msg: NW6, say (Trenton's North Ward location six, where he'd make the night's next pickup—Methyl didn't trust anyone out with more than three deliveries at a time).

Dick stayed out later the later in the night he was called, and so on a three A.M. delivery to a party that had run out that a colleague, *Rex*, had delivered earlier that evening, a party pumping for six or seven hours already through music playlists both popularly appropriate and of someone's step-dad's collection of Dylan bootlegs and whose mixer juices and tonics had been exhausted, *Dick* would not be moved, especially not when a girl—the same girl who'd called Methyl, who'd told his deliverer to expect a female customer—threw arms around him and said:

They sent *you* this time!

Dick, who prided himself on remembering all his customers, couldn't be sure whether this girl, Em, was pretending to remember him or just wasted—and this should have been his first warning.

The couch, the absorbent couch, furniture in appearance like a corkscrew coil of shit—brown cushions, black backing worn shiny—soaking in the boozy spill and smoke of years, intaking fumes and fluids through the spongy membrane of its upholstery. They sat there, he and this girl who knew him only as *Dick*—this townie fake gownie and though he didn't know it yet the daughter of a Midwestern appliances manufacturer who maintained, this daughter did, upwards of thirty anonymous Weblogs: *Stuff to Cook When You're Hungover*, *Movies I Recently Saw About Niggers*, *My Big Gay Milkshake Diary*, *The Corey News* (which warned of the depredations of child stardom), *What I've Heard About Bathrooms in North America*—all irregularly updated but all updated.

They sat doing lines—is that my line? that's your line? this line's mine— and all was weightlessly intimate until Em turned to him and said:

This is from yours right?

Dick didn't answer immediately so she asked again.

This is on you?

Dick said, Sure.

Sure?

Whatever. We'll figure it out.

Em said, No, not whatever. No figuring. Say it for me!

He felt like he had to stop himself from peeling her lips off her face as if they were price stickers, like they were designer labels as she said again:

Say it for me! This is your supply.

He said, This is *your supply*.

Em smiled.

Okay, this is my shit. This shit is mine.

And she laughed and said, Dick! I'm so glad they sent you!

And he said, Actually only people who work for me call me Dick. My name's really Rich.

Rich?

Richard.

Rich hard what?

I'd show you my license, if I had it.

He'd been craving this opportunity to brag.

I was jumped last month in Philly, rival dealers, took my narcotics and wallet (a lie: he'd been drug-free on his way to a job interview as a bartender, the muggers barely pubescent, three kids as stubby as their switchblades).

You don't carry ID?

He reached into a pocket, found his passport, passed it around.

Em flipped through it, Did you enjoy Mexico?

I went with my parents.

You were an ugly child.

Discussions were: over changing the music and so changing the mood, about what band was good or bad in which years and with which personnel—is playing the bass harder than it looks? does a true lead singer have any business playing guitar?

Anyway what kind of person would say which—*personnel* as opposed to *lineup*? *lead singer* as opposed to *frontman*?

Is this coke cut? Is all coke cut? And how is that not the same as *lacing*?

What innocents they were, *Dick* thought—the purity was theirs, not the drug's.

This one guy said, There was this girl I used to go out with who was the transitional girlfriend of a kid who starred in like every fucking movie.

Who was it? the party wanted to know. What every fucking movie was he in?

The guy told them.

Famous right? Crazy crazy famous? Girls saved his face into screen savers, produced ringtones out of his voice. She was with him for three months off and on. Then I was with her and after our third or fourth date we had sex and you know what she said to me after?

What?

She said: *Peter, before you having sex was just like staring at the ceiling.*

Like what?

Again: *Like staring at the ceiling.*

And that night that coital praise became an inside joke, like, whatcha-callit, a party trope.

When someone went to the kitchen, opened the fridge, and retrieved another beer for you it was, Before you drinking beer was just like staring at the ceiling, when someone tapped out a thick fat line for you with their parents' Platinum Plus Visa card on the glass slab tiered above the baize bottom of the house's three-quarter-size poker table it was, Before you coke was just like staring at the ceiling, then that prefatory endearment was dropped with the tense and it was only, This couch is just like staring at the ceiling, This floor is just like staring at the ceiling, This ceiling's just like staring at the ceiling.

You had to be there, but you're lucky you weren't.

Somebody left to buy the ingredients to bake a pie, somebody left to buy a pie, somebody left.

Cakes v. pies were debated, cupcakes v. muffins were, too, the salient differences between them, the identities of the world's greatest lacrosse players were discussed, various names proposed both at the college level and pro. Pressing questions asked and answered: What's more degrading, working as a stripper or working as a maid? What's the best position to have re: Iran—preemptive strikes or sanctions inevitably targeting women and children? What's the best sexual position for vir-ginity loss—for a man, for a woman, for a child? Is there a future for campaign-finance reform after the veritable abortion of *Citizens United v. FEC*? If you could repeal any amendment to the Constitution, which (no one allowed anymore to pick the first ten, whichever amendment repealed Prohibition, or the thirteenth, fourteenth, and fifteenth)? If you were a fart, what type (how wet, what smell)? Ten Most Mortifying Moments? Most egregious party foul? If you could describe your entire life in only one word to only one dead grandparent, which grandparent and what word?

Etc.

Mono's apartment had been advertised as a one-bedroom but having remitted the deposit he admitted to himself, why not, it was a studio. What the realtor maintained made it a one-bedroom was a small little nothing nook by the door so minuscule that whenever Mono wanted to open the door he had to move the television onto the bed. His TV slept better than he did. The door's peephole had been blackened for a robbery. The window opposite gave onto parking lot, he never kept it open, gas. On the floor, lotto stubs, scratchers he'd scratch with teeth. Under-labeled whiskey under the label. Flies at the bottom of a liter of cola. In the bathroom clothing hung from the showerhead smelling alternately feculent and moldy. The sink was mustached with shavings. He'd been using takeout napkins as toilet paper for a month. The sounds he'd hear by morning were those of mice the size of his pinky sprayed newborn from the walls or, once, the whining die of the smoke detector's batteries. The apartment had no light because the bulbs had burnt out and he never remembered to replace them. Anyway Mono was rarely home at night and the television was enough light and the computer was sufficient, too.

Mono was ISO work. He was perpetually interviewing and applying himself to applications because what's life for a man in the middle?

Interrupting binges where if you didn't have what they wanted you yourself weren't wanted.

Only feared.

Meeting people furtively but trying to be kind. Yet having that kindness misinterpreted.

I don't care what you think about the Yankees' outfield, one kid said, I just want my fucking drugs.

Yankee wants his fucking drugs? Mono unsure of what to say.

The kid apologized.

Accidental, his initial involvement. Mono had begun delivering when he began owing Methyl money—short one night on an eightball he was supposed to have split before a food court coworker bailed (that one week Mono worked at Quaker Mall).

He knew he had to get out when this past New Year's down the Shore at a condo shuttered for the season a fierce former valedictorian who'd strolled with him along the snowy beach had said, Let's continue this conversation some other time—a convo about renewable energy—like when I'm sober and you're not my dealer.

Mono had had sex with her lesbian friend that night: she was stretch mark-mangled, solicitous. She'd feigned abandon, collapsed on the bed, but just when Mono wanted to fall asleep she went to the bathroom to brush teeth, which was tender. The next morning she picked his jeans up from the floor and turned the pantlegs rightside out while Mono repositioned the pair of athletic socks in his jacket's breast pocket—an advertisement for his packing a gun. That was the only time he'd had sex this year.

The résumé he'd been sending around he'd falsified: his experience including six months as executive assistant in a film production company he'd created, a year as a consultant to a pharmaceutical consulting firm for whose HR hotline he gave his own phone, figuring he could talk drug distribution with the best—while his other references tended toward the suspiciously familial: his cousin who'd developed a dating Web site and was too lazy busy getting laid to pick up the phone, another cousin who did the ordering for but did not own as Mono had stated Trenton's North Triangle Liquors—though when it came to education he demurred: granting himself only a B.A. if cum laude, supplemented vainly by a Dean's Award in English.

Despite this, he'd become inured to rejection: Never called back by that Suburban Poverty Task Force that needed someone with a liberal-arts background to disorganize their archives, bend paperclips into helicopters and swans. Refused by that talent management agency requiring a front-office rep, or receptionist (he was overqualified, they qualified). A limousine driver, a limo dispatcher (ditto). Each being the juniormost position each business offered.

Monday punctually at noon the phone rang and Mono answered and a voice said, Mr. Monomian (the pronunciation was passable), I'm calling from Skilling Militainment Solutions.

Mr. Skilling, Mono said.

There is no Skilling. This is O.J. Muggs, recruiter, ret. capt. Marines.

Mono, sitting up in bed, said, Sir.

I'm afraid we can't offer you the position.

You can't? The position? But I haven't even been interviewed.

You won't be. This does not constitute an interview. Please say yes, indicating your understanding.

No, I don't understand.

Don't fool yourself, son. Not even civilians are exempt from civility. Security isn't just armed convoys, it's also a sound reputation.

What's unsound about my reputation?

What you do in private is your business, until it becomes public, and then it's your employer's business, especially if your employer's employed by the government of the United States. War's all about image—and effective chaplaincy and counterinsurgency.

Come again?

You need to clear your profile, son.

My profile, what about it?

Your presence, you need to clean your presence.

I'm not following, and Mono canvassed his apartment, wondering whether the man had a camera focused on him or was just intuitive.

The Internet, Muggs said, are you aware of your Internet?

Mono was not aware of his Internet. He'd never made a habit of googling himself—it was too depressing of a venture.

Previously his life had passed undetected by bots. His life too modest for hits, too meek for the concerns of blog postings and tweets.

Mono had always taken such paucity personally—virtual presence being, to him, presence nonetheless.

Whenever he searched there were only two results, two matches found: the first listing his name along with others of his class from Princeton High, the second aggregating what had to be all the names of all Jersey high-school graduates ever to redirect them to wealth-management services and medical-tourism sites.

But now still abed, after ending the phone call, tugging his computer close and keying in *monomian*—typeable with two fingers, every letter but one kept to the right of the keyboard—he found a third.

The blog was called *Emission*.

The link was that optimistic bright blue that after Mono clicked would turn to the drab abused and nameless color of vomit.

The post's heading RICHARD MONOMIAN.

Mono withheld his vomit.

246

He scrolled to the end and the post was signed with that single name, Em, time-stamped midday the day before.

But just as he was about to read the whole post from the top his computer emitted a pop—his father was messaging him over chat:

Greetings, Diran!

That was Mono's birthname, before Richard.

Why are you not returning my calls?

Mono messaged:

cant talk now dad, then deleted.

Mono messaged:

its rich dad, then deleted again.

His father messaged:

Diran, it is my hope you are not ignoring me.

Mono clicked the chat box shut, blocked his father from chatting.

He read on:

Friday night @ party with RICHARD MONOMIAN. *He brought 'snax.'*

Wink! wink!

Thats what he does for a living. He brings snax that are OK priced but also of crackhead quality.

Anyways.

Were all just hanging out smoking getting our drink on telling stories about former bfs and gfs when RICHARD MONOMIAN *tells us this story.*

About another party he went to.

A highschool party.

Now when the guy who brings the snax begins doing the snax and telling stories about highschool you know its time to bag for home but for some reason we didnt.

This was spring break, end of senior year.

Before P'ton, obvs.

It was a big houseparty at a big house with the hosts parents away—remember those?

It ended with everyone oblitermerated passed out on random beds in random rooms and RICHARD MONOMIAN *searching around for an empty bedroom to crash in.*

And he found like a guestroom or spare for using the computer or phone in room and there was a bed in the corner or like a foldout sofa.

A girl was sleeping.

RICHARD MONOMIAN *said he didnt remember her name but even if he had remembered it and told me I wouldnt repeat it, thats not my style.*

RICHARD MONOMIAN *said this sleeping girl was cute, I guess not cute enough to rape.*

Instead he pulled his pants down below his ass tits and pulled down his underwear also.

RICHARD MONOMIAN *grabbed his penis and stroked—he stood over her and stroked it!!*

Dick fisting his shit! Dick fisting his shit!

Dick grabbed his hard dick hard and below him the girl kept sleeping.

He was on MDMA I think.

I think ecstasy and weeds.

Highlarious!

Suddenly he came: RICHARD MONOMIAN *blew a load that landed in her hand.*

RICHARD MONOMIAN *said he didnt wipe it up because he didnt want to wake her, he just pulled up his underwear and pulled up his pants and fell downstairs and out the door for home.*

Thats it.

All the deets I have.

Retardedly I didnt take a pic of him last night and cant find a pic online but Im sure one of my readers can and if you can then fwd: because I sometimes need a pic to look at to get less horny, Subject line: because I sometimes need a pic to look at to get less horny,

(And if youre that girl who woke one morning on a strange sofabed in a strange house with a jizzy palm worried about what happened, maybe you ran out to get tested, maybe you ran out to get the pill—this is it, youre welcome, be careful where you fall asleep, sista.)

At least his pic wasn't available. That was the best benefit of his previous anonymity.

Mono tried to remember what pics of him were around. Not many, few digitized. School portraits, a few snaps with friends moved away to colleges and family poses, most of which his father had storaged. Easier to imagine a picture of yourself than to imagine yourself. He thought, why is it so hard to remember colors? And did anyone else think of death while being shot for an employee ID? (Besides the passport the only photo of himself he had was just that, from that week pretzeling at Quaker Mall.)

He stayed in bed, blowing through what cash he had left ordering to his door medium pizzas and Asian noodle decoctions waiting for Methyl to call with his next assignment as the legitimate world with its legitimate rewards stopped calling, stopped responding to his calls—him sitting up in bed, with the pillow verticalized between his legs as stuffed buffer between computer and any Monomians to come, searching himself, researching his name, "within quotes."

Three results went to four when another blog he suspected this Em of hosting linked to the *Emission*, then four upticked to six when two readers of those blogs linked up from blogs of their own.

Sometimes it was just an embed singly described, *Disgusting*, at other times it was a capsule blurb that transclused: *Em, a college girl from Jerzee who's been keeping a party diary, writes about a guy masturbating on top of a sleeping girl . . . NSFW.*

But that was a particularly responsible example and most of the keywords were rather: *Wrong, Sinister, This is just totally scrotally insane.*

People thinking this funny precisely because it was legend, social lore—it didn't happen to them:
next time sleep with an umbrella
next time my girls not in the mood im gonna give her a monomian cumbrella lol!
wear rubbers!!

Within a week a hundred-plus results all replicated his name as if each letter of it—those voluble, oragenital *os*—were a mirror for a stranger's snorting, reflecting everywhere the nostrils of New York, Los Angeles, Reykjavík, Seoul, as thousands cut this tale for bulk and laced with detail, tapped it into lines and his name became a tag for abject failure, for deviant, for skank.

To pull a Monomian.

To go Monomian.

Fucking Monomial.

No one, had you asked them, would have thought that he was real. Only he knew he was real. And he only knew that, he thought, by his suffering.

Mono was on the Internet all day but did not masturbate. Porn sites went unvisited. He'd type in half their addresses then stop and delete, hating himself because the computer couldn't hate him instead. The nonjudgmental nature of technology, if technology could have a nature—that struck him as unfair.

He restrained himself from leaving comments on Em's blog or from responding in any way by starting to blog himself because already people were posting under his name, were posting as *him*: Richard_Monomian, Rich_Monomian, Dickhardmon, Monosturbator69, each claiming to be "the real meatspace Monomian."

IRL I jerked in my own hand then inseminated her preggers (wrote Modick).

Actually the bitch was so passed out I gave her an anal alarm clock (wrote Dicknass).

The more the commenters commented, the more accurate even their inaccuracies felt, the more their elaborations felt essential.

The weekend after losing out on a janitorial job then failing to obtain two other minimum-wage positions (jeggings folder, organic waiter), Mono began searching for something else, not for this proliferating porno about himself but for a number of basic variations: "how to get something off the internet," "how to remove stuff from the net," "slander on the web," "info on online defamation and how to fight it," "how to destroy a website entirely forever," "is destroying a website technically legal if the work is contracted to someone in another country," "how to knock out someone's server if you don't know anything whatsoever about hacking or even what servers are."

He found a forum dedicated to cybersecurity that counseled a girl whose ex-boyfriend had uploaded a sex vid to contact a lawyer and sue for removal plus compensation.

One chat room included a comment from a genuine lawyer—"A Verified User"—advising a man whose wife had put up a Web site accusing him of being a compulsive gambler and not paying child support to contact him, he'd send a Cease & Desist for cheap.

That must have worked because the link www.myexhusbandrandy isalyingdegenerateteenfuckinggamblerwhosbadinbedanddoesnotpay forhisonly childsfoodandmedication.com was no longer functional.

Also the lawyer advised him to pay his child support: Buddy, that's just Christian.

Mono searched for lawyers in his area by typing "lawyers in my area." The number-one result was a Web site called "What Is a Good Web Site to Find Lawyers in My Area." Like digging a hole to find a buried shovel to use to dig a grave.

Then Mono typed in "how to get people to take down libel from online," adding the local zipcodes.

At the bottom of the first page of results, the tenth hit, was a link to a digital paralegal.

That's what the header said, Da Digital Paralegal.

Mono didn't hesitate, his connections did: B$_4$UGO Network gave two bars, Chuck's Den gave three, Sally Sally Wireless Home—finally full-strength.

He arrived at a site either terribly low-tech or trying to keep the lowest of profiles: a page all blank white like paper with only a single address centered, the contact, *dp@dadigitalparalegal.com*, not even clickable—it had to be typed into the To: line of an e-mail.

What Mono sent this address was tentative, vaguely worded: *Hello, my name is Richard and I am inquiring after your services*, and though it was very late at night—though these were his normal working hours, beginning around midnight when, if Methyl had called, he'd be commuting the speed limit down U.S. 1 South between campus and the strip joints of Trenton—the DP wrote him back within the minute, before he had the chance to sign off, amid a last reloaded scan of the news:

Climate change was being called a sort of temperature socialism—it redistributed warmth to the colder months. This winter had set records. A woman gave birth to triplets, her twin to quintuplets. The father of all—the nondescript fertility doctor.

Elections don't end wars.

The DP's e-mail, terse:

U still up—just call me, then it gave her number. Her name, appearing not as a signature by dully fonted macro but as if by regular typing, was *Majorie*.

Hello, *Majorie?*

No reason she'd let it ring ten times.

Yes, the voice lidless, up, what time is it?

You asked me to call.

No, I know. I'm aware of my e-mail.

This is Dick.

Dick who?

Reluctance then because he'd have to say it anyway, Richard Mono-mian, and then he spelled it out.

It's good to meet you M-O-N-O-M-I-A-N.

Behind her voice he could hear a toilet flush.

How does this work?

You were rather unclear in your initial query. But let me tell you to start, investing in taxi medallions is 100 percent safe and legal—a burgeoning business. I myself own ten I've leased at absurdly favorable terms.

You've lost me.

I have a comprehensive information packet if you'll only give me your mailman address.

My mailman's address? I'm calling about the Internet.

A pause and then, *Mailman's address* is just a code, of course—if you were active in the Celebrity Privacy movement you'd have answered *my mailman has no address*, then we'd be talking business. I take it you're no technophile.

No, I'm a courier.

A courier. Is that your only problem?

Now after the toilet a sink ran. Majorie might've been washing her hands. Which Mono chose to take as the mark of a professional.

And you're a paralegal?

In the interests of disclosure I'm a paraparalegal. It's the same difference pretty much.

And where are you located? Could I come by your offices and talk?

Majorie gave a cough or burp, an unforthcoming eruction.

Excuse me, she said, I'm out-of-state.

Don't you realize we have the same area code?

I prefer to do business over the phone.

Why?

Security.

Are you recording this?

It's a federal law that you have to tell someone when you're recording their conversation.

Are you telling me that you're recording our conversation?

No.

Mono suspecting now that her office was her residence, which was a disaster, had to be. He heard—suspected he heard—junk-food wrappers crunch under slipper as she stalked around, as if testing the echoes of a floor's worth of partially furnished rooms in an old drafty inherited house: from the reverberant bathroom she, they, seemed to be now in a larger room or long hallway.

She told Mono she could help him, that she did this type of freelance all the time.

Her voice was backed by clacking keys or particularly strident cicadas.

Do what?

First I customize a letter for your situation then I e-mail it to the Webmaster or mistress of the originating offending URL—that's Uniform Resource Locator.

What does this letter say?

It's your standard-issue unequivocal demand: remove the original post from both Web site and cache and post instead a short retraction.

Saying?

This post has been removed. Or would you prefer a public apology?

I think the less said about it the better.

Then I'll ask the Webmistress to sign her name to another e-mail acknowledging the site falsified its information before sending that around to every linking site asking them to likewise take down content and threatening suit if they refuse to comply.

Every linking site?

Tell me this: is what Em wrote true—did you really spray all over that girl?

Mono, stymied, asked, We can't be sure that Em's her real name, can we?

Doesn't matter.

How long is this going to take?

There's no guarantee—the Web's like sweaty footwear: stuff lives in there forever.

Mono imagined the smell of her slippers—sweat: ammoniac, uriniferous, vinegar, chipotle sauce.

How much do you need?

I won't accept payment in narcotics.

Could you get started tonight?

I'll get started the moment you transfer $1000. Paypal to my e-mail.

I'm on it.

Don't worry, she laughed, I won't fall asleep on the job, and only the next morning did he realize she was making a joke about him splooging all over women in their somnolence, which wasn't funny.

Hey Kidderoos guess what Mama got today?

Re: that salacious stroking tidbit of earlier last week? . . . Just a note, below, after the jump.

Toward week's end the *Emission* posted not any scripted retraction but a screenshot of the retraction request itself, accompanied by Em's commentary:

This type of coercion has no legal basis whatsoever, Im not even pre-law and I know this.

So let me make this as clear as clear as clear can be, which on the Internet MEANS CAPS:

I WILL NOT PUB A RETRACTION, Online Fidelity Fixers or whatever your ridongculous company is called that has no history anywhere, I dont think has ever been incorporated or registered or you get what Im saying and certainly has never filed taxes in the State of New Jersey [this hyperlinked to a state taxation page that said, "terms: 'Online Fidelity Fixers': No Record(s) Found"].

This story Richard Monomian told me is TRUE.

He knows it is TRUE.

That he knows it is TRUE and nothing but the TRUE is why he hired you, Online Fidelity Fixers.

I looked you up globally, suckers!

What have you ever done? Your website hasnt been updated in two years [hyperlink to Web site]

Who designed it, a retardy chimpanzee [hyperlink to vid of chimp, unclear as to whether retarded but still slurping its own feces]?

This email of yours is just a smear of yours truly. Funded by a desperate assaulter of women named Richard Monomian.

Who is also a dealer!

Whose coke is also BAD!

And you Mrs. J.K.M. Jorie, LA—l.egal a.ssistant requires an abbreviation, are you queerious?

This is amateur hour, yo.

By that later Thursday afternoon, the last waning work hours when bored deskbounds log on and comment to do anything but improve their own existences, tidy the file chains, or disburden the inbox, this post had racked up over three hundred and fifty responses like:

MunchieZ: right on girl!

anonymous: u tell it!

anonymous: I am a practicing lawyer in the city and you Em are cor-
rectamundo as always.

jd: Im with u. I call bullshit.

m@jd: Bullshit!

bullshit: Bullshit! (first!)

anonymous: this letter is not even worth the paper it is not
printed on.

{*Hugger89* and *go_deep* like that comment.

That comment had a comment—*see one reply*: monomaniacal wtf!?)

Friday morning after googling himself and finding that post Mono
called Majorie and got a voicemail that said: You've reached Broken
Wings: Last-Minute Frequent-Flyer Miles Broker to the Bereaved.

He waited for the beep, Call me. This is unbereavable.

He lay back in bed perusing a magazine he'd found weathered wet
and unsubscribed to in the hallway last week, read from the cover in a
whisper— *revista feminina*—as if a foreign language had the power to
save him from what he did understand (was the Internet as virulent in
Spanish or Italian, in German or French?).

He flipped the pages, past the makeup styles and recipe tips—what
Mexicans had the kitchens for this? had the flatware, stemware, and
jobless hours?—heading into an article headlined ¿QUÉ ES LA DEPILACIÓN
LÁSER?

Mono wondered if he'd ever be able to masturbate again. Not above
a sleeping stranger and not even to the Internet, which had been sexually ruined for him—but perhaps to this *revista*, that tan woman of
thumb proportions depilating herself on page thirty-four?

The phone rang and Mono picked up.

It wasn't Majorie but Methyl.

Which was good news—Mono having had no income in over a week.
Had all of Jersey stopped getting—depilated?

I'm coming over, Methyl said.

Under the cashmere overcoat Methyl wore only a wife-beater, the chest
hair coming in spirals like @ signs. Below were baggy jeans and between the jeans and beater was a full foot of red boxers exposed.

He came swaggering into the apartment, sat on the bed—there was
nowhere to sit but alongside Mono, Methyl waiting as the TV was repositioned, returned to the floor.

This all? he asked.

Mono asked, That mean you're giving me a raise?

Methyl had in his hands a gaming console as gray as a desiccated brain strangulated in black cords attached to two controllers.

It's a new game, he said, still in development. I gave these city guys some tips on how to make it rawer, they gave me a copy of the Beta.

He bent to fit plugs into sockets.

Balancing the console on top of the screen.

The TV showed a brick wall.

A man walked past the wall. Another man passed by the wall in a car. The man in the car lowered his window, yelled something indiscernible—*Hooooooo!?!?*—pumped one shotgun round that struck the walking man in the no-longer-walking head. The car continued, drove offscreen. The man's head broke apart, spattering the wall in seven spots of sanguinary graffiti that dripped down to form a word with seven letters: *Corners*.

Kids crept up to the corpse, pulled spray cans from the pockets of puffies and tear-away trainers and tagged the brick.

One wrote *1 Playa*—effective aerosol sound effect—the other scrawled *2 Playas.*

I play the dealer, Methyl said, you play the snitch.

The screen was splitscreen so there wasn't one wall now but two and they were different.

I'm gonna let you walk free for a while, Methyl said. Try and get a feel for the controls.

Mono the snitch walked to the end of the wall, which was the end of the sidewalk. He walked to the end of the screen but there was more screen. The next block was crowded with bodegary. Fat mamas pushed pushcarts stacked fat with bags of laundry, bags of rice. Hot mamacita hissed. Stolid old guy swept a stoop. Kids, rather trainee cholos, junior bangers.

A red blur burst from behind a tenement's billboard—pigeon graphics flying wildly out of frame as Methyl lunged at his controls, pressed Pause.

This billboard's trying to kill you. Playa's from a rival gang.

Mono asked, What gang am I in?

You used to be in my gang but you snitched me out so I'm trying to kill you too. But also the red niggas want to kill us both. And then the cops. You stay away from cops. I'm taking us off Pause. The second I do just cross the street. Red nigga won't get a clear shot.

Where's the map? Mono asked.

Ain't no map. Just gotta memorize the streets.

Memorize them how?

Lady Liberty knish take the A train, motherfucker! Don't you know New York?

Not the outer boroughs.

We in Manhattan—me uptown, you down. I have it saved in memory to start my every game on 145th and Amsterdam—Playa 1 starts by default down at Delancey but you can program any block.

Then Methyl quieted and said, Ain't like we in Staten Island.

Snitch heading north up Orchard.

Trendoid gastronomes. Theme outlets that had paid to be included in the game.

Methyl spinning sewer lids like record platters. The sound track robotic cucaracha.

Then the snitch stood and did nothing because Mono was watching Methyl's screen half. The dealer was covering major blocks at a major clip shooting everything that moved—everything that moved that was malevolent. He took out pimps in parked cars, slaughtered whole drug deals and arms sales in dumpstered alleys and basements. Wasted lookouts execution style. Then stole the drugs and arms for later resale. He stopped by a restaurant, ate soul food. He helped himself to seconds, a double order of biscuits to go. He stole a Mercedes coupe and drove off his half of the screen until the two screens converged with the car pulling up on Mono's block.

Mono managed to turn around, fumbled.

Methyl, stepping from the Merc, held his gun sidewise, shot Mono in the face (button A to draw, B to cock to tricksy side, C to pull the trigger).

Screen nasty black with game blood.

You dead, Methyl said.

Me?

You fired, too.

I am? I thought you'd come with work.

Methyl sat up, turned to him and said, Any other business you survive this. But the cops today, they online all the time.

People don't know I'm him.

They will.

I'm fucking broke, bro.

The Internet says you just that guy who whips it out. But I say you an onus.

257

Instead of unplugging the gaming console Methyl unplugged the TV, put the controllers atop the console on top, boosted the entire package.

Then he stood on the bed while Mono, getting the silence, got up to get the door.

With the TV's powercord pocketed, Methyl stepped to the floor and walked out to the hall, saying without turning around, I was you I'd start thinking about how to change your name. Bro.

Without the television Mono's apartment seemed both bigger and smaller, and worse.

He should've handled this himself, Mono decided Sunday night when he was down to his last thousand dollars and applying for credit cards online: should've found Em's address or phone through pleading at keggers and honor-society socials, then handwritten a letter or called personally, throwing his future on her mercy or just paying her off, throw her a couple hundred or even a thousand—that would've cost the same if not less and less worry.

He shuddered whenever the phone rang.

Majorie? He didn't think Ms. Airline Miles Mogulette ever intended to return his call.

She sputtered, I hope you're not recording this.

I last asked that of you.

Never mind. I've been talking to Tech.

Who?

My support guy.

Who guy?

My computer person.

Okay.

But this is mondo illegal, shaky shaky ice. I never said that. I've never done this before.

Done what?

He lit a smoke.

I'm liaisoning with my liaison, my hacker. He's going to hack into this Em woman's blog and erase the original entry then he's going to do the same to all the other sites, I think.

You think? trying to stabilize the ashtray on a knee.

Or else he's going to send them all a virus that destroys everything but leaves no trace, I don't know, I'm no gearhead, just a paraparalegal.

We're talking additional costs?

The tray teetered, heaping.

It's a sliding scale.

A slide beginning where?

We're not prepared to quote just now. We'll send you an e-mail with the figure.

We?

Myself for project management but mostly the Tech for the tech stuff.

And who is he or she exactly?

Richard, when it's against the law, I'm against naming names.

What are the risks?

We assume more risk than do you—that's also why it's expensive, if it's traceable it's to us.

But then you're traceable to me.

Plus it's time intensive—there are worms to code, firewalls to crack.

You sure you know what you're talking about?

It's not a minor undertaking, having to stealthify kludge all that daemon javascript and such—Tech was explaining it all just this morning.

Mono's cigarette was finished except for the filter, the foam pellet he thought of popping into his mouth as if a pacifier, chewy.

I'll call you back when the process is in process, Majorie said. Do you have any pay phones in your neighborhood?

I have pay phones in my neighborhood.

Find the number of one, making sure it's not the most convenient but pick one a ways far out then e-mail that number to me spaced over ten e-mails, one digit per e-mail, you with me?

With you.

Then intersperse each digited e-mail with other e-mails containing links to, I don't care, hardcore penetration, but none of the e-mails can be sent from your address—be sure to open other accounts with multiple providers.

Didn't I tell you I'm through watching porn?

Then send me more better news, Rich—I have no idea what's happening.

There are wars on.

Mono sent her links.

On Wednesday it felt like winter was finally breaking. The ice could crack for the grass to sprout and a warm breeze could balm the parking lots and roundabouts and it was fine—winter would be back next year. Mono would be shattered forever.

He put on his coat and walked to the only pay phone he was sure of, located just outside the university's main library—every student body could use that phone every day though they never did, they all had phones of their own that didn't require booths. He'd recently forwarded Majorie a link to an article—a Web exclusive, never printed in hard copy—about the phone book's disappearance. They were going to stop universal distribution—this, the one book everyone could be in.

Students were coming out of the library but none clutched books, they held each other.

And a new beverage for a new generation, not bottles of water but *bottled water*, plastic, perspirant.

They didn't need books because of the bags on their shoulders, which contained computers—tablets and pads on which they could read all that'd been written by anyone ever and also Em on Richard Monomian.

The phone rang but his rush to pick up was unnecessary.

Students, children essentially, pedestrated past as blithe as projected light.

He said, My mailman has no address.

Pigeons alighted on the pathway slabs, pecking at butts and clots of gum.

Was that the password?

You tell me.

We're on track but also delayed.

Which is it?

Both. Plus I need that second thousand.

Behind her speech Mono made out the riddling whirr of her computer's cooling fan, the high screech of either passing sirens or neglected pets.

It wasn't that it wasn't spring enough yet or that it was sunset already—he was chilled from being scared, feeling himself recognized by all who passed. He remembered there had been another phone by the gym. Nothing remained besides a stanchion tumescent from a speck of foundation.

Can I call you back from my mobile?

And subvert our subversion—what kind of subterfuge is that?

I'm paying you—so you find a pay phone, e-mail me the number, set a time, and I'll also call ten minutes late.

That's precisely what I wanted to talk about. You have my invoice. I have material expenses.

Must be a reason I didn't respond to your e-mail about the next installment.

Richard, it might be better if we talked about this once you're comfortably at home.

Mono had begun to suspect that this hacker of hers, this gensym guru he was never allowed to talk to, was not a person, not a man or woman and so not her lover as Majorie let on, claiming access to him at all hours: when Mono called from home bonged stuporous slack drunk at three A.M. on Thursday asking to be reminded whether they were trying to infiltrate the sites to remove the posts or just crash them with a Trojan she said, Let me ask him. He's sleeping just right next to me. Then there'd be a murmur that had to be her respiration—Mono got the idea she never even took the phone from her mouth to imaginarily rouse this imaginary partner—until she'd say, Tech's grouchy, not getting up. He had a rough day yesterday. I'll ask him over breakfast and check in with you tomorrow.

Mono wondered how delusional Majorie really was, whether she'd invented an illusory male or, worse, she actually regarded her desktop itself as her lover: wedging its switches between her lips and flicking.

On the Friday noon call, which Mono also instigated—Damn, you missed him again! Techie just stepped out for frogurt!—Majorie was saying these blogs had incredible security.

These blogs that were just default regular and free for anyone to setup and whose platforms required no training for operation and were entirely intuitive to maintain—their protections were just top-notch.

It's amazing, she said, all my attacks are repelled (she'd already slipped into the singular).

Mono grunted.

No offense works, I don't know what's wrong. I've followed all the instructions, took that extra class online, even signed up for the personalized tutorial.

Feels good I'm not the only one being scammed.

Which reminds me, Monday at the latest. Are you sending me my cash?

Monday I'm sending you a sympathy $100.

But there's a program I need.

Your invoice said it was for a line of code.

I need both. Also have to pay the Internet bill. Three months over-due. Not everyone's a signal thief.

$100. No more payments after that.

Richard, we're in this together, both our reputations are at stake. She posted my name! my real name!

Her name was Marjorie Feyner.

It was a Wednesday again, a new credit card had arrived, was activated by the ordering of Mexican *muy picante*, and Mono had begun to think about that name change. His computer booted to Word, the .doc scrolled boldly with his mothers maiden name: *White, Richard White, Rich White, R. White*.

In search results for just the word *monomian*—unenriched by Richard—he was still the sixth or seventh, the first five or six being the man who'd named him.

But *Richard White* was limitless—it was a nothing name, a nothing being. There was a Dr. Richard White OB/GYN, a Richard White, Esq., "Rick" White the builder/general contractor, Richard White the ac-countant, the actor/voiceover artist, the character in multiplatform franchises, movies, and television shows (the Internet tending to cata-log other media and not differentiating between an actor's name and a character's), even a Catholic martyr or errant knight—Richard the White?

One self-declared as a pre-op transsexual.

Mono wondered had his father heard about this yet.

This was encouraging, this purity—reboot, restart. But Mono didn't know what the process was, what documents were needed to make such an alteration official, was about to search for the answer—after anyway replacing his appellation on his most current CV—when the phone rang.

Only one person called anymore, who said, Rich, I have another solution.

Try me.

I've had enough of this cracking crap—this password guess where you're given ten attempts at access then the account's frozen when you fail. Let's get back to the proven methods.

Which methods would those be?

Mono got out of bed, determined he needed more room for his cyn-icism, opened the door and walked out to the hall. A dull clatter at his sneaks, he swerved to avoid the neighbors' leaky trash bags, greasy bikes.

What's that noise? she asked.

I'm going out for air.

He walked down the hall to the door to the staircase, down the two tottering flights to parking—entirely vacant at midday, it was a lot of lot.

The stairs and landing were also cluttered with bikes—inextricably engaged, their wheels, pedals, and gears—locked to the railings. Mono maneuvered, steps following him, steps just behind him.

Suddenly he realized he'd ripped his phone from the wall with the charger still attached. He'd been dragging the cord behind him and turned to pick it up, stashed the scraping prongs and whatever length he could into his jeans' pocket.

Rich, she said, I finally decided to forgo the protocols and searched around for variations on Em—any Emma, Emily, Emilia, and Embeth @ princeton.edu. You're not supposed to do that. Every resource says it's better to abstract the adversary, best to keep them symbols: IP or an e-mail. Person-to-person, face-to-face, that's the nuclear option—no other way to go.

I searched that two weeks ago, Marj. You know how many Emmas and Emilys go to Princeton?

I found about a hundred possibilities.

Ninety-nine more than necessary. And before we go any further, tell me this, there was never any tech guy—it was all you just studying up.

Rich, forget Techie. He's over. Moved out. I've moved on. The circumstances have become exponentially more dire. My name's all over the Net. Another blog even uploaded a pic of me fatass at the beach. From Richter, Richter, Calunnia & Di'Famare's summer Law Lounge back when I was still employed.

Mono had to restrain himself from running inside, finding the image himself.

You checked all one hundred? he asked.

I plugged all their names into the usual social sites, opening a few false accounts to lurk. I took pains, signed in strictly from public connections. One persona joined the Princeton Jell-O polo team, another a networking group committed to combating squirrel chlamydia on campus. Then I got inspired: I opened an account under the real name and title of a real person who didn't have an account—an associate dean of academic affairs who taught undergrad humanities—who'd turn down a friend request from her? She asked to be friends with all the Ems, which gave me access to their profiles.

Impressive, Marj, but what did you find?

She's an Emmanuelle. I've e-mailed you her profile pic. When you get home I want you to verify then delete.

I'll be home in a second, Mono hurried back upstairs.

If you don't respond I'll know it's her.

You can just stay on the phone with me for another minute and I'll tell you right away.

Mono quickened through the hall.

First he googled for images of "Marjorie Feyner," uncovered that shorefront snap. She engulfed a bikini, held a plastic coconut, a fake hairy ball stuck with a straw. People were laughing in the waves—waves of surfboards and tubes—not laughing at her.

Everyone but her was tattooed.

Mono said, Bad strength of connection today. xxxprslaptop-BCrib, what a weakling.

In a new window a pic unfurled, Mono tugging its edge taut.

So? Marj asked.

It's her.

Here Em was, but pixilated younger, with shorter blonder hair hanging in wiry bangs. Braces like microchips programming an exaggerated dentition.

She was deep jawed, Mono recovered the memory—a mouth of gluttonous proportions.

She's a sophomore, major undeclared. I called the school, said I was her grandmother.

You should go easier on yourself.

I told school I wanted to send her a surprise package but lost her address—said I'd found her baby booties, stuffed them silly with favorite candy. The work-study brat said it wasn't their policy to relay that information. She suggested I call her parents—be in touch with your daughter, with your son-in-law, she said.

How responsible.

So I searched her friends and identified her high school, searched the local phone listings and called who I thought was her mom.

You what?

Said I was a high-school acquaintance of Em's just transferring schools—I positively detested it at Georgetown—and did you have her address as I wanted to get together?

You know—for a drink, take some pills, go to a club, have some seat down bathroom cunnilingus?

The mother offered her e-mail but I said I'd prefer her street address as my computer had just crashed—it's tragic, I lost everything.

You're jinxing yourself.

She asked, wouldn't you rather I gave you her phone?

Wouldn't you?

I was afraid it'd be a mobile but she gave me her landline, too.

And you did a reverse lookup?

I had to look up how to do a reverse lookup. You'll find them on my next invoice itemized separately.

And you're going to call or send a postcard? Or go over there yourself?

No.

Don't tell me I should go.

No, I've met a new man. I call him Alban. He's Albanian. He works security at my multiplex for the big crowds on the weekends. I'm always wasting Sundays and we talk. He lets me into a double feature no problem. I made a quiche for him last week.

Not Alban, his real name was Enver. He was a recent immigrant, born in Tirana. He worked for a security company that had classified his language skills as Minimal. Before moving to the area he'd lived in New York, which is where all immigrants live until they sleep with their brother's wife. Enver was not even attracted to her.

His brother's couch was three-cushioned, comfy. And his job, his first job his brother vouched for him, wasn't bad. Enver worked for a friend of his brother's at a pizza joint called, coincidentally, Two Brothers. Albanians being swarthy and proximal to the Mediterranean by birth pretending they knew their dough and cheese and sauce. But Enver wasn't allowed to make the pies. He was supposed to sit on a stool by the back door, held ajar by cinderblock, waiting until his brothers friend's minivan appeared on his monitor. Then he was to open the door all the way, accepting from this man, Arben, whatever he was handed. Electronics, often bags containing something that looked like flour but was not—it was heroin—and less often, bags filled with cash (the entire ring was busted).

Enver was lonely in Brooklyn. His brother came home late from Manhattan. His cousin in Staten Island hated Brooklyn. His cousin in

New Jersey hated Staten Island. Enver understood no relevant geography. Across the way was a hair and nail salon. That's it. No other fact or germane sensation.

He tried to make friends. Like when that one time he was allowed to work the register he didn't charge three kids for three slices plus diet grape sodas.

They looked hungry, Boss, he said to his boss, a taciturn elderly American with an erratic scar across his neck in the shape of a dollar sign who was the only employee permitted to make the pies and the next time Enver was in back watching the monitor and the minivan pulled up, when he opened the door Arben smacked him in the mouth and said, You looked hungry.

Arben said that in this language.

One night Enver spun home, spread himself like a fine crust on the couch and started watching—the TV, like the fraternal oven, was always on.

Appropriately disappointing: it was a cooking show, the woman in it was cooking.

Liridona, wrung from the shower, sat next to him.

The recipe was just some simple stir-fry.

Peel your vegetables, but lose your nutrients.

By the time the show had cut to commercial Liridona's robe was floored.

Next morning he left for Jersey, pawning himself off on a cousin. His brother never found out, that's why Enver was still alive with intact knees.

Enver said to his brother, Time for you to have babies, as if that explained his abandonment of the couch.

He went to sit for that test at a security company his cousin's friend moonlit for, went to a strip mall themed Early American Grange, sat at a desk exposed to a recently foreclosed storefront's glass—a former florist's, still perfumed—and pondered the questions.

They could use him, they explained, as store security—that was the best job, requiring some sort of intelligence and special training—with the worst being crowd control: bars and nightclubs, live events. Almost everyone was retired law enforcement. The proctor, a tubby Hispanic kid who taught communication skills at a community college (a frustrated stand-up comic), kept calling him "Erven," then "Mile High" because the corrected Enver sounded like *Denver*. They laughed through the exam. "Juan will be back _____ fifteen minutes." A) in; B) on; C) with; D) about.

Freshly flowering bushes and trees went out of their ways to impress beauty on the youth—the scads of polished khaki kids stalking the kempt paths, groping in the topiary. A frisbee flew overhead. Birds high up enough resembled frisbees. Another class earning credit by punting at soccer. Extraneous jackets were laid out for impromptu picnics. Water bottles wafting clarifying alcohol. A girl smoked a cigarette wedged between her girlfriend's toes.

She came out of Reading Freud PSY 23090, unbound from Green Hall and onto the green, headed toward Chancellor for a coffee. Did she want it iced? Indubitably. Anything to go with that? No, that will be all. It was like a phrase book come to life. What a terrifically executed textbook exchange, why thank you.

Emmanuelle wore mosquito-eye sunglasses, a T-shirt whose logo read *Brand*, her skirt never showed lines, no underwear map.

While she waited for change her phone rang, she took the call (from friend R., poli-sci major, public health minor, in the midst of a shaming crawl back from a date the night before with a thirty-three-year-old I-banker in the city), skimmed milk into her coffee and half a packet of artificial sweetener without bothering to stir.

At the testudinal traffic light she crossed.

College students driving adult cars, vehicles actually too fancy for any adult and perhaps better never driven. They drove them impulsively, alternately absent then reckless as if they already had jobs to get to.

Nassau Street laid the boundary of campus.

Em caffeinated while walking, hollowing her cheeks, pursing for suction then chatty again. Such oversize overactive labials. Let's imagine the waves radiating from her phone—what if they were visible? what if they were colored by her mood? Rainbows, refractive rainbows. Wavelets of talk coursing through the air, coursing daily through our own ears and mouths and minds—yet we're never privy to that talk. Or we'll become privy only when it develops into tumors on the brain.

Retail gave purchase to the quieter suburban.

At a corner with a receptacle she stopped, sipped her last, tossed the coffee inside—not a trash can but an empty newspaper vending machine.

267

The day was warming, still not warm enough for flip-flops—Em's thongs to soles athwack.

She took two more blocks then rounded the corner: Victorians—two floors, three floors—windows that hadn't been cleaned in failed semesters, porches in a slump. Stoops stooped. The lawns diseased.

Em stopped to tuck phone between ear and shoulder, scratched in her handbag for keys.

Enver crossed the street and waited at the bottom of the stoop until Em turned the key in the lock then he took the stoop in two steps and once on the porch gave her a smile of glittering fillings.

She kept the door open for him with a flip-flop. Thinking he was the roofer?

She was still on the phone but on hold. (Her friend's banker date had called, the slut beeped over.)

Enver entered, held the door.

She had a teensy stud in the left naris, a diamond pimple.

He waited for her to check mail.

Yes? Em turned to say, flicking hair into a quote behind the uphoned ear.

Enver closed his eyes. He couldn't talk while looking at her sunglasses.

What do you want?

She flipped shut her phone.

He said, I want you to change your blogs—opening his eyes only after remembering what Marjorie had told him—I want you to take what you say on your blogs about Mono Man down.

Excuse me?

She dropped the coupons received to the vestibular rug.

And then, he said, to send e-mail saying this was wrong and made up by you to everywhere also.

Also?

Linked, he was straining, posted.

That's impossible! flipping open the maw of her phone, with hard-bitten pink polish pressing three buttons then the most commodious, Send—and when she repeated, I want you to know how impossible that is! Enver knew she was stalling, for time, to call, the police.

He swiped at her phone, knocking it to fade its ring through the air as she kicked him with a flipper all gawky, sending her off balance—tricky this kicking in a skirt—and though he put out a hand and caught her before she fell, which must've been his attraction to her, which

268

must've been his, he knew the word from the only other language he knew besides this minimal language and Albanian, *tendresse* (there was so much his brother didn't know that came to light in court: he'd labored a full year in Marseille), with his other hand he made a fist and punched her, driving his knucks into her skull cradled by his hand.

From the floor the ringing continued.

A CCTV camera awning a deli two blocks east caught him on the run—add that to the testimony of Ems neighbor, a spooked Korean grad student Enver thrashed past on the stoop, spilling the kids' bachelor cold groceries: fruit and cereals, sprouts, soy yogurt.

Ludicrous to go back to campus—cameras, everywhere, had him everywhere, running between surveillances. Cutting between frames.

He was as big as a movie to the cops, who had him in custody within three hours (picked up hiding in a basement playpen at his cousins in Plainsboro).

At the Biergarteni paid for Mono's beers then checked my phone. I'd missed a few calls, had a few messages. Parents, delete. My landlord wanting to make a final Prussian inspection of the premises once my duffels had been shipped then get my keys. Girls, including one Amsterdam video artist with whom I had one unfilmable night. Do not del. The more attractive waitress, the Turk, was attempting Russian with the Russian, saying their *do svidanya*. A foosball careered across its tabled pitch. A slot machine clanked from the interior dank.

Mono said, Naomi.

She was Mono's cousin on his mother's side. They hadn't spoken in years—Mono had last seen Naomi at his mother's grave—yet it was she who saved him.

Both sets of parents had emigrated together, had already settled into Jersey and Ph.D. programs by the time they were Mono and Naomi's age, both had graduated together (1982), had bought their houses and had their children at the same time (Mono and Naomi were born the same month, 1984), bought their BBQs, bought their inground pools, opened their e-mail accounts—Mono related the success of this parental relocation, especially successful when compared with ours.

Though Naomi, unlike Mono, was said to have matured.

She was to marry a man so incidental to even his own self let alone to this tale that his name shouldn't be recorded—let's have tact, let's try for it.

About two months before Mono's exploits went viral Naomi's mother called to announce the nuptials and guilt him into being there—there being New York—the tacky boathouse in Central Park.

She jotted his address for a formal invitation, said, We'll catch up at the ceremony.

Mentioning, There's a girl I'd like to introduce you to. She's a nurse. She looks like A. Jolie.

I'm excited, was all he could say.

She said good-bye with: I called your father for your number. Don't worry, the Poz is not invited.

Poz being Armenian.

Mono, who did not speak Armenian, knew it meant *dickhead* or equivalent.

Imagine gripping the back fat of that nurselet for the slow dances, or having to replay the act behind his meme fame for his smuttier uncles in the bathrooms between the entrée and dessert—Mono didn't want to go, but he had to go: he'd already RSVP'd.

Still he procrastinated, waited until the Friday before the event to ball his only suit into his backpack—the suit black crisp funereal, worn to his college interview—and drive out to find the dry cleaner's.

He remembered a cleaner's adjacent to a tanning salon or ye olde historic sandwich shoppe.

Or else adjacent to both.

He didn't google, wished to locate by memory alone.

An hour later returning, having stopped at a diner to park a reuben in his gut.

His suit would be ready only on Sunday, they opened at noon. He'd have to crawl into the suit in the car on the way to the bus or the train.

Out on the patio it'd become a clear summer night—not cloying anymore but breezy perfection—I couldn't believe I had just a week of this left.

The smoke of our cigarettes the only clouds of the moon—closing time.

We were the only customers.

I wanted to offer Mono to pick up his suit, send it to him—airmail? or boat rate?

On me.

We haven't been in touch.

Mono said:

Squad cars surrounded his building. He knew they were idling for

270

him. For dealing, for whatever Marjorie Feyner had done—he didn't know Em was in a coma until resettled abroad, his second night insomniac in Paris when he'd checked that life online at a café.

Circling back, circling the lot.

His backpack was slung over the back of the passenger seat and inside the pack was his passport, which clinched it (the last codex, his last account, those durable blue covers).

They could have his computer, have bed and bare walls. His password, his password for everything, was *sdrawkcab* (remember it "backwards").

He drove his mother's car to Newark International, abandoned it in Parking. He wasn't in any databases yet. A ticket would be sold.

Nominated by The Paris Review, Don Waters

EVERYTHING IS SEXUAL
OR NOTHING IS. TAKE THIS
FLOCK OF POPPIES

by DIANE SEUSS

from BLACKBIRD

smoke-green stems brandishing buds the size of green plums,
      swathed in a testicular fur. Even those costumed in the burlesque
         of red crepe petals have cocks under their skirts, powdered
            with indigo-black pollen,

staining everything they touch. Either the whole world is New
      Orleans at 3 a.m. and a saxophone like a drill bit or it's all clinical
         sunlight and sad elementary school architecture, circa 1962,
            no broom closets opening into escape

hatches, no cowpokes with globs of sap skewered on hickory sticks.
      Either it's all New York in 1977, the Pan Am building lit up like a honey
         hive and erecting itself out of the fog, and one of us is a junkie
            and one of us is naked under a gold

skirt safety pinned at the waist and the material melts in the rain, either Kinky
      is playing the Lone Star and Earth is the women's john at the tail end
         of the bar and the stall doors have been blow-torched
            at the hinges and dragged away

by horses, either cunnilingus is an ocean salting every alleyway
      and lifting every veil or the French teacher did not masturbate
         beneath the desk as he taught the subjunctive, and lightning
            did not cleave the cherry tree and pleasure

its timbers. Either straitjacket, or shock treatment orgasm igniting
the dinner theatre, the actors cradling and hair-pulling, kissing
each other so deep some might call it brain surgery, the wigs
slipping, chintz curtains aflame, codpieces bursting

into flower, or what's left is a book of wet matches, my dear,
and it's all been for nothing, for didn't Jesus say you are
either with me or against me, from out of his blossom
of bloodshot dust?

Nominated by Blackbird, John Rybicki, Chad Sweeney

LUCKY ONE

by CHRISTÍAN FLORES GARCIA

from AMERICAN POETRY REVIEW

U.S./Mexico Borderline

There is only he, sister and I. And the moss green '86
Ford Granada running is our ride.

He says he's the one taking us to our parents. Orders
we hand over our belongings.

He reminds us that *we've never met*, if we get caught
again. He demands water, cigarettes,

extra matches and sanitary pads from the girl tending
the counter at the liquor store.

He talks on the phone about us. *Got the girls. Yes
wearing jackets. Yes*

*running shoes. Got their birth certificates. Yes, I know, I am
taking care of it. Yes, I'll feed them now.*

We wait. We sit. We hold hands, sister and I. He asks
which one is the lucky one?

Dropping a pink *Stayfree* and two chocolate bars
on our hands. He whispers *change, eat.*

He warns *it's time to go, it's the only one you get.* I count
sudden aches. I am ready.

He opens the trunk and the tears come to me. I don't
let them escape me, I breathe.

Get in, is our next task. I go first and then sister. She shapes
into my shape. And then a blanket

and other things are loaded on top of us. I don't like
this casket blackness

so I close my eyes instead and pretend this is only hide
and seek. It is forbidden to talk

so I move my lips, hold back sound. Refusing stillness
I sing: *todo esta bien, todo esta bien.*

Everywhere sweat escapes me and I get nauseous
with my own odor.

My made-up lyrics are boring so I count facts instead:
tonight, the moon doesn't shine,

I am cold, something is jabbing at my ribs, we stop
and go, stop and go, the sun is rising

somewhere. Stop. And go. I am cold, my sister's ass
is warm against my thighs.

I brush the tip of my shoe against the nape of her neck
so she knows I'm awake.

We stop. The muffled voices whisper *checkpoint.* Stop.
Stop. Go. The sun, freshly out, is brutal

on our eyes when the trunk is open and we are unburied.
We have to be pulled out—

breeched, with our muscles asleep, the tingling
makes it painful to move.

Like shaky foals we sway from side to side. We are safe.
He explains that we are hours away

from our parents. We have five minutes to stretch.
Back in the dark I hold her hand and smile

thinking *Disney, yellow school bus, Madonna,*
McDonald's here we come.

Nominated by Maura Stanton, Richard Cecil

THE HAWK

by BRIAN DOYLE

from THE SUN

Recently a man took up residence on my town's football field, sleeping in a small tent in the northwestern corner, near the copse of cedars. He had been a terrific football player some years ago for our high school, and then had played in college, and then a couple of years in the nether reaches of the professional ranks, where a man might get paid a hundred bucks a game plus bonuses for touchdowns and sacks. Then he had entered into several business ventures, but these had not gone so well, and he had married and had children, but that had not gone so well either, and finally he'd taken up residence on the football field, because, he said, that was where things *had* gone well, and he sort of needed to get balanced again, and there was something about the field that was working for him, as far as he could tell. So, with all due respect to people who thought he was a nut case, he decided he would stay there until someone made him leave. He had already spoken with the cops, and it was a mark of the general decency of our town that he was told he could stay as long as he didn't interfere with use of the field, which of course he would never think of doing, and it was summer, anyway, so the field wasn't in use much.

He had been nicknamed the Hawk when he was a player, for his habit of lurking around almost lazily on defense and then making a stunning strike, and he still speaks the way he played, quietly but then amazingly. When we sat on the visiting team's bench the other day, he said some quietly amazing things, which I think you should hear:

The reporter from the paper came by, he said. She wanted to write a story about the failure of the American dream and the collapse of the

277

social contract, and she was just *melting* to use football as a metaphor for something or other, and I know she was just trying to do her job, but I kept telling her things that didn't fit what she wanted, like that people come by and leave me cookies and sandwiches, and the kids who play lacrosse at night set up a screen so my tent won't get peppered by stray shots, and the cops drift by at night to make sure no one's giving me grief. Everyone gets nailed at some point, so we understand someone getting nailed and trying to get back up on his feet again. I am not a drunk, and there's no politicians to blame. I just lost my balance. People are good to me. You try to get lined up again. I keep the field clean. Mostly it's discarded water bottles. Lost cellphones I hang in a plastic bag by the gate. I walk the perimeter a lot. I saw some coyote pups the other day. I don't have anything smart to say. I don't know what things mean. Things just are what they are. I never sat on the visitors' bench before, did you? Someone leaves coffee for me every morning by the gate. The other day a lady came by with twin infants, and she let me hold one while we talked about football. That baby weighed about half of nothing. You couldn't believe a human being could be so tiny—and there were two of him. That reporter, she kept asking me what I had learned, what I would say to her readers if there was only one thing I could say, and I told her, What could possibly be better than standing on a football field, holding a brand-new human being the size of a coffee cup? You know what I mean? Everything else is sort of a footnote.

Nominated by The Sun, Mark Irwin, Nancy Richard, Naomi Williams

NOTHING LIVING LIVES ALONE

fiction by WENDELL BERRY

from THE THREEPENNY REVIEW

I. FREEDOM

Andy Catlett was a child of two worlds. At his house down at Hargrave, at the river mouth, going by car was taken for granted. But at his Catlett grandparents' place, in the summer of 1945 and for yet a few more years, there was not a motor-driven implement or vehicle, except for the elderly automobile owned by Jess Brightleaf and his family, who lived down the creek road on the back of the farm. Andy's Grandpa Catlett, at eighty-one, less than a year from his death, still rode horseback when he had any distance to go, though now he had to mount from the well-top. The farmwork was still done by the Brightleaf brothers, Jess and Rufus, and by Dick Watson, with teams of mules. They were good mules too, as Grandpa Catlett would have added: mules well conformed and matched, well broke to work.

What he thought of as the town-world of automobiles Andy had known from his first consciousness and was accustomed to, though until the war's end and a little after, some farm people still drove into Hargrave in horsedrawn wagons and buggies. Every summer one of the last of those, a sweet old woman, as Andy's mother called her, with her nice grandson always in his Sunday clothes to come to town, drove her horse and buggy through the streets, peddling jams and jellies, vegetables from her garden, and fresh-picked wild berries.

But with no more deliberate choice than he had invested in the town-world, Andy had given his heart entirely to the older world of what his father, and Andy and his brother Henry also, would always call the "home place" as it was until the great alteration that followed the war. Until then it belonged to the motorless world of stones, streams, and soil, plants and animals, woods and fields, footpaths and wagon tracks, all of it infused still by his grandpa's still-excitable passion for good land, good livestock, good horses and mules, and good work.

The town of Hargrave, charmed by its highway and motor connections to everywhere else, thought itself somewhat worldly, but at the home place, with its broad open ridges falling away and steepening to the woods along Bird's Branch on one side and Catlett's Fork on the other, Andy felt himself in the presence of the world itself, in the world's native silence as yet only rarely disturbed by the sound of a machine, its darkness after bedtime unbroken by human light, its daylight as yet unsmudged, its springs and streams still drinkable. It was a creaturely world, substantial and alive. Even the rock ledges of the slopes, even the timbers and planks of the buildings seemed to him to be alive in the vital presence of the place. In those days he simply lived in it and loved it without premonition. Eventually, seeing it as it would become, he would remember with sorrow how it had been.

From the farmers he was kin to, and from others who were his influences, Andy learned that there was a difference between good and bad work, and that good work was worthy, even that it was expected, even of him. He wanted to work, to work well, to be a good hand, long before he was capable. By the time he became more or less capable of work, he had become capable also of laziness. Because he knew about work, he knew about laziness. Though he could not always resist the temptation to be lazy, he knew that laziness was what it was, and he was embarrassed by it even as he indulged in it.

His father, whom he knew familiarly, but also by reputation as Wheeler Catlett the lawyer, who had his law practice and other duties to attend to, had never been able to wean himself from farming—if he had ever tried to do so. As Grandpa Catlett got older, Wheeler had assumed increasing responsibility for the home place. And also, in partnership with his brother Andrew, he had acquired two other farms, which he carried on alone after Andrew's death in 1944.

Because he was a lawyer by profession, but a farmer by upbringing and by calling, Wheeler always had farming on his mind. He went to the farms before and after his day at the office, on Saturdays, on Sunday afternoons, and he would sometimes take a day off from the office to work with the cattle or the sheep, or to break a team or two of young mules. Or he would be up long before daylight, waking his sons to help, to meet a trucker at one of the farms to load a load of spring lambs, or of hogs, or, late in the fall, the year's crop of finished steers, for the trip to the Bourbon Stockyards in Louisville.

And so the first, the most continuous, and the dearest fabric of Andy's consciousness was provided by the home place, its life and work and the creatures, human and not-human, tame and not-tame, who lived there. And the home place belonged to the countryside around Port William and Port William itself, which was the native country of both his father's and his mother's families.

The home place, his father's home place, was about four miles, by road, from Port William. On one of the far corners of Port William stood the old house where his mother was born and grew up. At the houses of their Grandma and Grandpa Catlett and of their Granny and Granddaddy Feltner, Andy and his brother Henry were as freely welcome and as much at home as they were in the house of their parents down at Hargrave, the county seat. But for Andy, the Catlett home place was the focus of his consciousness and affection because, of the three places, it was the most creaturely, the quietest, undisturbed by the comings and goings of even so small a center of trade as Port William. And it was at the home place that he was most free.

As he looks back across many years from his old age to his childhood, it seems to him that there was a time, from when he was eight or nine years old until he was fourteen, when he experienced intervals of a freedom that was almost absolute. This freedom came to him mostly in the neighborhood of the home place, mostly when he would be alone. Sometimes, when he was with his brother Henry and their friend Fred Brightleaf, they would be sufficiently free, by default of the watchfulness of their elders. They were capable then of exploits beyond the powers of a single boy. But sometimes they would get at cross purposes, and would squander their freedom in arguments over what to do with it. Alone, Andy was free sometimes even of his own plans and intentions.

Grandpa and Grandma Catlett were the older of Andy's grandparents. He was freest at their place, maybe, because he got over the ground faster than they did, but also because they were not much inclined to worry about him. When he was with them he sometimes tried their patience, but he liked their company and their talk. Their memories went back almost to the Civil War, to a time long before the internal combustion engine, when the atmosphere of the Port William country would be pierced only occasionally by a steam whistle. For most of their lives the country had been powered almost entirely by the bodily strength of people and of horses and mules, and the people had been dependent for their lives mostly on the country and on their own knowledge and skills.

Without intending to do so, Andy learned much from watching his Catlett grandparents and from listening to them. From his grandpa he gathered knowledge of land husbandry, and of the proper conformation and good management of livestock. These were things that Grandpa Catlett passionately knew, and he enforced them in his grandson's mind by his naked contempt for anybody ignorant of them. From his grandma he became familiar with the economy of the household: the keeping and care of the old house, the uses and re-uses of all the things that could be saved, and all the arts and refinements by which food made its passage from the ground to the plate.

From the house and barns and other outbuildings clustered on the hilltop, he passed beyond the supervision of his grandparents into the open fields on the ridges, or down into the woods on the steeper land along the creeks. On these travels he would often be alone, on foot or riding Beauty the pony. Sometimes he carried a cane fishing pole and a can of worms to the pond in the back field or to the holes along the creeks, coming home on his lucky days with strings of small perch or catfish that his grandma fried in batter. He might swim in the pond, which he was not supposed to do, or spend a long time watching the tumble bugs rolling their dung balls along the cow paths. He loved the mown fields and the croplands open to the sky. Even more, he loved the woods, where it seemed to him that every life was secret, including his own. Of the secret lives of the woods and the tall grasses he did not learn much, for he lacked the patience to sit still. But the place itself he learned so well that when he went to bed at night, then and for the rest of his life, he could see it all in his mind. In thought he could follow the paths and the wagon tracks. In thought he could walk over it and see how it looked from every height of the ground.

And there were hours and days when he hung about the men at their work, to watch, to listen, hoping to be given some bit of real work to do, sometimes proving able actually to help, but more likely than not told to watch himself or get out of the way, or he would be assigned to some drudgery that the men preferred to avoid: go to the spring or well, for instance, to bring back a fresh jug of water. But sometimes when he begged to drive a team, they would hand him the lines and then watch to see that he drove correctly and kept out of danger. And so he learned to do what he was capable of doing, and he imagined himself grown big and strong enough to cut swiftly and accurately with an axe, or to lift great forkfuls of hay onto the loading wagon, or to unload corn into the crib, the metal ringing as the mounded ears flew off the scoop.

As the men worked they talked, and their talk was wonderful. They told jokes and stories, some of which were full of grownup knowledge. Andy especially liked the talk of Rufus Brightleaf, who had a poetical and profane answer for everything.

One day, coming upon Rufus working alone, Andy asked, "Where's Jess?"

And Rufus replied without stopping or looking up, "He went to shit and the hogs eat him."

Or sometimes, When they had had a good day at work and he was feeling fine, Rufus would sing one of the songs of his extensive repertory. He would sing to the tune of "The Great Speckled Bird," raising his voice over the rattle of chains and wheels, maybe, as he drove a wagon home to the barn:

Did you ever see Sally make wor-ter?
She could pee such a beau-ti-ful stream.
She could pee for a rod and a quar-ter,
And you couldn't see her a-ass for the steam.

And he spoke of doctors who treated certain troublesome swellings with hairy poultices that never failed, healings that to Andy seemed veiled in a mystery almost biblical.

But rowdy as Rufus was, as he enjoyed being and was gifted to be, he was also a man perhaps of many small regrets and certainly of one great sorrow. His great sorrow was for his son whose death in a logging accident Rufus had witnessed, knowing on the instant that there was "not a thing I could do, not a thing." He had told Andy of this, as old Andy supposes, because he needed to speak of it to somebody, because he and the boy Andy were friends, and the boy was a listener. Knowing this, Andy was aware also that there were other hard things to know

283

that came to Rufus's mind, causing a look to pass like a shadow over his face.

They were artists, the Brightleaf brothers, their work in all its stages beautiful to see. Like artists of other kinds, and like a considerable number of their neighbors in that country at that time, they held before themselves an ideal of perfection that every year they approached and every year inevitably failed and yet attempted again the next year, year after year.

They were of the kind known as "tobacco men," a title not bestowed upon every grower of tobacco, but only upon the most select, the best. In those days, just after the war when cigarettes had been standard equipment for the men fighting overseas, long before the proof of the unhealthfulness of tobacco, and tobacco's consequent decline in public favor and in quality, the premium at sale time was absolutely upon excellence.

The crop itself was in every way exceptional. It was intricately and endlessly demanding in the ways it was cultivated, handled, and prepared for market. In the time before tractors and chemicals, the tobacco crop was made by the work of mules and men and, when needed, women, the man-hours far exceeding the mule-hours. All crops then, of course, were dependent on such work, but tobacco was unique in the intensity, skill, and length of the work it required. Its production then, as Andy Catlett now thinks, looking back, involved higher standards and a greater passion for excellence than any other practice of agriculture, excepting only that of the better livestock breeders.

For the Burley tobacco of these parts, the crop year lasted from early spring, when the plant beds were burnt and sowed, until late winter, when at last the crop of the summer before would have been stripped, tied into "hands" according to grade, compacted in presses, loaded, hauled to market, and sold. The requirement for informed attention, care, judgment, and work was unremitting. Some of the work would be more or less solitary. But especially at the times of transplanting, harvesting, and stripping, crew work was necessary, and the crew was supplied by family members and hired help, both men and women, and by exchanges of work with neighbors. At these times the difficulty of the work was relieved, in some measure even compensated, by the sort of talk that people do for pleasure, the telling of jokes and stories, and by dinners at noon that were daily banquets, the food bountiful in variety and quantity, capably prepared, and joyfully eaten. Many a wife then received and deserved the highest praise: "As good a cook as ever I ate after."

Jess and Rufus Brightleaf, and Jess preeminently, had a high reputation throughout that part of the country. They put their characterizing marks upon their crops at every stage. Their finished work on the warehouse floor would be recognized on sight by any bystanders who knew what to look for.

Often when Andy would be riding with his father through the fields, Wheeler would stop the car at some point of vantage to watch Jess Brightleaf at work in a tobacco patch, for Jess was a man worth watching. At his work he moved carefully, thoughtfully, with authority, and yet swiftly and gracefully, surrounded by his own work well done.

And always, a moment or two before putting the car into motion again, Wheeler would say quietly, "Beautiful, isn't it?"

"Yes," Andy would say. For it was in fact beautiful, and unforgettably so.

That was a good time for farmers. During the war and for several years after, farmers received prices that were something like just. And this, in expectation, brightened the mood of the work.

From their first year as tenants on the home place in 1939 until their last in 1948, Jess Brightleaf and his wife, by their work and their thrift, saved ten thousand dollars with which they bought a farm of their own.

II. IN THE OLD TIME

In his latter years Andy Catlett has tried to use appropriate hesitation and care in speaking, in any way particularly personal, of the diminishment of the world. He dislikes hearing old men, including himself, begin sentences with such phrases as "In *my* day" or "When *I* was a boy." But when he thinks of the freedom he enjoyed during the five or six years of his boyhood that were most active and carefree, he recognizes that he is setting up a standard of sorts by the measure of which the world must be seen to have diminished. It has diminished by the standard of a boy's freedom, but that freedom has diminished necessarily in association with other diminishments, both social and material.

His freedom then had little to do with home or school, but everything to do with a home landscape which was, as he can see now, an inhabited and a human landscape. On the farm of either set of his grandparents, he could walk within a quarter or half an hour from some spot in the woods where he imagined that no human had ever stood before to places where he knew he walked in the tracks of elders and companions, some of whom had died in his own time.

He could walk as quickly, moreover, from solitude that had lasted as long as needed into the company of men and women at work, who were doing work that they did well and even liked, that they expected to continue to do for the rest of their lives, in a place or a part of the country that they did not expect to leave. They were leading lives that were capable and settled. This was mainly true even of Jess Brightleaf's hired hand, Corky Dole, whom Jess paid off every Saturday night and bailed out of jail every Monday morning. They knew their work. They did not dither. It was a settled culture, and there was a certain freedom for a child in that alone.

It was hardly a perfect place or time. Like any of the past, it was not a time that a person of good sense would consider "going back to." But that time, to the end of the war and a while after in that part of the world, had certain qualities, certain goodnesses, that might have been cherished and enlarged, but instead were disvalued and discarded as of no worth.

Its chief quality can be suggested by the absence from it of a vocabulary that in the last half of the twentieth century and the beginning of the twenty-first would become dominant in the minds of nearly everybody. Nobody then and there was speaking of "alternatives" or "alternative lifestyles," of "technology" or "technological progress," of "mobility" or "upward mobility." The life that Andy knew then in Port William and its neighborhood was not much given to apologizing for itself. People did not call themselves, even to themselves, "just a farmer" or "just a housewife." It required talk of an infinitude of choices endlessly available to everybody, essentially sales talk, to embitter the work of husbandry and wifery, to suggest the possibility always elsewhere of something better, and to make people long to give up whatever they had for the promise of something they *might* have—at whatever cost, at whatever loss. You might of course have heard somebody wonder toward the end of a long, hard, hot day of work, "You reckon you'll ever get anywhere without changing jobs?" But that was weariness and wit such as might come from anybody at any work in the midst of the hardest of it. You might have heard the same self-critical humor from somebody who had danced or coon-hunted half the night before a hard workday. Andy has no record of this time except his memory, but he does not remember that anybody who spoke so of "changing jobs" ever spoke of the job he wanted to change to.

Rather than alternative jobs or lives, the ordinary talk in barns or at row ends ran to the best remembered or imagined versions of things that were familiar: harvest dinners, capable mules or horses or hounds or bird dogs, days or nights of hunting or fishing, good crop years and crops, good days and good hands. Or they told jokes or stories in which there was an implicit recognition and acceptance of the human lot.

Such settled and decided people are parts of the world, as the unresting, never-satisfied seekers of something better can never be. The boy who wandered away alone into a new world newly discovered by himself could return to a familiar world communally known by people he knew who were at work or at rest in it. And in both worlds he was free. He was free not only to ramble at will and at large when he was beyond family supervision or had not been put to work, but he was free also in the company of Dick Watson, the Brightleafs, and any other grownups, who treated him as a child only when he was in the way, in danger, or in need of correction. Otherwise, they made no exceptions. They spoke to him as they spoke to one another, as a familiar.

Home to him, then, was a home countryside, one place with the limits of one place but limitlessly self-revealing and interesting, limitlessly to be known and loved. It was precisely in that limitlessness that he was free, a limitlessness inherent in the nature, the "genius," of the one place, free then of the litter of alternatives.

This was a freedom undoubtedly more apparent and available to a boy than to a man. But Andy would remember it. It would be the enabling condition and the incentive of his choice finally to leave off his wanderings and come home, to make his own life indistinguishable from the life of his place. And this was his choice, by the terms and standards of his time, to become "odd," as one of his most reticent old friends told him at last that he had chosen to be.

But the young Andy Catlett was free in another way that he did not know when he was young, that he has learned in all the time he has spent in growing old. In those years he thinks of now as the years of his freedom he was free of a fear that has since grown greater in every year

287

he has lived. He was free of the fear of the human destruction of the world, a freedom that no child will again enjoy for generations to come, if ever again.

If Andy's regret for the loss of the old creaturely world of Port William in his childhood were only nostalgic or sentimental, then it would be merely a private feeling, properly to be ended by his death. His regret is considerable and worth talking about because it is applied to real losses, tangible and significant, some of which are measurable: the loss of the economic integrity and neighborly collaboration of rural communities, the loss of independent livelihoods, the loss of topsoil, the toxicity of air and water, the destruction by mining of whole mountains, the destruction of land and water ecosystems—so much destruction in the interests of machines, chemicals, and fuels to replace the people who have been displaced, by the same interests, from the home places of the world.

We can brush away the past, as we like to do and feel superior in doing, but the nightmare of Andy's old age is to *know*, wide awake, the destruction of many and of much not only pleasing and desirable, but of lasting value if they had lasted, and, for all we can yet know, necessary.

And suppose, to elaborate the nightmare, that we had decided even as late as 1950 to grant a proper stewardship and husbandry to the natural world. Suppose we had refused to countenance the industrialization of everything from agriculture to medicine to education to religion. Suppose we had not tolerated the transformation, in the official and then the public mind, of vocation to "a job," which is to say the transformation of the farmer, the tradesman, even the sharecropper (all subsistence-based) to an "employee" helplessly dependent on an employer and "the economy" and interchangeable with any other employee. Suppose we had not stood for the displacement of people who once functioned as parts of the creaturely world, working members of their places—-the *quality* of their work always, of course, in question— to the "labor pool" and the placelessness of modern life.

Andy by now has lived and watched long enough to know the reality of the ongoing human destruction of the world. He knows that he himself is involved inescapably in its destruction. But he can remember, to further elaborate his nightmare, wandering in the woods or working in the fields early in the year, when he drank from wet-weather springs, the water cool and tasting of the ground, with no thought of chemical contamination. His experience of that time was decisive for him. It was luck, perhaps a blessing. It was an unaccountable gift, for the place and the way of life he learned then was in fact a sort of island: a small, fragile, threatened order in the midst of a world war and all its dire portent.

Freedom, then, existed. Andy knew so from his early travels and his early work in his home country. Along the way he learned too that freedom, when it happened, was an interval with responsibilities at either end. He knew long before he understood, or could choose to act on the knowledge, that neither freedom nor responsibility existed alone, or could exist alone very long, but that each depended on the other.

He was late in acting on that interdependability, partly maybe because of school, but certainly because he would remain a boy for a long time, a boy either in deference to the authority of grownups or in rebellion against it. His early experience of freedom, anyhow, prepared him poorly for school, and for prolonged enclosure of any kind. School, before it had taught him much else, taught him to be a critic, though it did not intend to do so, and though "critic" was not even a word he knew. He was in school when he made his first conscious objection to something he read in a book.

He read in a book (maybe it was a reader; maybe it was from the small library the teacher kept in her classroom) a story of two children, brother and sister, who visited their grandparents' farm where there was a wonderful woodland. The children played happily among the trees. They had a pet crow and a pet squirrel that accompanied them on their visits to the woods—and this, to Andy, was a charming thought, as was the thought of the beautiful woodland itself, as was the thought of the woodlands around Port William.

And then, without explaining why, the story told how the grandparents sold the trees to a logger, who cut them down. The logger cut them *all* down, every one of them. In proof there was a picture of the boy and girl standing in a field of stumps, and the crow and the squirrel perched on a stump apiece. The story then explained that, though the children and the crow and the squirrel would miss the woods, this was really not too sad because the woods would grow back again.

Until then, Andy had thought that anything printed in a book was true. And so it was a considerable shock to him when he realized that he knew—though he could not then have said *how* he knew: he knew from intuition and experience; maybe he knew, Heaven help us, by premonition—that the story had told a lie. The story was in fact too sad, it was a story of great loss and sorrow, and it could say nothing to make itself happy. To know that grownups, even writers and teachers, were questionable did not smooth Andy's way through his formal education.

III. A TIME OUT OF TIME

The old man, Andy Catlett, does not believe that the mind of any young creature is a blank slate. But he knows without doubt that young Andy Catlett, in the years of his boyhood, was being formed. He was being in-formed. He was being shaped, and this was his dearest education, as a creature of his home place, his home country, by his growing knowledge of it. He was sometimes deliberately taught by his grandparents, his father, and the other elders who in one way or another were gathered around him. He was learning by their example, instruction, and insistence the ways of livestock, of handwork, of all in the life of farming that would make him, beyond anything else he might become, a countryman. But he was also shaping himself, in-forming himself, by knowledge of the country that he got for himself or that the country itself impressed upon him.

In the winter of 1947, after Grandpa Catlett died, Grandma Catlett wintered in a room in the Broadfield Hotel down in Hargrave. And then, early in April, when Elton Penn came in his truck to load her and her spool bed and her bureau and her rocking chair to take her home, Andy loaded himself and his bundle of clothes and books and went home with her. Now, as Andy thought, as she allowed and maybe encouraged him to think, her ability to live at home depended on him. He took a deep pleasure in the sense of responsibility that filled him then, and he was steadily dutiful and industrious. Grandma was cooking as always on the wood stove, and in the mornings, sometimes all day, they still needed fires for warmth. Andy kept the kitchen supplied with firewood, and carried in coal for the stove in the living room. When the cow freshened, Andy did the milking, night and morning. Later, Grandma said, they would need a garden, of course, and Andy would need to help with that.

On school day mornings, after he had done his chores and eaten breakfast, he got himself out to the road in time to catch the school bus. But he had a little initiative in this. Because he was considered an occasional or temporary rider of the bus, he apparently was not officially expected by the driver. And so if he got to the road ahead of the bus, he would put up his thumb. If he failed to catch a ride for himself, then he rode to school on the bus. This was a freedom he cherished, and he told nobody about it. The people who gave him rides also apparently kept his secret. He shirked his lessons, antagonized his teachers, stored up trouble for himself. On days of no school, as long as he showed up for meals and did his chores, and as soon as he was out of sight of the house, he was free.

One warm spring Saturday afternoon, when he had fished his way from pool to pool down Bird's Branch and had caught nothing, he came to a large, dry, flat rock. He propped his fishing pole against a tree and lay down on the rock. The rock was unusually large and flat and smooth, and he felt that something should be done about it. And so he stretched out on it for some time, looking up into the treetops of the woods. He was no longer on the home place then, but had crossed onto the more or less abandoned back-end of a farm that fronted in the river valley. He was at the mouth of a tributary dell known as Steep Hollow, whose slopes you could not climb standing up. The woods there was an old stand of big trees. Whether because of the steepness of the ground or the dubious benevolence of neglect, the stand had never been cut. But now, remembering it, he is obliged to remember also that a few years later it was cut, and is forever gone.

The woods floor was covered with flowers, and the tree leaves were just coming out. Andy's eyes were quick in those days, and he could see everything that was happening among the little branches at the top of the woods. He saw after a while, by some motion it made way up in a white oak and not far from the leafy globe of its nest, a young gray squirrel that, except for its tail, appeared to be no bigger than a chipmunk.

The squirrel was just loitering about, in no hurry, and Andy studied it carefully. The thought of catching and having something so beautiful, so small, so cunningly made, possessed him entirely. He wanted it as much as he had ever wanted anything in his life. He knew perfectly that he could not catch a mature squirrel. But this one being so young and inexperienced, he thought he had half a chance.

The tree was one of the original inhabitants of the place. It had contained a fair sawlog in the time of Boone and the Long Hunters. By now it was far too big to be embraced and shinned up by a boy, or a man either, and its first limb was unthinkably high. But well up the slope from the old tree was a young hickory whose first branch Andy could shinny up to, and whose top reached well into the lower branches of the oak. Andy was maybe a better than average climber, and he had spent a fair portion of his life in trees. He was small for his age, and was secure on branches too flimsy for a bigger boy.

He went up the hickory and then into the heavy lower limbs of the oak. The climbing was harder after that. Sometimes he could step from one thick limb to another up the trunk. Sometimes he had to make his way out to the smaller branches of one limb, from there into the smaller branches of the one above, and from there back to the trunk again. Finally he was in the top of the tree, a hundred or so feet from the ground. Just above him was the little squirrel, more beautiful, more perfect, up close than it had looked from the ground. The fur of its back and sides was gray but touched, brushed over, with tones of yellowish red and reddish yellow, so that against the light it seemed surrounded with a small glow, and the fur of its underside was immaculately white. Its finest features were its large, dark eyes alight with intelligence and the graceful plume of its tail as long as its body.

Andy knew with a sort of anticipatory ache in the inward skin of his hands and fingers what it would feel like to catch and hold this lovely creature and look as closely at it as he wished. He climbed silently, and slowly from one handhold and foothold to another, up and out the little branches that held him springily and strongly until he was within an easy arm's reach of the squirrel. He reached almost unmovingly out, and at the approach of his hand, the squirrel leapt suddenly and easily to another branch. It did not go far, but the small branch it was now on belonged to a different limb from the one Andy was on. And so he had to go back to the trunk and start again.

About the same thing happened for a second time. The almost-catchable little squirrel waited, watching Andy with a curiosity of its own, until it was almost caught. This time it ran a little farther out on its limb and leapt onto a branch of another tree, another oak. Now Andy had to climb a long way down to find a limb that crossed to the second tree, make his way out to limbs still affording handholds and footholds, limber enough to lean under his weight until he could catch a limb as strong in the other tree, swing over, go to the trunk of that tree and up and out to the highest branches, where again he almost caught the squirrel.

That was the way it happened so many times he lost count. The squirrel seemed to wait for him, watching him with interest, imaginably even with amusement, taking its rest while Andy laboriously made his approach, and then at the last second, without apparent fear, seemingly at its leisure, leaping beyond reach, never far, but always too far to be easily approached again. In fact, Andy and the squirrel must have been at about the same stage of their respective lives: undoubting, ignorant, fearless, curious, happy in the secret altitudes of the treetops and the little branches, neither of them at all intimidated by the blank blue sky above the highest branches, the outer boundary of both their lives.

It was a time out of time, when time was suspended in constant presence, without past or future. It began to move again only when the squirrel finally leapt onto the snag of a dead tree and disappeared into an old woodpecker hole.

And then it was late in the day, past sundown, and Andy was still high up among the tall trees. He had not thought of getting back to the ground for a long time, and from where he had got to he was a long time finding a way. The trunks were too large to grip securely and were limbless from too high up. He finally made his way to a grapevine, and slid down it slowly to ease the friction on his hands and legs. When he stood finally on the ground again, it seemed at first to rock a little as if he had stepped down into a boat. He was sweating, his hands and arms and legs bark-burnt and stinging, and he was a long way from home. He recovered his fishing pole, now deprived of its charm and the sense of adventure he usually invested in it, and started back.

When the screen door slammed behind him and he stepped into the back porch, his grandma opened the kitchen door.

"Where," she said, drawing the word out, "on God's green earth have you been?"

"Fishing," he said, which was true as far as it went.

But he was late. He was too late. It was getting dark. In coming back so late he had betrayed not only her trust but his own best justification for staying out there in the free country with her and not in town.

"Oh," he said, "I'll go milk right now. I'll hurry. I won't be long."

She said, "I did it."

So while he had been up in the tree tops with the squirrel, forgetful of the time of day and where he was, she alone had done the evening chores and milked the cow. She said no more. She left him, as she would have put it, to stew in his own juice, which he did. He would not forget again, and he would not forget the lesson either.

Nor would he forget for the rest of his life his happiness of that afternoon. What would stay with him would not be his frustration, his failure to catch the squirrel, but the beauty of it and its aerial life, and of *his* aerial life while he tried to catch it among the small, supple branches that sprang with his weight as if almost but not quite he might have leapt from one to another like the squirrel, almost but not quite flying.

He had not wondered how, if he had caught the squirrel, he would have made his way back to the ground. It would take him several days to get around to thinking of that. The heights of that afternoon he had achieved as a quadruped. From where he had got to he could not have climbed down with his two feet and only one hand. If he had caught the squirrel, he would have had to turn it loose.

Nominated by The Threepenny Review

IN A KITCHEN WHERE MUSHROOMS WERE WASHED

by JANE HIRSHFIELD

from PLOUGHSHARES

In a kitchen where mushrooms were washed,
the mushroom scent lingers.

As the sea must keep for a long time the scent of the whale.

As a person who's once loved completely,
a country once conquered,
does not release that stunned knowledge.

They must want to be found, those strange-shaped, rising morels,
clownish puffballs.

Lichens have served as a lamp wick.
Clean-burning coconuts, olives.
Dried salmon, sheep fat, a carcass of petrel set blazing:
light that is fume and abradement.

Unburnable mushrooms are other.
They darken the air they come into.

Theirs the scent of having been traveled, been taken.

Nominated by David Baker, Ellen Bass, Michael Bowden, Joyce Carol Oates

I SEE MEN LIKE TREES, WALKING

fiction by JAMES ROBISON

from WIGLEAF

At dusk funnels of frayed rags whirl from the barn lofts, bats pouring up to feed on summer mosquitoes. I shoot a white lariat of hose water; it loops my cabbage garden. My daughter fires hardballs at her mother who catches them in a piepan leather mitt, *thwock*. Later, my wife is saying how hard to love all things, hard to take the sense of fleas or the cottonmouth that blinded the little girl out Route 9, near Bonner's Black Angus farm. Crickets roar. Silent lightning. Downhill, the bloated creek crashes in its channel. In the Union cemetery on our property, beyond the north pasture, in a windbreak stand of ash trees, each mossed tombslab, (there are seven), leans for a soul perfectly forgotten.

Nominated by Wigleaf

CIVIL TWILIGHT

fiction by TIMOTHY HEDGES

from THE GETTYSBURG REVIEW

Augie Salvatore slid the remote from his sleeping father's hand and hit the button to call the nurse. A young black lady with Crystal on her nametag walked into the room and touched the foot of the bed. "How's Mayo this morning?" she said, not looking at Augie.

"The pain," Augie said. "When he talks. It sounds like he's swallowing gravel."

"Well, then," Crystal said. "Maybe when Mayo wakes up, he should take his doctor's advice and stop talking." She spoke the last two words as if she were a teacher tapping a chalk board.

Mayo's eyelids fluttered, and he said, "Not sleeping."

If Augie hadn't been standing next to the man, he'd have sworn the noises came from a creature covered in fur, a bear, perhaps, or a moose. It was far from the imperial voice he remembered booming throughout his father's bus, announcing the cross streets at each stop: Van Dyke, John R. In that vision, Augie was the kid sitting by the door, trying to catch his father's eye, proud that the man in uniform with his hands firmly turning the wheel was his dad.

"You should be," Crystal said. "Sleeping. I heard you were up all night buzzing Michelle like you were a puppy in love." She shook her head and stepped out the door.

Augie's father laughed, a grating burst, and the terrible noise made Augie want to press a pillow over his ears, his eyes, anything to block the signs that his father was going to die. It had been twenty years since his mother's passing, and Augie had learned to live in the spaces created by her absence. But those spaces didn't include Mayo, his father, the man responsible for her death.

"I'm driving tonight," Augie said, raising a hand. "Don't speak. I'm just telling you. I picked up the route for a buddy. Wife's having triplets. Christmas miracle, I guess. But I'll be back."

Mayo nodded, his shaky hand lifting a plastic water bottle as if it were a twenty-pound barbell. Augie looked his father in the face, noted the milky cloud in Mayo's right eye, the hearing aids, like puzzle pieces, jammed in his ears. Augie grabbed his coat from the chair, and his father's cane, which had been leaning against the wall, clattered to the floor.

Augie had been driving the extra Woodward route for the last five days, ever since his father arrived by ambulance at Beaumont for the fourth time that year. Today was Augie's first visit. "This one's it," Dr. Morgan had said to Augie over the phone last night. "You need to understand that your father isn't going home."

"Twenty-five years and you're driving Christmas Eve," Mayo said, closing his eyes, the words like broken glass crushed beneath a radial tire.

Augie tensed for the explosion, waited for the familiar critical barrage, but held his tongue. If he stayed in his trench, kept his head down, no one could touch him. Mayo had taught him that.

Mayo nodded with each breath, and Augie could see how difficult it was for his father to swallow. The nurses had told him that the drugs kept Mayo groggy from seven until daybreak. If the weather held, if his route ran smoothly, he'd make it back in time. And then? And then tomorrow would be Christmas, and his father would still be dying.

The sun was sinking when Augie pulled his bus to the curb on Big Beaver. He was ahead of schedule, obligated to kill a few minutes before heading south on his final run. He flipped a switch, and the doors collapsed, sucking inward with a hiss.

"Yo, can we get some heat back here? Damn." The voice came from a teenager in the back row, a kid with a chain dangling from his gigantic jeans. When the passenger load was light, Augie would play a private game, try to predict where each rider would get off. On southbound Woodward he'd use the mile markers as they descended into the urban jungle: Fourteen Mile, Eleven Mile, Eight. Most white folks got off before Ten Mile, unless they were students at Wayne State. The kid in the back was a Six Mile; Augie knew it.

Augie made eye contact in his rearview mirror but did not turn around. "Heater's broke," he said.

The kid folded his arms in his puffy black coat, the kind Augie saw the thugs wearing on TV, a coat bulky enough to conceal a gun, three of them.

"Bullshit, man," the kid said. "I need to get me a refund."

Augie slid from his vinyl seat and eased down the steps, stiff fingers gripping the handrails, ankles creaking with each extension of his foot. Not even fifty, he thought, and barely hanging together. As he landed on the pavement, a cold wind ripped at his cheeks, and he turned his head. The traffic rushed along, headlights spearing the darkness outside the mall. In the bus shelter—a transparent igloo perched near the icy sidewalk—a bearded man slurped chunky soup out of a Styrofoam bowl, overstuffed Macy's bags at his feet. Augie caught the man's eye and raised his cap. The man put down his spoon, leaned forward, and used his tongue to push a gob of meat between his lips where it lingered briefly before dropping to the ground, a pile of waste that seemed to smolder with each red flash of Augie's parking lights.

The windows of the mall glowed white. Wreaths hung from every lamppost, red ribbons frenzied in the wind. Augie stepped back on the bus and looked toward the skywalk spanning Big Beaver, where people in striped sweaters rode the moving walkway from one side of the mall ("where the rich assholes shop," his father always said) to the other ("where the rich assholes' bosses shop"). Augie could only see their torsos as they coasted along, their bodies floating unnaturally, like angels, hovering above an earth they were too elegant to touch.

He didn't mind the Woodward route—"The Cruise," his fellow drivers called it. "The Fade to Black." North to Troy, the ritzy mall—the Somerset *Collection*—then back into the warzone of twenty-first-century Detroit. Augie settled into his seat, his legs squeezing beneath the giant steering wheel, and waited.

He scanned his shivering passengers, bundled-up souls who'd gotten on in Birmingham to escape the cold even though they knew the bus was not yet heading in the direction they needed to go. He figured he had a few Twelve Milers, a couple of Tens. Momentarily, he knew, they'd be joined by a troop of black people wearing janitorial jumpsuits

299

and Sbarro aprons under their winter coats. They'd settle in for the sixty-minute ride to Seven Mile, the fairgrounds, Highland Park.

"It's freezing, man," yelled the kid in black. "You wanna close the damn door? Fucking bus. When we gonna move?"

If the heater had been working, Augie would never have heard the complaint. Noise from the back row would have been swallowed by the gushing roar of the booster fans. He raised his eyes to the mirror again and held up three fingers to signify the minutes until departure, then he pointed to the sign next to his mirror: No Offensive or Abusive Language. He pushed a button, and the doors rattled shut. He scratched his thigh through two layers of pants, pulled at the sleeves of his ribbed military-style sweater. He flexed his hands on the wheel, white fingertips wiggling at the ends of his leather fingerless gloves.

A minute later, a fist pounded on the glass door, and Augie's head jerked forward. A string of riders stood on the curb. One by one, each swiped a card or fed crumpled bills into the machine before claiming seats near the back.

When Augie had started as a driver, when he'd had more responsibility—such as counting change—he'd talked more. Now he just stared forward and let the money machine rattle and hum. Periodically he'd push a button to release the tray of coins into the lockbox, and, every time, the crashing noise reminded Augie of a slot machine.

As soon as the clock blinked 4:20, Augie pulled the bus into traffic and headed west toward Woodward. Over his right shoulder, one of the women started to sing softly, a song about buckling shoes and death knocking on the door. She had a man's voice, the timbre of a stringed instrument, Augie thought. A cello, maybe. It was, he considered, a Christmas voice. It was bound to make him sleepy as he headed toward the setting sun, so until he turned south on Woodward, he recited in his head the fifty U.S. states and their capitals, a trick he'd learned from Mayo, a colorful map forming in his head.

By the time he was done, the woman had begun an ultra-slow version of "We Three Kings." Augie thought of his father lying in room 3042, the records he used to play when Augie was a kid: Bobby Darin, Perry Como, Lou Monte. His father had been a driver, too, back in the '60s when the SMART service was known as SEMTA, the South Eastern Michigan Transportation Authority. He'd been one of the only white guys who stuck with the job after the Twelfth Street riots in '67, continuing to drive the 92 Warren route five days a week. In a union full of black drivers, Augie's father, Maurizio—light skinned despite his

Italian heritage—quickly became Mayo, short for Mayonnaise, and Augie had rarely heard anyone refer to his father without using the nickname. Even the nurses at Beaumont had caught on, and the whiteboard on the wall of his father's room read "Mayo's Meds."

Augie caught sight of a waving hand and pulled toward the last stop in Birmingham. A black lady wearing a fancy purple hat climbed in, biting off her mittens and reaching into her pocket. A handful of quarters clanked into the money box, and the woman said, through clenched teeth, "Merry Christmas."

As she stepped past, Augie waited for the box to register her fare. When he didn't hear a click, he checked her coins and saw that she was short. "Ma'am," he said, "you didn't pay the full fare."

"What?" the woman said, spinning, her hat dipping like a bird. "I paid right there."

"Not enough," Augie said. He tapped the fare table on the console to his right. "Fare hike. December first."

The woman squinted at the windshield. "You think I'm lying? I paid the full damn fare," she said, her head moving like a plate spinning on a stick. "Go on and drive the bus."

Long ago, Mayo had taught Augie not to make exceptions. "You let this one go," he'd said. "You let that one go. Pretty soon, you're running a charity. Let me tell you one thing, Augie. You are not responsible for the world's misery. You're going to get nickeled and dimed every day of your life. That means every nickel and dime counts. Everyone pays their way, you got me? This is a full-fare world. Even God up in heaven keeps his receipts. You understand?" Augie had nodded, his brand-new driver's cap slipping a little on his forehead.

"You need to find some more coins," Augie said to the woman, closing the door. "Or you're getting off at the next stop." He spun the wheel and stepped firmly on the accelerator. In his mirror, Augie saw the woman stumble backward and collide with a girl whose face was swallowed by a scarf.

The woman dragged herself back to the money box where she breathed heavily in Augie's ear. Looking sideways, Augie saw the woman pull a plastic Baggie from her coat pocket. It was full of wadded bills and bulging with coins, though the lack of shine seemed to indicate most of them were pennies. "Here's your full fare, Cracker Jack," she said, slamming her hand onto the money box. The coins clinked into the bin. "I didn't hear nothing about raising them rates. I pay my *taxes*."

"Thank you, ma'am," Augie said.

The woman huffed. "Now where's my change?"

Augie stared at the road and pointed to the top of the money box where he knew the words Use Exact Change were featured four times. "I can't make change," he said. "Please take a seat."

The woman stood in the aisle, swaying as the bus shuddered down Woodward. "I put in an extra quarter," she said. "And I want it back *now*."

"Ma'am. Please." Augie's hands choked the wheel.

"You didn't even look me in the eye when I got on this bus, and now you want to argue with me," the woman said, loud enough for the entire bus to hear. "I don't need attitude from no white man."

Augie let the words settle, let the bus go silent.

Every year since he'd been a driver, he'd had to attend daylong "sensitivity" workshops, been forced to sit through role-playing games in which a variety of "challenging" passengers disrupted a route. He'd always thought the acting a waste of time. His real sensitivity training had come from Mayo. "Don't drive around thinking you're better than people," his father had said, pulling Augie close to his face. "You think you're smart. You better dig deep and find some respect." He'd released Augie and sat back in his chair, taking a deep breath. "Augie," he said, his face settling into a familiar impassive mask. "One day you'll learn: when it's dark, all sheep are black."

"Hey," yelled the kid from the back row. Augie glanced in the rearview and saw the boy moving up the aisle, his hand inside the front of his coat. Augie reached for the radio.

He'd imagined the scenario before: a shooter on the bus. Augie knew to keep his foot on the gas, knew that no one wants to kill the driver of a moving vehicle.

The kid stopped and spread his arms, grasping the ceiling bars on either side of the aisle. "Take it easy, lady. Your bus operator is a trained professional," he said, and Augie knew he was reading one of the signs posted above the side windows. "SMART bus operators receive nearly two hundred fifty hours of classroom and on-the-job training. God damn, that's right." He burst into laughter. "Too bad they don't teach 'em how to fix the heat, yo."

Augie released the radio, and the woman shuffled a few steps back, muttering words he couldn't hear. Everyone else on the bus pretended not to have noticed the scene, a familiar phenomenon on public transportation, one that Mayo used to describe to others as "injustice in daily operation."

302

"It's amazing what we choose not to see," he'd say whenever he drove Augie through the crumbling neighborhoods surrounding old Tiger Stadium.

Augie understood this desire to avoid looking the devil in the face. For years after the crash, he'd not known how to talk to Mayo, how to understand the pain of a man whose momentary lapse had caused his wife's death. When Mayo stood charged with aggravated driving while intoxicated, when he'd faced fourteen years in prison, Augie had been unable to look him in the eyes. His father had pleaded guilty, accepted eight months behind bars, asked for it, even, and, upon his release, moved into a tiny apartment in Warren, right down the street from a bus stop. Augie had let him suffer alone. And now, more than a dozen years later, his father, too, was going to die. Augie knew his father wanted forgiveness, wanted Augie to absolve him for destroying their family, but Augie wasn't sure he could say the words, wasn't sure whether the words even existed.

The boy in the puffy coat leaned toward Augie's shoulder. "What time is it, Pops?" Augie waved a hand at the console clock. The boy whistled low and said, "Yo, Pops, you better watch out. That lady was about to tear you up." His shoulders bobbed in a quiet laugh.

Augie had always been amazed by Mayo's ability to work his passengers, to riff with regulars while trundling down the road. On Warren 92, Monday through Friday, Mayo Salvatore held court, and his riders always knew the law.

"My name's not Pops," Augie said.

"My name's Give-a-Shit," the kid said, pulling up his hood. "Good to know you, Pops."

Augie watched him retreat down the aisle, exchange an intricate handshake with a Latino boy who'd hopped on at the last stop.

With the heater broken and the sun going down, Augie could see his breath if he exhaled heavily. In the mirror, he observed his passengers squeezing themselves tightly, leaning away from the cold walls.

He'd ridden with his father lots of times as a kid. Between shifts, his father walked with him down to Hart Plaza and bought him peanuts, which Augie shelled, dropping the pieces, one by one, into the river. On the walk from Capitol Park, Augie skipped down the sidewalk, careful to avoid each sewer cover, which some of his classmates had identified as the entrances to hell. Augie had a perpetual fear of being sucked downward into the terror that existed below the city streets, and his father had done nothing to alleviate his fears, instead placing a hand on his shoulder and saying, "What the earth swallows is soon forgotten." Augie could still hear that stony voice, mixing with the rumbling memories of his father's old diesel bus, and he shivered in his seat.

On the benches behind him, Augie heard the purple-hatted lady talking to an older man wearing a Semper Fi baseball cap. "I got a boy, Royal, in Iraq," she said. "Corporal, he is. Gets to do some bossin' these days."

"Good for him," the man in the cap said. "All I did was take orders for three years. Vietnam."

"But you made it home."

"Yes. I made it home. That's my burden."

They were crossing Thirteen Mile, and Augie could see Beaumont Hospital off to his right, behind the Kroger Grocery where the sun was going down. The clouds in the west were red and swollen, an unnatural winter sight. They reminded Augie of animals battling in the sky. His father was in that distant building, his hardened lungs barely able to inflate. Augie braced for the pothole he knew was ahead, and when he hit it, just past the McDonald's, the rearview mirror shuddered and bounced, the reflection of the bus's interior quivering.

As the image blurred, Augie saw himself riding his father's near-empty bus, eight years old, Sunday afternoon, bored. He was standing in the aisle practicing Willie Horton's batting stance, working on his glare out to the imaginary mound, the one that meant, "Go on, I dare you." He was picturing the ball floating toward the plate, the invisible pitcher—Catfish Hunter, maybe—holding his breath. Then the bus jerked to a stop, the floor rolled beneath his feet, and Augie spilled forward onto his face.

"Sorry, folks," his father said, eyes raised to the mirror as people reached for dropped packages. "Cat."

Augie climbed into his seat near the door, dabbing a finger at the blood on his lip and trying not to cry. His father looked over his shoulder and hissed, "There was no cat."

Augie leaned forward, tried to see out the windshield.

"When you ride the bus, you *sit*," his father said. "When you can't sit, you hold on to something. Boy, you never know when the world might throw you."

He remembered the advice even now as clearly as he remembered the smell of his father coming through the front door: sharp diesel fuel and smoky fingers bathed in Murphy's Oil Soap. It was the advice that he'd clung to when his mother died, when Lily, his second wife, childless and bitter, had finally given up on him and moved to Cleveland last fall. The world, it seemed, was heavy on the brakes.

"My son, the one in Iraq," the purple-hatted lady was saying, "he says you wouldn't believe the sandstorms. Megahurricanes, he calls them. Shards of glass splitting his skin."

"I believe it," said the man next to her. "I got a chemical burn once when I was working for Ford. Felt like a jagged thumbnail ripping me open from elbow to wrist. Shoulda sued their asses. But that's not how we did it back then. If I had, I'd be rich."

"Everyone can't be rich, some has got to be poor."

Augie snuck a peek in the mirror at his cargo, the souls he was carrying south. They continued to huddle in the cold, many of them with headphone cords dangling from their ears as if desperate to drown the noise of the world in wave after wave of thumping beats.

The lady in the purple hat shifted to gaze out her window. "That sun," she said. "Would you look at that? That fire. That glow. That's the road to heaven. See that? That's the bridge. Even when it sinks away, it'll light up the world. You watch."

Augie raised his voice but continued to stare straight ahead. "Civil twilight," he said. Then louder, "You're looking at civil twilight."

"Whatever you call it," the woman said. "It's God."

Augie wanted to keep talking. "My father was a good man," he wanted to say. "He was in the army. Inchon. Korea. He used to talk about how quiet the beaches got during civil twilight, how the ghosts were scared of shadows." If he was driving his normal route, if his regulars were seated nearby, he'd tell a good Mayo story, maybe account for one of his father's medals.

Here, surrounded by strangers, he cleared his throat, spoke as if reciting an answer in a long-ago science class. "Civil twilight. The last point in the day when the horizon can be defined. But it'll be over soon," he said, his voice lowering. "You can always count on darkness."

The lady in the purple hat got quiet, let out a weird moan, the sound of a nervous dog. The light of the world became diffused, like a blanket slowly descending. Augie studied the scene. His father was dying. He was driving a bus into the heart of a dead city. It was Christmas Eve. It was getting dark. This much he knew.

Augie had been raised Catholic, but it had been years since he'd received the Host. Before his first communion, he'd asked his mother what it would feel like. She'd rested her hand on his forehead and said, "Softness . . . compliance . . . forgiveness . . . grace." What it had actually felt like was a stale potato chip.

Civil twilight, Augie thought. *A fancy way to say it was getting dark*.

The lady in the purple hat signaled to get off at Lincoln. Ten and a half, Augie noted. A loss. He'd had her at Nine. As she stepped into the dusky air, her hat blew from her head and cartwheeled in front of the bus on Woodward. She clutched at her uncovered head and spun to see her hat blowing into northbound traffic. Then she clasped her hands over her ears and moved stiffly into the shadows.

An angry voice shot from the back of the bus as Augie shut the door and slid back into traffic. "Damn, I'm about to get pneumonia on this bullshit ride. I can't even feel my fingers and shit. This is fucked up." The boy. Mr. Give-a-Shit.

At Ferndale Plaza, outside a bar named the Stolen Pear, Augie lowered his ramp to allow a man in a rickety motorized wheelchair to roll aboard. The chair looked like it had been rigged together in someone's garage, different colors of metal for the wheels and the frame, black electrical tape wrapped around the control box where the man's chapped fingers squeezed a knobby joystick. The man wore a baseball cap with *8 Mile* stenciled on the front, and around his neck hung a cardboard sign reading Jesus Saves. A tray stretched across his lap, and on it a red plastic cup was held in place by several strips of duct tape. Inside the cup Augie saw dozens of tiny American flags attached to toothpicks.

In April of his senior year, he'd opened the thin envelope from West Point, his official rejection letter. When he turned the envelope upside down, as if the real notification, the acceptance, was somehow stuck inside, a sticker of the stars and stripes had floated to the ground, turning end over end like a strip of ticker tape.

"There's always enlistment," Mayo had said, reaching down to retrieve the flag. "You'll be better off getting your boots dirty." Augie had waited three weeks before telling him he was taking the grunt job with GM, that if he couldn't go through the academy, he didn't want to serve.

"You need to be strapped in?" Augie said to the man in the wheelchair. Augie couldn't tell if the man's bobbing head was a nod or a tick, but he hopped up and watched the man steer his chair into the handicapped space behind the console in back of the driver's seat. Then Augie knelt and pulled the C-Straint safety straps from the compartment in the wall. He slid the bolts into the floor grooves, hooked the clasps under the chair, and pulled the belts tight. The man smelled of fry batter.

"Okay?" Augie said. "Your brakes on?"

The man put his hands in his lap. "Good," he said, not looking at Augie. "Good. Thank you."

When Augie spun the wheel and headed back into the travel lane, he could hear the bus laboring. The noises were angry: squeals, bursts, grumbles, growls. Each release of air while braking or shifting gears reminded Augie of the sound of a breathing machine, a noise he associated with his mother's final days.

His father, too, had spent time hooked to rhythmic machinery as the throat and lung cancer attacked his ability to speak. Ten years ago, after his first major surgery, Mayo, his hands too shaky to hold a pen and his throat stitched and swollen, had balled his fists at Augie, made wild gestures at various objects in the room, the IV stand, the medical cart by the door. Finally Augie had gone to Workplace Warehouse to type a list of words, to have the sheet laminated. He had imagined holding the sheet in front of his father and letting him jab his trembling fingers at the words. *Tired. Happy. TV. Window. Lights. Pain.* Mayo had taken one look at his new vocabulary and tossed the sheet like a Frisbee back into Augie's chest.

Twilight was turning into darkness as the bus hurtled through Ferndale and neared Detroit's city limits. At the Eight Mile stop, the back exit door stuck without Augie realizing the problem until angry voices yelled, "Back!" Augie pushed the button again, but the door remained closed. "Open the damn door!" a voice yelled, and, on the third try, the signal went through, and the panels lurched open like a closet door wobbling on its hinges. Up front, a man with half a bushy beard heaved himself aboard. One cheek was bare, the other covered in white bristles as long as worms. Behind him on the sidewalk, a girl waited under the streetlamp, her hand resting on a stroller in which lay a baby boy wrapped in a dirty beach towel. Augie kept the door open for another few seconds until the girl looked up at him and shook her head.

"Trouble is in the world, Augie," Mayo had announced during one of Augie's childhood rides. "And these people, they've seen it. I've seen it, too. I'd change that if I could. But I'm just a driver. My job isn't to solve anyone's problems. My job is to get people where they want to go."

307

Augie's old bus moved like a leaking ark, and Augie felt the sink in his chest. They were behind schedule. Against regulations, he reached for the cell phone in his pocket. Though he hadn't felt any vibrations, he was sure the hospital had called. There were no messages, and he placed the phone in his lap. To his right was the Machpelah Cemetery, where, according to Mayo, the Jewish bodies were buried upright to save space. As a boy Augie had not known whether this was a joke or a lie, but it had always made him think of zombies. Further south, across from the fairgrounds, Woodlawn Cemetery was full of leafless trees and large digging machines, like vultures, silhouetted against the dusky sky.

The bus had grown quiet; the passengers, as usual, were lulled into silence by the disappearing sun. The only noise was a steady hum, like the drone of a refrigerator, coming from the man in the wheelchair. Augie's buddy, Manley, had a name for this stretch between Highland Park and midtown: "The Infinite Descent." Augie knew the scenery by heart: the Hennesy billboard, Red Sammy's Barbecue, the XXX Uptown Bookstore beside the BNB Candy and Snack Shop. He stopped outside the old Temple Beth El, now a Baptist church, and opened the door. A man with an uncovered head faced the bus. Even without the white cane, Augie knew the man was blind. "What bus this is?" the man said, his Afro creating a perfect circle around his head. He poked the ground with a golf umbrella. "Four fifty. Local," Augie said.

The man stuck the umbrella through his belt and pulled himself up the steps, his fingers wiggling to find the machine where he could swipe his card. Most people with impaired vision sat close to the driver, but as Augie shifted gear, he saw the man reaching hand over hand on the overhead pole, making his way to the rear bench. Augie realized the man hadn't told him where he needed to get off. *His problem*, Augie thought. *The world's misery*.

A shattered-glass rain began to hit the flat windshield. These new roadboats are like a face without a nose, Mayo would say whenever discussing the superiority of the old diesel fleet. Augie had to agree. In the new models, he felt off balance, liable any minute to pitch forward through the windshield and land on the roof of the vehicle up ahead.

The rain was making the road shine, the angry eyes of the approaching headlights laserlike in the gloom. In the middle of a vacant lot, Augie saw the sign for the Historic Holiday Home Tour and, behind it, the brick mansions whose plywood windows were covered in graffiti.

Cars were braking ahead of Augie, testing the slickness of the road, and the bus slowly emptied of passengers, energy, life. The frozen kid in the back seemed to have fallen asleep next to the blind guy. *Jackass probably missed his stop*, Augie thought. Out of sight behind the driver-side console, the wheelchair man continued to hum.

Crossing Warren always felt like coming up for air after a long underwater swim. Augie could once again detect the city's faint heartbeat. Up ahead in JFK Square, the world's tallest Salvation Army kettle towered over the temporary ice rink. It was almost 5:30. Two more stops until he could swing west to the Transit Center. There he would hop the shuttle out to the site of old Tiger Stadium, where his '89 Spectrum (minus three wheel covers) was parked. Augie might still make it to Beaumont before his father fell asleep, before the nurses patted Augie's back and told him to come back tomorrow.

A glance in the rearview told him only three passengers remained: the puffy-coat gangster, the blind guy tracing half circles on the floor with his umbrella, and the wheelchair man making noises like a dial tone. At Congress the bell dinged, and Augie pulled to the curb. The downtown streets were deserted, the rain crystallizing into fat, feathery flakes that stuck to the sidewalk. The wheelchair man cleared his throat, the phlegm breaking up violently, the sound of a fist squeezing a bag of popcorn. "Help," he moaned. "Stop." Augie hit a button, and the bus flooded with artificial light.

In the mirror, Augie saw the angry kid waking up, looking around as if he'd just landed on a new planet. Augie smiled a little when he heard the boy say, "Where the fuck?"

Augie slid his legs from under the wheel and stepped toward the wheelchair. *Where the hell are you going?* Augie thought, kneeling to undo the C-Straint harness attached to the wheelchair's thin frame.

"Yo, Pops," the boy yelled from the rear doorway. "Open this shit up."

The wheelchair man reached into his cup of flags and held one out to Augie. "Just a second," Augie called over his shoulder, tugging at the belt. "Let me get you out of here." The procedure should have been simple. Squeeze the release, slide the anchor, unhook the clasp. He'd done it dozens of times.

"Two dollars," the man said, tapping Augie's shoulder with his fist. "Help your brothers."

The belt would not release. Augie straightened his back, then pulled off his gloves and bent forward to try again. "Two dollars," the man said, his hands raking at Augie's forearm, nearly throwing him off balance.

The boy in the puffy coat was moving toward them. "Let me off this god-damned bus," he said. "Now."

"Just . . ." Augie said, dropping to his knees and jerking at the restraint. "I can't—"

"Let me go," the man said, banging his hands on the wheelchair's tray. "Let me go."

The puffy coat brushed past Augie's head, and he looked up to see the boy reaching across the driver's seat.

"Get away from there," Augie yelled, rising to his feet and placing his hand on the wheelchair's tray. The man was humming, rocking in his seat.

"Open the mother-fucking door," the boy yelled back, kicking at the glass. Once. Twice.

Augie looked toward the back of the bus, as if for help, but all he could see was the blind man's Afro, a great dark spot on the back wall, silent, unmoving. Up front, the boy's puffy coat had come unzipped, and it swished with each twist of his body.

The man in the wheelchair squeezed Augie's fingers, and Augie looked down. The man held a flag in his fist, and Augie realized, too late, what was happening as the man rammed the toothpick down into the back of Augie's hand.

A burst of pain rippled up Augie's forearm, and he jerked backward, falling into the seats across the aisle. The man was screaming now, "Let me go. Let me go. Let me go." He had activated his chair, and its motor was whining as the frame jerked forward three inches, the restraint tightening like a fishing line.

The boy had stopped kicking the door and was standing above Augie, watching the frenzied man in the chair. "Whoa," the boy said, holding his arms out as if to ward off a blow.

Augie looked at the back of his hand, at the toothpick sunk into his skin, the American flag sticking out of his flesh. Blood was trickling from the puncture, and the knuckle was already starting to purple. He plucked at the toothpick and pulled it free. "Calm down," he said, untucking his shirt and pressing it to his wound. The chair continued to buzz and whir, a needle caught on a skipping record. The man's screams became a low-pitched moan as he hunched forward, the Jesus Saves sign dangling into his lap.

Augie stood up, clutching his right hand over his left. The man in the back of the bus was a shadow, his umbrella balanced on his lap like a set of scales. Augie took a step forward and kicked at the harness, the wheelchair, the man. Anything to set him free. To Augie's right, the boy's leg shot forward and slammed into the strap. Side-by-side, the two of them hammered at the trapped wheelchair. With the heel of his boot, Augie stomped at the restraint and connected with the hook at the edge of the chair's frame. The frame bent slightly, and the hook broke loose, dancing in the air for a split second. The chair, untethered, slid free and collided with the console behind Augie's seat. The man lurched forward and slumped onto his tray. The wheelchair's motor fizzled, then died.

"Shit," Augie said, pressing his bloody left hand into his thigh. The boy reached out and dragged the man back into his seat. The man's *8 Mile* cap was crooked on his head, and his sign was spun backward, revealing the words This Side Up.

Augie wrapped his right arm around the man's chest and pulled. The man sat crookedly in his chair, legs crossed like twisted branches. "Home," he said without looking at Augie. "Home."

Augie felt the throb in his hand, the clenching pulse of pain, and he again kicked the man's chair. "Get off my bus," he shouted, bringing his face close to the man's, their noses almost touching. "You fucking stabbed me." His mouth was filled with salt, his ears full of burning water. It was the feeling he'd known when he refused to visit his father following his mother's death, when he'd offered the broken man no repair.

The boy in the puffy coat stood silently, hands in pockets, observing the scene. Augie faced him. The boy seemed much younger, a child, really, a kid trying to make sense of the world. "That was messed up," the boy said. "Your hand okay?"

Augie nodded and took a step toward him. The boy flinched as Augie reached past and flipped a switch to open the front door. They looked at each other for a few seconds before the boy lowered his head, stepped to the curb, and backed away from the bus.

Augie pressed the button that would extend and lower the access ramp and turned to the wheelchair, the pitiful man slumped in his seat. He looked over his shoulder at the blind man silhouetted against the wall, as still and quiet as a corpse. A pile of tiny American flags lay scattered across the aisle. Spots of blood formed constellations on the floor. When the ramp clicked into place, Augie reached for the chair's control mechanism and found the motor switch. The man was staring straight ahead, repeating the word *sleep* over and over. Augie pictured the man sinking his teeth into Augie's arm. "Shut up," Augie said. Then softer, "Shut up." He placed the man's hand on the control box and shoved the stick forward. The chair accelerated with a shudder, moving out into the snow, the right wheel wonky, like a top. The chair puttered onto the sidewalk, then kept going in a straight line past the No Parking signs and a row of potted trees. It continued its slow path toward the glass siding of the J.P.Morgan building. Augie stared, his hand at his side, blood on his fingertips, as the chair bumped directly into the wall and stopped, like a remote control car, like a child's sorry toy.

"It's an honest job," his father had said twenty-five years ago, Augie's first day behind the massive wheel. "This city may be the auto capital of the world, but it ain't nothing without the people who ride the bus."

Augie looked at the clock. He looked at his hand. He reached up and pulled the wire. The Stop Requested sign glowed above the driver's seat, and the familiar chime echoed down the empty chamber. "Hey, buddy," Augie said to the blind man. "This is your stop."

The man stood without speaking and pushed his umbrella down the aisle. Augie thought of his father on the shores of Lake St. Clair, his metal detector strapped to his back, the sensor sniffing the ground for treasure. As a child, Augie had never understood his father's joy at unearthing a filthy earring, a crud-encrusted dime.

The man did not even ask where they were as he descended the back steps. Augie leaned out the front door and watched him float north, back in the direction they had come. To his left, the wheelchair remained next to the building, flakes blanketing the man's hat and shoulders, covering him in white. The boy in the puffy coat was gone, swallowed by the empty spaces of downtown Detroit, the forest of office towers and cement. The blind man crossed Congress and continued up Woodward, and then Augie saw him turn around as if looking back.

A wave of warm air passed over Augie, as if the heater had somehow burst to life. "Hey," Augie called, snowdrops melting on his cheek. "You know where you are?" He wanted to race to the man, wrap a blanket around his shoulders, steer him, peacefully, to his home. He wanted to find out where the man was going and where he had been. He wanted to know the man's name.

The blind man clasped his hands together, then pulled them apart, a gesture Augie did not understand. A car rose from an underground garage, its headlights exploding in Augie's eyes, and he was sightless in the sudden illumination. After the car turned left and Augie blinked away the ghosts, he saw the blind man moving again, his back to Augie, his umbrella—Augie could almost *see* it—making crescents in the snow.

Nominated by The Gettysburg Review

A FABLE FOR OUR ANNIVERSARY

by ALAN MICHAEL PARKER

from SUBTROPICS

You asked to be surprised, so I
traded our last sack of rice
for a little knife curved into a question,

the knife for a bit of cloth
embroidered by a prisoner,
the cloth for a monkey who was never nice,

the monkey for a bowl of sayings,
the sayings for a pair of silver candlesticks,
the candlesticks for a goose.

The goose bit the dogs in the courtyard,
so I traded the goose for a pink bonnet
that makes the wearer invisible.

Who would want to be invisible?
I traded the bonnet for a sheaf of wheat
that shone in the garden for a little while

like a giant piece of golden jewelry,
the wheat for a desk, solid as a bad idea,
the desk for a couple of tickets to a show.

Love, we could go to the show, but the show would end.
I traded the show tickets
for an old trousseau, the linens flush with lavender,

because I knew a man who
would give me a magic goat
for the smells kept between those sheets.

But first the man made me fetch
a cup of coffee from the deli, which I did,
cream, no sugar, an epic quest.

It was one of those dawns that didn't
and then was. The crows were calling
in their office across the street,

all that old business of the soul and such,
but don't you worry, I wasn't scared.
And now I have a goat:

I lead him home, pat his head
and say the words I'm supposed to say—
careful, those words are powerful—

until the goat begins to float into the air,
bleating a bit, and huffing
outside our bedroom window.

Wake up, sweetie!
We've been married for twenty-five years!
I brought you a magic floating goat!

Nominated by Jane Ciabattari, Kevin Prufer

SKYDIVE

by SARAH DEMING

from THE THREEPENNY REVIEW

"When you are in free fall," Utah warned me, "you may feel like you can't breathe. You can. Just close your eyes and smile."

The tips of my sneakers were at the airplane's open door and the wind was in my face. I was strapped into a kind of spooning position with Utah, since New York law requires novices to skydive in tandem with an instructor. I had decided this was my favorite New York law. Utah was about six-foot-four, of Paul Newmanish appearance, and had possibly been genetically engineered to reassure me. He was, he'd informed me, the instructor they sent out with paraplegics and the elderly.

"Look up at the wing!" he yelled.

I averted my eyes from the reeling landscape and fixed them to the wing of the Twin Otter. We were the last ones to jump. I had already watched the other skydivers tumble out, howling with joy and followed by videographers. Everyone at Skydive the Ranch seemed to be there with a birthday or bachelor party, except me, which might have been why I got the special needs instructor. I wanted to tell Utah that I really did have friends. Peekaboo wanted to come, but she had to pole dance, and Colin backed out because of Hummel's Piano Trio Number Five.

Skydiving was the last thing on my Two-Kidney Bucket List. For a year, I had been taking the tests required to be a living organ donor for my mother, whose kidneys were barely functioning after sixteen years of lithium for bipolar disorder. A prophylactic transplant would save her from, in the words of a friend, "the living death of dialysis." Finally I'd finished all the bloodwork, urine tests, pap smears, mammograms,

CAT scans, and EKGs. Our transplant was scheduled for the following week.

I had gotten the idea for the Two-Kidney Bucket List while surfing the Web for surgical horror stories and morbidity rates. A page on the Kidney Foundation website offered the following advice:

> activities best avoided by people with only one kidney include: boxing, field hockey, football, ice hockey, lacrosse, martial arts, rodeo, soccer and wrestling . . . may also include extreme activities such as skydiving.

Some of these I'd already gotten out of my system: soccer as a child, field hockey and lacrosse in high school, martial arts and boxing in my twenties. Over the last month, I'd been checking off the rest of the list. My football experience consisted of lunch with Everson Walls, the great NFL cornerback, who had donated a kidney to his former Dallas Cowboys teammate, Ron Springs. I had originally asked Mr. Walls to throw a football around with me, but he clearly considered this request ridiculous and possibly inappropriate, so I settled for a stimulating discussion about interceptions, racial politics, and Tom Landry. I wasn't being rigid about the Bucket List; "ice hockey" was a survey of classic and contemporary video games curated by my brother Dan. We scored the games on a ten-puck system, the winner being NHL Slapshot with its authentic icy feel. For rodeo, I rode the mechanical bull at Johnny Utah's in Midtown.

I covered my bases with both amateur and professional wrestling. First I ran the food concession at a girls' freestyle tournament organized by a non-profit called Beat the Streets. This was a surprisingly moving experience. Next, I traveled to Atlanta for a professional wrestling lesson with "Number One Cocky" Sonny Siaki, a muscle-bound Samoan who had retired from the ring to give a kidney to his brother Bernard. Sonny was adorable and chivalrous; at no time during our lesson did he slam me to the ring neck-first in his signature move, the "Siakalypse Now."

All that remained was skydiving, which I had considered skipping. I am crushingly afraid of heights, and I do not like sports that involve speed. I would never have entertained the notion of jumping from a plane had it not been included on that Kidney Foundation list.

It was hard to tell where my husband stood on this issue: whenever I brought up skydiving, he began radiating the benign indifference he normally reserves for housework. Everyone else was horrified. My mother didn't know, and I wasn't going to tell her until I was safely on the ground. When I'd broached the topic a few weeks prior, she'd sounded stricken.

"What if you die?" she asked. "What will happen to my kidney?"

This made me a tiny bit mad. It wasn't her kidney yet. I had a week left with Odysseus, and I intended to show him a good time. I had named my left kidney Odysseus, because he was going on a heroic journey back where he came from.

My right kidney, the one I was keeping, was called Mike Tyson. People don't think of him this way, but Tyson was small for a modern heavyweight, just five-eleven and less than two hundred and twenty pounds in his prime. My right kidney only weighed a pound, but it could take out kidneys twice its size.

When Mike Tyson talks about Cus D'Amato or pigeons or fighters of the classic era, he reveals an intelligence that is startling, even to those of us who know that intelligence is required to throw a great left hook. Sure he's bitten some ears. He's bipolar, like my mom. Bipolar people do crazy things sometimes, but that doesn't mean you stop loving them.

Mike Tyson, Odysseus, and I were perched to jump at the airplane's edge.

Utah was yelling over the wind: "We go on three! One . . ."

On the flight up, I'd confessed my fear of peeing my pants, or worse.

"You can't physically pee," Utah had replied. "And you can't poop, and if you were having sex in the airplane—pardon my language—but when you get to that door, you're not having sex any more. It's fight or flight. The blood goes to your muscles and brain."

"Two . . ."

He had also said my crushing fear of heights would not be an issue, since we were thirteen thousand feet up, too high for accurate depth perception. I was shocked to find that this was true. I felt none of the bodily terror I experienced on high ledges and rooftops. The ground looked distant, abstract.

"Three!"

You don't fall from the edge, and you don't jump. You push your feet back and arch, leaving the airplane behind.

That's when the terror hit. It was like an orgasm, only bad. I became a blind animal, flipping and twitching as the air screamed by. I did not remember what Utah had told me about being able to breathe. I did not remember to close my eyes and smile. Luckily, like an orgasm, this was brief.

I breathed.

I felt Utah unhook my arms from their death grip on the harness. He moved them into ninety-degree angles, like the arms of a cactus.

"Skydive!" he cried.

The overpowering sensations were of noise and cold. Utah's hand appeared in my blurry peripheral vision. He yelled single words over the wind's roar.

"Look!"

He pointed to trees.

"Beautiful!"

He pointed to fields.

"Look!"

He pointed to trees.

"Skydive!" he cried.

He moved my cactus arms to the left and then to the right so we spun in freefall. We plummeted for six thousand feet, but it didn't feel like falling. It felt like being suspended in a vast wind tunnel, like being the man in that old Maxell ad, blasted back by sound. My eyes watered beneath the goggles and my hands went numb within the double-layered gloves. I was relieved when Utah guided my right hand back to his hip. Together, we grasped the golf-ball-sized handle of the ripcord. We yanked.

The only way I knew how fast we'd been falling was by how fast we stopped. In the sudden silence, the unfurling parachute sounded like flying birds.

Utah removed my goggles, and I blinked at the vista.

"Now we can talk," he said softly. "Congratulations, you did a wonderful job."

He loosened something, and I sat back into the parachute harness. I was slack with aftershock and could not stop giggling. I thanked Utah, again and again. I wanted to thank everyone I had ever known.

All around us, other skydivers hung suspended from their primary-colored chutes. I gazed down at the darling meadows of New Paltz, a village in upstate New York that I would later describe as "somewhere on Long Island"; once I leave New York City, I never know where I am.

When I was six years old, I asked my mother what religion we were, and she told me, "We are Jewish atheists," an answer that got me into hot water with Girl Scout management. To this day, if you put a gun to my head and asked my faith, I would probably say, "None," but as I floated above the farmland of what I believed to be Long Island, I felt somehow religious. After thirty-seven years, Odysseus was going home, but first I had taken him for a ride.

Utah said, "Let's go in for a show landing."

We did some fancy spins in front of the other skydivers.

"Lift your legs!" he commanded. "Press down!"

We skidded to earth on the seats of our jumpsuits, and I saw a white and yellow parachute land in our wake. As he helped me to my feet, Utah announced my kidney donation to all the other skydivers. Everyone applauded. I got embarrassed and cried.

Utah said, "The Buddha loves you, Sarah."

Strangers came up and hugged me, and one of them said, "You could shoot a bus full of nuns and still go to heaven."

Nominated by Alice Mattison, Jessica Roeder

THE BUTTERFLY EFFECT

by JENNIFER LUNDEN

from CREATIVE NONFICTION

METAMORPHOSIS

It was cold in Maine. Cold. And the snow was heaped in dirty piles on the side of the road. And the sidewalks were icy. And it got dark at 4:30 in the afternoon.

It was the dead of winter, and I wanted out, so I flew to California—to Pacific Grove, aka Butterfly Town, USA, to see the monarchs. It was a journey home, really, though I had never been there.

I grew up in a box-shaped house on a well-manicured lawn in the suburbs of a mid-sized Canadian city in Ontario. Across the road and abutting the river was a patch of city land, untended, wild, a field of tall grasses flecked with milkweed and Queen Anne's lace. There, I discovered my first monarch caterpillar. I was 9 years old, and I had never seen anything like it. Boldly ringed in concentric stripes—black, yellow and white—it was stretched out on a milkweed leaf, eating. I plucked it off, held it in my hand, touched it with my fingers. Its skin was smooth, leathery. It did not roll up in a ball. It did not seem afraid. Docile. I broke off the milkweed near the top and carried my find home.

I scoured the fields in search of more. I filled jars with milkweed and caterpillars. I pounded nail holes in the lids. I spent hours watching them.

They ate voraciously. I could see their mandibles working. I could

321

see the chunks they took out of the leaves, bite by bite. They grew fast, and before I knew it, they were climbing to the lids of their jars. They spun small mounds of silk and attached themselves to the mounds and hung there in the shapes of J's for a long, long time. And then, when the moment was right, they split the skins on their backs, wrestled with themselves and turned inside-out, and, suddenly, there they were, something wholly different: an emerald green chrysalis with little golden flecks and a gold crown.

Miraculous.

They would hang for days, for what seemed like forever, and nothing changed. And then one day, I could see the darkening. The butterfly was forming. Soon, I could see the outline of a wing. The orange. The black veins. The white polka dots.

The waiting for what would come next. . .. It seemed interminable.

I didn't want to miss it.

MIGRATION

When a monarch butterfly sets off on its journey to its winter destination, it does not have to pay a $ 100 fee because its suitcase is 25 pounds over the limit. It does not have to take off its shoes, its watch, its coat and scarf, in case of bombs. It does not have to put its carry-ons in the overhead compartment or under the seat in front of it. It does not have to watch the flight attendant demonstrate how to put on a seatbelt or an oxygen mask. It does not worry about going down. It does not worry.

It's 11 degrees Fahrenheit and a cold, clear day when my flight departs, and it's hard to imagine what a monarch does experience on its own winged migration. It experiences, certainly, the view. It experiences a silence I cannot imagine. It experiences, I think, a certain peace, a free tilting. It knows nothing but how to ride the waves of the wind.

It is the opposite of me, crammed here in the stale air of this "Freedom Air" Embraer EMB-45.

HABITAT

I have a carbon filter mask. If I were to give it a name, I think it would have a male name. Tom. Something strong and protective.

My mask is battleship gray. It shields me from perfumes and colognes, air fresheners, cleaning products, pesticides, fumes from fresh

322

paint. I carry it in a baggie in my purse, and I take it out now, on this airplane, and strap it on.

I wear it when I can feel the headache coming on. When it hits, it feels as though my brain has swollen inside the cradle of my scalp. A fog rolls in. My capacity to juggle a number of thoughts at once, an ability most people take for granted, dwindles. It alarms me when this happens, when my brain gives way.

I have it easy compared to some people. I know people who suffer seizures when exposed to chemicals. Closed airways, joint and muscle pain, nausea, insomnia, disabling fatigue. Panic attacks, mood swings. I know people who could never hazard the bad air on planes. Some of them live in ceramic trailers in the deserts of Arizona. Some of them are homeless; they live in their cars or tents. They can't find anyplace safe to breathe. They can't find habitat.

We call ourselves "canaries in the coal mine." We have multiple-chemical sensitivity, and our numbers are growing.

BUTTERFLY TOWN, USA

Everywhere, all over the little town of Pacific Grove, population 15,522, there are butterflies. And not only the real live fluttering kind: There's a monarch emblem in bas-relief on the Chamber of Commerce plaque hanging at the Butterfly Grove Inn; there are 22 wooden monarchs of various sizes adorning the town's Shell station; even the bakery's cookies come in the shape of monarch butterflies. This place, this magical little place, is indeed Butterfly Town, USA.

I did not know, when I was 9 years old, that it would come to this. I didn't know that the magic would stay with me, all these 30 odd years. That I would fly across the country to see the monarchs. That I would finally—or ever—get to see the overwintering monarchs clinging together in their clusters of thousands.

TORPOR

When the monarchs hang clustered together, paralyzed by the cold, that is called "torpor." They are clasped to each other, holding the heat between them. They wait for the sun to warm them. You wouldn't know they are so beautiful, hanging in the trees like dead leaves. Wings closed, their brilliance is disguised. They wait for the mercury to hit 55 degrees, and then they open their orange wings to the sun. Some of them flutter aloft; others stay together, warm and close in their safe clusters. They cleave to each other like family, like best friends, like a community.

The earliest record of the monarchs in Pacific Grove dates back to 1875, the year the town was established as a Methodist resort, when several hundred people first assembled there in worship. But as far as anybody knows, monarchs have been migrating to Pacific Grove for thousands of years. It is their home.

As recently as 1997, there were 45,000 monarchs overwintering in a little 2.7-acre grove of eucalyptus trees behind the Butterfly Grove Inn. When I am there in early January 2008, however, we count only 4,000. It is a bad year for monarchs.

In fact, annual counts show the monarch populations all over California in a rapid downward spiral. What is happening to the monarchs? Why are their numbers plummeting?

THE BUTTERFLY LADY

In 1987, Ro Vaccaro was a high-powered secretary at a high-powered law firm in Washington, D.C. She could type 130 words a minute. She typed for four lawyers and answered the phone for nine. She made a good living.

But four years earlier, Ro had been diagnosed with lupus, and her symptoms—joint pain, sensitivity to touch and depression, to name a few—were flaring. It had gotten so bad she had to wear braces on one arm and one leg to get around, to keep going. The stress was aggravating her symptoms. She worked in a 12-story building, and she was thinking of jumping off it.

One day, her sister Beverly called. Beverly knew how butterflies buoyed her sister. Twelve years earlier, at an estate auction, Ro had found her first butterfly—in the shape of a beautiful, jeweled pin. She was in the middle of a divorce at the time, and she told Beverly, "I feel better just holding it." In that moment, Ro Vaccaro was transformed.

So when Beverly learned of the Pacific Grove monarchs, she called her sister and suggested they make a pilgrimage.

That October, the sisters found themselves celebrating the butterflies' return with the rest of the town at its annual Butterfly Parade, a Pacific Grove tradition since 1939. There were all the kindergarteners decked out in their bright orange monarch wings. There were all the town's children dressed in costume, marching down Lighthouse Road.

There were the school marching bands, the baton twirlers. Monarch cookies! Monarch cinnamon rolls! There were all the happy people, celebrating the return of the monarchs.

Ro was touched by the magic. She knew she needed to come back to this place.

A year later, she did just that. And when she looked up into the butterfly trees, she told her sister it was like a cathedral. Later, she wrote, "They are nature's stained-glass windows, flying high between us and the sun."

She found a job there and took a $10,000 cut in pay. Appointing herself Pacific Grove's first butterfly docent, she joined a small cluster of monarch aficionados, and, together, they organized Friends of the Monarchs, an education and advocacy group. Many years later, one February, she told a National Public Radio (NPR) reporter her story:

> "I surprised even myself by sending my letter of resignation by Federal Express. I said, 'Consider my two-week vacation your two-week notice. I'm moving to live with the butterflies.' And I did. As you can see, there's no brace on my leg, there's no brace on my arm, and I haven't wiped this silly grin off my face since I got here."

MIGRATION

How do they know where to go? How is it that they trace the same route, the great-great-great-grandchildren, year after year, and end up in the selfsame trees? Scientists have found 40 genes that help monarchs use the sun as a compass to guide them to warmer climes. Still, it seems to me there is mystery in it.

It's possible that some of the monarchs I raised as a girl migrated down the coast and all the way to Mexico. East Coast monarchs flock to Mexico by the millions, as they have for thousands of years. Until recently, only the Mexican locals knew about the magnificent "magic circles" where the butterflies overwinter. There, millions of monarchs hang from the oyamel firs—Latin name: *Abies religiosa*.

They fly about 12 miles per hour, 46 miles a day and as high as 11,000 feet. They migrate as far as 2,200 miles. In early November, millions of monarchs stream into Mexico.

On Nov. 2, my birthday, Mexicans celebrate "Dia de los Muertos," Day of the Dead, honoring friends and relatives who have passed on.

In Michoacán, where the monarchs come to roost, the locals say the spirits of their beloved return in the shape of bright, fluttering butterflies.

The locals call the butterflies "las palomas," which translates as "the doves" or, according to Robert Pyle in *Chasing Monarchs*, as "the souls of lost children."

DIAPAUSE

There are approximately 200 roosting sites along the coast of California. None of them attracts the millions of monarchs that the Mexican sites see. One or two may count as many as 100,000 in a good year. Pacific Grove averages 20,000. The monarchs cluster there for five months, arriving in time to be fêted at the annual butterfly parade, then mating and departing around Valentine's Day. These butterflies live as long as eight months, much longer than the summer generations, which enjoy the bright flowers and summer breezes for a mere two to six weeks. They are in a state of diapause, these migrating monarchs: Their reproductive functions are switched off. They are conserving their energy. They are waiting for the right moment.

Around Valentine's Day, as milkweed starts poking through the earth north and east of Pacific Grove, something changes in the small enclave where the monarchs have spent the winter. The butterflies come to life. There's energy in the air.

Here is how Ro Vaccaro, the Butterfly Lady described it on the Valentine's Day 2005 NPR broadcast:

> "They chase in spirals up into the sky, and there are chases going on all over the grove as the male butterflies try to choose their Valentine sweethearts. And when he finds the girl that he thinks would be just perfect, he zooms in front of her, and he sprinkles her with this wonderful perfume, and she is just dazzled. And he grabs her in midair with his feet, and so, like a little maple seed, they come twirling down out of the sky. He strokes her body, and then he puts his head right down next to hers, and it looks just like he's whispering sweet things in her ear. But he's going to trick her. He stands on his head and flips her, and if he does it correctly, he'll have the abdomens aligned, which is the only way he can make the connection. Then she becomes very docile, and she folds her wings

together. He runs two or three steps. He lifts her up underneath his body, and he carries her all the way up to the top of
the trees where they'll be the warmest, and they'll stay together till the sun comes up the next morning."

CHRYSALIS

One day this past summer, at the park where I take my dog, I spotted
a monarch fluttering around a milkweed plant. I stopped and watched.
The butterfly dropped down to the top leaf, touched the tip of her
abdomen to it and then flew off. I bent over the leaf and beheld something I had never seen in all my years of monarchs: an egg, gleaming
like a small gem.

The butterflies lay them one at a time—400 in all—on milkweed all
along the migration route north. They mate repeatedly. Each egg is
sired by the female's most recent mate. Each is fertilized only when she
deposits it on a milkweed leaf. Only milkweed. Nothing else will do.

When the caterpillar hatches, three to seven days later, it is two millimeters long. Tiny. Its first meal is the egg it comes from. Then, the
fine, hairlike filaments of the milkweed. Finally, as soon as it is large
enough, it begins its leaf-feast. It eats and eats. It's as though the monarch caterpillar were born to eat. It grows 2 inches in two weeks, fattens
to 2,700 times its birth weight. It outgrows its skin four or five times
and molts to accommodate its expanding girth.

And then, one day, it is time. Who knows how the caterpillar decides?
It attaches a little silk fastener to the underside of a leaf. It pierces the
silk with its "cremaster"—a small, hooklike appendage at the end of its
body—and wriggles hard to make sure the connection will hold. It
hangs . . . still . . . in the shape of a J, and then, when the moment is
right, it splits the skin on its back, miraculously transforming itself into
an emerald green chrysalis with a crown of gold.

MYSTERY

What happens inside a chrysalis?

One day, I decided to find out. Nine years old and aching with curiosity, I took one of my chrysalides to the side of the house and set it down
on a large rock. I held it gently with my thumb and forefinger as I cut
into it with my jackknife.

No butterfly no caterpillar: just black ooze.

I'd made black ooze out of something that could have become a butterfly.

What I didn't know, what I was trying to find out, was what Kathryn Lasky describes in her lovely little book, *Monarchs*: "The body of the caterpillar melts away into a solution of transforming cells and tissues."

Something magical happens inside.

ECLOSION

It hangs, this gem of nature, for nine to 15 days. When it is almost ready, the "imago," or butterfly, can be seen in outline. The orange wing, the black veins, the white spots—they darken. The chrysalis is now translucent.

Finally, one day, in one small moment, the butterfly breathes. Its intake of air splits the chrysalis open. This is called "eclosion," when the butterfly emerges from its chrysalis. It hangs there, stunned, perhaps, by its new form. The world looks different through its new eyes. Its abdomen is fat with hemolymph, which it pumps through the veins into its wings.

FLIGHT

A 9-year-old girl is closer to the ground. She sees things up close. She watches. She waits for miracles to happen. And sometimes, when she is really lucky, she witnesses one with her very own eyes. The chrysalis cracks open. The monarch, fat and wet and crumpled, bursts into the world.

A 9-year-old girl takes the time to lie down on the burnt orange rug in her parents' living room, holding the new monarch on her finger above her. It clings to her. It hangs, drying. Her arm gets tired, but still, she holds the butterfly aloft. She wants to watch its wings unfurl. She wants to see its abdomen slim. She wants to watch it get strong.

When it starts to open and close its wings, it is almost ready for flight. The girl stands up. The butterfly clings to her hand. Carefully, gently, she walks out of the living room, pushes the screen door open, carries her monarch to the middle of her weedless, grassy yard. She holds her hand out to the sky.

She expects the monarch to fly away in an instant, glad to be set free. But it clings to her hand for a long time, opening and closing its wings, waiting. And then, suddenly, it lets go. It lifts itself up into the blue sky and flutters off into the distance and out of sight, leaving the girl down below with her hand over her brow, shielding her eyes from the sun.

MICROCLIMATE

Ro Vaccaro decided the butterflies needed an advocate. So, she began showing up at city council meetings, using the three-minute public comment period to talk about the butterflies. Soon, everybody was calling her the "Butterfly Lady." It was here, at these meetings, that she first laid eyes on Mrs. Edna Dively the woman who owned the Butterfly Grove Inn and the land beside it—the magical place where the monarchs roosted every year. Mrs. Dively was fighting for permission to develop her property. She wanted to build houses and an apartment building. And one day in 1989, the city granted her wish.

Mrs. Dively swore that she had no intent to take down the butterfly trees, that she would build around them. But Ro Vaccaro was dubious. Any change in the microclimate might make the monarchs decide the grove was no longer fit for their needs.

So Ro Vaccaro set about to stop Mrs. Dively.

CHRYSALIDES

I can't help it. When I see milkweed, I look for monarch caterpillars. And when I find them, my heart leaps with that familiar joy and excitement, and the impulse to take them home is too strong to deny. One year, long before I flew to California to see the monarchs, I found three caterpillars in the park and brought them home. Despite all my best intentions, I killed every one. Each died in a different stage of metamorphosis. The first, a caterpillar, got sluggish and simply stopped eating. The second died with only a little triangle of green on its back where the splitting had begun. I found it, finally, hanging vertically, its J depleted: done. It simply didn't have the strength to complete the transformation. The last died in chrysalis. It simply turned black. No orange of the wings, just black, and finally, I gave up waiting and took it outside, laid it in a pile of brush.

The next year, I found two caterpillars munching away on separate leaves of the same milkweed. My heart leapt. Then I hesitated. What if I had become, somehow, an angel of death for monarchs? I should not take these caterpillars, I thought.

But.

I uprooted the entire milkweed and brought it, and them, home.

What could it be? What was killing my monarchs? Was it my loss of innocence—the simple fact of my adulthood—that left me incapable of supporting the magic to completion? Or was it something more sinister?

I built a screened cage for them. I avoided city milkweed. I doted. A few days later, both caterpillars hung themselves in J's and turned into green chrysalides. I waited. I waited.

And once again, the chrysalides turned black.

MEMORABILIA

She saved monarch memorabilia the way a mother saves all of her first-born's artwork and school assignments. Boxes and boxes of letters, handouts and newspaper clippings. If it had to do with the monarchs of Pacific Grove, Ro Vaccaro put it in a box and kept it.

"I wear a butterfly every day, at least somewhere—but usually multiple butterflies," she told the NPR reporter. "I have a butterfly watch, butterfly earrings, butterflies on my shoes and socks."

She had monarchs on her hat, monarch pins and buttons and patches on her coat. She decorated her house with them. The walls, the pillows, the rugs, the shower curtain. And she blazoned her car with bumper stickers about saving them.

Ro Vaccaro, the Butterfly Lady of Pacific Grove, lived and breathed monarch butterflies.

BREATHING

My other mask—my special occasion mask—is a flowery lacy affair, skin-toned, with a little rose appliqué by its left strap. Feminine. Or as feminine as a fume-deterring mask can be.

It's not any better, really, this flowery, lacy mask. What I really want is a mask bearing an appliquéd symbol that stands for "your toxic products are making me sick." It would be nice if the symbol could point out, too, that 62,000 chemicals used in the United States have never been tested for safety. That we are human guinea pigs. That while we think our government would surely protect us from egregious toxins, we are wrong.

But what would that symbol look like?

330

If I have to wear something that makes me stand out in a crowd, I'd rather it not be something that stands for "crazy" (think Michael Jackson) or "communicable" (think SARS). I want people to know that this mask isn't about me so much as it is about us.

THE BUTTERFLY GROVE INN

The Butterfly Grove Inn is a pink motel nestled right next to the stand of eucalyptus trees where the monarchs have been overwintering for generations. In the lobby, someone has cut out a newspaper article about the monarchs and posted it on Bristol board next to the front desk. There are butterfly pins and postcards for sale. I buy an extra-long postcard depicting, in five photographs, the stages of metamorphosis. I have arrived at dusk, too late to find the monarchs.

I have always loved motels. The thrill of opening the door. Fresh space. But my love for an empty motel room comes fraught, now, with doubt and anxiety. Will the room be safe? Or will it be toxic?

I swing the door open and take a whiff. Inside, the walls are painted beige, and framed photo prints of waterfalls hang over the two beds. The room smells fresh at first sniff. But is that chemical fresh or clean-air fresh?

I drag my big suitcase through the door. Inside my head, the alarms begin to sound. Get out! Get out! The air is not good. But I have paid to stay the night at the Butterfly Grove Inn. There's nothing to do but open the window and let in the cold, clean air. The room is frigid. I put an extra blanket on the bed. The brain fog rolls in; the glands in my throat swell; I'm rubbing my eyes. The headache is on its way. Cleaning products, must be.

THE BUTTERFLY EFFECT

In the 1960s, meteorologist Edward Lorenz made a discovery that would change the way we view the world. He found that even minute discrepancies between two starting points could produce vastly disparate outcomes. For instance, if a little boy took two identical balls to the top of a hill and released one just a fraction of an inch away from where he let go of the other, they would probably end up in two very different places. The scientific term for this was "sensitive dependence on initial conditions." More poetically, it came to be known as "the

Butterfly Effect," and Lorenz suggested the possibility that something so seemingly innocuous as the flap of a butterfly's wings in Brazil could create changes in the atmosphere leading to something as momentous as a tornado in Texas.

What happens, then, when there are no butterflies left?

MONSANTO

Almost 50 percent of this country's landmass is cultivated for agricultural purposes. Not so long ago, Midwestern corn and soybean fields furnished about half of the breeding grounds for the Eastern monarchs. No longer. Now, thanks to crops made "Roundup Ready" by genetic-engineering monolith Monsanto, 100 million acres of monarch habitat have been annihilated; milkweed has been virtually extirpated from American farmland.

Roundup, advertised on TV in mock-Old-West-style, with suburban "cowboys" wielding Roundup "guns" while a little boy rides past them on a bicycle, is the herbicide of choice not only for homeowners and public works departments, but also for farmers. "Roundup Ready" crops can withstand heavy doses of the herbicide, which kills most every plant it touches, including milkweed.

Over 18 million pounds of glyphosate—Roundup's active ingredient—are sprayed annually on U.S. crops, sidewalks and yards. The "clean field" ideal of industrial monoculture farming—no weeds, no insects and no diseases, thanks to insecticides, herbicides and genetically engineered crops—is wiping out the monarch caterpillar's only food source.

GLOBAL WARMING

California is heating up. Most areas in the country, in fact, are getting hotter. Insect ecologist Dr. Orley R. "Chip" Taylor, director of Monarch Watch—an educational outreach program whose mission is to create, conserve and protect monarch habitats—has demonstrated a correlation between rising temperatures in California and lower West Coast monarch populations.

Taylor reports that monarch numbers crash every time temperatures above 90 degrees combine with low water availability for a week or more. The hotter it gets, the shorter the lifespan of flowers, so nectar is less available. And while the need for water increases in hot weather, availability decreases. So monarch butterflies don't live as long in the heat, and they lay fewer eggs. This is called "decreased realized fecundity" and what it means is that populations take a nosedive.

Temperatures have increased 1.4 degrees Fahrenheit; nine of the ten warmest years on record occurred in the last decade. Precipitation has declined 0.25 inches per decade.

I feel a weight in the pit of my stomach when I read these numbers.

DEFORESTATION

In 1976, a National Geographic article revealed, for the first time, the location of the East Coast monarchs' Mexican hideaway. All of the East Coast monarchs, millions and millions of them, flock to the oyamel firs and other trees in seven to 12 sites (depending on the year), spread across the state of Michoacán's Transvolcanic Mountains. But there is a problem: logging. Although 217 square miles of these mountains are now a designated Monarch Butterfly Biosphere Reserve (MBBR) and protected by government decree, still, at a rate of 2 percent to 5 percent a year, the trees keep coming down.

Illegal logging strips away the butterflies' particular roost trees; it also puts gashes in the forest canopy. As Chip Taylor describes it, "These gaps are like holes in your winter coat, as far as the monarchs are concerned. They let in snow and rain, and the roosting monarchs are more vulnerable to freezing." In 2002, millions of monarchs froze and dropped to the ground. Witnesses described wading through dead monarchs, knee deep.

Shortly after he took office in December 2006, Mexico's new president, Felipe Calderon, promised to protect the MBBR, and in December 2007, the government conducted what amounted to the largest illegal-logging sweep ever seen in the vicinity of the Reserve. Nineteen sawmills and lumberyards were raided, and at least 45 people were arrested and charged. Logs and lumber from as many as 1,750 trees were confiscated.

Of course, those trees could not be taken back to the forest. And although the World Wildlife Fund in Mexico and the Michoacán Reforestation Fund have planted a combined total of more than 4.8 million trees over the past 10 years, even these aren't enough to keep up with the rate of deforestation.

HABITAT

Every day in the United States, new subdivisions, malls, condominiums and parking lots consume 6,000 acres of natural habitat. This adds up to 2.2 million acres per year. At this rate, an area of habitat the size of Illinois is razed, then paved, every 16 years.

Soon, the butterflies will have nowhere to land.

WAYSTATIONS

Chip Taylor had an idea. It was a simple idea, really: If enough people would create way stations in their backyards or on their rooftops, then perhaps, despite the clear-cutting and the Roundup and the development, the monarch migration—one of the great natural phenomena of the world—might be saved.

The Monarch Waystation Program encourages people all over the country to create garden sanctuaries to sustain breeding and migrating monarchs. Monarch Watch sends starter kits that include seeds for six kinds of milkweed and six nectar plants favored by the butterflies. The nonprofit's Web site, http://www.monarchwatch. org, also lists noninvasive milkweed-host varieties, as well as monarch nectar plants, including tithonia, cosmos and echinacea. Butterfly gardeners can register their way stations online and even order a weatherproof sign identifying their habitats as official Monarch Waystations.

Since the program was introduced in 2005, more than 4,000 Monarch Waystations have been registered.

"Loss of habitat is pinching all species," says Taylor. "It's hard to figure out how to help the larger species, but for the butterflies, there is something we can do. The individual citizen can do a lot."

PETITION

She rallied the schoolchildren—that's what Ro Vacarro did. She went into the schools and told the children about Mrs. Dively and the houses she wanted to build on the monarchs' land. She handed out petitions and urged the children to take them door to door and get signatures. The Friends of the Monarchs also canvassed the town. They needed 6,000 signatures to get it—a resolution to stop the development, buy the land and grant permanent sanctuary to the monarchs— on the ballot.

And sure enough, one day, Ro Vaccaro strode into the town hall, bearing her pages of signatures. Next, she had to write a ballot bond and convince Pacific Grove's voters to pass it.

So the Friends of the Monarchs marched in that year's annual Butterfly Parade, handing out "Vote Yes" flyers. Scholastic Review got wind of the butterflies' plight and published a cover story about it, and students from all over the country sent letters in support of the monarchs. The story ran on the "CBS Evening News" and in *The Wall Street Journal* and *The New York Times*.

In the end, the citizens of Pacific Grove voted to raise their own taxes. For what amounted to about $30 per person, per year, they purchased the $1.2 million plot of land.

Years later, Ro's sister said, "The monarchs saved her. She was just returning the favor."

CONVALESCENT

Her last two years as a docent at the sanctuary, the Butterfly Lady used a walker.

Finally, her body could no longer hold her. On top of lupus, diabetes, fibromyalgia and emphysema, Ro had contracted lymphoma. She had no choice but to move into a convalescent home.

That is where she was living when I first made contact with her friend Sharon Blaziek, head docent at the monarch sanctuary. Sharon told me Ro was in good spirits and would probably be delighted to do an interview once I got to Pacific Grove. I wrote Ro a letter, sent it by U.S. mail, told her I was on my way.

"LUPUS ERYTHEMATOSUS"

The first part of the name, "lupus," derives from the Latin for "wolf"; the second part, "erythematosus," refers to the red rash that is a frequent symptom of the illness. This is also known as the "butterfly rash," so called because it spreads across the bridge of the nose and over the cheeks in the shape of a butterfly's open wings. For obvious reasons, Ro Vaccaro preferred the latter designation.

One day, at the convalescent home, she rolled up her sleeve and showed her sister a bruise. It was 2 inches wide and in the shape of a butterfly. "I'm so gung ho," she said, "even my bruises come out like butterflies."

MONARCH MADNESS

Nothing could stop Ro from joining the festivities at the annual "Monarch Madness" family fun day. That November, she secured an all-day pass from the nursing home. She refused to miss a moment of the fun—the butterfly storyteller, the 5 M's band ("Mostly Mediocre Musical Monarch Mariposas") singing butterfly lyrics to the songs of the 60's and '70s, the craft table and face painting, the monarch caterpillars and chrysalides on display, the milkweed seeds for sale.

She refused a chair. She stood all day—happy, talking butterflies.

E-MAIL

Four days before I was to meet Ro Vaccaro, I got an e-mail from her friend Sharon Blaziek. Ro had died.

I slumped in my chair. The Butterfly Lady was gone.

TAGGING MONARCHS

To tag a butterfly you must first grasp it between your fingers, making sure you have a snug hold of the closed forewings as well as the hindwings. You hold the butterfly in your left hand, with the abdomen toward you. Your partner hands you a tiny, round sticker preprinted with a phone number and an ID. You place the tag on the underside of the right hindwing. You look for the small black dot of the scent gland that is in the vein of only the male's hindwing, and you report the sex to your partner, who writes it down on the log. You note any damage to the wing, and she jots that down, too. Then you put the tagged butterfly in a paper bag and wait for the sun to rise above the trees.

I have arranged with Jessica Griffiths, wildlife biologist for California's Ventana Wildlife Society—a nonprofit whose mission is to conserve native wildlife and their habitats—to spend the morning after my arrival with a handful of other volunteers who will count and tag monarchs in the Pacific Grove Monarch Sanctuary. As a kid, I had dreamed of tagging my monarchs and releasing them so that when they fluttered around the house, I would know they were mine, and when they flew away for good, I would maybe someday know where they had gone.

At 8:00 a.m., I open the door to my room and step out into the cold, damp air. It is 48 degrees. It feels colder. I walk around the corner to the sanctuary walkway and hang a right. Most of the trees in the grove are eucalyptus trees, and their scent hangs heavy and rich in the air. I look up into the trees, searching for clusters. I have been told it is a bad year for monarchs. I see one cluster, two. There they are, way up in the highest branches, hanging quietly, waiting for the warmth to come.

A small knot of people stands watching as Jessica and an intern reach high up into the trees, using an unwieldy 8-meter telescoping pole with an attached net, collecting the torpid butterflies. Jessica is bundled up in a knit hat, a scarf and black mittens with pink butterflies on them. I introduce myself, and she pairs me up with Irene—a sanctuary docent for the past 11 years—and puts me to work. Irene and I are sitting on lawn chairs, and there is a paper bag between us. Inside are the sleepy butterflies.

When the thermometer hits the magical 55 degrees, some of the monarchs high up in the trees liberate themselves from their clusters and flutter around against the blue palette of the sky. Jessica gathers the bags of tagged butterflies and steps off the walkway. One by one, she picks the monarchs up by the wings and tosses them into the sky.

SANCTUARY

On Feb. 10, 2008, in a private nook of the monarch sanctuary, in the place that Ro Vaccaro had always described as a cathedral, a small cluster of people, about 30 in all, gathered to pay their last respects to the Butterfly Lady. It was a warm, sunny day, and the monarchs, just heading into their breeding season, were preparing to take off and head north to Canada and east to Idaho, Nevada, Utah, Arizona.

As Sharon Blaziek read the memorial tribute to her friend, orange and black monarchs lit from the surrounding trees and fluttered and soared behind her for everyone to see.

Ro Vaccaro was a good Christian woman, but she had confided to her sister that she hoped to be reincarnated as a monarch.

"I told her to make sure it's in September," said Beverly, "so she can come here and tell these monarchs about the people."

FRESH PAINT

My bags are checked, and I'm waiting for my flight home when a sharp taint suddenly permeates my consciousness. I turn around. Forty feet away, the maintenance man is painting, in vivid royal blue, the doorway to the jet-bridge. The headache starts behind my eyes. My brain fogs in.

I pick up my bags and lug them as far from the paint as I can get. But the fumes are everywhere. I stand up, look for somewhere to go. A little Japanese girl toddles up to me and grabs my legs in a bear hug. I can't get away. There is nowhere to go.

SUSURRUS

It is magic, this orange fluttering, this quiet fluttering. It is peaceful. Free. Surely, even the most cynical can't help but feel it, watching. One finds oneself breathing deeply, from the belly, in the presence of it.

"A soft whispering or rustling sound: a murmur or whisper"—that is the dictionary definition of "susurrus." It is the word used by entomologists to describe the sound of hundreds, thousands, millions of butterfly wings, suddenly bursting into flight.

Nominated by Creative Nonfiction

LANTERN

by TED KOOSER

from THE KENYON REVIEW

In the predawn cold and darkness,
it was only a pinch of light,
not more than a cup of warmth,
as a farmer carried it over the snow
to the barn where his dozen cows
stood stomping, heavy with milk
in the milky cloud of their lowing.
But that was many years ago,
and his lantern has rusted,
its last fumes lost on the seasons
like the breath of those cows.
But at the last he thought to leave
a fresh ribbon of wick coiled up
in the chimney in case it was ever
needed again, a dollar's worth
of preparation. And, getting prepared
for a later winter, a pregnant mouse
was able to squeeze through a vent
and unravel that wick and make
a cottony nest with dusty
panoramic windows, and there to raise
her bald and mewling pissy brood,
and then for them to disappear,
the way we all, one day, move on,
leaving a little, sharp whiff
of ourselves in the dirty bedding.

Nominated by Joan Murray

THE BARGE

fiction by LAURA KASISCHKE

from THE FLORIDA REVIEW

One Wednesday a barge got stuck beneath the bridge. We were children, and we loved this fateful accident, this trouble occurring to others, this summer entertainment conducted under a bridge, just for us. We stood on the bridge all day looking down, waving our little stripes and stars at their hammers and sickles.

The men on the barge were patient with us. They had children of their own. They'd been stuck many times on barges under bridges in their own country in the past—which was a gray woolen blanket behind them, sodden with memories, like the sea.

They smoked cigarettes, ran their hands over the tops of their heads, waited for something to happen.

Rag-Anne was with me on Wednesday on the bridge.

Rag-Anne had been with me since the beginning.

I'd woken up in this world behind bars in a crib with Rag-Anne beside me—back when she was new and all her stitches were pulled tight and her yarn hair was blonde and I wore a ribbon and called my father Daddy. She was as real to me as the friends around me on the bridge that day—with their dirty faces, eating candy they wouldn't let me taste on sticks—but she was a doll. Gray and limp and made of thinning cloth. I'd long since swallowed her button eyes. There were grease-spots on her apron.

But, of course, I was also growing older. I had dirt on my knees that

340

no amount of scrubbing could wash off. One day when I crawled into my father's lap and called him Daddy, be pushed me off.

"Ugh, does that thing have to sit at the table with us?" my father would ask, looking at Rag-Anne looking at him from her seat at the end of the table.

"Oh, just a little longer," my mother said in the small voice she only used when he was in the room. "Someone's birthday's coming up!"

Oh, the birthday, the *birthdaycomingup*. There was a doll I'd seen at the department store and wanted and been assured I would have. That doll's human hair reflected the department store light, and her eyes were made of human glass and her skin of human plastic, like all the dolls at the department store I'd always wanted and had yet to have.

But the doll on the bridge above the barge with me that day was named for my grandmother Anne, who'd died alone in a back room of our house two winters before, unraveling like a sweater or a shadow in her bed as I played with the doll by the fire and turned up the volume on the television so I couldn't hear the other Anne struggle for breath on the other side of the wall.

Anne, and Anne.

On and on.

But everything came to an end in the end.

"Your doll's never been on a barge," my friend Rachel's older brother said in a false-baby voice. "She wants to give it a try."

Once, this boy had snatched a piece of watermelon out of my hand and eaten it in front of me while I screamed. Once, he'd grabbed the tail feathers of a dead bird in a ditch, and flung it at me. Once, he'd stuck a handful of snow down the front of my pants—keeping the hand there as the snow melted, staring into my eyes as if he were seeing into my brain.

That bird he'd flung managed to fly, flapping its wings mechanically over my head for a few seconds before it fell in front of me in a soggy heap to die a second time, and the soggy heap of that bird was what he saw inside my brain.

And the snow—I told my mother about the snow, and she put her dishtowel to the side of her head and said, "Oh dear, oh dear, don't say another word about it. You don't want Daddy to find out."

I expected Rachel's older brother to grab the doll from my hands and toss her over the bridge. I realized in that moment that I had been prepared since the day I was born for this boy to grab my doll and throw her over a bridge. I wouldn't even gasp, I knew, when he did it. I would let him. I would watch.

But he didn't.

He just looked at Rag-Anne, at me, and then down at the men on the barge. They were patient down there, but they were also tired. This was no longer a game to them. The air was maritime gray. Rag-Anne looked at me with no eyes. *Please*, she said, speaking to me with no eyes. *Please?*

She meant the bridge, the barge, the men below us. Please.

What?

Please, you know what.

Please.

She was trying to explain to me what I already knew but had not entirely believed. That she was getting older, as was I. That everything was about to change—whether we accepted the change, whether we set it in motion ourselves, or tried to prevent it, or not. That there was *birthdaycomingup*. That there would be a new doll with blonde hair and human eyes, and what would become of Rag-Anne then?

We knew. We knew. We knew.

Why not?

Why not, while there was still this chance? While there was still this barge below us on this bridge? Who knew how long until this chance, this barge, was gone forever from our lives? Could she not just, perhaps, please, give this other life a try?

No, I thought, clinging to her more tightly.

Rachel's older brother smirked. The others watched.

No.

No eyes.

When he touched her with a finger, she didn't even flinch. His smirk, his dirty finger. It seemed she didn't even mind.

"Just let her try," he said, almost kindly.

Please, she said. Oh, please. How long anyway is any doll's life? How long, anyway could any life go on? My grandmother had finally been taken from our house on a stretcher borne aloft by a muscular woman and a small man. They'd burned her up. I knew that much. I saw the urn, and overheard.

"Toss her over," my friend's brother said. "Go on."

He didn't need to speak to me like a baby now. Now, I understood the language we were speaking. *Toss me over, Please*. It was what she would have said with eyes if she still had eyes, if her eyes were not lodged deep inside me. I looked at her, at him, and then—

Then she slipped, feathered death, over the railing of the bridge, sighing into the oncoming twilight below us, and my friend's older brother poked me gently between my legs with his finger—a burning branch unfurling itself all through my body and sprouting out of the back of my skull when he did—while the other children laughed, and he said, "Good job, idiot."

For whom did I cry all the way home and into the bathtub that night? Rag-Anne?

No.

I'd cast her off on purpose. I'd hated her, and her decay, her frayed gray petticoat, her grease-stained apron, even her name.

Rag-Anne, and also Anne.

I'd hated them both—but especially my grandmother, who'd burned a hole in me by dying, by allowing herself to be burned alive. I could stick three fingers into that hole, wiggle them around—bloodless, pain-less, but also terrible. I'd wanted those two out of my sight.

And, yet, I felt afraid. The men on the barge seemed not to have noticed that a doll had fallen into their midst. Who knew what they might do when they did? They might cast her into the water. They might set her on fire.

That night, an enormous hairless zoo animal made of silence slipped into my dream, lay down on top of me, and stayed there, like a warm snow-pile, until morning. Then, we all went back to the bridge and saw her:

Anne!

I knew it was her by the expression on her face. I had been looking at that face for years, and it had never changed, even without eyes.

The boys whistled, but not loud enough for the men smoking on the barge to hear. The men on the barge were watching her, paying no at-tention to the children overhead.

She was blonde now, again, in a thin fresh flowered dress. No under-wear, it seemed. I could see a black triangle between her legs, the button-eyes of her nipples. There was a smear of fiery lipstick on her mouth. Where had she gotten it? Even my grandmother had never worn lipstick.

She was laughing as she sat on their laps. One man's lap, and then another's. She was barefoot, black-eyed, very young. When one of the men on the barge pointed a cigarette in our direction, she looked up, holding a hand to a forehead.

Was she saluting, or blocking the sun?

She waved at us with her other hand, and we waved our little American flags back at her, and the boys stuck out their tongues. The men on the barge grabbed at her small breasts, and she just laughed and let them—and then she was gone, and then she was gone, down in the bowels of the barge.

Anne, my grandmother, my rag doll animated by their new world down there below the bridge, on the barge, their wild new life, which was entirely my fault, my hideous idea entirely, my brave idea that had saved them from the fire.

You know the rest.

The bridge. The barge. A church bell clabbering in the distance along with the echoing sneeze of a metal tool banging on a metal roof— as if it were a competition between heaven and earth, as if heaven had the slightest hope of winning.

It was hot down there, and they took turns, and they came back out into the sun, pulling on their shirts, zipping up their pants, one by one, one by one, until each of them was done, and then the barge began to pull away, and all of it was gone.

And all of it was gone.

And I started to cry again, and he touched me with his finger between my legs again, almost tenderly, my friend's older brother, and he said, "Shut up, you idiot."

It was Thursday. Nothing like that ever happened again.

Nominated by David Baker, Pinckney Benedict, James Harms,
Jane Hirshfield, Mark Irwin, Jim Moore

SECTION 8

fiction by JAQUIRA DÍAZ

from THE SOUTHERN REVIEW

The same summer the magic city strangler Started Cruising South
Beach men's rooms, before the Section 8 projects were dismantled and
we were all forced out, I did my last stint in juvie. I was sixteen, and I
went in pretending I owned the place, bragging to all the younger girls
that it wasn't my first time. I'd been locked up twice before. Once, for
stealing a bottle of Mad Dog from a local bodega, and another time, for
breaking into that same bodega with my homeboy, Cabeza. That much
was true. But I didn't tell them that both times I'd only been there
overnight, until my hearing. That part I kept to myself. Didn't think I'd
be there long, even if it was my third strike. I had my hearing the same
afternoon, and I was sure the judge would send me home again. After
all, it was no big thing. All I did was get into a fight with some girl from
Treasure Boulevard. But the judge didn't see it that way. I needed a
wake-up call, she said. I looked over my shoulder at the benches behind
me, at the families of all the other juvenile delinquents, the empty spot
where my people were supposed to be. A wake-up call was the last
thing I needed.

Then she sentenced me. Twenty-one days.

I didn't get out for another month, though. They wouldn't release me
until a parent or guardian came for me, and it took my mother that long
to convince one of her asshole boyfriends to take a drive down to JDC.

The first time my homegirl Boogie and I heard about the Strangler, we
were in my room, knocking back a six-pack of my mom's Colt 45. We

were watching *Deco Drive* when the show was interrupted by the local news, a report about the third body found in one week. All the victims had been professional, openly gay men. Strangled.

"Are you hearing this?" I said. "There's a serial killer in South Beach."

"Yeah," Boogie said. "Well, I hope he kills me." She was all drama. Her father had just left her mom for some *sucia* who worked at a tollbooth on the 836, and now her mom got served with custody papers. He was going back to Jersey, and wanted to take Boogie with him. He had family there. In Miami, Boogie had no one except for her mom, who was always threatening to send her ass away if she kept acting up.

"I ain't going nowhere," Boogie said, lying back on the bed. She slammed both fists on the mattress, grinding her teeth, squeezing her eyes shut as if trying to push back the tears.

"Don't worry" I said. "You can stay with me." We thought we were grown up, invincible. That we could take on the world as long as we were together.

"What about your mom?" she asked, wiping her face with the backs of her hands.

"She won't care."

Boogie and I had been friends for so long, I couldn't imagine she'd let them send her away. She was strong. She wouldn't let them get away with it.

"He only wants me so he can avoid paying child support."

"Fuck him," I said. I lay next to her and took her hand.

She rolled onto her side, buried her face in my neck. Moments like this made me nervous. As long as I could remember, there had always been this thing between us, the way we looked to each other for comfort. And afterward, we wouldn't talk about it. The last time she slept over, we were in bed, and I had this feeling, but it was just a feeling. And now I was having it again. I thought of my mother in the next room, partying with her man, how she could walk through that door at any time. Maybe it was the way we were raised, the way we were programmed to think of two men, or two women, as simply wrong. Maybe we were excited by the wrongness of it. Or by the danger. Either way, it didn't matter. I thought of the possibility of losing her, Boogie up in Jersey without me, lying like this in someone else's bed. And so I kissed her. Not the way they kiss in the movies—eyes closed, bodies entangled and throbbing in a heated embrace, hands in all the right places—but it was still a kiss. My whole hand grasping two of her fingers, my lip trembling, the stink of my armpit sweat in the back of my throat. And she kissed me back.

We were friends. Just friends. On my first night back in the Section 8 projects, the thought repeated itself in my head. Me and Boogie were sitting around on the milk crates on the rooftop of my building, watching a bright red sky turn dark, listening to N.W.A. on Power 96. We were finishing off a quart of St. Ides, waiting for Cabeza to show up with a bag of haze.

"What was it like?" Boogie asked. She lowered the volume on her radio.

I'd spent the better part of the day listening to gossip about who got caught making out behind the portables at school, who got arrested for beating down their mother, or evicted, all the things I'd missed while I was locked up. Not once had I volunteered anything about my time in juvie. Didn't want to make a big deal, just wanted everything back to normal.

"You know," I said. "Thirty days of bad hair."

"That's not what I meant."

Usually Boogie and I talked about everything. But then the kiss happened, right before I got locked up. It was just one kiss, but we never brought it up. Didn't want things to get weird.

"It was fine," I said. "Got into a couple fights at first, but that's it."

I was relieved when Cabeza showed up.

"Nena," he called out to me. "You fucking delinquent!" He brought another guy with him. Looked just like him, except he was fine as hell and his head wasn't as big. "You remember my cousin Junito, right?"

I did. He used to spend summers with Cabeza and his dad when we were kids. But he was all grown up now. Boogie and I said what's up, and I wondered if he could tell I was nervous. It had been an entire month since I'd been around guys, locked up with twenty other girls. And Cabeza didn't count since he was more like a brother.

"Long time," he said, gave us both a kiss on the cheek and handed us each a brand-new quart.

"He just moved in, " Cabeza said, sitting on one of the crates. He pulled out his baggie and a dutch, starting rolling on the spot. That was Cabeza. Always took care of business first. "Maybe you can show him around, introduce him at school. Hook him up with one of your homegirls."

"Don't listen to him," Junito said, shaking his head.

"Fine," Cabeza said. "Then hook *me* up."

"Like hell we are," Boogie said. Cabeza was our boy, but every girl we introduced him to turned out to be a stalker, or tried to get him to stop hanging with us.

Cabeza lit the dutch, took a long drag, and passed it to Boogie. When it was my turn, I just held up my hand, shook my head no.

"I'm good," I said.

"What, they put you in the program?" Cabeza asked.

"Yeah," I said, even though I had no idea what he was talking about. I just didn't want to get too fucked up with Junito around, say something stupid.

"What program?" Boogie asked.

"Some at-risk youth intervention shit," Cabeza said. "They make you piss in a cup every week."

"So why did you move?" I asked Junito, changing the subject. It was darker now, but I could make out his loose T-shirt flapping in the wind.

"My mom got locked up." He passed the dutch back to Cabeza.

"What'd she do?" Boogie asked.

Cabeza shot her a quick look, mouthed the word *don't*, shook his head from side to side. Junito looked straight ahead, across the street at Normandy Park. I wanted to tell him that I understood, but kept my mouth shut. I hated when people thought they knew what I was going through.

We sat in awkward silence for a moment, until Cabeza started coughing.

"This weed," he said, "is shit."

Junito started school with us that fall. At lunch, instead of playing basketball with the rest of the Section 8 boys, he'd go turn wrenches in the auto shop. Sometimes me and Boogie would hang by the handball courts, laugh at all the girls who would gather outside the auto-shop bays to see if they could catch a glimpse of him shirtless. The other girls were fascinated by Junito because he was new, and because he was from Philly, and to Miami girls that meant he was exotic, like he could take them away to some other world where they would be exotic, too.

One afternoon, as we headed to our usual lunchtime hangout, we spotted Amanda Lopez and Junito talking. I stopped in front of our table. They were out by the bays, and every time Junito made a gesture like he was heading inside, Amanda touched him on the shoulder or grabbed his hand. I watched them until she kissed him on the cheek and strutted away.

When I turned back to Boogie, I realized that she'd been watching me, not them. I sat at my usual spot, placed my bag on the table in front of me, didn't even touch my lunch.

"What's up with you?" Boogie asked.

"What do you mean?"

"Nena . . ." she started saying. Then, "Never mind."

I knew where she was going, but like me, Boogie decided it was better to let things be.

When I got home that afternoon, the living room was littered with half-empty beer bottles, and my mother was asleep on the couch. She was lying on her side, one dirty sofa cushion covering her naked body. Her face was wrinkled and ashy, smeared with black mascara, and her forearm was hanging over the armrest, a lit cigarette between two fingers.

"What the fuck is wrong with you?" I reached for her hand, swiped the cigarette, and dropped it into one of the bottles. "One of these days you're gonna burn down the whole damn building."

But my mother never heard a thing when she was sleeping off a *borrachera*. She just turned over, her back to me, as if I wasn't even there. I left her on the couch. Didn't bother cleaning up after her anymore.

I was in bed, plotting ways to get Amanda Lopez kicked out of school, when Boogie showed up. She came in through the window, which I never bothered to lock.

"Are you crazy?" she asked as soon as she got inside. "I could've been the Strangler."

"What? The Strangler only kills men."

"Haven't you been watching?" She turned on my TV, tried adjusting the rabbit ears, but couldn't get a picture that wasn't scrambled.

"They just found another body," she said. "A woman. Set on fire."

"Then it wasn't the Strangler," I said.

"Yeah? How do you know?"

"Because she wasn't *strangled*."

Her eyes narrowed like she was considering this. "Am I sleeping over?" she asked, changing the subject. Before I got locked up, she slept over all the time when her mom worked the graveyard shift.

"Don't know," I said. "Are you?"

"If you want me to," she said.

It had been nothing, but we were still dancing around it. I didn't want to hurt her feelings. I took her hand, and we sat there for a while, our fingers interlaced.

"I want you to," I said finally.

We slid under the covers, neither of us saying what we were both thinking. We lay next to each other for a while, and I could smell the Newport she smoked before coming over.

The first time had been in juvie. It was Ethel, a girl from an Opa-locka crew. My first cell mate, Estrella, gave me the rundown. Don't give away any food in the mess hall, 'cause they'll think you're soft. Don't let the *morenas* braid your hair, cause then you'll owe them. And whatever you do, don't fuck with Ethel. She's a *pata*.

At first I was down with the rules. But then, everywhere I went, there was Ethel. I could feel her eyes on me, in the yard, in the mess hall. Until one day she caught me looking at her. It was one of those things, you know. We were in the shower, and I didn't even realize it until it happened, and by then it was too late.

After that I avoided her. It was easy at first, since they kept us locked up most of the time. But then one of the other girls asked for a new cell mate, said she couldn't handle being locked up with a *pata*. And who ended up with Ethel?

A week later I was home again.

After Halloween, the Strangler was all over the news. Bob Blackwell, some famous South Beach music producer, went missing after leaving a party alone. He was a rich, gay man, so everyone assumed the Strangler got him, that it would only be a matter of days until they found his nude, lifeless body in a Dumpster somewhere.

I was getting on the metro when I spotted some kids from school. Nestor Socarras, Alvin Jean Pierre, and their boys.

"Just the other day," Alvin was saying, "I was crossing the street and I saw two of them holding hands. *Nasss*-ty."

I walked all the way to the back of the bus, as far away from them as possible, even though all the seats were taken. The other people on the bus acted like they couldn't hear them, looked straight ahead or pretended to see something out the window.

"Miami Beach is overrun with them," someone else said after a while, and I was glad we were getting closer to Normandy Park.

"The Strangler's just cleaning up the city," Nestor said. "Doing us all a favor." The rest of them smiled or nodded in agreement. I rang the bell for the next stop, even though it was two stops before mine.

Halfway home from the bus stop, I ran into Junito. He was bouncing a basketball in front of his building.

"Headed to the park?" I asked.

"Waiting for Cabeza," he said. He started walking with me, bouncing the ball. Then he stopped. "Nena, can I ask you something?"

"What's up?" We were at the light, waiting for it to change so we could cross the street. He balanced the ball on two fingertips.

"What's up with your homegirl?"

"Boogie?" I asked. "What about her?"

"I mean, you know what they say about her, right?"

I knew what he was getting at. "I don't give a shit what people say," I said, knocking the ball out of his hand.

"Damn, Nena." He took off down the street, chasing after it, and I kept walking. I wasn't in the mood for this shit.

"My bad," he called out, running up beside me. We were already in front of my building.

"It's not true," I said. "Whatever they say is bullshit." I sped up until I reached my door, then turned to him. "Who?"

"Who what?" he asked.

"Who said that?"

"I don't know. People."

I looked him dead in the eye. "Well, you and those people can go fuck yourselves," I said, and shut the door in his face.

Later, I locked myself in my bathroom and let the shower run until steam filled the room. When I couldn't see myself in the mirror anymore, I undressed slowly, imagined someone was watching me. It was Junito first. Then Boogie.

The next morning they found Bob Blackwell, strangled, in the trunk of a stolen taxi.

That Friday, Boogie and I went roller-skating at the old rink on Collins. Between the two of us, we'd polished off one of the bottles of strawberry Cisco we got from the bodega around the corner. I had two more in my backpack, but I didn't think we'd need them since we were already pretty fucked up. We were hanging on to each other, and Boogie was getting stupid, so I tried dragging her off to the bleachers. I put one arm around her waist, and threw hers over my shoulder, trying to keep my balance. We were almost to the sitting area when I saw Cabeza and Junito walk in. I was trying to play it cool, like I didn't even see them, when Boogie noticed them and started waving her arms in the air.

"Yo, Cabeeeza!" she said. I lost my balance and fell flat on my ass. Boogie fell sideways on top of me, then rolled onto her back and burst into laughter. I laughed, too. I had no choice. It was either laugh or cry.

Cabeza was hunched over, laughing and pointing at us, but Junito came over right away. It was then that I noticed they were with a group of other guys from the neighborhood, but they spread out, ready to scam on a crowd of girls from Saint Brendan's Catholic High School.

"You okay?" Junito asked.

"I'm fine," I said. I was dusting myself off, avoiding his eyes. Then I pulled off my backpack, checked that the bottles hadn't cracked.

"You sure?" He was helping Boogie to the bleachers. She was still laughing, and Junito smiled at her, then looked back at me, shaking his head.

I sat on the bleachers, next to Boogie, and she laid her head on my shoulder and closed her eyes. I wished she wasn't drunk so he would see that there was nothing weird about us.

While she was untying the laces on her roller skates, Junito found a spot next to me. Then she took off, wearing only socks, toward the rental counter to return her skates.

"Nena, I didn't mean to offend you," he said. He was looking into my face and I could tell he meant it.

"Why would you say some shit like that?" I asked. He was leaning forward, looking down at his sneakers like he was considering what to say. Until that moment, I had no idea that a simple question would be so hard for him to answer. Or maybe it wasn't that at all. Maybe he could see right through me.

"You know why," he said. He leaned toward me, gave me a peck on the cheek, then pulled back slightly, waiting for me to make the next move. I considered what it would mean, Cabeza and all his homeboys watching, Boogie at the rental counter, what it would lead to. I could've said no, could've pulled away. I made a choice. I closed my eyes, pressed my lips against his, and waited.

The next thing I knew we were kissing. When I finally pulled away, Boogie was standing right in front of us, looking sober as hell.

"Just getting my sneakers," she said. She picked up my backpack and got her Nikes and a bottle of Cisco. "See ya." She tossed the backpack at me, turned for the exit.

I should've called her back. Should've asked her to wait up. But I thought of Junito, of Cabeza, his homeboys, all the other kids from the barrio I'd have to face day after day, and I let her go.

I was running late for my Health class when I saw them again, Nestor and Alvin, standing in front of Boogie's locker. There was a cluster of kids gathered around them, watching as Nestor shook a can of spray paint, the marble inside beating against the metal. Then he popped the top and painted the word *tortillera*. Bold black letters against the red steel.

Then Alvin snatched Nestor's can, a smile forming on his face, while the crowd cheered and called out, "Do it!" and "Oh hell yeah!"

His first word was *madivinez*. I didn't know what language it was, but I knew what it meant. He kept writing. *Faggot, eat pussy, cunt.* Then he turned to the crowd. "What else?" he called out.

"Dyke," someone yelled back.

That was the last word. *DYKE.* In capital letters.

As quickly as the crowd had formed, it vanished. All of them, Nestor and Alvin also, took off laughing down the halls. One of the security guards, Mr. Boyd, was coming over to see what the commotion was about. I stood there, reading the slurs over and over.

Then I saw her. Boogie was walking slowly toward her locker, toward me. She was already late for class, so she should've been in a hurry, but she walked slower and slower the closer she got, fixed her eyes on the locker door. She stopped where Alvin and Nestor had stood a moment before, jaw clenched, chest rising, falling. I thought she would burst into tears. I thought I should hug her, say, "Fuck those assholes. They don't even know you."

But I didn't. I didn't say one word. Just turned and walked away.

353

I avoided Boogie for about a week after that. At lunch, I hung out with Junito at the auto-shop bays. I didn't even meet Boogie for our usual Saturday, when we pretended to be turistas on Miami Beach. I took Junito with me instead, spent the entire day browsing the electronics and T-shirt shops on Lincoln Road, then snuck into the pool at the Carillon on Collins. When we got back to Normandy Park, the street-lights were coming on. I didn't expect to see Boogie, but there she was, sitting at the bus stop in front of my building when Junito and I rolled up.

"What's up, Boogie," Junito said. For a moment I thought she would blow up on him, since I'd stood her up to spend the day with him. I hoped she knew that he didn't mean any harm.

"Hey," I said. I couldn't look her directly in the eyes.

"I came looking for you," she said to me. She avoided looking at Junito, pretended he wasn't there.

I couldn't think of anything to say, no explanation for the way I'd acted the last few days.

"I wasn't home," I finally said. I tried to make out Junito's expression from the corner of my eye.

"Yeah. I noticed," she said. She got up, headed for her place, and I could feel the heat of her as she brushed past me into the night.

I was waiting for the metro after school a few days later when I spotted Boogie headed my way. She saw me, then turned around, pretended she was checking for the bus. When she glanced back at me, I looked the other way, pretended I didn't see her either. We'd stood there for a while, not seeing each other, when Nestor, Alvin, and their friends showed up.

Alvin did the talking while his friends surrounded her.

"Hey, baby," he said. She looked him up and down, then checked for the bus again.

Alvin glanced at me, but didn't seem to have any interest.

"Where's your girlfriend?" he asked her.

"Fuck off," Boogie said. She stepped around him.

Alvin inched closer to her, put his face next to her ear, whispered something I couldn't hear. Boogie pushed him away, tried to break from the crowd, but Nestor blocked her.

"Get out of my way, asshole," she said, but Nestor was laughing.

Alvin came around again, made sure I was watching, then turned to Boogie. I thought he would touch her, of what I'd do if any of them laid a hand on her.

"Maybe what you need is the feel of a man," Alvin said, grabbing himself. "You ever been with a man?"

She let out a chuckle, and I could tell she thought he was lame as hell.

Then Nestor pulled something out of the pocket of his jeans. It was a water gun.

"Are you fucking serious?" she said.

He aimed directly at her face and sprayed. She turned away and lifted her forearm to protect herself, but Alvin and his friends pulled out their own guns and sprayed her, too. I wanted to jump in, but didn't. I was frozen. She took a few steps back, but the boys moved with her, Alvin hopping around on the balls of his feet.

That's when I saw it. The wet spots on her jeans were changing color, getting lighter. There were spots on her green T-shirt that were already fading to amber. They were spraying her with bleach.

For a moment I stood there, not moving, not breathing, just letting it happen. Alvin stopped spraying, stepped back to get a better look at her. He was pleased.

"Fucking dyke," he said.

I lunged at him. Pushed him back as hard and fast as my body would let me. He took a few steps, tried to steady himself, fell on his ass. The crowd backed off, but Nestor turned his water gun at me and sprayed. I didn't care. I went directly for him. He inched away, backward, laughing at me, and kept spraying. I didn't see it coming, and neither did he, but when he stood, turned on his heel and started to run, he ran right into Boogie, and she kneed him hard in the balls.

The boys took their friends and their guns and walked off, Nestor clutching his stomach. They turned the corner, disappeared behind the Ocean Bank building.

Another crowd had formed, kids waiting on their buses. I looked around at familiar faces. Some of them lived in our neighborhood, but none of them had stepped in.

"Are you okay?" I heard myself ask, but didn't wait for an answer. Just kissed her. It didn't even matter that people were watching.

I'd like to imagine that she kissed me back. That we didn't care about the rumors starting right there on that sidewalk, didn't notice the whis-

pers, the judgment. Later, we would head back to the Section 8 projects. We would watch the news, holding hands, and praise the Lord that
they finally arrested the Magic City Strangler.

But she didn't.

She grabbed hold of my shoulders, her eyes narrow. "Don't you fucking touch me," she said, before pushing me back against the bus stop.

That night, right outside of the Section 8 projects, someone set another woman on fire.

Nominated by The Southern Review

FIRST HARD FREEZE

by DAVIS MCCOMBS

from INDIANA REVIEW

The first hard freeze, an owl beyond the twig
at the window like the shadow of a thought
across the mask of a face, and whatever it is
that will unmask the girl who masks the old
woman who is turning the tap, comes crawling
up from timber on a night like this, comes
wandering like wind when everything else
is frosty and still: the deer, unbuckled, the field
a matted bulge, and the flashlight's beam
that will not come to light the fires of their eyes.
On a night like this, the old woman will think
secretly of the dead in their graves, of satin
and of wood and of a dark that pours itself
into a vessel it will never fill. On a night like this,
and in thoughts like these, she is not alone.
The compost hoards its clump of heat; frost
welds the chain to the gate, throwing sparks.
She will lie down to dreams that scatter ahead of her
like snow, but not before she turns the tap one turn,
a hammered metal drip drip drip she'll wake to
when a hand not made of hand tests the latch.

Nominated by Indiana Review, Michael Heffernan

LAUGH YOUR TROUBLE AWAY

by PATRICIA SMITH

from SUGAR HOUSE REVIEW

Motto, Riverview Park, 1904-1967, Chicago

I.

Every city had one, a palace with a fried tint to its air,
a hurting-hued screech of no underneath, everything
plummeting or ascending, a monument to hazy flailing
and sudden fun vomit. Swing the Riviera onto Belmont,
and you see the Pair-O-Chutes rising to heaven on dual
strings, headed for the pinpoint and release, then the sick
whip and fall, the little public murder, a blaring grace
so storybook gorgeous, suddenly flood in the throat.

Revelers board creaking Fireball cars and slice the August,
mistaking acid bubbling in their bellies for symptoms
of glee, then stop to stuff quavering guts with plastic
and syrup. Their quick sustenance has wafted all day
on a river of grease. They hunger for white cakes
curled stiff with sugar, sausages that pop huge heat,
pink candy of cotton chomping rot down their throats.
The jagged stains of compromised fruit circle screaming
mouths and paint shadow across the teeth, making them
horrible. Bulbs flash. Wet Polaroids are lifted and waved
like church fans to etch and clarify in the summer steam.

The aged horses are dizzied, diseased. Chained to a tilting
stake, they blur through the drag, deferring to their brutal,
squirming burdens. Potbellied flies, nasty to the point
of charm, nibble passages toward the horses' blue hearts.
Above it all, the freak show MC—his shout an odd mixture
of pity and sex—dares us to witness sweaty sloth, tiny floating
corpses, so much skin unlike ours, more legs than allowed,
and a Negro who can separate himself from his eyes.

While on the midway, your father will never win the thinly
stuffed neon grinners—the bears, dolphins, curlique serpents,
kewpie dolls and counterfeit Mickey Mice that leer from shelves.
He hurls balls at weighted milk cans, blasts at a measured parade
of bobbing ducks, guns water into a pinpoint, guesses a woman's
weight. Finally, he just buys something soft and ugly, a token
you will clutch and sing to until, too blackly loved, it melts.
At dusk, he steers you away from the midways squalling edge,
where everything seems to be happening, where the hooting
and laughter have a raw, unmeasured throat. You pout, he pulls,
and, not for the first tune, you wonder what he hides.

II.

I am their pickaninny, dressed in a repeating river.
All of me is droop and sustain.
My drenched dungarees are gravity on me.
I have learned to smile at the several versions
of my name, my face is complete in its teeth
and studied dumb ogle. *Oh, woe is me* I say
while the white boys wind up, and damn if they
don't always smack that huge disc, dead center.
I rise laughing from my clockwork baptisms,
the canned river funked with my own spit and piss,
just to see another man clutching the red ball,
his eyes harder than the first of these. Sometimes
an awed Negro dots the crowd, his numbed smile
a link chained to mine. I spot one using his body
to block his little girl's view of me, so I make
my voice louder: I *oh sweet jesus kind suh no,*

I lawd ham mercy suh I I believes I might drown
I please let me dry off in this sun a little I mercy
me you sho does look strong suh until she twists
hard away from her daddy and full unto me.
I have just enough time for her to sound it out:
D-D-D-unk-unk Dunk a N-N-N-ig-ig-Nig-ger
and then I salute, and hold her father's eyes as I fall.

Nominated by Sugar House Review

MATCH.COM/MATTHEW LIKES BUTTERED TOAST, VULNERABILITY . . .

by ELIZABETH POWELL

from NEW OHIO REVIEW

My love lives in a little tiny box
Made of pixels and engineering. When I write him
He writes me back and when he writes me
Back, I write him. Even though we exist
Me/him, here/there: one day our band
Of consciousness will grow outward,
When science puts chips in brains
So all mysteries can be known—
Delusions, proclivities, sentences.
For now imagination, a gangly vine,
Grabs for a life. He has been so busy
Writing a narrative where he has no wife
That she has disappeared. So much first-person
Construct and banter. He has
A vixen schoolteacher held down
On the bed of his mind. And when he
Writes me he makes me
And when I make him I write him.
We are invented, in part,
By the wanting and not having
Of others. Soon someone else
Will pick him out of his little box
And begin again, wait for him

In the rain in front of the coffee shop
Where inside the donuts harden like
He can't, and the red counter chair swirls empty
As if trying to conjure something so close.
But so close is almost, and almost is really
Far, still. She tries to pick him out of the crowd,
Ever hopeful, though night comes on like emergency.
And he is two places at once, virtual and real.
My love lives in a little box. Someone
Is making him
Into something else now.

Nominated by New Ohio Review

ANIMALCULA: A YOUNG SCIENTIST'S GUIDE TO NEW CREATURES

fiction by SETH FRIED

from THE KENYON REVIEW

THE ELDRIT

When observed, the eldrit changes. Once its characteristics and tendencies are documented, it adopts new characteristics, new tendencies. A researcher observes through a microscope that the eldrit propels itself by means of long, translucent flagella. The researcher writes:

> *Flagella, translucent,*
> *means of locomotion*

But as soon as he returns his attention to the eldrit, he finds that it now propels itself by means of a slight undulation of its belly. The flagella, now bright orange, are being used to expel waste. The researcher makes a note of this and then finds that the eldrit in question is suddenly stationary. Its flagella have disappeared altogether.

It will most likely be surprising to you that the scientific community has no idea how the eldrit is able to accomplish such dramatic mutations. However, keep in mind that the mechanics of an ant walking along the vein of a leaf is enough to make all the technological advancements of the last three centuries look like the output of an eighth grade woodshop: wobbling tables, misspelled signs, precarious rocking horses unevenly stained. Human achievement and understanding are constantly being dwarfed by the complexity of the natural world.

So how do scientists address this question of the eldrit's ability to alter itself? We step around it, nodding politely as we pass. As a scientist, it is often the only acceptable method to ignore an impossible question, which, if history serves, will most likely be answered on accident by someone setting out to answer something else.

Rather, most research regarding the eldrit is concerned not with how it changes itself, but why. Because if one accepts the assertion that the first priority of all living organisms is self-preservation, then one must conclude that the eldrit's very existence serves as an argument that there is something caustic in being identified, in having the boundaries of one's physical and behavioral make-up established.

In fact, this seems almost intuitive. Once characteristics of a creature are fixed, it is given a role to fill as a result of those characteristics. Through the act of being itself, a creature becomes either the one forced to attach itself as a parasite to a lower intestine, where it will depend on that organ for the most foul sustenance imaginable, or else it becomes the one whose lower intestine is thus infested. Certainly, neither position could be said to inspire envy. But because each creature allows itself to be itself, both positions are unavoidable.

The evolutionary adaptations that creatures undergo in order to alleviate their circumstances are—at best—only half-solutions and—at worst—further provocations of hardship. The haunch muscles that aid the antelope in its flight from predators are also an excellent source of protein. The bear's massive strength also betrays its equally massive capacity to starve to death.

But while other creatures change themselves in response to the environmental pressures that affect their various roles, the eldrit seems to change in order to shun the notion that it has a role to fill in the first place. Furthermore, the eldrit does not depend on a Punnett square in order to carry out these changes. Instead, it changes instantly. So in the exact moment that one creature is just beginning to realize, after hundreds of thousands of years of genetic alterations, that an elongated snout is not nearly as useful as perhaps its ancestors had supposed—the eldrit is growing two dozen snouts per minute, stretching them out farther and farther. Just as quickly, the eldrit allows its snouts to fall off and desiccate.

Though, before we regard the eldrit's position as being totally advantageous, it should also be mentioned that, on account of its compulsive tendency to change, the eldrit misses out on one of the most pleasing aspects of being a creature, which is, simply put, *being* a creature.

Among all living things, there is a certain joy in being recognizable as oneself. Even those of us whose bodies are a constant source of apprehension and awkwardness take comfort in seeing our faces in the mirror at the end of the day. As young scientists, you are all no doubt very unattractive. Yet, there is something reassuring in knowing that you have taken a shape, however unfortunate. It is something that is utterly yours, and no matter how miserable you might look while standing in your underwear or how ill at ease you might be in a bathing suit, when you are being honest with yourself, you enjoy your shape; you take solace in it. Think: when people feel dejected and forlorn, they often hold their own heads in their hands. Why do they do this, if not to take consolation in the fact that they have a definite form, that they are in the possession of something entirely their own.

This notion that all creatures possess inalienable qualities, which represent an incorruptible sense of self, exists on an evolutionary scale as well. Just look at the transformation of dinosaurs into birds. The dinosaur might not mind diminishing in size or growing wings, but to stop laying eggs? To begin shaping its skeleton differently or its heart? To give up the beautifully vacant eyes of a reptile? The savage waggle of its neck? Unthinkable. That is why researchers are now attempting to determine if, in all the eldrit's responses to the observations directed at it, there are any qualities that refuse to change and are quintessentially itself.

A common approach is to have a live video feed of an eldrit's magnified image broadcast onto a large monitor where it is then viewed by a room filled with observers, all of whom stare intently at the image and direct as many observations at it as possible. The manic and prolonged ripple of changes that this exercise produces in the eldrit is recorded for posterity and then viewed repeatedly by researchers attempting to establish some sort of constant in the eldrit. The hope is that if a great enough number of observations is directed at a single eldrit for a long enough period of time, the creature will eventually become over-whelmed and begin to falter, inadvertently revealing its secret consis-tencies.

No such breakthrough has occurred.

As the number of observations directed at an eldrit increase, so does the eldrit's ambiguity. On a monitor in an observation room, an eldrit takes on a series of indescribable shapes, splits itself in two, reabsorbs itself, becomes bright pink. It trembles slightly, and then explodes. It reassembles itself. Explodes. Reassembles itself. Explodes.

One must admit that even the meekest creature ends up seeming bold in comparison. Consider the gazelle. There is an unmistakable bravery in its implicit admission that, through being a gazelle, it is a gazelle. And even though one can hardly look at its long, delicate neck without immediately thinking of the powerful jaws that will inevitably snap it in two, the gazelle does not shirk its post. It manages to take responsibility for what it is, while the eldrit can only change uncondi-tionally, a slave to its wild, untouchable freedom.

THE KESSEL

The lifespan of an average kessel is four one-hundred-millionths of a second. To put this figure into perspective: If you were to fire a .30 caliber rifle at an opposing target fifty feet away, 462,963 generations of kessel would pass by the time the bullet reached the target. If you were to hold a handkerchief six inches from your nose and sneeze into it, 8,522,727 generations of kessel would pass in the time it took for the mucus to reach the handkerchief. But numbers do little to convey the extreme brevity of a kessel's life. Rather, imagine a newborn infant flashing from its mother's womb like a lightning bolt and arriving in the doctor's arms as a full-grown skeleton already crumbling to dust.

Naturally, observing the kessel is rather difficult. Its death follows its birth so closely that it is impossible to distinguish one process from the other. In fact, the three major acts of a living creature (birth, procreation, and death) are so compressed in time that the kessel seems to accomplish all three by means of a single exertion.

Even the experienced observer, aided by recent technological developments in high-speed photography, will find it impossible to differentiate the characteristics of a dying kessel from one that's just been born or a sexually mature kessel from one not yet fully developed, because it is all these things at once. In the kessel, each stage of life informs the other simultaneously.

Though strange, this quality of simultaneity should not be considered altogether remote from human experience. Who has not occasionally seen death as a weary nod toward birth and vice versa? Who has not occasionally recognized the link between sex and death? Young lovers, as they embrace, are often already able to sense the coming of a private apocalypse in the thumping of their lovers' hearts. Ailing men and women, as they lie on their deathbeds, are often said to feel as if they are being slowly undressed, as if they are expecting a release, which, as it first approaches, is at once frightening, painful, and secretly exhilarating.

Throughout the ages, human beings have viewed the transition from birth to sexual maturity to death as a necessary progression. The notion that these things are distinct from one another, that they form a grand narrative, is a social construction that many people have internalized as an indisputable fact. So it is understandable that the existence of the kessel happens to make many people uncomfortable. What kind of parents would want to be told that their newborn child is an aspect of death? Or, worse, that their child has sexual implications beyond the gentle copulation that produced it.

The manner in which the kessel's existence informs our own can be incredibly disheartening. Its cells begin to form and break down at the same time, and so, when successfully recorded and played back on video streams slowed to infinitesimal proportions, these cells produce a tesseractic movement, folding down into themselves continuously without altering their shape. This motion would be hypnotic if it weren't so brief. Even with the video slowed, the cells disappear in an instant. This sight is, in a word, depressing. It is so abrupt and senseless that it makes the sight of a suicide jumping off a bridge festive in comparison. The amount of time it takes for the suicide to hit the water ends up seeming generous, more than any one person could deserve. It makes us—who are fond of saying to one another under various circumstances that life is, in fact, too short—seem like the worst sort of gluttons.

On the other hand, the smallness and brevity of a kessel's existence begins to remind one of how small and brief our existence is on a universal scale. Stars die. Galaxies collide. And everything in the universe that is human, the sum of all our ambitions, histories, fears, achievements, and failures exists on the head of a needle.

In consideration of the kessel, human nature seems to be open to two conflicting criticisms. The first is that we see our average lifespan as being insufficient, despite the fact that the time afforded to a stillborn seems decadent when compared to the life of a kessel, and despite the fact that we still find time enough to be bored and to wish for time to move faster. While the second criticism is that we see our average lifespan as sufficient and that the actions contained therein are significant. We flatter ourselves with the assumption that anything of importance can be accomplished in our seventy to eighty years when the earth has been around for billions of years and has been known to change dominant species as if they were hats. Our pity for the kessel is revealed as naive in that, if you judge a kessel's existence by the amount of time that elapses in the human world and judge a human's existence by the amount of time that elapses in the universe, then we disappear from our surroundings even faster than the kessel disappears from its own.

This is particularly disconcerting because, though at odds, both arguments seem valid. And so, along with the already grim content of these criticisms, comes the hurtful reminder that human beings are riddled with absurdities and contradictions even with respect to something as simple as our faults.

The whole issue of the kessel as it relates to our existence is ultimately filled with so much unmitigated glumness that many consider it to be an inappropriate topic for polite conversation. Details regarding the kessel are among the type of cold-hearted facts that are inevitably mentioned at parties by angry young men, who wish to impress upon anyone who seems to be having more fun than themselves that the world is, in fact, little more than a brutal joke. Most researchers who specialize in the kessel end up adopting this air of arrogance and scorn. They are typically unkempt, wild-looking. Their faces are ravaged by distrust, and they are always ready with a discouraging remark.

It makes sense that researchers who watch that sad footage again and again—the kessel fluttering briefly and then vanishing—would eventually give in to despair. Further, it makes sense that those who are confronted on a daily basis by those criticisms of our nature mentioned above would eventually begin to despise our nature. But based on their studies of the kessel, these people are ready to conclude that everything we hold dear is futile and amounts to nothing. However, the fact remains that such a view of the kessel and of human nature is incomplete.

For example, the kessel mates for life. At first, this might seem unimpressive, owing to the fact that life for a kessel is a brisk four one-hundred-millionths of a second. But because it is sexually mature even before it is born, the average kessel spends a greater percentage of its lifetime with its mate than any other creature on earth, a relationship which is strictly monogamous and, again more than any other creature on earth, most resembles our understanding of romantic love.

Granted, some researchers argue that it maintains one mate because it simply does not have the time to take on another. Dr. Richard Koch—unkempt and wild-looking, Koch is a preeminent figure among the kessel specialists mentioned briefly above—is a strong proponent of this theory. In a recent study, Koch examined the mating practices of the kessel, focusing on the kessel's speed and urgency in an attempt to establish its promiscuity.

But Koch's own study contains evidence to the contrary. Buried in indexes and supplemental figures are instances of kessel who chose somewhat older mates, outlived them, and then spent the rest of their short lives in mourning. In fact, this is rather common. A kessel that is two one-hundred-billionths of a second old might select a mate that is one one-hundred-millionths of a second old. When the latter dies, the former does not seek a replacement but spends the rest of its life in solitude. There are also instances of kessel, which, seeking an ideal mate, have waited in absolute celibacy a staggering three one-hundred-millionths of a second.

These instances of self-imposed isolation are remarkable, especially when one considers the fact that the kessel tends to crave desperately the company of its own kind. Experiments have been conducted in which a single specimen has been separated from a larger group by a tenth of a millimeter. These experiments show that the lone kessel will spend its entire life moving back toward its fellows despite the fact that a tenth of a millimeter—for a creature, which, in addition to being so small and short-lived, is not particularly fast—is like the distance between two stars. In some primal fashion, the kessel must understand that that is an impossible distance. And yet, it persists.

So, yes, it's true: the universe is massive, whereas we are small and quickly fading. But things are never as hopeless as people like Koch would have you believe. There are still opportunities for happiness for those willing to accept existence for what it is. Even a creature like the kessel seems to understand the transformative capabilities of something as simple as affection. It fixates on companionship in what seems like deliberate ignorance of the fact that it is surrounded by larger and larger worlds. When it finally finds its mate, the kessel exhausts its life in that purest intimacy, without a care, as its one moment goes rushing past.

THE PRINCIPLES OF OBSERVATION

In the same way that it is difficult to think of a distant planet as being an actual place—as real as the ground beneath your feet—it is often difficult to think of most animalcula as being actual creatures. Like a planet viewed through a telescope, one tends to recognize an animalculum viewed through a microscope not as a thing, but as an image of a thing. Though both instruments manipulate reality in only the most rudimentary fashion, bringing objects closer or making them larger, we still understand that what we are seeing is a deception. Our minds take in what is seen by means of those instruments with the same reflexive disbelief with which we have learned to greet the computer-generated monsters in the summer blockbuster, the map of Texas behind the meteorologist, the digitally altered photograph in a magazine of JFK drinking a Pepsi.

At this point in history, a healthy sense of skepticism with respect to images is increasingly necessary. Otherwise, every single soap commercial would break our hearts. Every advertisement featuring a beautiful woman lying on a white-sanded beach in the ecstasy of whatever product would corrupt us not only with a desire for that product but also with the belief that our life is pale and undesirable, something that needs desperately to be fixed. And so we lean on our skepticism as if for balance. We roll our eyes at that woman on the beach. We hold at arm's length all the deliberately phony images of the every day, the pervasiveness of which so harasses us that we are no longer able to differentiate false images from true ones.

Likewise, when students first observe the characteristics of an animalculum through a microscope, it is as if they are only taking note of the ridiculous assurances in yet another commercial or parsing a news broadcast for its biases and inconsistencies. Even those few students who do feel a connection with their subject [SEE DAWSON] will readily admit to the limitations and frustrations that are involved in dedicating oneself to what is, for all practical purposes, little more than a moving picture.

However, before you allow this skepticism to taint your research, keep in mind that your own vision manipulates reality more than any microscope ever could. Far less distortion takes place between the objective lens and eye piece of a microscope than takes place in your own mind when you stare at your feet in the bath. This is by no means an exaggeration: your mind interprets the retinal input of your feet soaking in the tub by means of a complex system of inference, using its accumulated knowledge of how far away from your eyes your feet tend to be, of where the source of light in your bathroom tends to come from, of how light tends to move through soapy water. In short, your mind cross-checks all the combinations that could create this retinal input against the input's given context, so that what you experience as the image of your own feet has less to do with the reality of your feet at that moment than it does with your brain's efforts to provide you with an image that makes sense.

So if the era in which you live has made you skeptical with respect to manipulated images, then you must accept that this skepticism applies to the visual world as a whole, and that there is no real difference between a computer-animated dinosaur and your own hand held out in front of your face.

After embracing this, you have two options: 1.) You can reject everything and regard the world as a baseless fiction, or 2.) You can take the information that your senses give you, albeit incomplete and interpretive, and attempt to derive from it rules and principles. You can accept the fact that science is an operation of faith, and that in order to participate in it you must first reject the fear that a false image could make you foolish.

THE HALIFITE

Before the discovery of the halifite, the scientific community was in agreement that an emotion was a response to a state of being. In the same way that the concept of time is used to keep track of objects moving through space, it was believed that the purpose of emotion was to help individuals keep track of themselves as they moved from one state of being to another. Just as it is easier to delineate one's physical existence by means of the artificial units of hours, minutes, and seconds—quantities which are significant only because they have been widely agreed upon—our prehalifite understanding of emotion maintained that quantities such as happiness and sadness were likewise only artificial, convenient points of reference.

This view of emotion as a mechanical response to the progress of our fortunes seems immediately naive to those of us who experience emotions on a daily basis. Contemporary readers, such as yourselves, will have difficulty understanding how the prehalifite view was ever taken seriously. However, before you condemn those who came before you for their ignorance, keep in mind that without the insights afforded to us by the halifite, the prehalifite view would still be unassailable fact. From the water cycle to the validity of bivalent protein substructs, everything seems like common sense once it has been established.

The halifite tends to be found on the bodies of large mammals. Subsisting on dead skin cells, it goes generally unnoticed. It is oval in shape with a pale-blue outer cuticle. It most resembles and is often mistaken for an exceptionally small variety of dust mite. However, in addition to its size, the halifite is distinguished by its uncanny ability to emote.

One does not have to observe a halifite for long before it begins to exhibit behavior that is altogether singular and which, to the uninitiated, might seem delightful. A halifite stands upright on the tip of an eyelash while happily doing a sort of soft-shoe routine. Another halifite is on its knees, beating its chest and pulling melodramatically at its antennae. These exhibitions of emotion tend to be entertaining to lay observers in the same perverse and universal way that it is often considered funny to see a farm animal dressed in women's clothing or a dog smoking a pipe. Halifitic expressions of emotion contain elements of the same mad-cap anthropomorphism which is the ruling principle of Saturday morning cartoons and children's books. For this reason, much like the ridiculous-looking frilled-neck lizard and the overtly adorable panda cub, images of halifite have become a staple for the covers of elementary school science textbooks in their belabored attempts to convince children that science can be fun.

But presenting the halifite's behavior to students in this way drastically undermines its importance. It is also extremely disrespectful to the inner experience of such a sensitive creature. Not pictured on the cover of those textbooks are all the halifite that, overwhelmed by their own emotional experience, have hanged themselves to death from a host's earlobe or deliberately bashed their own heads open on a patch of dry skin. When studying the halifite, keep in mind that there is no difference between its joys and your joys, between its sorrows and your sorrows. If you perceive a difference, what is it? That the halifite is small? That it does not have language or a higher intellect? Don't be a snob. Feeling is feeling. Also, remember that it is only on account of the halifite's inner experience that we are beginning to better understand our own.

In this respect, the halifite initially seems to confirm the idea that emotion is a direct response to a state of being. That is, the halifite seems to use its emotions as a way of processing external stimuli in a way that adheres to common sense. Pleasant stimuli correspond to happiness, unpleasant stimuli to sadness.

Example: An adult, female halifite returns to her nest to find that her eggs have been destroyed by a competitor. The halifite probes the ruined eggs with her antennae and shows obvious signs of mourning.

However, when the observer increases the level of magnification, the emotion exhibited by the halifite in question suddenly changes. In response to the demise of her eggs, the halifite is now expressing a guarded sense of relief, as if she has been freed from a tremendous burden. When the level of magnification is increased again, the halifite is consumed with guilt. As the magnification is increased again, the halifite is convulsing in a kind of laughter, which is unmistakably at her own expense. As the magnification is increased again, the halifite is bowing her head toward the destroyed eggs in the grips of some bizarre and reverent joy. As the magnification is increased yet again, the halifite's expression is frozen in a mask of grotesque horror.

With every incremental adjustment to the level of magnification, the observer will discover a new, discernible emotion in the halifite. The emotion being expressed at the lowest level of magnification—in this case, mourning—is actually a composite of all the emotions being expressed at the greater levels of magnification. Far from a being pure, clear-cut phenomenon, the halifite shows us that a single observable emotion is really only the most obvious facet of the complex interplay between all possible emotions.

On account of this insight, many inner-events which would have been regarded as insane under the prehalifite view are now understood to be perfectly natural. In an unexpected moment, the widow laughs into the casket. The businessman grieves over his profits. The assassin swoons for the king. Our emotions never wholly reflect our state of being, because we are experiencing every possible emotion at all times, just in varying proportions. So it is when we are sad that our happiness most surprises us. It is when we are pleased that our sadness most perplexes us. It is when we are prepared to slit the king's throat that our love for him is the most startling.

But if emotion is not a direct response to our state of being, then what function does it serve? This question that the prehalifite view perceived as being so crucial is, of course, ridiculous. It neglects the fact that the universe is a hairy, tangled mess filled with purposeless digressions, of which our entire emotional framework is most likely just one among the uncountable. At any rate, be wary of those who would attempt to judge things solely by their function. The world is not an implement.

We must begin to approach the idea that, perhaps, emotion exists for emotion's sake, and that what makes our inner-events so intense and manifestly difficult to understand is that the end toward which all emotion is moving is unknown even to its own components. And if this uncertainty troubles you or leaves you feeling depressed, then examine your feelings carefully and take note of the fact that you are also thrilled by it.

THE KIRKLIN

All kirklin currently occupy a space no larger than an acorn. This arrangement should be impossible, as there are currently ninety-five trillion kirklin in existence, and each is roughly the size of a grain of rice. The compression of their entire species into such a small space is an incredible feat, and, in terms of understanding it, the scientific community is at a loss.

In 1988, a physicist at Yale by the name of Dr. Josephine Klemp attempted to duplicate the kirklin's compression using two hundred thousand popsicle sticks in a pressurized chamber. The resulting explosion killed the thirty-eight graduate students who had been working under Klemp and destroyed the better part of Yale's historic Abbot Building where the study was located.

Klemp was not in the lab when the explosion occurred and went on to publish a somewhat controversial paper based on the data she collected regarding the force with which the popsicle sticks had blown through the skulls of her former assistants. While many found the paper to be in poor taste, the fact is that by extrapolating that data and applying it to the kirklin, Klemp was the first to raise the question of the potential force that might be implicit in the kirklin's compression. Klemp pointed out that because the level of compression achieved in her study was only a fraction of that which exists within the kirklin population cluster, the explosion that occurred in her study was only a fraction of what would result if the cluster were to suffer a similar instability. In short, Klemp raised the fear that a kirklinic explosion would cause our entire planet to share a fate similar to that of Yale's Abbot Building.

However, over the years, many experts have argued against this view. Prominent physicist Dr. Quentin Butler describes Klemp's explosion theory as foolishness. According to Butler, the notion that Klemp's compression of popsicle sticks is any way analogous to the current state of the kirklin is unfounded. Butler contends that given the extreme density of the kirklin cluster, the creatures are far more likely to implode, creating a giant black hole that would consume our solar system and go on to gnaw away at the surrounding universe.

Others maintain that Butler's view is no more realistic than Klemp's. Dr. Alfonzo Delgado, former director of the Conklin Institute, derides both views as pseudo-scientific. He claims it is far more likely that instability in the kirklin cluster would spark a chain reaction, in which the kirklin would cause everything that came in contact with it to become similarly compressed. Dr. Marie Cabot-Berger, at the Trevor Laboratories, describes a theory in which the kirklin might corrupt the vacuum of space, causing the entire universe to disappear at the speed of light.

While opinion varies greatly as to how it would happen, all experts seem to be unanimous in the assumption that the kirklin is on the brink of ending the world. The popular press has seized on this anxiety, and every two weeks there is a new theory being put forth in which the kirklin will destroy life as we know it. And while some theories are more difficult to disprove than others, it is important to remember in each case that because what is being feared is without precedent, there can ultimately be no real evidence to support it. What is being expressed in these conjectures is simply the natural human fear of catastrophe, the perennial concern that the sky will fall, that the earth will open up, that all the aspects of the universe that we cannot control will finally come to bear. These fears are ancient, and science has simply put new words to them, given them a new, compressed shape.

THE ROLE OF CREATIVITY IN SCIENCE

If a stranger were to approach you with a box of crayons and ask you to draw a clown, how would you respond? Would you pluck out a crayon at random and draw a stick figure, adding only a few wholesale gestures meant to indicate in the laziest, most basic way possible that what you have drawn is a clown—large circular feet, the hurried scribble of a fright wig? Or, worse, would you scorn the exercise altogether? Would you roll your eyes, as if to suggest that drawing a clown is beneath you, that your very inability to perform such a task stands as proof that you have dedicated yourself to far worthier, far more challenging pursuits? If either of these reactions seems plausible to you or correct, then you are not a scientist. Nor is it likely that you will ever become one.

However, if, despite the fact that you are not a gifted artist, you try to draw a clown with enthusiasm, if you ask the stranger with his box of crayons to be patient while you carefully determine which colors you will use, if you approach the absurd names of the crayons—Antique Brass, Aztec Gold, Electric Lime, Jazzberry Jam, Smokey Topaz—not as examples of obscene cutesiness but as units of a true and exhaustive taxonomy, signifying fundamental components of expression which will need to be deliberately selected and arranged so as to achieve the perfect image of *CLOWN*, if you manage to come up with a handful of creative flourishes—the distinctive head of a seltzer bottle, a bright pair of button suspenders, a certain, waggish look on the clown's face—which, despite your aforementioned lack of artistic talent, not only evoke the viewer's concept of *CLOWN* but enrich that concept—then you are most definitely a scientist. Congratulations.

To pursue a career in science, the level of reflexive creativity described above must be the foundation of your personality. The reason for this is that science does not take place in the physical world but in the framework of your mind.

Example: You are watching a combination of chemicals sputter and foam in a dish. As you do so, you are confronted with a mental image of a floating placard upon which is written the formula for the chemical reaction that is just now taking place in the dish. This formula is either written in the penmanship of a long-forgotten teacher as it was first glimpsed on a chalkboard years ago or else simply in the indescribable scrawl of your own thoughts. Whatever the case, it is this placard, containing that formula, which helps you to distinguish the sputtering taking place in that dish from all other sputterings.

What's more, all the sensory details attached to this chemical reaction—the bright white foam, the sound of a gentle crackling, the pinched, acrid smell—are not taking place in the physical world, which cannot see or hear or smell. All these things are taking place in your mind. So the act of observing the contents of this dish involves interplay between at least two abstractions: 1.) The floating placard and 2.) Your mind's interpretation of the physical world.

It is for this reason that science depends on creativity, because grasping the relationship between abstractions is essentially a creative act. Such mental dexterity depends on the same imaginative leaps of faith as art, the same lightning-strike intuition, the same ability to draw connections between dissonant quantities.

"That's all well and good," one might say, "but do you mean to suggest from this that when approached by a strange man and asked to draw a clown, I must automatically submit myself to his whim?" Yes! You must! It is not enough that scientists be creative only when it suits them. Unlike the artist, whose creativity is narrow and self-interested, a scientist's creativity must be all-consuming. Childlike tasks must be immediately appealing, because the way in which a scientist approaches the world must be the result of a sense of wonder that is intrinsically childlike.

When you take a young boy to the zoo, he wants to know everything. Looking at the gorilla, he asks you what kind of things the gorilla eats. But before you can answer, he asks you who is responsible for feeding the gorilla. What's more, he asks you if that person has a family, and, if so, where do they live. The boy wants to know if there are any children his age in this family and where do they go to school. Also, he asks, who made the gorilla's cage? How did the people who made the cage know that it would be able to withstand a gorilla? Does the gorilla like it here? Why am I a little boy and not a gorilla? When you inevitably lose your patience with the boy and tell him to stop asking you these questions that you perceive to be pointless, the silence that follows will be loaded and urgent as he does his best to hold back his unyielding necessity to look at the world and ask *how* and *for what reason*. Likewise, a scientist must confront the world with questions hanging off questions hanging off questions.

Now, draw a clown:

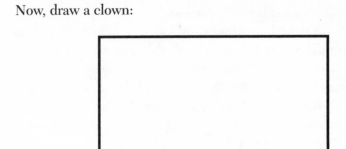

THE ERNOTH

The social order that exists between all ernoths is incredibly complex. There are countless parallel and overlapping hierarchies within which ernoths are all constantly gaining or losing power. Because they are all more or less the same, when an ernoth elevates its status it is through sheer confidence. Likewise, it can only diminish in status on account of its own anxiety and doubt. This confidence level does not depend on its temperament but simply on its position within its given hierarchy. The ernoths in the lower echelons are all convinced that they belong at the top, whereas the elite ernoths are nagged by fears that they secretly belong at the bottom. It is for this reason that an ernoth never holds a position in a hierarchy for long, as its current position—whether in power or out—is always a source of anxiety. The only thing that changes is in what direction that anxiety is compelling it to strive.

THE LASAR

Bloodshed between species is constant and essential. Without it, predators would starve for want of food, and prey would collapse under the weight of their ever-expanding populations. However, violence within a single species is comparatively rare. When it occurs, it is typically restrained and ritualized. For instance, a rattlesnake does not make use of its deadly poison when fighting another rattlesnake. Instead, it will wrestle with its opponent in a predetermined ceremony, in which each snake harmlessly attempts to pin the other to the ground.

So while rattlesnakes will not hesitate to kill an unsuspecting child or a curious dog, when it comes to one rattlesnake pitted against another, the two will typically choose to settle the thing like gentlemen. The same is true when two elk deliberately clap antlers or when two elephants lock tusks or when an African saplid empties its ink pouch onto a rock adjacent to a competing saplid's egg mound.

Unrestrained conflict between animals of the same species is not unheard of, but, through the logic of natural selection, it is far from being the rule. In addition to the fact that it is a costly expenditure of energy, the risk of being seriously injured is as real for the attacker as it is for the animal being attacked. If such conflict can be avoided, most creatures do just that.

However, a notable exception to this is the lasar. A stout, round little creature, it will attempt to kill any other lasar it comes into contact with by ramming into it repeatedly. Since the other lasar will conduct itself in the exact same way, the probability of any lasar surviving one of these contests is roughly the same as a coin toss. Existence, for the lasar, is little more than a succession of purposeless murders ending inevitably in its own.

The ritualized righting of other creatures is typically attached to disputes over territory, resources, and sexual dominance, whereas the all-out conflict that exists between lasar is attached to none of these. Therefore, the lasar is thought to be the only creature on earth other than man capable of governing itself by means of an ideology—by which it is simply meant that its behavior has somehow been elevated above common sense.

There is no way to determine the content of the lasar's ideology, as ideologies, in general, have no content. They are only indications of a failure to incorporate oneself into the natural world. That the lasar insists on killing other lasar is merely an example of this kind of failure. Unsurprisingly, it is an endangered species. This is seemingly of its own accord, and the fact that there might one day be no more lasar to speak of seems less the result of its shortsightedness than of whatever vague promise it perceives in its own vicious and unstoppable cruelty.

THE FEAR OF ERROR

There is no greater boon to a young scientist than a healthy fear of error. If you double- and triple-check your measurements, if you anxiously reexamine your calculations, it is because you believe that your research is important. In turn, people who claim to be fearless are only saying that they do not consider anything they do to be important. Such people are doomed to wander the earth like ghosts, listless and vacant. After all, fear is a natural consequence of hope. The reason that fearful people are ultimately the best scientists is that they are all secretly filled with the hope that their research will answer some fundamental question. They nurture in themselves the desire for their work to produce some tremendous breakthrough, for their efforts to unlock singlehandedly the next wing of human history. With this ambition comes the inevitable fear that their work could possibly be meaningless, that their lives up to that point have been histories of unflinching error.

THE PAGLUM

The paglum is compelled to imitate whatever creature is closest to it. If you place one in a specimen dish next to a kyrnsite, an animalculum known to propel itself by the awkward groping of its crablike claws, the paglum—though clawless—will begin moving its slender, delicate legs in a manner which evokes perfectly the clumsy, disorganized scramble of the kyrnsite. If you place that same paglum next to a feltspire, a tight little ball of a creature known for its tendency to zip quickly from one place to the next, the paglum will gently curl its body in on itself in order to appear similarly compact. And though it is not as fast as the feltspire, it will stretch its antennae in the direction opposite to the one in which it is moving, as if, propelling itself at incredible speeds, its antennae are being blown back.

During these imitations, the paglum does not alter its physical appearance radically. In fact, what is so remarkable is how subtly it is able to depict its fellow creatures. The paglum singles out defining movements, unconscious gestures. It is this sense of nuance in the paglum's mimicry that distinguishes its behavior from other creatures known to engage in similar behavior. Unlike the stick-bug or the chameleon, it is not the goal of the paglum to disguise itself. And while its impressions are uncanny, no one would ever mistake it for anything other than a paglum.

It is because its performances are never wholly convincing that they are so compelling to watch. An impressionist in a nightclub does not transform completely into the impressionee. Such an act would be more startling than entertaining. Rather, the impressionist arranges his or her own features in a way that cleverly characterizes something essential about the impressionee. What is remarkable about this feat is that the features being used to evoke the impressionee are recognizable at all times as belonging to the impressionist. The personality of the paglum, like that of a good impressionist, remains present even as it takes on the characteristics of another creature.

The paglum seems to understand that what is pleasing about an impression is not what is included, but what is deliberately left out. In other words, an impression reveals to us how much of reality can be discarded with reality still being successfully expressed. In the end, an impression is not a depiction of reality, but a seeing-through, a shutting-out of everything that is not essential. In this sense, seeing the paglum do a spot-on imitation of a klempate or a feltspire is rather freeing. As if you were in a nightclub, watching some desperate, ugly little man in a powder-blue tuxedo flawlessly impersonate a matinee idol, you will experience a sense of exhilaration as you observe the paglum. Your first instinct will be to applaud.

THE ADORNUS

Because there is only one adornus in existence, studying it is ultimately pointless. Without the benefit of observing more than one specimen, there is no way to determine whether it is acting in a way that is natural to its kind or in a way that is specific to this adornus in particular. Certainly, it is a vibrant little creature and there is a great deal of behavior to describe, but why bother? The only thing of value that can be said is that the adornus is unique in the purest sense of the word.

By way of comparison, what we praise as uniqueness and individuality among human beings is, upon serious consideration, only an improvisation that exists within set parameters. And while it is possible for our improvisations to be wonderfully rich and complex, our capacity to be dissimilar from one another has definite limits.

What's more, in order for a person to be recognized as being an individual, that person has to have a great deal in common with the group that he or she is attempting to be distinguished from. This may seem counterintuitive, but consider the words *hot* and *cold* in relation to one another. Both are adjectives referring to extreme temperatures. The reason that we recognize these words as being opposite of one another is that except for one distinction their meaning is identical. Likewise, in order for a person to stand out as an individual that person must first adhere to an untold number of social conventions. If anyone were to be purely unique, that person's existence would no longer make sense to us.

That is why studying the adornus is useless. If there is no context to judge its behavior against, no conventions for it to adhere to or reject, then it is impossible for anything it does to have meaning.

THE PERIGITE

The large green rings that circle the earth are still a relatively new development, but it is already difficult to imagine the sky without them. Those two broad rings that intersect one another like the gimbals of a gyroscope are now as commonplace a sight overhead as the flight of birds. Already forgotten is the widespread anxiety that occurred when those rings first appeared—a strange, claustrophobic feeling as the once wide-open sky was suddenly imposed upon by those immense swaths of green. The initial sense the rings provoked was that the living world was being hemmed in. Now, of course, we know the exact opposite to be true.

Unlike the rings of cosmic dust that circle the gas giants of our solar system, the earth's newly formed rings are comprised entirely of small creatures called perigites. These are the first organisms known to migrate successfully outside of the earth's atmosphere. So while the impression one first had was of the living world being closed off, it is now understood that these large bands are a sign that life has begun to expand out into the universe.

The common reaction to this fact was excitement. It was, after all, a triumph for the race of the living. The perigite had learned to thrive in a new medium just as our animal predecessors had risen up out of the sea and learned to live on dry land. Life, it was generally agreed, was marching forward, was preparing itself to populate the universe with its creative might.

However, within this celebratory mood, it was difficult to deny the simultaneous realization that, in this next glorious stage of life, mankind was being left behind. As earth's dominant species, we had up until that point assumed that life's potential for progress rested on our shoulders. But once the nature of the perigite was understood, it became quite clear that this potential rested elsewhere.

Just as we tend to look back with pity and condescension on all the creatures that are still bound to the ocean, we as a people began to understand that the next stage of life would look back in the same way on us, still bound to this floating palace of dirt.

That is why, though the sight of those rings is quite common, many still tend to regard them curiously. Naturally, as a species, our thoughts are conflicted. On one hand, we feel usurped and irrelevant. Excluded, and jealous. Yet, we also cannot help but maintain that first touch of pride we experienced upon learning of life's great journey out into the universe. Despite ourselves, we regard those far-off rings affectionately. We wish them well.

Nominated by Michael Czyzniejewski

TO THE RAINFOREST ROOM

by ROBIN HEMLEY

from ORION

PART ONE

THE ALLURE OF EASY CHEESE

I'm in favor of Authenticity.

Maybe I should rephrase that.

I want everything in my life to be Authentic. I want to only eat Authentic Food and only have Authentic Experiences. When I travel, I want to travel authentically (hot air balloon, camel, steam railway). I want to meet Authentic People (family farmers, I think, are authentic; people you meet in the Polka Barn at the Iowa State Fair; members of lost tribes; chain-smoking hairdressers named Betty). I want to think Authentic Thoughts.

Actually, Authenticity baffles me. I first wrestled with the notion about ten years ago, when I was researching a book about a purported anthropological hoax. The Tasaday were "discovered" in 1971 in the southern Philippines leading an authentically Stone Age existence. They lived in isolation in the rainforest, had no metal or cloth except what had been given them by a local hunter, wore leaves, carried around stone axes, and, most authentically, lived in caves. The Western world fell in love with them and soon the Tasaday graced the cover of *National Geographic* and were the subject of countless breathless news accounts. No one could be more authentic than the Tasaday until 1986, when a freelance journalist from Switzerland hiked unannounced into their forty-five-thousand-acre reserve and was told through a translator that the famous Tasaday were nothing more than a group of farmers who had been coerced by greedy Philippine government officials into pretending to be cavemen.

My task was to unravel the mystery, to discover whether they were in fact a bald hoax or a modern-day version of our Pleistocene ancestors.

Before giving you the definitive answer, I'd like to interrupt this essay to bring you a word about Easy Cheese. If given a choice between the inauthentic (Easy Cheese!) and the authentic (cave-aged cheddar cheese from Cheddar, England, where it was invented a thousand years ago), I usually go for the authentic, unless of course I want Easy Cheese because sometimes that's what you want. This problem dates back to when I was in boarding school in 1974 and someone handed me a Triscuit (Original Flavor) topped with a vivid orange floret extruded from a can. What can I say? It tasted great. How can we hope to live authentically when we have been compromised by prior experience?

With that out of the way, we may proceed.

The Tasaday were neither Authentic Cavemen nor a hoax designed to fool the naïve public. They were, in fact, a poor band of forest dwellers whose ancestors had fled into the rainforest a hundred and fifty years earlier to escape a smallpox epidemic. They became Pseudo-Archaics (a term used by Claude Lévi-Strauss) and lived more or less unmolested until they were "discovered" and made poster children for authenticity, chewed around for a while in the imaginations of the fickle public, and then shat out onto authenticity's midden.

From time to time, I read sentiments like this: "For a few hours I lived in an alternative Africa, an Africa governed by a quiet glee and an innocent love of nature," and I think *your* quiet glee, buddy, *your* innocent love of nature. This sentence, by the way, is an authentic quote from an actual essay that appeared in a recent travel anthology. When I read it, I could get no further. I wondered what the writer thought he was doing experiencing his quiet glee in this alternative Africa? This sentimentalization of "Primitive Man" in harmony with nature seems akin to a hunter praising the pristine beauty of an elk head he's shot and mounted. The hunter can move but the elk can't. The authenticity tourist can and will depart the rainforest, leaving behind his tourist dollars and those irrepressibly authentic Africans twittering their gleeful songs on their kalimbas.

Nature declawed, stuffed, mounted. What then do we really want from the Authentic Destinations of our imaginations? And how do our perceptions of them differ from the Real Thing? When we think of an unspoiled place, how much do we need to strip away before we reach the desired level of authenticity? Strip Hawai'i of its inauthentic fauna and you're left mostly with bats.

The idea of an authentic place implies an unchanging one, which also makes it an impossibility.

My experience with the Tasaday has rendered me hyperaware of the aura of desperation and melancholy surrounding our common need for the Authentic, especially in regard to Place and People. Call it a sixth sense. If I were a superhero, this might be my special power, though it might also be my singular weakness, my kryptonite, which was, after all, the only thing that could kill Superman, a chunk of authenticity from a home planet he could barely remember. And no wonder—because neither he nor his home planet ever existed, except in our minds, where they continue to exist, and powerfully so.

And so I present for your further confusion, if not edification, three rainforests.

PART TWO

LIED RAINFOREST: OMAHA, NEBRASKA

Overlooking the second-largest waterfall in Nebraska, I wish that I could meet the plumber of this fifty-foot marvel. I asked to meet the plumber, but my request, I guess, was not taken seriously, and so I've had to make do with the director of the Henry Doorly Zoo, Danny Morris. I suppose I had some doubts about visiting one of the world's largest indoor rainforests before I showed up (yes, there *are* others). So what if a paradise tanager settles on a branch here? It's still Omaha outside.

Why would anyone go to the bother of bringing the rainforest to Nebraska? It's my theory that Nebraska has developed a severe case of landscape envy.

Arbor Day: invented by a Nebraskan.

The only man-made national forest (Halsey National Forest) is in Nebraska.

The word *Nebraska* originates from an Oto Indian word meaning flat water.

People of my generation will remember with fondness the weekly TV show *Mutual of Omaha's Wild Kingdom*, starring Marlin Perkins, which ran from 1963 to 1985 and gave most Americans their first exposure to the conservation movement. Perkins might not have been from Nebraska (though he was a midwesterner), but Mutual of Omaha, the show's proud sponsor, certainly was. It may be the most logical thing in the world that a state as mono-diverse as Nebraska would be infatuated with exotic flora and fauna. If the rainforest is the closest thing on Earth to the Garden of Eden, to which we always hold out hope for our eventual return, Nebraskans may simply be looking for a shortcut.

Perhaps that's what drove the Henry Doorly Zoo's former director, Lee Simmons, to bring the rainforest to Omaha. Simmons had traveled to many rainforests around the world, because a zoo such as Henry Doorly typically has a research component to its mission. In fact, in the actual disappearing rainforest of Madagascar, the zoo's staff and interns have discovered twenty-one previously unknown types of lemurs. One day, Simmons and others, including Danny Morris, taped two whiteboards together, set a perimeter, and started drawing things they'd like to have in their rainforest, including of course, the waterfall and a swinging bridge, de rigueur in any rainforest worth its mist.

Yes, it was planned, and yet planned to look unplanned, so that you might experience the rainforest as authentically as possible without the fear of lawsuits. In the jungle you hardly know what is in front of you and then you turn a corner and see a waterfall or monkeys in a tree, and Simmons wanted to replicate that sense so that you'll never be sure what you'll find. Yes, of course, it's simulated, but at the same time "accurate." Simmons sent his "tree artists" to the Costa Rican rainforest. "You could tell the difference when they got back," Morris says. "Their trees were a lot better."

Consequently, in the Lied Rainforest there are no surprises, and yet everything is surprising.

The white noise of water cascading from the waterfall is designed to mask the shrill voices of schoolchildren on their outings, as well as the many life-support systems required by the ninety or so subtropical species living within its 1.5 indoor acres. The eighty-foot tree in the center of the rainforest, cutting through its various levels, is made of polyurethane-reinforced concrete and is hollow, acting as a giant air duct, recirculating warm air from the ceiling of the eight-story-tall rainforest in the winter and venting it in the summer. The paths, a mixture of dirt and rock wool, which acts as a stabilizer, are roto-tilled. Walk up an artificial cliff to Danger Point, lean against the bamboo fence, and it wobbles to give the impression that it might give way at any minute. It won't. The bamboo is set on steel pegs. Gibbons, hidden in the foliage, hoot like kids. Scarlet macaws perch on palm logs beside the epoxy tree they've vandalized by chewing on its branches. Bats fly free in the building, and arapaima, grown from twelve inches, loll in their pools, resembling manatees.

All of it seems authentic in most respects but happily inauthentic in others. At six p.m. or so, when the zookeepers open the doors of the holding pens, the animals are there waiting patiently to go in for the night, clocking out, as it were, for supper. And no one's threatening to put a road through Lied jungle. No one's mining for gold. If we lost as much of the Lied Rainforest today as we will of the Amazon, the Lied would be gone by tomorrow. And that, of course, is a large part of the point.

"You can watch all the National Geographic and Discovery Channel you want," Morris says as we pause in front of a curtain fig with its labyrinth of roots that kids can climb through. "But you need to smell it, hear it, and feel the heat. When you put all that together, it makes a more lasting memory."

So what if this tree is in finely fitted segments that are keyed for easy removal and reassembly?

Morris frets that, in the age of Google when everything is at our fingertips, nothing is actually touched, and the idea of the rainforest will become ever more remote to Nebraskans, as will the notion of anything authentic at all. He's noticed fewer field trips from the local schools (Morris himself started at the zoo over thirty years ago as a volunteer Explorer Scout). And the zoo staff has been talking recently of adding to the exhibits a Nebraska Farm because so few Nebraskans have ever set foot on a real farm.

But doesn't the word *authentic* lose all meaning if applied too liberally? What is an authentic cup of decaffeinated coffee? An authentic polyester suit? What are the essential properties of an authentic family farm? An authentic family farm would seem to need—now I'm just speculating here—a family running it, rather than the well-meaning staff of a zoo. But that might just be me.

Morris and I walk effortlessly from the rainforest canopy to the riverbed, across three continents, passing pythons and other creatures we wouldn't likely see in the real rainforest and would actually hope to avoid. In this rainforest, the one thing you must not do is step off the path, but if you do step over the little rope you might just turn a corner and find something completely unexpected: an EXIT sign above a garage door big enough to drive a truck through.

We walk across a bat guano minefield, through a smaller door next to the garage door, and come upon a wide tunnel ringing the complex that seems straight out of a James Bond film. We've dropped into an entirely different realm now. The green EXIT sign, the garage door, and suddenly we're confronted by, what? No evil henchmen, no jungle drug lab, but wading pools, animal toys, a reverse-osmosis system, and doors that seem like metaphysical portals: one says "South America," another, "Malaysia." It's here in these rooms, the holding pens for the animals, that the pretense of authenticity drops away. These rooms are the Lied Rainforest equivalent of the actor's dressing room and Morris enters respectfully, not wanting to encroach on the animals' down time, but also concerned that a Francois' langur monkey might snatch my glasses. But the black monkey with its bulging abdomen regards me from its wildness, sees that I am of no importance to its world, and ignores me. Somehow, this moment of disregard strikes me as the most authentic of the day.

PART THREE

ARAJUNO JUNGLE LODGE: ECUADOR

From a motorized dugout canoe on the Arajuno River, I see a mostly unbroken screen of foliage on either bank. A woman does laundry on one muddy bank while her naked toddler squats and plays. A couple of men run a machine in the water, dredging for gold. They can make up to $150 a day for about six grams. The river flows swiftly after several days of rain. A young man perched in the bow of the canoe, barefoot, wears a muddy t-shirt and shorts. He sees the same scene every day, and yet he seems mesmerized by it, as though the river is someone he has recently fallen hopelessly in love with, or perhaps he's daydreaming of his real beloved, waiting for the right spot where he can get a signal on his cell phone and text her. We pass a young man in the river fishing with a net. Ten years ago, before my companion in the canoe, Tom Larson, arrived, the man might have used dynamite to fish instead.

A wheelbarrow and two giant bamboo saplings that Tom is donating to the community of Mirador for erosion control lie in the canoe beside us. The canoe is the local taxi service, so we're also joined by a woman in her twenties who has been to the market. We pull up to a heavily forested bank—her stop. The woman, a Kichwa Indian like most of the locals here, gathers her belongings: a backpack, a large white sack, a live chicken she dangles by its ankles in front of her. Two children and another woman descend the fern-lined embankment to give her a hand, one child reaching into the canoe and grabbing the real treasure, a liter bottle of Coke.

We pull away again and soon pass a sight that seems nearly as incongruous as a garage door in the middle of a jungle. A billboard protected with a thatched roof sits in a mostly denuded spot on the sandy bank, a few desultory banana plants growing beside it. The billboard shows a local official nicknamed Ushito, smiling broadly and giving the thumbs-up sign. Behind the trees, barely out of sight and parallel to the river, bulldozers have recently carved out a muddy track that will someday be a road connecting indigenous communities that until now have been connected mainly by the river. The road is one of Ushito's campaign promises. And today is Election Day. In jungles like this, roads tend to lead to deforestation, formerly inaccessible tracts of old growth being too tempting for illegal loggers to ignore. But labeling them "illegal loggers" makes them sound foreign. For the most part they're locals, though the buyers they're selling to are not.

When we reach Mirador, invisible from the shore, the bamboo plants are unloaded with the help of the canoe's pilot and a couple of local boys. Tom, wearing his typical uniform—Arajuno Jungle Lodge cap, t-shirt, cargo pants, and sturdy rubber boots—instructs the men in Spanish what to do with the bamboo. The fastest-growing bamboo in the world, these saplings, already seven feet tall, will grow into bamboo Godzillas in a short while.

In his mid-fifties and wearing wire rims, Tom speaks softly and has the bearing of someone who has nothing to prove but can easily prove anything he wants to prove, a lifetime of conservation knowledge always at the ready. When Larson first landed in the area in the late '90s and purchased the eighty-eight hectares that became Arajuno Jungle Lodge (sixty-five hectares of primary growth and the rest secondary), a multihued paradise tanager landed on a nearby branch, and Tom took this as an omen. This is paradise, he thought. A former U.S. National Park Service employee and Peace Corps official with a master's from the University of Idaho in environmental interpretation, Tom Larson has been trying to balance the books between paradise and "progress" ever since. Over time, the Arajuno Jungle Lodge has transformed from a personal project to save a small swath of rainforest to an eco-lodge and now a nonprofit foundation dedicated to helping the locals earn a living while not destroying their birthright in the process.

Hence, the fast-growing bamboo that we've transported to Mirador, which not only controls erosion, but can be used as building material and its young shoots eaten. Several days before my arrival, some university students from Canada and the U.S. planted this same variety of bamboo on the western edge of Tom's eighty-eight hectares as a clearly visible boundary. "You'll probably be able to see it from satellites when it's grown," he says. His property abuts the Jatun Sacha Reserve, two thousand hectares of rainforest, where on any given day you can find people cutting down trees (and through which cuts yet another road, this one eight kilometers long, despite a toothless legal ruling saying it shouldn't be there). Tom's bamboo boundary is in part to let everyone know quite clearly that this is Tom's part of the forest. No one, no one local at least, would cut one of Tom's trees.

In the Make-of-It-What-You-Will Department: Tom Larson was born and raised in Omaha, Nebraska.

The center of Mirador is deserted when we arrive after a short hike along a muddy and tangled path. Tom thinks perhaps they've formed a *minga*, a work party, and are off helping someone build or paint something. A field of grass defines the place, surrounded by a sparse and unevenly spaced ring of huts, some thatched, some roofed with tin. Tom points out the local school. A couple times a year, a group of students from the U.S. comes to Mirador and adjacent Santa Barbara to do projects. This year the students painted the school. Tom leads me across the field to check on some solar panels languishing inside the small building. The residents used the panels, donated by a Spanish group several years ago, to power their cell phones, but the storage batteries have since died.

Along a muddy path cutting through waist-high grass, we hike back to the river and hitch a ride in a canoe across to Santa Barbara, where Tom wants to show me the results of the aquaculture project he initiated. Tom started the project because, well, the dynamite blasts were "scaring the shit" out of the eco-tourists at his lodge. First rule of eco-tourism: keep dynamite blasts to a minimum.

What would it take to stop you from blasting the river? he asked the locals, and they said they'd stop dynamiting the fish out of the water if they had their own supply of fish. So Tom, in partnership with the Peace Corps and with help from local residents, built twelve fish ponds in four communities. The Arajuno Jungle Foundation and the Peace Corps supplied the first five hundred fingerlings of *cachama* (a native fish) and tilapia (the ubiquitous supermarket fish), plus two one-hundred-pound bags of fish food. After that, the communities were on their own. Tom sent out word that anyone caught fishing with dynamite would never get assistance of any kind from Arajuno. Dynamite fishing has been reduced by 90 percent, he claims. Additionally, the Arajuno Jungle Foundation (whose board is made up exclusively of Nebraskans) built the water system for the ponds with Peace Corps assistance and built another system to bring water to the village.

When you imagine a rainforest pool, it's almost certain that you do not imagine the fish ponds of Santa Barbara. These utilitarian holes have been gouged between huts with planks and muddy paths running between them, PVC and hoses snaking all around. One woman wears a t-shirt with the smiling face of Ushito! She scatters fish food on the still surface of her pond, and hundreds of two-month-old fingerlings swim to the surface—all tilapia, because cachama fingerlings cost more and are somewhat more difficult to care for. The people in Santa Barbara don't really seem to worry that cachama are indigenous (and thereby authentic) while the tilapia are not.

A couple of ponds look dirty. One that wouldn't hold water has been turned into a muddy volleyball court. Another is empty because its drunken owner fell out of his canoe and drowned.

In the center of the village, we sit with a few local men and chat. The most talkative is Jaime, who has a reputation as a drunk, but he's a good-natured drunk. He offers us *chonta*, the red palm fruit that appears once a year, about the size and shape of a Roma tomato, and begins thanking Tom profusely for helping them with their fish and saying how proud he is of his community that they have stopped dynamiting the river. Jaime, who appears to have been swilling local hooch all afternoon, gives me the thumbs-up sign. So do his companions. "Ushito!" they all yell in unison.

Back at the Arajuno Jungle Lodge, I'm enjoying an afternoon of quiet glee, swinging innocently in a hammock overlooking the river. Tom flips through a copy of *The New Yorker* I brought with me. He asks if I'd like to watch Pink Floyd's *The Wall* sometime this week? Sure. Why not? That's what I came to the rainforest for. The guide who brought me here from Quito, Jonathan, who grew up in Ecuador, but whose parents are American, lolls like me in a hammock.

"You hear that?" Tom says.

At first I don't, but then a faint whine separates itself from the birds and the river. "That's the sound of progress," he says.

Jonathan looks up, listens, says, "There's three of them at least," meaning three men working chainsaws somewhere in the forest.

"I used to stop what I was doing when I heard chainsaws and investigate," Tom says, bringing beers for all of us to two long picnic tables near the hammocks. "But why should I put my head on the chopping block when they're not going to do anything anyway?"

By "they," he means his neighbor and much bigger reserve, Jatun Sacha. By "chopping block," he means getting shot or blown up. He's found dynamite on the hood of his car before. Last year, a park guard was shot. A bullet grazed his head and when the police came to arrest the gunman, they found themselves in a standoff with the man's many armed supporters, most of them from Santa Barbara. The police turned and ran.

"I've gone to Jatun Sacha how many times?" Tom says. "If you go on any Thursday they're cutting down trees to sell at the bridge in San Pedro on Friday. I've told Alejandro, 'I don't even mention this to you anymore because you never do anything.' 'I don't do anything,' he says, 'because I can't do anything. The police don't do anything. The Ministry of the Environment doesn't do anything.'"

Alejandro, whom I've met, is the director of Jatun Sacha. With his shoulder-length hair, thin mustache, and tired eyes, he looks a bit like Don Quixote, which is probably not an entirely inappropriate comparison. Jatun Sacha sold the right of way for an oil pipeline to run through the reserve, and, in exchange, two community internet centers were constructed that allowed eighteen people to finish high school. He's doing the best he can. And by "the best he can," I mean he wins Pyrrhic victories.

But if the notion of compromise isn't native to the rainforest, it has certainly taken hold here, kicking notions of authenticity from the nest. The tourist who clings desperately to the latter might console himself briefly with the idea that authenticity is a man-made concept (like Easy Cheese!). Before this was a rainforest, it was an ocean. Was it more authentic then? Notions of authenticity themselves are a kind of invasive species.

In any event, there's no way to keep commerce and its insatiable appetites at bay for long. A new international airport in Tena, fifteen minutes from Arajuno, is slated to open soon. Ushito's road will continue being built across the river, but won't likely be finished before the next election. Once the road is complete, Tom contends, the forest will go.

"If I were to oppose that road," Tom says, "my name would be mud around here." Instead, he effects what positive change he can. His teeming fish ponds are stocked with giant cachama and *handia* as well as native turtles he plans to restock in the river. And Arajuno bustles with projects for the community. A ceramics workshop. A workshop to train rainforest guides. A project to create medicinal plant gardens for indigenous communities. Even a French chef, training local women to cook meals using native plants for eco-tourists at the various lodges in the region. My imagination takes flight and I envision pan-seared cachama with a chonta ragout. In this way, it's not just bellies that get fed, but fantasies, too, what we might call the Paradise of Cell Phone Coverage for the people of Santa Barbara, and what we might call the Paradise of Accessible Inaccessibility for the rest of us. A Paradise of Roadless Places with a way for us to enter. A Paradise of Contradictions.

PART FOUR

THE GREATER BLUE MOUNTAINS WORLD HERITAGE AREA RAINFOREST AND SCENIC RAILWAY: KATOOMBA, AUSTRALIA

The *Indiana Jones* theme song welcomes me to my third and final rainforest, as I and about sixty other tourists, the largest contingent from China, crowd into a funicular that is open on all sides and covered with a green, cagelike mesh. To gain access to the Greater Blue Mountains World Heritage Area Rainforest and Scenic Railway, I purchased a ticket in the gift shop that entitled me to plunge, via the steepest funicular railway in the world, down to the forest floor and ride the Sceniscender, the steepest cable car in Australia, back up whenever I have seen enough to warrant the price of admission. And that will be whenever that invisible gauge in me that craves authenticity hits full.

I consider this a Bonus Rainforest, like an offer in which you buy two rainforests and get the third for free. Truthfully, I stumbled upon it. An hour ago, I was in suburban Australia, on a pleasant and tame street in the town of Katoomba, in a house overlooking a garden. But now I am caged and strapped into my seat on my way down the side of a mountain. In the spirit of adventure, I'm even wearing my Arajuno Jungle Lodge souvenir cap.

I'm visiting Katoomba on a retreat of sorts, the nature of which isn't important, except that it involves spending most of my time indoors, chatting amicably with a group of Australian writers, most of whom ask me daily if I've had the chance "to take a stroll down the path to the overlook!" Not one of them told me there was a rainforest there. You'd think this was something one ought to mention. Admittedly, one of them did describe it as "like the Grand Canyon but with trees."

Until now, Katoomba has seemed like another tourist town the likes of Park City, Utah, or Asheville, North Carolina, with sloping streets, pleasant houses, grocery stores, boutiques, and restaurants, and quaint architectural landmarks, in this case the grand Carrington Hotel, built in the late 1800s. To learn why it has the feel of a tourist town, go down Katoomba Street to Echo Point Road until you find yourself, almost without warning, facing an overlook as impressive as any in the world. Suburbia suddenly ends and a kind of prelapsarian fantasy begins as you gaze out upon seemingly endless miles of mountains, replete with rainforests and waterfalls and the giant stone pillars known as the Three Sisters. It is indeed like the Grand Canyon but with trees.

If someone had just uttered the magic word *rainforest*, I would have dropped everything to experience its majesty.

The exhibit, if we might refer to nature that way, can be found at the end of the funicular ride, where, upon disembarking, I find myself on a boardwalk surrounded by railings to protect the flora and fauna from me, as one sign admits. The forest floor is dominated by gum trees and a Chinese tour group with a harried, flag-waving guide who wants everyone to stay together. I want to get away from them, not because they're Chinese, but because they're human, and one of the reasons I go to the rainforest is to get away. I don't want to hear Chinese or English or French spoken. If in Ecuador, I want to hear the three low whistles of the undulated tinamou, a floor-dweller the size of a pheasant, answered by the longer and higher whistle of the little tinamou. If in Omaha, I want to hear the roar of a fifty-foot waterfall drown out hordes of schoolchildren. Here, I'd like at least a kookaburra with its almost stereotypical jungle call, the avian equivalent of *Ooh ee ooh ah ah, ting tang walla walla bing bang*.

I run down the boardwalk, pursued at a brisk pace by the Chinese. Signs along the path identify various plants, but I hardly have time to note them. I stop briefly at a blueberry ash, with its cluster of drooping white flowers, and also at a gray mound, a giant termite's nest, "home to a million termites or white ants." Ahead of me, a man speaks softly into his digital camera's microphone while jogging at a good clip and pointing the camera at the forest canopy. His efficiency and his lung capacity impress me, and I run after him just to see if I can keep up. His wife, also jogging, glances over her shoulder at me, seemingly alarmed, and I fall back. I would love to chat with them to ask why they're jogging as they film, how they think they'll remember this experience, but I'm too out of breath.

At a crossroads, one sign points to the Sceniscender, which will lift me away from this place and back to suburbia, but I'm not ready to be lifted. TO THE RAINFOREST ROOM, another sign proclaims, pointing in the opposite direction, and I think yes, "Tally ho! To the Rainforest Room!" I imagine a jungle glen, a stream, a twittering canopy in dappled light.

Ahead of me is an octagonal, open-sided building made of the kind of wood you'd build your back deck out of, with twelve benches and a trash can in the middle. I sit down on one of the benches across from three young Australian women and one man, taking a breather.

"I think she's pretty," one of the women announces.

"No, not at all," the man beside her says.

"I think she's pretty in a European way," she says.

"No, not at all," he insists.

A sound separates from the conversation—faintly in the distance, not a chainsaw, but a plane, its insect whine claiming the empty space it glides across.

The Australians stand up to leave.

"I'd come back here," one of the women says.

"Not me," says the man. "No toilets."

I spot, a little way up the path, a flag waving frantically, drawing closer.

Half an hour later, the Sceniscender lifts me and about fifty other people back to the familiar world. We ride up and out of the jungle—past the Three Sisters, past a defunct roller coaster that was built over the gorge but never officially opened—and are delivered directly into the maw of the inevitable gift shop. Here, I can purchase any number of didgeridoos, placemats, and coffee mugs decorated with aboriginal art, stuffed toy wallabies, and outback hats. I resist.

Stepping out into the parking lot, I find myself thinking about how often our idea of what's real differs from what's actually there. And about how certain concepts persist in our consciousness long after they've disappeared. When the Dutch killed the last dodo on Mauritius in the 1600s, the idea of the dodo did not cease to exist. It became the poster bird for all creatures that are too stupid to save themselves. Still, any loss over time becomes more bearable. I can't authentically experience a dodo, but I can imagine it. I can Google a dodo, and in this sense get closer to a dodo than most people did who were alive when dodos still existed. And though dodos no longer walk the earth, I saw a real dodo foot at the British Museum when I was eleven.

Maybe everything authentic eventually winds up an exhibit. Worse, maybe everything authentic eventually winds up depicted on a shot glass in a gift shop. Maybe the very idea of authenticity implies extinction. For the record, I'm not in favor of extinction. Here's one test if you want to replicate it but can't, it's probably authentic. So maybe authenticity is something to be wished for, catalogued, but never owned. Something we can't quite pin down, but nevertheless yearn for. Something that, for a while anyway, can keep at bay the nightmare of a globe covered with polyurethane trees and inhabited by wild animals who clock out every evening.

Nominated by Orion

PREFACE

by JILL MCDONOUGH

from HARVARD REVIEW ONLINE

Hand and foot, from head to toe, the body we know
like the back of our hands, we say, patting our palms
since we don't know back from front, don't know our ass
from our elbow. I help Liz find her vagina to use
a tampon her first time, Brooke tells me what to expect
during a blow job, Jeff says to let the funneled
force of Coors hold open my throat, a stranger
gives me Valium when I reach for her hand
on a plane. Now Depo, condoms, the Pill
make way for FSH and BBT, how the sperm
that makes boys goes faster, dies sooner,
like boys, says Joanna, holding her little girl.
Laura's fingers flick to show how the dye popped open
her fallopian tubes. Rita Mae says a forty-eight-year-old's sperm
could cause autism, Esther says *kids are nice but they
do ruin your life*. Billy's friend announces,
out of nowhere, *I am so happy with my decision
not to have children* and none of us believe her.
X shopped around for the perfect Jewish eggs, Y
injected her belly, evenings, with little syringes, the bruises
blooming black, now purple, now yellow and green.
During implantation the nurses played soft eighties hits—
*I bought a ticket to the world, I know I know I know
this much is true.* She says in the ultrasound her ovaries
looked *like bunches of grapes.* Z has a baby at forty-two—

in vino she and her husband joke, *in vitro*
a no-no in the Roman Catholic Church. Encyclicals entitled
Donum Vitae, Dignitas Personae say why: *the human person
is objectively deprived of its proper perfection: namely, that
of being the result and fruit of a conjugal act.* The church,
thank god, is soothing, confident, ready to clear all this up. Life
a gift, human persons dignified. And we, most of us,
are perfect, because fathers put their penises in moms.

Nominated by Gail Mazur, Lloyd Schwartz

THE ART OF POETRY

by MARIANNE BORUCH

from PILOT LIGHT

isn't sleep. Isn't the clock's steady
one and one and one though seconds eventually make
an hour. And morning passes
into a thing it might not recognize by afternoon.

Or you practice the ordinary art
of shrinking strangers back to children, who they
could have been: bangs cut straight across,
boys and girls the same.
I blink kids into grown-ups too, who they
might become, the exaggerated gestures we do,
the weight on each word
a warning, kindly
or just so full of ourselves
we can't help it. But this odder

elsewhere not old or young, male,
female, this century
or that. It simply visits, this who, this
what. This art
of suspension. Wait.

If you've ever acted, you understand what it is,
standing in the wings, the dark

murmur out there. Every dream
for days you nightmare that. Saying or not saying.
Then wake to lights, the other
pretenders on stage bowing, happy enough.
Except it's not

like that, this wish
being small: to make emptiness
an occasion, the art of calling-it-down.
To wonder for the first time as I write it. And elegant
is good. Wild, edgy, half-uttered in fragments is

good. And always that sense of the dead overhearing.
Or simply: voice I never,
not once in the world, give me a sign.
I'll pick up the thread. Dally with it, sit in its coma,
wait for its news in the little room
off the nurse's station. Don't be

maudlin, says the garden, don't
be pretty pretty pretty, and don't think whimsy
unto irony disguises.
Because it is
a garden. You walk and walk and twilight now,
its darker half
half floats a yellow still visible in high spiky things.

There's a dovecote where nothing nests. There's an expanse
orderly as blueprint but flowers get wily, and only
make believe they agree the best place
to stand or lean. It's not the sun.
I can't decide anything. Can't decide.

Begging bowl, ask
until asking
is a stain. Any garden's a mess.
Am I poised at an angle? Am I listening?
A stillness in summer
so different than winter's. Lush and forgetful though

all the lost summers lie in it, ones
in old photographs. Children a century ago, a few
who never thought to leave, still busy
in certain pictures making houses in the yard out of
porch chairs tipped over,
and sheets. Their worn shirts, their hair every
which way. Someone loved them.
She raised a camera.

But I don't,
don't mean that. It's the art of the makeshift
almost house. Or how the children
don't see her, so aren't
dear yet.

Nominated by Alice Friman, Jane Hirshfield, Brigit Pegeen Kelly,
Donald Platt, Grace Schulman, Eleanor Wilner

JUNIPER BEACH

fiction by SHANNON CAIN

from THE COLORADO REVIEW and THE NECESSITY OF CERTAIN BEHAVIORS (University of Pittsburgh Press)

Charlie works as an auto travel counselor in the Cranston, Rhode Island, branch office of the American Automobile Association. Mostly her job involves the assembly of TripTiks. Charlie's parents are newly dead, their car having run off the road three weeks ago outside Tucson, Arizona. Upon her return to work after their funeral, she began creating TripTiks that send Triple A members to destinations different from those they'd asked for.

There have been complaints. But this week Charlie rescued a pair of newlyweds from a hackneyed Niagara Falls weekend, sending them instead on an off-season bargain honeymoon in the turret of a renovated French Canadian chateau overlooking Lake Ontario. Yesterday a father showed up at her counter in the hope that a White Mountains fishing trip would separate his teenage sons from their Xboxes; Charlie saved him from KOA campground monotony and sent him and the boys to a grouping of National Forest log cabins on the Tioga River.

The TripTik Request Form now at the top of Charlie's inbox has been submitted by Ruth and Geoffrey Leaf, who report that they would like to travel to Orlando. They want her to reserve for them a Premium Campsite at Disney's Fort Wilderness Resort. The brochure Mrs. Leaf has attached to the Request Form, presumably as a caution against Charlie's being unable to find Disney World on a map, describes the campground's recent improvements, including "enlarged paving in many sites."

Charlie tosses the brochure into her wastebasket. If Ruth and Geoffrey Leaf carry out their plans, the Leaf children will not, during this vacation, run squealing into the waves of the great and friendly Atlantic. They will not bite into tuna sandwiches gritty with sand. They will not squint into the clear sky and engage in thrilling speculation about Gulf Coast hurricanes.

A TripTik consists of a series of map strips, printed on narrow slips of paper. If you clipped a particular section of American interstate—fifty miles, say—out of a typical road map and enlarged it tenfold, you'd have a TripTik strip. Each strip opens like a pamphlet and has a map detail inside, upon which appear popular landscape features, human-made monuments, secondary roads.

Charlie pulls strips of map from their cubbyholes, creating a little pile, and sits down at her desk. She runs her orange highlighter over the interstate. At the end of each strip she draws an arrowhead, to redundantly indicate that it's time to turn the page. Charlie's mother used to say that one mustn't take a paycheck for granted. Charlie twirls the rubber stamp carousel on her desk, plucks off the stamp that says SPEED LIMIT RIGIDLY ENFORCED and thumps it onto strip C-122, between exits 14 and 7 in southern Georgia, where the interstate crosses Rose Creek Swamp. In fifty-one years Charlie's mother never earned a dollar she could call her own. She died when Charlie's father, traveling drunk at top speed on a perfectly straight road in the shadow of a place called Tumamoc Hill, ended their vacation by driving their tinny rented Ford Fiesta into a two-hundred-year-old giant saguaro cactus, top-heavy with six tons of monsoon-season moisture. It collapsed onto their car, crushing it. It would be nice if the circumstances of her parents' death didn't remind her of a scene from a Wile E. Coyote cartoon, but she keeps imagining the Road Runner, that wicked little witness to all manner of coyote injury, speeding from the scene.

The Leaf family will take Interstate 95, straight south. There's a tricky exit, however, where the 287 intersects the New Jersey Turnpike: Mr. Leaf will need to make a quick left-lane merge, otherwise he'll end up on Route 440 to Perth Amboy, descending into a nightmare of auxiliary roads. Charlie turns to the map detail on the inside of the strip and draws a loop to demonstrate how to navigate this cloverleaf. After this point, it's smooth sailing, as long as he watches the signs. Nobody really needs a TripTik to get to Disney World. But to know your route is a comfort, a pleasure, a bit of security. Charlie finds nothing wrong in ministering to those with an impaired sense of direction. A good map tells you where you are, where you're going, and where you've been.

Via highlighter, she diverts the Leaf family to Juniper Beach. It's the off-season; they won't need reservations. At Juniper Beach, oceanside cottages painted in pastels overlook the sea. They are equipped with Formica dinette sets and 1950s pale green iceboxes only slightly rusted around the edges and Adirondack chairs on the porch meant for sipping rum mojitos in the slanted evening light while chicken with jerk sauce roasts on the grill and pink-skinned kids wreak mischief with water balloons. At Juniper Beach there are no super-smooth roller coasters or six-dollar hotdogs.

Although rolling in money—the degree to which Charlie learned only after their deaths—her parents believed in accomplishing family road trips on the cheap, via the old-fashioned purity of the American station wagon; the state park campground; the family-owned roadside diner. Her father took back roads when he could and interstates only at night: darkened two-lane highways were overrun with Indians and drunken rednecks, especially west of the Mississippi. "During the day they're in bed with their hangovers," he said.

Before she turned to guerrilla travel planning, Charlie spent six years suggesting stimulating vacation alternatives to Triple A customers. She pointed out secondary highways to nature preserves, trails through state parks, roadside curiosities. She shared scenery, historical interest, local quirks she remembered from a childhood strung together by road trips. Members would lean on the counter as she talked. They would touch the map with their fingertips. "But if you could get us straight to Miami Beach . . . ?" they'd say. They'd open a Tour Book, search for a Holiday Inn. Most often they were concerned with the availability of high-speed internet access and discount coupons to Sea World. They'd speak of driving all night, sleeping in shifts. Why must Americans travel across their country as though they were being chased?

When Charlie is done marking the strips for the Leaf family, she takes the pile to the back of the room and places them between glossy cardstock covers bearing the Triple A logo. Recently the Triple A research and development department launched web-based software that allows members to make their own TripTiks online. Charlie slips a plastic spine onto the binder machine and pulls the lever to open the comb. She works the die cuts at the top of each strip onto the row of curved plastic prongs. You can't create a book on your personal computer. An internet TripTik is nothing more than a sheaf of office paper, cluttering up your car. It won't even fit in the glove box.

405

Charlie and her girlfriend, Heather, have been together for six years. Recently they seem headed for dissolution, a fact Heather seems unable to face.

"You're in shock," Heather says. "Don't make any big decisions right now." She pushes Charlie's bangs off her forehead. Which is an annoyance, given that her forehead is the area over which Charlie has configured her bangs to fall.

"Small decisions aren't doing the job," Charlie says. She removes herself from the couch, from Heather's proximity. Charlie is feeling emotionally ungenerous. Heather discovered this phrase in a book titled *Making Same-Sex Relationships Work*. But ever since a cactus crushed Charlie's parents, the term has disappeared from Heather's vocabulary, along with negative sentiments generally. Whatever interesting edginess that existed in Heather's personality has disappeared. She has become gentle and kind and philosophical. She offers *resources*.

"There's humor in it, you know," Charlie says. "Honestly, a saguaro? It's slapstick."

Heather regards her mournfully. "It's okay. You should laugh if it would help."

"Haven't you always wondered about the children of people who died doing something stupid?" Charlie says. "Can you imagine? Going back to sixth grade and sitting there in math class, everyone knowing your father broke his neck diving into shallow water?"

"Nobody was doing anything stupid," Heather says. She strokes anxious finger furrows into the pelt of their German Shepherd, Ralph. "Except driving drunk, I guess."

At the funeral, Charlie's brother, Larry, downed a six-pack in their parents' kitchen and informed her that the old man had become pretty much a full-time drunk starting the Easter Sunday six years ago when *standing on this very linoleum* she announced she was in love with a woman.

"Quit being an asshole," Charlie told her brother. They both knew her parents turned out to be crazy about Heather. They saw her as a positive influence on their gloomy kid.

Larry stared into his bottle for a minute, crying some more. "I'll quit being an asshole when you quit being a queer."

She looked past him, past the arched opening through which their

406

mother handed probably three thousand casseroles for delivery to the dinner table, at the crowd in the living room trying to pretend the children of the deceased weren't bickering. "I guess that makes you pretty much a permanent asshole," Charlie said.

When Charlie gets back to her desk from her lunch break, she unwraps a new Triple A members-only, free-gift tote bag from its plastic. Inside she places her lunchbox, her spare shoes and toothbrush, and the personal effects on her desk, detritus of summers past: a framed photo of herself at the rim of the Grand Canyon, taken when she was four; a petrified rock paperweight from Utah; a tiny but authentic Hopi Indian basket in which she keeps change for the soda machine; and a carved wooden mermaid purchased at an artists' cooperative on a rainy day in Asheville, North Carolina.

She packages the TripTik for Ruth and Geoffrey Leaf together with large regional fold-out maps of the Northeastern and Southeastern United States, upon which she's convincingly marked the route they requested, the route to Disney nirvana. This, Charlie hopes, together with their trust in Triple A, will ease them into the complacency required to accept that she, their auto travel counselor, possesses superior knowledge; to accept with only the briefest moment of confusion (perhaps even shrugging in a way not unlike a lemming might, if lemmings had shoulders) that the best access to Orlando comes by way of Juniper Beach.

Because members always flip to the back of their TripTik to check the destination—who can resist a destination?—Charlie has finished the Leafs' booklet with the strip of map that contains Disney World. She has omitted, however, the piece that would get them there from Juniper Beach. For good measure—and in defiance of Triple A policy— she has written a cheerful *Have a Great Vacation!* in heavy black marker over a critical section of the Southeastern US regional map, obscuring the route away from Juniper Beach. She places the Leaf Family vacation plans in the Completeds drawer. Ruth Leaf will arrive tomorrow to pick it up.

The Leafs' TripTik finished and her boss in the parking lot with his afternoon beers, Charlie begins a scrapbook containing automobile fatalities. She clips articles from the newspaper and prints some more off the internet. On a slick curve on remote Highway 2, fifty miles southeast of Billings, Montana, a pair of teenagers, twin sons of a single mother who'd raised them on her salary as a rural paramedic, rolled their Toyota pickup. The twin in the passenger seat was thrown through the windshield. It took the ambulance thirty-five minutes to arrive, and when it did, the mother performed CPR on her dead son for another forty. The other twin, the driver, survived unhurt.

A retired couple on vacation near Puerto Peñasco, Mexico, hit a truck carrying firewood head-on at sixty miles per hour on a dark stretch of MR 8, twenty minutes south of the border. The husband had attempted to pass a Volkswagen Bus on an uphill curve. The kind local woman driving the vw, knowing the *federales* routinely imprison *turistas* who cause accidents until insurance paperwork is filed and authenticated, put the stunned and bleeding *americana* into the bus and drove her away, leaving the husband's body on the side of the road.

Charlie glues the articles onto pages and snaps them into a three-ring binder she's gutted of the Triple A employee handbook. She finds the spot on a TripTik strip where each accident happened and she marks a cross in pink highlighter. She pastes these strips next to the articles. Charlie's mother had had a hard time with maps. She couldn't reconcile the paper highway with the actual one. On a road trip to Colorado Springs the summer after fourth grade, her father tossed the Rand McNally to the back seat and appointed Charlie family navigatrix.

That night she takes Ralph to a new car dealership. It is midnight. She parks her fifteen-year-old Hyundai on a side street and steps over a knee-high gate. She's come in the dead of night to avoid the car salesmen. Ralph sniffs the curb at the edge of the lot. Charlie and her brother each received seventy-two thousand dollars in life insurance money from their parents. More will arrive when the estate settles. She and the dog stroll up and down the aisles. Under the neon floodlights the cars sparkle. Broken glass, or mica, something shiny, has been mixed into the asphalt. Ralph's aluminum tags clink together cheerfully, although the air is clammy with moisture and gnats.

Someone is employed here whose job description is to wash and shine all these vehicles. Whoever it is takes pride in his work. Still, the cars fail to dazzle her. They hulk malevolently in their spaces, a grid of death machines.

On the way home she spots a miniature RV parked in a vacant lot under a yellow streetlamp. A banner made from a bed-sheet says For

Sale. It is now one o'clock in the morning. She circles the RV, finds herself actually kicking the tires. She climbs the front bumper and peers inside: compact, economical. Blue plush. The front seat is like a recliner. She calls the number on the banner. When she says she'll pay cash, the owner stops squawking over having been awakened.

Charlie pulls into the driveway in the RV. "Are you breaking up with me?" Heather asks when Charlie climbs down.

"Not really," Charlie tells her.

"Just because you're experiencing a loss doesn't mean you get to treat me badly," Heather says.

"I wish for once you'd just be clear," Charlie says. "Don't you mean that just because my parents are dead doesn't mean I get to be a bitch?"

"Sweetie, isn't that what I just said?" She squats down and lets Ralph rub his big, black snout against her cheek. "We could go with you," she says. "Me and Ralph."

"I'm coming back," Charlie says.

"So you say," Heather replies.

A family of three, driving through Yellowstone National Park, pulled over to watch a brown bear and her cubs. The mother bear approached their car, reared up on her hind legs and sniffed at the groceries inside the carrier on top of the car. Excited, the parents unbuckled their seat belts for a better view. A tourist bus with a distracted driver sideswiped the car, plunging them into a ravine. The infant daughter, still strapped into a rearward-facing child safety seat installed by trained firemen, was the only survivor.

From Cranston, Rhode Island, one's interstate options are limited to north or south. After you've gone south for a while, your choices expand significantly. Charlie takes I-95 through New London, switches to the 287 at Westchester, and heads over the Tappan Zee to New Jersey. Just south of Parsippany she changes to the I-80 and settles in for the straight, unchallenging haul lengthwise across Pennsylvania. The seat in her RV cradles her so comfortably it's a hazard: a person could fall asleep.

Her TripTik would have you believe the landscape alongside the interstate is an expanse of flat, white nothing. Strip R-33, which covers this stretch of highway, is a filler strip, a connector through which her highlighter used to race, uninterrupted, to the next turnoff. Charlie is halfway surprised to discover actual scenery outside her enormous windshield: purple mountains, fruited plains, et cetera.

She passes exits for state parks: Rickets Glen, Little Pine, Cook Forest, Oil Creek. She crosses the Susquehanna, the Allegheny. She planned to stop for the night at Shenango River Lake, six miles off the interstate, which according to her Tour Book features a number of campsites overlooking the water. Nearby is an 1854 Greek Revival mansion, renovated to mimic Tara in *Gone with the Wind*. Tour guides wear Civil War-era costumes. Charlie is tired, though, too tired to drive on.

Summer 1996, central New Hampshire: In a rare moment of sibling unity, Charlie and her brother conspired to wheedle their parents into a KOA campground for the night. "They've got pinball machines," her brother said. "And a lounge with a TV."

"*Friends* is on tonight," Charlie added.

"No dice," their father said. They ended up gazing, heavy-lidded, at the stars through an open skylight in the vaulted ceiling of a Forest Service knotty pine cabin, exhausted from an evening of chasing crickets, tossing pinecones into a blazing campfire, and skipping flat rocks into the water as a full, orange moon rose over the Tioga.

Charlie sleeps in the parking lot of a Burger King at exit 4A in West Middlesex, at the intersection of State Route 760. In the morning she sits at the RV's fold-down table and watches the sun rise over a strip mall. She expected to feel different. She expected to know more about where she is going. She consumes a Styrofoam cupful of coffee; a sausage, egg, and cheese Croissan'Wich; and French Toast Sticks. She dips the sticks one by one into a tiny plastic tub of delicious imitation maple syrup and waits to see what will happen next.

On a breathtaking stretch of the Alaska Highway, thirty-four miles southeast of Tok, three brothers on a summer road trip from Portland discovered the beer in their cooler was growing warm. They encountered a glacier they judged to be within climbing distance. On his way back to their Jeep, a four-pound chunk of prehistoric ice in his backpack, one of the brothers slid down the rocky hill and broke his ankle. As the others were carrying him across the road, a logging truck emerged around the bend. To avoid hitting the men, the driver plunged his truck over the cliff and was killed on impact.

Charlie keeps to the interstate. She stops at outlet malls, strip malls, shopping malls, multiplexes, big-box superstores, franchise restaurants. She is in America: it is the same everywhere. Before the trip she hadn't appreciated the beauty of this monoculture. She'd taken on her parents' disdain as her own. But in this America, everything is clean. Neon signs are never missing their letters. Toilets flush. Restrooms feature maintenance charts encased in plastic, employee initials indicating the frequency with which traces of human biology have been wiped away. Food arrives quickly and is hot or crispy, soft or cold, as appropriate, packaged in paper, delivered on clean plates by servers in the same uniform as the place eighty miles ago. At cinema multiplexes adjoining five-lane highways, she watches movies of minimal artistic merit. She saves the popcorn bag in Akron and smuggles it in for a free refill in Cleveland. She is at home, rootless yet ensconced, held in place by her movement across strips of landscape.

Charlie affixes a map of the contiguous United States to the wall above her bed in the RV. She records her progress each day with a blue highlighter. The American interstate system is a miracle of engineering and resolve. If she were a philanthropist she'd give her fortune to the federal Department of Transportation. Behind the wheel, she ponders the notions of equal opportunity and freedom of mobility and such American proverbs as *Home is where the heart is* and *Everything happens for a reason*.

The sun sets over Oklahoma wheat fields. Her windshield is bug-splattered. Ahead she spots a Denny's sign, rising fifty feet into the pink prairie sky. Some camping mornings, when they were up with the sun and her mother said she couldn't stand to cook one more meal at another dirt campsite, they'd leave their tent pitched, their equipment at the site, and drive to town for a greasy-spoon breakfast. Their father would order tomato juice and ask the waitress for Worcestershire and mustard and a lemon wedge and a stalk of celery and some Tabasco. Other diners would look sideways at him, grin when the vodka appeared from his coat pocket. In a schmoozing voice that would mortify Charlie, he'd offer to mix up a few for the people in the next booth.

The detail inside the TripTik strip for the hundred-mile stretch of southwest Montana is clear and accurate, in keeping with Triple A standards. Charlie locates the stretch of road where the twins died. She'd have preferred to be there at night, to drive the S-curve in the dark like the boys did. She parks at the opening of a long dirt road, the RV straddling a cattle guard. She's purchased a Polaroid at a Target somewhere. The sky is cloudless; asphalt snakes away into mountain foothills. The twins must have ridden this curve a thousand times in the back seat of their mother's car. She would have warned them, when they got their learner's permits, to exercise caution here. She might have instructed them on the moment at which a good driver accelerates through a turn. She might have railed against the landowners who'd refused to grant right-of-way to the state, requiring road builders to construct a nonsensical corner on an otherwise straight prairie road. She might have told them stories about her own high school friends crashing their cars here. The boys would have rolled their eyes.

Charlie walks the road. The accident occurred eight months ago. The weeds have regrown, skid marks have worn away, bloodstains long gone or scrubbed off the pavement by some rancher's wife. The paint on the wooden memorial marker has already begun to flake. Water has seeped between the plastic laminate protecting the boy's photo. Charlie takes a picture and stands at the side of the road, waiting for it to develop. She is eighty-six miles from the nearest interstate.

Near Boise she stops at a Kinko's. Three hundred e-mails fill the screen, mostly junk. Eight are from Heather; one for each day Charlie's been gone. She prints them and pays the cashier fifty cents per page.

There are miles and miles of road; thousands, potentially millions. There is friendliness on the highway, reliability. Weeks can be lost in the hum of tires; in the movement of the sun across the sky; in the traffic, the vacationers, the eighteen-wheelers, the traveling salesmen. Roadside, wildflowers blur into brushstrokes of yellow on the prairie, blue in the mountains, white everywhere. The RV runs; drinks its gasoline, its wiper fluid, its oil; excretes its exhaust, its gray water, its sewage. Accident sites are different and the same. It is nighttime, it is morning, there are markers, there aren't, there are five miles between sites or five hundred.

Charlie's map is crisscrossed with blue; she doesn't chart a course. She's in Utah; ten days later she's in Utah again. At a truck stop in northern Louisiana she stands transfixed before a swiveling display stand of insignias shaped like the fifty states. Now they're just ordinary stickers, but she remembers when they were decals, packaged in cellophane bags. Her mother would buy two in each state: one for the car and one for the road trip scrapbook. When she and Larry immersed the decals in water, they would slide off their paper backing, the glue coming to life slippery and thick. They would fight over who got to apply a new one to the station wagon's rear window.

Heather's e-mails wait for her at various Starbucks. Charlie collects them, reads them at night on her foam mattress. *Ralph has fleas*, Heather writes. *I got a raise. I'm writing until you tell me to stop.* Charlie has always been lousy at knowing what needs to be said. Heather has seized on this communication deficiency, stubbornly establishing for them both that Charlie's silence means only that the relationship isn't over.

Summer 1997, nearing sunset in northern New York State, fifty miles from the Canadian border: "You got the Tour Book back there, Charlene?" her father said. "Find us a room."

"There's a Howard Johnson's in twenty miles," Charlie told him. She was dying for a Jacuzzi, dying to find people her own age, dying to sit at the pool and drink diet soda. To make friends with a girl who came from somewhere interesting.

"Howard Johnson's, pish!" Charlie's mother said. "Find us a mom-and-pop. Find us a Shangri-La Motor Inn. A Pink Owl Motel!"

Which is how they ended up at a renovated French Canadian château overlooking Lake Ontario. No Jacuzzi, no soda machine, no possibility of meeting another traveling girl. Just a tiny, round bedroom inside a turret that her parents, with a wink to the proprietor, rented just for Charlie, where she gazed happily through a skinny fortress window at the lake below, like a teenage *princesse* waiting for her life to begin.

In Mexico, Charlie waits an hour to cross the border back to Arizona. She found a white cement shrine at the site where the husband of the *turista* had been abandoned. A Virgin of Guadalupe statuette stood under an arch, protected from the sun. A plastic bag whipped in the wind, snagged on a bouquet of plastic flowers. The Polaroid developed with a bright, dusty haze. She cannot stand the feeling of vulnerability caused by traveling outside the Triple A map system.

The Ruth and Geoffrey Leaf family will be in Florida any day now, wandering a narrow coastal road in their minivan, Ruth in the passenger seat frowning over her TripTik and muttering, *This isn't what we*

413

asked for. In the back seat, the kids will turn away from their headrest DVD players to wonder at the synchronicity of pelicans coasting low over the waves. The little girl will open her window and cup the breeze in her hand to capture the feel of flying, her wingtips kissing the water.

At a Circle K on the western edge of Tucson, Charlie buys a topographical map and finds the Globeberry Wash where it intersects Greasewood Road, at the base of Tumamoc Hill. The fallen saguaro has a dozen arms, some of them longer and wider than Charlie herself. The stench of decay is astonishing. She bends over the corpse of the cactus, examining. Its thin, green skin is blackened and cracked; an oozing, gelatinous substance seeps from the fissures.

Yosemite. New England in the fall. Manhattan for Christmas. Chesapeake Bay for the Fourth of July. The Redwoods, Four Corners, Mount Rushmore, Big Sur, Death Valley, Hollywood, Lake Michigan, the Florida Keys. Her father took them to every state in the Union connected by asphalt. He exceeded the speed limit, cared not a whit about seatbelts, drove under the influence of fatigue and bickering children and sips of whiskey from a silver flask nestled between his legs. He showed them miracle after miracle.

A pack rat scurries into a thicket of creosote. Earth is disturbed, evidence of heavy machinery having been used to shove the cactus from the roadway. Charlie's Triple A Tour Book tells her the State of Arizona prohibits tampering with fallen saguaros, in defense of the ecosystem that thrives inside the carcass. Another decade will pass, it tells her, before the outer casing decomposes to reveal the woody ribs beneath. On the same page is a photograph of an actual roadrunner, which looks nothing like the cartoon. *I'm here until you come home*, Heather also wrote in her last e-mail, an earnest dispatch from her imperfect, codependent heart.

In twenty-nine hours Charlie arrives in Juniper Beach. A Holiday Inn Express stands where the cottages once were. The girl at the front desk tells her those old huts were infested with termites anyhow. She asks for the Ruth and Geoffrey Leaf family, but they've already checked out. Charlie's room has a postcard view of the Atlantic Ocean and its wide empty shoreline.

Nominated by The Colorado Review

A ZEN ZEALOT COMES HOME

by SHOZAN JACK HAUBNER

from THE SUN

A Zen Buddhist monk in my tradition gets exactly one week off a year. This time is specifically designated for a "family visit." I always take my week at Thanksgiving, and every year I prove right that old Zen adage: Think you're getting closer to enlightenment? Try spending a week with your parents.

This year I flew in on a Friday, going straight from balmy Southern California weather to a heart-stopping Midwest ice storm. My father picked me up at the airport. I saw him first, standing beside the bank of arrival monitors, looking distinguished but weathered in the same clothes he'd worn last year: a flannel button-down from Mills Fleet Farm (Dad's the kind of guy who buys his boxer shorts, power tools, and pretzels all at the same store) and washed-out jeans, in the collapsed seat of which I could see the deflated future of my own behind.

"Mr. Magoo!" he cried. I received this moniker as an infant. Something about the size and shape of my head.

Pops is pushing seventy. His eyes are magnified by ever-thickening lenses, and his upper body is a pale reflection of his bodybuilding years, but he's still six foot and solid, with the laconic, winning presence of a small-business owner who's punched adversity in the gut a few times and never cheated on his wife or his taxes. We hugged, and I smelled the rifle-barrel business all over him: metallic, rusty, and wet. Instantly I was transported back to my scrawny, scowling youth. The combination of my father's machine-shop musk and coffee breath retarded any and all spiritual progress I had made over the past year, and I was, like the hero of some Hollywood time-traveling comedy, fourteen years old again.

We went home. I hugged Mom, but my eyes were on the fridge, a frost-fogged treasure chest of sweet, rich, fatty foods, the kind I never get at the monastery. Within minutes these treats had found their way into my gut in alarming quantities. Pleasantly nauseated, I collapsed on the leather La-Z-Boy in front of a flat-screen TV the width of an RV windshield. Naturally it was tuned to Fox News. My parents are the Fox News constituency. They voted for George W. Bush in 2000, had four years to think about it, and then voted for him again. Guns hang on every wall in their home: ancient guns, modern guns, guns for dropping a rhinoceros or a fleeing Navajo woman at a hundred yards. I longed to pull one down and silence forever this TV, which was as loud as a helipad, its sound waves rippling my cheeks.

My father entered the room and hovered over me, a silent reminder that I was sitting in his chair. I moved to the couch. Dad navigated the channels from Fox News to a dramatic medical reenactment of a seventeen-inch tapeworm making its exit from a woman's tastefully blurred behind, and I wondered why in the hell I had come home.

Years ago my father was roughing out a rifle stock on a table saw when he buzzed off the top half of his right index finger. (Yes, his trigger finger.) In its place now is a curiously malformed combination of flesh and scar tissue that bears a striking resemblance to a typically less visible part of the male anatomy. "My pecker," he calls it, waving the stubby appendage up and down in a suggestive manner.

The smartest anti-intellectual I know, my father has many favorite sayings. We call them "Dad-isms." One is "We Germans think with our hands." If Germans think with their hands, I ask my father, what does his phallus-like finger imply about his thought process? We laugh about this.

I once tried to tell him about *takuhatsu*—monastic begging rounds. Once a week a monk from the monastery drives down to the produce market in Los Angeles and partakes in a Buddhist mendicancy ritual with a husky-voiced Italian vendor from Brooklyn, who then loads our pickup with produce. My father could not hide his horror.

"Phew," he said, studying me to see if I was for real. "I can't imagine anything worse than having to beg for my food." He gave it some thought. "Maybe having to beg for a place to crap, but that's about it."

Dad does not like to rely on others. He's proficient in plumbing, electricity, machining, carpentry, tile work, flint-knapping arrowheads, and just about anything else that requires intelligent hands. Not only would this ultraindividualist, self-made man never beg for lunch, but he keeps a large food stash in his concrete-walled bomb shelter in case he needs to survive in a postapocalyptic Wisconsin.

"Begging is a lesson in humility, Dad," I tried to explain.

"Yeah," he said, "I'll *bet* it is."

More than God, America, or the Green Bay Packers, my father loves guns. He is known in his trade as the "Gun Guru." "I like to make things go bang," he says, but it's more than that. The firearm is a key metaphysical prop in his eminently conservative belief system. To him a life worth defending, perhaps even shooting someone dead for, is a life that *means* something, that is singular, precious, and real. But for the practicing Buddhist a life finds true meaning only in union with others. My 104-year-old Japanese Zen master explains it thus, in broken English: "Being Buddhist monk means you look at others, you see yourself." Hard to see yourself when you're looking at others through the cross hairs, in my opinion.

My dad has argued before a special subcommittee of the U.S. Congress that firearms are necessary to protect one's family. Yet, in my experience, it's often each other that family members need protection from. Whenever I come home, politics and religion are the arenas in which my father and I slug out all of our unresolved father-son issues, most of which can be traced back to a few key episodes when my old man blew his fuse and displayed the violence I've come to see, fairly or not, as inherent in his gun-loving mind-set.

I have five distinct memories of receiving severe physical punishment from my father. The last time was when I was twelve and I flung my younger sister Helen into a snowbank. I was practiced in the art of inflicting just enough punishment on my siblings to fly under my parents' radar, but not this time. I was busy jamming sidewalk slush into her nostrils, ears, and eye sockets when I felt myself lifted off the ground as if by magic, and I was suddenly on my back, gagging on fistfuls of snow myself. It was my father, teaching me a lesson, asking, "How do you like it?"

We were on the sledding hill in front of our old farmhouse, which topped a butte overlooking white-blanketed cornfields and snow-wigged treetops. This was our final showdown—the last time I was going to let him touch me. A congenital wimp, I wasn't really capable

of fighting back. It was more an explosion of maniacal energy, screaming, spitting, and flailing, like a kitten when you step on its tail. But I
got my point across. He rolled off me, his own temper cooled, as though
I'd sucked the hot anger right out of him. I sprang to my feet and shot
off into the wind-bitten woods, losing myself in its spiny thickets.

In many ways I am still stumbling through the moonlit thickets of
our relationship today: feeling furious with my father, loving him, resembling him, and being as baffled by him as he is by me. I thought I
had found my own path and left him far behind, but with each family
visit I come boomeranging back, determined to resolve the unresolved
issues he has passed along to me from his own glacial relationship with
his "hard-assed old man."

Not that I'm holding a grudge or anything.

On Thanksgiving, six days after my arrival home, relations were still
cordial between the Gun Guru and Mr. Magoo—no meltdowns over
the Second Amendment or "flaky" Eastern religions. Around mealtime
several hefty SUVs pulled into the driveway, and eleven nieces and
nephews flooded my childhood home. My father tossed off a vintage
Dad-ism—"There's more kids around here than *people!*"—and all
twenty-three members of our family sat down at a pair of dinner tables
to increase our collective body weight by a hundred pounds or more.

My mother, a pint-size but commanding matriarch with olive skin
and silver-tinseled ebony hair, said grace with tears in her deep Hun-
garian eyes. *What could possibly go wrong tonight?* her expression said.

Then I brought out the sake—Japanese rice wine, the alcoholic drink
of choice for naughty Zen monks when they jump the monastery wall.
This seemingly innocuous gesture was actually a ploy in my ongoing
mission to expose my parents to new things and so juxtapose my world-
traveler sophistication with their hunkered-at-home philistinism. *Warm
wine?* I imagined my father saying. *What in tarnation?* Then he would
take a sip and marvel: *Wine the temperature of soup! Who'da thunk?*

Made from rice, *no less*, Mama would cry, snapping her suspenders.

Holiday dinners in my family don't involve inebriation. We're too
busy carefully loving each other Wisconsin-style, with lots of head nods
and "you betchas," and consuming as much sugar and fat as possible.
(Everyone is always either eating, exercising, or talking about one or
the other in our house.) And so I, the Buddhist monk, introduced a new
tradition this year: drinking!

Ever allergic to direct conflict, like most Midwesterners, my dad communicates criticism with snippy, offhand comments that slowly leak into your bloodstream like a time-release poison. At lunch he'd dropped one that still had me enraged: "Boy, free groceries and a free roof over your head. Sounds to me like you're on Zen welfare!" At dinner I guzzled my unappreciated sake, allowing my voice to rise in volume. In-laws carefully looked away. My favorite little kewpie-doll niece, sensing a priceless opportunity to trick an adult into making an ass of himself, suggested I dust off the old "flatulent tarantula" routine from my long-retired stand-up-comedy act, and I did, spraying imaginary web and flatulence—and spilling my drink—all over Dad's prized pool table.

"Sake," my Zen master once noted: "Sometimes medicine. Sometimes poison."

My father swung his granddaughter Ella into his lap. Ella is one of those unbearably cute toddlers who are not happy giving their love to one adult unless they're noticeably denying it to another. My father pointed to me. "See that? That's your uncle Jack. He's a monk. Know what *he* does all day?"

"What he does?" Ella asked, looking down her little button nose at me.

"He stares at his navel!"

They laughed and pointed at me.

I sobered up instantly. Rage will do that to you. Whether he'd meant to or not, my dad had finally tipped his hand. How many times had I calmly and patiently—and perhaps condescendingly—explained to him the intense challenges and rewards of my life on the misty mountain-top? Many were the verbal portraits I'd painted of the American Zen monastic experience, Rockwellian in detail with surreal, Daliesque flourishes. I'd wanted him to understand in his gut what it means to watch yourself grow old in robes. He had nodded and smiled, but he had not understood.

Anger filled me like molten lead: *So he thinks I'm just some saffron-swathed cipher, as sexless as a Ken doll, grinning his life away on a* zafu *cushion at a year-round, Japanese-themed summer camp.* (It didn't help that the monastery is a former Boy Scout retreat.) As the Gun Guru roared and tickled Ella with that ghastly penile finger, I saw with besotted clarity that he'd knocked something loose in me those times he'd hit me, and Mom hadn't loved it all back together again like she was supposed to, and so the pain and brokenness inside me had grown to mythic proportions until I could fix it only by dedicating my life to religion. Now he refused even to respect the lifestyle that he'd driven me to with all those blows to my backside—and once to the side of my face.

None of my five brothers and sisters had ever caught it from him the way I had. Why? Because I reminded him of himself. "Here's the last thing you want to hear, but it's true: You and I are a lot alike!" he used to proclaim. And so he'd tried to beat out of me all the parts of himself that he despised: the weakness, the confusion, the fear. But he'd only driven them in deeper. And now, after seven years of intense Zen practice, that boyhood self was surfacing, black souled and mutilated from decades of subconscious lockdown.

I knew then, with the absolute certainty of the truly drunk, that I would never become my own man until I stood up to my father and defended the nobility of bald, berobed Buddhists everywhere, preferably with four-letter words. I stumbled to my feet. Then I had to sit down again. I got back up, determined to make a statement this time, but I was facing the wrong way.

Miraculously, before I could do permanent damage to my liver or familial relations, I was struck by a migraine so crippling I worried I was having a brain hemorrhage. I belched my good nights and pointed myself upstairs.

As I tried to decide which of the two blurry staircases was real, Dad's voice boomed behind me: "There he goes. He's off like last week's underwear."

A night's sleep healed no wounds. I woke up feeling foul and ready to spill blood.

My parents were already eating lunch. "Good morning, sunshine," my dad called out from behind his copy of *Shotgun News*.

I fell to the table and gripped my veiny skull, inside of which a small elf with a big drumstick was beating out a very fast rhythm. I wanted to go back to bed, but then I remembered that I was flying out that afternoon. Time to strap on the plastic smile and make nice. I wasn't going to see my parents again for a whole year.

Mom closed her newspaper with a groan and said two words that flew at me like a pair of killer bees coming in ass-first: "Climate change."

This is how it works during family visits. Everyone can fake it for a while, but eventually your true self wrangles to the fore, and what you're really thinking comes out. You just can't hide around your loved ones. That's what makes them so impossible to get along with.

My parents suspect that global warming exists solely within the fervid imaginations of liberals (unlike such proven realities as guardian angels and Noah's ark). So it didn't surprise her at all that environmental scientists in England had just been caught manipulating data on global warming.

"They're calling it 'ClimateGate' on Fox," she told me, and she launched into an impersonation of Al Gore, painting him as a bloated cyborg who waxed robotically about environmental doomsday. "Welcome to the *Al*-pocalypse!" she said, doing her best stiff-armed Gorebot.

This was more than I could bear. Snarky political satire was the forte of *my* people—the creative liberal vanguard—not string-cheese-eating Wisconsin housewives!

"Damn liberals," my dad added, never looking up from his reading. "Useless as tits on a nun."

You have only three hours before you're on a 747 flying back to your true *family,* I told myself, *with their beautiful black robes and glistening bald heads. Don't do it.*

But I did.

"So," I began, grinding my teeth, "you don't honestly think global warming is a hoax, do you?"

It got ugly quick.

When arguing with my parents, what I lack in facts I make up for with opinions delivered at increasing volume. Like a boxer getting the shit kicked out of him, I lumbered around the rhetorical ring with my mother, that nimble welterweight, taking bigger, sloppier, dizzier swings while she landed blow after stinging blow. For every "fact" I produced about melting ice caps and homeless polar bears (things I know nothing about), she asked for references, opening her laptop and patiently waiting to Google them. She did this jovially, without a trace of attitude and with the frightening certainty of a woman fortified by a year of daily lectures at Glenn Beck's blackboard.

My father put his magazine down and folded his hands over it, but he did not participate. And so my mother became the target of all my pent-up rage at him. But wasn't she my adversary in her own right? After all, what kind of matriarch stands around and watches her husband beat her son? Pickled overnight in sake, my thought processes were cloudy and sour. I concluded that, because she had long ago subjugated her mothering nature to my father's will, she was now projecting this onto the environment with her belief that Mother Nature was subservient to—and protected by—God the Father. Sure, carbon-dioxide emissions were a problem, she said, but not a lethal one. Nature would always bounce back because "God made it that way."

A deep discontent with monotheism had been brewing in me since my college days, when I'd hated authority of any kind. God was the Great Idea that had failed Western civilization, just as my parents had failed me. And for the same reasons! The angry God in the sky was the classic template for the abusive parent. It was all coming together with brutal clarity. Just as my father, through his violence, had sent me on a quest to understand why we suffer, so, too, Westerners were being driven to Eastern forms of spiritual expression by an intolerable deity whose all-too-human shortcomings—anger, jealousy, spite—were matched only by the implausibility of his existence. How closely my personal problems mirrored our culture's deepest spiritual malaise! (As it is writ in the Gospel of Dad: "Just 'cause your own ass aches doesn't mean the whole world's got hemorrhoids!") This was shaping up to be one of those monumentally bad mornings, when the ground under a relationship finally shifts, opens along a fault line, and swallows everything on the surface.

"Let me get this right," I began. "You think the earth has some kind of eternally regenerative essence? That it'll just magically go on forever?"

"As long as we need it to, yes," my mother replied. She was in her kitchen, pretending to be busy elbow-greasing away invisible counter stains.

"And you think that *you* are going to go on forever?"

"I believe in an eternal soul, yes."

"Because you believe in God, the super-duper being in the sky?"

"If I didn't, life would be unbearable."

A trapdoor opened within me, and the last of my patience disappeared through it: "I've got news for you. For the most part, life *is* unbearable! It's called the 'First Noble Truth' in Buddhism: 'Life is suffering.' And your religion only takes a hard world and makes it worse!"

For decades my parents' kitchen table has hosted a Virgin Mary plant holder in which we kids used to hide the numerous vitamins our mother gave us. As I spoke, I gestured wildly and upended the botanical Virgin and her trailing vines, which I could hardly be bothered to then right.

"This illusion of a supreme being," I continued, "which leads to your illusion of an eternal human soul, which leads to your illusion of an indestructible planet, is *destroying* this very vulnerable planet and pretty much everything decent on it!"

"I don't see the connection."

"That's exactly the problem. You don't see how things are connected."

"I don't understand," she said, wiping soil from my place mat.

"Well, let me spell it out for you, then," I cried. "If we're all dependent on a miracle from God to save us and this planet, then we're conveniently excused from being responsible for each other, and life becomes every man for himself! Frankly, to me, that's the very definition of hell on earth."

Here I turned my puny wrath on my father, who was studying his scuffed work boots, unable to meet my bloodshot gaze: "You people believe that this earth was just *given* to you by God, and that it's yours to do whatever you want with. It's like *you're* on welfare, and God is the nanny state, and you just take and take and take!"

It was an inspired bit of cruelty, and I took what I can only describe as sexual pleasure in saying it. I closed my eyes and waited for my dear mother's tears. I'd exploded dynamite at the very foundation of her religion, but it had to be done.

She sighed deeply and said with a shrug, "Yeah, that *is* basically what I believe. God as a Divine Parent, watching over us, taking care of us and this planet."

Was there no stopping this woman?

I then delivered an anti-Catholic diatribe about delusion and projection and witch hunts and book burnings and gays and women's rights and abortion and pedophile priests. It was as though I'd stuck my finger down my throat, and up came every complaint I'd ever had against the religious tradition in which they'd raised me.

"Take a good look at the world around you," I concluded. "Religious wars are going to destroy this planet. They are going to *destroy this planet.*"

My father looked up, and our eyes skidded into each other. Then he spoke: "Yes, they are—starting with our family."

My ears rang. I couldn't pull air into my lungs fast enough. My throat was pinprick thick, like those of the hungry ghosts of Buddhist lore. I was asphyxiating myself with rage.

Finally my mind caught up with my mouth—always an awkward moment for those of us with tempers. My apoplexy ceased. My fury lost its redness. And, for the first time that trip, I really took them in: Dad's once-chiseled face, collapsing with age. Mom's hair, pinned up in a bun, one step closer to hoary and desolate white. How old they'd become. How many more visits would I even be blessed with? How many more chances to make things right?

In an attempt to prove their religion violent and insane, I'd manifested those same qualities myself. Here I was, the Zen zealot, screaming at my parents to think of the planet as their close relation while shattering the precious harmony of our own family in the process. All the fight went out of me. I slid into my seat at the table. Snow was falling outside, light flakes that filled the air.

These were not the same people who had raised me. Those people existed only in my head, caged and rotting behind my tight, unhappy grin for decades while my actual parents got older, gentler, wiser; while their bodies fell apart and their souls grew deep. I felt the grace of my mother's God just then, a surge of the sacred that bore a distinctly Christian imprint. *Forgive them*, some part of me cried.

But it ain't easy, replied another. Why had my father never apologized for beating me? A fair question. And here was another: Why hadn't I apologized to my five siblings for all the noogies, nipple twists, and occasional drubbings with a pair of foam-padded nunchucks that I'd subjected them to? The sins for which you cannot forgive yourself are the sins for which you will never be able to apologize. Such is the Catch22 of extreme guilt: I can't come to terms with the violence I've committed until I can admit that I did it, but I can't admit that I did it until I can come to terms with the violence I've committed.

Suddenly I felt a twinge of kinship with my father. We were both at war with ourselves, not each other.

As I watched the falling snow become one with the snow that had already fallen, I thought of familial love as the planet's most precious, limited resource, a delicate system of checks and balances, of giving and receiving that must be protected against the toxic human ego the way the oceans and sky must be protected from pollution. I saw how my father's unhappiness had spilled into me, just as he'd been the vessel for the unhappiness that had spilled from his own "son-of-a-bitch old man," who had been the vessel for *his* father's tears . . . and on and on, all the way back to the first single-celled organism, which split in two, turned around, saw itself in another, and started the first family argument.

I was about to rend the long, clean linen of silence with a heartfelt apology when my father, a master at misreading the moment, said, "Well, we'd better get you to the airport, Magoo." Then he turned to his wife of forty-five years, raised his finger-phallus, and declared: "We're off like a turd of hurdles. I mean, a herd of turtles."

The conversation on the way to the airport was freighted with my desire to take back every single infantile accusation or comment I'd made. I felt a lump in my throat as my best intentions dissolved in wisps of forced small talk.

"They have a Hummer dealership off I-94 now?" I asked.

"Yeah, it's the biggest one in the Midwest."

"Wow."

Futzing with the air-conditioning vent, I thought, *C'mon. I'm more enlightened than this!* But of course I'm not. And that's what my parents are there to remind me of for one week every year.

As I stepped through the airport metal detector, I stole a look back at my father. In a year he would be standing in roughly the same spot to pick me up, wearing the same flannel and denim, and posing the same challenges to my inflated opinion of my spiritual progress. I felt like a frightened twelve-year-old heading off to church camp all over again. I was sick and tired of the home behind me, but also terrified to fly, terrified to land, terrified to invest another year of my life in that wintry, patriarchal monastery, where the principal pleasures were lukewarm showers, the occasional cheese condiment, and masturbation—not necessarily in that order.

Lacking any other option, I tried to do my Zen practice right there while getting x-rayed—to be in my body, to inhabit the actual real-time situation instead of my head full of ideas. But it was no use. The week had been too rough. My heart was a raw wound.

Then it occurred to me: maybe I *was* in the actual real-time situation after all, and pain was just a part of it. I was in the moment, and the moment sucked. Just because you hurt doesn't mean you're doing something wrong. It may simply mean that you're alive. I'd been numb to my parents for decades, denying my rage and resentment. Now I was finally feeling something. I was feeling like shit, actually. But it was a start.

I gathered my shoes and wallet on the other side of the metal detector and took a last glance at my father, who was still there, still waving. That mangled finger had always been a symbol of his shortcomings and deformities to me, but now I saw it was also a testament to all that he'd sacrificed for our family. He'd lost that trigger finger building the business that had fed and clothed me. I imagined he was not only waving me goodbye but waving me forward with that symbol of his own woundedness.

Nominated by The Sun

ELEGY FOR KENNETH KOCH

by FRED MORAMARCO

from POETRY INTERNATIONAL

d. July 6, 2002

It seems too crazy, like one of your mad, funny poems,
that you're not with us any more, not here to point out
the *thisness* of things, like mountains, circuses, and fresh air.
You were always the court jester of poets,
toppling pretension from its granite and marble heights.
"Look," you would say, about this or that,
"how absolutely strange, marvelous, and ordinary it is,
like everything else you will meet on your daily rounds."
You noticed the blueness of blue, the curvature of the round,
the still beats of silence within seconds.
One of my favorites of your lines is
"To learn of cunnilingus at fifty
Argues a wasted life." This from your poem,
"Some General Instructions," which pings in my head even today.
Ah, Kenneth, the obit said it was leukemia and you were 77.
Hard to imagine either. You, a frail old man, eaten by blood cells.
I rarely saw you when you weren't laughing, darting here and
there.
I remember we wrote a sestina in your class,
each student writing a line as the poem went around the room.
I wrote the last line of that poem, and remember it forty years later

because you thought it was the perfect ending:
"Who would have guessed at such a meaning for summer?"
And I say that again, for this summer, when you're no longer here:
Who would have guessed at such a meaning for summer?

Nominated by Poetry International, Michael Bowden

RESURRECTION

by LAURA RODLEY

from THE NEW VERSE NEWS

Never again will a tsunami
come silently out of the unknown,
it will be tracked by radar
so there will be just enough
time to run.
Never again
will people walk unaided
by the spirits of those
drowned by the tsunami;
smell this rose for me
they will say, dipping
their head closer as
if for a kiss,
taste this smoked eel
for me, as they lean
by your cheek
to hear you chew,
touch this they will say
willing you to lean towards
the magnolia bud
ripe with the wish to burst,
but not yet the pink halo erupts.
Carry this, they ask,
carry this load of bamboo
tied with rope upon my back

take this load to my mother,
tell her I got lost upon the way
and now in deep waters of the ocean
I have not forgotten.
Untie the bundle for her,
her hands knotted with age,
lay the bamboo in a neat pile
for her to use as she wishes.
She had so admired the way
I cut the stalks without
braising their ends;
it takes a clean, sharp knife.
Tell her I am calling her name,
speak it for me,
Mamasan, my little Rebecca,
speak it for me
so she can dry her tears.
And for my brother,
pull his hands away
from the damp soil
tell him I am not here,
he will never find my bones,
but you have found me,
oh kind stranger,
walking beside you
and you will tell him
what I say; I beg you,
and I am not ashamed of that.

And take these slippers
for my sister, red with
embroidered flowers, beaded.
They were for her birthday,
tell her I have not forgotten;
I was just looking for a way
back in to bring them to her,
a way back in.

Nominated by The New Verse News, Pamela Stewart

TIGER

fiction by NALINI JONES

from ONE STORY

The trouble with the cats, Essie believed, was entirely her son-in-law Daniel's fault. They first turned up on the day that Gopi was expected to come shake the coconuts down from the trees. It was mid-morning, a January day without too much Bombay haze, and early enough for the children to play outside without Marian worrying about the heat. Still, she insisted on hats for them. Essie said nothing when her daughter called the girls to the front veranda steps, just sat and helped Marian rub their limbs with lotion to protect them from the sun. Both were fair-skinned, though darker than Daniel, whose pale, pinkish skin reminded Essie of chicken not cooked long enough.

Marian went upstairs to help the servant Ritu wash the children's clothes, but Essie stayed to keep an eye on the girls. They were five and six only, babies still by Essie's reckoning, and it was her belief that Daniel did not pay close enough attention. She knew better than to approach him directly, of course; he would only turn to her with his blank American look and smile his blank American smile. It was all too soft and spongy for Essie, who had wondered when she first met Daniel whether he fully understood her. Who was this man her daughter had married? Did he know proper English? Were his mental faculties intact? She had adjusted her speech in his presence, talking loudly and slowly, using smaller words. But her efforts had no effect and eventually she realized that conversation with her son-in-law would always have a shapeless quality, like sinking her fingers in a lump of dough.

She had prayed for guidance and patience, as she had once prayed

431

for her daughter to come home again and marry an Indian Catholic boy from their own neighborhood. Such nice-looking boys! Essie had kept her eyes open to suitable possibilities. And then, the shock of this Daniel and his soft American answer: "Well, not exactly Catholic." There is no exactly in this matter, she'd informed him. A person is Catholic or not. She had confessed her disappointment to all the parish priests. But one after the other, they disappointed her too. What to do, they said, but accept?

Now when Essie was troubled by his American ways, she took her concerns straight to Marian. But her daughter, so clear-eyed in her girlhood, so close to Essie that they had seemed two limbs of the same living thing, had gone a bit soft herself after so many years in the States. When Essie pointed out that Daniel was too relaxed with the girls, Marian looked down, or away, or said, "Oh, Mum," as if Essie were one of the children, acting up and tiring her.

For a little while, the girls practiced badminton, a game their grandfather had played when he was young. Daniel, Essie noted, did not have good form with his swing. But everything had to be cleared away before Gopi arrived and coconuts came pelting down into the compound. Daniel pulled up the stakes of the net and the girls were collecting shuttlecocks. Nicole, who was older, flung her racket onto the lawn and ran up and down the garden wall, checking under leaves and behind the roots of trees as though hunting for Easter eggs. But it was Tara, a year younger, who found the cats behind a thick clump of bamboo and called everyone to come and see.

"Look at that! Kittens!" Daniel peered into the corner where a mother cat and two half-grown kittens had been hiding. All three were alert and staring.

"Don't touch!" Essie said quickly, drawing Tara back. "They'll scratch."

"No, they're nice," Nicole decided. She squatted on the ground and held out her hand. One of the kittens made a tentative move closer and Essie inhaled sharply, a sound meant as a warning.

"So dirty, baby! See their fur? They don't live with people."

"They don't look too bad," Daniel said. The mother cat was thin and dingy, with white fur that reminded Essie of yellowed muslin and patches of gray and ginger. One of the kittens was spotted, half its face shadowed in gray, and the other was ginger-striped, as if the mother had poured some part of herself into each of them.

432

Nicole extended her arm as far as she could and Daniel put a hand on her shoulder.

"Not too close, you'll scare them." He began to call the animals with a whispery noise.

"These aren't your American cats," Essie said. "They could carry disease."

But Tara was spellbound. "One kitten for each of us . . ."

"Your grandmother's right. These cats don't like to live inside with people."

Nicole looked up at her father, stricken. "But we have to take them inside. Gopi is coming!" The danger of the falling coconuts had been impressed upon her all morning; she must hold someone's hand when Gopi did his work, she must stay safely beneath the veranda roof. Otherwise, tuk! Her grandfather's fist had knocked against her head. (Essie had watched this display with disapproval and scolded her husband. "Such a thing to clown about, Francis! Have some sense.")

Now she hastened to reassure Nicole. "These cats are wild, darling. Like tigers. They like to look after themselves. See the mummy cat? She won't let anything happen. She'll hear Gopi and they'll all go running."

"Where?" Tara was solemn, all eyes and wonder.

"They have places they like to go." The girls were clearly unconvinced, Tara's eyes reproachful. Essie spoke brightly. "Maybe they'll go to the fish market, for a nice piece of fish!"

"Maybe Ritu has a little fish she can give them," Daniel suggested. "Let's see if they want something to eat."

"Not in the house," said Essie at once, but the girls were already scrambling up, naming the cats, begging them not to run off, promising to be back in another minute, *stay, stay*, their voices high as fevers as they called from the staircase and Essie watched while Daniel followed, letting them run up the steps without holding the railing, not saying a single word to slow them down.

The next hour was given over to the cats. They were easily lured into the garden with pieces of cheese, and step by step, the girls coaxed them up to the outdoor landing with saucers of milk. This was the main entrance to the upper storey, by means of a staircase that began on the far side of the veranda and ran up the side of the house beneath a narrow wooden roof. The small square landing at the top led directly into the front room, and the heavy wooden door was kept open all day long to let in light and air. The cats, Essie thought grimly, were literally at her doorstep.

It was some small satisfaction, at least, that Marian greeted this development with dismay.

"Babe, what could I do? Their father told them to feed the cats. I cannot contradict him. All I can do is tell him the way we live here, but," Essie paused. "What could I say?"

"Well," Marian said. "At least they don't look like they have fleas."

"Fleas are too small to see. We'll only see the bites."

The girls were alone on the landing, the kittens playing near their feet while the mother cat perched a few steps below. Daniel joined Essie's husband Francis, who had switched on the test match the moment he returned from a morning at his club. Daniel was new to cricket. He leaned forward to ask a question, a glass of beer in one hand, and Essie eyed him sharply to be sure he didn't put it down on the wooden arm of the chair.

She raised her voice to be heard over the television. "Marian, you were scratched by a cat when you were small—you don't remember. A bad scratch, on your cheek. I had to rub oil every day so you wouldn't scar."

Daniel did not turn from the screen but Marian sighed. "The kittens seem harmless enough." One had been lured into Nicole's lap. Tara, warned to be gentle, was stroking the other with exaggerated softness.

Essie grunted. "They've been eating in rubbish piles, God knows what they might pass on. And what is keeping Gopi? Maddening, these fellows! *Yes, yes, I'll come*, he says, and what? I've let the whole morning go waiting for him!"

"Let them play awhile." Marian said. "When Gopi comes, the girls will want to watch and the cats will run off on their own."

But Gopi never came. By lunchtime, the girls had names for all three cats—even the mother, a wild, skittish creature who kept her distance until she saw a chance of food and then came creeping up the stairs, low on her haunches as though she were hunting.

"That one is Tiger," Nicole told Essie. "She's the mother."

"What is this one called?" Essie tried to enter the spirit of things. "Is this Panther?"

"No," Tara said. She was squatting, perfectly balanced on her heels. "That's Smoke."

"And the little ginger one is Fire?"

"That one is Ritu."

Essie felt strangely dissatisfied. She had never liked cats, all hiss and tooth and claw, slinking like vermin among the market stalls. She would not want the girls to name one for her, but it did not seem right that Ritu should be singled out.

The real Ritu was bringing plates of food to the table, a chicken dish from the day before, a new fish curry. She heard her name as she was setting down a steaming bowl of rice.

"Who is Ritu? Oh! See, bhai, chota Ritu! Thank you, Baby, thank you, Chota Baby." She laughed, using the same sing-song the girls used when they remembered their manners. Ritu called both little girls Baby, but Tara, smaller, was Chota Baby. "Baby is taking care of Chota Ritu, and Ritu is taking care of Chota Baby. Come, food is waiting." She stooped to pick up Tara but Essie stopped her.

"Have you brought the curds to the table?" she said, picking up Tara herself. Ritu made fresh yogurt daily, which the little ones ate with their meals to cut the spice. "Come, darlings. Come and eat."

Nicole held one of the kittens to her chest, her voice pleading. "Can't we eat out here?"

"Girls." Marian used her warning voice. "Grandma says lunch is ready. Let the cats be, they've had enough."

The girls did not disobey but dragged themselves to their feet.

"Come," said Essie. The men had got up from their seats near the television but were still focused on the screen, standing as though anchored. She spoke in a loud, ringing voice. "We'll clean your hands first, lots of soap. Those cats must have been filthy."

That was the beginning. The cats returned the next day, just as lunch was being served, and again the day after. By the third day, Essie had agreed that the girls could leave milk for them on the back balcony. "At least let them be out of our way," she said. She could not have people coming up and down with stray cats on the landing, and the days were filled with visitors, neighbors, tradesman. But even after she had banished the cats to the kitchen balcony, they seemed to creep into her days, pushing from one minute into the next, curling around the arms and legs of the children as though they were entwined. There were ten days left, a week, five days. Already the children had gone to the market for the last time, and the beach at Juhu. The banana man had come on his weekly round and had given the girls a full bunch as a present; he would not meet them again. Marian had begun to arrange all her packing in piles, and Daniel had taken the suitcases down from the tops of the wardrobes. The cases lay on the floor, flopped open like wide hungry mouths. Francis began to stay home from his club in the evenings, waiting for the girls to be bathed so they could pad out in bare feet and flowered gowns and say good-night. Essie read to them from the Bible at bedtime, longer and longer stories, until they had collapsed against her shoulders or across her lap. Still the girls went running whenever the cats appeared, no matter what other treats Essie planned for them. In the late afternoons, while she and Marian entertained guests in the front room, she could hear the sounds of the girls' voices drifting in from the kitchen balcony as though from someplace other than her house, as though the balcony had torn free and no longer belonged to her but to the cats—the pirate cats with their patches and hooked claws, their grinning white teeth, their narrow eyes, floating slowly away with Ritu and the children, who were laughing as they left her.

Four days before Marian and her family were set to depart, Essie was soaping herself and felt the lump, a hard knot where her breast sloped toward her under-arm. She checked again and again, feeling the way it seemed to roll beneath her fingers. Then she checked her other breast: nothing. She stood for a moment, still and dripping, in the afternoon sun. They bathed out of buckets, one hot and one cold; now both faucets were off and instead of running water, Essie could hear the clear bright calls of birds. She leaned against the tile wall, slick but not cool. It was a thick afternoon, unseasonably warm, and she had come for a quick bath before the girls woke from their naps. She had not intended to wash her hair so she'd caught it back in a braid and flicked it over one shoulder or the other, out of the water. Now she pulled the damp tail of it to the front, over her breast, and slowly removed the elastic. She kept her hair carefully dyed, a flat tarry color that did not quite take on the living quality of her youthful black, but she was not yet willing to be gray. She had only two grandchildren, after all; her sons, one living abroad, one posted in Delhi, had not yet married. For the first time, she thought of letting the dye fade. She poured a dipperful of water over her head. Another. Another. Then she seized handfuls of her hair and wrung them like fruit, imagined the dye running down her chest and thighs in rivulets, staining the floor, pooling at the drain where a rubber stopper kept the cockroaches from climbing up the pipes. Slowly, carefully, she washed her hair. She did not rush, even when she heard the children wake and call for her.

She waited until the girls were asleep that night—dinner and baths and wet hair combed, heavy heads against her chest, both children in her lap, one last story, a moment's pleading, one more last story. Grandma, tell us about trains, tell us about Gopi, tell us about Mum when she was little. She went with Marian to tuck them into bed and pull the mosquito netting down like drapes.

She waited until Daniel had taken her suggestion and accompanied Francis to his gymkhana, Francis puzzled but with the same foolish bland smile on his face as Daniel's. Off they went together, to cards and whiskey and long-running tabs and friends Francis didn't bring to the house. Essie leaned out the front window and watched them go with relief. What help could the men give her? Let them at least be out of the way.

She waited until Marian sat quietly, writing letters to aunts and cousins in other parts of India, letters Essie would post for her. Essie watched her daughter. Even now, folded into a chair, no proper jewelry, Marian was a beautiful girl. She had lovely skin, a delicate jawline. She might have married anyone, might have had her pick of the best neighborhood boys. She might have lived all her life only a few steps away.

"You must cancel your ticket," Essie told her.

Marian stopped writing, looked up briefly. "We can't, Mum. You know that. Don't make it harder."

"I'm not making anything!" her voice rose against her will; she wanted to stay calm, a woman prepared for whatever came next, a woman with her daughter beside her. "I have something here," she put a hand near her breast.

Marian's voice sharpened. "What do you mean, something? A pain?"

"Not a pain." Essie considered. "Perhaps it's a little tender. But not a pain only. I can feel something hard, under the skin. This is just what happened to Aunty Ann, you remember? One day she was fine and six months later she was gone. Totally diseased. Nothing the doctors could do."

"You have a lump? When, Mum? When did you find it?"

"Today only." Essie's eyes filled with tears; here, at last, was the daughter she had been missing, Marian alert and focused keenly on her, Marian sharing her secrets. "What to do, babe?"

"We'll go to the doctor. I'll take you tomorrow, we'll go first thing."

"But I have no appointment—"

"We can wait until he sees you. Daniel can watch the girls."

"No, babe, no need. We can make an appointment properly and go later in the week, you can extend a week or two and take me."

"Mum." Marian came to sit next to Essie on the couch, put an arm around her shoulders. "We should see him right away, okay? It could be nothing. But let's get it checked as soon as we can. I don't want you to worry."

Essie felt Marian's arm tightening around her, Marian's head resting softly on her shoulder. The letters lay abandoned in Marian's chair. Essie wondered, she truly wondered, if she was dying. She believed she was. But it was a distant idea, more faint than she expected. The more palpable question was how long her daughter might stay.

The doctor pierced her with a needle, extracted fluid, sent it off to the lab. "In a few days we'll know more," he told them. Marian sat next to Essie, holding her hand, her face tight.

The plane tickets could not be changed without exorbitant fees. Daniel had to go back to work. The girls could not miss another week of school. "We may hear from the doctor before the flight," Marian said, a limp offering.

Essie did not bother to answer.

"Mum, let's sit down with Dad and tell him."

Essie shut her mouth firmly, again said nothing.

"I can tell him if you're nervous. But he should know what's happening. Maybe he can help."

Essie snorted. Marian crouched on the floor before Essie's chair, looking up at her like a child. "The doctor says there's a good chance nothing is wrong. But listen—" she held Essie's knees—"I don't want you to feel alone while you're waiting."

Essie could think of nothing to say to this beyond the obvious. So she said nothing.

Marian put her forehead on her mother's knee. "You understand I have to go? I wish I didn't, Mum. I wish I could stay."

"What good is wishing?" Essie asked, and her daughter didn't answer.

The night Marian and her family flew home, Essie hired two taxis to take them to the airport so that there would be room for her to see them off. She held Nicole in her lap until the last moment— after Daniel had unloaded all the suitcases, even after Daniel said, "Come on, girls," and Marian counted all the tickets and passports.

"Check again," Essie told her, kissing the top of Nicole's head, her arms tight around the child's chest. "Check the date to be certain."

The girls were dressed in blue jeans and long-sleeved shirts, as though they had already left her for another climate. It was nearly eleven o'clock, long past their bedtime, and in the harsh lights flooding the airport entrance, they looked pale and drawn. They had already said goodbye at the house: to neighbors who had come to wish them goodbye; to their grandfather; to Ritu. *But where are the cats? Where are the cats?* Both began to cry. It was no good explaining that cats come and go, that the mother cat must put the kittens to sleep, that Grandma would find the cats tomorrow and deliver all their messages. "We have to say goodbye to the cats!"

They had stopped crying by the time they reached the airport but their faces seemed strangely hollow and serious, as if the past few hours marked the onset of a wild acceleration and they had already begun to grow older—girls Essie would hardly recognize in a year or two when she saw them again, if she saw them again. Did she have a year or two? They had not heard back from the doctor. When Marian called his office that afternoon, she was told the results weren't yet back from the lab.

"Mum, you'll be fine," Marian kept saying. "I'll come back. I'll come back if anything happens."

"Something has already happened," Essie told her.

"Just see what the doctor says, Mum."

Essie shook her head, a parrying motion. What was the point? She knew where things could lead. Daniel, she noted, said nothing.

"I'll come back."

Her daughter was crying, the way she cried sometimes as a girl, streaming tears and silence. For a long while she clung to Essie, shoulders shaking, then she moved away, a sleeve to her face. Essie's spectacles were useless, the airport lights blurred and flaring through the wet lenses. She took them off and tried to rub them dry. She must have a last good look at her daughter. By the time she put them on again Marian and her family had moved the few steps from the curb to the departure hall. No visitors were permitted inside but Essie watched the doors swallow them up, the girls looking small and forlorn, Marian still in tears, turning to wave a final time. After a few minutes, Essie climbed back into her cab.

At home the mosquito netting was still draped over her bed, where the girls had slept with her for their last nap. The cotton cover was rumpled from their bodies. Francis had slept in another room for years but Essie could hear him snoring and the evidence of his peaceful rest at such a time filled her with bitterness. The windows were thrown open and outside she could hear cats brawling, a tangle of raw-throated screeches and howls.

A few hours before dawn she switched on the light to begin a letter to Marian. She tried to chronicle all that had happened in the scant time since they had parted: the impatient cab driver, rushing her departure from the airport, the vacant hours sitting up by the telephone in case the flight was canceled. She described the dark house and Francis's useless snoring, the cramp in her hand from writing, her prayers for their swift return; she described the way the knowledge of her own death was stealing over her, a certainty she could feel in her bones and her muscles and yes, in her breast—she did not have to wait for the doctor to tell her what her body already knew—and even then she could not stop. Here was the way to keep Marian tethered to her, a stream of confidences no one else could share, a comfort mother and daughter might only find in each other. Words poured from her, a spill she could not check—her fear that she would slip away before seeing her daughter or sons again, her dread of disease, of her body rotting away from the inside—did Marian remember visiting Aunty Ann in the nursing home, did she remember the rattling cries, the smells? She wrote about the solace she found in placing herself in the Virgin Mary's hands. *You too might have done this, my girl—place yourself at the mercy of Mary and not worry so much about the costs of things. Who knows how God would have provided if you had decided to stay?* She wrote about her faith in being reunited with both her parents, the father she had lost when she was only a girl, the mother who had raised her; she leapt ahead generations and wrote about all her hopes for her granddaughters. *You must bring them up in the church, so that they too*

440

have a light in these darkest times. Eventually she began to reprise the terrible shock of Marian's decision to marry an American—the fainting spells, the long nights of weeping, the visions of this very moment, sick unto death with no children beside her. *Even now I can hardly believe you are wrenched from me at this crucial hour,* she wrote. *We may never see each other again. But these are the nights I foresaw when you married, which you did not.* She filled twenty pages before her eyes began to ache, and even when the room was dark again, Essie lay in bed, her mind turning with what she was too tired to write.

The late night at the airport had upset Essie's routine and she woke later than usual, the departure lingering like a hangover. Her ankles seemed swollen, her calves like rods, her limbs so heavy they might have been waterlogged. The world made its swollen turn, slow and stupid, senseless with miles. The day throbbed with hours. Everywhere she looked, something needed cleaning or putting away, but she sat in her chair, a pad of letter-paper in her lap, and watched dust tumble through dry shafts of sunlight like tiny shavings of wood. She imagined that splinters, fine as hair, worked their way into her skin every time she pushed through the air of the empty house.

She was alone. Francis had disappeared to his club, frowning at nothing. Ritu had dressed in salwar kameez and gone to the shops, viewing this as a treat since Essie usually insisted on going herself. Essie had intended to continue her letter to Marian but her efforts in the middle of the night seemed borne of a feverish energy, a kind of blood-letting. She sat in her chair now, depleted and drained, and listened without interest to whatever passed beneath her window, the mild traffic of a morning underway. Women's chirping voices, cars moving slowly past the rut in the road, a stiff volley of barking from the dog next door. Birds screeched like policemen with whistles, squawking over nothing; a motorcycle stuttered past, the sound loose as a chest cough. Essie ignored the long drifting calls of vendors, flung out like fishing line. She ignored the bell at her gate which set off the neighbor's dog again, and eventually she jotted down a few desultory lines. But the letter began to seem flat and useless. It would not reach Marian for two weeks at least. Marian herself would not arrive home for another day—that's how wide the world was. And even in her passion the night before, Essie found she could not express the full sweep of her thoughts. Each memory had eight or ten more at its back—a dozen, a hundred—too many to record so that anyone would understand how quickly and powerfully they came upon her. She could write and write, letters enough to span the globe; she imagined the lines of longitude and latitude in her own handwriting, floating gently over green and blue. And still it would not be enough to record the longings of even a single moment. Everything she hoped for was connected to everything she remembered and everything she had lost—a web spreading in all directions. Words moved in single file.

Essie pushed the letter aside and closed her eyes. She fell briefly to sleep, upright in her chair. When she woke she was still alone but light blazed in the window. Francis would soon be home and she was not up to cooking. *I have very little appetite*, she thought of writing to Marian. *This may be a sign of what is to come.* She must see what could be warmed for lunch.

The refrigerator was old, full of jars she had not labeled, but on the top shelf was a glass of fresh yogurt. *The house is full of reminders that you are gone*, the letter in her mind continued. *Everywhere I look I find something that pains me—even the curds I made for the girls.* She paused, wondering how best to convey the pathos of the uneaten yogurt. *I should not have made more with so little time left. But it is so difficult for a mother not to feel hopeful. Up to the last minute, I felt certain, in the circumstances, you would change your mind. Daniel had to go back to work, that is one thing. But would a few days more have been such a sacrifice, knowing what I am going through?* She imagined the way she would describe her pleasure in seeing the girls eat, how much she already missed pulling chicken from the bone to feed them by hand.

Now here is the chicken dish they liked. I've shown you how to make it but I don't know what spices you can get there. Last night, you remember, Daniel took three big pieces so there is not enough for today. Never mind, I can go without.

A faint scraping jolted Essie from her thoughts. She turned, expecting to find a rat. Instead she saw the ginger kitten, scratching an empty sack of rice. The gray was close behind, sniffing the whisk broom Essie had left in the corner; the mother was nowhere to be seen.

"And what are you doing back again?" she said aloud. "No one wants to see the likes of you," she told them. "All your friends have gone." Still she made no move to chase them away. The gray cat abandoned the broom and began to investigate the rough black surface of the grinding bowl. The ginger, the cat named Ritu, stood perfectly still and stared up at Essie, one of its claws still hooked in the burlap. Essie had the strange and unwelcome impression that the cat was awaiting instructions, or perhaps the opening of negotiations.

A sudden soft leap, and the ginger perched on top of Ritu's grinding stool.

"Tcha! Get down from there."

The cat drew its legs together on the small surface.

"Go on. Get down." Essie clicked her tongue and after a moment's hesitation, the cat dropped to the floor. The gray sidled closer, reminding Essie of the way Tara sometimes reached for Nicole's hand.

"Such nonsense," she said, but in a warmer tone. The gray stretched up its head on its thin neck; the ginger made a plaintive noise. "Little beggars, the both of you." The cats watched as she returned to the refrigerator and snipped open a container of milk. "Outside," she told them, and they followed her onto the balcony, crowding near her heels as she stooped to leave the bowl for them.

For the next several days Ritu was permitted to feed the cats. The kittens always turned up first, leaving the mother cat to brood below in the shady corner of the garden. She would only join them after a slow, stealthy advance. Essie would not admit to her own part in this uneasy truce; she refused to pay any attention to their comings and goings and made a point of complaining about the price of milk. When Marian called to say they had arrived safely, Essie reported that the cats were sleeping on the balcony.

"You see, babe, what happens? Every day they come, bold as you please."

"What about the doctor? Have you called the office again?"

"Why should I call? He can call when he has his results. Until then, I know what I know."

"Mum—"

But she refused to discuss the knot in her breast, refused to give Marian that satisfaction. Birthdays, anniversaries, feast days, school concerts, sports matches—the parade of moments she might have shared with her family if they lived near—all thinned to voices on a phone line. But she was not willing to accommodate such distance in the matter of her dying. Marian had left; very well, let her feel the consequences. The Marian of her letters, the Marian to whom she revealed all the movements of her soul, seemed a different person than the Marian on the phone. The Marian of the letters was the daughter Essie thought she had raised, the daughter who would have stayed.

"The girls miss you so much," Marian told her. "They loved being in India. On their first morning home Daniel made them tea but both girls cried. They said the tea didn't taste the same."

"Use the tea I packed for you," Essie urged. "Make it yourself. Your husband doesn't know how to do it properly."

They could not talk for long; the rates were too high.

"Wait, babe—so much to tell you! Daddy is up to his old tricks, every night at the gymkhana, so everything falls into my lap. Even the coconuts—this fellow Gopi still hasn't come."

Marian had begun to say goodbye, her voice hollow.

"Just let me say a quick hello to the girls."

But Marian had put them to sleep. The connection was scratchy with a slight delay; words tumbled into their echoes. "Tell them I send tight hugs. I pray for them every night. Tell them to read their Bibles. The breast is paining a bit, but only slightly. Pray I'll be taken quickly, without too much pain."

"Please call the doctor, Mum. Don't put yourself through this."

"Ask the girls to pray for me."

"The girls will write soon. Lots of love."

Essie's voice rose, high and cracking over the static. "Tell them not to worry, Grandma is looking after their cats. Only they must come back soon."

"Goodbye, Mum."

Essie held the receiver until she heard the click. "Hallo? Hallo?" she said loudly, just in case, but the line had gone dead and after another moment she put down the phone. She went into the kitchen, where Ritu was washing up with a bucket of hot water and where Essie could see the cats on the balcony, napping against the balustrade. The mother shot instantly to her feet, whisking down the stairs, but the kittens only yawned, showing small sharp teeth, and stretched up their heads to greet her.

Days passed slowly, sagging with heat. Blossoms dried to soft brown skins and trees hung heavy, fruit swelling like goiters. Essie bathed her limbs each night with cold water and slept on top of her bed. *This heat wave has given me a rash. You remember your brother used to have them as a baby?* By now addressing her thoughts to Marian had become habit, as though all that passed through Essie's mind was part of

444

a letter she was composing to her daughter. *I should stay out of the sun but then who will do the marketing?*

A batch of notes came from Marian and the family, all in a single envelope. Marian's was rushed and glancing; she was busy with programs for the girls' school, she would call again soon. Daniel had enclosed a postcard he wrote during their layover in the Frankfurt airport, which Essie examined but decided was not pretty enough to save. Nicole wrote on colored paper that was printed with flowers, each word with round, careful letters. *How are the cats?* Essie read. *We have no cats here. We love you.* Tara drew a picture of the cats with sharp triangle ears and whiskers stiff as bristles.

A week later, another fat bundle arrived from Nicole's first grade class. Marian had just visited their classroom, wearing a sari and telling the children about life in India. The teacher hoped Mrs. Almeida would not mind if the children wrote to her with some of their questions.

Essie emptied the packet onto the dining table. All the letters were written on rough, grainy paper, scored with solid and dotted lines to guide the children's pencils. Essie sifted through them, looking for Nicole's and picking out a line here and there.

What do you eat for breakfast?

How many languages do you speak?

Do saris[printed over a streak of grimy erasure marks] *ever fall off?*

Dear Grandma, she found at last. *Have you ever seen a real tiger?*

Essie put down the letter. Yes, she thought. Once when Marian was nearly two, they had gone to visit Essie's uncle, a conservator of forests in the south. They were driving through a protected stretch of jungle with six others packed in a small car, moving slowly, cautiously, around the blind turns. *Do you remember, my girl?* Essie sat with Marian on her lap, hot and sweaty, tired of jolting along bad roads when they suddenly rounded a corner and saw a tiger reclining in the center of the road. It lifted its huge head to stare at the oncoming car. *Quiet! Everyone, quiet.* They braked, not daring to pass. Essie could still remember the feel of Marian struggling to stand on her lap and see. She had caught the child's fists in her own hand, preventing Marian from thumping on the window. For three hours they waited while the tiger slept. After a time Marian fell asleep, her skin sticking to Essie's. The tiger had stretched in a shady patch of the road, protected by a thick canopy of trees until the sun bore down overhead. *See,* Essie's uncle whispered. The tiger remained in the sun a few minutes, so still it seemed dead,

445

then suddenly, with a lazy roll, it stretched, rose to its feet, and ambled back into the trees, out of sight.

You only woke up when we were driving again and then you wanted to go back and find the tiger! It seemed to Essie that she could still feel her daughter sleeping against her chest, the hot breath against her neck, the sure damp weight of one who belonged to her.

That evening the phone rang while Essie was in the kitchen with Ritu. Marian, she thought at once. Her fingers were oily; she looked for a rag and couldn't find one, then tried to hold the receiver against her ear with just the palm of her hand. "Hallo?"

It was the doctor. "So sorry for the delay, Mrs. Almeida. The results were misplaced in the lab. But they've come at last and it's good news. Nothing malignant, totally benign. Come back in again this week and we'll drain the fluid. You see, Mrs. Almeida, I knew you'd be a good patient!"

She shifted the phone against her ear and nearly dropped it. "But the pain, doctor? And you don't know the history. This very thing happened to my aunt and she—"

"No, no, I'm telling you. You're in perfect health. The pain is from the fluid only. It's very common. There's no danger at all, you mustn't worry. Okay? Right then, come by this week. That will be that." He laughed and rang off.

Francis had drifted to the table, the way a dog might sniff at its empty bowl. Essie found she could not bear his expectant air. "Dinner's not ready," she snapped. "Another twenty minutes at least."

"Who was calling?"

She shook her head, too annoyed to answer.

"Was it the doctor?"

She stared at him.

"Marian said you had a . . . pain of some kind. A lump. What did the doctor say?" When she didn't answer, he moved closer and put a hand on her arm.

"I'm covered in oil." Her voice was frayed; she was on the verge of tears she could not explain. "The doctor says it's nothing serious. I have to go back next week to remove fluid, or some foolishness, I don't remember exactly."

He grasped her arm for a moment, then let his grip loosen and patted her gently. He kept his eyes on the place where his fingers touched her skin. "I can go with you."

"No need," she said. They stood quietly. When he released her she moved past him to the kitchen. "Twenty minutes," she said. "Go find something to do until then."

The phone rang again after Francis was in bed. Essie had been waiting in her chair. For a while she had watched television, then she turned it off and waited in the dark. It was all over, she would tell her daughter. A fright, nothing more. They had prayed and their prayers had been answered.

"Have you spoken to the doctor?" Marian asked.

Essie paused. She felt the phone lines between them like tight ropes, felt the moment sharpen to a single shaved point upon which she must balance. She felt herself falling.

"There's no news, babe. He hasn't called."

"Oh, God, Mum. It's been two weeks! Give me his number, let me call him myself."

"No, no! No need! I—" but she stopped. "I'll go myself next week. He's out of the office now, on leave, but after the weekend I'll go myself and ask."

"You promise, Mum? I mean, this is crazy, making you wait so long. I'm sorry I'm not there to go with you. Maybe Dad—"

"Stop pulling your father into my affairs," Essie said. "I'm perfectly capable of going on my own."

"Mum." Marian's voice was suddenly so small, so close to tears, that for a moment Essie imagined Nicole or Tara had come to the phone. "Mum, tell me honestly. Do you think it's serious?"

Later she wished there had been time to pray, time to beg Mary for an answer or for the strength to answer. How badly she wanted to reassure her child, to promise, no, no, nothing will happen—but how badly she needed to say yes, to show her daughter some part of the strain she had endured alone. "I don't know," she said, and her voice broke, and she began to weep.

It would only be a little while, Essie told herself after they had said goodbye. In a few days she would tell Marian all was well, and nothing

447

more need come of it. But she felt jittery, agitated, a churning in her stomach. She went to the kitchen for a glass of water, moving quietly. Ritu slept on a roll of bedding in one corner of the kitchen balcony, just beyond the spiral steps that led to the garden.

She heard the cats before she saw them, a dark rustle, and flicked on the light. Blinding yellow for a moment, then the kittens twining near the empty rubbish pail, sniffing the rich dark stains. She could not see the mother at first, but then the cat leapt from the counter to the floor with a soft thud and stared up at her, so impudent, so fearless that Essie felt a surge of unaccountable fury. She caught up a whisk broom and beat the cat away with it.

"Out, go on, out! Back you go!"

"What, bhai? What, what?" Ritu had woken, lifting her head from her pallet and rubbing her eyes in the moonlight, but Essie kept after the cats—"Away with you!"—poking the broom until she had driven them onto the metal stairs. The mother cat dropped down two steps, turned and hissed before she retreated, her tail lashing, her body curling sinuously around the central pole of the staircase, her half-grown kittens close behind her. At the bottom she leapt softly into the damp patch of earth where wash-water was thrown and stalked slowly, fearlessly into the garden.

The next day only one of the kittens appeared. It sat, thin and piteous, near the threshold of the kitchen and made a noise that sounded like crying.

"The mother is gone," said Ritu, looking worried. But by midday Tiger had emerged from a tangle of undergrowth. She could not, however, be lured up to the balcony.

"Offer a bit of chicken, she'll come."

But the cat remained in the garden. Finally Ritu took food down to her, moving slowly down the spiral steps. The cat hissed when she ventured too close, but ate hungrily once Ritu had gone back up to the balcony.

"See, bhai, Mummy is hurt." Ritu pointed to a fresh wound on the cat's shoulder.

By late afternoon, the ginger kitten had curled to sleep in the corner where Ritu kept her bedding but the gray kitten had still not returned.

Essie felt a dull certainty that there was nothing to be done and that she herself was culpable. "Just go and look for it," she told Ritu. She waited until the girl had gone down one side of St. Hilary Road before she set off toward the shops in the other direction.

The sun was still unseasonably hot and St. Thomas Road was in a state of upheaval. Men were shoulder high in pits, putting in new pipe, while women carried away baskets of rubble. Shoppers clambered past as though on river banks and Essie had to slowly pick her way past clots of clay and bits of broken pavement. At the juncture near St. Jerome's, three cows were ravaging a rubbish pile and she thought of what the girls would say to that, the funny, loud, slow, American way they would say cows. She walked as far as the market and back along the shore where the Varuna fishermen lived, narrow winding streets that teemed with cats. She searched the next day and the day after that, but they never saw the gray kitten again.

At the end of the third day, she sat in her chair and tried to answer Nicole's letter. She described the tiger in the road, other tiger hunts she had seen with her uncle, and then she stopped writing, not certain how to continue. The evening had rusted to night. Marian would not call.

She had given her daughter the good news. Perfect health, Essie said, and listened to Marian's flood of love and relief. She had tried to take pleasure in her daughter's words, tried to catch and hold them, to savor them later, but whatever Marian said had slipped away. The whole episode hardly seemed real. Essie felt empty and drained, as if the doctor's needle had taken more than he intended.

I never saw a tiger family, she wrote in reply to Nicole's question. *A tiger likes to live alone.*

Ritu came from the kitchen to clean the front room. Usually Essie would leave her to her task, but she felt rooted to her chair. She watched as Ritu brushed the dust and crumbs into cottony piles and flung them from the stair landing. Then, with a damp rag in one hand and the tail of her sari draped over the other, Ritu squatted on her heels and began to swab the floor. Essie sat in silence, listening to the soft kiss of the rag dipped into her pail, the trickle of water as it was wrung, the whisper of cloth sponging over the tile. The wet floor met the dry floor in a scalloped line, lapping forward as Ritu advanced on her toes. She crept just behind the slick edge, pressing it further along the tile, fanning her arm in wide swaths before her. Essie thought of the tiger hunts she had seen as a girl, with beaters who tamped down the grasses for the rifle-bearers.

Once I saw a tiger killed, but that—She stopped. What could she tell a six-year-old about population control?—*was a big and old tiger. A naughty tiger who liked to frighten children.* Would she give the child nightmares? *There are no tigers in America. And none in Bombay, so you can come back soon. Only in the jungle.*

Dip and wring, dip and wring. At times, the scratch of the bucket as Ritu dragged it behind her. Her toe ring clicked against the floor like a fingernail tapping; past the table, the sofa, Essie's own feet in slippers, all the landmarks of the room until she had reached the kitchen and then she peered onto the balcony.

"Chota Ritu is staying, bhai. But Mummy is gone."

Ritu hung the rag over her wrist and picked up the bucket to swab downstairs, her bare feet leaving cloudy marks on the floor which had already begun to dry in streaks.

Essie wrote, *The only tiger here is* your *Tiger.*

Not true, of course. *What to do, babe? I've looked and looked.* But there was no one to witness all her searching, no one to appreciate her effort and penance, no one to share what she had always imagined she would share with her daughter. It came to Essie then, as she had not felt since she was a child, that there were parts of her nobody would know or understand, thoughts too numerous to record, adrift and orphaned, with no one to hear them. She closed her eyes and tried to pray, to imagine God the keeper of all her secrets, but all she could think of was the sleeping tiger. She had wondered then if God could see her and what exactly He saw: the light picking through a tangle of trees, her uncle's hands, tense on the wheel, her own gold cross at the base of her throat, the child asleep in her arms. She wondered if He saw all that would happen once the tiger had awakened, if He knew now where the gray kitten had gone, if the mother had died.

A few minutes later she picked up her pen again. *Your cats are well and happy, darling*, she wrote to Nicole. *All three are fast asleep, happy here with me.*

The next day, nearly a month after he'd promised, Gopi turned up at last to harvest the coconuts. Essie had been sitting upstairs, replying one by one to the letters from Nicole's class, when he arrived: a small, dark-skinned man from Kerala, his leather strap slung over his shoulder. He waited until she had finished scolding him and then he lifted his hands. His wife just had a baby, he told her in Hindi. The baby came early—so small. Gopi held his hands apart, the size of a breadfruit. For three weeks, no one knew what would happen. But now—he smiled suddenly, a flash of light in his dark face—the baby was fine. A son, his first son. A son will stay, he told her. Daughters grow up and marry and go, but a son will stay with his family.

A few minutes later Gopi climbed the first tree. Essie had imagined standing with the girls beside her, watching the way he shimmied up, the strap looped around his waist, his bare feet curved around the trunk until he was lost in the thatch of palms at the top. She had already counted out the money she would give Gopi as a gift for the child.

For the first time in years, she did not oversee the coconut harvest. Instead she went to the back of the house, down the narrow winding steps of the kitchen balcony. The sun never penetrated that one shady corner of the property, and she sat on the lowest stair, elbows on knees, feeling the cool soft mud on the hard skin of her feet. In the front yard, she could hear Gopi climbing, the leather strap slapping against the tree as he hoisted himself up. The gray kitten, Smoke, was gone, the Tiger-mother nowhere to be seen, but the ginger, Ritu, was picking a delicate path along the garden wall, and Essie had brought a piece of fish down from the kitchen especially. She lured the kitten right to her, caught safe in her lap when the coconuts came raining down.

Nominated by Nancy Richard

HELEN KELLER ANSWERS THE IRON

by ANDREW HUDGINS

from THE KENYON REVIEW

Though I'd rather have been one of the boys who could smack a base-ball solidly with a bat, my talent was telling jokes. I was fascinated in them as mechanisms—machines made of words, to use William Carlos Williams's definition of poetry. I tinkered with them as obsessively as other boys enjoyed taking apart radios, jack-in-the-boxes, and frogs to see what was inside. In bed at night, walking home from school, sitting in church, I sharpened the details of jokes, changing the settings, nam-ing the characters after kids in my classes, and altering elements that had flopped the last time. I didn't even have to try to memorize jokes. After I heard a joke, I, like an elephant, never forgot.

Other kids knew a few elephant jokes, but I knew them all. I even convinced my mother to buy me a book of elephant jokes. I had to cash in my birthday wish to do it, and still it took some lobbying, arguing, and whining because Mom did not—emphatically *did not*—see the point in spending good money on books. That's what the library is *for*.

"But, Mom, it isn't in the library yet. I checked."

"They'll get it sooner or later." She always said that. "Now, hush. You've got a birthday coming up and maybe we'll see about it then."

I still remember the cheesy black-and-white drawings of elephants with machine guns and elephants hiding in the cherry trees. I was em-barrassed by the drawings. They took the jokes I was enthralled with and treated them as if they were just something dumb for kids, even though I was a kid and I loved the jokes and I knew they *were* stupid. But that was the point, wasn't it? I remember asking other kids, "How do you kill a blue elephant?" They hesitated, and before they could even say, "I don't know," I said, "Shoot it with a blue elephant gun." Then, quickly, "How do you kill a red elephant?" When they said, "Shoot it with a red elephant gun?" With real glee and false scorn, I screamed, "No! You squeeze its trunk till it turns blue and then shoot it with a *blue elephant gun*"—and we all cackled together.

Elephant jokes mock logic, deliberately deranging the senses of sense. They are an adolescent intellectual's version of spinning around till you fall down. The jokes partake of surrealism, which was famously defined by the Comte de Lautréamont as "the chance meeting on a dissecting table of a sewing machine and an umbrella." What's gray, stands in a river when it rains, and doesn't get wet? An elephant with an umbrella. Determinedly capricious, elephant jokes are an inside game—much funnier if only one person doesn't know the joke and everyone else yells the answer in his face. If you ask someone why elephants can't be policemen, the punch line is not really funny, but it's funny to inflict your private knowledge on a listener: because they can't hide behind billboards! I was interested to see who'd go along with the absurdity of the initiation into false knowledge and who twisted his lips, sneered, "That's just stupid," and stalked off. The rejection stings briefly, sure; but the sneerers were declaring themselves serious people, nonlaughers. It's useful to know who those people are.

Traditional riddles are difficult, but fair. But the *echt* elephant jokes deconstruct riddles. They are so arbitrary that you have to know the answer to get it, which is eerily reminiscent of being a student when the teacher asks one of those questions you couldn't possibly know the answer to, a question whose whole purpose seems to be to make you admit your ignorance. Answering the unanswerable question for his listener, the joke teller is a teacher correcting a dim-witted student.

In school, I learned that many countries counted bauxite as their chief export without my ever being told what bauxite was. Ditto milo. Flying buttresses? Doric, Ionic, and the other kind of column? "The mitochondria are the powerhouses of the cell," I wrote on test after test, wondering what it meant. Though I knew iambic pentameter was what Shakespeare wrote, I had no idea what it was, how it worked, or why I should give a flip—and I doubted the teachers knew either. Just what did Paul Revere, Molly Pitcher, Betsy Ross, Patrick Henry, Sojourner Truth, Buffalo Bill, Annie Oakley, Walter Winchell, and Abner Ducking Fubbleday actually *accomplish* that was so damn great? John Hancock had a cool signature that I tried for a couple of weeks in sixth grade to imitate, but Hancock's John Hancock seemed to be the only reason he was included on posterity's pop quiz. Virginia Dare, Crispus Attucks, George Armstrong Custer, Davy Crockett, Jim Bowie and what's-his-name Travis's renown derived from obstructing the paths of armed men who outnumbered them. I was unimpressed with George Washington Carver's wizardry with peanuts, whatever it was, and though I thought it was just fine that Helen Keller could spell "water," I couldn't for the life of me figure out why that made her important.

I knew that the trivium and quadrivium were very, very important, but if I'd ever been asked what they were, I'd have had as much chance answering as I did when I was first asked how an elephant is like a banana. They are both yellow. Except for the elephant. I did love to say *twivium* and *quadwivium*, over and over again in an Elmer Fudd voice, much to the annoyance of my teachers, and long past the time when even my most easily amused friends had hardened their hearts against these particular *bon mots*.

The elephant riddles spoofed not just the questions the teachers asked and the whole experience of education, but thinking itself. At first, I was impressed with logic, this "thinking clearly," that teachers and my parents made such a big honking deal about. Logic was, I first thought, like a train. Get on it and the rails would carry everyone to the same destination, and when they got there they'd see it was the only place to be. But I soon understood that, outside arithmetic class, logic was more like a taxi. You told it where to take you, and it took you there. If you were in favor of the death penalty, it found a street that led to the electric chair and nailed the accelerator to the floorboard. If you hated the death penalty, it took the same street just as fast, but in the opposite direction. Sure, I could see that logic was useful, but it never did anything surprising. But messing with logic—thinking things that were antirational—now *that* lightened the leaden step of dialectics, put swan's wings on reason's nine-pound hammer, and made causality turn off the interstate and careen down a dark dirt road with the speedo's needle pegged into the triple digits. Why do ducks have flat feet? From stomping out forest fires. Why do elephants have flat feet? Stomping out burning ducks. A joke gets you a roller-coaster-with-a-Möbius-strip-twist thrill ride of antilogic, ending in a laugh, because you return to where you started, but upside down. What does logic get you? A disquisition on how ducks have, over many millennia, evolved flat feet to help them swim.

At school, you learn to be a member of the group of people who know certain stuff—science, history, literature, and who Abner Doubleday

454

was. Elephant riddles were a *reductio ad absurdum* of that process. You subject yourself to the joke-teller's arbitrary knowledge so others will then come to you for answers. To be superior, you first have to be subordinate. To be active, you must first be passive. The pure caprice of elephant jokes gave me the sense that we jokers were enrolled in a free-floating and oddly democratic club, and yet exclusive, too, because the jocks, hoods, and class officers, who didn't care for the silliness we valued, excluded themselves.

If jokes were my first step out of social isolation, they were also my way out of books. My language, even by the time I was eleven, had grown bookish and artificial. The vocabularies of Robert Louis Stevenson, Walter Scott, or Sir Thomas Mallory rocketed around my head and occasionally burst from my mouth. I noticed the startled look on my fifth-grade teacher's face when I asked permission to go to the restroom because I needed to make water, but I didn't know why she was startled. I suffered awkward moments before I learned that *zounds, nay, nary, grand,* and *bloody* were best left on the pages where I had met them. "I had nary an inkling that such a grand idea could go so bloody cockeyed" is a sentence I never uttered, though I did make, separately, every single gaffe in it.

A year or two later, when I was deep in the hard-boiled thrillers of Hammett, Chandler, and Ross Macdonald, it seemed natural, until I actually said it, to tell my friend that going trick-or-treating was jake with me, to inform my mother that I couldn't go to the matinee if she didn't give me some scratch, and to warn a Dumb Dora in my seventh-grade class I was going to smack her in the puss if she didn't stop ragging me and vamoose. These slips drew looks of strained forbearance, like the overly patient expressions on adults' faces when five-year-olds explained the plot of a cartoon or when the retarded boy in my Sunday School class took off his shoes and socks and started counting to ten on his toes while the rest of us were singing. But as soon as I started telling jokes, I began paying more attention to how the kids around me talked. People drew back from you if you pitched your vocabulary too high, wound your sentences too tight, or recited the joke from memory.

I also paid attention to what the jokes were about. A joke can be well-told or poorly, but it has to be *about* something. The more nervous-making the subject matter, the tighter the spring is compressed in the jack-in-the-box—and the more forcefully jack leaps out. So of course I liked best the edgy jokes, the ones that sidled up against the taboos that I was just becoming conscious of.

The elephant joke I thought funniest was: "What's that black stuff between an elephant's toes?" "Slow natives." I see now that the joke built part of its hilarity on racism, and I indistinctly sensed then that the smug superiority of an American schoolboy toward the squashed natives drove some of my laughter. Tarzan and Jungle Jim movies, which I'd watched intently as a younger kid, were affirmed in their naive racism. Natives run in wild panic ahead of stampeding elephants, saved only by their speed, despite having lived around elephants all their lives. At the time, though, I focused on the black stuff between the elephant's toes. I was a boy. Gross stuff enchanted me. After a day with my feet bound into dark, damp shoes, I wrenched off my sneakers, peeled off my socks, and found black lines of sloughed skin between my toes.

It was filth, filth made from my body. It represented the corruption of the flesh that preachers sorrowed over in church, but it was also farcical. Toe jam fell below the solemnity of Saint Paul's animadversions of the "works of the flesh": "fornication, uncleanness, immodesty, luxury, witchcrafts, enmities, contentions, emulations, wraths, quarrels, dissensions, sects, envies, murders, drunkenness, revelings, and such like." But it symbolized all those uncleannesses, and if the Apostle had continued *"and such like, including toe jam, snot, spit, mucous, eye buggers, gnawed fingernails, peeled blisters, dingleberries, and both number one and number two,"* he would have resolved some theological implications that had vexed me as a boy.

Toe jam was oddly sinister then, but also gross, comic, and mysterious. The joke about the poky Africans reduced human life to sloughed skin, and I feared that, in life, I was a slow native, one who'd be trampled by the ambitions and talents of other people. And of course I was afraid of death itself, the elephant that tramples and smashes us all to black stuff between its toes. My mind careened through these possibilities, never settling on any one for long, and the unsteady equation of myself with natives, toe jam, failure, and death, along with the image of a ridiculously outsized elephant who didn't even notice people smushed between his toes, made me laugh. In the shifty joke, I glimpsed fears that I didn't want to think about nakedly because they were too frightening without some clothes thrown over them. I was just becoming a teenager, a time when taboos are as fascinating as they are frightening, and they're a potent force in jokes.

Death, religion, race, and sex make jokes funny because fear, tripped as it stalks toward us, makes the reversal of expectation more powerful.

It's funny when a clown trips over his big shoes, funnier when a banker in a bowler slips on a banana peel, and funniest of all when a boogeyman jumps out of the bushes, skids on wet leaves, and falls on his face as he's shouting "boo." Our relief at not being harmed makes us laugh even harder because we know we might not be laughing at all the next time the boogeyman jumps at us.

Death was a fine taboo, but sex is finer. My joke about elephants and their dislike for black lace panties went over so well at the junior-high lunch table because it nudged up against the naughtiness of sex, though I was myself as sexually uninformed as it is possible to be. I affected a jaunty knowingness that in retrospect is funnier than the joke, which worked despite the fact that the boy telling it didn't really understand it. But I knew enough to evoke the taboo subject of sex and twist it for a laugh. The joke, though small, lived larger than its medium.

Neither did I, as a teenager, entirely understand this joke: What does an elephant use for a tampon? A sheep. I told the joke a time or two, uneasily, and laughed at it, when I did laugh, uncomfortably and self-consciously. Until I was married, menstruation was a mystery. I understood the physiology, but not what it meant in practical terms. So, though I seldom repeated the joke, I thought about it a lot. I was tickled by the image I concocted of an elephant grabbing a sheep with its trunk and jamming it up under its tail, and the white sheep turning red. But when the mysterious sexual opening was enlarged to the point that it took a sheep to cover it, I squirmed, nervous both about what the joke implied about the largeness and bestial nature of sex, and afraid that someone more honest than I would say, "I don't get it" and ask me to explain a joke I couldn't explain. I could have babbled something like, "See, elephants and sheep don't go together naturally, and so it's funny that an elephant would have to use a sheep for something an elephant doesn't need, and take it and jam it into her private parts." True enough, as far as it goes. But isn't the point of the joke that human fastidiousness about sexual taboos, like the "uncleanness" of menstruation, is unknown to animals, and our ideas of civilization are mocked when we see an elephant try to find a natural equivalent to a tampon? That was a possible truth I was not ready to entertain, or be entertained by.

Despite my queasiness with the sheep, most elephant jokes were getting a bit tame for my changing taste. Before long, elephant jokes were on TV and in magazines. They were printed in the newspapers. What was the fun of knowing something that everybody already knew?

By then I'd moved on to the dead-baby jokes, mutilation jokes, and Helen Keller jokes that boys began telling when I was in junior high and high school. I laughed at them hysterically, in both senses of the word, with a sense of pleasurable fear that approached panic. I was thrilled as what could be said slid toward the unsayable, the unthinkable, and the forbidden. These subversive jokes were thoroughly disapproved of by adults and squeamish kids, unlike the Little Moron, Polack, and elephant jokes—and having to keep them secret from adults sharpened the edge of laughter.

At the dinner table, over the salmon croquettes and string beans, you could ask your little brother, "Hey, how do you get an elephant up an oak tree? You plant an acorn under him and wait for it to grow." He might ask back, "Yeah, well what time it is when an elephant sits on your fence?"—and you'd shout, "It's time to buy a new fence! Everybody knows that one, you dork!"

Your mother might or might not chuckle. Your dad might grumble that the jokes were stupid or he might just say, "Be quiet and eat your beans." But he wouldn't yell that he wasn't going to have that kind of talk at his table, young man, and if you couldn't keep a civil tongue in your head you could go to your room, and your mother wouldn't shake her head and say, voice trembling, that she doesn't know where you heard such nasty things, but she didn't want you bringing them into her house and ruining everyone's appetite.

Dead-baby jokes, quadriplegic jokes, and Helen Keller jokes were over the line. They could get you yelled at, smacked, wept over, prayed for, and sent to bed hungry. At least in my house. I loved having the power, even if I knew better than to use it, to provoke such a passionate response. I loved being wicked without doing anything mean. The jokes were so far beyond common decency that they always startled me, no matter how often I told them, and the more graphic they were the better I liked them. My favorite was "How is a truckload of dead babies different from a truckload of bowling balls?" "You can't unload the bowling balls with a pitchfork." Because I was familiar with both bowling balls and pitchforks, I reveled in the tactile uneasiness that trembled along my nerve endings every time I told the joke and imagined, without intending to, the difference between the tines of a pitch-fork clinking against a bowling ball and sliding into baby flesh. It was unthinkable, and I thought it. Nobody else, not even the hardened thirteen-year-old joke-tellers I hung out with, thought the joke was as funny as I did. I suspected they had never held a pitchfork, much less tossed hay with one, and so the visceral disgust the joke evokes was lost on them. I was thinking of myself on both sides of the pitchfork, pushing the pitchfork into the body and being the body the pitchfork slid into. I was beginning to see in myself the power to harm awfully and the power to be harmed awfully.

For some of the same reasons, I adored the pun in "How do you make a dead baby float?" A: "Two scoops dead baby. Fill with root beer." The gross—or is it sentimental?—image of a dead baby suddenly becomes grosser—cannibalism played for laughs. Sure, the idea was revolting. But by disgusting ourselves, we boys were assuring ourselves we'd never do something just because we could imagine it. Basic as it seems, the point was important to me because in church I sat through many sermons that, quoting Jesus, assured me that to think something was the same as doing it. All that stood between thinking and doing was volition—as if volition was nothing! To be pure, I had to make myself an unblemished vessel, untainted in thought or deed. But my thoughts, I knew, moved in their own ways, logic clumping along on its path and imagination buzzing erratically from lilac to honeysuckle to rosebud, as well as violet, dandelion, red clover, morning glory, and all the other weeds I spent long afternoons prying out of the yard with a forked cultivator. I saw no harm in seeing where logic went—or imagination either, as long as I didn't *do* anything dumb or immoral.

With these adolescent jokes I was separating myself from the world of adults, who would be appalled, and from little kids, who wouldn't be mentally tough enough to take them. I loved the jokes as things in and of themselves—not things of beauty exactly, though I can imagine a definition of beauty that includes their linguistic efficiency, their powerful imagery, their probing of social norms, and their provoking strong, often conflicting, emotions. Because I loved them and admired them as art and as craft, my emerging sense of discretion was balanced, and all too often outweighed, by my desire to share them. Who would laugh? How far could people be pushed? How far could I push myself? I knew not to tell them to my father, but did I dare tell them to my mother?

I sprawled across the vinyl recliner, legs flung over the arm, watching my mother, who sat in a child's rocker by the sliding glass door, using the natural light to see the sock she was darning. She loved the small, cane-bottom rocker because it was the perfect size for her small body

459

and it was easy to pull around the living room, from the TV set to the glass door to the telephone. I was sixteen, hesitating on the edge of a joke, trying to decide if I could tell it to her. Mom liked to feign a southern tomboy toughness since she was raising a houseful of boys, four of us that she'd called "rug rats," "house apes" "yard monkeys," and "carpet munchers" when we were younger—she'd heard that last phrase and absorbed it into her vocabulary, thinking it meant something other than it does. But how tough was she with jokes?

"How do you stop a kid from running in circles?" I asked her. I paused a moment to let the question sink in.

"I don't know. How?" she said, once she determined that I was not asking for advice.

"Nail his other foot to the floor," I said.

The moment between the last words of the joke and the laugh, if there is a laugh, is a fraught and complicated expanse of time. The listener has to resolve the confusion of the poem's antilogical logic to "get" the joke and then assent to it, if she finds it funny or clever. But the teller depends totally on the listener's willingness to go along with the joke, to play with absurdity instead of rejecting it, and then to laugh with you. It's asking a lot. Even friends who know you well might suddenly, instinctively, decide a joke about abusing and mutilating a child is revolting—and you are a pervert for telling it. I did not want my mother to think I was a perv, but damn, I wanted to tell my joke. I'd already told it to everyone I could find to tell it to and it was burning a hole in my brain.

Her blank look crumpled into laughter, which she tried to suppress. That joke shouldn't be funny! But the natural impulse won out. She laughed, stopped to sputter, "That's terrible!" and then laughed some more. The joke surprised her with its amoral logic. For a parent who'd nailed one of her child's feet to the floor, it makes sense to solve the problem of his running in circles by nailing the other one down. Myself, I was always a bit startled to imagine a house in which it was acceptable to hammer nails into the floor—a revelation about how I perceived the rules of the rented houses that, as a military family, we lived in.

I suspect my mother also laughed because these jokes couldn't be shared with my father. The anarchy of jokes troubled his sense of a moral universe. A lot of serious people assume that anybody telling a cruel joke is in fact a perv, advocating cruelty instead of flinching from it. My mother, thank God, wasn't one of those always oh-so-serious people. Actually, I've always thought the jokes affirm established morality by imagining a world so amorally unaware of our deepest convictions about the integrity of the body that we can't help laughing. Without knowing it, I'd been testing to see if my mother and I could share a laugh behind my father's back, and it was an illicit pleasure to discover that we could laugh with one another almost like adults, just for the pure joy of laughing.

I already knew I wasn't a perv, though. I'd learned that two years before when my ninth-grade world history teacher played a recording of *Medea*, and I failed at listening to it. When the scratchy LP of Euripides' play spun around to the scene in which Medea kills her children, I began to giggle. I fought the giggles, but they burst from my throat in snorts and liquid sputters. Soon I was laughing desperately. Holding my sides, head down on my desk, drooling, I jerked with laughter and hated myself. Why was I helpless with amusement at a mother's anguished determination to slaughter her sons and feed them to her unfaithful husband?

The teacher raised the needle from the black groove, and the whole class, already silent, stared, waiting for me to compose myself. I expected to be slapped and shipped off to a secure facility where I Could not hurt myself or others. The only place I'd ever seen people laugh the way I was laughing was on movie screens, and those laughers were homicidal lunatics with spectacular and obviously flawed master plans for world domination.

The teacher, a tall woman with a pixyish face and short chic black hair, walked to my desk, paused, and gently touched my head with one finger. I was still snorting, trying to squelch my laughter. "When we hear an event too horrible for our minds to comprehend," she said to the class, "we sometimes laugh. We refuse to accept it. We treat it like a joke." Aspirating snot, still half slobbering, I sucked my humiliating cachinnations to a halt, and wiped the desktop with my shirtsleeve. She was doing me a great kindness while also teaching me something that would be useful for the rest of my life. If I could remember the name of that magnificent woman, that splendid teacher toiling at a high school in France for American military dependents—and I have tried for decades to call it up—I would send her a spray of white roses every year on her birthday, and then randomly from time to time, just to surprise her.

I seized her explanation gratefully; it let me off the hook and made me look good too: I had responded so crassly to the play because I was really more sensitive than anyone else in the room. I suspected she was right, mostly right—but later I wondered if there weren't more to it than that. I was also laughing at the stilted language of the two boys when they figure out Mom's going to chop them into stew-sized bits. It didn't sound like anything my brothers or I would scream if we saw our mother racing toward us with a sword in her hands and crazed determination in her eyes:

First son: "Ah me; what can I do? Whither fly to escape my mother's blows?"

Second son: "I know not, sweet brother mine; we are lost."

"Sweet brother mine" started my giggling, but I lost control entirely when the second son cried out in terror, "Even now the toils of the sword are closing around us." The languid and archaic way the boys were discussing their imminent murder was what triggered my laughter. The ungraspable idea of an infanticidal mother was what kept it going.

From my involuntary laughter and the teacher's shrewd interpretation of it, I glimpsed how life and art can be horrifying and comic at the same time. That inchoate perception grew into an aesthetic appreciation the following year, when at Sidney Lanier High in Montgomery, Alabama (our football team was the Sidney Lanier Poets), my sophomore English class read *Macbeth*. The teacher went into agonies of explanation about how, though we might find it jarring to move directly from the murder of a sleeping king to a rowdy porter's answering a knock at the gate, we should think of it as an opportunity to recover from the intensity of the murder. The scene was, then, a palate cleanser, pineapple sherbet for our literary taste buds.

It had not occurred to me to worry about the scene. I instinctively loved the dazzling shift from high drama to low comedy. (I didn't know, but my understanding of the scene was similar to Thomas de Quincey's in his famous essay "On the Knocking at the Gate in *Macbeth*.") The comedy does not just let us recover from the dramatic intensity and prepare us to accept more of it later, it enlarges the vision of the play. The porter's grouchy wit and drunken mockery remind us that the world goes on, more or less happily, unaware for the moment of Macbeth's crime. The two realities exist side by side: the undiscovered body of the king and the porter's tipsy stand-up comedy routine on events in the news. The release of emotion from the murder powers our laughter at the comedy, and the porter's innocent joking heightens our knowledge of how horrified everyone will be when the dead king's body is discovered. Even though one of the points of the scene is that the porter's trivial complaints about being awakened will soon be dwarfed by the consequences of Duncan's murder, the vision of the play grows much larger because it includes comedy (and comedy's very different ways of seeing) inside the tragedy. The two are bound together in art, as they are in life. Most of us don't live in a literary genre, but in a world that swerves between the tragedy and comedy, as it famously does at weddings, where we often find ourselves weeping when we expect to be laughing, and laughing at funerals, where we expect to cry.

The teacher's kindness when I cracked up during *Medea* opened a deeper and stranger world of laughter than I had known before. When I discovered the almost maniacal, intoxicating laughter of the desperate, I dove into it as if it were a drug. And it was that, an intoxicant. It altered my consciousness; it made my world larger, richer, weirder, more frightening, and truer to what I saw.

While my mother was still laughing at the joke about the boy running in circles, I asked, "What do you do with a dead dog?" "Take it out for a drag." She doubled up. The pile of blue socks and the needle, black thread dangling from it, slipped off her lap and onto the carpet. She was completely lost inside the silliness of the joke, the grotesque and oddly naive—even innocent, if deranged—image it evokes. For the next couple of days, she looked at me from time to time, said, "Take it out for a drag," and giggled.

It was risky to tell these jokes to a woman who had lost a child, something I fretted about before I told them, but my craziness to laugh and share the laughter overwhelmed my always weak sense of discretion. This time I was right. I didn't, though, ask my usual lead-in to the dead-dog joke: "What do you buy a dead baby?" "A dead puppy." And I certainly didn't ask her, "What's red and sits in a high chair?" "A baby eating razor blades." And I did not ask, "What's black, bubbly, and taps at the glass?" "A baby in a microwave." I knew these jokes were too graphic for her, but I'm afraid my discretion grew as much out of knowing they aren't very funny as sensitivity to her sorrow.

At school being insensitive was the point. Most girls winced and left the room when we boys asked one another, "What's blue and squirms?" A baby in a plastic bag. Their gasps, their flutters of indignation, their flouncing away from us, muttering, "You're sick," confirmed our sense of being *outré*, of being boys, especially since the guys I hung out with weren't athletes. We didn't have the athlete's socially acceptable way of proving our masculinity on the football field or basketball court.

Not long ago, I read a critic who said that the dead-baby and mutilation jokes arose as abortion was first being debated openly in America. The jokes, he argued, were the country's way of beginning to work through its ambivalence and unease about abortion. Perhaps. But not for me. Growing out of childhood, physically weak, uncertain of who I was, I wanted to be a tough thinker, if not a tough guy, and what better way to show you're not soft-minded than to make fun of the most sentimentalized people that exist: babies and cripples? And Helen Keller.

I was enchanted with Helen Keller jokes from the first time someone asked, "How did Helen Keller burn her fingers?" "Trying to read a waffle iron." The joke was merely absurd, with a cruel edge, and to this day I can't find the slightest sparkle of wit in it. The pleasure mostly resided in mocking a woman who had been used as a bludgeon to shame and taunt us kids. If Helen Keller, who was blind and deaf, could overcome all the terrible obstacles life had thrown in front of her, surely you, Andrew, with all the advantages you've had, could learn your multiplication tables. You could spell "Mississippi," read Tolstoy, earn at least a B+ in algebra. Even when Helen Keller's moral superiority wasn't stated—and it usually was—the point was implicit in every classroom performance of *The Miracle Worker*, every assigned reading of Keller's autobiography, and every book report on yet another children's book about her. Still, with all the praise that was heaped on her, all the saintliness attributed to her, I was never certain what Helen Keller had done other than be blind and deaf and learn how to read. What was I supposed to do? Poke my eyes out and jab a pencil in my ears so I could get credit for doing normal things? (Apparently blind kids had it even worse than the rest of us. Georgina Kleege in *Blind Rage: Letters to Helen Keller* gets down to business in her very first paragraph, telling Keller, "I hated you because you were always held up to me as a role model, and one who set such an impossibly high standard of cheerfulness in the face of adversity. . . . 'Yes, you're blind, but poor little Helen Keller was blind and deaf, and no one heard her complain.'")

Mom laughed when I told her the waffle-iron joke. As a country girl from Georgia, she bore a chip on her shoulder against the celebrated and the intellectual. So I asked if she knew how Helen Keller's parents punished her. They rearranged the furniture. How did Helen Keller burn her ear? Answering the iron. How did Helen Keller burn her other ear? The guy called back. Mom laughed less enthusiastically then. But I ploughed ahead with the irritating tenacity we jokers are famous for. How did Helen Keller burn her face? Bobbing for french fries.

Mom pursed her lips and darted me a cautioning look. The joke had gone too far. Yes, that's why I liked it. It was so grotesque that it became a parody of cruelty jokes. It established a boundary by crossing it and scuffed its feet on the line as it crossed. It showed that even jokes that make a point out of going too far can go too far. But that joke inside the joke was a pleasure I could not expect others to share.

More idiosyncratically, I laughed at the joke about Helen Keller's burned face because I was fascinated by deep-fat fryers, which are dangerous and therefore potentially funny. In high school I worked at a hamburger joint, and one of my jobs was to man the deep-fat. On my first day on the job, when I casually plopped down on a metal bench next to the fryer, the shift foreman slipped a handful of ice into the hot fat. Everyone jumped back, and before I registered what was happening, scalding grease sprayed a nasty archipelago of red islands up my left arm, to the merriment of everyone, including, eventually, me.

As new workers came on the payroll, I obsessively repeated the joke. I was a jerk about it. Hell, I'd laughed at being hurt: so could they. But in lulls between rushes of customers, I sometimes stared into the hot grease, watching it roil and sizzle around a load of frozen potatoes. The terrible image of Helen Keller plunging her face into the fryer leaped to my mind, and with it came the empathetic vision of my own face submerged in the boiling oil—and I shuddered at what the imagination was capable of, and at the frailty of human flesh.

In "What to Do with Helen Keller Jokes" (in *New Perspectives on Women and Comedy*, 1992), Mary Klages says that telling Helen Keller jokes "makes us feel safe, adequate, and competent, as we realize that we can successfully perform tasks, like shopping and answering the phone, that left this noble American heroine completely bewildered." It's not a coincidence, I think, that jokes ridiculing the competence of a famous role model became popular just after baby boomers like me learned how to answer the phone, walk to the bathroom without a night light, and make waffles, and right before we learned to hold jobs and make french fries. From time to time, throughout childhood and well into high school, I'd clench my eyes shut when no one was home and wander around the house—go to the bathroom, maybe try to make a bologna sandwich—testing out what it must be like to be blind, imagining I was Helen Keller. But I could never do it long. Going backward and relearning skills I'd already learned strained my sense of transparent mastery of everyday life; the exercise in infirmity was too frightening.

The sick jokes—dead baby, Helen Keller, and mutilated-boy jokes—mock human frailty. They became popular when we boomers were, as adolescents, starting to grasp that our bodies weren't invincible and our lives would have a terminus, even if we couldn't yet see it over the horizon. And we, some of us, had to toughen our minds to that knowledge.

Those of us who grew up in evangelical churches were reminded almost every week, sometimes two and three times a week, that we were mortal and we would die. We were steeped in the Apostle Paul's fierce insistence on the weakness and evils of the flesh. As a practical matter, our preachers knew they could more easily convince apprehensive teenagers to walk down the aisle and accept Jesus if the sermon hammered home what they were beginning to comprehend with new emotional force: life is fleeting and death eternal, and the body begins to decay while we're still in it.

We may be proud of our strength, they preached, but strength could be taken from us in an instant by a car wreck or a fall from a bike, and we'd be left dead or imprisoned in a bed or a wheelchair. Even in the normal course of life we'd weaken as we aged, until even breath itself was taken from us.

We may be proud of our intelligence. Yes, we might think we were so smart that our intelligence couldn't be taken from us. But time and chance happeneth to all men. The nursing homes are full not just of broken bodies. Also there, and even sadder, are men and women with perfectly sound bodies, staring into space. They look just like you and I, but they do not possess the wit to feed or wash or wipe themselves. Everything can be taken from us in the blink of an eye.

Morbid? Sure. But true, too, and after one of these sermons I, like almost everyone I knew, staggered down the aisle, blubbering in terror, to be baptized and saved from the terrible fate of living in a body made of perishable flesh. I came almost immediately to doubt that anything was eternal, while still frantically hoping I was wrong, but I could see my body was a terribly flimsy abode for my soul, a house made of straw, not brick, and I was only renting it, not buying.

Real life was every bit as morbid as my jokes. The year my family moved to Alabama, 1966, Charles Woods ran for the Democratic gubernatorial nomination against George Wallace. In rambling half-hour commercials that he bought with his own money, Woods appeared regularly on television, and I watched, horrified and fascinated. Charles Woods looked like a half-melted blob of shiny, pitted pink plastic, splotched with red. I'm not sure how I extrapolated the colors. On our black-and-white TVs, Woods looked, as one of my friends said, like Mr. Potato Head without some of the plastic facial features, as he talked calmly, if stiffly, about how sound business practices would solve all of Alabama's problems.

Later, I learned he was born in a shack in Toadvine, Alabama. After his father deserted the family when Charles was five, his mother placed her two sons in a state orphanage because she could not support them. At twenty, Woods joined the Royal Canadian Air Force and later transferred to the U.S. Army Air Corps. By the time he was twenty-three, he had already made hundreds of trips from India to China, "flying the hump" over the Himalayas, to supply the Chinese forces of Chiang Kai-shek. It was extraordinarily hazardous duty, and on December 23, 1944, loaded with twenty-eight thousand pounds of aviation fuel, Woods crashed on takeoff and was burned over 70 percent of his body. According to his surgeon, James Murray, who later received a Nobel Prize for his work in organ transplants, "The fire erased his face, destroying his nose, eyelids and ears. . .. Over the next two years, we operated 24 times to build Woods a new face—a new nose, eyelids and ears—but he still looked like no one you have ever seen."

He does not say that Woods's new ears were barely more than small ridges of flesh and the black eye patch over his right eye was held in place with a black strap that sometimes went around and sometimes over his head. His good left eye was so oddly prominent that, when I watched him, I always thought of Poe's "The Tell-Tale Heart": "One of his eyes resembled that of a vulture—a pale blue eye with a film over it. Whenever it fell upon me my blood ran cold." Despite his terrible scars, Woods, a hero by any measure, went on to make a fortune from house construction and a television station in Dothan. He also fathered a large brood of children—seven or so—whom he once arrayed before the TV cameras, leading many of us callous souls to speculate how one particular appendage survived the fire.

Only fifteen years old and new to Alabama, I failed to grasp that he was running to unseat George Wallace, which would have been a service to America greater even than his military service. What I knew was

467

that a man who looked like Death's own horrifying self took over our TV from time to time. So I was not surprised when one of my friends at school asked, "Why can Charles Woods never be governor?"

"I don't know."

"Nobody'll let him kiss their baby."

Another friend showed me a joke that I liked so much I took it over as my own. I drew an eye patch on my thumb with a jagged mouth under it. Holding my inked thumb before people, I said, "Hi, I'm Charles Woods. Friends, Alabamians, countrymen, lend me your ears." Mom, shocked, laughed at that.

Now I'm nearly appalled at my callousness. Any joker has to be worried about the truth behind Goethe's chilling judgment that "Nothing shows a man's character more than what he laughs at." But I'm only nearly appalled because I remember what I was thinking then. I could have *been* Helen Keller. I could *still* be Charles Woods. I could be the dead baby or the armless and legless boy whose parents tossed him on the porch and called him Matt, hung him on the wall and called him Art, threw him in the pool and called him Bob. Anything that happened to them could happen to me. By telling the jokes, I sneaked up on acknowledging that life was harsh, unfair, and temporary— and that my time in the world was unlikely to culminate on a positive note. By laughing at cruelty and fate, you could pretend to be superior to it, and yet what fueled the laughter was the absurdity of laughing: nothing tames death. So you might as well laugh, brother, and strengthen your mind against your own vanishing.

Nominated by Jay Rogoff, Pamela Stewart

"OYSTERS WITH LEMON IN MONTMARTRE"

by DIANE WAKOSKI

from FIFTH WEDNESDAY JOURNAL

I found this line jotted on a scrap of paper, thin as
Dover Sole, written in black fountain pen ink
that made the words seem as if they
had been torn from a letter.

And all this autumn afternoon, with the deciduous
trees glowing like glasses of freshly poured Meursault or
Nouveau Beaujolais, I have smelled the lemon,
picked once in California, then cut into wedges and squeezed over
the oyster, itself bathed in a liqueur
of thick brine,
   I, who don't eat oysters,
yet remembering Brittany, not Monmartre,
  and Wilton telling me, as my husband just smiled—knowing me
  so
  well—"Diane, you can't leave here without tasting
  these oysters."
It was a shower of meteors. Summer Perseids.

Eating an oyster
  is like standing in front of a mirror
  wearing the Helmet of Darkness
  while swallowing your pride—you, a California girl who
  got a tan over her oyster-white skin,
  but could not swim, who wanted to

change the rules of beauty but could not accept
the consequences.

In any mirror, you always face the loss
of memory; mirrors retain
nothing of what they have seen.
That loss is not only the taste of the oysters in my mouth in
Brittany.
It is always imagining the oysters' textures,
not as old cobwebs, but as
Wilton's or Robert's salty slurp,
each mouthful, embellished with the liquid wink of a California
lemon.

Those numinous words,
        "oysters with lemon in Monmartre,"
like David's footprints on Pavese's lawn
are a scrap of the missing
        from my un-oystered world,
their black-as-deliquesced-mushrooms-ink,
scripted
on an errant fragment of paper, chalky as the Cliffs of Dover.

Nominated by Fifth Wednesday, Christina Zawadiwsky

WHAT WE KNOW OF HORSES

by REGINALD DWAYNE BETTS

from RIVER STYX

& when my brother says Swann Rd. is the world,
he ignores boarded vacants, broken windows - this place's
shattered glass? He tells me to believe the world
is a tenement house, a pocket full of stones, a world
of ghosts, & what's left of ash & smoke after each inhale.
I visit him now that a prison cell holds his world.
Dead men circle every block we know, thread this world
with quotes from psalms, *"the sorrows of death embrace
me," "some trust in chariots and some in horses."* They embrace
metaphor, disbelieve gravity, breathe in a haunted world.
& what of my brother? Running these streets, he was a horse —
graceful, destined to be broken. Why admire horses?

Why compare everything fast and beautiful to horses?
My daddy's generation had a saying for men lost in the world,
it was true of my uncle, my cousin — men strung out on horse,
men *chasing the dragon*, shivering with the memory of horse,
that stallion gone postal in their veins — called them lost in place,
stuck *on the nod* — with cities buried inside them — horses
inside them stampeding. My brother put all his faith in horse,
& there is no map to find him now. He tells me he inhales
the funk of men doing life sentences & knows he is in hell,
knows that he is no better than the foul smelling dung of horses,
that he has dug his own grave amongst bricks that embrace
him. He is an exile, with only rusted iron bars & bricks bracing

471

his two hundred pounds. Who will admit this cage embraces
him? His life taught me *"history is written on the back of the horse"*
broken by the world. We all in prison now, we all bracing
for a cell. I stare at this man, my kin ruined by embracing
night. Call this place a horsecollar, a way to redefine a world,
& watch how it cuts into skin, how the leather embraces
all of our necks. Even as a visitor behind plate glass I brace
myself for cuffs. This is not Swann Rd., this burden placed
on me, these memories of courtrooms and the places
where bodies were found. & still, I want to stop and embrace
my brother, to hold him close to me and pause to inhale
the scent of prison, to tell him what I smell, what I inhale,

is still the body of a man. He says, "lil Bro my spirit is in hell."
He say, "I know the whole story." He's lost in memories he embraces:
the dope, the capers, the dice games. How can a man inhale
so much violence and not change? I light my Newport, inhale.
Think on how his voice has changed. My man, now a feral horse
wearing kick chains, unable to sleep, always on guard, inhaling
the air for prey, as if he is still the predator, as if he can inhale
death & keep on living. Death is the elephant in this world.
I imagine the other men here, all in a world of hurt, a world
filled with a casket's aftermath. How much grief can you inhale?
My brother tells me he prays at night, he wants to leave this place.
Who blames him. But we know all his wild hours placed

him in this mural of blood on a stained glass. His hunger placed
him in C-block, cell 21. He tells me it suffocates him, makes inhaling
fresh air harder and harder to believe in. Nothing replaces
time. "You okay in here," I ask my dude. But he's in a place
that only he knows. When he walks away from me he embraces
the kind of rage I fear. A man was killed near him, placed
on a gurney and rushed down a sidewalk. Dead in a place
where no one gives a fuck if you're breathing. To be a horse
galloping away is what I want for him, he wants horse
trundling through his scarred veins. Prison has taken the place
of freedom, even in his dreams. This is not a "world
where none is lonely." & I know, he is lost to the world,

& I know he believes this: "I shut my eyes and all the world
is dead," & I know that there is still a strip, a place
that he believes is the world: Swann Rd., where he can inhale
& be free. Sometimes his cuffs are on my wrists & I embrace
the way they cut, as if I am the one domesticated, a broken horse.

Nominated by River Styx, Eleanor Wilner, Maxine Scates

SONNY CRISS

fiction by JEANNE SHOEMAKER

from THE IOWA REVIEW

Sonny Criss was named after his father, William Henry Criss, called Sonny for the obvious reasons, and lived with his mother, Delpha Mae Criss, and his father on a fifty-thousand-acre spread halfway between Chugwater and Wheatland, Wyoming. His best friends were his horse, Spider, a 15.3-hand chestnut quarter horse, and his blue heeler dog, Red. Sonny was lean-legged and slim from the waist down, but his top half was thick and broad like someone had sewn the bottom half of one guy onto the torso of another. Sonny was in his forties, had never dated girls, though he himself could not say why, and had developed diabetes two years back: fell into a coma one afternoon baling hay in the shimmery heat—turned pale, crumpled, and met the ground hard. He recovered, got his blood sugar under control, and was, more or less, healthy again. But some residue, or premonition, he couldn't tell which, lingered in his mind, and Sonny couldn't shake the feeling that everything he was accustomed to and took for granted was now tentative and flimsy. Though he had always been a good son, he was kinder to his mother and more patient with his father. He patted his horse and dog more.

Spider was copper-penny colored, had a sloppy wide blaze that veered over one nostril, and was narrow shouldered with a big rump—best cutting horse Sonny ever owned, but spooked at water. Even a rainbow trout could set him off, and when it did, Spider twirled so fast Sonny flew over his shoulder into the rocky churn of the Laramie River.

"God dammit," Sonny said. He grabbed his soaking cowboy hat and slammed it against the thigh of his wet jeans. Red waded into the river and barked his head off, adding to the commotion. Sonny looked over to a copse of cottonwoods where Spider ran to get himself out of that water, and Spider gave him a white-rimmed fearful eye, a look horses have when they're both scared and disdainful, and when Sonny sloped through the water and grabbed the reins, Spider widened his eye more and sidestepped. Sonny had to stroke his neck, right up under his mane, to assure him he wasn't that mad, so they could carry on. He led him back through the river, talking the entire time, saying how there was just some nice tasty fish in there and a few rocks underneath—nothing big or scary—to the far side where the other cowboys, Colin and Moe, sat on their ponies, forearms resting on the saddle horns, laughing.

"Just shut it."

"Didn't say a thing."

"Heard you thinking," Sonny said and swung a soggy leg across the worn saddle.

They rode on, over the hills to where the cattle grazed in the scrub brush. Red went first, nose in the dirt zinging this way and that, looking to scare off rattlers; but they all looked down and ahead, careful to rein their horses through the perils and potholes, and avoid the cactus spines and sun-bleached bones of animals killed by wolves, coyotes, diamondbacks, forked lightning, and plain old hard luck.

The Criss Ranch was impossible to find if you didn't know where you were headed. There was a black mailbox with their Circle CR brand paintbrushed in red and a barbed wire gate—that was the first obstacle—then a long meandering rutted road, cattle grates, more barbed wire fences to yank open and get around, more cattle grates, sharp rocks, and deep potholes. The road was impassable part of each winter, and in the spring spear grass grew so high a regular car was a liability. City folks had a hell of a time.

The house was covered in tarpaper and chiseled into a fold of hills. Its roofline was so low Sonny stooped when he went through the door. The entire front was kitchen, and from the window, before dawn and again at dusk, herds of white-tailed deer loped across the far hills, to and from the river, springing, delicate, in single file—like reindeer pulling a sleigh. The backside of the house was built into the hill, and the bedroom and parlor had no windows. There was a wood stove for cooking and another for heating, and the tiny house was airless and hot all winter. The only plumbing was cold water piped in for washing up. They pumped drinking water from an outside well, kept it in a wooden bucket in the kitchen, and drank it from a ladle—the water was cool, tasted of granite, best water in the world.

The bedroom had a twin and a double bed, a dresser, a treadle sewing machine, and a closet with a curtain for a door. The space between the beds was so narrow a person had to step sideways to get through. When Sonny turned ten, he moved out onto the sofa bed in the parlor to get away from his mother's snoring. In the summer months, to get out of the heat, he slept on a quilt on the patch of lawn. Under the moon-and-star speckled sky, Sonny's sleeping form looked like a giant cocoon, shed on the grass by an alien creature. Red slept curled at his feet, gave the creature a seahorse tail.

The Criss Ranch ran Herefords, more than a thousand head, had six dairy cows, three horses, including Spider, and the two ranch hands, Colin and Moe. Sonny did all the cowboying. He looked after the beef cattle and let his dad milk the cows. Fifty acres were irrigated, and they grew sugar beets, field corn, alfalfa, and wheat each summer.

Delpha Mae Criss was in her mid-seventies, a few years younger than her husband, Will. She wore size twenty-two dresses and underneath, flesh-colored laced corsets ordered through the Sears catalogue. She was impervious to the cold, had a stern expression but a generous heart. Delpha had a manly face, little squeezed eyes, and wore wire-rimmed bifocals bought off a rack in the Coast-to-Coast hardware store. Her big rough hands could break a chicken's neck, harness a horse to plow, pump water, milk cows, dig graves. If they were short-handed, she could still saddle and ride a horse, wore a funny kind of apron over her dress when she rode.

Will Criss was a head shorter than his wife. He had small hands and feet, and his hair was white like a toddler's. His people came from Missouri, and he retained the speech patterns and charm of a Southern gentleman. Twenty years earlier, he'd been trampled by a bull in a stockyard. His hip ached when the barometer fell, predicting rain and weather changes with remarkable accuracy. Will had no teeth, poured his coffee into his saucer, blew on it until it was cool and then sipped it in. Six days a week Will wore bib overalls and a flannel shirt buttoned up tight. Sundays, he wore his dress pants, white shirt, suspenders, and a grey sweater with patch pockets to read his Bible. His health was frail, and he'd fallen ill many times to pneumonia and infections of one sort or another. Delpha got him through it all. When he was down, she did his work and her own like it was the most natural thing in the world.

Sonny Criss took after his mother. He had her fleshy face and bulbous nose. His hair was tight-curly and peppered with grey. His ears stuck out like a bat's. He was not a good-looking man, but like his mother, kind and formidable.

That last winter Will's hip got worse. It hurt something fierce in the cold, and the ice and snow were a treachery for an old man with a cane. Navigating was just too hard for Will now. He could barely get out at all, had to pee into a Mason jar he kept under the bed. He worried about Sonny and Delpha working too hard—milking cows twice a day on top of all their other chores. It didn't make sense. He made a deal to sell four of the cows to a farmer, Pruitt, who lived down the road.

"Pruitt wants the cows but he won't take them 'til spring. He's got a nice barn and all those kids, could use the milk," Will said.

"You sure about this, Dad?" Sonny knew how much his father loved those cows. "Which ones?"

"Just the babies." Will meant Queenie's offspring, though not Bosie.

"Don't seem right selling Queenie's girls."

"Like to give your mom a rest, let her watch her program in the afternoon."

Delpha had a little black-and-white TV, a Christmas present from Sonny, and watched a soap opera in the afternoon, when she could. She sat in the parlor on the sofa, attentive and still for thirty minutes, before resuming her chores.

"Can't use all that milk," Delpha told Sonny. "Half of it goes bad now, and in the summer, with the heat, just goes to waste." She'd had more than one dizzy spell in the past year. She nearly fainted lugging a milk can into the creamery.

"You could go out on a Saturday night if it weren't for the cows, stay out even."

Delpha wanted Sonny to meet a nice girl and stop being such a good son. She'd mentioned it many a time, but got no response then either. She poured Sonny coffee and set the mug down a little noisier than she needed to.

"Never spent a lonely day in my life," she said.

Sonny and Delpha did all the milking that winter. It was dark in the morning and in the evening when the cows started to moan. They milked by kerosene lamp, steam rising from the pails and the cows' moist nostrils. They wore fingerless gloves and warmed their hands with the lamp so not to startle the cows when they commenced.

Sonny trudged stiff-legged to the barn, shivered in a flannel jacket buttoned over his buckskin coat and two layers of long johns. He carried the lamp and steadied his mother's arm, while she looked into the sky and pointed out constellations and other planetary activity: comets, Orion's Belt, the North Star. Delpha wore Sonny's oilskin greatcoat, slung it over her shoulders like a cape or an afterthought—only because he insisted—and underneath, a short-sleeved dress. She never bothered to button the coat or stick on a hat. She was the most rugged person Sonny ever met; he felt effeminate by comparison. He'd talked to his dad about it.

"Ever seen Mom cold?"

"Nope."

"Seen her sick?"

"Nope."

"Heard her complain?"

"Nope."

"How'd you get so lucky?"

"Praise the Lord." Will Criss believed his wife was a gift from God, though wasn't sure what he'd done to deserve her.

Delpha lived in a state of perpetual amazement. Standing in the snow, she looked like photographs Sonny had seen of opera singers, regal and grand, a Valkyrie with a long coat draped over her broad shoulders and her face turned to the night sky.

In the inky-black milk stall, the lamp cast a feeble halo, and the thick cold sucked it in. Sonny did the milking by feel, closed his eyes, rocked the wobbly milk stool side to side, rested his forehead on the cow's warm cinnamon flank, and more than once dozed off from the sweet creamy scent and rhythm. When Sonny was a boy, Delpha told him ghost stories while they milked. On the coldest, worst mornings, he still asked for one. Delpha told it in a singsong voice, loud, like there was an entire audience to hear it, not just Sonny, Red, the cows, the barn cat, Mopey, and her kittens.

The Crisses were accustomed to the isolation of winter. They hunched around the kitchen table by the wood stove, played cards, crazy eights mostly, penny-ante poker if they had company. Sonny read Zane Grey and old *Western Horseman* and *National Geographics* his mother collected from the church donation bin. They listened to the radio, got one scratchy station out of Guernsey. Sonny wasn't particular to country music, he didn't like the lyrics, but Delpha sang along in her gospel voice. Will was partially deaf, he couldn't hear the radio at all, but he heard his wife's sweet voice and closed his eyes and nodded when she sang. If it was an upbeat number, he tapped along with his cane. Delpha made quilts, sewed baby clothes with tatted lace collars, and produced paint-by-number pictures she was proud of: three landscapes lined the parlor wall, and her masterpiece, The Last Supper, hung in the kitchen.

Winter months on the ranch were like one long tunnel you couldn't get out of. Sonny worked and slept hard, dreamt wild dreams. He was asleep by seven, up at five—took his insulin each morning while he sat on the edge of the sofa bed in his boxer shorts, jabbed the needle into his thigh with a quick motion like he was throwing a dart. He ate slabs of fried mush and bacon drenched in sorghum, milked, shoveled paths to the chicken coop, then to the creamery, and down to the barn. He hauled round bales out to the horses and beef cattle—if the snow was too deep for the truck, he had to roll the hay onto an old barn door and drag it out to the field with the tractor. The cattle grew thick winter coats like woolly mammoths, and Hondo, the bay thoroughbred, got so skinny Sonny had to double-blanket him. He used two heavy New Zealands and ran a roll of duct tape around Hondo's belly to keep them on. Spider and Pal, Moe's pinto, grew so much coat they looked prehistoric.

At the end of the day, Sonny milked the cows once more, separated the cream and the milk, and lugged it into the house in big silver cans. When he stumbled inside, feet and hands numb, for his supper, Will Criss would be sitting at the head of the table reading old newspapers with his magnifying glass. Delpha'd be standing at the stove, eyeglasses steamed up. Will and Sonny'd go over things, and Sonny kept his father apprised of any heifers or steers lost to predators or the deadly chill of winter.

If it weren't for his mom and dad, Sonny feared he'd go crazy. When he stamped his boots on the mat and ducked through the front door, Delpha had supper ready, and they sat down to a roast or fried chicken, mashed potatoes, snap beans boiled with onions and bacon, biscuits, and pie. Like God's heavenly bounty, Delpha cooked each day like she was preparing a feast. She slaved all summer to keep the root cellar full: slaughtered chickens and made soup with broad egg noodles, put up every kind of pickle—dill, bread and butter, watermelon, and sweet (she added a dot of food coloring, liked to make them bright green)—and whipped up batches of pickled beets and chow chow and picadilly relishes.

The garden she planted each spring burst with beefsteak tomatoes, sweet peas, cucumbers, strawberries, radishes, Grand Rapids lettuce, beets, dill weed, and the biggest, sweetest watermelons in the world. Rhubarb grew wild under the cottonwoods by the irrigation ditch, and Delpha turned it into compote, cobblers, and pies. Sonny bought a one-hundred-pound bag of sugar each year, and Delpha made candy: divinity, fondant, pralines, sea foam, fudge, and nut brittle. Sonny couldn't eat any of it now.

In August, Delpha hiked along the Laramie River bank to collect choke cherries for jam and jelly and big ripe Bings she canned in syrup—in the days before Sonny's diabetes he ate the purple cherries for breakfast, poured a mountain of them into a bowl and drowned it with cream so thick it lay on the syrup like a snowcap.

The Crisses had a freezer locker in town full of beef but when they couldn't make it in and ran low, Sonny rode out on Spider, picked off a white-tailed deer, brought it home slung over the saddle. Hated to do it. Delpha skinned and butchered it in back of the chicken coop, tossing the entrails to the hens.

And then finally, come spring, Colin and Moe arrived, and they moved the cattle from one section of grazing land to another, spent the slow months of summer riding the range, camping out.

"Winter's the price we pay for spring," Will Criss liked to say.

Delpha took the call—party line, two longs and a short was them. Mrs. Pruitt said her husband would be over directly, and Will Criss started to cry before the farmer pulled up with his flatbed truck.

Sonny suspected his mom knew this was going to be a hard day for her husband. She had made milk gravy, baking soda biscuits, and chicken-fried steaks. They finished their dinner, the midday meal, with a big piece of sugarless rhubarb pie and coffee. Delpha had to help Will from the table and walk him out the front door. Sonny sat a bit longer. He went out when he heard the tires crunch and watched the wobbly wooden sides of the truck shudder as Pruitt's rig came to a stop by the loading chute. It was like watching a hearse pull up. Sonny felt the meal he'd eaten fall in his stomach and drop somewhere into his bowels.

Will stood outside the corral, waving his handkerchief goodbye to

Whitey, Roberta, Roberta Junior, and Daisy, while Pruitt tried to move them toward the rickety chute. Bosie and Queenie, the cows that weren't leaving, wouldn't get out of the way, wouldn't let Pruitt separate them. Bosie was Queenie's daughter, her firstborn, and the two ran the herd. They made the cow decisions: where to graze, when to lie down, when to get up.

Sonny stood by Will and watched. Pruitt held his arms out like a stick man and came at the cows. Roberta Junior sniffed the air in his direction. Bosie lifted a back leg, like she was going to move, then brought it to her ear and scratched. Pruitt found a lead rope and slapped it lightly across Bosie's hind end. When Bosie turned to face Pruitt, she stretched her neck out and made herself bigger.

"Pruitt doesn't know a thing about dairy cows, didn't even ask their names." Will had both hands on his cane, feet wide apart for balance, and stood in the dry clay of a tractor tire rut.

"They'll never come when he calls them. He'll have to go out and lead each one in with a halter." Sonny made his father laugh.

The cows came when Will called them. No matter what time of day or where they were, when they heard his thin girlie voice stretching over the pasture, "Come on, come on now," they raised their heads and shuffled single file, resolute, near-to-bursting udders swinging, along the path they'd worn coming and going twice a day for years, into the corral. They stood chewing hay and looking at nothing, the way cows do when they eat, while Will milked Queenie and Bosie first—there was an order to it—and then the rest, in twos.

Sonny had tried it, tried to imitate his father's call.

"Come on, come on now," he crooned like a lovesick castrati.

Nothing. The cows wouldn't even raise their heads. When Sonny did the milking he had to send Red to roust them.

Whitey wouldn't go into the chute, backed away from Pruitt with a haughty look on her curly face. The others followed, moved into a far corner, and fanned out like a squadron.

"Get a bucket of oats. See if that'll do it," Sonny suggested.

It didn't. The cows were in formation, like they'd suddenly acquired the ability to plan, defend, and conquer. Bosie shook her head fast like she had flies in her ears, and the others stood with their eyes fixed on Pruitt.

"Think they'll kill him?" Sonny said, not altogether joking.

Colin and Moe came from somewhere, probably the barn-board shack they lived in when they weren't out with the herd.

"Anything we can do, help out?" Moe asked.

Will took a few wobbly steps closer to the fence, hung his cane, and rested his hands on the top. Pruitt moved to one side and tried to creep up on Whitey. He acted like he'd turned invisible.

Whitey lowered her head and neck—she was half albino, front half—and went for Pruitt so quick that he lost his footing in the deep muck of the corral. He went down hard on his side. The cow stopped just short of gouging him with one of her blunted horns when Red slid in. She circled on her back legs, threw her big head at the dog and stamped the ground, but Red kept coming at her, yipping, twisting, aiming to get at her hocks and tail. The stub of his tail swished so fast, you could barely tell it was moving.

Colin pulled Pruitt up. "Hurt any?"

Pruitt slapped at the muck on his clothes. "They always like this?"

Sonny called Red off Whitey, and now the dog had Pruitt's baseball cap in his mouth and was loping around the corral like he'd won a prize.

"Pruitt, got an idea," Will said.

Pruitt followed Will over to the lawn by the house. It took a while for Will to get somewhere. Pruitt was clean-shaven, a nice-looking young fellow with short, clipped hair. His dirty jeans looked city-bought, and he wore tennis shoes—new to farming. He had purchased the land, house, and equipment at auction two years ago and was growing field corn and alfalfa. He didn't know what he was doing. Sonny felt sorry for him. Pruitt had a wife and kids to feed and had one problem after the other with his crops—the land hadn't been properly rotated before he got hold of it.

Delpha came out carrying a tray with two slabs of pie and mugs of coffee.

"Get squared away with them cows?" she asked.

She'd no doubt watched the whole fiasco but knew better than shame Pruitt further by letting him know. She wore the fancy dress with the pineapples on it that Sonny had bought for her birthday—he reckoned it'd go well with her sombrero—and a starched apron tied around her big waist. Will and Pruitt settled into the flimsy aluminum chairs.

After Pruitt drove off in his rattletrap truck, Sonny, Colin, and Moe came over and plunked down. Thunder sounded close by. There were windstorms and forked lightning every afternoon. The wind came across the prairie sudden, fierce—blew the lawn chairs clear across the yard, scattered the chickens, and caused the cows to clump together tail end out.

"Made a deal. Told Pruitt I'd keep the cows if he'd come over to milk. Says he can fix that old separator, get it working right. Glad he knows how to do something." When Will laughed, his shoulders moved up and down inside his bib overalls and his eyes grew shiny and wet.

"Sounds about right. Go on in Dad, we'll do the milking." Sonny helped Will out of his chair, though it tipped over in the process, and handed him his cane.

Sonny waited for the others to go ahead. He felt close to tears, like something monumental had happened that afternoon, but couldn't understand exactly what. Maybe I just need something sweet, he thought, and pulled a butterscotch candy from his jeans pocket and unwrapped the gold foil.

The cows stood behind the granary, out of the storm, blinking their white eyelashes and swishing their broom-like tails at the buffalo gnats.

"Let's go, girls," Sonny said. "Come on Bosie, Queenie, get this over with."

The cows strolled into the milk stall and poked their necks through the slots in the feed trough. Sonny dragged a milking stool over and sat down. Mopey and her kitties appeared like magic, sliding their fur along the wooden sides of the stall. Sonny aimed a pink teat and sent an arced spray of milk into a black and white kitten's mouth, and it rose up on its twiggy hind legs and pawed at the air.

"You're a crack shot. Regular Annie Oakley," Moe said and pulled a stool over toward Bosie.

The Criss Ranch paid more than most, and the same Mexican family came back each year with more kids and grandkids. They brought Delpha a present one year, a big yellow sombrero. She wore it when she hoed the garden. But the Crisses had to cut back now. They couldn't afford migrant workers. They had to turn the Mexicans away that spring when they showed up in their rusted-out, muffler-less vehicles. Will tried to explain about falling sugar prices, how they weren't going to put in sugar beets and wouldn't be needing help with weeding and picking. He wasn't sure how much of it they got.

"A shame, just a shame." Will's eye sparkled with tears. "Y'all stay for dinner though, least we can do. Stay in the bunkhouse as long as you want."

The bunkhouse was a shack on the far side of the corral. It had glass-less windows, barn-board walls, no electricity or running water, a wood floor and two bed frames with rusty springs. The wind blew through. Delpha saved burlap feed sacks for them to hammer over the windows or line a corner where a baby would sleep.

The men took their hats off before they came in, and they crowded around the kitchen table, passing the babies back and forth while they ate. Will and Sonny took a turn too. No one spoke much. Sonny knew three or four Mexican phrases. The women were shy, their men small and thin. The older kids knew English pretty well but weren't much for conversation.

After dinner Sonny went out and peered at their cars. He helped change a flat and pounded out a dent in a fender—wished he could do more. They spent the night but left early the next morning. Delpha packed them sandwiches and pie for the road. Will shook his head as he watched them leave, felt so bad. Sonny had to remind him they were barely getting by themselves.

Moe was short for Maurice, not a true cowboy name, but Moe wasn't someone you made fun of either. He was wiry—five-feet-five tops—with rock-like biceps that made his shirt sleeves bulge. Moe liked to show off. He mounted his pinto-horse, Pal, Indian style—grabbed the saddle horn and swung up without putting a foot in the stirrup. Sonny had tried it once, when he was alone, but swung short and kicked Spider in the flank. "Sorry, boy," he said and patted him. He tried pretending that it was an accident, like he stumbled somehow. On the next try, he got his foot over the saddle but without enough momentum and fell back hard on his butt. It was tougher than it looked.

Colin was lanky, with curly hair. He borrowed Delpha's flatiron once a week to press his shirts, wore scented aftershave, and did the camp-fire cooking when they were out with the cattle.

"You'd make someone a good wife," Moe told him more than once.

"Marry you myself if I was so inclined."

Moe and Colin worked at a dude ranch near Douglas when Sonny didn't need them. They made good money and met lots of girls. Moe was especially lucky in the romance department but kept quiet about it. Colin bragged for him.

"Do better for a short guy than anyone I ever met."

"Ain't short 'cept when I'm standing."

"Moe tells them the jackalope story, works every time."

Jackalopes were taxidermied, moth-eaten, jackrabbit carcasses with antlers glued onto their little marble-eyed heads. The back legs and hooves of an antelope were attached to the torso, and it was usually propped up in some oddball pose. The worst one Sonny ever saw held a wooden rifle in his paws and wore a camo vest with an NRA button pinned to the pocket flap.

There were signs all over Douglas that said, "Welcome to the Jackalope Capital of the World." Even the nicest restaurant, The Cattleman's Steakhouse, had jackalope in glass cases with printed placards full of jackalope lore.

Colin rode the liver-colored horse, Hondo, a hot-blooded thoroughbred some guy gave Will and was glad to be rid of. Hondo had raced in his youth and was so eager to go out each morning that he sidestepped and pranced for the first hour. They had to let him go first or he laid his ears back and got so lathered up that he was useless. But if a cow wandered off or something caused the herd to stampede, Hondo could outrun anything, cool off for two minutes, and do it all again. Moe and Sonny wouldn't ride Hondo. Sonny was surprised Colin'd taken to him.

"Colin likes a horse that matches his hair color," was the way Moe explained it.

Colin and Moe helped Sonny move the cattle to graze in higher ground, helped round up calves for doctoring and, in past years, for branding. But Sonny had convinced his dad to stop. He hated the smell, hated the way the cows looked at them as they burned their Circle CR brand into their calves' tender flesh and fur. He hated the way the calves bawled and ran to their mother's side and licked themselves with their meaty little tongues.

"When's the last time you heard of anyone rustling cattle?" he said to his dad one spring, and Will nodded, knowing the truth when he heard it.

"Price of beef these days, barely give cattle away."

When Sonny, Moe, and Colin caught up with the herd, they were grazing on the north section where cottonwood and lone pine provided a few dots of shade. They needed to move the cattle back to the ranch for auction. It had been a long, hot ride and the horses and men were tired. They camped out that night and set off early the next morning. In the afternoon, they took a break by the river, letting the horses and cattle drink and rest a bit. Moe had a nap. Colin produced a meal. Sonny stripped off his shirt and washed in the river.

485

They mounted up again and headed through a gully. The horses had to walk on the slant. Sonny kept his weight uphill for balance. Red, never happier than when he moved the herd with purpose, tore around nipping at the back legs of stragglers. But he went too far, he took a bite out of a young steer, and off it went with Red scooting after it. Sonny let it be a minute, happy to sit. His back was sore from Spider tossing him into the river the day before, and his leg ached from pushing on the downhill stirrup. He wanted to dismount and stretch, but knew he'd be sorer getting back up, so he let the reins hang on Spider's neck, untied his neckerchief, and slopped water on it from his canteen. He swiped at his face and neck and took a swig.

He heard barking, a short *yip, yip, yip*. Rattler no doubt. Red would keep at it until it struck, jump out of the way, just in time, and grab it by the neck. Then he'd rat-shake the thing until it drooped from his mouth like a thick strand of spaghetti. When Sonny lifted the reins, Spider took off at a gallop. He pulled his .22 from its case.

The snake struck as Spider came to a sliding stop. Red jumped in an arc as Sonny's leg swung over Spider's back. Sonny'd remember this: how his leg felt, sore from riding on the uneven terrain, how bright it was—he lost his hat in the gallop—how Red sprung up to meet the snake and whipped his muzzle back so it would travel past his mouth. But, the snake moved mid-air, changed its course like a heat-seeking missile, and drove its fangs deep into the dog's cheek. Red shook his head, flung it back and forth, desperate to get the thing off, and the snake's body gyrated in a nasty dance with a two-beat rhythm. Sonny was off Spider and on the ground running, grabbed the snake below its head and squeezed. He had both hands on it, one over the other, and through his buckskin gloves felt the scaled body and its fearsome, Biblical strength. It hardened like a piece of rebar, then bucked like a horse, used its entire length to build momentum. The second time it bucked it sent a shudder through Sonny's spine, sudden and hard, and then the white, bloodied fangs slipped out of Red's fur and the snake turned its hideous eye and mouth on Sonny.

"Throw it," Moe yelled, and Sonny pitched it like a javelin. The snake sailed in the air, snapped its tail around like a bullwhip, and landed with a rubbery thud twenty feet from the dog. Sonny heard Moe crash through the sagebrush and dirt, heard a scuffle as Moe jockeyed around and got ready, then the shot that killed it.

Sonny hauled Red onto his lap. He worked quickly, picking through the fur, looking for puncture marks. The blood formed two small pools but there wasn't much of it. Red licked Sonny's hand like he was sorry, like he'd done something wrong. Sonny squeezed the skin to get the blood to flow but it didn't work.

"Got to get him to the vet's," Sonny said.

Spider hadn't moved through any of it. He stood with his weight on his hind legs, ready to spin and run. Sonny laid Red across the saddle and swung up. He scooped Red and settled him across his thighs, and moved deeper into the saddle. When he lifted the reins, Spider took off in a flying start.

Sonny heard Hondo whinny as they headed back into the gully. He softened his shoulders and belly to absorb the motion, using his fore-arm as a cushion so Red wouldn't bump against the saddle horn. He stood up in the stirrups, as best he could, to let Spider's back muscles work and stretch. Spider drew his neck out, kept his topline low, found his own path, and lengthened his stride.

It was a half mile or so to the truck. Colin and Moe had been repairing fence posts, and the bed of the pickup was filled with lumber and tools. Sonny was off Spider before they came to a full stop. He laid Red on the ground, then reached up to unbuckle the noseband and throatlatch of the bridle. Spider's head nearly touched the ground, his sides heaved, he was lathered like soap. Sonny undid the cinch, yanked the saddle and saddle pad off in one motion, and left it tilted on the ground. He pushed Red under the lower strands of the barbed wire fence, then wormed his big body through. Red looked at him but didn't move as Sonny laid him on the cracked leather seat and pulled himself into the cab.

Sonny drove into town without letting up on the gas, the lumber and tools banging hard. A shovel and two fence posts fell out as he sped through the town's only stop sign and turned onto Pine Road. The folks on the sidewalk that day stopped and swiveled their heads as the truck rumbled by. The sheriff, Wayne King, instinctively put a hand on his holster.

The vet was new to town, had only been there a year, did it all, little critters for the town folks, big critters for the farmers. Sonny had met him when he'd come out to see about some udder infection Roberta Jr. refused to give up. He was usually out on barn calls, but this day he was standing in his exam room with an orange cat on the slick table. Eye infection. Its owner was an elderly lady, Mrs. Smith, a cousin of Sonny's mother. Her husband, in a dark suit and string tie, was there too, sitting in a chair, when Sonny shot through the door with the dog hanging in his arms.

Mr. Smith jerked his head back—he'd been reading a magazine—and Dr. Lockman's hand was poised mid-gesture, about to apply some antibacterial goo to the cat's puffy eyelid. Mrs. Smith tilted her head sideways and then held her hands out, as if to take the dog or ward Sonny off, it was hard to tell. "Why, Sonny?" was all she said.

Lockman handed the cat to Mrs. Smith and made a sweep of the table with his arm. Sonny laid the dog on the cold surface. Red's eyes were open too wide and his breathing was wrong—he made *heh, heh, heh* sounds. His gums had gone from pink to ash.

"Rattler got him." Sonny's legs didn't feel right. He hung onto the table.

Mrs. Smith took hold of his arm and Sonny felt Mr. Smith on his other side. Sonny had known them all his life, yet suddenly felt he knew nothing about them. They had no children. They always called each other Mr. Smith and Mrs. Smith. Was it a Southern custom? Sonny realized he didn't even know their first names or why they'd remained childless. And he was sorry he'd never asked his mother about them, sorry he'd never taken much interest.

Mr. Smith's three-piece suit gave off a whiff of cherry pipe tobacco as he reached into the pocket of his vest. He pulled out two pink Canada Mints and fed them to Sonny from the flat of his hand. Sonny's shirt was soaked through. Red's blood dotted the front, and the back was shredded from barbed wire—like a cougar swiped him.

"Treat him for shock, start an IV, get that going." Lockman worked fast. He pulled an electric razor from a drawer, shaved the fur off Red's foreleg in one quick motion, jabbed a needle in and taped it down. He had Mr. Smith hold the IV bag while he filled a syringe with clear liquid from a tiny vial.

"Antivenin's only good if you get it in right away. Be awhile before we know." He shot the fluid into the IV.

The orange cat was on the floor where Mrs. Smith dropped him and wove between the legs of Sonny and Mr. and Mrs. Smith, eyes closed tight as if in reverence.

Red didn't run cattle much after that, and when he did he looked troubled, like there was somewhere else he needed to be. He liked to stay with Delpha now, and she let him snooze in the kitchen on a bed of empty feed sacks—dropped him bits of this and that while she cooked.

Sonny hurt his back in the commotion, from the fistfight with the snake, getting thrown, bending low to get through the fence. He laid up on the sofa bed with the hot water bottle for two days, had to increase his insulin for the week.

Lockman called, a few weeks after the rattlesnake got hold of Red, about a litter of Border Collie pups that needed homes. Sonny took the runt—had a dark circle over one eye like a circus dog—named him Blackie. Red mothered him and taught him to herd. He showed off for the pup. It made Red young again, at least for a while.

They had the year-old Blackie with them at the end of that last summer and he was doing a fine job. He came when Sonny called him, responded to whistles and hand signals. They kept an eye on him, didn't let him get out of sight much. Sonny put him up on the saddle part of the day to make sure he didn't get too tuckered out. The cattle didn't respect him yet, but it'd come.

That summer the Criss Ranch let their herd numbers fall to a hundred, and Sonny tried to lay off Colin and Moe.

"No way we're gonna miss your mom's cooking," Moe said. "Besides, Colin's got decorating ideas for the bunkhouse, make curtains or something."

"Get up to no good if we stay in town. It's you doing *us* the favor," Colin told him. Conversation was over.

And life as they knew it went on. Sonny, Colin, and Moe spent the summer on horseback, moving the cattle from one scrubby locale to another, washing in the river, eating Colin's cooking, and sleeping on the ground. The Criss Ranch was so vast they discovered new parts every year. They found an oasis, that last perfect summer, with willow trees that provided a canopy for their tents and a place to rest out of the wicked hot sun. With the reduced herd, that summer was the best Sonny remembered, less work, and more time to do nothing.

Will found her, thought she'd fallen, rolled her over and then sat holding Delpha's work-calloused hand. He didn't speak when Sonny rode up on Spider, and later Sonny had no idea how long the two'd been out there. Hours maybe, possibly all day. Sonny needed supplies and was planning on going back out when he found them. He had Blackie slung across the saddle. Red ran to meet them, but barked funny, made that *yip yip yip* sound like he found a rattler, and twirled over and over again. Sonny kicked Spider into a canter and they loped into the yard.

He saw his dad sitting in the dirt, thought he'd fallen, then the over-

489

turned wash basket and his mother's stout legs. She went quick, efficient and perfect, if there is such a thing, dropped down on her knees as she was coming back to the house, wet clothes flapping on the line behind her, and lay down softly on her side in the summer grass. Sonny dismounted, set the pup beside Red, and let Spider's reins drop.

The funeral was at the Criss Ranch. Colin and Moe organized a cowboy tribute, and Delpha's coffin was on the picnic table, under a white tent the mortician had rigged up, piled with a mountain of white lilies, carnations, and baby's breath. She'd had a stroke.

The womenfolk commandeered the kitchen, set up card tables with freshly ironed tablecloths. There was plenty of good hot food for later. The sheriff, Wayne King, used his cruiser to bring Delpha's cousins, Mr. and Mrs. Smith, out to the ranch for the funeral. He abandoned his duties for the day. He went into the Coast-to-Coast that morning and spoke to Sam Granger, the owner.

"Anyone cause trouble today, tell them I'll shoot 'em when I get back," the sheriff said before he stomped out.

Sam was just about the only person not going to the funeral. He had to stay in on account of the store being the post office and the Continental Trailways bus station. He wore a black armband, felt awful about not being there.

Delpha Criss had been a big part of things in this small town: President of the County Fair and Rodeo Auxiliary, and she had organized the Ladies' Rest Room in an empty store so farm women had somewhere to sit and talk while their husbands bought feed and drank in the saloon.

The cowboys trailered in their horses, had on their best gear and parade tack, and processed, hats off, heads bowed, sidestepping their horses in a continuous line the length of the tent and the seated guests. The beef cattle came in from the range, stood against the fence line, silent. It was an elegant, holy moment, man and beast paying tribute.

Will Criss wore his dark suit and grasped his fancy cane, the one with the silver top. He looked bewildered. His unshaven jaw trembled. Will Criss was suddenly smaller than he'd been; the shoulders of his suit stuck up, dwarfed his head and neck. His toothless mouth looked even more caved in, and his lips moved like he was trying to talk, but no one could make it out. His turquoise eyes darted from side to side; he didn't know where to look. He couldn't look ahead at Delpha's coffin, or to the line of cottonwood trees where they'd bury her after. He tried looking up, but didn't have the strength. His wispy hair floated in the breeze.

Will sat on a folding chair between Mr. and Mrs. Smith; each had a hand pressed on his shoulder. Mr. Smith held his free hand to his heart.

Sonny stood behind his father's chair, chin out, stiff. He had Red and Blackie on lead ropes to keep them from running around. Red was worked up, knew Delpha'd gone missing. He'd been looking for her for the past three days. Sonny had to drag him into the house to get him to stop running and barking.

The service was conducted by the Baptist minister, who was so overcome with his own grief and loss that he had a hard time getting through it—Delpha had been exceptionally kind to him and his wife when their first baby died. He read the twenty-third Psalm, led them in the Lord's Prayer, and tried to talk about Delpha's life, but had to stop. He took a drink of water, looked down at his feet, then took a deep breath before he could continue. When it was over, he closed his Bible and stood before Will Criss.

"Sir, I truly am sorry . . ."

Will clasped his wrist and held on like a man about to fall off a cliff.

Sonny stood ramrod straight through the whole thing. He longed to say something, praise his mom, thank his friends, and curse the God that had taken his perfect mother away. He felt his throat was twisted up, feared he might strangle.

They'd never prepared for this day. His father seemed certain of death's imminent arrival, and being a religious man, he had talked about his new life in the sweet hereafter. He had it all planned, said he was ready to go when the Lord wanted him. Delpha had never spoken of death, and Sonny never imagined she'd die at all, let alone go first. But she must have talked it over with Will. The morning after she died, Will pulled a sheet of lined paper from the Whitman's Sampler box that Delpha kept her special things in—photographs and birthday cards—and on it she'd written, in pencil, My Funerel.

Delpha Criss wanted to wear her pineapple dress on her journey to God's immortal home and the fake garnet earrings Will gave her for their fiftieth wedding anniversary. She wished to be laid to rest in the Criss cemetery next to her two babies: she had one stillborn and one sickly child before she gave birth to Sonny. She had dug the graves herself. Will told Sonny he couldn't do it for nothing, said it was the saddest thing he ever saw. He felt terrible about it still.

"Your mother was always the strong one."

As they laid her to rest, two women from the church choir sang "The Old Rugged Cross," like Delpha wanted.

Sonny dug the grave the night before, after it was dark. He wanted to do it alone, with the stars shining down, but Colin and Moe came out and helped. They used a pickaxe on the rocky parts. Will insisted on being there too. They had to hold him up to walk, take both arms and then sit him on a chair. Red and Blackie got involved. Sonny set up two kerosene lamps. The moon was nearly full. It took most of the night. When they finished, Moe built a bonfire, brought the lawn chairs over, and they stared up at the heavens where they knew Delpha would be.

"God must have needed her back," was all Will managed to say.

A week after the funeral, Colin and Moe fixed up the bunkhouse. They put in a generator and tarpapered the outside. Sonny bought a cast-iron stove and plugged panes of glass into the windows. They all ate together in Delpha's kitchen. Colin cooked. Will was quiet, hardly ate, claimed Delpha visited with him every day. The root cellar emptied out.

Sonny, Colin, and Moe had one last cattle drive—drove the dairy cows over to Pruitt's place. It took most of the day. Pruitt had a nice barn with a hayloft. His kids learned the cows' names right off the bat. Sonny told them to feed the cows watermelons in the summer, and they promised they would.

Red stayed in the kitchen nearly all the time, sleeping on the same old burlap sacks Delpha had put out for him. Sonny got a job driving truck and took the pup along for company when he was on the road. His paycheck supplemented his dad's old-age pension, and they made out okay money-wise. Moe and Colin did the farm chores and looked after Will when Sonny was away. They'd do it until Will passed. Wouldn't be long. Kept the ranch, that was the important thing.

Nominated by Ron Tanner

AZEROTH

by JENNIFER PERCY

from AGNI

In the summer, the people in the mountains smell of the mountains.
They smell of onion, flowers, manure, *ćevapi*, butter, goat, petrol, spring
water, spiderwebs, wet wood. In the winter they smell of something
else.

We seek a village in the mountains. No one knows its name. The village is so isolated, so small, that the roads are simply the names of the
people living at their ends: Šimić, Tatarčík, Uroš. At the top of the
mountains, if you look to the west, you can see the meeting place of
Bosnia, Serbia, and Montenegro. The mountains are blue. They are
sleeping women, their curves as multitudinous as piled fruit. The old
man we visit here, in this village, is of unknown relation to the man I'm
traveling with, Aleksandar, my lover. We believe the old man is Aleksandar s great-great-grandfather's cousin, and so we will say he is that.
This cousin, his name is Gjorko, found a book about Aleksandar's family and discovered a myth. The myth says Gjorko is a descendant of
three brothers from Montenegro who owned a store by a lake. One
evening, the oldest brother shot a Turkish chieftain's dog, to show his
hate for the empire. But the brothers were discovered and they were
attacked, and they fled to Bosnia with money in their socks. They settled in these mountains.

Gjorko has dark skin and I don't know if it's from the sun or from the
earth. He lives with a big woman with a heavy sausage nose stuck between bruised, hurt-colored eyes. Her toenails are yellow and uneven,
like pieces of chewed bread. Gjorko says he married her for her bigness. She is twice his girth, twice his height. She has ankles the width

of his thighs. She dresses poorly and he dresses sweetly. He wears tweed pants and a buttoned-up shirt and keeps a black shiny *šajkača* on his head. He rides a motorcycle.

When he broke both his legs after falling from an electric pole, she found him in the flowers and carried him to the hospital. She carried him for six months. She carried him to the bathroom, to the toolshed, to the cow barn. She carried him to town and to the bars. She carried him to sleep. This is how he knew he had married the right woman.

Gjorko talks to me and laughs and I nod as Aleksandar translates between us because I don't have the words to say otherwise. I say nothing, laugh too.

Amerikanka, Aleksandar explains, *ona ne govori srpski*, pointing at me. Gjorko pauses and tilts his head to light a cigarette. He repeats *Amerikanka* very slowly, chews on his cigarette as if to eat it and wipes some tobacco off his tongue. He waits before speaking the same way one waits after trying a strange food, deciding whether or not it is palatable. His hands are on my face. I am his first *Amerikanka* and the village's too. He cheered for Obama, and when he won the election, Gjorko wrote him a letter of congratulations. Later, he realized he did not have Obama's address. He never sent the letter.

His home has hardwood floors and gold velvet couches with orange flowers on their pillows. The TV shows a woman in a spandex jumpsuit, singing. In the glass cabinet above the TV are two eight-by-ten portraits of war criminals Radovan Karadzic and Ratko Mladic. After the war, Karadžić went missing. In 2008 authorities found him in Belgrade, running an alternative clinic known as Human Quantum Energy under the name Dr. David. The newspapers reported that people in town were "shocked" at the news.

Gjorko looks at me looking at the photos. "I'm not a nationalist," he says. "I want to collect the portraits of all the bad guys plus Tito so that I can show my children how things have devolved. Clinton and Bush too," he says, and points to an empty spot near Mladic. "They will go here."

Lunch is a pile of barbequed goat meat, cut radishes, a soft white cheese, milk from the cow in the yard. After we eat, we sit on the couch and Olga puts her arm around me. I feel her bigness.

Gjorko tells us how the land gives him and Olga everything. He won't eat from restaurants or grocery stores and he won't eat any food whose land he has not seen. He shows us the farm. A small shed with a silver cow and its yellow calf. He stands in front of the cow. The cow is shitting while he speaks, an endless shit that steams, and the steam gets into our clothes and deep into our lungs.

Each animal has its own space, its own shed. He finds a chicken in the chicken shed. It has feathers on its head arranged like a hat. He plucks one of its chicks from the sun where it sleeps and hands it to me. He says it's a gift. I tell him America is far away and that they have security systems to check for things like chickens. He tells me to leave it on the side of the road. Let it be a wild chicken.

The steep hills that rise on each side of his farm are overgrown with corn. During the war, the Serbian soldiers slept in the valley below. At night their camps were a dark fog he watched rise in the mornings from his bedroom window. One day Gjorko walked down to the valley to greet the men. They pointed their guns. Gjorko waved his hand dismissively and left to pick corn from the hillside.

With his bags full, Gjorko started a fire near the soldiers, close enough so they could see, and began cooking. He let the smell of corn fill the valley. Finally, one soldier, overtaken with hunger, came to Gjorko and together the men sat down to eat. The soldier smiled and told Gjorko that the corn tasted like smoke. After the first soldier finished his meal he called out to the rest of the men. By evening the whole Serbian army was eating corn with Gjorko.

When he tells me about the soldiers, Gjorko touches his arm and pulls on a piece of loose skin. The skin sags like a hammock. I'm human, he says. But they still pointed their guns.

In the early evening, on top of the mountain, in a graveyard of crooked headstones, we set out trays of cheese and smoked beef and sausage and boiled eggs. The cheese sweats and the bees and flies crawl over the food before we can finish. A man and his child are also here. He pours us beer. He is crying and crying. His eyes are red and when he cries he leans back and exposes a stomach covered with black hair. I make a sandwich and the crying man stops me. He digs his thumb under my meat and pulls out a black hair identical to his own.

If the dead smoked in life, you light a cigarette and put it in the ground. We put many cigarettes in the ground. Most of the dead have the same surname as Aleksandar but he says he does not know who they are.

We eat burgundy cherries from the trees and drink cold springwater from the ground. We walk for miles down a dirt road, just Gjorko, Aleksandar, and me. We find an abandoned house, its roof burned black and slanted low like two tired wings. The couple died, Gjorko says.

We don't speak, we don't touch anything. The wood floors are rotted in places with mold, dark holes showing earth. The bed is still covered in unwashed sheets and the metal frame is bent in the places its owners had once slept. The quiet fridge holds old, dry food.

"Everywhere," Gjorko says, "towns are disappearing."

"Why?" I ask.

"There are no new people to replace the old."

We came to these mountains from Višegrad, a village nearby, where Aleksandar was born. The Serbian army arrived in Višegrad in the spring of 1992 and killed 3,000 Bosniaks. Some were locked in houses and burned, some were tied to cars and dragged along the street, some had their kidneys ripped from their backs like wet stones, some were raped and then killed privately in hotel rooms, some were gunned down and then dumped in the river. Children were thrown over the bridge and shot midair.

Aleksandar left when the Serbian army came. I never learned the details. He moved to Germany when he was fifteen and has lived there ever since. We met in the Midwest a few years ago, and during the time we were together he rarely spoke of the war. If I asked, which I did, he only said: *It's in the book. Didn't you read the book?*

He wrote a book, a novel. I read most of it, or I tried. It is about a boy forced to leave Višegrad because of the war. He told me he didn't like it when people asked what was true and what wasn't. And he especially didn't like it when I asked. For three years, I felt I only knew about him—his childhood, his parents, his interests, his loves— from a novel. His name is not Aleksandar. I have given him the name of his novel's protagonist because that is the man and the boy I felt I knew.

Even the book is about storytelling. The young protagonist writes his own version of history. He writes his own book, tucked in the middle of the novel, another layer, an alternate account of the war. He gave me an advance copy of the English translation a month after we met. It was flimsy and full of typos. We were both students, and when he went back to Germany, I missed him so I stopped reading it because I believed he was the protagonist and that these were his words and his thoughts and his war. It was too close. Instead, I read reviews and summaries and when I visited him in Germany I went to his readings, and that is how I began to learn about the war and his life. Sometimes the readings I attended were in German and I had to imagine the story. My favorite chapter is one I've never read.

Because of the distance, our relationship existed mostly through stories. I told him I wanted to visit Višegrad but I didn't tell him it was because I wanted to know the truth about his past or because I thought he was hiding something from me. No. I told him I needed to travel to former Yugoslavia to research a group of Serbians who write satirical aphorisms about the war. "We might as well go to Višegrad too," I said. And so we did. First, we traveled to Belgrade and found the aphorists. They told us their work explores the depths of reality and discloses its true, ugly face. They admitted that their country has a problem called mythomania: a tendency to build and maintain a prettier, idealized image of its own people as warlike and chosen, envied by all. Aleksandar Baljak, their leader, recited an aphorism to me in a busy square in Belgrade: "We had to kill them—imagine what they would have done to us!"

When we arrive at Aleksandar's grandmother's tall apartment building in Višegrad, she leans out the window, boobs resting like cooled bread on the sill. "Call her Baba," he says. Everyone in Baba's building is a grandmother. When Baba wants something from one of her friends, she just calls out the window and another grandma's head appears. They speak in this way.

The building has no lights but the sun. By the time we drag our suitcases to the fourth floor, she is already waiting in the hallway, one foot propping the door. Before I can greet her, she takes the water bottle I'm holding. *Pijanica*, she says. "Drunkard."

"Only the town drunks drink from bottles," Aleksandar explains. She runs the bottle under her nose, sniffing for vodka. When she smells nothing she sets the bottle down and hugs me.

The apartment is small. Baba sleeps in the living room. I wonder if I have already been here, traveled to the couch where Aleksandar's grandfather died of a heart attack, or to the kitchen where his grandmother cooked plum cake. In Florida, when we visited Aleksandar's parents, also refugees of the Bosnian War, his mother said: "You know that scene in the book? The one where his grandfather died? That really happened!" Then she whispered: *Don't tell him I told you*.

Baba invites us into the living room and pours shots of peach schnapps. They speak and I listen. Keeping track of time in a foreign country is hard. A few minutes of untranslated conversation and the isolation grows deep. I begin to imagine what they are saying, wondering if it is about me. After another round of schnapps, Baba turns to me and says something. I do not speak Baba's language and she does not speak mine.

"What?" I say.

"You sit like a Muslim," Aleksandar says. "You sit with your legs crossed."

After the massacre in Višegrad, anthropologists were able to distinguish Muslim remains from Serbian remains based on bone structure. The Muslim femur is bent just slightly in an arc because they squat.

Aleksandar excuses himself to go to the bathroom, leaving Baba and me alone. She makes a sound, waves her hand in the air and looks out the window. We stay this way.

"Don't do that again," I tell Aleksandar when he returns.

He does not sit by me on the couch but moves to the table. He opens his computer. "I'm going to work for a bit, okay?"

"We just got here," I say. He says nothing.

I get up to sit on his lap. He minimizes the open webpage.

"What are you doing?"

"Nothing," he says.

"I want to see the bridge." I'm talking about the bridge over the river Drina. It's where the Serbians brought the Bosnians to be slaughtered and dumped.

Aleksandar closes his computer. "Okay."

I go to the other room to change, and when I return to the living room Baba begins talking to me in a screaming voice again.

"You're dressed like a man," Alexandar explains. "You'll embarrass us."

I'm wearing a wife-beater and jeans. "I didn't know I had to dress up in a place like this."

"I didn't know either," Aleksandar says.

"But you were born here."

"I thought things would be different."

Baba follows me into the room and digs through my suitcase and throws a blouse at my chest. I change, put on lipstick, put on heels. I brush my hair and tie it in a knot.

On the way down the stairs, a corpse-like woman steps into the hall. "I was bored," she says. "I just heard someone so I thought I'd come out." Another door opens. Light spills. A grandma with a giant mole on her face, wearing cutoff sweatpants and a yellowed shirt, grabs my arm, drags me and Aleksandar inside, shuts the door. She tells me her name many times but I cannot remember. The Serbo-Croatian words are a complicated mess to my ear, and when I try to speak my tongue cannot shape itself to their sounds. She feeds me cake and then more cake and then cookies and more cookies and then juice. She feeds me until I beg her to stop and then she lets us leave.

Aleksandar pauses before we step outside. He points to the dark space where the stairs curve endlessly down. "We hid there, in the basement, when the bombs came."

All the village people are outside, sitting and drinking coffee. It's August and hot and everyone hides in the shade. Sports lottery stores line the streets like mini casinos. Each one we pass is filled with men betting on soccer games. The unemployment rate in Višegrad is seventy-five percent.

We take the long route to the bridge, and on the way, stop at Aleksandar's old home. It's a stone building next to what I first see as a fruit stand, because that's what it was in the book. Now the stand sells plastic dogs and candy. He points to his room and I imagine him there as a child, looking down at us.

His elementary school is up the hill. Here the clouds are not flat but rise upward like trees. Near the school is a graveyard. The Serbian graves are marked with stone and the Muslim graves are marked with wood. There are no names carved into the wood, just numbers.

We walk down the curving streets. "Here is the house where soldiers locked up women and children and then burned the house."

"What if they tried to leave?"

"If they tried to leave, the Serbian soldiers were waiting outside with guns and they would shoot them. They had to decide."

"What did they decide?"

"I don't know."

"What would you decide?"

He doesn't answer.

"I'd rather be shot," I say.

It takes thirty minutes to circumnavigate the city. Everybody knows everybody. Mountains rise several thousand feet on all sides, blue in the day, black at night. At the sports bar, a man wearing a tracksuit sits at a table drinking alone. Before the war, he was a friend of Aleksandar's family. Later he decided to join the Serbian army, and after he did, he shot people in town, people he knew, friends and neighbors. "It's different with a uniform on," the man told Aleksandar during their first encounter after the war.

We find the jail where Aleksandar's uncle was tortured. Today his uncle is a quiet man who lives in Croatia and dives deep into the Adriatic to bring his wife purple urchins which he cracks and feeds to her—their orange insides—on sunbaked rocks, her hands spread on his face.

We take the path along the river and look into its depths. Milk jugs surface in the rapids like ghost fish. A ravaged plum tree, carrying the names of lovers, dips its roots into the river.

He shows me the chickens that stopped clucking after the first bomb fell.

The Serbian soldiers must have looked at the bridge over the river Drina, at its Ottoman arcs, plaques of Arabic prayer, and thought it was a good place for killing. In the center of the bridge is a circle of stone where Aleksandar once came to hide from adults, where lovers now come to kiss, and where the Serbs executed women and children. The river has two layers of bodies on its silt floor. Wehrmacht soldiers from Nazi Germany are the first layer. The second, Muslims from Višegrad. The river is lined with rosebushes and I wonder if they are for the dead. Baba won't walk on the bridge. "Too much blood," she says. Every year Višegrad hosts a flotilla. Men float under the bridge, gnawing the bones of sheep.

Aleksandar has six friends who survived the war. We gather one night in Ivona's pink-walled room eating pizza with ketchup instead of tomato sauce. She lives in the same building as Baba, among the grandmothers, the last of youth to stay in town. She's a volleyball player, and has just returned from a championship game in Uzbekistan.

"Who's Serbian?" I ask. They all raise their hands.

Aleksandar has a Bosnian mother and a Serbian father. Half Serbian means you are not Serbian.

A man named Goran, Aleksandar's best friend from childhood, takes us to the top of a mountain, the highest in Viegrad. He tells us his wife is in labor across the border. "It's cheaper to have a baby in Serbia," he says. The mountain is covered in purple flowers, blossoms big as fists. A clump of trees make angled silhouettes in the sky. A man and his sheep hide in the trees. At the mountain's top, we are 3,000 feet above the village. "The snipers used to come here," Goran says, crouching. "I was playing soccer in the streets." He points and lifts an imaginary gun. "When the shots came . . . I don't know if the shooter was trying to kill us or scare us . . . but one of the bullets hit the ground in front of my friend, bounced, and then"—Goran lets his hands take over the story by making two fists and then opening them quickly.

Aleksandar and Goran sit on the edge of the mountain, their feet kicking above the city. I sit above them, ripping apart clover.

When the sun is gone and we return to the village, hundreds of people are in the street, walking in orderly opposite directions. The women are wearing heels: Prada, Gucci, Versace.

Aleksandar notices me looking at them. "They are not really happy," he says. "They want everything to appear okay, even if it's not. They save all their money to buy brand-name clothes but they don't have money to buy food."

The Bosnians have a phrase, *idemo šetati*, or "let's go walking." Every evening the villagers come out of their homes to walk from one side of town to the other. "They look at each other," he says. "It's like a catwalk."

We join them, and in an hour, only the very old and the very young remain; everyone else is standing around Club Metro. The women hold their drinks with weak wrists.

We follow them, order beer. We find a table outside. Aleksandar squints. "Look, there's a bullet hole."

I stick my finger inside the hole and the building fits like a ring.

After midnight, we go to the only restaurant still open, a closet-sized burger place, halfway underground. On the wall above the grill is a McDonald's menu. I tell them I want a Big Mac. A pregnant girl wearing pink sweatpants takes my order. She gives me a mayonnaise sandwich with cucumbers.

"That board is just for show," Goran says. "There's no McDonald's."

At home, Baba sleeps. The windows are open, the TV is on, burning white. I see her feet, curled over the end of the living room couch

501

which is her bed. We walk quietly but she hears us pass. *You little shits*, she yells.

We shut the door and have sex in the back room.

Aleksandar tells me it's the first time he's had sex in Višegrad. This makes me happy because I am invading his past, making it different from the one I had imagined.

I imagine each country—Bosnia, Germany, America—is a different self, a contained version of who he wants to be.

In Germany, the cultural differences seemed small. Germany was like living in an America with smart urban planning and black socks.

Love was another issue. He shared an office with his translator. They went on trips together to Sweden, to islands made entirely of rock. Then, two years into our relationship, I learned they had a relationship before me. "No," he corrected me. "Not dating—just sleeping together."

Six months later, I found photos of them in his parents' house.

"It's normal in Germany," he said.

We blamed everything on culture.

When we were staying in a cabin in the mountains of Switzerland, two years into our relationship, I found condoms in his bag. I dug my hand in the pocket to lift them and they slipped through my fingers like blue candy.

He held one to the light. "Strange," he said. "I never use that pocket. They must have been there for years."

In the end I believed him because we were in the mountains and he invited me to drink *glühwein* in the center of an igloo that by summer would melt and become the water we drink.

Bosnia was still only a story, and in this story I imagined he loved many women before me—women like Ivona, who he sometimes visited while I napped in the afternoon. I think about how the war ended their love and how this is the only time I am glad there was a war. I imagine, too, that Višegrad is a place he didn't really want me to ever know or see. I imagine that is why he offered me his book—a different version of life, a better one.

We lie together in Baba's apartment without speaking. The gold-striped wallpaper turns white from the moon, illuminating the painting of a bearded man, a frilled lampshade, the rows of books on Tito.

"What happened when you got to the Serbian border?" I ask.

"It's in my book," he says.

"It's a novel."

He puts his hands together. "In the book the soldier stops Aleksandar and his father. He asks if they have any weapons. The father says, 'We have a lighter and a tank of gasoline.' This makes the soldier laugh and he lets them through. We left the day before the border closed. No one got out the day after we left."

I turn on my stomach, look at him. "Lucky."

"I know."

"Is that true?"

"I don't remember. Ask my father."

I hear Baba breathing. She whispers in her sleep: *I will kill you like kittens.*

Seven kilometers southeast of Viegrad is the Vilina Vlas hotel. This is where the Serbian army brought detainees from Viegrad to be raped, tortured, and murdered. It's most famous for the rape.

Down the road from the hotel, in a small stone building covered in moss, is a Turkish bath. It uses water from hot springs in the mountains. In the heat, in the sickly light filtering through stained glass, we undress. Our bodies look bruised. We put our clothes on the ground in small piles and slip into the water. We are quiet. We swim in circles.

"Who swam here?" I ask.

"The people of Višegrad."

"Did you?"

"No."

"It's not very warm."

"It has healing powers."

"You're sure people weren't raped here?"

"Not here. Only down the road at the hotel."

"We are very near the hotel."

He dives underwater and emerges near my body. He puts his hands under my arms and lifts me on top of him. When he kisses me I'm drinking water from the mountains. When he fucks me I'm thinking of the women being raped and whether they were allowed to drink the water for healing.

After Bosnia, we have three months, maybe four, before we see each other again.

"How is he?" everyone asks. "Who knows," I say. Our time apart is more than our time together.

I'm in the Midwest and I can't find a job. A friend tells me about something called medical pretending.

"Sounds easy," I say.

I'm hired on the spot. The other pretenders and I meet in a building called MERF for two weeks of training with the University of Iowa's Carver College of Medicine. We're officially called Standardized Patients, or SPs. We act out the roles of patients so that medical students can get hands-on experience making diagnoses and talking to "real" people. Everything is filmed and observed by the Quality Control Team. To train, we watch old videos of SPs acting out their assigned roles. In one, the pretender fake-vomits and the medical student runs out of the room, arms flailing. In another, the medical student asks the pretender what his feces smells like and the pretender says: *My feces smell like shit.*

Once they had a case where the pretender was required to flirt with the medical student. After a month, the case was cancelled. The medical students couldn't distinguish what was real from what wasn't.

My boss has long blond hair, wide eyes, and in sunlight I can see the powder on her skin. "My kids," she says, "always end up getting the illnesses that our SPs have."

We each get a case or two based on our age. I'm 26-year-old Hannah Duncan from Washington, Iowa, and I keep having seizures. They started when my friend died two years ago. I'm depressed. My dad fell into a grain silo when I was six and my uncle got sucked up by a tornado while traveling with his band to Des Moines. My mom takes Xanax. I had to stop working at the grocery store because I was worried I'd have a seizure in front of people.

I have something called conversion hysteria, meaning my repressed emotional conflicts are changed into sensory, motor, or visceral symptoms, such as blindness, anesthesia, hypesthesia, hyperesthesia, paresthesia, involuntary muscular movements, paralysis, aphonia, mutism, hallucinations, catalepsy, choking sensations, and respiratory difficulties. They say the disorder is caused by a conscious or unconscious desire to obtain sympathy.

"Is everyone feeling depressed and spacey today?" my boss asks every morning of me and the five other Hannahs. To warm up for our roles, we speak with *la belle indifference* for an hour.

We call our time with the doctors the "encounter."

Before the encounter, the medical students linger in simulated waiting rooms, holding clipboards, being nervous. The Hannahs wait in simulated exam rooms.

We have a script, but it's basic. The students can ask us anything. Sometimes, if we don't know the answer, we have to imagine ourselves fully as Hannah and decide what she would say. Sometimes they ask questions and I want to tell them my own story and not Hannah's. I'm usually thinking about Aleksandar, how I'm not sure if I really know him or not. I wonder, during these sessions, if I have spent more time imagining him than living in the world with him. After months apart, when I see him again, he is always unfamiliar. I'm always surprised by how different his face looks from the one I had been holding in my mind.

I wish Aleksandar were my doctor. I fantasize about him entering the simulated examination room, touching me, asking me things about my life that I've never told anyone else—all on film, so we can go back and check things.

"I think there's something wrong with your brain," the medical student says. "I mean *mentally*. I mean *chemically*. I mean *scientifically*."

He will be a researcher in a lab, I decide.

One day I get a letter in the mail from the Quality Control Team. On a scale of one to five, one being the worst, I get a one for accuracy.

"Hannah doesn't have a cat," one of the QCT men explains to me in the MERF hallway. A few "advanced pretenders" wearing hospital gowns shuffle quietly across the hall. "That could lead the doctors in the wrong direction. They might think you have allergies. You do a great job being depressed though. It's totally convincing."

After I'm Hannah Duncan, I have trouble getting out of character. I'm depressed the whole day, her life and mine intertwine. I get the facts confused. I cannot separate her script from my own. I don't like that there are other Hannahs. I want to be the only one.

"What seems to be the problem?" the doctor asks.

I stare at the floor and don't say anything. "Sorry," I say. "I'm a little out of it."

"Why did you come here?"

I tell him about my best friend who died in a car accident and how I got there too late. She was already dead. I tell him that I wish I had been in the car—that imagining the event is much worse.

One day the Hannahs and I are sitting in the waiting room when a woman of seventy walks in. "What's wrong with you guys?" she asks.

"Conversion disorder," we say, "with seizures." She tells us a story about her daughter who had a seizure right in front of her. "I had no idea," she says. "She went completely still—the seizure made her numb. She couldn't move." She says she can't believe that something so violent can happen silently, internally.

For a long time, I couldn't have sex with Aleksandar without imagining that he was having sex with another woman. It was always the same woman, the translator, the girl he traveled with to Sweden. I never told him this. The phantom of this woman grew more and more powerful. I flew all the way to Germany one weekend to meet her so that the real person could destroy the image I had created in my mind.

When I saw Aleksandar again after I started my job as a pretender, he kept asking: "What's wrong?"

And I wished that, like Hannah, I had a script. "I have the feeling you're hiding something," I finally told him.

We would often fight over e-mail, over text, in chat rooms—always virtually. I'd get e-mails with the subject line: "Better in writing."

"You're the crazy one," he said. Then back in Germany he finally e-mailed me to tell me what he'd been hiding. An online game addiction, he said.

For the three years we were together, he played. The game he loved was called World of Warcraft. Every time he visited me in America, he said, he was secretly playing on his computer. He always had "work" to do. Sometimes he would have "work" to do all night. He would "work" while we were eating breakfast and at lunch and at dinner and in fancy restaurants. "I was playing video games," he said.

I remembered that once he had invited me to play. His computer showed a cavernous world. A man breathed in its center. He let me pick the man's sidekick, a chicken. I ran through the world at high speeds and ended up in a snowy country, beautiful and blue. I killed three wolves.

He played for twenty-four hours at a time without stopping, until sleep took him, and then even in sleep he dreamed the game and awoke to play.

He played other games too, but would beat them. And that is why he loved World of Warcraft, because in its world—in Azeroth—the war continues, and one doesn't finish a level, but only grows endlessly more powerful.

I wonder when he played if he imagined he was at war—the war he had fled—now, virtually, slaughtering Serbian soldiers himself. I wonder if it was an act of revenge, a way to return to a world and rebuild it, conquer it on his own.

When he said he married another character, it felt like cheating. At the time, I thought about creating my own character, entering the world and making him fall in love with *me*—a virtual me. If he didn't have the time to love me in the flesh, I wondered if he could love me there, indefinitely, as a product of our collective minds.

He tells me he is going to the Black Forest with his friends. He will be gone for a long time. When he says they will be "role playing," I don't know what that means.

"We tell each other stories," he says. "We invent characters in an imaginary world. I am the main narrator. I build the world. The others take what I give them and add to the story from there."

"Are the stories long?"

"Sometimes they last for months. Sometimes they never end."

I go deeper into the character of Hannah Duncan. I'm sitting at my desk, looking out my window, at the blue light that comes with dusk. I imagine that he is here, watching, and I close my eyes and let my body tell a story for me—the arching of my back, the stretching of my small mouth, the quick contortion of my arms and legs.

The letters from the Quality Control Team pile up in my living room, all with poor scores. I'm too embarrassed to return to work. I keep Hannah's script in a drawer near my desk. Sometimes I look at it at night when I am alone.

Nominated by Agni

BELOVED

by MICHAEL WATERS

from GOSPEL NIGHT (BOA EDITIONS)

Romania, 1989

She cradles the rag-swathed, 40-watt bulb
Like a hand-painted egg in woolen gloves
With holes scissored at forefinger and thumb
For turning pages in the icy nook.
The library looms beyond gritty drifts,
Past blood-soaked slats and the empty, grease-glossed
Hooks beckoning from butcher shop windows.
Last week she began reading *Ethan Frome*,
A donated copy—some Fulbright prof's—
And felt that New England snowscape her own,
But the volumes vanished between visits.
She hopes Ethan chose love over duty.
Still, she can't bring herself to steal a book;
Ceaușescu won't be shot until Christmas.
She scours shelves for American novels—
Overhead bulbs fizzled out years ago—
Then finds the harrowing tale of a slave
That makes her bulb seem to surge with power
Hour after hour in the cold cubicle.
(A decade later she'll meet the author.)
Sixteen now, she can't anticipate much,
Except to be loved as she loves these books.

for Mihaela

Nominated by Michael Bowden, William Heyen, Nancy Mitchell, BJ Ward, David Rigsbee

FROM YOUR HOSTESS AT THE T & A MUSEUM

by KATHLEEN BALMA

from THE CAFE REVIEW

If you will not tip me for my dance, tip me for daring to ask. Or if, having stared at me directly for the duration of a song or two, you still did not manage to see me, as you claim, then tip me for what you see now: the perfect circumference of twin areole, one torso a la Aphrodite statue, one triangle of cloth bundling *The Origin of the World* and pointing like an arrow to the masculine earth. Do you doubt that the artist tipped *his* model? Ah, but you're right: there is that old understanding between painters and nudes. Tit for dab, so to speak. Similarly, artists and restaurateurs have sometimes exchanged a mouthful for an eye feast. (Dab for tidbit; slapdash for tiddlywink.) Tip me, then, in calories; offer me a slice of lime split wide over the edge of a beverage. Tip me for staring back so hard it puts even *Olympia* to shame and makes her *chat noire* slink ever closer to her overlooked and underrendered black maid. Tip me, at least, for carrying so many geometrician's tools: the circle, the triangle, the rectangular bills tucked beneath such finite and measurable bikini lines. Tip me for my burlesque, crescent-shaped ass. Tip me for what you don't see: the abstract; the invisible; the squiggly outline of a model's brain matter in silhouette; the negative space plastered between fleshy objects like some happy vacuum, giving form to the nothingness between us.

Nominated by Cafe Review, Maura Stanton

A MAN FOUND AN ANGEL

by TOON TELLEGEN

from THE MANHATTAN REVIEW and RAPTORS (CARCANET PRESS)

A man found an angel, in some out of the way place,
let's fight, said the man,
good, said the angel

the man fought with him,
gained a victory over him,
tore him apart,
swept him up, threw him away,
scrubbed the floor
                    until there wasn't a trace of him left,
rubbed his hands
and stopped thinking about him

and the angel smiled
and lifted the man up, between two ringers,
looked at him with surprise
                    and some emotion too.
dropped him into an abyss

and the man fell and fell,
thinking that he was walking
and that it was summer
and that his future was full of promise.

translated from the Dutch
by Judith Wilkinson

Nominated by The Manhattan Review

THE OLD PRIEST

fiction by ANTHONY WALLACE

from THE REPUBLIC OF LETTERS

1

The old priest is a Jesuit, brainy and fey. He smokes Pall Malls fixed bayonet-style in an onyx and silver cigarette holder, and he crosses his legs at the knee. He tells stories as if he is being interviewed for a Public Television special on old priests. A small, guttural chuckle serves to launch one of his very interesting anecdotes: it's a kind of punctuation that serves as transition, like a colon or dash. You bring your latest girl to see the old priest, you always bring your latest girl to see the old priest.

"Mildred, what are you doing with this rascal?" asks the old priest, ordering a Tanqueray martini "standing up."

Mildred squeals at the idea of you as a rascal. Everything is very jolly. The old priest's hair is the same shade of silver as the end of the cigarette holder, a prop which fascinates Mildred.

"This cigarette holder was given to me by the mother of one of our students," explains the old priest. "She didn't think priests should smoke non-filtered cigarettes, and she objected to the bit of tobacco that became occasionally lodged in the corner of my mouth. Later that same mother, emboldened by one too many *grappas*, tried to seduce me in the sitting room of the country house where I was to spend the weekend."

Your latest girl is rapt at the stories of the old priest, they are always rapt, the old priest does half the seducing for you.

Back in the room Mildred says, "That's some old priest. Is he gay?"

"What do you think?"

"I think all you Catholic school boys seem gay."

511

Another girl and the old priest, always ready to be bought lunch or dinner. He smokes, drinks, laughs, tells stories—makes people feel as though they are participating in the history of their own time. The old priest is a monologist of the old school, tossing brightly colored balls into the air and keeping them aloft.

"Another time, we were in Madrid and wanted to get out and see the night life," recalls the old priest. "We concocted a story that the American Ambassador had invited us to dinner, but the Prefect said that in order to receive permission to leave the house after nine we'd need the permission of the Provincial. The Provincial said, 'If the American Ambassador really wants to see you, he'll invite you to lunch.' My friend Arthur Ramsay thought we were sunk right then and there, but I convinced him that we should go through with it anyway, even though it was against the rules. We danced the Flamenco till three."

Everything is very jolly. Your girl is from the South this time and refers to the old priest as a "sexy old queen."

Time and again you meet the old priest. Years fly by the way they used to mark time in the movies: wind and leaves, the corny tearing of the calendar page, the plangent tolling of Time's own iron bell. You either bring a girl along or, if you're depressed, you go by yourself and expect to be consoled.

"I want to write but I can't write," you say.

"It will come," says the old priest. "Give it time. But the pattern is that you should have written your first stories by now. You're a bit behind schedule, you know."

You can almost convince yourself that he knows what he's talking about. He speaks with the authority of a grammar book and is relentlessly optimistic.

Life takes you through a couple of twists and turns, you do things you never thought you would be doing. You live in a rooming house, you drink a lot in the evening, you work a day job as a blackjack dealer in Atlantic City. You wear a white tuxedo, red bow tie and matching red buttons, which your fellow croupiers refer to as "the clown suit." Nobody, not even you, can believe it.

In summer the old priest comes for a visit. You shake martinis in your third floor efficiency. The heat is stifling, oppressive. Through the walls comes the scent of frying meat, and a loud conversation that goes on and on.

"This is a house of failure," the old priest says, jaunty in his white polo shirt and Madras shorts.

"It's experience."

"So is being bitten by a shark."

"I need a membership card that provides entrée into the historical moment."

"Dear child, I have no idea what you're talking about," the old priest says, pausing for the transitional laugh. "When I was your age I was going to the bullfights in Spain. We actually saw Ava Gardner one time. I went beforehand to ask for permission but the Prefect said, 'Jesuits don't go to bullfights.' When we got there the place was crawling with Jesuits in mufti."

2

In your spare time you read Rimbaud and crave poetry, mystery, illumination. You find an old fish tank somebody has left at the curb and in it, according to the directions of a mail order kit, you raise a crop of hallucinogenic mushrooms. Two weeks before Christmas you visit the old priest at his sister's house on Cape Cod, in Wellfleet, where you plan to spend the weekend breaking into the ancient mysteries. Poetry, mystery, illumination: you'd like to get to the bottom of it.

The old priest says to you as you're unpacking: "Be careful not to leave anything behind. A friend of mine left a pair of black briefs in the guest bed and now my sister says she is beginning to believe everything she reads in the papers."

"Just from a pair of black briefs?"

"Well, apparently he had *Booty on Board* embroidered into the rather narrow seat. Oh dear heavens!"

You drink a pitcher of martinis accompanied by three slices of American cheese and a box of stale Ritz crackers. For dessert you chew the mushrooms, one or two at a time, unsure of the proper dosage.

"This is a fine delicacy," the old priest says. "It's a first-rate cocktail snack."

You nibble the mushrooms, dried and crumbling in your fingertips. The pattern and texture of the desiccated stems and tiny caps become increasingly interesting until, without much warning, the old priest has sprouted tufts of white hair on his face, and his pinkish hands also have sprouted coarse white hair and the hard dull grayish-black points of two cleft hooves.

"Don't look now, but you've turned into a goat-man," you say to the old priest.

"Is that true?" wonders the old priest, lighting a cigarette. Even as a goat-man the old priest has not lost his taste for tobacco.

"Just look for yourself in the mirror."

The old priest stands to look into the gilt-framed mirror that hangs full length above the red velveteen sofa.

"I suppose I have," remarks the old priest, vaguely amused. "Is it permanent, do you think?"

"For the next eight hours or so, anyway." You laugh. The idea of the old priest transformed into a goat-man is hilarious.

He examines himself in the glass, puffing his cheeks and shaking his oversized head. When the cigarette is finished he shakes the cigarette holder and the final few filaments of burning tobacco fall to the floor. He stands before the glass with the empty cigarette holder and begins to wave it in front of him in frantic, cross-like motions.

"You take life, but you can't give it," says the old priest, his hand trembling but his eyes fixed steadily forward.

"Who are you talking to?" you ask.

"I have to chase these demons away," is his response, but after a few more swipes he sits down on the sofa, places the cigarette holder in his shirt pocket, and laces his fingers together. "We're not supposed to see this," says the old priest, plainly worried. "This is a sin we're committing."

"It's just in our heads," you laugh. "It's the power of the human imagination."

That's what you intend to say but it comes out, *It's the power of the fungus humungination.*

"Oh no it's not," is his answer. "It's even worse for you if you think it is."

He gets down on all fours and in the process the cigarette holder drops suddenly to the ground. He clatters goat-like back and forth in front of you on his knuckles and knees, shaking the walls and knocking his sister's knick-knacks from the mildewed shelves.

"Look what you've done to me now," says the old priest, goat-like and forlorn. "Look what you've done to me now."

"Where's your God now?" you say, laughing, in your best Edward G. Robinson, then are immediately sorry to have said it. You are sorry to have turned the old priest into a goat-man. You are sorry to have spoiled his religion, to have brought him pagan-low. You are sorry for everything. This is something you've been taught, something that will not go away. You are sorry for *everything*.

The Baltimore Catechism: "O my God I am heartily sorry for having offended Thee, and I detest all my sins, because of Thy just punishments, but most of all because they offend Thee, my God, who art all-good and deserving of all my love. I firmly resolve, with the help of Thy grace, to sin no more and to avoid the near occasions of sin."

"This is a bad trip," you say, then add that it is his religion, not a handful of dried mushrooms, that makes one sorry about everything. Then you are sorry for that, too.

3

You find a new girl, it's been a while, things have cooled a bit between you and the old priest since the magic mushroom incident. The three of you get dressed up and go to the best French restaurant in Boston, where the old priest is taking a year's sabbatical at a Jesuit house in Cambridge. He is wearing his Roman collar and all signs of the goat-man have vanished. He looks a bit less puffed around the edges, and his sea-glass eyes are sparkling. It occurs to you that the old priest has been consigned to a drying-out facility.

"Wine," the old priest says, lifting a full glass of Nuits St. George. "Bringer of *ekstasis* to pagans and Christians alike."

"What's *ekstasis*?" your new girl Ruthie wants to know.

"Well, it's a bit different than ecstasy as you probably know the definition of that word," explains the old priest, and it occurs to you that he is making a pronounced effort not to leer. "It's the state, literally, of standing outside oneself. Of being able to step outside the prison of one's own body, if only for a moment or two. Isn't that what everybody wants, after all?"

"I guess I've never thought about it that way," your new girl admits, leaning in.

"I dined with a Swiss Jesuit one time," the old priest chuckles, passing Ruthie a bite of his Veal Oscar. "He ordered beef and I ordered duck. I wanted a taste of his beef and do you know what he said? He said, 'If you wanted beef, you should have ordered it, and if I wanted duck, I would have ordered it.' Oh dear heavens! The Swiss, well, you know what Harry Lime says: the great product of their civilization, the cuckoo clock!"

"Were you in Europe a long time?" Ruthie asks.

"Seven years. I wanted to stay and earn a doctorate at the Sorbonne, but the Society of Jesus had other plans for me. I came back to Washington just in time for the Kennedy years, which was quite a spectacle."

"What do you know about anti-Semitism in Europe?" Ruthie asks, a bit pointedly.

"The place is crawling with it, I know that much." He puts down his knife and fork. "Once, during my novitiate, I stayed for a time in a Jesuit house in Vienna. This was in the early fifties, not even ten years after the War, and the city looked it, too. The Jesuit house where I was to spend the summer was an old castle with parapets and ramparts, battlements and whathaveyou. In the first few weeks of my stay I made friends with a Jesuit from Argentina. He liked to joke that so many people from this part of the world had relocated to Argentina that he had to come to Vienna for a while, just to balance things out a bit. Father Madero hated the Viennese Jesuits, though. He told me one time about how he'd been in this house during the War, had in fact been there for almost ten years. In the evening after supper we used to go up on the roof to smoke and watch the sky change colors, flocks of swallows darting and diving among the chimneys, and one night he pointed down to a side street—I suppose we were up about eight stories—and said, There used to be a synagogue down there, where that kiosk is now standing. One night we were all gathered out here after dinner, smoking cigarettes and chatting, and from this roof we watched a group of men come down the street with sticks and bats. They broke every window in that synagogue then beat the Jews as they tried to run away. And do you know what your fellow Jesuits did?' asked Father Madero. Well, I don't suppose there was much they could do,' I offered, for I knew by now that Father Madero hated the Society of Jesus. They cheered,' was his reply, and he began clapping and whistling. Dear sweet Jesus."

"An honest man," Ruthie says, and for a few moments nobody says anything.

"An honest man," Ruthie says once more, reaching with her fork for another bite of his Veal Oscar.

The old priest, it seems, will stop at nothing to impress one of your girlfriends.

You go back up to Boston, this time alone. The new girl once more has not worked out and you are feeling depressed, ahistorical.

"I'm feeling depressed, ahistorical," you tell the old priest.

"Well, so you're making a pile of money, anyway," the old priest says, exhaling cigarette smoke.

"Not a pile, exactly."

"If you're not making a really large sum of money, then I don't get it."

"It's a job to do like any job. I'm not writing anything, so what's the difference?"

"What's the difference with anything?" the old priest wants to know. "Are you living your life or are you not?"

"I have no sense of my life as a part of the historical moment."

"*Idiot*," he says, as if the French pronunciation will soften the blow.

"Maybe I should go to graduate school."

"I was a contrary student myself," the old priest says, though you were in fact a very good student, bursting with promise and the will to please. "If they told me to read *Hamlet* I'd read *Macbeth*, and if they told me to read *Macbeth* then I'd read *Hamlet*. My junior year in high school I despised my English teacher. One time I handed in an E.B. White essay on skating in Central Park, except that I changed it to Boston Common. I got a C. I wanted to write E.B. White and tell him he'd gotten a C in high school composition. They kept me back a year, and I started to wise up."

"They kept you back with C's?"

"There were other factors."

"Such as?"

"Unbridled contempt. They told me I'd never be accepted at an accredited school, so one day at the end of my senior year, only a couple of weeks before graduation, I walked over to Boston College. They asked me where I was going to high school, and when I told them they simply had me sign the forms and I was admitted at once."

4

The old priest, who was built like an oarsman when you first met him, is nicotine thin. He is in Philadelphia for the time being, visiting with friends and trying to convince his superiors to reassign him to Boston, where he still has some family in Southie. He eats hardly anything and insists that the second martini be on the table before dinner can be ordered. He likes to drink in tablecloth restaurants because it is more seemly than standing at a bar. However, the new smoking regulations land you at a table near the bar most of the time anyway. The bars are noisy and the old priest hears not so well. The evening ends when you get tired of shouting and pantomiming.

The new girl is a red-haired gold-digger named Tanya who has the cheek to order beluga caviar whenever the opportunity presents itself. You eat the caviar on toast points and wash it back with iced Russian vodka. The old priest says, "I was once the guest of a woman who took us to a restaurant in Paris where the waiters came out with great crystal trays of caviar in crystal bowls that were somehow illuminated from the bottom. The lights were extinguished, they brought the caviar out in a procession, a long line of waiters holding the trays aloft on their right arms, the bowls rising up, lit by candleflame, unreal."

The red-haired girl sits rapt, convinced she's stumbled onto a pile of money and that the aristocratic bearing of the old priest proves it. However, this is the third or fourth time you've heard this story, and your attention, like the candleflames beneath the caviar, is quavering.

"The old priest the old priest!" the red-haired girl says, back in the room. "I've never met anybody like that, a character out of a Waugh novel!" The gold-digger is a gold-digger, but at least she's not an illiterate like some you've brought round. "It's interesting," she says, "the urge toward self-creation. I guess it's what most intelligent people do," she says, then stares at herself in the hotel mirror.

"Whatever happened to the gold-digger?" asks the old priest, raising his martini glass. "I liked her. She spent all your money and told you you were a pompous ass when she was through with you."

"The gold-digger hit paydirt, packed her shovel. Is off to another dig, I suppose."

"You shouldn't be so hard on women," says the old priest. "It's their nature to be acquisitive."

"You should have it happen to you sometime."

"Oh dear child, if I were not in the Society of Jesus I'd be prey to every manner of boy hustler." He fixes a cigarette in the holder. "As it stands, I have God on my side and they line up to buy *me* dinner."

"God and history," you say.

"They're not exactly the same thing. Tolstoy calls on us to end the false and unnecessary comedy of history and to dedicate ourselves to the simple act of living."

"Joyce calls history a nightmare," is your response.

"I'm inclined to agree with Tolstoy," laughs the old priest, waving his cigarette in the smoky air.

5

The next time you see the old priest he is in Washington, living in a Jesuit house in a sketchy part of Capitol Hill. The Boston plan, it seems, has not worked out, but neither of you mentions it.

"I'm teaching slum children how to speak French," says the old priest. "I must say it's better than working for the man. But what about you? How's the writing going?"

"I haven't written anything in years. A false alarm, I guess."

"A velleity."

"Huh? How's that?"

"A wish for a wish. But what *are* you doing these days?"

"I left the casino business, finally. I'm waiting for my teaching certificate to come through."

"Congratulations, you've finally done something sensible. But don't be like that English teacher I had. He was giving me C's, so one time I handed in an essay by E.B. White. It was on ice skating, and I changed the location from Central Park to Boston Common. Have I ever told you this one?"

"No, I don't think so."

"He gave me a C. I wanted to write E.B. White and tell him he'd gotten a C in junior composition at Saint Francis Xavier High School."

"I won't be that kind of English teacher."

"Good."

6

A year later there is a female English teacher, and the two of you take the train from Philadelphia to Washington. Her name is Dawn; she is twenty-three years old and very pretty and also economy-minded, the way natural-born high school teachers always are. When the old priest starts talking about caviar she blenches, orders a tossed salad with low-fat dressing.

"The bowls were themselves of carved ice and illuminated from the bottom, luminous in the dark against the black sleeves of the waiters' jackets and the gleaming white of the doubled cuffs."

"Such extravagance," Dawn says. "Another time in history."

"The woman who threw that party became attached to a gigolo from Argentina who used her, took her money, and left her addicted to prescription drugs."

"Now *that's* a good story," Dawn says.

The old priest comes to Atlantic City for the wedding, even though you've insisted on a civil ceremony, and the two of you have a bachelor party at one of the casino buffets.

"I remember the last day of my first year at Boston College," the old priest tells you, exhaling cigarette smoke. "Have I told you this story?"

"I don't think so."

"My friend Pat Dempsey was waiting for me in a car with the top down. I went into the office and there was this Jesuit behind a desk and I said, 'I want to sign up here. I want to sign up now.' He told me to finish college first, and I told him that if he did not get me right then and there, on that particular day and time of day, he would not get me at all."

"What did he do?"

"He signed me up at once."

"So why didn't you just turn away?"

"It's a vocation. That's what I'm trying to tell you about: something you absolutely have to do, regardless of what anybody thinks. You have no choice in the matter. Like you with your writing."

"But I don't write—haven't written anything. I told you before. I stopped all that."

"You're young yet. It will come to you. You can make a pile of money in the casino business and then retire."

"That's what I'm planning on, yes. I'm considering teaching high school English after I retire. What do you think?"

"That's good, as long as you leave yourself time to write."

"I think I can work it in."

"Sink roots down like the roots of old trees."

At the reception the old priest tells stories to Dawn's parents.

"My friend Itchy and I wanted to go to the movies but you had to go to Confession on Saturday nights, so Itchy said to my mother, 'He can go to Confession in my neighborhood, it's on the way to the movie house.' On the way we met this girl Itchy knew and she said, 'Suckenfuckenickel.' I said, 'What?' And she said, 'Suckenfuckenickel.' As we walked away I said to Itchy, 'What did that girl just say to us?' What she'd said was that she would suck and fuck us for a nickel. Oh, dear heavens! Then Itchy took me to his church and pointed to a confessional box and I went in. There was an old German priest in there and he said, 'Who ist das? Is you boy or girl? Speak up! Speak up!' Oh, it was dreadful. I told him my small few sins and he cried, 'Oh you bad boy, oh you wery bad boy!' and began to beat his hands violently against the wooden walls of the confessional box. When I came out Itchy was in the vestibule of the church, leaning one elbow against a holy water font and roaring with laughter. We went to the movie but could not contain ourselves. Every time there was a break in the dialogue one of us would shout, 'Oh you bad boy! Oh you wery bad boy!' The third time we started up, the usher came and threw us out the fire door."

"Where'd you get that old priest?" Dawn's mother asks when you come back from the honeymoon.

"He was my French teacher in high school. French and senior guidance. We've stayed in touch."

"He's a scream," Dawn's mother says.

"He is that."

"You should take a page or two out of his book," Dawn's mother suggests.

7

A year later you go down to Washington by yourself. Your English teacher, you've just found out, is having an affair with the school nurse—a pair of lipstick lesbians is the word in the halls —and you want to be consoled. The old priest seldom leaves his room, which reeks of tobacco and is heaped with dirty clothes and cardboard boxes. Wads of crumpled Kleenex are strewn about the floor and heaped atop the dresser. His hair is greenish in a certain light, and his eyeballs and fingertips are different shades of yellow. He wears a mauve crewneck sweater, loose black corduroys, and bedroom slippers with the toes snipped off. His knees, as he stands for a moment to greet you, open and close stiffly as a churchyard gate.

"This is my last weekend in this room," explains the old priest.

"They're moving me to Assisted Living. Father Lemmon was behind it. I helped him through his novitiate and this is the thanks I get. But I shall die as I have lived, safe within the arms of the Society of Jesus!"

You bring Chinese takeout from around the corner and almost get mugged on your way back to the rectory. You set up all the little cartons on his desk, festive as can be, but he barely takes a bite. His hearing has dimmed considerably, and to communicate with him you have to shout. Tufts of coarse white hair sprout from his nose and ears.

"My wife is a lipstick lesbian," you shout.

"How's the cat?" is the old priest's reply.

"I have dogs."

"How are the dogs, then?"

"Fine."

He stares at you, blinks, stares some more.

"I said they're fine. The dogs are just fine."

"Dear child, why are you shouting?"

"I'm passionate about my dogs."

"How's the writing?" the old priest asks.

"I haven't done any writing since I was a young man."

"But you're a young man still."

"That's a matter of opinion, but whatever the case I haven't done any writing for quite some time."

"Well then, how's the casino business?"

"I got out of it years ago. I teach English at Atlantic High. 'Stopping by Woods on a Snowy Evening,' that sort of thing."

"There you are, I knew you'd come to your senses. And you've had children?"

"No, not yet. Maybe soon."

"Don't wait too long: you'll shorten the time you have with your grandchildren."

"That's a point."

"My brother got married at fifty, a very Irish thing to do. He died when his only daughter was still in her teens."

"I didn't know you had a brother."

"Oh, I had two of them, one still alive."

"Why did you never say anything about them?"

"How's that?"

"Why did you never tell me that you had two brothers?"

"I don't suppose it ever came up. But Itchy was more like a real brother to me anyway."

"Whatever became of Itchy?"

"Have I not told you that story? Itchy's mother ran off with a man who arranged a *ménage a trois* between himself, the mother, and the daughter. Itchy stayed with his father, who became very bitter and drank all the time. I think he beat poor Itchy. I came to the door one time and Itchy said, 'Oh, it's you again. Go 'way,' he said, and I went away. I never saw him again."

"Why do you think he did that?"

"He was embarrassed by the situation, I suppose."

"That his father beat him?"

The old priest gazes at you, and again you realize you have to speak up. *"He didn't want people to know his father was beating him?"*

"That I loved him." The old priest leans forward to take your free hand, the hand not holding the drink, in his own two hands. He sits peering at you as if by lantern light. "Dear sweet beautiful child of light and grace. He was embarrassed that I loved him."

8

You picture the old priest in his ritual garments, his "vestments," lifting the host up high at the consecration, the process of transubstantiation, the moment when a dry disc of unleavened bread becomes the body of Jesus Christ.

Per omnia saecula saeculorum.

Amen.

Pax Domini sit semper vobiscum.

Et cum spiritu tuo.

You picture the old priest in Europe in the fifties, spotting Ava Gardner at a bullfight in Madrid. She is wearing a beret, he is wearing a *soutane*. This is history. No, wait, he is not wearing a *soutane*, he is wearing mufti. He is in history and he will lead you into the promised land of the historical moment, the instant in time in which history is happening and you are in history, you yourself present in that unique and meaningful moment: the moment in time when everything makes sense.

This is only theoretical, of course, but even so it seems clear enough to you that there are those who stand inside history and those who stand outside, like beggars at the gate. This is not a matter of money; it is a matter of something else, though it is hard to say exactly what. Whatever it is, though, the old priest seems to have plenty for everyone.

To penetrate time you must go outside of time. Outside of time is the world of myth, of eternal and meaningful recurrence. Even as the old priest tells his anecdotes again and again they acquire substance, a kind of permanence or narrative integrity that goes beyond their literal level. No longer does the old priest as a young boy simply knock at Itchy's door; he eternally knocks at Itchy's door. Itchy, perhaps having just come from a fresh beating, eternally answers the door. This is a cool trick. You'd like to try it yourself, but you keep steady contact with so few people that there aren't many whom you could repeat your stories to, if you had any stories you considered worth repeating. Well, you do, as it turns out. The stories of the old priest.

9

You call the book *The Old Priest* and you get an agent interested, and he gets a publisher interested. Priests old and otherwise are hot news that year because of the sex abuse scandal that is in all the headlines. In the popular imagination priests are rapidly becoming synonymous with pedophiles.

"I like the way you leave the whole sex thing ambiguous," your editor says. "That's really the heart of the matter. The idea of the priest as traditionally representing good is juxtaposed against the current idea or perception of the priest as representing evil. And you walk the fine line down the middle. Very 'Young Goodman Brown' of you. And of course your character is destroyed the same way as Young Goodman Brown. We don't know what or how much really happened. It could all be in his head. Was there sex between the main character and the old priest?" the editor wants to know. "I mean, just between us."

"I don't know. I left it up in the air, so I never really had to make that decision."

"Smart. Play both ends against the middle."

The Old Priest is a short novel that was formatted and marketed as a novel, on the supposition that some people would like to say they've read a novel but not spend a lot of time actually reading one. It is written in the second person; it is "mannered, overstylized, derivative," to quote one reviewer. As a writer you have some talent, most people seem to agree, but you also have an odd quirk that has proven a fairly severe limitation: you are only truly comfortable writing in the second person.

In fact, you wanted to change the title of your book to *The Second*

Person, but the publisher didn't want to do it and the book went out into the world as *The Old Priest*.

"Old priests are what sells," the editor told you, "not witty references to grammar books and Graham Greene. Let your character be the sap and you be the smart one."

He was smart, that editor, but he missed the reference to Jesus, the second person of the Holy Trinity. Also perhaps the second person as the conscience or moral self, now that you think of it. All the same, you liked that: "Grammar Books and Graham Greene" should really be the title of something, though nothing you will ever write.

10

Somewhere along the line it occurs to you that you should let the old priest know you've written a book about him. Well not about him, exactly, but a book in which he served as the artist's model. You don't, though; something stops you whenever you think about it. The last time you saw him was right after Father Lemmon had him moved to the Assisted Living facility outside Baltimore, and the room and his condition were even more depressing than they'd been when he was fending for himself in the Jesuit house on Capitol Hill.

"They seem to have taken the assistance out of assisted living," you observed dryly.

"They come in once a week to give me a shower, shave me, comb my hair. Then I sit here for a week, smoking and doing crossword puzzles, until they come back again. I get a carton of cigarettes and some books, two meals a day brought to this room. Oh dear sweet Jesus." No irony, no dry twist: no guttural colon or dash.

"Are you getting any visitors? Any family members dropping in?"

"My brother Jack came by two weeks ago and brought me a crab cake," said the old priest, and gave you a sharp look.

He also mentioned the name of former student X, who'd arrived the week before with a six pack of beer, drank all six cans, then went off to the National Gallery for an afternoon of Vermeer. You've dined with former student X on a few occasions, have even bought him dinner once or twice. He is one of those people who are always working on their dissertations. Sometimes if you came with a new girl the old priest would bring former student X. You always wondered if he and the old priest were having an affair, although that might not be the right term. Illicit sex, in any case, since priests young and old take a vow of celibacy,

525

and also since homosexual behavior is considered sinful by the very organization which the old priest claims to represent. At these dinners there would always be too much drinking, and sometimes former student X would sit across the table and leer at you in the manner of a gothic double. He is six or seven years younger than you, athletic, not as bright as you but possessing an ingenuousness the old priest seemed to consider a highly valuable quality: an ingenuousness that liked to flirt with disingenuousness. The old priest would frequently say about former student X, "Oh, he is like a big kid! Oh, he is like a big big kid!" You asked one time, rather pointedly, why big-kiddedness should be such a desirable quality, but the old priest waved the question away with a puff of cigarette smoke and the hoarse, watery laugh. "Oh dear heavens!" he laughed. "Oh dear heavens!"

It occurred to you in the Assisted Living facility outside Baltimore that you would be happy to see former student X never again.

11

The old priest appears to you in a dream. He is eating duck liver *pâté* and drinking a glass of *Meursault*. The grayish-brown *pâté* froths at the corners of his mouth. Then he turns into a goat-man, cloven hooves and wispy white fur on his hands and cheeks. Then he uses the cigarette holder to subdue the goat-man. When you wake up you think you finally know the secret of the old priest, but as the day wears on you see that you were mistaken. The idea of the old priest is a mass of sticky contradictions and reversals. The old priest is a kind and gentle man, a good and considerate friend. The old priest is a pedophile who enjoys the company of high school boys or their equivalent. The old priest is old as sin. The old priest is witty as redemption.

12

In the Catholic grammar school you attended as a boy the priests kept at a distance while the nuns ran the show, dour and plentiful in their identical costumes, as if they'd tumbled out of a machine that vended them a penny apiece. If a priest came into the classroom on the odd Tuesday it was like Jesus Christ almighty had come down from the cross to tell a few jokes or riddles. One priest was a fanatic for spelling, another asked questions plucked randomly from the *Baltimore Catechism*.

Who made us?

God made us.

Who is God?

God is the Supreme Being who made all things.

And so on.

Another priest, an older man, the pastor, came into the classroom a few times a year and claimed to be able to read everyone's thoughts. As he went through the catalogue of what all the children were thinking he threw his arms around and paced violently, in the manner of Bishop Sheen. He scared the bejeesus out of you, you have to admit. Then too, that was the whole idea.

At a certain time of the year the parish priest came to bless the house. You remember your grandmother kneeling down in the cramped living room, her head bowed, the priest intoning the words and sending sprinklets of holy water flying from a small, occult-looking bottle drawn from his inside pocket. You like to remember his black suit, his black hat with its short brim, his small black cigar balanced nimbly on the railing just beyond the open doorway. The priest reeking of cigar smoke and spewing holy water on the dated furniture. Your grandmother kneeling on the spinach-colored carpet, kerchiefed head bowed low. Years later this memory or set of memories was triggered by the climactic scene in *The Exorcist*: the two priests standing in the room with the possessed girl, throwing holy water and chanting, "The power of Christ compels you! The power of Christ compels you!"

There have been other movies, other movie priests:

Pat O'Brien as Father Jerry Connelly, the slum priest who has turned away from a life of crime in *Angels with Dirty Faces*.

Bing Crosby and Barry Fitzgerald in *Going My Way*.

Bing Crosby once again as kindly and melodious Father O'Malley in *The Bells of St. Mary's*.

Spencer Tracy as fighting Father Flanagan in *Boys Town*.

David Niven as the ambitious but unhappy Episcopal bishop in *The Bishop's Wife* (helped to a deeper level of spirituality by Cary Grant's angel Dudley).

Karl Malden as the two-fisted activist priest in *On the Waterfront*.

Oskar Werner as the tormented and dying theologian in *The Shoes of the Fisherman*. Also of course in that same movie Anthony Quinn as the Pope who opens the coffers of the Church to the world's poor and hungry. The Pope, don't forget, is also a priest (he roams the streets of Rome, gives tender counsel to an English woman whose marriage to David Janssen is on the rocks).

A not very well known actor as the priest who believes Jennifer Jones has had a true vision of the Blessed Virgin Mary in *The Song of Bernadette*. (The same actor played the father-in-law in *The Days of Wine and Roses*, if that is any help.)

Rex Harrison as the Pope who commissions the painting of the Sistine Chapel in *The Agony and the Ecstasy*.

Thomas Tryon, before he became a novelist, in *The Cardinal*.

Richard Chamberlain as the priest with the untamable lust in *The Thorn Birds*.

Robert DeNiro as the priest who tries to play the complicated game of church politics in *True Confessions*.

William S. Burroughs as the junkie priest in *Drugstore Cowboy*.

There should be more movie priests, priests we have yet to see upon the silver screen.

The priest who solicits oral sex in the sacristy, then absolves the altar boy when he is finished with him. *Absolvo te* blah blah blah. There has never been a language better than Latin when it comes to being an old priest. Mysterious, arcane, dripping of the long ago.

The cheerful parish priest who lives a decent life, ministers to his parishioners, likes to treat himself to a good dinner, likes even better to be treated by his well-heeled parishioners. He is affable, physically soft, a guy who knows how to go along to get along.

The priest lost in the mysticism of his own religion, sitting alone in his room, chanting gibberish. If he were not a priest he would be on the street, living in a cardboard box. His illness is legitimized, yet who is to say he is not a true mystic? Then too, who is to say the guy living in the cardboard box is also not a true mystic?

The priest who leaves his order and breaks his vows to marry the woman he met working behind the counter in the pizza shop. The priest who leaves his order to marry the nun he met in the grammar school. The priest who leaves his order to marry the priest he met in the seminary or, much later perhaps, the one who reminds him of that charming young fellow.

There was an old woman, one time, the grandmother of an acquaintance, who said that you should be a priest, you had just the right look. You pretended to wonder what she meant by that, but you knew right away exactly what she meant.

There are decent priests there are dreadful priests there are so many priests under the sun. You are sitting in a bar in downtown Atlantic City on a weekday afternoon.

"The Catholic Church," somebody says.

"Yeah, the Catholic Church," somebody replies.

"The Gay and Lesbian Society of North America," the first man sniggers.

"So it would seem," is the only thing you can say.

"They take their training in the *semenary*," another man chortles.

"They're just like anybody else," someone else says.

"But they say not," another man, all the way down at the end, puts in. "They say they're in the know."

"Who says that?"

"*They* say. They themselves."

"Someone should be in the know, don't you think?" you wonder out loud.

"Sure," the first man says. "But we all know nobody is."

13

The old priest no longer answers his phone, he does not have voice mail, he does not have email. A few years go by, a few years then a few years more.

Once, when *The Old Priest* was first published, you did a reading at a Barnes and Noble in Philadelphia and former student X turned up, leering at you from the back of the room.

"This is great," said former student X, coming forward after the reading to have his copy of the book signed. "This is absolutely fantastic."

"Thanks. I guess my writing has finally come to something, though I'm not expecting much from this financially."

"Does he know?"

"Who?"

"Who!"

"Oh, well, no, I've lost track of him, actually. He's become fairly re-clusive, it seems." Then you looked at the book in former student X's hand, the book jacket with its illustration taken from the *Baltimore Catechism*, the three milk bottles that illustrate the soul in its various states: the full milk bottle is the state of grace, the empty milk bottle is mortal sin, the milk bottle with some spots in it is venial sin.

"Oh—oh, I see—you're jumping to conclusions there, but of course I can see the impulse. I can definitely understand—"

"He mentioned you, you know," said former student X. "Last time I was down there, in that terrible place in Baltimore. He was wondering why he never hears from you anymore."

"Oh, was he, now? I'll have to be sure and give him a call and tell him all about this, though of course the character of the old priest is a composite of a lot of priests I've known over the years. Some that are now in jail, actually!"

You broke into a loud, obnoxious laugh then moved to sign the flyleaf of your book for the next person in line.

That was the last time you saw former student X, thank God.

14

After his novitiate in Europe the old priest came back to run a Jesuit high school in Georgetown, beginning in the early sixties, the Kennedy years through "We Shall Overcome" and "Burn, Baby, Burn" right into the middle of Watergate, the old priest always one to stand with both feet planted squarely in the historical moment. He came to Philadel-phia in the fall of 73, he was your senior guidance counselor and also became your French teacher when the original Jesuit who was your French teacher left midyear to marry a woman he'd met in a pizza shop. Those were somewhat different times, the seventies, when a man might suddenly drop whatever he was doing and run off with a woman he'd met in a pizza shop. (Of course that is still possible, but it no longer seems quite so commonplace.) Love was in the air, also anxiety, depres-sion, the mounting dread brought on by Vietnam, Nixon and Watergate, Black Power and Women's Rights, the death of the patriarchy that seemed likely to accompany the gradual breakdown in faith in govern-ment and religious institutions, a return to individuality and the pleasure principle, the inevitable victory of subjectivity and moral relativism, blah blah *blah*—

You remember how he seduced you, the old priest, how he charmed the David Bowie pants off you. Maybe that was part of it: '73, David Bowie and Rod Stewart, a little later Mott the Hoople and Queen: androgyny was just then having its fifteen minutes. The David Bowie pants? Oh, well, they came up really high at the waist and then billowed out in an exaggerated three-pleat, descending to two-inch cuffs designed to go with platform shoes. You had two pairs of each, an interesting style for a skinny seventeen-year-old prep school student, it lasted about fifteen minutes.

One day smoking cigarettes in his office after hours he told you all about William Peter Blatty and the young Jesuits of Georgetown, in a smoky pub one afternoon merrily gathered round a mongrel-brown Lester spinet. Stories were told. Some information was leaked. Classified information about the Devil got out. There really was an exorcism, though it was performed on a Lutheran boy by not one or two but an entire team of exorcists. The exorcism itself went on for months, the whole thing audio taped and the tapes themselves locked away in some vault in the Vatican.

The best parts of the book, according to the old priest—the best parts, of course, being the scariest parts—were taken directly from the secret transcripts. He knew people who knew people who knew the Devil! Talk about being on the inside track!

The old priest told his stories—he always told stories—which meant of course that he had stories to tell. You fell in love, *whatever that means*, can you just admit that much? People fall in love: kids and old ladies, middle aged bachelors and hot young kindergarten teachers. The heart has its own secret life, like the family cat, and what it might drag home is anybody's guess.

Not love, perhaps, but a schoolboy crush. Something glandular but at the same time completely non-glandular.

Can you admit *that* much?

Of course you can. Sometimes. Once in a while.

15

You remember your childhood, the lower middle class Irish neighborhood in South Philadelphia, the corner tap rooms with their blacked-out windows, Krause's bakery each Sunday morning after eight o'clock

Mass. You remember polishing your shoes for Easter Sunday, the church the next morning filled with fresh white lilies, the pews and the side aisles, all along the stations of the cross, overflowing with parishioners there to perform their "Easter duty," which is another way of saying that they didn't go very often but neither did they wish their membership to lapse.

When you were eight years old you watched *The Song of Bernadette*, in rerun, on your grandmother's black and white TV. You looked up at the dark place at the top of the stairs, hoping that the Blessed Virgin Mary would suddenly appear to you. Wanting that to happen more than anything else in this world. Also not wanting that to happen more than anything else in this world.

You think sometimes of the candy store lady, whose response to everything was JesusMaryandJoseph JesusMaryandJoseph JesusMaryandJoseph JesusMaryandJoseph JesusMaryandJoseph JesusMaryandJoseph.

   One day a punk of the neighborhood came barreling into the store and knocked your pinball machine on tilt. You backed down, of course, the boy took your machine, and the old woman sent up a fervent chorus of JesusMaryandJoseph JesusMaryandJoseph JesusMaryandJoseph JesusMaryandJoseph JesusMaryandJoseph JesusMaryandJoseph.

Then there was the time with the little girl in the alleyway, exposing yourselves as little children do. You were both five: tiny Adam and miniature Eve. The girl, you've heard, has grown up to be a junkie, a prostitute, a queen of the do-it-yourself porn industry. "Her name was Grace," you say out loud. Her name *is* Grace, you correct yourself, though not out loud. But you don't know if she is among the living or the dead.

16

One time, very drunk, as drunk as the two of you have ever been together, the old priest said: "I send this one out to live in the world. This is the one you see. You like this one. But you wouldn't like the other one."

"How do you know?"

"Trust me, you wouldn't."

"Just give me a peek."

"I'm afraid I can't do that. He can't be trusted. No, I'm afraid it's absolutely out of the question. He's locked up safe and sound as The Man in the Iron Mask. Ha ha."

You went home, thinking of the real old priest bound and tossed into a dungeon, the iron mask locked securely to conceal his face, the brutal, ignorant guards to glimpse only his wry mouth and sea-glass eyes. Of course the question then becomes which old priest is out in the world and which one locked away? It occurred to you then and has crossed your mind a few times since that the old priest is an arch fiend, an imposter who walks the earth while the true old priest—well, it's too horrible to think of.

Years later it occurs to you that you have done much the same thing with the old priest, or rather with the simulacrum of the old priest. He imprisoned the real old priest while you imprisoned the fake one. He's in a book you wrote called *The Old Priest*. He's in there, drinking *Tanqueray* martinis and telling his charming anecdotes. He's locked up, safe and sound.

17

The Old Priest, as it turns out, pretty quickly became a period piece. It went almost at once to the remainder tables, probably due to its lack of explicitness. Old priests are what sell, but only if you catch them *en flagrante*. Once in a while you take a peek at the book yourself. It is not very good. It is "mannered," as one reviewer pointed out, and it is also derivative, a retelling of the old priest's stories combined with some mildly ambiguous hints at homosexuality, a strange and self-conscious amalgamation of *The Power and the Glory* and *Brideshead Revisited* by way of *A Separate Peace* and *The Trouble with Angels*.

It is as outmoded as those lace things they used to place on the tops of parlor chairs so that one's head wouldn't stain the fabric. Why would one's head stain the fabric? Hair oil, perhaps, or dye the color and consistency of shoe polish. The old priest would know what those things are called, were called. But you don't, although among your students it is well known that when asked your favorite book your immediate response is the OED. Nobody, not even your colleagues, seems to remember that that was Auden's famous reply. You've got your tweed, your manners and your mannerisms, a few chestnuts in the one hand, a couple of shibboleths in the other.

Still, it was your dream, publishing a novel, the dream of your youth, and since you have a novel, albeit one that has not done very well and is currently out of print (alas), you now have a job, comfortable enough, in which you will live out the rest of your days, professionally speaking. Teaching English in a posh New England boarding school, well talk about mannered! Tweeds, rep ties. For a joke on the first day of school you sometimes wear a boater!

And so once again you are back in Boston, this time without the old priest, a strange and portentous reversal to have ended up where he would like to be but is not. You are getting on in years, living by yourself in a large but shabby one-bedroom on Washington Street, the bedroom itself facing the street so that you have to protect your sleep with a white noise machine or an air conditioner, depending on the time of year. The white noise machine, which looks like something designed for a low-budget sci-fi movie, sounds like the endless slosh and chop of some eternal ocean. The air conditioner sounds like the void: empty and metallic and without variation.

Whatever has become of the gaiety of the old priest? Sitting at a dinner table, enraptured with the present moment, seeing and being seen, fine clothes and expensive bar drinks and first class victuals, all of life's possibilities laid out before you like a flight of oysters. Now you are getting old and have resigned yourself to bachelorhood. Your talent, paltry at its best, has left you; you walk the cold streets of Beantown in shabby clothes, a denizen of the pubs and second hand book stores.

Your students like you all the same. You are an affable old failure who is nevertheless a tough old bird, an eagle's eye for the misplaced comma and the misused semi-colon: some of the hipper students call you "Old School" behind your back, or you wish they would. The truth is you give them all B's, and the girls with pert breasts get B plusses. Oh, even the girls without pert breasts get B plusses, who are you kidding? The poor sad pimply-faced freshman boys, arms and legs askew, get the B minuses, and they deserve them, too. They themselves admit as much.

"Walk among them," advised the old priest when he found out you'd become a high school English teacher. "Always teach standing up. Be a presence among them. Let them feel your presence as you walk among them."

You walk among your own students and wish to tousle their hair or

534

to trail your fingers across their downy arms as they sit, scribbling in their notebooks. And what would be so wrong in that?

In your free time you tinker with a second novel, which you call *The Western Gate* after a line from "Luke Havergal." These days if you can only get to twenty thousand words they'll package it some way to make it look like a novel, or at least they will if they think they can sell it that way. *The Western Gate* is the story of a dissipated novelist, a drunk and a womanizer who is his own worst enemy. He drinks, adulterizes, insults powerful people while he is going about his drinking and adulterizing. Once again the material is a combination of thinly veiled biography and heavy-handed fantasy. You use the details of your own boarding school and place within those details yourself as an idealized creation, a writer talented but with a checkered past and an unreliable conscience. You yourself have neither—at least not to a degree anybody would find interesting. You have never adulterized, have rarely insulted anyone, and go quietly home from the pub after two pints. You have no illusions about leading your students into the promised land of the historical moment; in fact, you have no illusions about anything at all.

18

Life goes on this way—wind and leaves, the corny tearing of the calendar page—until one October afternoon, after explaining to your A. P. seniors the theological underpinnings of "Everything that Rises Must Converge," you go to check your e-mail and there is death—exactly where you expected it would be.

> (Salutation,)
>
> I am sad to inform you Fr. passed away. He has a viewing this evening in Philadelphia and then a mass tomorrow morning at St. Ignatius Church in Baltimore and then afterward is being buried at the Woodstock cemetery, also in Baltimore.
>
> I think of you often, and gather you are a quite successful writer.
>
> Be well,
> (Former Student X)

You write back, describing what you were doing on the day of the old priest's passing—the conversation you had with your students about "the world of guilt and sorrow" just moments before reading of the old priest's death—expressing regret that you were not present and asking the obvious questions. What you really want are the details that will allow you to form a resolution—the resolution that will allow you to close the book.

(Salutation,)

The viewing was in Philadelphia at Manresa Hall on Friday, October 27th. A place for old and dying priests. There were about 10 really old priests in walkers and wheelchairs, as well as former student Y and former student Z and myself from the class of 1982. There was also one gentleman from Gonzaga's class of 1961, who is an architect in Bryn Mawr now, and one other impaired middle-aged man present. I overheard the gentleman with a short leg and hearing aid tell another priest that when he was at Georgetown Prep he was bullied because of a speech impediment and his limp, and Fr. helped put an end to it. The day was cloudy, cold, and drizzling wet. After the viewing he was taken to Baltimore. Fr. Lemmon did the ceremony (I was not there) at St. Ignatius Church. Apparently, there is a Woodstock cemetery in Baltimore, and that is where he will be buried.

As for not seeing him. . .no one knew how sick he was. I saw him in mid-September. My wife Susan (I recently got married) and I went to the Provincial's House in Baltimore where he was living and took him out for lunch. We showed him our wedding pictures. Of course he had his cigarettes and martini. He was frail. When I inquired to his health, as I always did, he said "not bad for a man of my age, don't you think?"

In early October, he was sent to Manresa Hall in Philadelphia. They could not care for him at the Provincial's House in Baltimore any longer; for the last year he had been struggling with throat and neck cancer. Yet even his sister and niece, nor anyone close to him knew until a week or two before he died. He was in Philadelphia, 15 minutes away from me, and I did not even know. His sister remarked that it was the typical Irish way, not to talk about illness and dying. That is all she could understand of not knowing, and she would be likely to do the same, if she was dying.

As for "the world of guilt and sorrow," remember Flannery O'Connor also said "All is sacred, nothing profane," and as Fr. used to quote to me from Teresa of Avila, "All is well, all manner of things are well, and all manner of things will be well." Fr. would not want us to spend any useless time on guilt and sorrow.

In the last month, the cancer became extremely aggressive, and he developed a large tumor on his neck and left chin. It was visible, although I did not see it a month ago. On his last day, Friday, October 20th, he got up, although hard to eat and talk at this point. He got dressed. At lunch went outside to smoke and had a drink while reading the New York Times. After lunch he told the head nurse he was going to take a nap. She went in to check on him, because that was not typical, and after a time, he appeared to wake up abruptly, got halfway up from the bed, looked her way, collapsed to his side and died. He went without pain, quickly, doing what he loved—smoking, drinking, and reading. He said to me, he thought of death as a perfectly open door, with bright light radiating, and that one day he would casually walk through the door. He also told me he cared about this life, and that he did not give a shit about death because it was completely unknowable.

It is particularly strange that you were teaching Flannery O'Connor and the underpinnings of theology. I am sitting here with Fr.'s Master's Thesis from Louvain completed April 2, 1954, entitled "Theology and Prayer."

In it Fr. writes, "A book is a machine to think with. In a good book this statement is verified both for the reader and writer alike. I do not flatter myself that this short paper offers that advantage to any reader it may have. My problem is too personal, as is the solution I have worked out for myself. This paper is a nothing more than a machine for thinking out a problem that has long troubled me. It were better compared to a loom upon which I propose to weave some of the unraveled elements of science, service, and prayer. My problem in its simplest form was this: how to integrate the elements of prayer, theology, and daily routine into a unified whole? Or more exactly, what is the point at which theology can become the living source, the principle of prayer and action? If such a point of insertion existed, and I did not for a moment doubt that it did, I wanted to find it and to formulate it as accurately as possible. Because, above all, my solution had to be a practical solution. I wanted a principle that would be operative beyond the walls of the Theologate, that would prolong, not only the effects of our four years of study, but would keep theology as the central point of reference from which all flowed and to which all returned, so that no phase of my life as a priest would not know its permeating presence. I think I have found such a principle in that method of theological reasoning we call the 'Argumentum ex Convenientia.' I look upon the 'Agumentum ex Convenientia' as the summit of theological reasoning, that towards which all the rest of theology is ultimately oriented; and I find that it is at the same time a form of prayer, a method, if you want to place it in a category, which partakes of the nature of contemplation.

"If the objection were raised at this point that I am assigning too large a place to Theology in the life of prayer, that the spiritual life can be lived on the highest level without any reference, explicit at least, to theology, I would reply that although this might be true, it should not be true in the case of a Jesuit."

Fr. goes on to say that "To highlight one aspect of this interdependence of Theology and Sanctity is my purpose here." Much of the writing is in French and hence I am unable to translate, given my poor skills as a French student.

As for my life, I am a tenure track assistant professor of counseling at Community College of Philadelphia. I love my work. I hear Fr. in my work every day as a teacher and counselor. I got married in June and live in Collingswood, New Jersey with my wife Susan, a medical writer from a Nebraska farm of strong willed German stock. She has a Ph.D. in food science and an MBA, was in the Peace Corps in Ghana, and lived in Tunisia for a year doing research. She is a fascinating woman, and she makes me a better man.

I struggle every day with good and evil in my life, but it is a worthy fight. I am not a very good Christian or Catholic, but I never give up the fight. Sometimes I make the fight harder than it needs to be, but I guess I fight better as an underdog.

Life is beautiful, fleeting and tragic, and I love every minute of it.

I have attached a picture of Fr. a little less than a year before he died, and a wedding picture.

I hope you are well. Thank You.

Your brother through Christ,

(Former Student X)

20

In Maytime of a certain year, in the auditorium of your Catholic grammar school, you attended a vocational fair hosted by the Maryknoll Fathers, who are missionaries. You saw a glossy illustration of a Maryknoll
Father who'd been tortured by savages, and you got an erotic charge. In
the same week you read *Dracula*, which was your favorite novel until
The Scarlet Letter came along a few years later. In Maytime of a certain
year you began to see the connection between sex and death. Sex is sin
is death. Then, as you continued to look, it really got confusing. Sex is
sin is death is the resurrection and the life. The old priest:

"Once, in that Jesuit house in Vienna, I found a room that was like a
medieval torture chamber. There were whips and straps, iron benches
and wooden racks. Good heavens!"

"But why would anybody want to do such things?"

"To abase the flesh, of course."

"But why would you want to do *that*?"

"*Idiot.*"

"Did you try it?"

"I went in there one afternoon, the room completely empty and still,
sunlight coming in through the barred windows and the little chinks in
the wall, and I thought of Itchy, and I flogged my bare back mercilessly
for one hour. There are some things lost to us in modern times that
ought not to be lost. Many things, actually, that most people would call
barbaric, or medieval, but ideas and practices we might need all the
same. Things lost to us which we can't do without, even if we don't
know we can't do without them."

In the end you are alone, a bachelor-teacher at a posh New England
boarding school. Not the worst life you could have imagined for yourself, though a suite of rooms at the boarding school would be better

539

than taking the train each morning from North Station. Your colleagues are entertained no end with the stories of your colorful past, the casino days of your profligate youth. Oh, how they wish they had lived such a varied and adventurous life!

In the end you are alone in your room, still thinking of the old priest, what to say about your friendship, your "relationship," what not to say, how to write an end to this, if the ending is yours to write. As a young man you were awkward and depressed, youthfully morbid but far from Keatsian. Women found you dull, ponderous—"bloodless," one of the cleverer ones called you from the other side of an open doorway—intelligent but without much style or imagination. The old priest alone took an interest in you. Years later you read a few newspaper articles that caused you to see this overweening interest in a somewhat different light.

In the rooming house in Atlantic City where you settled down after college the old priest came for a visit that very first summer, jaunty in his white polo shirt and Madras shorts. You sat up all night smoking cigarettes and drinking gin and tonics, the two of you talking with the drunken high-mindedness of fraternity boys. Later you found out from former student X that it was the real and true *modus operandi* of the old priest to stay up all night smoking and drinking with a former student, talking all that drunken, high-minded talk until daybreak, but then, at that moment in time when it was taking place, you thought it was the first time it had happened to either one of you. In the morning you walked the block to the beach and swam before breakfast in the gently breaking waves. He sang "O Mio Bambino Caro," plunging up and down in the easy current, and you can still see his face as it was in the early sunlight, spouting water from both nostrils and singing in Italian. Later you cooked cheese omelets then lay together side by side on the pullout sofa which was his bed, holding hands. As he drifted off to sleep his final words were not his own. They were Shakespeare's: "I will grapple you to my bosom with hoops of steel."

After he left you decided the whole thing had been a terrible mistake. A few months later you went to see him, in Philadelphia, to explain it to him. You walked along the cobblestone streets of Old City, sullen and intractable, refusing to hold his hand. "Bare ruined choirs where late the sweet birds sang," was his reply, gazing up into the leafless branches of the maple trees.

Two lines of Shakespeare (plus a little Puccini) to fix in place the simple but overwhelming fact: you loved another person, even though you did your best to cancel it out or turn it into something else, even if it was your right to cancel it out and even if it really was something else, something other than what you took it for at the time, whatever that was.

The ending, then: you loved him, something you were in a big hurry to forget but which he was in a bigger hurry to remember. For he loved you also. That is the one thing you seem most of all to avoid considering. Others he loved as well, perhaps—at least that has been your suspicion all these years, supported mainly by the leering presence of former student X—but he loved you, or at least the person you were in your youth. The handsome boy with the David Bowie pants and the nicotine-stained fingers, the frenetic teenager bursting with promise and the will to please.

All right, love is love but resentment is also resentment, and little by little you came to resent the way the old priest continued to look at you, as if he could fix you in a certain moment of your life and experience and keep you there. As if you yourself were a story to be told, and told the way he'd decided to tell it!

As if you alone could save him.

And so one day you went away, intending to return, as many another times you'd come and gone, but things happened, one thing and then the next, time and distance, and you never got the chance to go back.

You abandoned him, is what really happened.

Just face up to the ending, the real ending, even if that's not how your book ends.

The book ends with you and the old priest having martinis and Chinese takeout the evening before he is to be placed in Assisted Living. The book ends with the old priest, having gone a bit senile, drinking martinis and casting out imaginary demons between bites of tea smoked duck.

But this story does not end with imaginary demons and cold dim sum.

He betrayed you, is what really happened, following which you betrayed him. You abandoned him also, following which he abandoned you.

Just face up to it. Be honest. Admit what happened and move on

Nominated by Salvatore Scibona.

VECTORS 3.1 : APHORISMS AND TEN SECOND ESSAYS

by JAMES RICHARDSON

from HOTEL AMERIKA

1

In the long run there is only the short run.

2

Maybe what interests us in the mirror is not ourselves but that person who looks so interested in us.

3

Some are always naked, some never.

4

History repeats itself is roughly equivalent to *Language repeats itself*. And having heard all the words doesn't make it any easier to know what to say.

5

The frog eats flies but grows no wings.

6

I'm blissfully solitary for a few minutes, and then who shows up but myself?

7

Even words are beyond words.

8

The cycle of wars will end when the vanquished are properly grateful.

9

There's no reason for my discontent, but I'm sure I'll find one.

10

Zeal strikes not from conviction but in order to believe.

11

Not till I walk out of the sea of noise into the night do I know I'm drunk.

12

His anger is a mine happy to be stepped on.

13

Gods, too, get promoted to their level of incompetence.

14

She thinks her frenzy is a victimless crime.

15

When the Devil offers his restructured deal—*Everything you could possibly wish for, yes, even more wishes!*—just remember that the best things in your life are things you would not have known exactly how to wish for.

16

My resentment is a child who needs attention. *I'm out of here*, he says. *Don't let me go.*

17

You try to take it back, but the tape in reverse is unintelligible.

18

Suffering builds character? Or a mind tensed for more suffering that understands every touch as a blow.

19
Hatred, like love, thrives on silly details.

20
Credit says I may not have to pay it back. After all, I am really borrowing from my future self, and he is kind.

21
Let's not burn that bridge till we cross it.

22
Labor must be the opposite of laughter since the least funny thing is someone working hard to be funny.

23
Useless to try to do what the world tells you to, since what it really wants is something better than it knows how to say.

24
Democracy and individualism are inconsistent: everyone else is wrong.

25
That's a great point. Meaning *I have already thought of it and will now elaborate.*

26
Imperishable fame is one of the oldest phrases in language, and the first justification for literature. Did it wink out forever in my lifetime? Or is it just that it was always an idea of the young, who needed to believe that the work ahead of them would last forever? An idea more credible in the millennia when few lived long enough to see greatness forgotten, or to forget it themselves.

27
What they call creativity is just an accident we learn how to keep having.

28

Comforting how few of the stupidest things I've said anyone seems to remember. Apparently only I knew enough about what I was really thinking to know how monumentally stupid they really were.

29

The self does not exist. But just try to change it.

30

He was so slow to speak that even silence put words in his mouth.

31

Realism exposes itself by caring a little too much that you think it's real.

32

When the power goes off, the silence wakes me.

33

It's a baseball truism that left-handed hitters like the ball low. That's because the right hemisphere is best at tracking moving objects and it controls the left visual field of both eyes. Given the tilt of a lefty batter's head, the left visual fields are lower than the right. Where else was I going to publish this theory?

34

I'm far less likely to say *That's too young for me* than *I'm too old for that*, maybe hoping someone will tell me I'm not.

35

What's the name for the color of leaves at night, a black you cannot see as other than green?

36

Seems like the older I get the fewer reasons there are to do the things I don't want to, which makes them both harder and easier to do.

37

I like hanging out with kids, since youth is contagious. Only now—
like my colds, like the years—it's shorter and less intense.

38

The day is so bad I think *At least it will be a good story*. And then,
the worse it is, the better.

39

Somehow it's easier to believe people are better than I am than that
they are smarter.

40

Good thing I'm too ignorant to know this has already been said.

41

The unbeliever's prayer: *Help me so little I don't notice. Be the luck I
can take credit for*.

42

Our darkest secret is that we don't need each other. Though it's not a
secret. Though it's not true.

Nominated by Renee Ashley, BJ Ward, Richard Kostelanetz

I LOOK AT A PHOTOGRAPH

by ADAM ZAGAJEWSKI

from TIN HOUSE

I look at a photograph of the city where I was born,
at its lush gardens and winding streets, at the hills,
the Catholic roofs, the domes of Orthodox churches,
where on Sunday the basses sing so mightily
that neighboring trees sway as in a hurricane;
I gaze at the photograph, I can't tear my eyes away
and suddenly I imagine that they're all still alive
as if nothing had happened, they still scurry to lectures,
wait for trains, take sky-blue trams,
check calendars with alarm, step on scales,
listen to Verdi's arias and their favorite operetta,
read newspapers that are still white,
live in haste, in fear, are always late,
are a bit immortal, but don't know it,
one's behind with the rent, another fears consumption,
a third can't finish his thesis on Kant,
doesn't understand what things are in themselves,
my grandmother still goes to Brzuchowice carrying
a cake on her outstretched arms and they don't droop,
in the pharmacy a shy boy requests a cure for shyness,
a girl examines her small breasts in a mirror,
my cousin goes to the park straight from his bath
and doesn't guess that soon he'll catch pneumonia,
enthusiasm erupts at times, in winter yellow lamps
create cozy circles, in July flies loudly celebrate

the summer's great light and hum twilit hymns,
pogroms occur, uprisings, deportations,
the cruel Wehrmacht in becoming uniforms,
the foul NKVD invades, red stars
promise friendship but signify betrayal,
but they don't see it, they almost don't see it,
they have so much to do, they need
to lay up coal for winter, find a good doctor,
the unanswered letters grow, the brown ink fades,
a radio plays in the room, their latest buy, but they're
still wearied by ordinary life and death,
they don't have time, they apologize,
they write long letters and laconic postcards,
they're always late, hopelessly late,
the same as us, exactly like us, like me.

Nominated by Tin House, Naomi J. Williams

THE THING'S IMPOSSIBLE

by BRUCE BENNETT

from PLOUGHSHARES

> *Perhaps the single feature of the villanelle*
> *that twentieth-century poets made their own*
> *is the absence of narrative possibility. . .*
> *the form refuses to tell a story. . .*
>
> *—The Making of a Poem*

Don't write a villanelle to tell a tale:
they're not the form for narrative or plot.
It's pretty obvious why you will fail.

For instance, there's an island; you set sail.
The wind is perfect, and the day is hot.
Don't write a villanelle to tell a tale,

Because, well, you will have to see a whale,
a wonder, but it can't be caught, or shot.
You see? It's obvious why you will fail.

Say, you're with her, and you're both at the rail;
(I don't think I have mentioned it's a yacht—
don't write a villanelle to tell a tale!)

A magic moment. You'll embrace. The ale
your steward brought will just have hit the spot.
But wait. It should be obvious you'll fail

Since now her husband, who's been sprung from jail,
is in that sloop approaching, and he's got—
Don't write a villanelle to tell a tale.
The thing's impossible. You're bound to fail!

Nominated bu Jay Rogoff, William Trowbridge

MADE TO MEASURE

by SUE ALLISON

from THE ANTIOCH REVIEW

There was a period in my life when I knew the increments of an hour with pinpoint accuracy. What happened was this: my watch broke and when I didn't immediately replace it, for reasons I no longer recall, to my surprise, I soon discovered that I didn't need a watch at all. I started by clocks on buildings or the position of the sun or, when it was cloudy, the quality of the light. But though it happened gradually it seemed that all of a sudden I simply always knew what time it was. It was as if I had acquired a sixth sense. To be free of the tic of constantly checking my wrist was liberating. I always knew not only where in the world I was—41st and Madison, say—but also when. That was a time in my life when what time it was mattered and, without a watch, I told time the old-fashioned way: by physically moving through it in space. This is simpler than it sounds if you live in New York, which is an easy place to tell time if you are afoot. A Manhattan block running along the north/ south axis is about a twentieth of a mile, and since I knew it took twenty minutes to walk twenty blocks at a brisk and even pace, I could not only calculate my arrival at my destination, but also self-correct along the way, calibrate, as it were, the measuring mechanism that was me. Late, I speeded up; later still, I ran the lights. I may have been a point on a graph, a walking Cartesian equation, blithely mapping my day with precision, but the physics of being in time felt less like science and more like dancing.

But what was transformational was the sense I had of being constantly present. Liberated from telling time, I owned time. It wasn't really that I knew the time: I was time. And I cannot help but wonder if perhaps this is why I remember the ordinary physical details of that period of my life with uncanny, almost hyper-real, cinematic vividness. And that it is perhaps the reason we remember childhood with such clarity—that perfect, timeless, period of our lives before we were taught to tell time and time became our master. The old, who feel that the older they get the less time they have, say that youth is wasted on the young, but it is really time that is wasted on the old.

A fifth, a finger, a foe; a jerk, a jigger, a drop; a pottle, a pood, a parasang. A poppy seed, a barley corn, a scruple, a quintal, a quire, a parsec. The lexicon of measurement bounces and sizzles with sound, but look them up and they have meanings. A windle is 3-3 1/2 bushels of grain, a pottle half a gallon. But the particular beauty of measurement words is that they are more than signifiers of volume, distance, size. They are words, and as words are tropes, metaphors, small poems grounded in the human experience while reaching to describe the indescribable and somehow managing the job. They are windows through which we can view not only the past, but human nature itself, telling us what we measured and how. A cord of wood was a good amount, a cartload what a cart could hold, and the size of a hogshead depended on what was in it, oil, say, or wine, and where it had been filled: London or an outlying shire. A plethron was Greek for the amount of land a yoke of oxen could plough in a day; parasang was the Persian word for the distance a man could walk in an hour. The poppyseed was the elemental unit of length in Anglo Saxon England: four made a barley corn and twenty barley corns made a scruple, which was a unit of measure that would be about the size and weight of a small pebble. A scruple is no longer a measure, but what keeps us, as if we had a pebble in our shoe, to a measured step.

Why do we measure? "To put order and coherence into the picture of nature," said Aristotle. It is our nature; we have always measured; it is in all the recorded histories. We seek patterns, we tell stories, we make things—pillars, pyramids, paintings, poems—and we measure. And though we take it for granted, "in stride," as it were, clock-time and measurable space are man-, not nature-made. If not our earliest invention, it is perhaps our best, for it is the one that made all others possible. The history of man is the history of measure; of measure, man.

It starts with wonder. How far away is the moon? Aristarchus of Samos calculated the distance as 240,000 miles, which it is when it is closest to Earth in its elliptical, not circular, orbit. How many grains of sand would fit in the universe? After first inventing large numbers, Archimedes, the mathematics genius born in 276 B.C., and whom Horace called "the measurer of earth and ocean and numberless sand," came up with ten to the power of sixty-three. But he did not say ten to the power of sixty-three. The metric system hadn't been invented yet. One of the fiercest proponents for the creation of the metric system was Carl Friedrich Gauss (who ranks with Archimedes and Newton). Rather than praise Archimedes for all he achieved, Gauss took the ancient Greek to task for not also inventing the metric system. "To what heights would science now be raised if Archimedes had made that discovery!" he wrote in 1832 in a letter urging the French Republic to adopt decimals.

Standardizing measurement seems like a good idea, one naturally born, as it was, of the so-called Age of Reason, but as reasonable an idea as it is, we continue to inch along. We take a measured step. We weigh our words before we speak, our options before we decide. We raise or lower the bar, size up our adversaries, tell tall tales, gauge our progress. It is as if measuring, like making metaphors, is simply what the brain does as it tries to make sense of the world.

The beauty of words is that they are unstable—they change, they stretch, they have various and multiple meanings—but the beauty of numbers is that they are not. The move to metric measurement has meant a move from words—jigger, pottle, nip—and their maddening refusal to remain fixed as if to remain constant is death itself, which, it turns out, it is—to numbers. It has been a move, specifically, to numbers of ten. This is quite efficient. It means that the size of everything, from the diameter of a proton, which is 10 to the power of minus 15, to the size of the entire non-visible universe (according to cosmic inflation theory), which is 10 to the power of 53, can be described in one simple, systematic way. The whole world, from molecules on a DNA helix to the length of the Trans Siberian Railroad, can be described as a power of ten, as if we are all one family of Russian stacking dolls. Pretty neat trick, but does it work? Is it not too perfect? Are we really only a string of zeroes?

Nature is random, relative, uncertain, unpredictable, messy, cluttered, chaotic. It can be harsh, cold, difficult, unyielding. But does this diminish its beauty? Is it not in its so-called imperfection that its beauty lies? There must be a reason that a single imperfection on an otherwise unblemished face is called a beauty mark. Gothic cathedral builders knew the reason. They always added at least one mistake to make the building accessible; it was at the point of imperfection, they believed, that the human imagination could enter.

Brought forward to the twentieth century, Gauss's argument would claim that it was the metric system of measurement that allowed scientists not only to measure the size of a proton or the rate of the expansion of the universe, but to know these things at all. Measurement is an instrument to knowing. To know something, we measure it. Once measured, we know it. In the beginning, we measured what we knew: the length of Egypt, the perimeter of a pyramid, the height of a horse. Now we know because we measure. To measure is to know, to know is to measure. But measuring as a means to knowledge is limited. It is limiting because it is self-defining. Measuring to know, we know what we measure. Once we measure it, it is a thing measured, but is it anything more?

Or is measuring merely a compulsion? In 2002, Yasumasa Kanada led a nine-man team from the University of Tokyo to calculate *pi* to a trillion decimal places. It was Kanada's fifteenth calculation; in his first, in 1982, he calculated *pi* to 8,388,576 decimal places. He is probably still working on it, climbing his private Everest. How far can we go? How fast can we get there? How difficult can we make the route?

Pi is an irrational number. An inch worm is a measure worm. A meter is the length light travels in 1/2999,792, 458[ths] of a second. A second is the duration of 9,192,631,770 periods of radiation corresponding to the transition between the two hyperfine levels of the ground state of the cesium 133 atom. An inch is 0.0254 meters. It was in the Age of Reason, as it is called, that the metric system was created, passed by the French Revolutionary Assembly in 1795. On June 22, 1799, two platinum standards representing the meter and the kilogram were placed in the Archives de la Republique, where they remain. While most of the world has accepted SI, short for International System, or *Systeme Internationale*, the U.S. and Malaysia remain holdouts, though there is a strong argument for the standardization of measurement, and not only to ease global trade or even to defray confusion at the Olympics, where sprints are measured in meters but long jumps in inches. In 1999, the NASA Mars Climate Orbiter was destroyed on entering orbit due to the fact that different computer programs running the mission were using different measurement systems. In the same year the Korean Air cargo flight 6316 was lost on its way from Shanghai to Seoul when the crew acted on tower instructions given in meters as if they had been given in feet. It has never been found.

A bit is the fundamental measure of what in information theory is called information content and is a single digit having two values. Four bits is a nibble. Eight bits is a byte. Sixteen bits is four nibbles, or two bytes, or a half a word. A word is the information transferred from one system to another in a single package.

There are 615,000 words in the Oxford English Dictionary. One of the earliest dictionaries, or word lists, as they were called, was Robert Cawdrey's *A Table Alphabetical*, published in 1604; it had 2,500 words, which explains why Shakespeare had to add thousands of new words to the lexicon. There weren't enough to say all he had to say about the human condition, though Homer used a mere 1,500 different words in his odes and epics. Interestingly, both Globish, an international business language, and the Voice of America also use a vocabulary reduced to exactly 1,500 different words, though neither includes heart-grieving, swift-sailing, city-sacking, stout-hearted, silver-footed, wonder, wont, woo, wroth, weeping, pity, slay, spare, or sate.

Diction is the metrical arrangement of words. Meter, more or less regular rhythm, can be syllabic, meaning a certain number of syllables; accentual, meaning certain syllables are stressed; or accentual syllabic; or qualitative, which emphasizes duration over stress. In the 992-page *Princeton Encyclopedia of Poetry and Poetics*, the entry for "measure" occupies a mere fourteen lines. It is defined as "a metrical group or period." Period. Not the be-all and end-all of verse.

Galileo, who had more than a few inventions of his own, said that the alphabet was mankind's most stupendous invention of all.

Herodotus invented history. He is called the father of recorded history because he was the first to record it, but what Herodotus did, essentially, was take the measure of the known world, its sights, its stories, and its size. It is from him that we know that the walls of Babylon were 335 feet high and 85 feet thick. And that a distance of a three-day journey was the line keeping friend from foe. The distance from the Maeotic lake (today's Sea of Azov) to the river Phasis was "a thirty-day journey for an active traveler." The length of the Caspian Sea was a rowing voyage of fifteen days; its breadth, eight. Lake Moer, he said was, "7 days journey from the sea" and the coastal length of Egypt 60 schoeni.

Ten Egyptian schoeni equaled twenty Persian parasangs equaled 600

English furlongs, a furlong being the length of a furrow, intentionally made to be the distance a team of oxen could plow without a rest—or forty rods, or 10 chains, or 220 yards, or 660 feet, or an eighth of a mile: it takes twelve to round the track at Belmont. Herodotus explained differing measures. "Men who are pinched for land," he wrote, "measure by fathoms; those who are less pinched, by furlongs; those who have much by parasangs; those who have plenty, by schoeni. The parasang is thirty furlongs, and the schoenus is sixty furlongs." A Greek stadion was sixty steps, or about 200 meters, and a customary length, then as now, for a foot race.

"Man is the measure of all things" is more than probably the best-known aphorism. It is a cornerstone of Western thought. The saying was Protagoras' and comes to us from Plato, the wisest man in Greece of his time, and survives by way of Plato's dialogue "Cratylus," in which Socrates addresses the nature of truth and in which he repeats this saying. But what does it mean that man is the measure of all things? And what did Protagoras mean? Man is the measure of all things if by all things we mean what man can measure? Or did Protagoras mean that man is the standard by which all things are measured? The first recorded measurement, as a hieroglyph on Egyptian walls, was the cubit, the distance from a man's fingertip to his elbow. It was with the cubit, a square level, and a plumb bob the pyramids were built. The royal cubit was, of course, longer than the cubit. It was longer by three fingerbreadths. A fingerbreadth was the width of the middle of the middle finger. Using hands to measure, a digit was the width of the tip of the middle finger, called a nail in England. A palm was the width of four fingers held together; a span the distance from the tip of the thumb to the tip of the little finger on an outstretched hand.

But Protagoras was not talking about forearms, fingers, feet, or fathoms, the height of a man (six feet) and the customary depth of a grave. Protagoras was talking about truth, and the truth he was talking about was moral and the statement he was making was that there is no absolute moral truth, only what men believed and agreed to believe to be true, making each society's belief as true as another's. Today we call this moral relativism. Socrates and Plato, who believed in absolutes, disagreed fiercely.

If there are absolutes, who is the standard, against which others can measure themselves, for justice, for heroism, for beauty? The Trojan War was ostensibly waged to retrieve Agamemnon's wife, Helen, the most beautiful woman in Greece. She was "the face," as Christopher

Marlowe wrote in *The Tragical History of Dr. Faustus*, "that launched a thousand ships." But was the war really fought for Helen, who, Herodotus related, had not been behind Troy's walls at the time at all, but was in Egypt raising her sons? Which could be why *The Iliad* ends with no mention of rescuing Helen, only of the horrible death of Hector by Achilles. Helen remains the standard of beauty, Achilles of rage, Agamemnon of revenge, Penelope, who waited twenty years for her husband's return, of wifely fidelity, Odysseus of wiles.

In 1929, Moritz Schlick, the leader of the Vienna Circle, a group of cutting-edge physicists, published a booklet espousing the circle's credo, transforming Protagoras' saying from man to measure. "Man is the measure of all things. Whatever question is not susceptible to measurement . . . is no question at all." But we can measure nothing, too. Nullity is the mechanism by which scientists measure what they do not know, balancing what they can measure with what they cannot until the scale evens out and they know what they didn't know by knowing its measure. Nullity is the way our nervous system works, a nervous system that can register pain in limbs that are not there.

What do we measure? Everything. We measure IQ, we measure earthquakes, we measure wind chill, wrenches, wire gauge, tornadoes, comas, grit, type; we measure the brightness of lunar eclipses; the hardness of pencils, of gypsum, of talc. We measure the brain activity of meditating monks (very high). We measure brain size. The encephalization quotient is the size of a brain relative to the size of the animal it's in (humans 7, chimps 2); scientists think the measure has something to do with intelligence but they're not sure what. We measure shoelaces: a shoe with four pairs of holes takes a sixty-centimeter-long lace. We measure consumer satisfaction, carbon emissions, the rate at which the permafrost is melting. We measure justice. Themis carries a scale to make this point: justice is not some abstract value; it is something we measure. We measure what matters to us; once measured, it matters more.

The first person to measure the earth was Eratosthenes, in 276 B.C., the chief librarian at the great library of Alexandria, where he read on one of the library's papyri about a city in which a column at noon on the summer solstice cast no shadow. Wondering if a stick planted in Alexandria, a twenty-mile voyage up the Nile from Syene, would also cast no shadow, when the next summer solstice came around, he planted one and when a shadow was cast, he knew the earth was curved. This was interesting, but he wasn't trying to prove that the earth was round.

But knowing that it was, he knew he had to measure the earth, he needed to measure the curve. That the ratio of the circumference of any circle to its diameter was slightly more than three, the circular constant we call *pi*, was common knowledge in the ancient world, known independently in Egypt, Babylon, and the Indus Valley. So Eratosthenes was able to calculate that the Earth was 28,750 miles around. We measure it, at the equator, as 24,901 miles, making Eratosthenes' calculation remarkably close, given that one of his dimensions, the distance from Alexandria to Syene, was paced out, but Eratosthenes' great achievement was proving that the earth could be measured scientifically.

On a scale of one to ten, ten being the worst pain you can bear—I hate that question. I can never answer it. I don't know how much pain I can bear and I don't want to know. Even if I could bear a lot of pain, which when I don't have any I think I can, it doesn't mean it wouldn't hurt. What if we measured pain differently? If pain were measured in inches, how tall would your pain be? My pain is as tall as a house, a skyscraper; it is as deep as a primordial sea; as distant as forgetting, as near as loss. In 1940, James D. Hardy, Herbert G. Wolff, and Helen Goodell, all of Cornell University, invented what they called the dolorimeter to measure pain scientifically. It was a good idea, but it didn't work. Results could not be replicated. In 1971, Ronald Melzack and Warren Torgerson, psychologists of McGill University, invented what they called the McGill Pain Index, which broke ground by not using a machine and by not rating pain on a scale, but by providing patients with a vocabulary (organized in categories), with words to describe the pain they felt. These are the words doctors want to hear when they ask how it feels: flickering, pulsing, quivering, throbbing, beating, pounding, jumping, flashing, shooting, boring, drilling, stabbing, sharp, gritting, lacerating, pinching, pressing, gnawing, cramping, crushing, tugging, pulling, wrenching, hot, burning, scalding, searing, tingling, itching, smarting, stinging, dull, sore, aching, heavy, tender, taut, rasping, splitting, tiring, exhausting, sickening, suffocating, fearful, frightful, terrifying, punishing, grueling, cruel, vicious, killing, wretched, binding, annoying, troublesome, miserable, intense, unbearable, spreading, radiating, penetrating, piercing, tight, numb, squeezing, drawing, tearing, cool, cold, freezing, nagging, nauseating, agonizing, dreadful, torturing.

Justin O. Schmidt created the Schmidt Pain Index in 1984 to describe the pain caused by stings from saw flies, bees, and ants. The sweat bee's sting is, he wrote, "light, ephemeral, almost fruity, like a tiny spark has singed a single hair on your arm," while the sting from a tarantula hawk feels like "a blinding, fierce, shockingly electric pain, like having a running hair drier dropped into your bubble bath." And a bite from a bullet ant causes "pure, intense, brilliant pain, like fire-walking over flaming charcoal with a three-inch rusty nail in your heel."

In acoustics, a sone is the unit of perceived loudness, the range being from 0.02 sone, the sound of calm breathing or leaves rustling, to 676: the human threshold of acoustic pain. The misery index was created in 1960 by the economist Arthur Okun when he was an advisor to Lyndon Johnson to measure the state of the economy. It is calculated by adding the unemployment rate and the inflation rate; these should move in opposite directions, inflation easing when unemployment rises and climbing as people get back to work. Jimmy Carter won the 1976 presidential election by citing a national misery index of 13.57 percent and claiming that no one responsible for that had the right to be president; when he was running again, it had reached 21.98 percent, the highest it has ever been since the index was invented. He lost. The Misery Index is closely tied to the Consumer Price Index, which is closely tied to the Consumer Satisfaction Index, which measures consumer happiness. In 1972, Bhutan's King Jigme Singye Wangchuck dismissed criticism about his sluggish economy by claiming title to the index of Gross National Happiness to explain why his country was not as interested in developing manufacturing as it was in its Buddhist values.

How do we measure? In as many ways as there are things to measure. We measure in stacks and skeins and stories, a lovely word for a building's height that comes to us from Gothic cathedral builders who described the heights of their constructions by the number of stacked stained glass windows they installed. We measure horses by hands. We say pea-sized, dime-sized, walnut-sized and know what we're talking about. We measure by Eiffel Towers, Statues of Liberty, football fields, London double-decker buses. We measure by Belgiums. We give ballpark estimates. Australians use the sydarb to indicate volume. One sydarb equals the amount of water in Sydney Harbor. We escape by a hair's breadth, we need wiggle room, we keep an arm's length. A hair's breadth is 0.1 millimeters. It takes 48 to make an inch. A beard-second is the length an average beard grows in a second: five nanometers. One nanometer is one-billionth of a meter. We measure in steps. A blink is 0.864 seconds to a wink's 3,000ths of a microsecond, making a blink much slower than a wink.

We measure in steps. One step is thirty inches, though U.S. marching bands use a twenty-two-and-a-half-inch step—eight steps for every five-yard line of a football field. A pace is the measure of a full stride from the position of a heel when it is raised from the ground to the point it is set down again. In Rome, it spanned five feet. A mile got its name from the Latin *milliarium*, the name for military stones erected every 1,000 paces along the Roman highways. The odometer was thought to have been invented by Archimedes during the first Punic War. Chariots, whose wheels were four feet in diameter, turned four hundred times in one Roman mile. As the wheels turned, pebbles placed in a gear box were dropped one by one into another box, to be counted at journey's end.

In ancient Mesopotamia, there were twelve counting systems. One was used for slaves, animals, fish, wooden objects, stone objects, and containers. Another was used to count dead animals; another for tallying amounts of cereal, bread, fish, milk; still another for wheat, another for rations, another for fields; still another to count barley, and still another, malt. Before the Statute of England in 1592 defined the mile as 5,280 feet, the Irish mile was 6,721 feet, the Scottish mile was 5,951 feet, and the London mile was eight furlongs, each furlong being 625 feet, for a total of 5,000 feet.

Making measures uniform has value, to be sure, particularly in a world now almost completely one global community, without its idiosyncratic differences, but is there the same poetry in nano macro micro byte as there is in a bale, a bundle, a ball, a baht? Perhaps. Nano macro micro byte is cute, but like all cute things, lacks depth. They are powers of ten and tell no other tale. A bale is ten reams of paper or a bundle of hay left in the field until needed. A bundle could also be forty quires or twenty hanks of yarn or a package of shingles with which to roof a house; a ball is the measure for the degree of ice covering a polar sea; and a baht the weight of a silver coin in Thailand weighing 15 grams. There are stories in words that do not exist in numbers.

Metrology is a cold world and science itself seems bored by it. Physicists, it seems, like to name their discoveries with their human, not their scientific, natures. Reflecting the need to ground themselves in the real words, rather than abstract numbers, they talk in barns (1.0×10 to the minus 28 meters squared) and sheds (1.0×10 to the minus 24 barns) and outhouses (do you really want to know?), and shakes, the time it takes a lamb to shake its tail, which nuclear engineers have given as the name for ten nanoseconds. And it is how we got quark for the most fundamental particles of the universe and the "flavors" they come in: up, down, charm, strange, top, and bottom. Someone's going to have to straighten this out all over again someday.

Quark was coined by its discoverer, Murray Gell-Mann, winner of the Nobel Prize in 1969, when he happened across it, in *Finnegan's Wake*. In a letter dated June 27, 1978, he explained his epiphany. "I employed the sound quork for several weeks in 1963 before noticing "quark" in *Finnegan's Wake* when the bartender calls, "Three quarks for Muster Mark!" Gell-Mann measured a quark as being smaller than 10 to the minus 19 in radius, but with no actual size and no actual internal structure. Joyce is famous for his linguistic brilliance, so where he got the word is anyone's guess. It is a nineteenth-century word for what frogs and herons did before frogs croaked and herons cawed.

In the 1600s, a slug was a lump of metal shot from a cannon. Now it is the mass accelerated one foot per second per second by a force of one pound. Twelve slugs make a slinch, also call a mug, sometimes a snail.

How do you measure the coastline of Britain? The question was answered in 1960 by the Polish mathematician Benoit Mandelbrot, and the answer was: infinite. At one time, man thought infinity was farther than we could see, then farther than we could sail, then fly, then farther than we could send a rocket ship, and now it is as far as a telescope in space transmitting radio signals from the beginning of the universe. We went so far beyond where we could see that we got to where we began. How did we do that? Where, in the intervening space or time, between then and now so that then and now can coexist in time, is what we for so long called infinity?

But what is infinity? Is it merely farther than we can go? Until we get there? The conundrum about infinity is that there is both the infinitely far and the infinitely small. It was Zeno who in 450 B.C. theorized that if any line can be divided, as any line can be, then you can never reach your goal because first you have to go halfway, then halfway to that point, and so on, *ad infinitum*. The coastline of Britain is infinite, for every bay has an infinite number of inlets and every inlet an infinite number of coves and every cove its numberless nooks and within each nook are countless crannies, and so on. It is an example of randomness existing within a defined structure and is measured with scale.

The universe was once so small you would have needed a microscope to find it. Then, in one ten-million-trillion-trillion-trillionths of a second, it was one hundred billion light-years across, a moment in time and space coined as The Big Bang by Fred Hoyle in a 1949 radio broadcast in which the announcer was describing a theory he thought was a lot of flooey. The Hubble telescope has found that instant; it occurred 13.7 billion years ago. The Hubble telescope has also shown us the alarming news that all the galaxies, stars, and planets together, what seem to us to exist in infinite space, comprise a mere 4 percent of the known matter and energy in the universe. The rest is dark energy and dark matter, meaning we don't know what it is, only that it's up to no good, since it's causing the expansion of the universe to accelerate.

What does it mean to wonder of a thing how far away or how small it is? To wonder about what we do not know is to be human. It is the way our minds work. Freud wondered what was going on inside us and discovered the unconscious; rather, he discovered that by dreams and jokes and slips of the tongue the unconscious could be measured; measured, it could be known. What is it we are not wondering about? When scientists began to wonder why cigarette smoke curls, flames flicker, traffic jams the way it does, or even why nature, which appears random and messy and cluttered, is beautiful, they invented Chaos, the theory that describes a universe "in which there is instability at every point and in which small errors prove catastrophic over time." What subscribes to the theory? Art, asteroids, bees, bell-shaped curve, blood vessels, ferns, fireflies, mosquitoes, measles, Morse Code, rain, rivers, epidemics, insomnia, war. The twentieth century has been the century of tremendous scientific breakthroughs, but the names the physicists seeking to discover the absolute truth about the observable universe have given their theories is not exactly reassuring that we are achieving progress. The more precise our measuring becomes, the more the theories sound otherwise: the theories of Relativity, of Incompleteness, of Indeterminacy, of Uncertainty, and now, of Chaos are the great breakthroughs of the twentieth century.

When I was living in New York and meting my universe without the aid of mechanical devices, what I was doing was using physical reckoning. I was unconsciously, intuitively, and continually measuring, and I was as alive to the natural world and my place in it as if I were an Arctic hunter who knows exactly where he is, how far he is from home, and how long it will take him to get there. Whether one is crossing the tundra in caribou skins or pounding the pavement in four-inch heels, to measure is to make a personal connection to the perceived world. It is to literally meet the world—perhaps why *mete* is an old word for *measure*. While measuring, and mathematizing out measures in the numbers we create in our minds that miraculously correlate with what we see, gives structure to our perceptions, perhaps it is not measuring's answers that matter as much as the act of measuring itself, as the relationship between receiving and responding to the immediate world we're in. To measure is to make a connection. To do it without a net is thrilling.

Nominated by Antioch Review, David Jauss

FROM PROCESSION OF SHADOWS: THE NOVEL OF TAMOGA

fiction by JULIÁN RÍOS

from THE HUDSON REVIEW and DALKEY ARCHIVE

MORTES'S STORY

It was toward the end of September, when the drowsiness of autumn was beginning to make itself felt; the hours went by more slowly and time itself seemed to stagnate like the forlorn waters of the salt marshes around Tamoga.

"A traveling salesman," said or thought absentmindedly all the bored men gathered in the station with nothing better to do as dusk fell and they saw first the enormous suitcase and then the short man comically veering from side to side in his efforts to drag it along the platform. "A dung beetle," someone in the group joked, trying to breathe new life into their flagging conversation. They stared at the stranger for a few moments longer, but nobody could be bothered to add another comment. They watched the train disappear into the endless rain, feeling a twinge of disappointment, a nostalgia for times past.

That man, the stranger, perhaps never even knew himself why he had chosen this town. Or perhaps it was not he who had chosen it, but chance, fate, his lucky or unlucky star, one inevitability leading to another.

We learned afterward that he had agreed to meet a woman in the town, and that she—still young, almost beautiful, with the look of someone recently widowed—was his sister-in-law. We learned from Inspector Cardona the story of his flight, their crazy love affair. We also learned (she, the sister-in-law, allowed herself to be interrogated at length by the inspector; sad but serene, proud of her love, docile and disbelieving in the end, past caring about anything or anyone) that his name was Mortes and that he was a traveling salesman, that he was soon to be fifty, had a wife and five children, and a spotless past. Everything very ordinary and inoffensive, depressing. And yet it seemed that he, Mortes—the least mysterious man in the world—had come to our town to play out an apparently absurd little farce.

For us, for our curiosity, it all began one Tuesday in September at the start of autumn, the day he arrived. From the window of his second-class compartment, Mortes would have gazed out at the rain-swept platform, the faded sign with the letters *T* and *M* almost completely worn away, so that it read A OGA. He would have been greeted by a jumble of clouds and roofs. Seeing this, he must have thought the town was gloomy enough for what he had in mind. It's also likely that what persuaded him to get off the train at the last moment was weariness, boredom, the conviction that he had never been in this town before; the certainty that he would not be recognized, that he had never dragged his huge leather trunk through the streets of Tamoga or put on his professional smile in any of its stores or businesses. He must also have known and felt relieved that he had never leaned on any counter chatting to the inevitable old maid about ribbons and buttons with the restrained passion, the secretive air, of someone making an indecent proposal. It's also likely he was attracted by the town's location and the fact it was so close to the border (we came to suspect this later on, when the woman appeared), not to mention that from the start he thought he could rely on our stupidity and collective curiosity, our lack of foresight—although none of these suppositions help explain the end of this story, if it can be said to have an end. It might also simply have been that he was crazy or scared. Or possibly he got caught up in his own game, the impossible lie he wanted to believe.

As I said, he, Mortes, arrived in Tamoga at the start of autumn on a sad, rainy day. Despite the fact that he was only among us for a few hours, he is still remembered with great relish, especially because of how his story ended; many people swear not only to have seen him, but to have talked with him. He had the gift of metamorphosis, apparently, because each one of us remembers him differently—although it's possible that all of our impressions were equally correct: happy, timid, forlorn, a joker, sneering, respectful, cynical, dull, likeable: he is all those things in our accounts of him. In the end we're left with fascination, and the impossibility of telling his story, because in this case the words are more concrete than the facts, and a story is really only worth telling when words can't exhaust its meaning. We're also free to imagine and attribute multiple, contradictory, and obscure objectives to that rather short, rather skinny, rather ungainly stranger who chose Tamoga as the stage for his performance. Now Mortes is nothing more than words and a vague image already beginning to fade in our memory: a broad face with ill-defined features, dun-colored, as if made out of mud. His eyes were red-rimmed and his mouth a slash; his voice a nasal drawl that sometimes turned into a deep gurgling like the sound of water running through pipes. An unremarkable man who wore (not elegantly, but not shabbily either) a crumpled brown suit and a trench coat that was too big for him. That is how we see Mortes in our memory, and that is how Don Elío, the stationmaster, must have seen him that first afternoon.

"You get used to all kinds, especially at my age and this being a frontier station," old Don Elío will have said. "But there must've been something wrong with that one—he wasn't quite right in the head. Look: he was on the quarter past seven train, which that day was almost on time. It always stops here for five minutes, that's long enough. I rang the bell for it to leave and right across from me saw the man suddenly leap up from his seat and rush into the corridor with his trunk. He got off just as the train was pulling out. Because he was just absentminded, maybe? Well, listen: thirty seconds before, he had been staring calmly out of his compartment window. He looked at the people on the platform, at me, at the station, smoking as calmly as though he was going somewhere else, as if he wasn't at all concerned that this station was Tamoga, though the big sign was there right in front of his nose. He heard the bell as if it was a call to Mass and then, at the very last moment, he was in a rush, jumping off the moving train with his trunk and everything. He almost killed himself. You should have seen him: standing there on the platform as if he had fallen from heaven, arms out wide like a scarecrow."

In any event, he didn't stand there like a statue for long. He headed for the main exit and walked out into the rain and blustery wind of Tamoga. The taxi drivers sitting bored in their cabs outside the station watched him cross the square without any hope of a fare. He waved the porters away too and dragged his trunk over to the coach parked under the plane trees. He sat with the other few passengers in the ramshackle

566

bus, staring blankly out at the rain and the square, the dripping trees, and the showy sign by the side of the main road proclaiming in red letters: WELCOME TO TAMOGA, until One-Armed Gómez, the conductor, appeared in front of him. According to Gómez, the stranger looked like he was convalescing or completely exhausted, as if he had been in a hospital or was returning from a long trip. The stranger dried his face with a handkerchief and patted his shoulders to shake off the raindrops. He asked how much a ticket was, and how far it was to town. He seemed relieved at the answers, as though he was in a hurry and the three kilometers were one less thing to worry about. He sat examining his ticket, as if the small pink piece of paper announcing *Bus Service Tamoga/Station or Vice-Versa* was an object of great interest. After a while, he raised his head:

"Perhaps you can help me . . . Do you happen to know of a hotel without too many bedbugs or fleas?" he asked the conductor with a smile.

"I mentioned the London Hotel," Gómez said. "I don't know why, but I took a liking to him. Perhaps because he was different from the passengers I usually get. He put the coins in my left hand and made no fuss when he saw my stump. He seemed to find it quite natural that a conductor might have an arm or a leg missing, so long as he doesn't let anyone get away without paying. After that he said thanks, pressed his face to the window, and stared out at the marshes the whole time until we got into town."

He took a room at the London, wrote his name and all his details in the hotel register, putting up the whole time with Doña Milagros's rude stare. As usual, she was sitting bolt upright on her wheelchair throne behind the counter, knitting. (In our sentimental way, some of us suspected that Doña Milagros opened the hotel not simply to show everyone in Tamoga how resilient and capable she was—that she was in no way an invalid and would never accept pity from anyone—but also in the secret hope that one day her husband would make a nostalgic leap back to Tamoga. He had abandoned her in the middle of their honeymoon when she had her accident; terrified at the thought of all that this implied—with no money or job, and unable to bear his wife's temper a day longer, in a moment of panic and lucidity he must have glimpsed the inferno awaiting him. In those days they lived close to the Portuguese quarter, in a house belonging to one of Doña Milagros's uncles. An old bachelor, he was miserly and eccentric. He had sworn to leave everything to his niece if she looked after him in his last illness [like all old people, in his desire to go on living he must have promised himself a slow and difficult death], even though he steadfastly refused to give her a penny before then. Those were hard years. One morning like any other, her husband said good-bye in his usual unenthusiastic way, with his habitual forced smile: "I'm going down to the port. An English boat has arrived." That was the last time Doña Milagros ever heard his voice. A short while later, the old man died, as if he had only been waiting for his niece's husband to abscond to close his eyes in peace. With the inheritance money, Doña Milagros decided to open a hotel, rejecting the advice of those who told her she should live off her income. Ever since, she has sat at all hours in the hotel lobby, keeping a curious and watchful eye on everything, held upright in her wheelchair by hope and an ancient premonition—if her husband should come back one day, he might come to stay in the London, foolishly attracted as many visitors were by the hotel's cosmopolitan name, and unaware that the mummy-newlywed was lying in wait for him, knitting and unraveling her revenge—shamelessly studying everyone who comes to stay, trying to compare their faces with the features already fading in the old images stored in her memory or, perhaps, simply trying to assess how capable they are of paying their bill.)

So Mortes put up with Doña Milagros's piercing stare, asked for a single room with a bathroom, and said he had no idea how long he would be staying in Tamoga. "One day, two, or maybe a week. It depends on how things go," he said as he filled in the form. "Or perhaps I'll spend the rest of my life here," he added, winking at the old woman, trying to make a joke, which she didn't find funny.

After this comes the detailed report from Alcides, one of Doña Milagros's countless godsons. Enveloped in his customary black suit, funereal and anxious to please as ever, and with his fussy homosexual gestures and oozing the sickly-sweet rhetoric of a former seminarian, his head shining, perfumed, and pomaded, Alcides appeared in the lobby to take Mortes's suitcase, after a half-hearted struggle, then lead the stranger to his room on the first floor.

"The suitcase was heavy, like it was full of books or lead, or had a dead body in it," Alcides said in his exaggerated way.

"That'll do; you can leave it on the bed," Mortes told him.

He didn't seem disappointed by the small, dark room situated at the rear of the hotel.

He pushed back the faded lace curtain and peered out. From this height he could see the ground covered in puddles and piles of trash, and opposite, the warehouses and shacks where the Portuguese lived. Farther off were the bare, windswept hillsides, and the still, gray water lapping the horizon.

He walked around the room several times, carefully stuck his hand in the tear in the wallpaper, expecting to find a nest of bedbugs or something worse. Opening the wardrobe, he poked his head inside and with the back of his hand raised a sad arpeggio from the row of metal hangers. He continued his painstaking inspection: he went into the bathroom, pulled the lavatory chain, took a step back when he heard the water gushing ominously. He switched on the light, studied himself in the mirror for a few seconds, and rubbed his hands across his cheeks as if he needed to confirm he had several days' growth of beard. Finally, he turned on both faucets in the washbasin.

"There's no hot water," he said, with the look of someone who's just discovered he's been swindled.

"It only comes on in the mornings," sighed Alcides, weary of repeating the same phrase for the past eight years.

Mortes returned to the bedroom and saw with satisfaction that it contained two wicker armchairs, a portable lamp on the bedside table, a big china ashtray, and a bottle of water covered with a glass. Perhaps he wanted to seem demanding, as though he was going to spend several days in Tamoga and wanted to choose someplace comfortable.

"Haberdashery or fabrics?" asked Alcides, eager to earn his tip.

Alarmed at the cigarette burn on the bedspread and the patch of damp on the wall that looked like an enormous crab about to plummet onto the pillow, Mortes took a few moments to respond.

"A bit of everything," was his eventual unenthusiastic answer, aimed at the window or no one.

"I can give you information about the stores here," Aclides suggested, anxious to get to the point.

"He didn't seem interested," Alcides was to complain afterwards. "He pushed the crumpled edge of the rug straight, and turned toward me with an upset, almost disgusted gesture, as if I was trying to involve him in some dirty business.

"'Listen,' I said to him confidentially. 'Just listen. There are stores in this town that look very grand, look wonderful from the outside, and yet they've had the same stuff on show in their windows for half a century. I'm not exaggerating. How do they manage to survive? Don't ask: nobody knows. We have shops in the center of town (yes, you'll see them right outside) with windows as big as this, and signs that read Sons of So and So, Inheritors of What's His Name, House Founded in 1860, Latest Fashions from Paris, all very fancy. But if you go in, all you see is dust, fly droppings, and goods from the year zero, all of them moth-eaten or rotting away. They sell a few bits and pieces when the market is going and the country people from Páramos and Santa Cruz come into town, along with the fishermen from Providencia and Puerto Angra. But that's about all. Believe me: they're dead as doornails. You're wasting your time if you try to sell them anything novel or fashionable.'

"At this point I always pause for effect, with the salesmen passing through, before suggesting the names of shopkeepers who do have money and are interested in new products. But this had no effect on him, despite all my best efforts. He only grimaced, as though to say: well, what can you do . . .

"'Thanks,' he said, as if making excuses for himself. 'Thanks, but I don't need a guide . . . I like to survey the field of battle first, to work out for myself where I might bomb or make a killing, if you follow me?'

"What can you do with someone like that? By then I wasn't worried about my tip; it was a matter of pride, of being annoyed by his conde-scension. That's when I started to become suspicious. I've met more than enough salesmen, and all of them are curious, especially when they arrive in a town for the first time and don't know a soul. Show me a single one of them who isn't curious. Well, he immediately tried to make amends; he took a crumpled twenty-five peseta note out of his pocket, smoothed it and gave it to me with a smile.

"'We'll see in the morning,' he said, dismissing me.

"I was already out in the hall when I heard his nasal, world-weary voice once more:

"'What's there to do in a place like this in the evening or at night?' he asked, clearing his throat and jigging about comically.

"Aha! I thought. So he was one of those who like to put a brave face on things. A proper night owl, I'm sure.

"'This is a boring town,' I said without bitterness, but not wanting to lie. 'Though we do have three movie theaters. On Tuesdays only the Moderno is open. Today they're showing a Spanish film: *The Invincible Amada* or something like that, I can't remember exactly. We have too many bars and inns. On the weekends there are two dance halls. And then there's the Terranova. It's open every night until dawn.'

"By now he was listening closely, trying to imagine from what I was saying how sad a coastal town can be after the summer season. I went on listing the possibilities for amusement in Tamoga, thinking I was getting my revenge and that he was going to feel the depressing weight of the hours here, how long a night can be in this purgatory.

"'There used to be several houses where you could have fun down by the river,' I recalled, overcome by a sense of nostalgia. I remembered Materno the eunuch when he came with his five eternal virgins, and the love lottery in the ruins of the old salted-fish factory. Those were the good times, when the mineral-loading bay was functioning. 'But all that's gone now,' I told him, 'and our only house of ill repute is the Terranova. You can listen to music there, dance, have a drink or two, and if you're not too fussy, find some female company. You'll at least always have the comfort of seeing other faces as bored as your own—and, if you're lucky, you might make it back to the hotel with the memory of some not too horrible woman. Although I couldn't guarantee that, I must say.'"

Later on, when everything was apparently over and done with, Inspector Cardona, who was a stickler for routine and always wanted to discover a logical sequence of events in matters that quite possibly had none, tried to reconstruct the stranger's movements so that there would be no gaps in our knowledge of the short span of time that Mortes was among us.

He, Mortes, must have spent a couple of hours stretched out on the bed in his room (the imprint of his body on the bedspread was still there the next morning as proof that he had not spent the night in the London, but that, likewise, he wasn't a ghost, and had really existed in Tamoga for a few hours at least), going over his regrets and his plans, getting drunk on dreams, cradling his fear as he listened to the sound of the rain on the windowpanes, perhaps thinking as he lay facing the wall: "I'm here in a town surrounded by the sea and I have no idea what I'm going to do."

By the time he left the room he had probably already made up his mind, had understood (without rancor or regret) that he still had to perform the final act, had to show himself to his public, gather his strength so as not to have to be prompted, to take a bow as the curtain fell.

From the hotel Mortes must have gone directly to Prado's restaurant on Avenida Portugal. Perhaps he was tempted by the yellow lettering that falsely claimed: *Our Specialty: All Kinds of Seafood.* Perhaps he was hungry, or thought this was a reasonable time to have dinner and so pretend to be hungry. "He ordered a salad, sirloin with fried potatoes, fruit, and half a bottle of red," Prado reported meticulously. "He ate in a hurry, gobbling it down. Between each mouthful he stared at the pinup girl with the big backside on the calendar opposite him. He paid without leaving a tip, and asked where he could find a pharmacy open at that time of night."

He was seen in the town hall square, at the far end of town. He asked the night watchman which drugstore might still have a pharmacist on duty, and let himself be led to the street corner and then came to a halt beneath a metal sign reading "Rocha Pharmacy." Before going in, he peered at both the windows and at the lighted interior.

Severino the pharmacy assistant attended him. "He asked me for some sleeping pills," Severino said, "but first he wandered around the shelves, as if he was interested in all the pots with their gold lettering, or hadn't yet decided what he was after. Then he came and stood with his hands on the glass counter, his head tilted to one side as though he was still undecided or was trying to remember something. He looked bored and in need of conversation. He asked for some pills that would make him sleep properly: like a dead man, he added, with a wry grin. I don't think he often took sleeping tablets, because otherwise he would have asked for a particular brand. He offered me a cigarette and started to complain about the climate here. He said that by all rights the inhabitants of this region ought to have evolved gills by now, then asked how many pharmacies there were in town, and if people here were naive or trusting enough to believe in medicines and to see a doctor when they were dying. Jokingly, he asked me with that sly grin he had—twisting his lip—if in the provinces and in such a wet place as this there was much call for rubber goods, condoms and the like."

Now it was time for the love song. Either before or after visiting the pharmacy, Mortes went to the telephone exchange to call his sister-in-law and get her to come to Tamoga. At first we doubted the story that Señorita Serena, the operator, gave us. (She's completely senile and about to retire). We thought she was trying to sell us another of her fantasies, one of those incredible, grotesque rumors she gets into her head when she has one of her telephonic spiritualist sessions. You see, shortly after her sister died, Señorita Serena discovered that the dead—above all, friends and relatives of hers who had passed over—were trying to get in touch with her through the phone wires. Ever since, she's lived for the lengthy monologues, the weird and wonderful snippets of news that the dead of Tamoga offer her. She was encouraged partly by superstition and popular beliefs, but above all by the parish priest, Father Lozano, who once told his congregation in a memorable, moving sermon that he saw no reason why souls in purgatory shouldn't have recourse to modern means of communication.

That was why we didn't believe her. We thought it was another of her crazy ideas when she told us Mortes had been in the office that night, and had placed a long-distance call. "It was already very late, and I was saying my last prayers, though I don't know the exact time, when I heard flip-flop, the sound of footsteps on the stairs. Then, *ora pro nobis*, he came in like a phantom, whiter than the wall and soaked right through, dripping from head to toe, his hair plastered down over his eyes. He was groping along with his hands out in front of him, his hands and arms were covered in mud. He was a real sight to see," said Señorita Serena in her melodramatic style. "He could hardly speak, he made gurgling noises and sounded as though he was choking on every word. I thought he was a drunk who was going to throw up in front of me," she added.

"Srreaally uuurgen," he stammered. Later she, Señorita Serena, heard Mortes ask for someone to come and join him in Tamoga: ". . . ope you . . . com and . . . ook me in the eye and . . . ell me . . . ace to . . . ace you don . . . ove me," he said, his voice echoing down the line. From the far end came a continuous sobbing and then a woman's voice saying desperately, "Wait wait wait," before the line went dead.

But all this was later confirmed by the woman (Mortes's sister-in-law) when she came to Tamoga.

We also learned that he (Mortes) was in the Mezquita Café. At around ten, Barbosa, the waiter there, saw him cross the red earth courtyard, carefully stepping around the puddles, come to a halt to examine the deserted pergola with the chairs piled against the wall, uncertain or disoriented for a second or two, then push open the back door to the café and peer in at the almost completely empty room. At that moment the only customer was Doña María, from the old people's home. As usual at that time of night, Barbosa was arguing with her, refusing to serve her the second drink she invariably ended up ordering. "What can I get you?" the barman asked him. Tired or distracted, Mortes stared at the old woman, at the waiter's dirty white jacket, then at the row of bottles behind the bar. "I don't know," he said, leaning on the counter. "Yes, let me have a cognac and a glass of water," he said eventually. At that point Doña María insisted, "Pour me another anisette," pushing her empty glass to the edge of the bar. (She, the old woman from the home, receives a small pension every month. "My son sends it to me," she repeats proudly, to show us she isn't on her own, that someone remembers her; but by mid-month the money has evaporated or gone down the drain, and then, every day, Barbosa serves her a glass of anisette he knows he'll never be paid for. It's also likely that Doña María goes to the Mezquita not so much because she needs a drink, even if it is free, but for the pleasure and habit of arguing with the waiter, to see him refuse and then finally give in.)

"Another anisette," the old woman squawked.

"I said no," Barbosa told us. "I was annoyed she was taking advantage of the stranger being there, figuring I wasn't going to argue or refuse her another drink in front of someone we didn't know."

At that point Mortes himself stepped in: "Serve her the anisette if that's what she wants. I'll pay." Then Barbosa: "It'll be bad for her. She's already had a glass here, and I bet she had two or three more on the way over." Mortes: "Serve the lady." He bowed his head toward her, either shyly or insolently, leaning forward to study her wrinkled, powder-caked face, her tiny, lifeless eyes, the mangy fox fur hanging from her bony shoulders. He acted the perfect, gallant gentleman. Then he turned back to the barman. "If we're old enough, we get to the point where nothing is bad for us. Anything that lets us go on living is good for us, isn't that right, my dear?" he said, head tilted to one side, his voice low. He leaned back against the bar and listened politely to the old woman's chatter, as if he had already decided to court her.

He listened patiently, pretending to be interested and smiling pleasantly at everything she said, nodding slowly and reassuringly as she explained in a not altogether logical fashion that she was in the old age home to preserve her independence: "My children live far away and want me to go and live with them. Just imagine, young man, me in their house: it wouldn't be long before my daughters-in-law and I were at each other's throats. No, no . . ." she said, giving the excuse she had repeated so often she had come to believe it herself, entirely taken in by the convincing way she told it: "I live alone to honor the memory of my husband, there wasn't a man more in love in all the world. Many evenings after work he would say to me: *Ma, let's go and enjoy ourselves*, and we'd go out to dance. He really loved Viennese waltzes and French champagne. He could dance and still drink his glass down, what he called the champagne waltz. That's all there is for me, young man, the memory of my husband."

At this Mortes inclined his head once more: "Madame, would you do me the honor of accompanying me to the dance so that I can buy you a glass of champagne?"

"He was a comedian," said Barbosa, scandalized. "Either he was making fun of her or he wasn't right in the head."

"He was a gentleman, the first gentleman to set foot in Tamoga," the old woman retorted.

It is worth recalling Mortes's brief, unreal appearance at the Terranova. He had the old woman, who by now was quite tipsy, on his arm, as he solemnly rounded off the final act in his farce of love and compassion. As he led her over to a table, he tried to make the sailors and whores show her some respect, then he called out firmly for a bottle of French champagne, although in the end he had to settle for one from Catalonia. He raised his glass in a toast to her, smiling through the smoke and ignoring the deafening noise of the music and laughter. He went up to the bar and whispered in the barman's ear, slipping him a bank note while he was talking. Not wanting to look into the man's alarmed face, Mortes asked him to take off the boring, vulgar chachacha and put on a waltz instead. It's easy to say the words, but impossible to re-create the grotesque tenderness, the fantastical atmosphere of the scene. Slowly and considerately, Mortes led the old woman out onto the dance floor, gently put his arm round her waist, and began to move to the rhythm of the music. Clumsily at first, but increasingly light-footed, aerial even, her feet hardly touching the floor, his partner let him guide her, allowed herself to be carried away by the music, an ecstatic smile on her face and her eyes tightly closed, in the arms of this serious, ceremonious, Chaplinesque man, who turned and turned ever more quickly while in the suffocating gloom of the Terranova the whores and other clients looked on in astonishment, defending themselves with laughter and admiration, rubbing their eyes and asking themselves if what they were seeing was real, if they would be able to tell the story the next day when they had sobered up, if anyone would believe them.

That was all. This was the last that was seen of Mortes, although afterwards Doña María told her group of admiring, sighing old ladies that he had accompanied her to the door of the old age home and said by way of farewell: "Allow me to kiss you on the forehead, as though you were my mother or my first girlfriend, in memory of tonight." And, after all that had gone before, we might well believe it—fundamentally, it wouldn't be a lie, even if it never happened.

There's nothing else now except to draw this incomplete story to its close. We heard nothing more about him, Mortes, until the woman, a blonde with a drawn, scared-looking face, came and asked after him at the London Hotel. She arrived on the same train as Mortes had done two days before, just in time to identify the body, the corpse covered in seaweed that had been washed up a few hours earlier on the beach at Puerto Angra. She accepted the news with great dignity but would not accept what Cardona the inspector told her about Mortes's death. She said it was impossible that he would have committed suicide now, precisely when he had told her to come to him, that they were going to live together. She seemed proud of his love, which was all she had left. She stared at his body stretched out on the marble slab in the morgue, then kissed his face, eaten away by crabs. She stroked the hair plastered down on his forehead, stared some more, kissed his empty eye sockets, pressed her lips to his ear and whispered something to him, then caressed him again until she felt the inspector's kind hand on her shoulder. She turned to face him and said in her proud, terse way: "It must have been an accident, Inspector. There's no other explanation."

Possibly there is no other explanation, or we could accept several, really—any one will do. Possibly the ambiguous hypothesis Doctor Rey the pathologist put forward is the most plausible:

"This man could have committed suicide or had an accident, slipping and falling into the water. I don't know. Either way could have accounted for his drowning," Doctor Rey told the inspector in his concise manner. "What I do know is that he was condemned to die: he had lung cancer. I don't know if he knew this or had come to suspect it, even though it seems logical to suppose he had. Perhaps that's why he came to Tamoga (don't pay too much attention to what I'm saying, Inspector). Because, though it may be hard to live in this town of Tamoga, it's a better place than anywhere to come and die."

Nominated by The Hudson Review

TALLY

by ADRIAN BLEVINS

from THE GEORGIA REVIEW

The babies smelled like mixed-up milk and cotton dragged
through a little wax, but not like sugar or any amount

of caramel. Smelled like salty pee and skin swabbed slick
and the years forthcoming lit up by lemons. Smelled

like not-death—like the earliest of the early yield—like
kale and collards, maybe. Like lettuce? Smelled like

soil, though not so wholly-hearted—smelled more like
fallen apples, I would say, or melons rotting in baskets

made of a tincture of wheat and river water, and were thus
like sleep in an antique pantry. I mean, were like sleep

that much at last. Were sleep unchained from trees
and time and fire and time and hunger and time plus time

plus longing—were sleep cut loose from up and down
and this and that and therefore were—the asinine things—

life at its most extreme and comatose and dragging and slapdash—yes—but thunderstruck, all the same. And yes. And best.

Nominated by Rosellen Brown, Robert Thomas

WALKING THE DOG'S SHADOW

by DEBORAH BROWN

from WALKING THE DOG'S SHADOW (BOA Edition)

It's best to walk a shadow till he pants,
to let him roam a bit under the hemlocks
while you ponder the shade of boulders.
It's best to let grief enter you like this,
alone with your own black dog,
a drag on anyone's leash
along the logging road to the lake,
past loggers' landings and a clear cut,
across the brook's collapsing plank bridge,
past the neighbor's garden shrouded in plastic,
past no trespassing signs, a dried up vernal pool,
crisscrossed by trunks of grieving oaks.
Every night, eager as a pup,
this shadow leads you into the woods
and shows you how well it heels
at your side, this old black dog of grief.

Nominated by Genie Chipps

INTERNAL MONUMENT

by G.C. WALDREP

from MICHIGAN QUARTERLY REVIEW

A man was sad—for himself, maybe for someone else, maybe he had lost something, or someone—so he hired some workmen to erect a monument. He was not surprised when they came calling early one morning, while he was still in bed, but he *was* surprised when, with a practiced slash, the foreman opened his chest. "We build the monument inside," the foreman said. "But who will see the monument," the man protested. "It's a monument for feeling, not for seeing," the foreman replied.

The operation was unpleasant but was soon over. And sure enough, after a brief interval of recuperation, the man felt, he thought, a little less sad than before.

This lasted awhile, but then he felt the sadness returning, in spite of the dark, heavy space in his chest where the monument rested, nestled in flesh. He called the workmen again. They obligingly came and repeated the procedure.

Over the ensuing months and years, the man had cause to call upon the foreman and his crew repeatedly, as new life brought new losses, new sadnesses. His chest became a jumbled cabinet of monuments, the fatty tissue of his upper arms and thighs, his bowels: even his fingers and toes felt weighed down by his commemorations. At length, it was all he could do to lift the telephone receiver at his bedside. He called the foreman. "I can't get up," he said. "I can't even move." "An unfortunate side effect," the foreman told him. "Really, there's nothing we can do."

Bedridden, the man felt deprived even of what had been the most mundane pleasures of daily life: strolls down the avenue, the smell of bread baking at a neighborhood patisserie, autumn leaves. It was not turning out at all as he had expected, this life.

Inside his body the monuments huddled. Mutely, he thought, though sometimes, late at night, when he tried to shift position, they brushed against one another and made what could only be called sounds, though no one else could hear them, and he heard them, if he heard them, with his body, rather than with his ears.

When the man died, his landlord, his executors, eventually the city authorities all attempted to wrest his body from what had become his deathbed. No one could move it. Finally, they called the foreman, who agreed to try one last procedure on the corpse.

The foreman unzipped the body like a flimsy valise and, with the assistance of his workmen, slowly, carefully turned it inside out. Now everyone could see the monuments, but no one could see the man.

They were beautiful, his monuments. People traveled into the city from miles around to view them. The city graded and graveled lanes in what had been the sad man's body. Clerks and engineers began to take their families there for picnics. A bandstand was built. Lovers gathered at dusk for concerts and, later, laid out blankets on the generous lawns, over which the monuments stood like sentinels. "Look at the stars," the lovers whispered to one another. "Look up at the beautiful stars."

Nominated by John Allman, David Baker

SPECIAL MENTION

(The editors also wish to mention the following important works published by small presses last year. Listings are in no particular order.)

FICTION

The Enigma of Grover's Mill—Bradford Morrow (*The Uninnocent*, Pegasus Books)

The Fabulous Bestiary of Alton's Greek—Harrison Scott Key (The Pinch)

Wingman—Leslie Parry (Indiana Review)

Breviary—Jason Schwartz (New York Tyrant)

The Master of Patina—Miles Harvey (Agni)

Chametla—Luis Alberto Urrea (Tin House)

The Perfect Age—Kevin Moffett (Paris Review)

That's My Bike!—Paul Murray (Paris Review)

Is That You, Walt Whitman?—Therese Stanton (A Public Space)

The Teacher And The Revolution—Diane Chang (Glimmer Train Stories)

Open Mic—Sarah Frisch (New England Review)

The Dean And Mrs. Hess—Jamaica Kincaid (Little Star)

Motherfucker—Aimee Bender (Harvard Review)

Downstream—James Scott (Ploughshares)

Beach Vacation—Christine Sneed (Southern Review)

The Long Net—Anna Solomon (Missouri Review)

Atlantis—Richard Burgin (*New Jersey*, Akashic Books)

Blood Feud—Katie Chase (ZYZZYVA)

In The Zone—T.C. Boyle (Kenyon Review)

The Brother-In-Law and The Beach—Michael Czyzniejewski (Gulf Coast)

Dad Stuff—Benjamin Rybeck (Ninth Letter)

Welcome To The Authentic Trail of Tears—Michael Gills (Texas Review)

Champions of the World—Kristina Gorcheva-Newberry (Southern Review)

Panorama City—Antoine Wilson (A Public Space)

All Their Riches—David Yost (The Sun)

Here Is What—Robyn Parnell (Bellevue Literary Review)

Walk With Us—Askold Melnyczuk (Massachusetts Review)

Zero Gains—Bonnie Nadzam (Image)

1.7 To Tennessee—Jamie Quatro (Antioch Review)

Composite Body—Tony Tulathimutte (Cimarron Review)

The Letter—Miroslav Penkov (A Public Space)

A Family Matter—Keya Mitra (Kenyon Review)

Your Taxi Is The Greatest Movement—Mikael Awake (Witness)

I Looked For You, I Called Your Name—Laura Van Den Berg (Ploughshares)

Bread Alley—Sarah Tourjee (Anomalous)

The Boys Club—Maura Candela (The Common)

Summer, Boys—Ethan Rutherford (One Story)

Lust For Life—Susan Berman (ZYZZYVA)

Screen Test—Leslie Bazzett (New England Review)

The Associated Virgins—Rosalie Morales Kearns (Witness)

The Joy of Cooking—Elissa Schappell (One Story)

Felina—Rachel Swearingen (Mississippi Review)

The Fixed Idea—April Bernard (Little Star)

My Hand Is My Cub—Phong Nguyen (New Letters)

Dream Houses—Bonnie Jo Campbell (Notre Dame Review)

The Vandercook—Alice Mattison (Ecotone)

Life Among The Terranauts—Caitlin Horrocks (One Story)

Maybe We're The Angels—Jeff P. Jones (Five Points)

The Polish Bride—Tracy Pearce (Colorado Review)

But Now Am Found—Patti Horvath (Bellevue Literary Review)

The Miracle Worker—Mia Alvar (Missouri Review)

The Ranger Queen of Sulphur—Stephanie Soileau (Ecotone)

To Reach Japan—Alice Munro (Narrative)
Rothko Eggs—Keith Ridway (Zoetrope)
No Rabio—Tim Fitts (Gettysburg Review)
Want—Deb Olin Unferth (Noon)
Not Even Lions and Tigers—Steve Amick (Cincinnati Review)
The Anger Meridian—Kaylie Jones (Southampton Review)
Remain in Light—Gary Lain (Fiction International)
Ahmed's Wife—Scott Tucker (Alaska Quarterly)
The Reader—Nathan Englander (Electric Literature)
Beautiful Souls—Joan Leegant (Colorado Review)
Paolo's Turn—Karen Laws (Georgia Review)
Trash—Gilbert Allen (Southern Review)
The Showrunner—Frankie Thomas (At Length)

NONFICTION

The View from 90—Doris Grumbach (American Scholar)
The Labyrinth—Philip Appleman (Free Inquiry)
Born Again And Again—Joe Miller (New Letters)
The Special Populations Unit—Chanan Tigay (McSweeney's)
You Never Know Your Luck—Christopher Buckley (Packinghouse Review)
Resurrections—Christopher Dickens (Florida Review)
Next Year, For Sure—Zoey Peterson (Malahat Review)
Visions—Kristen Cosby (Normal School)
Coming of Age In Book Country—Bonnie Friedman (Ploughshares)
A Gyroscope on The Island of Love—Michael McGregor (Image)
A Beauty—Robert Boyers (Agni)
Dancing For the Bomb—Iraj Isaac Rahmim (Missouri Review)
The Room and The Elephant—Sven Birkerts (Los Angeles Review)
Speed Freaks—Ginger Strand (Orion)
The Death of The Book—Ben Ehrenreich (LA Review)
To Cèpe, with Love—E.J. Levy (Salmagundi)
One Message Leading to Another—John Berger (Massachusetts Review)
Night Piece—Judith Kitchen (Georgia Review)
Displaced—Norma Marder (Gettysburg Review)
My Mother's Burning Body—Jaed Muncharoen Coffin (The Sun)
The Currency of Love—Linda Lancione (New Letters)

POETRY

PRESSES FEATURED IN THE PUSHCART PRIZE EDITIONS SINCE 1976

A-Minor

Acts

Agni

Ahsahta Press

Ailanthus Press

Alaska Quarterly Review

Alcheringa/Ethnopoetics

Alice James Books

Ambergris

Amelia

American Letters and Commentary

American Literature

American PEN

American Poetry Review

American Scholar

American Short Fiction

The American Voice

Amicus Journal

Amnesty International

Anaesthesia Review

Anhinga Press

Another Chicago Magazine

Antaeus

Antietam Review

Antioch Review

Apalachee Quarterly

Aphra

Aralia Press

The Ark

Art and Understanding

Arts and Letters

Artword Quarterly

Ascensius Press

Ascent

Aspen Leaves

Aspen Poetry Anthology

Assembling

Atlanta Review

Autonomedia

Avocet Press

The Baffler

Bakunin

Bamboo Ridge

Barlenmir House

Barnwood Press

Barrow Street

Bellevue Literary Review

The Bellingham Review

Bellowing Ark

Beloit Poetry Journal

Bennington Review

Bilingual Review

Black American Literature Forum

Blackbird

Black Renaissance Noire
Black Rooster
Black Scholar
Black Sparrow
Black Warrior Review
Blackwells Press
Bloom
Bloomsbury Review
Blue Cloud Quarterly
Blueline
Blue Unicorn
Blue Wind Press
Bluefish
BOA Editions
Bomb
Bookslinger Editions
Boston Review
Boulevard
Boxspring
Bridge
Bridges
Brown Journal of Arts
Burning Deck Press
Cafe Review
Caliban
California Quarterly
Callaloo
Calliope
Calliopea Press
Calyx
The Canary
Canto
Capra Press
Carcanet Editions
Caribbean Writer
Carolina Quarterly
Cedar Rock
Center
Chariton Review
Charnel House
Chattahoochee Review
Chautauqua Literary Journal
Chelsea

Chicago Review
Chouteau Review
Chowder Review
Cimarron Review
Cincinnati Poetry Review
City Lights Books
Cleveland State Univ. Poetry Ctr.
Clown War
CoEvolution Quarterly
Cold Mountain Press
Colorado Review
Columbia: A Magazine of Poetry and Prose
Confluence Press
Confrontation
Conjunctions
Connecticut Review
Copper Canyon Press
Cosmic Information Agency
Countermeasures
Counterpoint
Court Green
Crawl Out Your Window
Crazyhorse
Crescent Review
Cross Cultural Communications
Cross Currents
Crosstown Books
Crowd
Cue
Cumberland Poetry Review
Curbstone Press
Cutbank
Cypher Books
Dacotah Territory
Daedalus
Dalkey Archive Press
Decatur House
December
Denver Quarterly
Desperation Press
Dogwood
Domestic Crude
Doubletake

Dragon Gate Inc.

Dreamworks

Dryad Press

Duck Down Press

Durak

East River Anthology

Eastern Washington University Press

Ecotone

El Malpensante

Eleven Eleven

Ellis Press

Empty Bowl

Epiphany

Epoch

Ergo!

Evansville Review

Exquisite Corpse

Faultline

Fence

Fiction

Fiction Collective

Fiction International

Field

Fifth Wednesday Journal

Fine Madness

Firebrand Books

Firelands Art Review

First Intensity

Five A.M.

Five Fingers Review

Five Points Press

Five Trees Press

Florida Review

The Formalist

Fourth Genre

Frontiers: A Journal of Women Studies

Fugue

Gallimaufry

Genre

The Georgia Review

Gettysburg Review

Ghost Dance

Gibbs-Smith

Glimmer Train

Goddard Journal

David Godine, Publisher

Graham House Press

Grand Street

Granta

Graywolf Press

Great River Review

Green Mountains Review

Greenfield Review

Greensboro Review

Guardian Press

Gulf Coast

Hanging Loose

Hard Pressed

Harvard Review

Hayden's Ferry Review

Hermitage Press

Heyday

Hills

Hollyridge Press

Holmgangers Press

Holy Cow!

Home Planet News

Hudson Review

Hungry Mind Review

Icarus

Icon

Idaho Review

Iguana Press

Image

In Character

Indiana Review

Indiana Writes

Intermedia

Intro

Invisible City

Inwood Press

Iowa Review

Ironwood

Jam To-day

J. Journal

The Journal

Jubilat

The Kanchenjuga Press

Kansas Quarterly

Kayak

Kelsey Street Press

Kenyon Review

Kestrel

Lake Effect

Latitudes Press

Laughing Waters Press

Laurel Poetry Collective

Laurel Review

L'Epervier Press

Liberation

Linquis

Literal Latté

Literary Imagination

The Literary Review

The Little Magazine

Little Patuxent Review

Little Star

Living Hand Press

Living Poets Press

Logbridge-Rhodes

Louisville Review

Lowlands Review

Lucille

Lynx House Press

Lyric

The MacGuffin

Magic Circle Press

Malahat Review

Manoa

Manroot

Many Mountains Moving

Marlboro Review

Massachusetts Review

McSweeney's

Meridian

Mho & Mho Works

Micah Publications

Michigan Quarterly

Mid-American Review

Milkweed Editions

Milkweed Quarterly

The Minnesota Review

Mississippi Review

Mississippi Valley Review

Missouri Review

Montana Gothic

Montana Review

Montemora

Moon Pony Press

Mount Voices

Mr. Cogito Press

MSS

Mudfish

Mulch Press

N + 1

Nada Press

Narrative

National Poetry Review

Nebraska Poets Calendar

Nebraska Review

New America

New American Review

New American Writing

The New Criterion

New Delta Review

New Directions

New England Review

New England Review and Bread Loaf
    Quarterly

New Issues

New Letters

New Ohio Review

New Orleans Review

New South Books

New Verse News

New Virginia Review

New York Quarterly

New York University Press

Nimrod

9X9 Industries

Ninth Letter

Noon

North American Review
North Atlantic Books
North Dakota Quarterly
North Point Press
Northeastern University Press
Northern Lights
Northwest Review
Notre Dame Review
O. ARS
O. Bl k
Obsidian
Obsidian II
Ocho
Oconee Review
October
Ohio Review
Old Crow Review
Ontario Review
Open City
Open Places
Orca Press
Orchises Press
Oregon Humanities
Orion
Other Voices
Oxford American
Oxford Press
Oyez Press
Oyster Boy Review
Painted Bride Quarterly
Painted Hills Review
Palo Alto Review
Paris Press
Paris Review
Parkett
Parnassus: Poetry in Review
Partisan Review
Passages North
Paterson Literacy Review
Pebble Lake Review
Penca Books
Pentagram
Penumbra Press

Pequod
Persea: An International Review
Perugia Press
Per Contra
Pilot Light
Pipedream Press
Pitcairn Press
Pitt Magazine
Pleasure Boat Studio
Pleiades
Ploughshares
Poems & Plays
Poet and Critic
Poet Lore
Poetry
Poetry Atlanta Press
Poetry East
Poetry International
Poetry Ireland Review
Poetry Northwest
Poetry Now
The Point
Post Road
Prairie Schooner
Prescott Street Press
Press
Promise of Learnings
Provincetown Arts
A Public Space
Puerto Del Sol
Quaderni Di Yip
Quarry West
The Quarterly
Quarterly West
Quiddity
Rainbow Press
Raritan: A Quarterly Review
Rattle
Red Cedar Review
Red Clay Books
Red Dust Press
Red Earth Press
Red Hen Press

Release Press

Republic of Letters

Review of Contemporary Fiction

Revista Chicano-Riquena

Rhetoric Review

Rivendell

River Styx

River Teeth

Rowan Tree Press

Runes

Russian *Samizdat*

Salamander

Salmagundi

San Marcos Press

Sarabande Books

Sea Pen Press and Paper Mill

Seal Press

Seamark Press

Seattle Review

Second Coming Press

Semiotext(e)

Seneca Review

Seven Days

The Seventies Press

Sewanee Review

Shankpainter

Shantih

Shearsman

Sheep Meadow Press

Shenandoah

A Shout In the Street

Sibyl-Child Press

Side Show

Sixth Finch

Small Moon

Smartish Pace

The Smith

Snake Nation Review

Solo

Solo 2

Some

The Sonora Review

Southern Poetry Review

Southern Review

Southwest Review

Speakeasy

Spectrum

Spillway

Spork

The Spirit That Moves Us

St. Andrews Press

Story

Story Quarterly

Streetfare Journal

Stuart Wright, Publisher

Subtropics

Sugar House Review

Sulfur

The Sun

Sun & Moon Press

Sun Press

Sunstone

Sweet

Sycamore Review

Tamagwa

Tar River Poetry

Teal Press

Telephone Books

Telescope

Temblor

The Temple

Tendril

Texas Slough

Think

Third Coast

13th Moon

THIS

Thorp Springs Press

Three Rivers Press

Threepenny Review

Thunder City Press

Thunder's Mouth Press

Tia Chucha Press

Tikkun

Tin House

Tombouctou Books

Toothpaste Press

Transatlantic Review

Triplopia

TriQuarterly

Truck Press

Tupelo Press

Turnrow

Tusculum Review

Undine

Unicorn Press

University of Chicago Press

University of Georgia Press

University of Illinois Press

University of Iowa Press

University of Massachusetts Press

University of North Texas Press

University of Pittsburgh Press

University of Wisconsin Press

University Press of New England

Unmuzzled Ox

Unspeakable Visions of the Individual

Vagabond

Vallum

Verse

Verse Wisconsin

Vignette

Virginia Quarterly Review

Volt

Wampeter Press

Washington Writers Workshop

Water-Stone

Water Table

Wave Books

West Branch

Western Humanities Review

Westigan Review

White Pine Press

Wickwire Press

Wig Leaf

Willow Springs

Wilmore City

Witness

Word Beat Press

Word-Smith

World Literature Today

Wormwood Review

Writers Forum

Xanadu

Yale Review

Yardbird Reader

Yarrow

Y-Bird

Zeitgeist Press

Zoetrope: All-Story

Zone 3

ZYZZYVA

CONTRIBUTING SMALL PRESSES FOR PUSHCART PRIZE XXXVII

A

A-Minor Magazine, 7C, 42 & 42A Hollywood Rd., Hong Kong
aaduna, 144 Genesee St, Ste. 102-259, Auburn, NY 13021
Able Muse Review, 467 Saratoga Ave., #602, San Jose, CA 95129
ABZ Press, PO Box 2746, Huntington, WV 25757-2746
Accents Publishing, P.O. Box 910456, Lexington, KY 40591-0456
The Adirondack Review, 107 1st Ave., New York, NY 10003
Agni, Boston University, 236 Bay State Rd., Boston, MA 02215
Airlie Press, P.O. Box 434, Monmouth, OR 97361
Airways, P.O. Box 1109, Sandpoint, ID 83864
Akashic Books, P.O. Box 46232, West Hollywood, CA 90046
Alabaster & Mercury, 5050 Del Monte Ave., #6, San Diego, CA 92107
Alaska Quarterly Review, 211 Providence Dr., ESH 208, Anchorage, AK 99508
Alice James Books, 238 Main St., Farmington, ME 04938
Alligator Juniper, Prescott College, 220 Grove Ave., Prescott, AZ 86303
American Arts Quarterly, NCCSC, 915 Broadway, Ste. 1104, New York, NY 10010
The American Poetry Journal, P.O. Box 2080, Aptos, CA 95001-2080
The American Scholar, 1606 New Hampshire Ave. NW, Washington, DC 20009
American Short Fiction, PO Box 302678, Austin, TX 78703
Amoskeag, 2500 No. River Rd., Manchester, NH 03106-1045
Ampersand Books, 5040 10th Ave. S., Gulfport, FL 33707
Ampersand Communications, 2901 Santa Cruz SE, Albuquerque, NY 87106
Anaphora, 163 Lucas Rd., Apt. 1-2, Cochran, GA 31014
Anatomy & Etymology, 173 Pasadena Place, Hawthorne, NJ 07506
anderbo.com, 270 Lafayette St., Ste 705, New York, NY 10012
Annalemma Magazine, 112 Second Ave., Ste. 30, Brooklyn, NY 11215
Another Chicago Magazine, MC 162, 602 So. Morgan St, Chicago, IL 60607-7120
Anti-, 4237 Beethoven Ave., St Louis, MO 63116-2503
The Antioch Review, PO Box 148, Yellow Springs, OH 45387-0148
Antrim House Books, 21 Goodrich Rd., Simsbury, CT 06070
Apple Valley Review, 88 South 3rd St, #336, San Jose, CA 95113
Apt, 70 Commercial St, #1R, Boston, MA 02109
Aqueous Books, P.O. Box 12784, Pensacola, FL 32591
Arcadia Magazine, 9616 Nichols Rd., Oklahoma City, OK 73120
Arctos Press, P.O. Box 401, Sausalito, CA 94966-0401
Arizona Authors, 6145 West Echo Lane, Glendale, AZ 85302
Arkansas Review, P.O. Box 1890, State University, AR 72467-1890

ArmChair/Shotgun, 377 Flatbush Ave., No. 3, Brooklyn, NY 11238
Arroyo Literary Review, 25800 Carlos Bee Blvd., Hayward, CA 94542
Arsenic Lobster, 1830 W. 18th St., Chicago, IL 60608
Arte Publico Press, 452 Cullen Performance Hall, Houston, TX 77204-2004
Asheville Poetry Review, P.O. Box 7086, Asheville, NC 28802
Ashland Creek Press, 368 Scenic Dr., Ashland, OR 97520
The Asian American Literary Review, P.O. Box 34495, Washington, DC 20043
Askew, P.O. Box 559, Ventura, CA 93002
Asymptote, 5737 Muirfield Br. SW, Apt. 1, Cedar Rapids, IA 52404
At Length, 47 Clifton Place, Apt. 2D, Brooklyn, NY 11238
At the Bijou, 71 Bank St., Derby, CT 06418
Atlanta Review, PO Box 8248, Atlanta, GA 31106
Atticus Books, 3766 Howard Ave., Ste. 202, Kensington, MD 20895
Autumn House Press, 87 1/2 Westwood St., Pittsburgh, PA 15211
The Awl, 875 Avenue of the Americas, 2nd Floor, New York, NY 10001

B

Bacopa, P.O. Box 358396, Gainesville, FL 32635-8396
Bamboo Ridge Press, PO Box 61781, Honolulu, HI 96839-1781
Barbaric Yawp, 3700 County Route 24, Russell, NY 13684
Barge Press, 3729 Beechwood Blvd., Pittsburgh, PA 15217
Barely South Review, Old Dominion University, Norfolk, VA 23529-0091
Barn Owl Review, Olin Hall 342, Univ. of Akron, Akron, OH 44325-1906
Bartleby Snopes, 917 Kylemore Dr., Ballwin, MO 63021-7935
basalt, Eastern Oregon Univ., One University Blvd., La Grande, OR 97850
Bayou Magazine, 2000 Lake Shore Dr., New Orleans, LA 70148
Bear Star Press, 185 Hollow Oak Dr., Cohasset, CA 95973
Bellevue Literary Review, NYU School of Medicine, 550 First Ave, New York, NY 10016
Bellingham Review, MS-9053, WWU, Bellingham, WA 98225
Beloit Fiction Journal, 700 College St., Box 11, Beloit, WI 53511
Beloit Poetry Journal, PO Box 151, Farmington, ME 04938
Berkeley Fiction Review, 10 B Eshleman Hall, UCB, Berkeley, CA 94720-4500
Bernheim Press, 5809 Scrivener, Long Beach, CA 90808
Big Lucks, 3201 Guilford Ave., #3, Baltimore, MD 21218
The Binnacle, 4 Kimball Hall, 116 O'Brien Ave., Machias, ME 04654
Birch Brook Press, P.O. Box 81, Delhi, NY 13753
Birkensnake, 559 30th St, Oakland, CA 94609-3201
Birmingham Poetry Review, 1517 Astre Circle, Birmingham, AL 35226
BkMk Press, UMKC, 5100 Rockhill Rd., Kansas City, MO 64110-2446
Black Lantern Publishing, P.O. Box 1451, Jacksonville, NC 28541-1451
Blackbird, PO Box 843082, Richmond, VA 23284-3082
Blank Slate Press, 2528 Remington Lane, St. Louis, MO 63144
Blink-Ink, P.O. Box 5, North Branford, CT 06471
Blip Magazine, 2158 26th Ave., San Francisco, CA 94110
Blood Lotus, 307 Granger Circle, Dayton, OH 45433
Blood Orange Review, 1495 Evergreen Ave. NE, Salem, OR 97301
Blue Fifth Review, 267 Lark Meadow Circle, Bluff City, TN 37618
Blue Mesa Review, UNM, Humanities #217, Albuquerque, NM 87131-1106
Blue Print Review, 1103 NW 11th Ave., Gainesville, FL 32601
Blue Unicorn, 22 Avon Rd., Kensington, CA 94707
Bluestem, Eastern Illinois Univ. (121400), 600 Lincoln Ave., Charleston, IL 61920
BOA Editions, 250 North Goodman St., Ste 306, Rochester, NY 14607
Bold Strokes Books, P.O. Box 249, Valley Falls NY 12185
Bona Fide Books, P.O. Box 550278, Tahoe Paradise, CA 96155
Bone Bouquet, 317 Madison Ave., #526, New York, NY 10017
Boone's Dock Press, 235 Ocean Ave., Amityville, NY 11701
Booth, English Dept., Butler Univ., 4600 Sunset Ave., Indianapolis, IN 46208
Borderline, 173 Pasadena Place, Hawthorne, NJ 07506
Bordighera Press, 25 West 43rd St., 17th Floor, New York, NY 10036

bosque, 163 Sol del Oro, Corrales, New Mexico 87048

Botticelli Magazine, 5982 Goode Rd., Powell, OH 43065

Bottom Dog Press, PO Box 425, Huron. OH 44839

Boulevard, 7507 Byron PL., St. Louis, MO 63105

Boxcar Poetry Review, 630 S. Kenmore Ave., #206, Los Angeles, CA 90005

Brain, Child, PO Box 714, Lexington, VA 24450

Brevity, English Dept., Ohio University, Athens, OH 45701-2979

The Briar Cliff Review, 3303 Rebecca St., Sioux City, IA 51104-2100

Brick, P.O. Box 609, Stn. P, Toronto, Ontario, M5S 2Y4, Canada

Brick Cave Media, P.O. Box 4411, Mesa, AZ 85211-4411

Brilliant Corners, Lycoming College, Williamsport, PA 17701

Brink Media, P.O. Box 209034, New Haven, CT 06520-9034

Broadkill Review, 104 Federal St, Milton, DE 19968

The Broadsider, P.O. Box 236, Millbrae, CA 94030

Brothel Books, 116 Ave. C, #17, New York, NY 10009

Bull, 343 Parkovash Ave., South Bend, IN 46617

Bull Spec, P.O. Box 13146, Durham, NC 27709

Burnt Bridge, 6721 Washington Ave., 2H, Ocean Springs, MS 39564

C

C&R Press, 812 Westwood Ave., Chattanooga, TN 37405

C4, 17 Cameron Ave., Cambridge, MA 02140

Caitlin Press, 8160 Alderwood Rd., Halfmoon Bay, VON 1 Y1, BC

Caketrain Journal, PO Box 82588, Pittsburgh, PA 15218-0588

Calliope, 2566 SE Bitterbrush Dr., Madras, OR 97741-9452

Calyx Inc., Box B, Corvallis, OR 97339-0539

The Camel Saloon, 11196 Abbotts Station Dr., Johns Creek, GA 36697

Camera Obscura, P.O. Box 2356, Addison, TX 75001

The Carolina Quarterly, Box 3520, UNC, Chapel Hill, NC 27599-3520

Carve, P.O. Box 701510, Dallas, TX 75370

Casperian Books, P.O. Box 161626, Sacramento, CA 95816-1026

Catfish Creek, Box 36, Loras College, 1456 Alta Vista St., Dubuque, IA 52001

Cave Wall Press, PO Box 29546, Greensboro, NC 27429-9546

Central Recovery Press, 3321 N. Buffalo Dr., Ste. 200, Las Vegas, NV 89129

Cerise Press, P.O. Box 241187, Omaha, NE 68124

Cervena Barva Press, PO Box 440357, W. Somerville, MA 02144-3222

Cha, Department of English, 3/F Fung King Hey Building, Chinese University of Hong Kong, Shatin, New Territories, Hong Kong SAR

The Chaffey Review, 5885 Haven Ave., Rancho Cucamonga, CA 91737-3002

The Chattahoochee Review, 555 North Indian Creek Dr., Clarkston, GA 30021

Chautauqua, UNC Wilmington, 661 South College Rd., Wilmington, NC 28403-5938

Chelsea Station Editions, 362 West 36th St., #2R, New York, NY 10018

The Chrysalis Reader, 1745 Gravel Hill Rd., Dillwyn, VA 23936

Cider Press Review, P.O. Box 33384, San Diego, CA 92163

Cimarron Review, Oklahoma State Univ., Stillwater, OK 74078

Cincinnati Review, Univ. of Cincinnati, PO Box 210069, Cincinnati, OH 45221-0069

Citron Review 631 S. Tularosa Dr., Los Angeles, CA 90026

The Claudius APP, 220 20th St., Apt. 2, Brooklyn, NY 11232

The Cleveland Review, 1305 Andrews Ave., Lakewood, OH 44107

Clock, 1203 Plantation Drive, Simpsonville, SC 29681

Clover, A Literary Rag, 203 West Holly, Ste. 306, Bellingham, WA 98225

Coal City Review, English Dept., University of Kansas, Lawrence, KS 66045

Codhill Press, One Arden Lane, New Paltz, NY 12561

Codorus Press, 34-43 Crescent St, Ste. 1S, Astoria, NY 11106

Cold Mountain Review, ASU—English Dept., Boone, NC 28608

The Collagist, 2779 Page Ave., Ann Arbor, MI 48104

Colorado Review, Colorado State Univ., Fort Collins, CO 80523-9105

Columbia Poetry Review, 600 South Michigan Ave., Chicago, IL 60605-1996

The Common, Frost Library, Amherst College, Amherst, MA 01002-5000

Common Ground, 40 Prospect St. (C-1) Westfield, MA 01085
Concrete Wolf, PO Box 1808, Kingston, WA 98346-1808
Confrontation, English Dept, C.W. Post Campus/LIU, Brookville, NY 11548
Conjunctions, Bard College, Annandale-on-Hudson, NY 12504
Connecticut Review, 39 Woodland St, Hartford, CT 06105-2337
Connotation Press, 117 Country Squire Village, Morgantown, WV 26508
Constellations, 127 Lake View Ave., Cambridge, MA 02138
Conte, 32000 Campus Dr., Salisbury, MD 21804
Copper Canyon Press, PO Box 271, Port Townsend, WA 98368
Copper Nickel, Campus Box 175, P.O. Box 173364, Denver, CO 80217-3364
Corium, 4328 Howe St., Oakland, CA 94611
Court Green, 660 South Michigan Ave., Chicago, IL 60605-1996
Crab Creek Review, PO Box 1524, Kingston, WA 98346
Crab Orchard Review, SIUC, 1660 Faner Drive, Carbondale, IL 62901
Crazyhorse, College of Charleston, 66 George St., Charleston, SC 29424
Creative Nonfiction, 5501 Walnut St., Ste. 202, Pittsburgh, PA 15232
Cross-Cultural Communications, 239 Wynsum Ave., Merrick, NY 11566-4725
Curbside Splendor, 2816 N. Kedzie, Chicago, IL 60618
CutBank, University of Montana, MST410, Missoula, MT 59812
Cutthroat, A Journal of the Arts, PO Box 2414, Durango, CO 81302
The Cyberpunk Apocalypse, 5431 Carnegie St., Pittsburgh, PA 15201
Cyberwit.net, HIG 45, Kaushambi Kunj, Kalindipuram, Allahabad—211611 (U.P.) India

D

Dahse Magazine, 86 Leonard St., #2C, New York, NY 10013
Daniel & Daniel Publishers, P.O. Box 2790, McKinleyville, CA 95519-2790
Dappled Things Magazine, 600 Giltin Drive, Arlington, TX 76006
The Darwin Press, P.O. Box 2202, Princeton, NJ 08543
Deadly Chaps, c/o Sarah Lawrence, 1 Mead Way, Bronxville, NY 10708-5999
decomP, 726 Carriage Hill Dr., Athens, OH 45701
The Delmarva Review, PO Box 544, St. Michaels, MD 21663
DemmeHouse, P.O. Box 2572, Brentwood, TN 37024
Denver Quarterly, 2000 E. Asbury, Denver, CO 80208
The Destroyer, 2640 N. Santa Rita Ave., Tucson, AZ 85719
Devil's Lake, UWM, 600 North Park St., Madison, WI 53706-1474
Diagram, New Michigan Press, 8058 E. 7th St., Tucson, AZ 85710
The DMQ Review, 16393 Bonnie Lane, Los Gatos, CA 95032
Drash, 2632 NE 80th St, Seattle, WA 98115-4622
Dreams & Nightmares, 1300 Kicker Rd., Tuscaloosa, AL 35404
Drunken Boat, 119 Main St., Chester, CT 06412
Dunes Review, P.O. Box 1505, Traverse City, MI 49685

E

Echo Ink Review, 9800 W. 83rd Terrace, Overland Park, KS 66212
Ecotone, UNCW, 601 S. College Rd., Wilmington, NC 28403-5938
Edge, PO Box 101, Wellington, NV 89444
Ekphrasis, PO Box 161236, Sacramento, CA 95816-1236
Electric Literature, 325 Gold St., Ste. 303, Brooklyn, NY 11201
Elephant Rock Books, P.O. Box 119, Ashford, CT 06278
Eleven Eleven Journal, 1111 Eighth St., San Francisco, CA 94107
Emerson Review, 195 Green St., Apt. 3, Cambridge, MA 02139
Emprise Review, 2100 N. Leverett Ave., #28, Fayetteville, AR 72703-2233
Encircle Publications, P.O. Box 187, Farmington, ME 04938
Engine Books, P.O. Box 44167, Indianapolis, IN 46244
The Enigmatist, 104 Bronco Dr., Georgetown, TX 78633
Epiphany, 71 Bedford St., New York, NY 10014

Epoch, 251 Goldwin Smith Hall, Cornell University, Ithaca NY 14853-3201
Erie Times News, 205 West 12th St., Erie, PA 16534-0001
Escape Into Life, 1380 West Truesdell, #5, Wilmington, OH 45177
The Evansville Review, 1800 Lincoln Ave, Evansville, IN 47722
Event, PO Box 2503, New Westminster, BC, V3L 5B2, Canada
Every Day Publishing, 1692 Windermere Pl., Port Coquitlam BC V3B 2K2, Canada
Exit 13, P.O. Box 423, Fanwood, NJ 07023
Expressions, MiraCosta Community College, 1 Barnard Dr., Oceanside, CA 92056
Exter Press, 116 Greene St., Cumberland, MD 21502

F

F Magazine, 3800 DeBarr Rd., Anchorage, AK 99508
FM Publishing, P.O. Box 4211, Atlanta, GA 30302
Failbetter, 2022 Grove Ave., Richmond, VA 23220
Fantastique Unfettered, 21 Indian Trail, Hickory Creek, TX 73065
Feile-Festa, 15 Colonial Gardens, Brooklyn, NY 11209
Fender Stitch, 9301 Fairmead Dr., Charlotte, NC 28269
Fiction Advocate, Oxford Univ. Press, 198 Madison Ave., New York, NY 10016
Fiction Fix, 370 Thornycroft Ave., Staten Island, NY 10312
Fiction International, SDSU, 5500 Campanile Dr., San Diego, CA 92182-6020
Field, 50 North Professor St., Oberlin, OH 44074-1091
Fifth Wednesday Books, Inc, P.O. Box 4033, Lisle, IL 60532-9033
Finishing Line Press, P.O. Box 1626, Georgetown, KY 40324
The First Line, PO Box 250382, Plano, TX 75025-0382
First Step Press, P.O. Box 902, Norristown, PA 19404-0902
5 AM, Box 205, Spring Church, PA 15686
Five Chapters, 387 Third Ave., Brooklyn, NY 11215
Five Points, PO Box 3999, Atlanta, GA 30302-3999
Fjords, 2932 B Langhorne Rd., Lynchburg, VA 24501-1734
Flame Flower, 3322 King St., Apt B, Berkeley, CA 94703
Flash Fiction, University of Missouri, 107 Tate Hall, Columbia, MO 65211
Flashquake, 804 Northcrest Dr., Birmingham, AL 35235
Fledgling Rag, 1716 Swarr Run Rd., J-107-8, Lancaster, PA 17601
Fleeting, 125 Lower Green Rd., Tunbridge Wells, TN4 8TT, UK
The Florida Review, P.O. Box 161346, Orlando, FL 32816-1346
Folded Word, 5209 Des Vista Way, Rocklin, CA 95765
Fomite, 58 Peru St., Burlington, VT 05401
Forge, 1610 S. 22nd, Lincoln, NE 68502
Fortunate Childe, P.O. Box 130085, Birmingham, AL 35213
Four and Twenty Poetry, P.O, Box 61782, Vancouver, WA 98666
Four Way Books, P.O. Box 535, Village Station, New York, NY 10014
Fourteen Hills, 884 Capp St, San Francisco, CA 94110
Fourth Genre, 235 Bessey Hall, East Lansing, MI 48824-1033
The Fourth River, Chatham University, Woodland Rd., Pittsburgh, PA 15232
Freedom Fiction Journal, Nirli Villa, 7, Village Rd., Bhandup west, Mumbai 400078, India
Freight Stories, Ball State University, Muncie, IN 47306-0460
Freshwater, Asnuntuck Community College, 170 Elm St., Enfield, CT 06082
Fringe Magazine, 93 Fox Rd., Apt. 5A, Edison, NJ 08817
Future Cycle Press, 313 Pan Will Rd., Mineral Bluff, GA 30559
Fwriction, 519 E. 78th St., Apt. 3G, New York, NY 10075

G

Gargoyle Magazine, 3819 13th St. N., Arlington, VA 22201-4922
Gemini Magazine, PO Box 1485, Onset, MA 02558
The Georgia Review, University of Georgia, Athens, GA 30602-9009
Gertrude Press, P.O. Box 83948, Portland, OR 97283

The Gettysburg Review, Gettysburg College, Gettysburg, PA 17325-1491
Ghost Ocean Magazine, 3650 N. Fremont St., Apt. 1, Chicago, IL 60613
Gigantic, 496 Broadway, 3rd floor, Brooklyn, NY 11211
Gival Press, PO Box 3812, Arlington, VA 22203
GlenHill Publications, P.O. Box 62, Soulsbyville, CA 95372
Glimmer Train, 1211 NW Glisan St, Ste. 207, Portland, OR 97209-3054
Globe Light Press, 8411 Cienega Rd, Mentone, CA 92359
Gold Man River, P.O. Box 8202, Salem, OR 97303
Gold Wake Press, 5108 Avalon Dr., Randolph, MA 02368
Good Men Project, 7 Wilson Ave., Watertown, MA 02472
Grain, Box 67, Saskatoon, SK, S7K 3K1, Canada
Granta, Grove Atlantic, 841 Broadway, 4th Floor, New York, NY 10003
Gray Dog Press, 2727 S. Mt. Vernon #4, Spokane, WA 99223
Graywolf Press, 250 Third Ave. No., Minneapolis, MN 55401
Great River Review, PO Box 406, Red Wing, MN 55066
Green Lantern Press, 1511 N. Milwaukee Ave., 2nd Floor, Chicago, IL 60622
Green Mountains Review, 337 College Hill, Johnson, VT 05672
Green Poet Press, P.O. Box 6927, Santa Barbara, CA 93160
The Greensboro Review, UNC Greensboro, Greensboro, NC 27402-6170
The Greensilk Journal, 1459 Redland Rd., Cross Junction, VA 22625
Greenwoman Magazine, 1823 W. Pikes Peak Ave., Colorado Springs, CO 80904
Grist, 301 McClung Tower, Univ. of Tennessee, Knoxville, TN 37996
Groundwaters, PO Box 50, Lorane, OR 97451
Gulf Coast, University of Houston, Houston, TX 77204-3013
Gypsy Shadow Publishing, 222 Llano St., Lockhart, Tx 78644

H

H.O.W. Journal, 12 Desbrosses St., New York, NY 10013
The Hairpin, 111 River St., Hoboken, NJ 07030
Hamilton Arts & Letters, 92 Stanley Ave., Hamilton ON, Canada L8P 2L3
Hampden-Sydney Poetry Review, Box 66, Hampden-Sydney, VA 23943
Harbour Publishing Co., P.O. Box 219, Madeira Park, BC V0N 2H0 Canada
Harpur Palate, PO Box 6666, Binghamton University, Binghamton, NY 13902
Harvard Review, Lamont Library, Harvard University, Cambridge, MA 02138
Haunted Waters Press, 1886 T-Bird Drive, Front Royal, VA 22630-9038
Hawaii Pacific Review, 1060 Bishop St., Ste. 7C, Honolulu, HI 96813-4210
Hawthorne Books, 2201 NE 23rd Ave., 3rd Floor, Portland, OR 97212
Hayden's Ferry Review, P.O. Box 875002, Tempe, AZ 85287-5002
The Healing Muse, 750 East Adams St, Syracuse, NY 13210
The Hedgehog Review, UVA, PO Box 400816, Charlottesville, VA 22904-4816
High Coup, P.O. Box 1004, Stockbridge, MA 01262
High Desert Journal, P.O. Box 7647, Bend, OR 97708
High Hill Press, 2731 Cumberland Landing, St. Charles, MO 63303
Hippocampus Magazine, P.O. Box 411, Elizabethtown, PA 17022
Hither & Yahn, P.O. Box 233, San Luis Rey, CA 92068
Hobart, PO Box 1658, Ann Arbor, MI 48106
Hobble Creek Review, PO Box 3511, West Wendover, NV 89883
The Hollins Critic, PO Box 9538, Roanoke, VA 24020-1538
Home Planet News, PO Box 455, High Falls, NY 12440
Homebound, P.O. Box 1442, Pawcatuck, CT 06379-1968
Honest Publishing, 21 Valley Mews, Cross Deep, Twickenham TW1 4QT, UK
The Hudson Review, 684 Park Ave., New York, NY 10065
Hulltown 360, 7806 Sunday Silence Lane, Midlothian, VA 23112
Hunger Mountain, 36 College St., Montpelier, VT 05602

I

I-70 Review, 5021 S. Tierney Dr., Independence, MO 64055
Ibbetson Street Press, 25 School Street, Somerville, MA 02143
Idaho Review, 1910 University Dr., Boise, ID 83725
Illuminations, College of Charleston, 66 George St., Charleston, SC 29424
Illya's Honey, PO Box 700865, Dallas, TX 75370
Image, 3307 Third Avenue West, Seattle, WA 98119
In Posse Review, 11 Jordan Ave., San Francisco, CA 94118
Indiana Review, 1020 E. Kirkwood Ave., Bloomington, IN 47405-7103
InDigest, c/o Nelson, 2815 34th St., 3A, Astoria, NY 11103
Inkwell, Manhattanville College, 2900 Purchase St, Purchase, NY 10577
International Poetry Review, UNCG, P.O. Box 26170, Greensboro, NC 27402-6170
iO: A Journal of New American Poetry, 3621 Kingman Blvd., Des Moines, IA 30311
Ion Drive Publishing, 6251 Drexel Ave., Los Angeles, CA 90048
The Iowa Review, 308 EPB, University of Iowa, Iowa City, IA 52242
Iron Horse, English Dept., Texas Tech Univ., Lubbock, TX 79409-3091
IsoLibris, 4927 6th Pl., Meridian, MS 39305

J

J Journal, 619 West 54th St., 7th Fl, NY, NY 10019
Jabberwock Review, Mississippi State Univ., Drawer E, Mississippi State, MS 39762
Jacar Press, 6617 Deerview Trail, Durham, NC 27712
The Journal, 17 High St., Maryport, Cumbria CA15 6BQ, UK
The Journal, Ohio State Univ., 164 West 17th Ave., Columbus, OH 43210-1370
The Journal of Experimental Fiction, 12 Simpson Ave., Geneva, IL 60134
Journal of New Jersey Poets, 214 Center Grove Rd., Randolph, NJ 07869-2086
Jovialities Entertainment Co., 521 Park Ave., Elyria, OH 44035
Juked, 17149 Flanders St, Los Angeles, CA 91344
Junk, 16233 SE 10th St, Bellevue, WA 98008

K

Kartika Review, API Cultural Center, 934 Brannan St., San Francisco, CA 94103
Kelly's Cove Press, 2733 Prince St., Berkeley, CA 94705
Kelsey Review, Mercer County Community College, P.O. Box B, Trenton, NJ 08690
Kenyon Review, Neff Cottage, 102 W. Wiggin St., Gambier, OH 43022
Kerf, 883 W. Washington Blvd., Crescent City, CA 95531-8361
Kestrel, 264000, Fairmont State Univ., 1201 Locust Ave., Fairmont, WV 26554
Kitsune Books, PO Box 1154, Crawfordville, FL 32326-1154
Kiwi Publishing, P.O. Box 3852, Woodbridge, CT 06525
Kore Press, PO Box 42315, Tucson, AZ 85733-2315

L

La Muse Press, 1 East University Pkwy, Unit 801, Baltimore, MD 21218
The Labletter, 3712 N. Broadway, #241, Chicago, IL 60613
Lake Effect, 4951 College Drive, Erie, PA 16563-1501
Lavender Review, P.O. Box 275, Eagle Rock, MO 65641
Leaf, Box 416, Lantzville, B.C., V0R 2H0 Canada
Levellers Press, 71 S. Pleasant St., Amherst, MA 01002
The Lindenwood Review, 209 S. Kingshighway, St. Charles, MO 63301
Lines + Stars, 1801 Clydesdale Place NW #323, Washington, DC 20009
Lips, 7002 Blvd. East, #2-26G, Guttenberg, NJ 07093

The Literarian, 17 East 47th St., New York, NY 10017
The Literary Lunch Room, 209 Riggs Ave., Severna Park, MD 21146
The Literary Review, 285 Madison Ave./M-GH2-01, Madison, NJ 07940
Little Balkans Review, 315 South Hugh St, Frontenae, KS 66763
Little Patuxent Review, 5008 Brampton Pkwy., Ellicott City, MD 21043
Little Red Tree Publishing, 635 Ocean Ave., New London, CT 06320
Little Star, 107 Bank St, New York, NY 10014
The Lives Yon Touch, P.O. Box 276, Gwynedd Valley, PA 19437-0276
Livingston Press, Station 22, Univ. of West Alabama, Livingston, AL 35470
Lookout Books, 601 South College Rd., Wilmington, NC 28403
Lorimer Press, PO Box 1013, Davidson, NC 28036
The Los Angeles Review, 10234 132nd Ave. NE, Kirkland, WA 98033
The Los Angeles Review of Books, 4470 Sunset Blvd., #115, Los Angeles, CA 90027
Lost Horse Press, 105 Lost Horse Lane, Sandpoint, ID 83864
The Louisiana State University Press, 3990 Lakeshore Dr., Baton Rouge, LA 70803
The Louisville Review, Spalding Univ., 851 South Fourth St., Louisville, KY 40203
Loving Healing Press Inc., 5145 Pontiac Trl, Ann Arbor, MI 48105-9279
Luminis Books, 13245 Blacktern Way, Carmel, IN 46033

M

The MacGuffin, 18600 Haggerty Rd., Livonia, MI 48152
Magnapoets, 13300 Tecumseh Rd. E., #226, Tecumseh, Ontario N8N 4R8, Canada
MAKE, 2229 W. Iowa St., #3, Chicago, EL 60622
make/shift, PO Box 27566, Los Angeles, CA 90027
The Malahat Review, PO Box 1700 STN CSC, Victoria BC V8W 2Y2 Canada
The Manhattan Review, 440 Riverside Dr., #38, New York, NY 10027
Many Mountains Moving, 1765 Lombard St, Philadelphia, PA 19146-1518
Marco Polo, 153 Cleveland Ave., Athens, GA 30601
Marriage Publishing House, 866 SE 10th Ave., Portland, OR 97214
Martha's Vineyard Arts & Ideas, P.O. Box 1130, West Tisbury, MA 02575
The Massachusetts Review, South College 126047, Amherst, MA 01003-7140
Matchbook, 31 Berkley Place #2, Buffalo, NY 14209
Matter Press, P.O. Box 764, Wynnewood, PA 19096
Mayapple Press, 362 Chestnut Hill Rd., Woodstock, NY 12498
McSweeny's, 849 Valencia, San Francisco, CA 94110
The Medulla Review, 612 Everett Rd., Knox, TN 37934
Memoir (and), 1316 67th St., #8, Emeryville, CA 94608
Memorious, 187 N. Harrison St., Johnson City, NY 13790
Menacing Hedge, 5501 31st Ave. NE, Seattle, WA 98105
Menu, 87-16, #501, Daejo-dong, Eunpyong-Ku, Seoul, South Korea 122-030
Metazen, Ulrich-von-Huttenstr. 8,81739 Munich, Germany
Michigan Quarterly Review, 915 E. Washington St., Ann Arbor, MI 48109-1070
Michigan State University Press, 1405 S. Harrison Rd., East Lansing, MI 48823-5245
Mid-American Review, Bowling Green State Univ., Bowling Green, OH 43403
Midway Journal, P.O. Box 14499, St., Paul, MN 55114
Midwestern Gothic, 957 E. Grant, Des Plaines, IL 60016
The Mighty Rogue Press, P.O. Box 19553, Boulder, CO 80308-2553
Milkweed, 1011 Washington Ave (A300) Minneapolis, MN 55415
The Millions, 107 Birch Rd., Highland Lakes, NJ 07422
Milspeak Books, 3305 Lightning Rd., Borrego Springs, CA 92004
the minnesota review, Virginia Tech, ASPECT, Blacksburg, VA 24061
Minnetonka Review, P.O. Box 386, Spring Park, MN 55384
Mississippi Review, 118 College Dr. #5144, Hattiesburg, MS 39406-0001
The Missouri Review, 357 McReynolds Hall, Univ. of Missouri, Columbia, MO 65211
Mixed Fruit, 925 Troy Rd., Edwardsville, IL 62025
Mixer.com, 3013 Woodridge Ave., South Bend, IN 46615-3811
MMIP Books, 416 101st Ave., SE, #308, Bellevue, WA 98004
Mobius, the Poetry Magazine, 14453 77th Ave., Flushing, NY 11367
Modern Haiku, PO Box 33077, Santa Fe, NM 87594-3077

Mojo!, 38 Exeter St., Arlington, MA 02474

The Monarch Review, 5033 Brooklyn Ave., NE, Apt. B, Seattle, WA 98105

Monkeybicycle, 206 Bellevue Ave., Floor 2, Montclair, NJ 07043

MoonPath Press, P.O. Box 1808, Kingston, WA 98346

Moonshot Magazine, 416 Broadway, 3rd Floor, Brooklyn, NY 11211

The Morning News, 6206 Wynona Ave., Austin, TX 78757

MotesBooks, 89 W. Chestnut St., Williamsburg, KY 40769

Mountain Gazette, P.O. Box 7548, Boulder, CO 80306

Mozark Press, P.O. Box 1746, Sedalia, MO 65302

Mud Luscious Press, 2115 Sandstone Dr., Fort Collins, CO 80524

MungBeing Magazine, 1319 Maywood Ave., Upland, CA 91786

Murder Slim Press, 29 Alpha Rd., Gorleston, Norfolk, NR31 0LQ, UK

Muse-Pie Press, 73 Pennington Ave., Passaic, NJ 07055

Muzzle Magazine, 700 Stewart Ave., #28, Ithaca, NY 14850

Mythopoetry Scholar, 16211 East Keymar Dr., Fountain Hills, AZ 85268

N

N + 1 Magazine, 68 Jay St., #465, Brooklyn, NY 11201

NaDa Publishing, 1415 Fourth St SW, Albuquerque, NM 87102

NANO Fiction, P.O. Box 667445, Houston, TX 77266-7445

NAP, 5824 Timber Lake Blvd., Indianapolis, IN 46237

Narrative, 2130 Fillmore St, #233, San Francisco, CA 94115

The National Poetry Review, P.O. Box 2080, Aptos, CA 95001-2080

Natural Bridge, English Department, One University Blvd., St Louis, MO 63121

Naugatuck River Review, PO Box 368, Westfield, MA 01085

New American Writing, 369 Molino Ave., Mill Valley, CA 94941

The New Criterion, 900 Broadway, Ste. 662, New York, NY 10003

New England Review, Middlebury College, Middlebury, VT 05753

The New Guard, P.O. Box 10612, Portland, ME 04104

New Issues, 1963 W. Michigan Ave., Kalamazoo, MI 49008-5463

New Letters, 5161 Rockhill Rd., Kansas City, MO 64110-2499

New Madrid, Murray State University, 7C Faculty Hah, Murray, KY 42071

New Mirage Journal, 3066 Zelda Rd., #384, Montgomery, AL 36106

New Ohio Review, Ohio University, 360 Ellis Hall, Athens, OH 45701

New Orleans Review, Box 50, Loyola University, New Orleans, CA 70118

The New Orphic Review, 706 Mill St., Nelson, B.C. V1L 4S5 Canada

New Plains Press, P.O. Box 1946, Auburn, AL 36831-1946

New Rivers Press, 1104 Seventh Avenue S., Moorhead, MN 56563

new south, Campus Box 1894, Georgia State Univ., Atlanta, GA 30303-3083

New Southerner Magazine, 375 Wood Valley Lane, Louisville, KY 40299

New Urban Review, Box 195, Loyola University, New Orleans, LA 70118

New Verse News, Les Belles Maisons H-11, Serpong Utara, Tangerang-Baten 15310, Indonesia

New York Tyrant, 676 A Ninth Ave., #153, New York, NY 10036

News Ink Books, 22848 State Route 28, Delhi, NY 13753

NewSouth Books, P.O. Box 1588, Montgomery, AL 36102

Night Ballet Press, 123 Glendale Court, Elyria, OH 44035

Nightblade Magazine, 11323 126th St., Edmonton, AB T5M 0R5 Canada

Nightwood Editions, Box 1779, Gibsons, BC, VON 1V0, Canada

Nimrod, 800 South Tucker Dr., Tulsa, OK 74104

Ninth Letter, 608 S. Wright St., Urbana, IL 61801

Noon, 1324 Lexington Ave., PMB 298, New York, NY 10128

The Normal School, 5245 N. Backer Ave., M/S PB 98, Fresno, CA 93740-8001

North American Review, Univ. of No. Iowa, 1222 West 27th St., Cedar Falls, IA 50614-0516

The North Carolina Literary Review, ECU Mailstop 555, Greenville, NC 27858-4353

North Dakota Quarterly, 276 Centennial Drive, Grand Forks, ND 58202-7209

Northwest Review, 5243 University of Oregon, Eugene, OR 97403-5243

Not One of Us, 12 Curtis Rd., Natick, MA 01760

Notre Dame Review, 840 Flanner Hall, Notre Dame, IN 46556-5639

Now Culture, 90 Kennedy Rd., Andover, NJ 07821

O

Oberlin's Law, P.O. Box 27, New Hampton, NH 03256
Obsidian, African Amer. Cultural Cntr, 2810 Cates Ave., Raleigh, NC 27695-7318
OCHO, 604 Vale St., Bloomington, IL 61701
Off the Coast, PO Box 14, Robbinston, ME 04671
The Offending Adam, 1225 Washington Ave., Unit 2, Santa Monica, CA 90403
Old Mountain Press, P.O. Box 66, Webster, NC 28788
Old Red Kimono, 3175 Cedartown Hwy. SE, Rome, GA 30161
1110, (One Photograph, One Story, Ten Poems), 54 Lower Rd., Beeston, Nottingham, NG9 2GT, UK
One Story, 232 3rd St, #E106, Brooklyn, NY 11238
Orange Quarterly, 3862 Hidden Creek Dr., Traverse City, MI 49684
Orchises Press, P.O. Box 320533, Alexandria, VA 22320-4533
Orion, 187 Main St, Great Harrington, MA 01230
Orphiflamme Press, P.O. Box 4366, Boulder, CO 80306
Osiris, PO Box 297, Deerfield, MA 01342
Other Voices Books, 2235 W. Waveland Ave., Apt. 1, Chicago, IL 60618
Out of Our, 1288 Columbus Ave., #216, San Francisco, CA 94133-1302
Overtime, PO Box 250382, Plano, TX 75025-0382
OVS Magazine, 32 Linsey Lane, Warren, NH 03279

P

P.R.A. Publishing, PO Box 211701, Martinez, GA 30917
PAC Books, 72 Tehama St., San Francisco, CA 94105
The Packinghouse Review, 1030 Howard St, Kingsburg, CA 93631
Palabra, P.O. Box 86146, Los Angeles, CA 90086-0146
Palettes & Quills, 330 Knickerbocker Ave., Rochester, NY 146155
Palm Beach ArtsPaper, P.O. Box 7625, Delray Beach, FL 33484
Palo Alto Review, 1400 W. Villaret Blvd., San Antonio, TX 78224
PANK Magazine, 1230 W. Polk Ave., #107, Charleston, IL 61920
Papaveria Press, 145 Hollin Lane, Wakefield, West Yorkshire, WF4 3EG, UK
Paper Nautilus, I-4 Bradley Circle, Enfield, CT 06082
Parallel Press, 728 State St, Madison, WI 53706
Parcel, 6 E. 7th St., Lawrence, KS 66044
The Paris Review, 62 White St., New York, NY 10013
Parthenon West Review, 1516 Myra St., Redlands, CA 92373
Passages North, English Dept., 1401 Presque Isle Ave., Marquette, MI 49855-5363
Paterson Literary Review, 1 College Blvd., Paterson, NJ 07505-1179
Pearl, 3030 E. Second St., Long Beach, CA 90803
Penmanship Books Poetry, 593 Vanderbilt Ave., #265, Brooklyn, NY 11238
Perugia Press, PO Box 60364, Florence, MA 01062
Phantom Drift, P.O. Box 3235, La Grande, OR 97850
Philadelphia Stories, 93 Old York Rd., Ste.1/#1-753, Jenkintown, PA 19046
Phrygian Press, 58-09 205th St., Bayside, NY 11364
PigeonBike, 611 Wonderland Rd. N. Ste. 379, London, Ontario N6H 5N7, Canada
The Pinch, English Dept., 467 Patterson Hall, Memphis, TN 38152-3510
Ping-Pong, Henry Miller Library, Highway One, Big Sur, CA 93920
Pink Narcissus Press, P.O. Box 303, Auburn, MA 01501
Pink Petticoat Press, P.O. Box 130085, Birmingham, AL 35213
Pirene's Fountain, 3616 Glenlake Dr., Glenview, IL 60026
Pleiades Press, Univ. of Central Missouri, Warrensburg, MO 64093-5046
Phoenicia Publishing, 1397 rue Rachel E., #102, Montreal H2J 2K2 Quebec, Canada
Ploughshares, Emerson College, 120 Boylston St., Boston, MA 02116-4624
Plume, 740 17th Ave. N, St Petersburg, FL 33704
Poecology, 1749 Kappa Ave., San Leandro, CA 94579
Poems and Plays, MTSU, P.O. Box 70, Murfreesboro, TN 37132
Poet Lore, 4508 Walsh St., Bethesda, MD 20815
Poetry, 444 N. Michigan, Ste 1850, Chicago, IL 60611

Poetry Center, Cleveland State Univ., 2121 Euclid Ave., Cleveland, OH 44115-2214
Poetry for the Masses, 1654 S. Volustia, Wichita, KS 67211
Poetry In the Arts Press, 5110 Avenue H, Austin, TX 78751-2026
Poetry Kanto, 3-22-1 Kamariya-Minami, Kanazawa-Ku, Yokohama, 236-8502, Japan
Poetry, 61 West Superior St., Chicago, IL 60654
Poetry Northwest, Everett Community College, 2000 Tower St., Everett, WA 98201
Poets and Artists, 604 Vale St., Bloomington, IL 61701
Poets Wear Prada, 533 Bloomfield St, 2nd Floor, Hoboken, NJ 07030
The Point, 255 Massachusetts Ave., Apt. 702, Boston, MA 02115
Post Road, Boston College, 140 Commonwealth Ave., Chestnut Hill, MA 02467
Potomac Review, 51 Mannakee St., MT/212, Rockville, MD 20850
Prairie Journal Trust, 28 Crowfoot Terrace NW, P.O. Box 68073, Calgary, AB, T3G 3N8, Canada
Prairie Schooner, UNL, 201 Andrews Halt, PO Box 880334, Lincoln, NE 68588-0334
Precipitate, 1576 Portland Ave., Apt. 10, Saint Paul, MN 55105
Presa Press, PO Box 792, Rockford, MI 49341
Press 53, PO Box 30314, Winston-Salem, NC 27130
Primal Urge Magazine, P.O. Box 2416, Grass Valley, CA 95945
Prime Mincer, 401 N. Poplar, Carbondale, IL 62901
Prime Number Magazine, 1853 Old Greenville Rd., Staunton, VA 24401
Printed Matter Vancouver, 910 T St, Vancouver, WA 98661
The Prose-Poem Project, Equinox Publishing, P.O. Box 424, Shelburne, VT 05482
Proverse Hong Kong, P.O. Box 259, Tung Chung Post Office, Lantau Island, New Territories, Hong Kong,
    SAR
Provincetown Arts, 650 Commercial St., Provincetown, MA 02657
A Public Space, 323 Dean St, Brooklyn, NY 11217
Pudding Magazine, 5717 Bromley Ave., Worthington, OH 43085

Q

Qarrtsiluni, P.O. Box 8, Tyrone, PA 16686
Queen's Ferry Press, 8240 Preston Rd., Ste. 125-151, Piano, TX 75024
Quiddity, Benedictine University, 1500 N. Fifth St., Springfield, IL 62702
Quill and Parchment Press, 2357 Merrywood Dr., Los Angeles, CA 90046
The Quotable, 520 W 21st St., #230, Norfolk, VA 23517

R

R.KV.R.Y Quarterly, 72 Woodbury Dr., Lockport, NY 14094
R. L. Crow Publications, PO Box 262, Penn Valley, CA 95946
Radius, 65 Paine St, #2, Worcester, MA 01605
Raintown Review, 5390 Fallriver Row Ct., Columbia, MD 21044
Raleigh Review, Box 6725, Raleigh, NC 27628-6725
Raritan, 31 Mine St., New Brunswick, NJ 08901
Rattle, 12411 Ventura Blvd., Studio City, CA 91604
The Rattling Wall, 269 S Beverly, #1163, Beverly Hills, CA 90212
Ray's Road Review, P.O. Box 2001, Hixson, TN 37343
REAL, P.O. Box 13007-SFA Stn, S. F. Austin State Univ., Nacogdoches, TX 75962
Rebel Satori Press, P.O. Box 363, Hulls Cove, ME 04644-0363
Red Alice Books, P.O. Box 262, Penn Valley, CA 95946
Red Hen Press, PO Box 40820, Pasadena, CA 91114
Red Lightbulbs, 4213 S. Union Ave., Floor 2, Chicago, IL 60609
Red River Review, 4669 Mountain Oak St, Fort Worth, TX 76244-4397
Redactions, 58 South Main St, Brockport, NY 14420
Reed Magazine, SJSU, English Dept., 1 Washington Sq., San Jose, CA 95192-0090
Referential Magazine, 8324 Highlander Court, Charlotte, NC 28269
Republic of Letters, Apartado 29, Cahuita, Costa Rica
Rescue Press, 1220 E. Locust, #209, Milwaukee, WT 53212
Resource Center for Women & Ministry, 1202 Watts St, Durham, NC 27701

Revolution House, 1117 Anthrop Dr., #12, West Lafayette, IN 47906
River Styx, 3547 Olive St, Ste. 107, St Louis, MO 63103-1024
River Teeth, Ashland University, 401 College Ave., Ashland, OH 44805
Rock & Sling, Whitworth Univ., 300 W. Hawthorne Rd., Spokane, WA 99251
Rose House Publishing, P.O. Box 3339, Grand Rapids, MI 49501
Rougarou, PO Box 44691, Lafayette, LA 70504-4691
Ruminate, 140 N. Roosevelt Ave., Ft. Collins, CO 80521

S

S.F.A. Press, P.O. Box 13007, SFA Station, Nacogdoches, TX 75962-3007
Saint Paul Almanac, 275 East Fourth St., Ste. 735, Saint Paul, MN 55101
Salamander, 41 Temple St., Boston, MA 02114-4280
Salmagundi, Skidmore College, Saratoga Springs, NY 12866
The Salon, 294 N. Winooski Ave., Burlington, VT 05401
Salt Hill, English Dept., Syracuse University, Syracuse, NY 13244
San Pedro River Review, P.O. Box 7000-148, Redondo Beach, CA 90277
The Sand Hill Review, 2284 Carmelita Drive, San Carlos, CA 94070
Santa Monica Review, 29051 Hilltop Dr., Silverado, CA 92676
The Saranac Review, 101 Broad St., Pittsburgh, NY 12901-2681
Scarlet Literary Magazine, 1209 S. 6th St., Louisville, KY 40203
Scarletta Press, 10 South 5th Street, #1105, Minneapolis, MN 55402-1012
Schuylkill Valley Journal, 240 Golf Hills Rd., Havertown, PA 19083
Scribendi, MSC06-3890, 1 University of New Mexico, Albuquerque, NM 87131
Sea Storm Press, P.O. Box 186, Sebastopol, CA 95473
Seal Press, 1700 Fourth St., Berkeley, CA 94710
The Seattle Review, Univ. of Washington, Box 354330, Seattle, WA 98195-4330
Seems, Lakeland College, PO Box 359, Sheboygan, WI 53082-0359
Serving House, 29641 Desert Terrace Dr., Menifee, CA 92584-7800
Seventh Quarry, Dan-y-bryn, 74 Cwm Level Rd., Brynhyfrd, Swansea SA5 9DY, Wales, UK
Sewanee Review, 735 University Ave., Sewanee, TN 37383
Shadow Mountain Press, 14900 W. 31st Ave., Golden, CO 80401
Shenandoah, Mattingly House, 2 Lee Avenue, Lexington, VA 24450-2116
The Shit Creek Review, 90 Kennedy Rd., Andover, NJ 07821
Shock Totem, 107 Hovendon Ave., Brockton, MA 02302
Shoppe Foreman Co., 3507 Homesteaders Lane, Guthrie, OK 73044
Short Story America, 2121 Boundary St., Ste. 204, Beaufort, SC 29907
Sibling Rivalry Press, 13913 Magnolia Glen, Alexander, AR 72002
Silk Road Review, 2043 College Way, Forest Grove, OR 97116-1797
The Single Hound, P.O. Box 1142, Mount Sterling, KY 40353
Sink Review, 95 Graham Ave., 2nd Floor, Brooklyn, NY 11206
Sixth Finch, 95 Carolina Ave., #2, Jamaica Plain, MA 02130
Slake Media, 3191 Casitas Ave., Ste. 110, Los Angeles, CA 90039
Sleet Magazine, 1846 Bohland Ave., St. Paul, MN 55116
Slipstream, Box 2071, Niagara Falls, NY 14301
Smartish Pace, PO Box 22161, Baltimore, MD 21203
Solas House, 853 Alma St., Palo Alto, CA 94301
Solo Press, 1555 Filaree Way, Arroyo Grande, CA 93420
Solstice, 38 Oakland Ave., Needham, MA 02492
Song of the San Joaquin, PO Box 1161, Modesto, CA 95353-1161
South Loop Review, Columbia College, 600 S. Michigan, Chicago, IL 60605
The Southampton Review, 239 Montauk Hwy., Southampton, NY 11968
The Southeast Review, English Dept., Florida State Univ., Tallahassee, FL 32306
Southern Humanities Review, 9088 Haley Center, Auburn, AL 36849-5202
Southern Indiana Review, USI, 8600 University Blvd., Evansville, IN 47712
Southern Poetry Review, 11935 Abercorn St., Savannah, GA 31419-1997
The Southern Review, Louisiana State University, Baton Rouge, LA 70808
Sou'wester Magazine, Southern Illinois Univ., Edwardsville, IL 62026-1438
The Sow's Ear Poetry Review, P.O. Box 127, Millwood, VA 22646
Southwest Review, PO Box 750374, Dallas, TX 75275-0374

sPARKLE & bLINK, 215 Precita Ave., San Francisco, CA 94110
Specter, One Market St., Apt 417, Camden, NJ 08102
Spillway, 11 Jordan Ave., San Francisco, CA 94118°
Spoon River, Illinois State Univ., Campus Box 4240, Normal, IL 61790-4240
Spudnik Press Coop, 1821 W. Hubbard St., Ste. 302, Chicago, IL 60622
Star Cloud Press, 6137 East Mescal St., Scottsdale, AZ 85254-5418
StepAway Magazine, 2, Bowburn Close, Wardley, Gateshead, Tyne & Wear, NE10 8UG, UK
Still, P.O. Box 1121, Berea, KY 40403
Still Crazy, P.O. Box 777, Worthington, OH 43085
Stirring, 114 Newridge Rd., Oak Ridge, TN 37830
Stone Canoe, 700 University Ave., Ste. 326, Syracuse, NY 13244-2530
The Stone Hobo, 16 Holley St., Danbury, CT 06810
Stone Telling Magazine, 200 Nebraska, Lawrence, KS 66046
Stoneboat, Lakeland College, P.O. Box 359, Sheboygan, WI 53082-0359
The Storyteller, 2441 Washington Rd., Maynard, AR 72444
String Poet, 10 Tappen Drive, Melville, NY 11747
Stymie, 1965 Briarfield Dr. Ste. 303, Lake St. Louis, MO 63367
Sugar House Review, PO Box 17091, Salt Lake City, UT 84117
The Summerset Review, 25 Summerset Dr., Smithtown, NY 11787
The Sun, 107 North Roberson St., Chapel Hill, NC 27516
sunnyoutside, PO Box 911, Buffalo, NY 14207
Super Arrow, 121 N. Normal, #3, Ypsilanti, MI 48197
Supermachine, 388 Myrtle Ave., #3, Brooklyn, NY 11205
Superstition Review, 3931 E. Equestrian Tr. Phoenix, AZ 85044
Sweet, 110 Holly Tree Lane, Brandon, FL 33511
Swink, 1661 10th Ave., Brooklyn, NY 11215
Sycamore Review, Purdue Univ., 500 Oval Dr., West Lafayette, IN 47907

T

Ten Thousand Tons of Black Ink, 716 Columbian Ave., Oak Park, IL 60302
10 X 3 Plus, 1077 Windsor Ave., Morgantown, WV 26505
Terrain.org, P.O. Box 19161, Tucson, AZ 85731-9161
Texas Review Press, Box 2146, Sam Houston State Univ., Huntsville, TX 77341-2146
THE2NDHAND, 1430 Roberts Ave., Nashville, TN 37206
Third Coast, Western Michigan University, Kalamazoo, MI 49008-5331
Third Wednesday, 174 Greenside Up, Ypsilanti, MI 48197
THIS Literary Magazine, 315 W. 15th St., #12, Minneapolis, MN 55403
Thought Publishing, 73 Alvarado Rd., Berkeley, CA 94705
Three Coyotes, 10645 N.Oracle Rd., Ste. 121-163, Tucson, AZ 85737
Three Mile Harbor Press, Box 1951, East Hampton, NY 11937
Threepenny Review, PO Box 9131, Berkeley, CA 94709
Thunderclap!, 1055 Thomas St., Hillside, NJ 07205
Tidal Basin Review, P.O. Box 1703, Washington, DC 20013
Tin House, PMB 280, 320 7th Ave., Brooklyn, NY 11215
Tipton Poetry Journal, PO Box 804, Zionsville, IN 46077
Toasted Cheese, 44 East 13th Ave., #402, Vancouver BC V5T 4K7, Canada
Toadlily Press, PO Box 2, Chappaqua, NY 10514
The Toucan Literary Magazine, 16519 Paw Paw Ave., Orland Park, IL 60467
Trachodon, P.O. Box 1468, St. Helens, OR 97051
Transition, 104 Mt. Auburn St., 3R, Cambridge, MA 02138
Transom Journal, 185 Vernon Ave., Apt. 4, Louisville, KY 40206
Traprock Books, 1330 E. 25th Ave., Eugene, OR 97403
Travelers' Tales, Solas House, 853 Alma St., Palo Alto, CA 94301
Treehouse Press, P.O. Box 65016, London N5 9BD, UK
Trinacria, 220 Ninth St., Brooklyn, NY 11215-3902
TriQuarterly, Northwestern Univ., 339 E. Chicago Ave., Evanston, IL 60611-3008
Truman State University Press, 100 E. Normal Ave., Kirksville, MO 63501
Tuesday, PO Box 1074, East Arlington, MA 02474
Tupelo Press, PO 1767, North Adams, MA 01247

Turbulence, 29 Finchley Close, Hull, East Yorkshire, HU8 0NU, UK
A Twist of Noir, 2309 West Seventh St., Duluth, MN 55806-1536
2 Bridges Review, NY City College of Technology, 300 Jay St., Brooklyn, NY 11201
Two Hawks Quarterly, Antioch Univ., 400 Corporate Pointe, Culver City, CA 90230
Tyrant Books, 676A Ninth St., #153, New York, NY10036

U

URJ Books, 633 Third Ave., New York, NY 10017-6778
U.S. 1 Poets' Cooperative, PO Box 127, Kingston, NJ 08528-0127
Umbrella, 5620 Netherland Ave., #2E, Bronx, NY 10471-1880
unboundCONTENT, 160 Summit St., Englewood, NJ 07631
Underground Voices, 4020 Cumberland Ave., Los Angeles, CA 90027
University of Arizona Press, 1510 E. University Blvd., Tucson, AZ 85721-0055
University of Nebraska Press, 1111 Lincoln Mall, Lincoln, NE 68588-0630
University of North Texas Press, 1155 Union Circle #311336, Denton, TX 76203-5017
UNO Press, University of New Orleans Publishing, New Orleans, LA 70148
Unsplendid, SUNY Buffalo, 306 Clemens Hall, Buffalo, NY 14260-4610
Unstuck, 4505 Duval St., #204, Austin, TX 78751
Unthology, P.O. Box 3506, Norwich, NR7 7PQ, UK
Uphook Press, 515 Broadway, #2B, New York, NY 10012
Uptown Mosaic, E Swan Creek Rd., Ft. Washington, MD 20744-5200

V

Vagabondage Press, P.O. Box 3563, Apollo Beach, FL 33572
Vallum, P.O. Box 598 Victoria Stn., Montreal, QC H3Z 2Y6, Canada
Valparaiso Poetry Review, English Dept., Valparaiso Univ., Valparaiso, IN 46383
VAO Publishing, 4717 N. FM 493, Donna, TX 78537
Versal, Postbus 3865,1001 AR Amsterdam, The Netherlands
Verse Wisconsin, P.O. Box 620216, Middleton, WI, 53562-0216
Vestal Review, 2609 Dartmouth Dr., Vestal, NY 13850
Victorian Violet Press, 1840 W 220th St., Ste. 300, Torrance, CA 90501
Vinyl Poetry, 814 Hutcheson Dr., Blacksburg, VA 24060
Virginia Quarterly Review, 1 West Range, Charlottesville, VA 22904
Virgogray Press, 2103 Nogales Trail, Austin, TX 78744
VoiceCatcher, P.O. Box 6064, Portland, OR 97228-6064
Voices, PO Box 9076, Fayetteville, AR 72703-0018

W

Waccamaw, PO Box 261954, Conway, SC 29528-6054
Wag's Revue, 811 E. College St., Iowa City, IA 52240
Wake, 1 Campus Dr., Allendale, MI 49401-9403
Walkabout Publishing, P.O. Box 151, Kansasville, WI 53139
The Wapshott Press, P.O. Box 31513, Los Angeles, CA 90031-0513
Water~Stone Review, MS A1730, 1536 Hewitt Ave., St. Paul, MN 55104-1284
The Waterhouse Review, 105 E Barnton St., Stirling, FK8 1HJ, UK
Wave Books, 1938 Fairview Ave. East, Ste. 201, Seattle, WA 98102
Wayne State University Press, 4809 Woodward Ave., Detroit, MI 48201-1309
Weave Magazine, 7 Germania St., San Francisco, CA 94117
Weighed Words, 1326 Sleepy Hollow Rd., Glenview, IL 60025
Wesleyan University Press, 215 Long Lane, Middletown, CT 06459
West Branch, Stadler Center for Poetry, Bucknell Univ., Lewisburg, PA 17837
The Westchester Review, Box 246H, Scarsdale, NY 10583
Western Humanities Review, Univ. of Utah, Salt Lake City, UT 84112-0494

Whispering Prairie Press, P.O. Box 8342, Prairie Village, KS 66208-0342
White Pelican Review, P.O. Box 7833, Lakeland, FL 33813
White Pine Press, P.O. Box 236, Buffalo, NY 14201
White Whale Press, 2121 Cleveland PL 1-N, St. Louis, MO 63110
Wicked East Press, P.O. Box 1042, Beaufort, SC 29901
Wilderness House Press, 145 Foster St., Littleton, MA 01460
Willow Springs, 501 N. Riverpoint Blvd., Ste 425, Spokane, WA 99202
Willows Wept Review, 17313 Second St., Montverde, FL 34756
Wilson Quarterly, 1300 Pennsylvania Ave., NW, Washington, DC, 20004-3027
Wind Publications, 600 Overbrook Drive, Nicholasville, KY 40356
Wings Press, 627 E. Guenther, San Antonio, TX 78210
The Winter Anthology, 2335 Lucerne Ave., Los Angeles, CA 90016
Winter Goose Publishing, 2701 Del Paso Rd., 130-92, Sacramento, CA 95835
Witness, Box 455085, Las Vegas, NV 89154-5085
WomenArts Quarterly, UMSL, One University Blvd., St Louis, MO 63121-4991
The Worcester Review, 1 Ekman St, Worcester, MA 01607
Wordcraft of Oregon, P.O. Box 3235, La Grande, OR 97850
Words without Borders, 3800 N. Lawndale Ave., Chicago, IL 60618
Work Literary Magazine, 8752 N. Calvert, Portland, OR 97217
Workers Write!, 2005 Brabant Dr., Plano, TX 75025-0382
World Literature Today, 630 Parrington Oval, Ste. 110, Norman, OK 73019-4033
Writecorner Press, PO Box 140310, Gainesville, FL 32614-0310

Y

Yale Review, PO Box 208243, New Haven, CT 06520
Yarn, 26 Hawthorne Lane, Weston, MA 02493
YB, 401 Zanzibar, Billings, MT 59105
Yes Yes Books, 814 Hutcheson Dr., Blacksburg, VA 24060
YU News Service, P.O. Box 236, Millbrae, CA 94030

Z

Zoetrope: All Story, 916 Kearny St., San Francisco, CA 94133
Zone 3, APSU, P.O. Box 4565, Clarksville, TN 37044
ZYZZYVA, 466 Geary St., Ste. 401, San Francisco, CA 94102

THE PUSHCART PRIZE FELLOWSHIPS

The Pushcart Prize Fellowships Inc., a 501 (c) (3) nonprofit corporation, is the endowment for The Pushcart Prize. "Members" donated up to $249 each. "Sponsors" gave between $250 and $999. "Benefactors" donated from $1000 to $4,999. "Patrons" donated $5,000 and more. We are very grateful for these donations. Gifts of any amount are welcome. For information write to the Fellowships at PO Box 380, Wainscott, NY 11975.

Carol de Gramont
Karl Elder
Donald Finkel
Ben and Sharon Fountain
Alan and Karen Furst
John Gill
Robert Giron
Doris Grumbach & Sybil Pike
Gwen Head
The Healing Muse
Robin Hemley
Bob Hicok
Jane Hirshfield
Helen & Frank Houghton
Joseph Hurka
Laure-Anne Bosselaar
Kate Braverman
Barbara Bristol
Kurt Brown
Richard Burgin
David S. Caldwell

Diane Johnsons
Janklow & Nesbit Asso.
Edmund Keeley
Thomas E. Kennedy
Wally & Christine Lamb
Sydney Lea
Gerald Locklin
Thomas Lux
Markowitz, Fenelon and Bank
Elizabeth McKenzie
McSweeney's
Joan Murray
Barbara and Warren Phillips
Hilda Raz
Mary Carlton Swope
Julia Wendell
Philip White
Eleanor Wilner
David Wittman
Richard Wyatt & Irene Eilers

MEMBERS

Anonymous (3)
Betty Adcock
Agni
Carolyn Alessio
Dick Allen
Russell Allen
Henry H. Allen
Lisa Alvarez
Jan Lee Ande
Ralph Angel
Antietam Review
Ruth Appelhof
Philip and Marjorie Appleman
Linda Aschbrenner
Renee Ashley
Ausable Press
David Baker
Catherine Barnett
Dorothy Barresi
Barlow Street Press
Jill Bart
Ellen Bass
Judith Baumel
Ann Beattie
Madison Smartt Bell
Beloit Poetry Journal
Pinckney Benedict
Karen Bender
Andre Bernard
Christopher Bernard
Wendell Berry
Linda Bierds

Stacy Bierlein
Bitter Oleander Press
Mark Blaeuer
Blue Lights Press
Carol Bly
BOA Editions
Deborah Bogen
Susan Bono
Anthony Brandt
James Breeden
Rosellen Brown
Jane Brox
Andrea Hollander Budy
E. S. Bumas
Richard Burgin
Skylar H. Burris
David Caliguiuri
Kathy Callaway
Janine Canan
Henry Carlile
Fran Castan
Chelsea Associates
Marianne Cherry
Phillis M. Choyke
Suzanne Cleary
Martha Collins
Ted Conklin
Joan Connor
John Copenhaven
Dan Corrie
Tricia Currans-Sheehan
Jim Daniels

609

Thadious Davis

Maija Devine

Sharon Dilworth

Edward J. DiMaio

Kent Dixon

John Duncklee

Elaine Edelman

Renee Edison & Don Kaplan

Nancy Edwards

M.D. Elevitch

Failbetter.com

Irvin Faust

Tom Filer

Susan Firer

Nick Flynn

Stakey Flythe Jr.

Peter Fogo

Linda N. Foster

Fugue

Alice Fulton

Eugene K. Garber

Frank X. Gaspar

A Gathering of the Tribes

Reginald Gibbons

Emily Fox Gordon

Philip Graham

Eamon Grennan

Lee Meitzen Grue

Habit of Rainy Nights

Rachel Hadas

Susan Hahn

Meredith Hall

Harp Strings

Jeffrey Harrison

Lois Marie Harrod

Healing Muse

Alex Henderson

Lily Henderson

Daniel Henry

Neva Herington

Lou Hertz

William Heyen

Bob Hicok

R. C. Hildebrandt

Kathleen Hill

Jane Hirshfield

Edward Hoagland

Daniel Hoffman

Doug Holder

Richard Holinger

Rochelle L. Holt

Richard M. Huber

Brigid Hughes

Lynne Hugo

Illya's Honey

Susan Indigo

Mark Irwin

Beverly A. Jackson

Richard Jackson

Christian Jara

David Jauss

Marilyn Johnston

Alice Jones

Journal of New Jersey Poets

Robert Kalich

Julia Kasdorf

Miriam Poli Katsikis

Meg Kearney

Celine Keating

Brigit Kelly

John Kistner

Judith Kitchen

Stephen Kopel

Peter Krass

David Kresh

Maxine Kumin

Valerie Laken

Babs Lakey

Linda Lancoine

Maxine Landis

Lane Larson

Dorianne Laux & Joseph Millar

Sydney Lea

Donald Lev

Dana Levin

Gerald Locklin

Linda Lacione

Rachel Loden

Radomir Luza, Jr.

William Lychack

Annette Lynch

Elzabeth MacKierman

Elizabeth Macklin

Leah Maines

Mark Manalang

Norma Marder

Jack Marshall

Michael Martone

Tara L. Masih

Dan Masterson

Peter Matthiessen

Alice Mattison

Tracy Mayor

Robert McBrearty

Jane McCafferty

Rebecca McClanahan

Bob McCrane

Jo McDougall

Sandy McIntosh

James McKean

Roberta Mendel

Didi Menendez

Barbara Milton
Alexander Mindt
Mississippi Review
Martin Mitchell
Roger Mitchell
Jewell Mogan
Patricia Monaghan
Rick Moody
Jim Moore
James Morse
William Mulvihill
Nami Mun
Carol Muske-Dukes
Edward Mycue
Deirdre Neilen
W. Dale Nelson
Jean Nordhaus
Ontario Review Foundation
Daniel Orozco
Other Voices
Pamela Painter
Paris Review
Alan Michael Parker
Ellen Parker
Veronica Patterson
David Pearce, M.D.
Robert Phillips
Donald Platt
Valerie Polichar
Pool
Jeffrey & Priscilla Potter
Marcia Preston
Eric Puchner
Tony Quagliano
Barbara Quinn
Belle Randall
Martha Rhodes
Nancy Richard
Stacey Richter
James Reiss
Katrina Roberts
Judith R. Robinson
Jessica Roeder
Martin Rosner
Kay Ryan
Sy Safransky
Brian Salchert
James Salter
Sherod Santos
R.A. Sasaki
Valerie Sayers
Maxine Scates
Alice Schell
Dennis & Loretta Schmitz
Helen Schulman

Philip Schultz
Shenandoah
Peggy Shinner
Vivian Shipley
Joan Silver
Skyline
John E. Smelcer
Raymond J. Smith
Philip St. Clair
Lorraine Standish
Maureen Stanton
Michael Steinberg
Sybil Steinberg
Jody Stewart
Barbara Stone
Storyteller Magazine
Bill & Pat Strachan
Julie Suk
Sun Publishing
Sweet Annie Press
Katherine Taylor
Pamela Taylor
Susan Terris
Marcelle Thiébaux
Robert Thomas
Andrew Tonkovich
Pauls Toutonghi
Juanita Torrence-Thompson
William Trowbridge
Martin Tucker
Jeannette Valentine
Victoria Valentine
Hans Van de Bovenkamp
Tino Villanueva
William & Jeanne Wagner
BJ Ward
Susan O. Warner
Rosanna Warren
Margareta Waterman
Michael Waters
Sandi Weinberg
Andrew Weinstein
Jason Wesco
West Meadow Press
Susan Wheeler
Dara Wier
Ellen Wilbur
Galen Williams
Marie Sheppard Williams
Eleanor Wilner
Irene K. Wilson
Steven Wingate
Sandra Wisenberg
Wings Press
Robert W. Witt

612

CONTRIBUTORS' NOTES

M.C. ARMSTRONG was recently embedded with SEAL Team 4 in Haditha, Iraq. He is the co-founder and co-editor of *Convergence Review*.

SUE ALLISON is the author of a book about the Bloomsbury Group. She received an M.F.A. from Vermont College and was included in *Best American Essays* of 2009.

KATHLEEN BALMA has been published by Café Review and elsewhere. She lives in Vernon, Connecticut.

BRUCE BENNETT teaches at Wells College, Aurora, New York. He is the author of dozens of books and chapbooks of poetry.

WENDELL BERRY lives, farms and writes at Lanes Landing Farm in Kentucky.

REGINALD DWAYNE BETTS is the author of the memoir *A Question of Freedom* (Avery, 2010). A founding member of the poetry collective The Symphony, Betts wan an NAACP Image Award and a Beatrice Hawley Award.

ADRIAN BLEVINS directs the writing program at Colby College in Waterville, Maine. Her poetry collections are published by Ausable Press and Wesleyan University Press.

MARIANNE BORUCH is the author of seven poetry collections, most recently *The Book of Hours* (Copper Canyon, 2011), and two books of essays. She teaches at Purdue University and Warren Wilson College.

DEBORAH BROWN's debut collection, *Walking the Dog's Shadow*, which includes this edition's poem, was published by BOA in 2011. She teaches at the University of New Hampshire.

SOMMER BROWNING lives in Denver. This is her first Pushcart Prize.

SHANNON CAIN is the author of *The Necessity of Certain Behaviors* (University of Pittsburgh Press) which includes "Juniper Beach." She lives in Tucson.

HARRY CREWS lived in Gainesville, Florida, where he taught at the University of Florida and where he died on March 28, 2012 at the age of 76. He was the author of nearly twenty novels, plus the first volume of his autobiography, and three essay collections. In 2001 he was inducted into the Georgia Writers Hall of Fame.

JOSHUA COHEN is the author of six books. "Emission" is reprinted from his latest—*Four New Messages* (Graywolf Press). He lives in New York.

SARAH CORNWELL was 2012 Writer-in-Residence at Interlochen Arts Academy. She was an investigator of police misconduct, a tutor, a psychological research interviewer, a toyseller, and a James Michener Fellow at the University of Texas.

SARAH DEMING is a former New York City Golden Gloves boxing champion. She is the author of the children's novel, *Iris, Messenger* (Harcourt). In 2011 she gave a kidney to her mother, Ruth. They are co-writing a memoir about the experience.

JAQUIRA DÍAZ studied at the University of South Florida where she also taught fiction and served as editor of *Saw Palm*. Her work has appeared in *The Sun*, *Slice* and elsewhere.

ANTHONY DOERR lives in Boise, Idaho. His awards include a Guggenheim, an O'Henry and two previous Pushcart Prizes.

BRIAN DOYLE is the editor of *Portland Magazine*. His *Bin Laden's Bald Spot and Three Other Stories* is just out.

JULIA ELLIOTT lives with her husband and daughter in Columbia, South Carolina. Her fiction has appeared in *Tin House, The Georgia Review, Fence* and *Puerto Del Sol*.

SETH FRIED last appeared in Pushcart Prize XXXV. He lives in Brooklyn, New York.

CRISTÍAN FLORES GARCIA lives in Hemet, California.

CHRISTINE GELINEAU is the author of *Appetite for the Divine* (2010) and *Remorseless Loyalty* (2006). She lives in Windsor, New York.

ELTON GLASER is Professor Emeritus at the University of Akron. Two new poetry collections are due in 2013 from Pittsburgh and Arkansas university presses.

MATT HART is the author of three books of poetry and several chapbooks. His most recent book is just published by Typecast Publishing.

SHOZAN JACK HAUBNER writes that he was "a former slave in the aspiring screenwriter salt-mines of Hollywood" before he escaped to a Rinzai Zen monastery. His book of essays will be published soon by Shambhala Publications.

TIMOTHY HEDGES lives in Detroit with his wife and children. He received a Hopwood Award from the University of Michigan, where he now teaches writing.

ROBIN HEMLEY is the author of ten books of nonfiction and fiction and the winner of many awards including a 2008 Guggenheim Fellowship and three Pushcart Prizes. He directs the Nonfiction Writing Program at The University of Iowa and is a senior editor of *The Iowa Review*.

JANE HIRSHFIELD's honors include fellowships from the Guggenheim and Rockefeller foundations, the National Endowment for the Arts and the Academy of American Poets. She is author of the collection of essays *Nine Gates: Entering the Mind of Poetry* (HarperCollins, 1997) and many poetry volumes.

ANDREW HUDGINS lives in Columbus, Ohio and teaches at Ohio State University. He is the author of *Diary of a Poem* (University of Michigan Press) and other books.

NALINI JONES lives in Norwalk, Connecticut. This is her first Pushcart Prize.

LAURA KASISCHKE has published eight poetry collections and eight novels. A book of short stories is forthcoming.

TED KOOSER served two terms as U.S. Poet Laureate and won the Pulitzer Prize for *Delights & Sorrows* (Copper Canyon). His books for children are published by Candlewick Press.

JENNIFER LUNDEN is the founder of the Center for Creative Healing in Portland, Maine. She lives in Portland and blogs at www.jenniferlunden.com.

MATT MASON won the Nebraska Book Award for Poetry with his first book, *Things We Don't Know We Don't Know*. He lives in Omaha.

DAVIS MCCOMBS is the author of two books of poetry—*Ultima Thule* and *Dismal Rock*. He lives in Fayetteville, Arkansas.

JILL MCDONOUGH is the recipient of fellowships from the Library of Congress, Stanford's Stegner program and elsewhere. She teaches at the University of Massachusetts, Boston. Her books include *Habeas Corpus* and *Where You Live*.

ERIN MCGRAW teaches at Ohio State University. She is the author of *The Seamstress of Hollywood Boulevard*.

FRED MOROMARCO was a founding editor of *Poetry International* and the author of seven books. He was Professor Emeritus at San Diego State University. He died in February of 2012.

JOYCE CAROL OATES won the National Book Award, the PEN/Malamud award and the Prix Femina, plus other citations. She lives and teaches in Princeton, New Jersey.

ALICIA OSTRIKER is the author of many books of poetry, history and criticism. Twice nominated for a National Book Award, she has received citations from the National Endowment for the Arts, the Poetry Society of America and elsewhere.

ALAN MICHAEL PARKER is the author of seven books of poetry, including *Long Division* (Tupelo Press, 2012) and three novels. His next novel is due soon from Dzanc Books. He teaches at Davidson College, Davidson, North Carolina.

ANN PATCHETT is co-owner of the independent store Parnassus Books in Nashville. She is the author of the recent novel *State of Wonder*, plus six other novels and two books of non-fiction.

BEN PERCY lives in Northfield, Minnesota. He previously appeared in Pushcart Prize XXXI.

JENNIFER PERCY is the author of *Demon Camp*, forthcoming from Scribner. She received a 2012 grant from the National Endowment for the Arts and a Truman Capote Fellowship from the Iowa Writers' Workshop.

ELIZABETH POWELL is editor of *Green Mountains Review* and teaches at Johnson State College in Vermont. Her book of poems, *The Republic of Self*, is published by New Issues Press.

JAMES RICHARDSON was the winner of the 2011 Jackson Poetry Prize. His *By The Numbers: Poems and Aphorisms* (Copper Canyon, 2010) was a finalist for the National Book Award.

JULÍAN RÍOS is published by Dalkey Archive Press. This is his first Pushcart Prize.

MARILYNNE ROBINSON is the author of the novels *Gilead* and *Home* and the recent essays collection *When I Was A Child I Read Books*.

JAMES ROBISON won a Whiting Grant for his short fiction and a Rosenthal Award from the American Academy of Arts for his first novel. He lives in Naples, Florida.

LAURA RODLEY is the author of two chapbooks, both from Finishing Line Press. She lives in Shelburne Falls, Massachusetts.

KAREN RUSSELL is the author of *Swamplandia!* and the story collection *St. Lucy's Home for Girls Raised by Wolves* (both from Knopf/Vintage). She lives in Philadelphia.

KENT RUSSELL reports that he is "kid brother" to novelist Karen Russell (also in this Pushcart Prize). He lives in Miami.

DIANE SEUSS is writer-in-residence at Kalamazoo College in Michigan. She won the 2009 Juniper Prize for Poetry.

JEANNE SHOEMAKER graduated in 2010 from the Iowa Writers' Workshop. "Sonny Crisss" is her first published story. She lives in Victoria, British Columbia.

PATRICIA SMITH's eight books include *Blood Dazzler*, a finalist for the 2008 National Book Award and one of NPR's top books of that year. She is a professor at the College of Staten Island, New York.

PAUL STAPLETON holds a Master's Degree in Classics from Fordham University. He has been a teacher since 1988 and lives in Raleigh, North Carolina.

MARY SZYBIST authored two collections of poetry: *Granted* (Alice James, 2003) a finalist for the National Book Critics Circle Award, and *Incarnadine* (Graywolf, 2013). She lives in Portland, Oregon and teaches at Lewis & Clark College.

TOON TELLEGEN is one of Holland's most celebrated poets. He is also a novelist and children's book author. "A man found an angel" is part of a sequence of poems entitled "A Man and an Angel" to be published by Shoestring Press in 2013. His translator, Judith Wilkinson is a British poet living in the Netherlands. Her poetry collection, *Tightrope Dancer*, is issued by Shoestring.

DIANE WAKOSKI has been Poet In Residence and University Distinguished Professor at Michigan State University since 1975. The most recent of her more than twenty poetry collections is *The Diamond Dog* (Anhinga, 2010).

G.C. WALDREP teaches at Bucknell University, edits *West Branch* and is Editor-at-Large for *The Kenyon Review*. A recent collection, with poet John Gallaher, is out from BOA.

ANTHONY WALLACE teaches at Boston University, Boston.

MICHAEL WATERS teaches at Monmouth University. His eight books of poetry include *Darling Vulgarity* (BOA, 2006). He lives in Ocean, New Jersey with his wife and son, Fabian.

BESS WINTER lives in Toronto. Her work has appeared in *Pank, Bellingham Review, Berkeley Fiction Review* and elsewhere.

RASHEDA WHITE is in the fourth grade. "A Shadow Beehive" is her first publication.

ADAM ZAGAJEWSKI, the distinguished Polish poet, has appeared in two previous Pushcart Prizes. He teaches at the University of Chicago.

INDEX

The following is a listing in alphabetical order by author's last name of works reprinted in the *Pushcart Prize* editions since 1976.

618

619

621

623

625

626

634

635

637

638

639

641